# EUROPEAN PLANT INTELLECTUAL PROPERTY

This authoritative new work analyses European plant intellectual property rights. Whilst the focus of the work is on Europe, and in particular the European Patent Convention, the Council Regulation on Community Plant Variety Rights and the EU Directive on the Legal Protection of Biotechnological Inventions, these provisions are discussed within the context of international legislation, including the Agreement on Trade-Related Aspects of Intellectual Property Rights (TRIPs) and the Convention on Biological Diversity. It is the first book to look at the impact of plant intellectual property rights on the European plant breeding industry and assess whether recent developments, such as the *Novartis* decision, will assist plant breeders, from all sectors of plant breeding, in the production of new plant products. In addition to a thorough discussion of the legislation, the book includes unique empirical research results obtained by the authors as part of a two-year research project funded by the European Union, which surveyed attitudes towards, and use of, plant intellectual property rights within the European plant breeding community.

# European Plant Intellectual Property

Margaret Llewelyn
&
Mike Adcock

·HART·
PUBLISHING

OXFORD AND PORTLAND, OREGON
2006

Published in North America (US and Canada) by
Hart Publishing
c/o International Specialized Book Services
920 NE 58th Avenue, Suite 300
Portland, OR 97213–3786
USA
Tel: +1 503 287 3093 or toll-free: (1) 800 944 6190
Fax: +1 503 280 8832
Email: orders@isbs.com
Website: www.isbs.com

Hart Publishing, 16C Worcester Place, Oxford, OX1 2JW
Telephone: +44 (0) 1865 517530 Fax: +44 (0) 1865 510710
Email: mail@hartpub.co.uk
Website: http://www.hartpub.co.uk

British Library Cataloguing in Publication Data
Data Available

ISBN–13: 978–1–84113–322–5 (hardback)
ISBN–10: 1–84113–322–1 (hardback)

Typeset by Hope Services, Abingdon
Printed and bound in Great Britain by
TJ International Ltd, Padstow, Cornwall

# Preface

The importance of plants, whether agricultural, medicinal, culinary, artistic, recreational or symbolic, resonates throughout history. Throughout the centuries man can be seen to place reliance on plants not merely to provide and maintain life[1] (or to secure death),[2] but also to designate status and define humanity.[3] From the earliest days man has also sought to use plants, whether by claiming plant material as territory or by influencing our perceptions by ascribing symbolic qualities to that material, but it is only with the advent of modern genetics that we have sought to secure rights not merely over but *in* the material itself.

In his book, *The Forgiveness of Nature: the Story of Grass*,[4] Graham Harvey details the way in which different types of grasses have been developed in order to meet different needs. From specialist amenity grasses for football pitches to grasses specifically bred to improve milk and beef quality, the book provides evidence of the fact that whilst most of us acknowledge the presence of grass, for 'it is a common everyday thing, scarcely worth a mention', few of us recognise its influence on much that we do and, in turn, on the lives we lead. Grass is not the only member of the plant world which serves as a silent player shaping the world we live in. In his two beautifully illustrated books, *The Plants that Shaped our Gardens*,[5] and *Dangerous Garden: The quest for plants to change our lives*,[6] David Stuart outlines the many different ways in which plants have been utilised from medicinal use to the purely aesthetic and yet, this use aside, most people give little thought to the plants around them, the diversity within species, or to the work which has gone into their production. Such thoughts as we do have tend to focus on individually localised issues such as whether a certain plant would be a desirable addition to a garden or if a particular vegetable would be suitable to serve at dinner—the innovation involved goes unnoticed and yet such enquiry and innovation is central to our ability to enjoy many of the plant products which surround us.

This fascination with plants and man's desire to make use of plant material can be traced back through the centuries. George Drower, in *Gardeners, Gurus and Grubs*,[7] provides numerous examples of little-known inventors who have

---

[1] Through agricultural usage.

[2] For example the use of hemlock.

[3] One only has to look at literature through the centuries to see nature, in both its natural and man-made guises, used to denote territoriality (for example 'this green and pleasant land') or to symbolise or represent man's state.

[4] (Jonathan Cape, 2001).

[5] (Frances Lincoln Ltd, 2002).

[6] (Frances Lincoln Ltd, 2004).

[7] Drower, *Gardeners, Gurus and Grubs, The Stories of Garden Inventors and Innovations* (Sutton Publishing, 2001).

made the gardening experience not only more enjoyable for the general public, but, in many instances, possible—such innovations including the wheelbarrow (Chuko Liang AD 231) and the classification of plants (Theophrastus circa BC 322–288—his first book, *An Enquiry into Plants*, attempted to classify all known plants; his second book, *The Causes of Plants,* concentrated on roses). Documentation from other civilisations also shows a reverence for plants. For example in Ancient Egypt the onion (which had been introduced into the country from Asia) was worshipped because it was thought to symbolise eternity and records show that frequently golden replicas of the vegetable were placed in the tombs of Pharaohs. Although other vegetables were less venerated they were still treated with great respect, and metal replicas of fruit and vegetables such as leeks, grapes, figs, radishes and pomegranates have been found.[8]

At a more general level, and concurrent with both the research into the transmission of characteristics undertaken by Mendel and Huxley as well as the refinement of national and international industrial property standards, there can be found the extensive descriptions of the exploits of those who could be termed 'plant explorers', who advertently placed the seeking out of new plants as the basis for their global wanderings. The delightful book *In Pursuit of Plants* by Philip Short[9] provides extracts from the journals of 19th and early 20th century plant collectors from around the world, each of whom describes the excitement felt in discovering new and wondrous plants. It is this desire to enquire together with developments in the capacity to utilise the material discovered through the enquiry which has produced the modern world of plant breeding. This work has provided society with many of the plants which it enjoys on a daily basis, including those used in non-obvious capacities such as textiles, medicines and engineering, although these uses often go unnoticed. Stuart 'Psycho' Pearce may be a much lauded hero to Nottingham Forest fans but it is doubtful whether many of the same Forest fans would pay similar homage to the Institute of Grassland and Environment Research which produces grass specifically designed for use on football pitches and was responsible for the playing surface at the City Ground which enabled 'Psycho' to play some of his best football.[10]

For the most part, plant breeding activity and its results go unnoticed and uncommented upon because it is uncontroversial. However, as has been well rehearsed elsewhere, this is no longer the case, and the activities of plant scientists are coming under increasing scrutiny. One of the reasons for this is the increasing awareness of the territorialisation of plant genetic material. This is

---

[8] http://nefertiti.iwebland.com/timelines/topics/agriculture.htm and http://www.aldokkan.com/science/agriculture.htm.

[9] Short, *In Pursuit of Plants* (University of Western Australia Press, 2003).

[10] This connection is particularly significant to one of the authors, as her grandfather, Professor ET Jones, was director of the Institute in the 1950s (when it was the Welsh Plant Breeding Station) and a founding father of the UK's plant variety rights system, and her partner, Professor Robert Bradgate, is an avid Forest fan.

nothing new—the use of land together with that which rests upon and below it to define and describe States and status can be traced back throughout history.

Land, and what it represents in terms of identity and power, stands as a single thread linking all nations, all peoples and every person throughout history. At the heart of this universal connection to the land lies the desire to own, and by owning, to define. States are defined via their borders and increase their power by extension of those borders often via the use of force. Individuals define themselves by reference to their property and to what they place upon it.

This connection to the land is not merely based on a physical association with it, it also resonates with perceptions as to what land represents. Simon Scharma in *Landscape and Memory*[11] provides examples of the roles land and landscape have played in religion, literature and art, amongst others, in shaping our, often unconscious, views of the world around us. In the past the global realisation of the importance of land came in the form of conquest. Today the physical annexation of another country is deplored and even the threat of such annexation can be sufficient to justify stern action from the international community, and land, and all that it represents has taken on what could be regarded as a heightened significance as countries and peoples seek to assert their identity.

Equally the colonisation of land, where no force is used, but indigenous peoples are nonetheless made subject to externally imposed rules and processes is frowned upon as colonisers are increasingly called upon to apologise for past practices, provide compensation and, arguably most importantly of all, to politically recognise the community(ies) affected. In the absence of other land to acquire in order to add wealth and power, attention has turned increasingly to the value of that which can be found upon and within it—and with this attention comes the concomitant issue of, if there is a value, who has the right to exploit it or, put another way, who owns the right to the value in the material. One of the main sources of this value are plants and the interest in acquiring the right to control the exploitation of both plants and the genes making up the plants has led some commentators to view this as a new form of colonialisation. This focus on the value of indigenous plant material and the issue of who can control access to any value residing within that material has meant that the control mechanisms, and more specifically intellectual property rights, have themselves come under increased scrutiny.[12] To a considerable extent the focus for the scrutiny has been the developing world, but as this book will discuss, there are also issues which arise which relate to policy and practice within a developed country context. This book will look at the way in which all aspects of plant material (from genes to species) have been increasingly regarded as private property over which a private property right can be asserted. The focus will be

---

[11] (Harper Collins Publishers, 1995).

[12] See, for example, the views expressed by leading genetic scientists such as Sulston and Ferry, *The Common Thread* (Bantam Press, 2003); Watson, *DNA: The Secret of Life* (Random House, 2004); and those of commentators on the possible impact of the science: Fukuyama, *Our Posthuman Future: Consequences of the Biotechnology Revolution* (Profile Books, 2002).

on European provision although it has to be understood that this must, ultimately, be looked at against international trends and practices.

In writing the book we have been greatly assisted by organisations such as the UPOV Office, the Community Plant Variety Rights Office, the European Patent Office, national plant variety rights and patent offices, organisations representing the interests, scientific and legal, of plant breeders, and the companies who are engaged in the research itself. In particular we would like to thank the following individuals who, over the years, have provided invaluable guidance and advice, John Ardley, Bart Claes, Deryck Beyleveld, Julyan Elbro, Jose Elena, Barry Greengrass, Joel Guiard, Bart Kieweit, Bernard Le Buanec, Peter Odell, Tim Roberts, Rene Royon, Bubpha Techapattaraporn, Roger Turner, Geertrui van Overwalle, Roger Walker and Sue Wigzell. We are also very grateful to all the plant breeders who participated in the diverse aspects of the EU project—they are unfortunately too many to mention, but we thank them all unreservedly.

Our biggest thanks go to those who, with us, ran the EU-funded Plant Intellectual Property (PIP) project, the project team Antoine Alegre de la Soujeole, Jean-Louis Talvez, Marc Lecrivain, Fintan Moran, Abdullah Sayegh, Geertrui van Overwalle, Martin Ekvard, Rosa Manjon and Alexander Krefft. Anyone who was involved in the PIP project will know that there was one person above all who made the whole project succeed and that was Marie-Josee Goode. As the third member of the Sheffield Triumverate she was responsible not only for the smooth running of all aspects of the project, but also for making it the most enjoyable experience imaginable. It is impossible to express our gratitude to her or our delight in having made such a great friend.

We owe an especial debt of gratitude to Richard Hart both for his belief in the value of this project but also for his patience (not least when the authors took a decision to delete the first final draft and rewrite from scratch).

Finally we would not have been able to write the book without the support of Rob and Diane. They have borne the brunt of our forays abroad, obsession with plants and bits of plants, the highs and lows of the PIP project and especially the trauma involved in writing it all up. Without their constant belief in our ability to write this book, this would still be a work in progress. The words 'thank you' seem so small and yet mean so much and we hope they understand the depth of our gratitude and love. We dedicate this book to them.

As ever, responsibility for the contents of this book remains our own.

# Contents

# Table of Cases

# Table of Legislation

## National Legislation

### Australia

# 1

# *Defining the Territory*

## I. INTRODUCTION

IN THE 21ST century, the provision of plant property rights (mainly in the form of patents and plant variety rights) is regarded as the norm. Indeed, for plant varieties international trade law mandates that such protection *must* be provided. The obligation to provide protection, which is contained in Article 27 of TRIPs (the Agreement on Trade-Related Aspects of Intellectual Property Rights),[1] has been the focus of considerable debate, particularly in respect of its implications for developing countries. What has been debated less is the effect of granting private property rights in and over plant material within a developed country context. As this book will discuss, protracted discussions took place in Europe during the 19th and 20th centuries as to whether plant material should be the subject of a private property right. As a result of these discussions the current position is that plant varieties can be protected via a plant variety right and all other types of plant material by patents. However, notwithstanding an apparent political consensus on protection, a number of important issues remain which, if unresolved, could have serious implications for the European plant breeding industry. Of critical importance are the relationship between the different rights (and, in particular, those points of tension which could arise as a result of the differences in function of each right including different practices relating to the limitations/derogations to the right) and those internal aspects of the rights which might pose problems for plant researchers (such as the threshold for grant and scope of protection conferred). It is these themes, in both their modern and original guises, which form the core of this book.

A problem facing the modern debate is the fact that because of the increasingly global nature of plant research, the issue of the protection of the results of that research has tended to focus on commercial concerns such as the removal of trade barriers by standardising protection, promoting investment through the promise of strong private property rights and maximising competition. In such an environment it has become easy to pass over those issues which were once the

---

[1] The TRIPs obligation will be discussed in ch 2. In essence it requires member states of the WTO to provide protection for plant varieties by the provision of patent protection and/or a *sui generis* right. Whilst micro-organisms must be protected under patent law, member states have the option of excluding plants from patent protection.

heart of the debate. These included the desirability of permitting private property rights over key material such as food crops, the need to foster a specific, socially desirable, research sector (such as plant breeding), and the function of any restrictions to such rights as are granted (and in particular the interface between the public and private interests in the material protected).

This change of focus could result in the belief that many, if not all, of those 'old' issues are now settled and, therefore, require no further discussion. Such a belief would, however, be misplaced. Clearly there are some issues which appear to be as hotly debated now as they were when the rights were first mooted—an example being the extent to which protected material can be used for research—however, it can be argued that over time the nature of the rights has changed significantly with the result that the rationales for certain key principles enshrined in the rights can also be said to have changed and this has significance for those who rely upon them. A key example of this is that the plant variety rights system was not introduced as an intellectual property right (with all the private property connotations which accompany these rights). Instead it was introduced to foster a specific sector seen as pivotal in securing the ongoing economic development of many countries, plant breeding. Because this sector was seen as having great social significance, limitations on the rights of the breeder were built into the system of protection to ensure that the rights were not used to overly monopolise key plant material. These limitations were firmly rooted in the public interest. Over time the plant variety rights system has, within certain jurisdictions (the EU being the most notable), been drawn into the intellectual property law family and the form of the right refined to mirror, in particular, its patent law counterpart. One of the basic tenets of intellectual property is the protection of the private property rights of the person who holds the right. In the case of patents this means placing minimal limitations or derogations on the right granted. Where such limitations/derogations do exist they are given a very restrictive application. In light of the inclusion of plant variety rights within the intellectual property law family it could be argued that the same restrictive interpretation and application should be given to the provisions within plant variety rights. However, to so do would be to refute the original intention behind the provisions—the question (which will be debated within this book) is whether it is appropriate to hold fast to the original intention or if it now appropriate to fully embrace the patent law approaches to such measures. To date this is not an issue which has been discussed much within the general fora of debate. As will be seen below, because of the Europe-centric nature of the background to the rights under discussion, this issue of the original justification versus the modern application is particularly resonant. Before looking at these issues it is worth attempting to define the geographical platform upon which this discussion will primarily take place and the problems encountered in providing a hard and fast definition.

## II. DEFINING EUROPE

At first glance, the term 'European plant intellectual property' would appear to be straightforward and uncomplicated. It implies firstly that there is communality of practices and policy which gives rise to a 'European' system. It is important to bear in mind that legal systems across Europe differ, with the most obvious point of departure being those jurisdictions which operate on a civil law basis (such as France and Germany) and those which are common law based (such as the UK).[2] Secondly it implies that this practice (predicated as it is upon the practice of permitting plant variety protection for plant varieties, with patent protection available for all other types of plant innovation) is based upon two sets of rights each of which fall within the intellectual property law family thereby carrying with them the same justifications and rationales for grant, extent of protection and derogation and that the justifications again find common ground within each European country as well as within the collective European Union. In addition, the fact of the two rights implies a division in types of research activity—that which may give rise to a plant variety right and that which could lead to a patent—and that it is possible to keep these divisions clear for the purposes of applying the rights. A further factor which has, if only subconsciously, served to differentiate between the two rights (and indeed those whose interests they are purported to serve) is the fact that the plant variety rights system is often also referred to as plant breeders' rights. The inference is that the right is intended to serve the interests of those who can be termed 'plant breeder' and this sector-specific nature of the right has tended to attach to the right irrespective of whether it is referred to as a variety right or a breeders' right. In an era where the boundaries between both types of plant subject matter and those who engage in plant research are increasingly blurred, not to mention the patentisation of the plant variety rights system provided (as will be discussed later in this chapter and in chapters 3 and 4) it is debatable whether it is accurate to distinguish in practice. That said, the sector-specific nature of the plant variety rights system remains important for this lies at the heart of the justification for the right. In particular, the public interest measures which resonate throughout the right (even within its modern guise) serve to provide a central point of demarcation between plant variety rights and the patent system. As these provide the central themes to this book, which will be discussed in greater detail alongside the substantive law, this chapter will provide some thumbnail definitions of Europe, the two intellectual property rights under discussion, and the science concerned, identify those organisations which are influencing policy and practice, and also outline some general issues relating to the operation of intellectual property rights in practice.

---

[2] There will be further references to these differences later in this chapter.

For the purpose of European plant property rights there are three main concepts which need to be taken into account when defining what the actual legal position is. We will only provide an outline of each here as these are investigated in more detail throughout the book.

The three systems are a) Europe plant protection law as defined by the European Union (EU), b) Europe plant protection law as defined by the European Patent Convention (EPC), and c) Europe plant protection law as defined by national laws conceived as a result of membership of international treaties (which may or may not mirror the principles enshrined under the first two headings).[3] Of course these are not separate from each other but are inextricably (for the present at least) interwoven with one another (not least for political reasons). The result is that there is a great deal of convergence, but equally there remains a degree of divergence (both across jurisdictions and within national and pan-national systems of protection) which needs to be borne in mind when determining the exact nature of provision within Europe.

We will begin in reverse order and start by looking at the international obligations.

### Defining the International Obligation

All European countries, and indeed the EU itself, are members of the World Trade Organisation (WTO). This membership carries with it an obligation to comply with the provisions of the TRIPs Agreement. As will be discussed in chapter 2, the TRIPs Agreement provides member states with a number of options as to the protection of plant material. Article 27(3)(b) permits members to exclude plants from patent protection, but nonetheless requires member states to provide patent protection for micro-organisms and/or *sui generis*[4] protection for plant varieties (the issue of defining a plant, a micro-organism and a plant variety will be dealt with below). Where members do provide for protection for plants (as opposed to plant varieties) the implication is that they will do so via the patent system, with only plant varieties being captured by the *sui generis* right (if that is the option chosen by the member state).

In terms of the provision of protection, European countries appear to be agreed. As a result of membership of the EPC, all European countries exclude plant varieties from patent protection; none excludes plants from patent protection. This would seem to indicate that all plants, other than plant varieties, are patentable. However, depending on the granting practices of the national

---

[3] A discussion of the substantive laws of each of the EU member states relating to plant property rights is outside the remit of this book. For this level of detail we would advise contacting bodies such as the European Bio-industry Association or European Seed Association, national granting offices or local organisations such as the UK's Chartered Institute of Patent Agents and British Society of Plant Breeders (each of which has a local equivalent in nearly all other EU member states).

[4] Of its own kind, this means a right which is individually tailored to a particular subject (the plant variety rights system is an example of such a right).

offices, the reality is not so clear, with some offices still refusing to grant patents over plant innovations on policy grounds—primarily that they do not fall within the technical notion of what is an invention. This means that on the face of it (and in the absence of an express exclusion of plants from patent protection) there may be local diversity as to whether protection will be actually forthcoming. (This issue will be revisited when looking at the concept of European patent provision under the EPC.) The second matter relates to the provision of a *sui generis* system. Because of the express exclusion of plant varieties from patent protection the implication is that all European countries will provide a form of specific plant variety protection, and that where they do so that protection will be uniform within each country. One of the reasons for the supposition is the existence of the International Convention on the Protection of New Varieties of Plants (UPOV). As will be seen in chapter 3, this Convention is generally seen as European in form and spirit essentially because it was introduced as a result of pressure from European plant breeders. The reality, however, is that not all European countries are members of UPOV (the most obvious absentee being Greece) and even where there is membership the nature of the membership might differ as a result of the substantive revisions to the UPOV Convention[5] which have taken place over the years with some countries adhering to a previous as opposed to a current Act (an example being France which is still a signatory to the 1978 Act). These differences in adherence are significant in respect of which species are protectable, the duration of protection and also the derogations provided to the right granted. These will be discussed at length in chapter 3.

### European Plant Protection as defined by the EPC

All European countries (including those who make up the EU) are members of the European Patent Convention. As will be discussed in chapters 5 and 6 this seeks to harmonise patent law across Europe thereby facilitating not only the provision of a single right enforceable in as many member states as the patent applicant wishes, but also ensures that the overarching grant mirrors the granting and enforcement practices of member states within which the right is to be protected. As mentioned above, the EPC expressly exclude plant varieties from protection (as well as essentially biological processes for the production of plants). The problem with stating that there is therefore a cogent and unified system of policy and practice regarding plant innovations within all member states of the EPC is that the EPC is overseen by the European Patent Office (EPO) which is primarily concerned with grant. This is crucial for three reasons.

The first is that anyone seeking to obtain patent protection in Europe has a choice. They can either seek a patent via the EPO or they can apply through

---

[5] The original UPOV Convention was introduced in 1961 and was revised (minimally) in 1972 and (substantively) in 1978 and 1991. These revised versions are referred to as 'Acts'.

national granting offices. As will be discussed later, in order to obtain a patent a certain threshold must be met. Both the EPC and national patent laws refer to the same threshold; however, the interpretation of what that threshold means in practice can differ. Whilst the EPO is vociferous in setting out its understanding of these common principles, its decisions are not binding on national offices and are merely persuasive in nature. This means that there can be differences in granting practices between the EPO and national offices.

Secondly, as already stated, the EPO is primarily concerned with grant. It is not concerned with matters relating to any limitations or derogations to the patent right once granted. Most national patent laws permit the use of patented technology for research purposes, but the issue of what constitutes 'research' may differ within jurisdictions. In addition, most patent systems permit third parties to seek a compulsory licence if the technology protection by the patent is not being appropriately disseminated—again there is local variation as to when such a licence can be sought. Serving as a further complicating factor, the national laws relating to the limitations and derogations may distinguish between types of subject matter (for example being more or less lenient where a pharmaceutical product is concerned) and alternative principles may exist which relate to material covered by a plant variety right which, when taken collectively with the patent law principles, may have an impact on the ability to protect/exploit a patent or conduct a plant variety research.

Thirdly, there is the issue of enforcement of the patent. As stated, the EPC is primarily concerned with grant—however, it does direct national courts as to how they are to interpret the scope of the patent once granted. This will be discussed in more detail in chapter 6; in essence, however, the courts are required to balance the interests of the patent holder with those of third parties. The nature of local jurisprudence may be such that there are differences of approach as to what constitutes an appropriate balance (this will be further discussed below when looking at the nature of a patent).

Finally, there is the issue of EU plant property rights.

### Defining EU Plant Property Rights

The EU has been extremely active in recent years and has introduced two key new pieces of legislation affecting the provision of a private property right over genetic material. However, the impact of these measures has been affected as a result of attitudes and practices brought about as a result of the issues identified under the two headings above. The two pieces of legislation are the Council Regulation on Community Plant Variety Rights (hereafter, variously, the Community Regulation, the Regulation, and Regulation (EC) No 2100/94) and the Directive on the Legal Protection of Biotechnological Inventions (the Directive). In respect of the former, this is intended to permit an applicant to secure, through one application made at the Community Plant Variety Office, a right which is enforceable across the EU. The right is based upon the 1991 UPOV Act.[6] The problems with Regulation (EC) No 2100/94 are two-fold.

The first is that, as mentioned above, not all EU member states have signed up to the 1991 Act. Whilst this does not create a problem for the enforcement of grants made under Regulation (EC) No 2100/94 it does mean that there may be a divergence between the rights which will be granted by a member state and its obligation to enforce as a result of a grant made under the Regulation (for example a member state may not permit national plant variety rights over a particular species, possibly for policy reasons, but nonetheless will have to enforce a right granted over that species within its national courts as a result of a Community right being granted).

Secondly, the 1991 Act introduces new concepts such as the essentially derived variety concept. As will be discussed in chapter 3, the determination of what is an essentially derived variety is to be left to the courts and, in the first instance, to national courts. It is possible that this will give rise to national differences. The same concerns arise over the restrictions placed on the ability of a farmer to retain seed from one year to the next for resowing. This was freely permitted under the first two main UPOV Acts (and therefore ostensibly remains freely permitted for farmers within those jurisdictions which still adhere to the previous Acts). However, it is not as simple as this, for these changes to the farm saved seed provisions appear to be compelling even within those jurisdictions where the previous Acts remain in force. In addition the fact that member states are free to decide the measure of any recompense to the breeder where the new limitations on the freedom to reuse are seen to operate means that there is likely to be diversity of operation notwithstanding the introduction of the Community system.

The same problems arise in respect of the Directive on the Legal Protection of Biotechnological Inventions. As is the case with Regulation (EC) No 2100/94, the Directive builds on an existing system of protection, in this case the EPC. However, because of perceived problems with a) the way in which the EPC was being interpreted in respect of biotechnological inventions and b) differences in national policy and practice, the European Commission felt it necessary to act at the Community level. The resulting Directive seeks therefore to provide a measure of good practice which national offices are to follow. The problem with the Directive is that a) it does not fully address the problem of national differences in the interpretation of the threshold for protection or enforcement, b) it does not provide any clarity on the limitations or derogations to the right (and for many most crucially there is no symbiosis between the Directive and the Regulation on the issue of research), and finally c) many member states have concerns over the ethical basis of granting private property rights over genetic material (and human genetic material in particular) and have, therefore, struggled to adopt it.

[6] In June 2005 the European Union became the first intergovernmental organisation to become a member of UPOV: UPOV Press Release No 65, 29 June 2005.

Thus, in a nutshell, one can see that whilst the term *European* plant intellectual property rights is a useful hook upon which to hang the issues relating to plant property rights within Europe, the term itself should not be taken as signifying that there is a single system of rights which can be defined as European.[7]

The next subject for definition is intellectual property rights and, in particular, the question of whether it appropriate to treat both patents and plant variety rights as members of the same family.

## III. DEFINING THE PROPERTY RIGHT

The World Intellectual Property Organisation (WIPO)[8] defines intellectual property as 'legal rights which result from intellectual activity in the industrial, scientific, literary and artistic fields'. The rights granted over this activity aim 'at safeguarding creators and other producers of intellectual goods and services by granting them certain time-limited rights to control the use made of those productions', with the rights traditionally divided into two branches, 'industrial property' and 'copyright'. Central to dictating the form of each of the rights, as well as the material protectable under them, are the Paris Convention on the Protection of Industrial Property (first signed in 1883[9] and last revised in 1979[10]) and the Berne Convention for the Protection of Literary and Artistic Works (first signed in 1886 and most recently amended in 1971).[11] It is noteworthy that neither the WIPO handbook nor the two Conventions mentions either plant varieties or the system for protecting plant varieties as intellectual property or intellectual property rights. The significance of this omission will be discussed later.

It is not proposed to discuss in detail either the origins of, or the justifications for, the grant of private property rights.[12] Suffice to say that the State grant of rights to reward the placing of new products, whether technological or artistic in form, into the market place can be traced back over several centuries. The objective is to both reward intellectual activity and provide an incentive for further such work by allowing the holder to prevent others from copying the protected material. Because the rights are essentially anti-competitive in nature (and there

---

[7]   There is another issue relating to the term 'European' which will be addressed in ch 8. This relates to the notion of what is a European plant breeder. In an era of take-overs and mergers, not to mention a research culture where the use of plant material knows few terrestrial bounds, it can be difficult to attribute use to any one jurisdiction or community of users. The relevance of this will be explained when discussing the Plant Intellectual Property project, funded by the EU, which sought to seek the views of *European* plant breeders.

[8]   The WIPO oversees the administration of both industrial property rights and copyright.

[9]   The first reported international conference looking at the provision of protection for inventors took place in Vienna in 1873.

[10]   20 March 1883, revised 14 December 1900, 2 June 1911, 6 November 1925, 2 June 1934, 31 October 1958, 14 July 1967, and 28 September 1979. The Convention currently has 169 members with accession dates ranging from 1884 (France) to 2004 (Namibia). See www.wipo.int for the full table of members.

[11]   And this central role is recognised within Part I of the TRIPs Agreement.

[12]   See Drahos, *A Philosophy of Intellectual Property* (Dartmouth, 1996).

is great resistance to anti-competitive activities), anyone seeking to use them has to meet certain criteria before the right will be granted—the level at which the threshold for protection is set depending on the nature of the material to be protected and the potential impact of the right granted. The distinction in economic function which lies behind the two general headings is key to understanding the different justifications lying behind industrial and intellectual property rights.

Industrial property rights are invariably sought to protect products (or processes) which have commercial value for commercial reasons. Because the rights are used to protect a market interest they have to be sought, they do not arise automatically, and are granted only if a certain threshold for grant is met by the applicant.

In contrast, those rights which purists refer to as 'intellectual' as opposed to industrial, for example copyright, have evolved to protect intellectual activity which has not necessarily been conducted with a market outcome in mind. The rationale behind the pure intellectual property rights is that the mere fact that intellectual effort has been expended, which is not directed towards producing a particular technical or technological result, gives rise to an invisible bond between creation and creator, and this relationship attracts automatic property rights.[13] The result of that intellectual effort is regarded as unique to the individual and unlikely to be produced in that exact form by another unless they copy it. In contrast, the industrial property rights reflect the fact that it perfectly possible for more than one person to come up with the same technical result. A person claiming a patent over that result therefore has to prove why they should be granted a right over it.[14]

It is not entirely clear why the collective name given to copyright, trademarks and patents is *intellectual* rather than *industrial*. One view, often expressed, is that as the nature of trade marks and patents is to promote competition in the market place by excluding competitors from replicating the protected material these rights are nothing more than state-sanctioned monopolies which most market-orientated societies shy away from sanctioning. It has been argued that the collective term 'intellectual property rights' is used to give the rights some credibility. The problem with this usage is that it implies some *intellectual* effort has been expended in the development of the material protected. Whilst this is not a problem for artistic works as such, and may not be a problem for

---

[13] This rather romantic distinction only holds true under limited scrutiny as these rights have developed in recent years to take account of predominantly commercial interests in the protected works.

[14] One final point of general comment is that those rights which are thought to be more easily acquired (copyright and registered trademarks) allow the holder to use a short-hand method identifying the existence of a property right through the use of the symbols © and ™. Neither patents nor plant variety rights use an equivalently simple symbol to denote that a right has been granted. Instead the more cumbersome 'patent pending', 'patent protected' or 'protected by plant variety rights' phrase is attached to either promotional material (eg the identification label) or to packaging. Some breeders see this as a problem, both for themselves and for other users, as it can make it difficult to know if they are using protected plant material—this is a issue which will be returned to in ch 9. For a further comment see Hamrick, *The State of Breeder's Rights* (FloraCulture, 2004).

many inventions which are the result of extensive intellectual endeavour, the intellectual element underpinning some inventions and all trade marks which justifies a right to monopolise the protected material is less easy to identify. However, the convention is that the term *intellectual* is used for all categories, and this has been adopted internationally as can be seen in the name of the World Intellectual Property Organisation and in the TRIPs Agreement.[15] For the purposes of this book, this convention will be followed.

The two rights with which this book is concerned are patents and plant variety rights. The origin for both can be found in the Paris Convention on the Protection of Industrial Property (which created the Paris Union).

## Defining Protectable Material

Article 1(3) of the Paris Convention states that the term 'industrial property' shall apply: 'to agricultural and extractive industries and to all manufactured or natural products, for example wines, grain, tobacco leaf, fruit, cattle, minerals, beer, flowers and flour.'[16] The use of 'for example' clearly shows that this is a non-exhaustive list. Although the principle of protection was included in the Convention, this did not mean that a) there was consensus on its inclusion[17] or b) that it was intended to include *all* the results of plant research activities. It is unsurprising therefore that following the introduction of the Convention this disagreement should be evident in decisions taken over whether (and how) to protect plant inventions. A number of reasons help explain this.[18]

The Paris Convention firmly established the principle that plant *products* could be industrial property; however, this did not mean that such patents were not sought *and obtained* prior to the introduction of the Convention.[19] The

[15] The Agreement does not contain the term *industrial property* and no explanation is provided as to why *intellectual* is used in preference to *industrial*.

[16] This definition remains in all subsequent revisions of the Convention.

[17] The records of the Paris Conference of 1878 show that '[b]atailles très chauds took place on whether chemical products, pharmaceutical preparations and foodstuffs should be patentable and, although the conference decided in the affirmative, an important minority was left dissatisfied.' Tilton Penrose, *The Development of the International Convention for the Protection of Industrial Property* (Johns Hopkins University Press, 1951), reproduced in Abbott, Cottier and Gurry (eds), *The International Intellectual Property System: Commentary and Materials, Part One* (Kluwer Law International, 1999) 642.

[18] Tellingly, however, such literature as exists indicates that those countries which did make early attempts to introduce some form of protection, for example France, invariably did so in response to pressure from their horticultural and ornamental breeding sectors and these were, even then, predominately privately funded. The calls for protection for the results of agricultural plant breeding (which remained mainly publicly funded until the latter half of the 20th century) came much later.

[19] There is evidence that patents over uses of plant material were being granted *before* the introduction of the Paris Convention, for example British patents were granted in 1637 to Amye Everard als Ball for a tincture of saffron and roses (PatGB104) and, in 1824, to Miss Lucy Hollowell of Neithrop, near Banbury, in Oxfordshire over the uses of seed imported from Connecticut to produce superior grass (source: Jaffe, *Ingenious Women* (Sutton Publishing, 2003)). The Paris Convention thereby merely endorsed existing practice.

language used within the Convention implies that it was already possible (and permissible) to protect plant products by one of the rights covered by the Convention—what the Convention did was to firmly establish any such practice as a general principle. Whilst the Convention refers to rights such as trade marks and the repression of unfair competition, the most obvious method of protecting the results of plant research was that which is used to protect the results of other scientific endeavours, namely either patents or utility models. However, access to protection was not forthcoming for, whilst the Convention recognised the industrial potential of plant products, the science itself was in its infancy and breeders were unable to demonstrate the level and type of engineering required to obtain industrial property protection. At the most general level, therefore, even where there was support for granting such rights, the nature of the property systems available at that time was such that protection was effectively out of the reach of any breeder.

The next factor to bear in mind is that in the period immediately following the Paris Conference, the main focus for plant research was the production of agricultural crops and much of this work was publicly funded.[20] Due to the public interest in both the work being undertaken and in the nature of the funding supporting it, it was felt that the provision of private property rights over the crops produced would not be appropriate. Two further factors served to support to this position.

The first was the fact that most of the plant breeders who were engaged in agricultural research had been trained as botanists. This predominantly requires an understanding of the external (phenotypic) features of a plant. Once the desired external characteristics are understood then the Mendelian principle of heredity can be applied using fairly basic tools (such as cotton buds or tweezers) and techniques (cross-pollination), not to mention a lot of patience, in order to achieve the desired result.

The second was that the focus of this research was on producing the agricultural plant *varieties*. These varieties might give rise to improved products such as grain, flowers or fruit, but the work which was to be encouraged was the breeding of the plants which produced those results. When this is set against the text of the Paris Convention it can be seen that the definition of industrial property refers only to end products (such as the flowers cut from a new variety or the grain harvested from it) and not to the plants from which these products are derived. A question can be asked whether the Paris Convention was intended to apply to the plants which produced the grain, flowers, and flour. This is a critical question for those seeking to open up the patent system to the research results of all plant breeding activities.

---

[20] For example, the first half of the 20th century saw the emergence of government-funded agricultural breeding institutes such as the German Max-Planck Institute for Breeding Research, the French National Institute of Agricultural Research, the Dutch Institute and Foundation for Agricultural Plant Breeding, the Swedish National Agricultural Research Centre, the British National Institute of Agricultural Botany and the aforementioned Welsh Plant Breeding Station.

From the perspective of those who believe Article 1(3) indicates that a patent is a 'desired objective for agricultural living matter inventions, plants and animals alike'[21] then it could be argued that the non-exhaustive nature of Article 1(3) enables an expansive interpretation allowing the use of 'includes' to extend the concept of industrial property to crops as well as crop products. On one level this is a persuasive argument: after all, the Convention specifically refers to agriculture as an industry and it also mentions specific types of plant products which are regarded as property produced by that industry—why should the definition not also be applied to the plants which produce the products? However, we would argue that it is more relevant to ask not how Article 1(3) can be interpreted, but rather, given the emphasis on agricultural breeding, why there is no reference to the results of this research work (a fact which has remained the case in all subsequent revisions of the Convention)?

This omission of the results of the work of the single biggest sector can be taken to mean that plant varieties (and agricultural crops in particular) were not intended to be protected by a Paris Convention industrial property right. Adding weight to this is the fact, as discussed earlier, that plant varieties could not meet the technical criteria for the grant of a patent and also the argument that the public interest would not be protected by allowing such rights to be granted over the result of work funded from the public purse. This interpretation indicates that Article 1(3) should be read as applying to plant end products but not to the plants which are used to produce them (as will be seen in the chapters on patent law and also in chapter 9, there is a fundamental problem with this interpretation when it is applied to the results of modern plant molecular biology). However, at the time that the Paris Convention was drafted, and its principles first applied by member states, the art of plant breeding was primarily based on external observational skills and there was also a closer link between the public purse and the production of agricultural crops.

This emphasis on agricultural plant breeding did not mean that work was not being undertaken in other areas involving plants, nor that such work did not garner government support. A number of countries also set up national institutes relating to these activities.[22] However, the public interest element in the research outputs was less than that for agricultural crops and there was a greater acceptance of both the investment of private capital into horticultural and ornamental plant breeding and the need to protect that investment by the provision of a private property right. Ostensibly the results of this work (the fruit and flowers produced) could be protected as industrial property under the Paris Convention. The problem was that, as with agricultural breeding, the art of botany prevailed and breeders could not rely, as many can today, on molecular

[21] Bent *et al*, *Intellectual Property Rights in Biotechnology Worldwide* (Macmillan, 1987) 41 (hereafter Bent *et al*).

[22] For example the German Institutes for Horticultural and Ornamental Plant Breeding, the Dutch State Institute for Horticultural Plant Breeding, and the Swedish National Horticultural Research Centre.

biology to assist in proving that their research results had been engineered to the extent necessary to secure a patent right.[23] This did not stop breeders from these sectors calling for their governments to provide protection for their end products.[24] The nature of the government response depended on whether it was a member of the Paris Convention and there was inconsistency in both provision and understanding of what could be industrial property.[25] Those countries which were not members clearly were under no obligation to regard plant material of the kind mentioned in Article 1(3) as industrial property. Even those which were members did not feel that the principle in Article 1(3) meant that property rights had to be provided for all types of material regarded by the Convention as industrial property.[26] However, a number of countries[27] did attempt to introduce protection but the lack of sophistication within the science was such that protection was only rarely available in practice.

It is clear that, post Paris, the issue of how to protect plant material, whether within any one jurisdiction or even across all member states of the Paris Convention,[28] was neither settled nor unified. However, the aborted attempts to protect plant material via patents did not necessarily mean that the objective of patent protection *per se* was necessarily being rejected, but rather that the subsequent failures speak more about the nature of the science involved and the attitudes towards patent law which existed at that time. Because of this, those plant products recognised as industrial property within the Paris Convention were failing to be protected. It was not until after the UPOV Convention had been introduced (with its emphasis on protecting the investment in producing agricultural plant varieties) that the science caught up with the Paris Convention principle, by which time the perception had grown that the only system of protection was that under UPOV, this view being reinforced by the exclusion of plant varieties within patent law, a provision which was interpreted in some jurisdictions as being short-hand for the exclusion of *all* plant material (as will be discussed in chapters 5 and 6). As will be seen in the next section, what arguably added insult to injury was the fact that those who had been most vocal in calling for protection both in the 19th and early 20th centuries, the horticultural and ornamental breeders, were those who secured least protection, as patent protection remained elusive and the UPOV system focused on

[23] The work of molecular biologists (particularly within the then emerging pharmaceutical industry) was key to the decision in the 1950s to remove the requirement that to be patentable an invention had to be a manufacture. This is discussed in ch 5.

[24] In most instances, the plant research was funded privately and the need to protect this individual investment played a central role in the demands to provide protection.

[25] For example France and the UK joined within a year, whereas Germany and Austria did not become members until the early part of the 20th century.

[26] The UK, for example, made no attempt to provide protection for any form of plant material until the 1950s.

[27] France being the most obvious example, as will be seen below.

[28] It is worth bearing in mind that territorial boundaries across Europe were, at that time, changing and indeed even in the 21st century the physical shape of the EU is still evolving.

protecting the plants which gave rise to the end products whereas their interests also lay in protecting the end products derived from those plants.

With the benefit of hindsight, the Paris Convention can be said to have created a conundrum. On the one hand, and with remarkable prescience given that it was not until the 1980s that patents over living material became widely available, the Convention refers to plant material and plant products as industrial property—the inference being that such property can be the subject of a property right. On the other, the reality was that, even at the time of drafting the Convention, patentable status would not have been forthcoming due to problems in applying the granting criteria and concerns over the monopolisation of key agricultural crops.

Whatever the thoughts of the draftsmen, the language of the Paris Convention and the legislative responses to it set the scene for the debate which is still ongoing. From the outset the legislative scene was set for potential friction between those staking the patent law claim to plant material and those seeking protection by alternative means (whether due to a belief that no plant material of any kind should be protected by an industrial right or because it was felt that the type of material (for example agricultural crops) could not be regarded as industrial property. Whilst it would be disingenuous to allege that each side sought to provide the *sole* form of protection, the result has been that the two sides have often been presented, and not always externally, as supporting an 'either/or' policy rather than embracing both forms.

At the dawn of modern plant breeding, the position appeared to be that the work of agricultural plant breeders should not be treated as industrial property (and protectable under the auspices of the Paris Convention) but rather be protected by a *sui generis* right and it was this belief which led to the creation of the UPOV system.[29] In contrast, members of the Paris Convention remained free to protect plant end products (such as grain, flour and flowers) as industrial property protectable by a patent. However, as the chapters on each of the systems will show, not everyone has been satisfied with the provision of protection under each system. As a result both have evolved to take account of a growing range of plant research products. This has meant that any original semblance of clarity of separation[30] has gradually become eroded as the two systems move closer together in terms of what they protect.

---

[29] It can be questioned whether the draftsmen of the UPOV Convention would have been able to take a non-Paris Convention route if they had been seeking to introduce specific protection for the types of plant material specified in Art 1(3) (flowers, flour etc, as opposed to varieties) or whether (as subsequent practice now appears to reflect is the case) Art 1(3) mandates that such plant products can only be protected by a right recognised in Art 1(2)—which, as the patent system is the one used to protect research results in all other areas of scientific endeavour, would indicate by patent protection.

[30] Although even at this early stage the potential for overlap between the two rights can be seen as the original UPOV right provided protection for the reproductive material of a variety (which can include flowers and fruit) and the later Acts permitted protection for the harvested material (flowers, fruit and grain) and derived material (which could include beer, flour and wine).

## Patents

As will be seen in chapter 5, the granting of monopolies over certain categories of 'invention' has a long history.[31] Originally, patents were granted to those who simply brought new material to the market place, and there was little emphasis on demonstrating inventive activity (other than the identification of a market gap) on the part of the trader. As the right has strengthened, and become the subject of more intensive scrutiny, then so too has the rationale developed to reflect the need for an additional, not necessarily commercial, justification for granting the rights. In this modern guise, the basis for granting patents has been well rehearsed elsewhere,[32] but can be summarised as intending to 'reward inventors who have contributed to the public good',[33] the twin functions being to act as a reward and to add to the public good. Inventions are regarded as industrial property which can be protected by a patent. As already mentioned the Convention which standardised patent practice is the Paris Convention.[34]

A patent is universally accepted to take the form of a private property right which gives to the right holder a time—(up to 20 years) and territory-barred (limited to the jurisdiction within which the grant has been made) monopoly over the invention as claimed in a written document known as the specification. In return for this protection the inventor has to demonstrate that the invention is novel, has resulted from an inventive step and is capable of industrial application. These are *legal* concepts and have to be recognised as such in order to appreciate the manner in which they are interpreted and applied within patent law. The objective is to provide protection the scope of which is commensurate with the level of inventive activity concerned which has produced a novel and useful result. Some patent systems (including those operating within Europe) do provide some limitations to the right; however, those which do exist are given a very narrow application.

Most patent laws operate on a presumption of patentability[35]—the only provision being that the invention has met the threshold for protection. This means that it is for granting offices to demonstrate why a patent should *not* be granted.[36] The emphasis on the threshold for protection reflects the fact that

---

[31] See Sherman and Bently, *The Making of Modern Intellectual Property Law* (CUP, 1999).

[32] The definitive text is Cornish, *Intellectual Property*, 5th edn (Sweet & Maxwell, 2003).

[33] White, 'Gene and Compound per se Claims' (2000–01) 6 *Bioscience L Rev* 239. The article can also be found in the journal of the Chartered Institute of Patent Agents, (2002) 31(2) *CIPA Journal* 80 and (2002) 31(2) *CIPA Journal* 134. The views sets out by White have been challenged, although not the principle of a reward for a contribution to the public good: see Crespi, 'Gene and Compound Claims: Another View' (2002) 3(5) *CIPA Journal* 255.

[34] The importance of the text of the original Paris Convention in shaping the protection of biological material will be discussed in later chapters.

[35] For example, Art 1 of the EU Directive on the Legal Protection of Biotechnological Inventions (discussed in ch 5) states that patents *shall* be granted over inventions concerning biological material.

[36] This is clear when looking at the guidance given to patent examiners—see, eg, the US Guidelines on the Examination of Biotechnological Inventions as published in the 66(4) *Federal Register*, 5 January 2001 (discussed further in ch 2).

patent law is, generally speaking, technology neutral[37] and this is also indicated in the designation given to the right.

The term 'patent'[38] simply refers to the thing granted rather than indicating a specific type of subject matter to be protected or industry intended to enjoy the protection. The fact that the granting office is primarily concerned with ensuring that the invention meets the threshold for protection (and in so doing it will operate on the presumption of patentability, which in turn places the interests of the inventor foremost[39]) means that little consideration, if any, is given to the interests of others who may working in, or are affected by, the field of technology concerned. The justification for this focus on the interests of the individual is the height of threshold to be met before a right can be granted, the argument being that the threshold is high enough to permit protection only for those inventions which merit a right being granted over them. For many this is what gives the patent system both its appeal and its rationale. It provides a strong right which, once grant has taken place, enables the holder to control virtually all uses of the protected material. The result is that the system serves to support and encourage investment and innovation. For others, the strength of the right (together with perceptions that only a minimal threshold for protection exists making the argument that the height of the threshold justifies the strength of right which follows) is precisely what is problematic with the system. At the heart of these concerns lie questions over the function of the public interest element within patent law, in particular, whether it is wholly appropriate to deem, as appears to be the present position, that this is served by protecting the interests of the inventor (who will place the patented technology into the public domain) or whether there are wider issues relating, for example, to access to the material which might require the use of a broader notion of what constitutes a 'contribut[ion] to the [greater/wider] public good'. These issues will be returned to later.

Many patent systems, including those within Europe, also exclude from protection specific categories of material because they are not regarded as inventions. These include discoveries and artistic works protectable under

[37] Although the fact that European patent law contains references to certain specified categories of excluded material, most notably certain inventions involving human genetic material, plant and animal varieties and essentially biological processes for the production of plants and animals, does indicate that the system is not wholly neutral.

[38] The word comes from the Latin *patere* meaning to lay open—this refers to the requirement that the person seeking the right must make available (or lay open) information relating to the protected material. In this can be found the requirement that an applicant must disclose his invention before a grant will be made.

[39] Some offices, the EPO for example, operate a notion of 'reasonable expectation' (a term which is used interchangeably with 'good faith'). In patent law terms this means that the office has a responsibility to give effect to the reasonable expectations of the applicant and subsequent patent holder. This can be contrasted with the concept which exists in other areas of law such as the law of contract which is far wider and captures the interests of all those involved in a bargain. If this were applied to the patent system then it could be argued that the reasonable expectations of those affected by a patent should also be taken into account. This could affect such matters as breadth of claims.

copyright, and inventions which are capable of meeting the threshold for protection but which are excluded for public interest reasons. These include inventions the commercial exploitation of which would be contrary to morality, plant varieties, and essentially biological processes for the production of plants.[40]

In order to acquire the right the applicant has to disclose all those elements of the invention (including where appropriate the precise route to its creation) to enable another skilled in that area of technology to both understand and reproduce the new technical effect protected using merely the specification as a guide. In addition to serving this 'teaching' function, the specification also defines the territory to be protected. This is done via the claims contained in the specification. In order to turn the invention into a legally recognised construct, most inventors employ the expert services of a patent agent who will usually have extensive knowledge of the scientific area within which the invention falls. As will be shown, the art of claims drafting is highly specialised and is key to both obtaining and enforcing a patent.

There are a number of issues within patent law which will require further discussion. The first of these concerns the function of the claims—do they act as fence posts which define the outer perimeters of territory protected or do they serve as sign posts which indicate where the protected territory can be found? In respect of the former, the concern is that whilst using the claims as fence posts might provide greater certainty as to what is protected by the patent, if the claims are too narrowly drawn then they might not give the patent holder protection appropriate to the inventive act. This is of particular concern where the invention involved is a 'blockbuster' or a significant breakthrough in the given technological area; in each instance this might warrant the inventor being given greater protection to reflect the magnitude of the innovative act. With respect to the latter, the worry is that if claims are too vague as to the protected territory then third parties will not know the full extent of the protection granted, with the result that a) they might unwittingly stray into the protected area or b) the patent holder might end up claiming more than he has actually invented. A strongly held concern which relates specifically to genetics is that whilst one of the justifications for the patent system is to encourage competitors to invent around—that is to innovate up to, but not enter, the patented territory—where the claims relates to material which has no alternative then the effect of allowing broad signposting claims could be to allow the patent holder to control vast swathes of territory. The effect of this could be to extend protection beyond the actual inventive act and prevent competitors from legitimately using that material for further research purposes.[41]

---

[40] These will be discussed in more detail in chs 5 and 6.

[41] See, eg, 'The Report of the Nuffield Council on Bioethics' (The Ethics of Patenting DNA, July 2002) at www.nuffieldbioethics.org/publications/pp_0000000014.asp; 'The Integrating Intellectual Property Rights and Development Policy Report of the UK Commission on Intellectual Property Rights' at www.iprcommission.org/graphic/documents/final_report.htm; and Cornish, Llewelyn and Adcock, *Intellectual Property Rights (IPRs) and Genetics: A Study into the Impact and Management of Intellectual Property Rights within the Healthcare Sector* (Department of Health, 2003) at www.phgu. org.uk/pages/work/IP.htm.

Two further issues relate to the extent to which patented material can be used for research purposes and to whether a third party can acquire a licence to use the protected material even where the patent holder is reluctant to grant such a licence.

One matter not mentioned in the above discussion is the question whether patents should be granted over plant material. This is an issue which will not be discussed within this book as the focus is on existing provision (which holds that plant material is patentable) and the implications (positive and negative) of permitting such protection for plant research.

In patent law the emphasis is on the individual, which contrasts with the plant variety rights system, which seeks specifically to place the interests of the rights holder *vis à vis* those of others engaged within the sector.

## Plant Variety Rights

Despite being mid-way through its fifth decade, the plant variety rights system is less well known than the high-profile patent law, with few texts on the subject of intellectual property rights making more than a bare reference to the right. As already mentioned neither the Paris Convention on the Protection of Industrial Property nor the WIPO refers to plant varieties as a form of industrial property nor do they seem to regard plant variety rights as a form of industrial property law.[42] As will be discussed further below, this omission is significant for it allowed those seeking to provide protection for plant varieties in the late 19th and early 20th century to seek alternative methods of protection which did not have to comply with the precepts of the Paris Convention.[43] The result of this work was the UPOV Convention introduced in 1961. Both the Paris and UPOV Conventions are central to European plant property provision.

Because of this flexibility, many of the early 20th-century plant protection systems were introduced under agricultural laws with provisions inbuilt to ensure that the rights granted to breeders did not counter-balance the broader interests of society in having access to important new crops. This did not mean that the Paris Convention has no relevance to the protection of plants—as will be seen it does specifically refer to grain, flour and flowers as industrial property—but the lack of specificity as to precisely which types of plant material were to be regarded as industrial property (not to mentioned old-fashioned notions of what is an invention) meant that its application to plant material was

---

[42]   There are two caveats to this statement which will be discussed below.

[43]   As will be seen in the discussion leading up to the introduction of the UPOV Convention in the 1950s, the option to introduce a right under the umbrella of the Paris Convention was offered but not taken up, mainly in order to placate those concerned about granting private property rights over plant material. The use of the Paris Convention might have led to a perception that the right was intended to be a form of patent, which was not the intention. There is a modern parallel with the attempts by developing countries to comply with the Art 27(3)(b) obligation under TRIPs.

treated flexibly.[44] Certainly both in the run up to the introduction of the UPOV Convention and in the first years of its operation, overt attempts were made to keep a clear distance between the Paris Convention type of right and that provided under UPOV. That has changed in recent years.

As the discussions over the relationship between patents and plant variety rights have intensified, so too has the tendency to refer to both using the shorthand term of 'intellectual property right'. As will be shown, questions may be asked as to whether it is wholly correct to refer to plant variety rights as an industrial property right (even though in some contexts, for example in Regulation (EC) No 2100/94, the right is now specifically stated to be an industrial property right) as that has potentially grave significance for the role of public interest provisions.

In contrast to the patent system, the plant variety rights system is not technology neutral but is overtly technology and sector specific.[45] The right is granted over plant groupings which can be shown to be new, distinct, uniform and stable—these criteria are subject specific and not capable of more general application as is the case with the patent granting criteria. Because the right is dependent upon a physical examination of the material, which means that whilst the application process involves some documentation it mainly relates to an assessment of submitted material, there is little need for the services of third parties (such as patent agents), although it should be noted that increasingly use is being made of third parties to draft and help enforce licensing agreements. The duration of the right depends upon the species concerned, with trees and vines being protectable for up to 30 years and all other species protectable for up to 25 years.[46]

As per the patent system, the right carries a presumption of protectability. Both the 1961 and 1978 UPOV Acts,[47] and Regulation (EC) No 2100/94[48] state that a right *shall* be granted if the conditions for protection are met. However, because the right is both subject and sector specific it is also intended to protect the interests of others engaged in plant research. As a result the right, contains some fundamental public interest limitations/derogations to the right (one of the issues which will be discussed later is the extent to which the public interest element has been possibly subjugated as a result of increasing pressure for the

---

[44] According to Tilton Penrose, the reason for including biological material within the definition of industrial property was in order to 'reflect almost exclusively the patentees' point of view': *The Development of the International Convention for the Protection of Industrial Property*, above n 17, p 639.

[45] This will be discussed in ch 3.

[46] The 1991 Act extended the duration. See ch 3.

[47] The language of the UPOV Convention can be seen to become increasingly emphatic on this matter through every revision. Art 6 of both Acts the 1961 and 1978 state that 'the breeder of a new variety or his successor in title shall benefit from the protection provided for in this Convention when the following conditions are satisfied', Art 5 of the 1991 Act, however removed the reference to the benefit to the breeder obtained where the conditions for grant are satisfied and instead simply states (in language comparable to that used in patent law) that 'The breeder's right shall be granted where the variety is (i) new, (ii) distinct, (iii) uniform and (iv) stable.'

[48] Art 5 states that 'Community plant variety rights shall be granted for varieties that' meet the granting criteria.

plant variety rights system to provide patent-equivalent protection for individual interests in plant innovation). This means that whilst the rights do protect the interests of the individual breeder, those interests have to be balanced against the broader public and sectoral interests. In patent law the interests of the patent holder are prime and there are few if any fetters on those rights.

A further factor, which reflects the singular nature of the right, is that the emphasis is on the physical material, the plants themselves, and not simply on a written description. This means that both the evaluation as to grant and also decisions relating to infringement are made by reference to the actual plants concerned. For those who support the use of plant variety rights over patents this has the effect of making the scope of protection more transparent then under patent law as it does not require professional interpretation in the way a patent specification might. However, for others the fact that only the actual material itself is evaluated means that such matters as demonstrating a level of inventiveness in order to acquire a right are overlooked, with the result that rights may be granted where there is effort but no innovation. In addition, the fact that a breeder is not required to describe the research path undertaken means that this can be kept secret and not placed in the public domain as might be the case when providing a sufficient disclosure in patent law.

When the right was originally mooted, in the 1940s and 1950s, there was a consensus that it should not be akin to a patent. The reasons for this are detailed in chapter 3, but in summary they are predominantly related to concerns over the monopolisation of key food products. As both the science of plant breeding has evolved, with the increased use of more sophisticated techniques, and acceptance has grown of the need for strong rights to protect research results, so too has the nature of the rights granted changed. In its latest guise (the 1991 UPOV Act), the right is closer to a patent than it has previously been. This evolution has in part been due to a desire to provide a viable alternative form of protection to a patent—the viability coming from providing an equivalently strong right; the pressure for this change has come about as a result of the marked developments in plant research. This has not only had an impact on the form of the right but also, by a less obvious change, on the function of the right.

One consequence of the modern bio-revolution has been the changes it has made to the nature of the plant breeding community and in particular to the concept of a 'plant breeder'. Plant breeding is no longer conducted by a dedicated group but is now wholly pluralistic. A side effect of this growth is that it is increasingly difficult to justify the existence of a right one of the main purposes of which is to foster and protect a specific sector where that sector is both increasingly diverse and privately owned. A little noted response to this has been the decreased use of the term 'plant *breeders'* right'[49] when referring to the

---

[49] For example, the UK Report which led to the introduction of the Plant Varieties and Seeds Act 1964 was entitled 'Plant Breeders' Rights Report of the Committee on Transactions in Seeds' (Cmnd 1092, HMSO, 1960), commonly known as 'The Engholm Report' after its Chair.

system of protection, and increased use of the term 'plant *variety* right',[50] the breeders' right simply being the form of right granted under that system.[51] What this change does is to direct attention away from granting rights to a specific industry and instead it focuses on protecting a particular product which, irrespective of who produced it, is, in itself and of itself, of value and in need of protection. This change is not merely a semantic one, but has great implications for the right itself.

As chapter 3 will discuss, plant variety rights were introduced to reward plant breeders for the time and effort involved in breeding new plant varieties because it was important to provide farmers with the best possible agricultural plant material. The object was not to protect inventive activity as such mainly because it was, at the time the right was introduced, difficult to demonstrate that a traditional breeding programme was inventive. It was, therefore, predominantly an *agricultural* right granted to breeders in order to encourage the development of beneficial new crops. The distinction between the function of an industrial property right, and patents in particular, and the agricultural right is apparent when a simple comparison of the two rights is made (discussed further below).[52]

It can take between 10 and 15 years to breed a new variety which both contains the desired traits, and breeds true following repeated propagation. Once produced, a non F1 hybrid variety (that is, a variety which can replicate as opposed to one which is sterile) was (and is) relatively easy to reproduce. As the economic importance of the agricultural industry grew, so too did the calls for the results of plant breeding programmes to be protected in the same way as the results of other types of scientific research.[53] For a number of reasons the patent system was not seen as conducive to either promoting the research or recognising the type of scientific endeavour involved,[54] and the decision was taken to introduce a right specifically designed with the needs of an individual sector in mind.

The decision to introduce a limited monopoly right over agricultural crops was not universally approved, even within the plant breeding industry itself. Many breeders felt that plant material should be freely available to those who could

---

[50] For example, the Council Regulation on Community Plant *Variety* Rights.

[51] There are notable exceptions to this trend—within the EU the emphasis on the right being a breeders' right is most noticeable in the Netherlands, for example, and, at the international level, the same is true in Australia.

[52] For a further discussion of this see Llewelyn, in Cottier and Mavroidis (eds), *Which Rules in World Trade Law: Patents or Plant Variety Rights in Intellectual Property: Trade, Competition and Sustainable Development*, vol 3, World Trade Forum (University of Michigan Press, 2002) 303.

[53] See 'International Conference for the Protection of New Plant Products' [1961] *Industrial Property Quarterly* 104; 'International Conference for the Protection of New Plant Products' [1962] *Industrial Property Quarterly* 5; Laclaviere, 'The Convention of Paris of December 2, 1961 for the Protection of new Varieties of Plants and the International Union for the Protection of New Varieties of Plants' [1965] *Industrial Property Quarterly* 224.

[54] The arguments put forward were that it would be difficult to demonstrate that either plant material or plant breeding practices were novel or inventive and that whilst the results were clearly capable of industrial application, it would not be in the public interest to allow a patent. It was also accepted that it would be difficult for plant material to meet the disclosure requirement.

make use of it for the development of other socially valuable crops. The persuasive justification for the right was to secure and promote a nationally important industry and not merely to provide rights over plant material. The introduction of the system of *sui generis* protection was, therefore, intended to underline that that which was being rewarded was the time and effort put in by breeders to produce valuable new crops. A key factor in the decision to introduce this right was that during the 1940s and 1950s there was an increased recognition of the social and economic value of the agricultural industries, and this industrial importance, which included recognising the value of the work of the breeders who provided the basic material for use by farmers, had to be protected. The rationale for the right was, very specifically, to recognise and reward the investment put into the production of new plant varieties by a specific category of scientists—hence it was referred to as a *breeders'* right. The determination of a form of protection suitable for the *type* of material concerned was, it is argued, a secondary consideration which naturally followed from the need to foster a specific, nationally important, sector. The fact that at this time the majority of plant breeding activity took place within the public sector is also relevant to this argument.

As the property, and market, value of plant material increased so the emphasis on the provision of a right for *breeders* correspondingly decreased. In addition, the growth in private plant breeding operation (not to mention the increased plant breeding activity of multi-national companies) has meant that it is less easy to categorise the right as being for the benefit of a discreet industry. What appears to be happening is an increasing emphasis on providing protection for the thing bred—in other words protecting the value of the plants themselves—and less on providing a form of protection specifically for plant breeders. The gradual removal of the term 'breeders' right' from references to the right, and the trend of simply referring to the right as a 'variety' right reflects a recognition of the economic value of the plant material protected.[55] In what could be said to be a reversal of emphasis, the issue now is not primarily on protecting a specific group but on protecting a specific type of valuable material irrespective of the sector involved in its production.[56] This is reiterated by the leading organisation representing the views of the seed trade and plant breeders, the International Seed Federation (discussed further below), which has stated that the scientific plant breeding based on new genetic knowledge and new technologies

> has rendered the development of new cultivars much more efficient than in the past leading to the emergence of a new category of people, professional plant breeders. Those plant breeders have created and are still creating new cultivars used by an

---

[55] A similar change can be seen in the change from another *sui generis* right which has seen a move from being termed a 'performer's right' to a 'right in performances'.

[56] A key factor was the growth in private plant breeding institutions. In the 1950s the sector was mainly publicly funded and there was a strong public interest in protecting it. With the growth in private plant breeding initiatives, the emphasis was arguably less on encouraging involvement in plant breeding but on protecting the valuable commercial assets resulting from breeding programmes.

increasing number of farmers world-wide. The new cultivars, integrating more and more genetic variability together with improved cultural practice, have resulted in a dramatic increase in food and fibre production, thus allowing feeding the growing world population whilst preserving marginal areas and wild habitats . . . the consequence of that necessary evolution is that plant breeding is no longer a by-product of agriculture, but a separate activity as such.[57]

What the Federation does not mention (but which must also be taken into account when assessing plant intellectual property provision) is that plant breeding is no longer primarily concerned with agriculture (although this is still its main area) and that it has expanded to include other uses of plant material for medicinal as well as cultural purposes.

As a number of key players in the plant breeding sector are closely involved with other forms of modern biotechnologies, it can be difficult to see why the plant breeding industry should be singled out from other areas of bioscience.[58] The change in emphasis is important as it could be said to result in a modification of the function of the right (discussed below). The issue now is not merely whether the protection provided is suitable for the sector concerned, but whether it is appropriate for the type of material involved. It is accepted this is a subtle shift in emphasis, but it is possibly one reason for the survival of plant variety rights. In other words, the right can be justified on the grounds that it is a more appropriate form of protection than patents for plant material. The question of whether it is suitable for what is an increasingly privately funded industry is almost a corollary to this. This reversal is perhaps not surprising given that a public interest justification in providing sector-specific protection is becoming more difficult to defend.

The importance of this subtle distinction is that an increased focus on the *subject matter* for protection as opposed to those who could benefit from that protection has meant that it is arguable that the policy and practice is losing sight of the original purpose of the right, namely to protect a vital economic and social sector.[59] The two issues which this in turn raises are a) whether the interests of plant breeders are still met by the right and b) if it is any longer either necessary or appropriate to protect the interests of a specific sector as opposed to protecting a specific type of subject matter. These issues will be discussed in the latter chapters of this book.

---

[57] 'Position Paper on Farm Saved Seed' (2002) at www.worldseed.org.

[58] This is the underlying ethos behind Art 27 of TRIPs. This requires firstly that patent protection must be available for all fields of technology (Art 27(1)) and then reinforces the need for protection (albeit not necessary by a patent) in respect of plant varieties in Art 27(3)(b). The explicit, and therefore primary, obligation is to provide protection for plant varieties; it is not to provide support for those breeding the varieties even though this is the hoped-for inevitable outcome of providing protection.

[59] For a further discussion of various economic factors which underpin the value in plants see Busch *et al*, *Plants, Power and Profit* (Blackwell Publishers, 1991) (although this book is years old the principles remain apposite in 2006) and Koo, Nottenberg and Parde, 'Intellectual Property Enhanced: Plants and Intellectual Property: An International Appraisal' (2004) 306 (5700) *Science* 1295–1297, 19 November 2004.

With regard to the right itself, for the purposes of this book we will use the term 'plant variety rights'. The next question, therefore, is whether it is appropriate to treat both patents and plant variety rights as intellectual property rights. Article 27(3)(b) indicates why this is a relevant question to ask.

When looking at the obligation to provide protection for plant varieties contained in Article 27(3)(b) of the TRIPs Agreement, and the juxtapositions of the requirement to provide either or both patents and *sui generis* protection, it would be easy to jump to the conclusion that the *sui generis* system is, like patents, a member of the intellectual property family. Caution needs to be exercised before making such an assumption because it is by no means clear that a plant variety right is a form of intellectual property right. If it is agreed that it is a member of the family (and modern convention would appear to indicate that it now is) then a second check must be applied—namely should that right be automatically connected with (and assessed against) the patent law side of the family.

## IV.  ARE BOTH INTELLECTUAL PROPERTY RIGHTS?

Clearly, patents are a form of intellectual property right. However it is questionable whether plant variety rights can or should be regarded as the same.

As previously mentioned, it is increasingly common to refer to plant variety rights as a member of the intellectual property law family. Indeed, both the UPOV system (post 1991) and Regulation (EC) No 2100/94[60] specifically describe the rights as such.[61] Notwithstanding these specific references, the actual classification of the right is more complicated than this. In contrast to the 1991 Act, neither the 1961 nor 1978 UPOV Acts referred to the right as being an intellectual property right and this is significant, for whilst the right clearly does have one foot in the intellectual property law family camp (in the sense that it takes the form of a private property right which serves to give the holder control over certain uses of the protected material), the right also has a foot firmly within the territory of plant breeding, and agriculture in particular. It is these two facets which have had the greatest impact on the way in which the right operates in practice. However, this dual footing has not, to date, proved particularly problematic (although arguably there has been some tension as to how the right should evolve from the perspective of non-agricultural plant breeding). However, as both sets of rights are increasingly used to protect plant material then it is possible to envisage a situation arising where the potentially ambiguous status of the right could cause problems.

The debate which took place in the 1970s and 1980s over how effectively and appropriately to protect plant material had the effect of placing plant variety

---

[60] Art 1 states that 'A system of Community plant variety rights is hereby established as the sole and exclusive form of Community *industrial property rights* for plant varieties' (emphasis added).

[61] See the Mission Statement of the UPOV Union (www.upov.org) and Art 1 of the Regulation on Community Plant Variety Rights.

rights under the intellectual property law microscope, with the consequence that it has been compared with these rights, and with patents in particular. For some the comparison was not a favourable one, and led to calls for plant variety rights to be either abolished or significantly revised. The latter route was chosen and along with it the decision to label the right an intellectual property right. This branding of the right is easy to understand. Not only does it have the effect of securing the right alongside patents, trade marks and copyright, thereby validating its use as an alternative to patent protection, but it also makes it more difficult to ignore or reject the right on the basis that it is not a fully paid-up member of the family. This magnification of the intellectual property aspect of the right has meant that there is a tendency to forget the other aspect to the right and yet, arguably it was this which led to the right being introduced in the first place. The ambiguous nature of the right becomes clear when looking at the background to the right and also at the way in which it is referred to in texts on intellectual property rights.

As already mentioned, the Paris Convention on the Protection of Industrial Property 1883 applies to patent law but it does not necessarily apply to plant variety rights. Indeed, when the discussions were held in the 1940s and 1950s as to how best to protect plant varieties, one of the issues for consideration was whether protection should be under the Paris Convention or not. The decision was to keep the protection of plant varieties separate from the protection of other types of scientific endeavour and this was underlined by the inclusion of a dual protection prohibition within the 1961 (and 1978) UPOV Acts which stated that a member states cannot provide both patent and plant variety protection for the same genus or species. Some patent systems (such as the EPC) mirrored this prohibition with an equally explicit exclusion of plant varieties.

As will be discussed below, 'dual protection prohibition' within the UPOV Convention 1961 was in part intended to allow member states the choice as to which route to follow (such choice being removed from European members of UPOV as a result of Article 53(b) of the EPC). In addition, the discussions which led up to the creation of the UPOV Convention involved a gamut of different organisations, including the Association Internationales Sectionneurs pour la Protection des Obtentions Vegetales (ASSINSEL), the International Association for the Protection of Industrial Property (AIPPI), the International Community of Breeders Asexually Reproduced and Ornamental Fruit Trees Varieties (CIO-PORA), the International Federation of the Seed Trade (FIS), the International Bureau for the Protection of Intellectual Property Law (BIRPI) and the Food and Agricultural Organisation of the United Nations (FAO).[62] The resulting Convention therefore sought to balance the differing needs of the various interested parties, bearing in mind that whilst there was strong support for proper protection for plant breeders, not all were convinced that this should be

---

[62] As will be seen later many of these organisations continue to play a vital role in the protection of plant material.

on the basis of existing forms of protection. As the right was intended to safeguard the interests of breeders as both producers and users of protected material it was decided that they would be the best gatekeepers of the right. Hence,
both the shaping of the right and its subsequent administration was placed into
the hands of the scientists. Because of this, the right was, for a long time, seen as
primarily an agricultural right and not a mainstream member of the intellectual
property family.

An example of the ambiguity surrounding the right can be seen in the WIPO
handbook. This does not include plant variety protection within its chapter on
the forms of intellectual property protection, (although patents, copyright and
neighbouring rights, trade marks, industrial designs, geographical indications,
and protection against unfair competition are included).[63] However, the chapter on international treaties and conventions on intellectual property does
include a section on the International Convention for the Protection of New
Varieties of Plants. It is perhaps pertinent to note at this juncture that one reason why the WIPO might take this approach is because it believes that activity
within 'plant biotechnology evokes first and foremost the patent system',[64] and
therefore the broader relevance of the plant variety rights system as anything
another than a niche right has not been addressed.

The inclusion of plant variety protection in a section entitled 'International
Treaties or Conventions on *Intellectual Property*' without any mention made of
plant variety rights as a *form* of intellectual property protection underlines the
apparently imprecise status of the right.[65] It is not a form of intellectual property right for the purposes of one chapter but it is for the purposes of another.
This confused status of the right is further enhanced by the fact that the UPOV
Office is based within the same building as the WIPO, making it seem, for the
uninitiated, as if UPOV rights are a form of intellectual property. For some, this
ambiguity is caused by the 'vagaries of history, which led to the creation of
UPOV as an independent organization next to the World Intellectual Property
Organization (WIPO)'.[66] These vagaries mean that 'plant variety protection is

---

[63] The same can be seen in *Introduction to Intellectual Property Theory and Practice* (World
Intellectual Property Organisation, Kluwer Law International, 1997).

[64] Comments made by the Assistant Director General of the WIPO at a Symposium organised by
both the WIPO and UPOV in October 2003 Gurry, *Plant Biotechnology Developments in the
International Framework*, Proceedings of the WIPO–UPOV Symposium on Intellectual Property
Rights in Plant Biotechnology (October 2003).

[65] This problem over the status of plant variety protection is evidenced elsewhere. In the UK, for
example, textbooks on intellectual property protection frequently omit any discussion of plant variety protection. Even the definitive work on intellectual property, Cornish, *Intellectual Property*,
above n 32, only alludes to plant varieties rights within the main body of the book (paras 5–70 and
5–83, which discuss Art 53(b) EPC), with the discussion of the law relating to plant variety rights
relegated to Appendix 3. This is true even within the most recent edition of the text (the 5th), which
does not discuss plant variety rights even within its new chapter, 'Intellectual Property and
Biotechnology' (ch 20). The right is clearly not seen as an industrial/intellectual property right.

[66] Heitz, *Intellectual Property Rights and Plant Variety Protection* (paper given in 2001) at
www.upov.int.

rarely mentioned in the lists of intellectual property categories,' but that should not detract from the fact that '[i]t is, nevertheless, a form of industrial property.' Another reason for the relegation of plant variety rights to an apparent after-thought in the minds of the WIPO is the view that 'plant biotechnology evokes first and foremost the patent system.'[67] The issue for the WIPO is not what form of protection should be available for plant innovations but rather whether, given the 'technology neutral evolution of the patent system, does the area of plant biotechnology raise any special questions that require specific attention and a deviation from the general rule of neutrality', the absence of any specific ascription of the right to the industrial property family therefore having no bear-ing on whether the right should be regarded as part of that family or not—its existence in itself and of itself indicates membership. In this the WIPO approach appears to be supported by the 1967 Stockholm Convention which established it, Article 2(viii) of which provides that:

> intellectual property shall include rights relating to:—literary, artistic and scientific works—performances of performing artists, phonograms and broadcasts—inventions in all fields of human endeavor—scientific discoveries—industrial designs—trade-marks, service marks and commercial names and designations—protection against unfair competition, and all other rights resulting from intellectual activity in the indus-trial, scientific, literary or artistic fields.

However, notwithstanding the WIPO stance this does not mean that the matter is settled and this continuing lack of clarity can be seen in the TRIPS Agreement. The Agreement, the stated aim of which is to 'promote effective and adequate protection of intellectual property rights',[68] makes no reference to plant variety rights *per se* implying therefore that they are not intellectual property rights for its purposes. However, mention is made of an obligation to provide protection for plant varieties within Article 27(3)(b). It is by no means clear if this obliga-tion means the right has to be an intellectual property right which accords with other provisions of the TRIPs Agreement or if could be another form of right, for example based entirely on agricultural considerations (this will be discussed in chapter 2).

There is additional evidence that the right cannot be solely regarded as an intellectual property right. Responsibility for administering local plant variety rights systems is principally a matter for agricultural departments (which in turn work closely with the appropriate scientific bodies). In the case of Regulation (EC) No 2100/94 the task of drafting and implementing the new legislation was given to the Agricultural Directorate within the European Commission. This can be contrasted with the patent system where responsibility for all aspects of the right invariably lies with governments' trade and industry depart-ments. There is, therefore, an argument for saying that, even if the right has

---

[67] Gurry, 'Plant Biotechnology Developments in the International Framework', above n 64.
[68] Preamble to the Agreement.

increasingly come to bear some of the characteristics of an intellectual property right (such as the provision of a private property right, it also has other antecedents which should be taken into account when affiliating the right. In terms of classifying the rights over plant material, it might, therefore, be more apt to talk simply about *rights* over plant material as opposed to *intellectual* property rights.

The second issue which arises out of the classification of plant variety rights as an intellectual property right is that this gives the impression that the rights either adhere, or are equivalent, to other intellectual property rights. As the discussion over plant protection invariably focuses on a comparison between plant variety rights and patent protection, it is unsurprising that the latter should be used as the main point of comparison for the former.

This comparison of the two systems in turn can give the impression that they are the same type of right, with the same justifications and presumptions. As will be seen, there are significant differences between the two systems and these differences go to the heart of what each is seeking to achieve and therefore their operation in practice. In assessing the relative values of each right it is important to take these differences into account and not to treat the rights as having the same rationales.

There are close parallels between the post-1991 UPOV-style of plant variety protection and patent law. Both provide private property rights which allow the holder to prevent others from using the protected material (commercially or otherwise) without permission. However, there are key points of departure, most notably the restrictions on what can be protected and the limitations to the right granted which are contained in plant variety rights. There are, for example, certain activities which the UPOV system does not consider should be up to the rights holder to control—these include the use of the protected variety in commercial breeding programmes and the ability of farmers to retain seed from one year to the next. When these elements are taken into account, then the right granted looks closer to copyright[69] than the notion of protection enshrined within patent law. Indeed, it has been argued that the plant variety rights system is, in common with much that it protects, a hybrid.[70] It is true that the post-1991 UPOV type of plant variety right is much closer to a patent than previously was the case (and indeed it is increasingly difficult to draw hard and fast lines

---

[69] In very basic terms this provides a right against copying, the right attaching only to the thing created, with minimal rights granted over the uses of substantial parts of the copyright protected work. Minimal variations on the copyright protected work can be sufficient to give rise to a wholly new work the exploitation of which may not be dependent on the authorisation of the original 'author'. There are also far more numerous limitations to the right granted.

[70] Reichman, 'Legal Hybrids Between the Patent and Copyright Paradigms' (1994) 94 *Columbia Law Review* 2432.

[71] For example, it has been assumed that the patent system is concerned only with the protection of plant inventions which result from genetic engineering or biotechnological research, with the results of conventional plant research being unprotectable. However, the reality is that the patent system can be used to protect both conventionally bred plants and breeding processes which produce those plants, the *only* barriers to protection being a) the need to meet the threshold for

between the type of material which is protected under each right[71]) but the right still retains those features drawn from elsewhere. The issue is whether those features should be invoked along intellectual property law lines (and patent practices in particular) which tend to place the emphasis on the rights of holder or if they are to be applied according to other considerations such as the needs of other breeders and end users. The move to describing the right as an intellectual property right not only means that there is cause for a direct comparison between the two rights, but also that it could be increasingly difficult to justify a wide-ranging application of the public interest limitations to the right. The reason for this is that the equivalent limitations in patent law serve only a narrow purpose, and a similar approach might now be expected within plant variety rights.

Despite these concerns, for the purposes of ease and conformity with other commentators, we shall use the term 'plant intellectual property rights'—but it must be stressed that the distinction drawn above between patent and plant variety rights is vital in understanding the full implications of the obligation set down in the TRIPs Agreement and also in analysing European provision.

## Contrasting the Rights

When the patent system is analysed it will be seen that its primary function is the protection of the interests of each individual patent holder. This is clear from the overarching presumption of patentability and the jurisprudence which has evolved around the substantive law. The effect of this is that any limitations or exclusions are given a restricted application.

In plant variety rights, whilst the interests of the individual breeder are clearly of importance, other considerations are regarded as fundamental to the system itself. This can be seen in the UPOV mission statement, which says that its object is '[to] provide and promote an effective system of plant variety protection, with the aim of encouraging the development of new varieties of plants, *for the benefit of society*' (emphasis added), and the substantive law itself expressly states that restrictions on the exercise of the right may be imposed when it is in the public interest.[72] On this basis it would be easy to draw, a superficial substantive distinction between the two rights as there is no exact equivalent statement in patent law.[73] However, this would be a disingenuous distinction to draw for whilst the patent system might not contain any overt reference to providing a public benefit it is generally held to have a public benefit element, as 'a reward to inventors who have contributed to the public good',[74] although the

---

protection and b) the exclusion of essentially biological processes, this latter being determined by reference to the extent of human intervention. This will be discussed further in ch 5.

[72] For example Art 17 UPOV and Art 29 CPVR.

[73] Unless one holds that the bar on the granting of patents over inventions for reasons of morality or *ordre public* is an equivalent—this will be discussed in ch 6.

[74] White, 'Gene and Compound per se Claims', above n 33.

precise form of that benefit is the subject of some debate.[75] What must be recognised is that, in patent law, the principle of public benefit is upheld by protecting the interests of each individual patent holder whilst in plant variety rights the principle encompasses protecting external interests as well as those of the holder of the right. This is of great importance when looking at the form of each right and in particular at limitations provided over each right.

It is important to bear these functional distinctions in mind when looking at the evolution of each right. The two systems are becoming increasingly inter-related and in an era of convergence it would be easy to ascribe the same objectives to both systems. This is important in respect of such matters as the presumption of protectability, the inviolability of the rights of the holder and especially use of protected material for research purposes and the role of compulsory licensing.

Because of this convergence it has become increasingly difficult to demonstrate clear blue water, either in functional or practical terms, between them. It is common for those discussing intellectual property rights and the protection of plant material to refer to patents and plant variety rights in the same breath as if they belong to the same family of protection. The consequence of this has been to imply that the plant variety rights system is a form of intellectual property protection with the same objectives and rationale as patent law. This makes it is easier to think of the right as an alternative to patents, the necessity for which is explicable by reference to the specific subject matter. It is worth noting, however, that at no time has it been formally agreed that plant variety rights should now be regarded as a member of the intellectual property family and it is likely that if the matter were to be debated, strong arguments would be presented by both sides as to why it should/should not be regarded as either an industrial or intellectual property right.[76] The reasons why this has been allowed to evolve without objection are two-fold.

Firstly, as discussed above, the plant variety right has been significantly amended following the revision of the UPOV Convention in 1991. In many respects the type of right now granted under plant variety rights is the same as that provided by a patent.

Secondly, as will be discussed in the next chapter, Article 27(3(b) of the TRIPs Agreement requires member states to provide either patent and/or *sui generis* protection for plant varieties. The Article does not apparently differentiate between the types of right and does not address the fact whilst patent protection is an intellectual property right and governed by the TRIPs Agreement, the other type of right is not and therefore, arguably, it is not governed by TRIPs.[77] The

---

[75] See, eg, in general, Drahos, *A Philosophy of Intellectual Property*, above n 12; and Sherman and Bently, *The Making of Modern Intellectual Property Law*, above n 31, pp 313–15.

[76] See Reichman, 'Legal Hybrids Between the Patent and Copyright Paradigms', above n 70.

[77] That TRIPs does not apply to UPOV-style plant variety rights is supported by the fact that whilst the Agreement refers to a host of international Conventions on industrial/intellectual property it makes no mention any of the UPOV Acts.

wording of Article 27(3)(b) provides an impression that the right(s) to be provided by the member state have the same basis and standing in law and, by extension and inference, that they are both intellectual property rights.

The critical question is whether, despite the tendency to refer to both rights within the same breath and notwithstanding the statement in Regulation (EC) No 2100/94, plant variety rights and patents can be regarded as essentially the same or if they are in fact very different legal animals.

The first point which has to be made is that the absolute monopoly provided by the grant of a patent is traditionally justified on the basis that the inventor has achieved something which colleagues working in the same area would not have thought of doing. The high threshold for protection therefore justifies the correspondingly strong protection and also the restrictive interpretation given to the limitations to that right. Whilst some commentators dispute whether the modern patent system does, in practice, continue to merit this traditional justification, there is nonetheless widespread resistance within the intellectual property community to sanctioning the existence of the patent system on commercial grounds alone. In contrast, the plant varieties rights system is firmly predicated on commercial grounds. As a result the system reflects the fact that, by sanctioning the grant of a right to monopolise commercialisation, such rights should be subject to clearly defined limitations.

The second point of contrast between the two rights relates to the notion of inventiveness. In patent law, it is necessary to show that another skilled in the relevant art would not have thought of engaging in the inventive activity which led to the production of the claimed invention. In order to determine whether the activity leading up to the production of the invention would have been obvious to another skilled in the art[78] it is necessary to demonstrate (or disclose) the steps taken in arriving at the invention. Disclosure is ensured if the specification describes what was known before and demonstrates why what the inventor did was not an obvious step forward given what had been known before. What the patent protects is the novel and inventive technical teaching disclosed in the patent specification.

In contrast, the plant variety rights system is not intended to protect non-obvious results. Most plant breeding activity involves trying the obvious—if breeders were required to show that what they had done would not be obvious to a person skilled in the art then few if any rights would be granted. The rationale for the grant of a plant variety right is therefore not to protect inventiveness. There is no need for the breeder to disclose information about how the variety was developed as s/he does not have to prove that the decision to pursue a particular line of research was unobvious. The key rationale for the grant of a plant variety right is the protection of the time invested in producing a new variety which is distinct from others of the same species, and which, over time, remains uniform and stable following reproduction. The corollary of this is that

---

[78] This concept will be explained more in ch 4.

the right granted is generally less extensive than that granted under patent law where inventiveness has to be demonstrated. The function, to protect the time invested in bringing a distinct, stable and uniform variety to the market, is further reflected in the fact that plant variety rights are available over discoveries.[79] This is in stark contrast to the patent system which, in Europe at least, explicitly excludes discoveries from protection. A further point, underlining the objective to foster a sector as a whole rather than individual interests within it, is that the use of protected plant varieties in commercial breeding programmes is not prohibited, whereas such use would be an infringing act under patent law.

Thirdly, plant variety rights are generally administered by governmental agencies responsible for agricultural matters and not by offices concerned with trade and industry, as is the practice with patents. This ensures that the operation of the right conforms with any overarching agricultural policy. This is embodied in the derogations, which are intended to ensure that the protection granted does not restrict ongoing research or interfere with the legitimate interests of the wider agricultural community. As will be discussed in subsequent chapters, the extent of these derogations has changed in recent years. The effect of these changes, however, differs according to whether the right is intended to operate according to the usual principles underpinning intellectual property rights.

A further point of contrast is the fact that, unlike in patent law where a paper assessment determines whether an invention is patentable, a plant variety is subjected to two years of practical trials before the right is granted. These serve to show whether or not the variety is actually distinct, uniform and stable, as opposed to simply relying on a written description provided by the breeder. The trials are undertaken by the granting offices in conjunction with plant research institutes, such as the UK's National Institute of Agricultural Botany (NIAB). A breeder may be requested to provide the reproductive material of the variety for retesting at any time during the period of grant to verify that it is still distinct, uniform and stable.

In addition, because of the inventive step and novelty requirements, patent protection will invariably only be available over plant material which has been produced using biotechnological processes—the use of essentially biological or traditional breeding processes not being sufficiently inventive to meet the threshold for protection. Plant variety rights, however, are available over any plant variety *howsoever* produced. Protection is available for plant varieties which have been discovered or bred using traditional methods such as the use of cotton buds to transfer pollen as well as for those which have been bred using the most sophisticated man-devised gene transfer devices. The ambit of protectable material is, arguably, wider than that under patent law. There is a

---

[79] Mere discovery of a variety is not sufficient to support the grant of a plant variety right; the applicant has to demonstrate that the variety breeds in a uniform and stable fashion over repeated reproduction cycles. A wholly naturally occurring plant grouping is unlikely to do this as it will naturally sport or mutate. These tendencies are controlled via plant breeding programmes.

caveat to this and this is that, in European patent law at least, the level of intervention by man necessary to turn the act of creation from one which is essentially governed by nature to one generated by man would now appear to be minimal. This does not lessen the need to show that the act itself gave rise to a novel and inventive result, but it does provide another indication of the continual reduction of the barriers to patentability. This will be discussed in more detail in chapter 5.

A potential flashpoint for future tension lies in what is protected once a right is granted. Both patents and plant variety rights draw a distinction between that which can be the subject matter of an application for a right and that which is protected by the right once granted. In respect of the subject matter of an application, protection may be accorded to those inventions or plant varieties which demonstrate that the requisite threshold has been met. However, once protection is granted a subtle change takes place and the right extends to material which would not, in itself, be capable of attracting protection under that right.

For example, in plant variety rights each of the genes which give rise to the distinct characteristics making up a plant variety would not be regarded as a plant grouping and therefore protection could not be sought for them. However, the right specifically states that constituent elements (which include the plant genes) of a variety are protected by the right once granted (as is material harvested from that variety, which again is unlikely to be defined as a plant grouping).[80] In patent law, plant varieties are generally not patentable, but where a patent relates to a process and that process has been used to produce the plant variety or where a patented gene has been placed into a variety, then the patent over that process or gene is held to extend to any material, including a plant variety, produced by that process or within which that gene is expressed.

There is, therefore, a clear distinction between that which can attract protection, for which a specific application for protection must be made, and that which can be protected, which merely needs to fall within the ambit of the protection granted. This will be discussed in more detail in later chapters.

## Reconciling the Rights[81]

One final point, which is important when looking at European plant protection provision, is that whilst each of the rights will be discussed separately they

---

[80] An extremely interesting discussion of this dichotomy can be found in Funder, *Biology, Information and Property: The Legal Appropriation of Plant Biotechnology* (DPhil, Oxford, 2001); see also Funder, 'Rethinking Patents for Plant Innovations' (1999) 11 *European Intellectual Property Review* 551.

[81] The question of whether the rights can be reconciled has existed since a) the introduction of the two systems of protection in the US following the adoption of the Plant Protection Act in 1970 and b) the increased use of patent protection to protect plant products: see, for example, Adler, 'Can Patents Coexist with Breeders' Rights? Developments in US and International Biotechnology Law' (1986) 17(2) *IIC* 195.

should not be treated as independent of each other. As will be shown in chapters 3 and 5, both the UPOV system of plant variety rights and the European Patent Convention resulted from discussions which involved the same set of individuals and organisations. Because of this, the principles upon which one system is based can only by fully understood if set against the other. This is most obvious in provisions such as the old 'dual protection prohibition' within UPOV and the exclusion of plant varieties in the European Patent Convention but is also important when looking at the exclusions and limitations to the rights granted. This inter-relationship is often ignored when looking at plant protection. The reasons for this are unclear but it gives rise to a picture of, at best, enforced co-existence and, at worst, actual conflict. In reality the two systems were intended to fulfil differing functions and each was designed to ensure that those functions could be fully realised. The rationale behind the UPOV Convention in 1961 was to introduce protection for agricultural crops whilst at the same time promoting these crops to both farmers and breeders for use on farms and in breeding programmes by limiting the right to commercial production of the reproductive material of the variety protected. In contrast, the provisions of the EPC built on existing patent practices which were increasingly predicated on providing strong, unfettered, protection for those who could meet the threshold for protection. Its function was primarily to consolidate these practices and to remove any ambiguities as to what could be protected—in particular, the Convention sought to remove the problems which had been encountered in national patent laws where protection was restricted to 'manufactures'. The removal of this term, and the emphasis not on the type of material which could be protected by a patent but rather on the granting criteria to be met before a grant could took place, meant that patent protection was no longer confined to mechanical types of innovation.

One reason why there has been some debate as to the ability of the two rights to co-exist is because of a misunderstanding as to the nature of one of the provisions within the original UPOV Convention—the so-called 'dual protection prohibition' contained within Article 2(1) of both the 1961 and 1978 Acts. Before exploring the issue of the rights themselves it is important to explode the myth surrounding this provision.

The Dual Protection Prohibition

As will be discussed further later in the book, throughout all the discussions within Europe which led up to the introduction of both the EPC and UPOV, concerns were expressed as to whether it would be appropriate to protect plant material under patent law. Both sets of discussions agreed that it would not and that plant varieties (at that time—the 1950s—varieties were the only plant constructs thought to be sufficiently designed by man to justify the grant of a private property right) would be better protected under a *sui generis* system designed specifically for that purpose. In particular, such a *sui generis* system could be constructed to ensure that the rights granted reflected certain over-arching public interest elements, for example including a right for other breeders to use protected varieties in commercial breeding programmes with the results of that programme being free from any rights granted over varieties used in that programme.

However, the systems diverged in terms of the absoluteness that plant varieties could only be protected under the *sui generis* system. The EPC introduced a total ban on protection through Article 53(b) because the draftsmen felt member states should be directed to using the plant variety rights system. The result was that no option was provided to enable the use of the patent system.[82] The UPOV system, however, provided its member states with a choice. Article 2(1) stated that member states could not provide protection for the same genus or species using patents and plant variety rights, where both rights accorded with the provisions of the UPOV Convention. It is the latter half of the provision which is crucial to understanding its effect. It merely prohibited the use of both rights where both rights accorded to the provisions of the UPOV Convention, namely used distinctiveness, uniformity and stability (DUS) as the criteria for grant and contained the same limitations to that right. If a member state provided protection under a system which did not conform to the UPOV provisions, for example ordinary patent law, then this was not, in fact, prohibited. In other words, the UPOV system never prevented the availability of patent protection for plant varieties. However, because of the juxtaposition of the introduction of the two new Conventions, and the perception that the two were intended to mirror each other in terms of the obligation regarding the protection of plant varieties, this perception grew that plant inventions were *only* protectable if they fell within the scope of protectable material in UPOV. This perception was exacerbated by the inability, at that time, of plant material to meet the patent law threshold for protection. For those who regard patent protection as the ultimate right, as well as those sceptical about the value of plant variety rights, this exclusion is an anathema, and the blame for the lack of patent protection is laid firmly at the door of the plant variety rights system.[83]

This misconception has dogged the plant variety rights system since the 1970s (and intellectual property law literature during the 1970s and 1980s is peppered with views such as of plant variety rights as an 'outmoded impediment'[84] and of

---

[82] As will be seen in ch 5, because of the manner in which the EPC came into operation this did not mean that member states were necessarily prevented from granting patents over plants or animals.

[83] This will be discussed in more detail in chs 3 and 5.

[84] Cornish, *Intellectual Property: Patents Copyright Trade Marks and Allied Rights*, 2nd edn, (Sweet & Maxwell, 1989) 148, paras 5–55. Other commentators writing in the mid-to-late 1980s also 'blamed' the plant variety rights system for denying a more expansive application of patent protection but, in our view, none encapsulated this generally held view (in patent law circles at least) as succinctly as Cornish nor did they so clearly show the potential threat to the plant variety rights system or the need also to rethink the patent law provision. We shall be using the Cornish quote throughout this book as short-hand for the prevailing views of that time and as an indicator of the flashpoint of opinion which underlined the pressure need for change but it is important to see this

the exclusion within the EPC being a 'sacrifice'[85]). These criticisms appear to be primarily directed at the differences in the strength of right granted and the impact on investment-intensive companies if only limited protection were available for the results of their plant research.[86] Such views appear to overlook the common heritage of the two systems. That the two systems should be thought unconnected with each other is perhaps not surprising given that once the two systems were established, with their diversity of granting criteria and protectable subject matter, there was no reason for them to interact. Indeed, the fact that there were separate granting offices, different personnel (with the plant variety rights system placing more emphasis on scientific rather than legal expertise) and mechanisms for litigating the rights has only served to emphasise the separation between the two. However, as the discussions relating to recent developments in both European patent law and UPOV will show, the original intention to provide a synergy between the two systems has not been wholly lost. In recent years both the European Patent Office and those charged with overseeing the revision of UPOV in 1991 (which saw the removal of the 'dual protection prohibition'[87]) have referred to the fact that the original intention behind the two systems was that they should co-exist—the problem has been that with the advent of genetic engineering and the increased commercial value of plant innovations the extent to which that co-existence is mutually supportive can be brought into question. In part this is due to the very different nature of those involved in both rights (this is discussed further below), but it is also due to an increased failing to recognise the very different rationales which lie behind the two rights and the need either to continue to support the differences or to explain why they no longer serve a relevant purpose. This problem is illustrated by the difficulties encountered by the European Commission when it

quote as indicative rather than individual. One of the reasons why there was such an anti-plant variety right view was the fact that before the 1980s little was known about the system. There was very little discussion of the rights within either intellectual property circles (other than within UPOV) or the academic literature. Those who did discuss the right tended to be versed in patent law and it could be argued that this coloured their perception of plant variety rights.

This is discussed further in chs 3 and 5.

[85] Straus, 'Genetic Engineering and Industrial Property' (1986) 11 *Industrial Property* 454.

[86] This was not the only criticism levelled at plant variety rights—there were others, generally speaking from outside Europe, who felt that plant variety rights were *too* strong and gave too much control to those who held them. The best example of this is Mooney, *Seeds of the Earth* (Mutual Press, 1979). The book argued that the use of plant breeders' rights was having the effect of reducing landraces, and key agricultural crops were being monopolised by a few multinationals to the disadvantage of the world's poorest. In order to counter this, the use of plant breeders' rights should be halted. Mooney's work was instrumental in rallying support for conservation which, eventually, led to the introduction of the CBD. His views were contested by various plant breeding organisations. For example, ASSINSEL published its response *The Attack on Plant Breeders' Rights Legislation and the Involvement of the Multi-nationals in Plant Breeding and the World's Seed Business*, www.worldseed.org

[87] With the effect that the only barrier to patent protection for those countries which adhere to the 1991 Act is that contained in Art 53(b) of the EPC. It is important to remember that not all European countries have signed up to the 1991 Act, and for those which adhere to the 1961/72 or 1978 Acts the 'dual protection prohibition' still remains a key part of their plant variety rights law.

attempted to introduce Community-wide legislation relating to patent law and plant variety rights.

At the heart of these problems lies a tension between providing strong rights which are of value to those who use them whilst at the same time ensuring that rights which are granted do not undermine plant breeding activity. As will be seen, the plant variety rights system has always regarded this balance as fundamental to its existence—however, as the right has evolved to provide a right equally attractive to that provided under patent law, the extent to which the public interest limitations continue to serve their original purpose may be questioned. Equally in patent law, as the system is increasingly used to protect a wide array of inventions involving genetic material, the extent to which the exclusions and limitations can and should be allowed to confine both the scope of protectable material and the impact of the rights granted needs to be examined. As will be seen, in evaluating the effectiveness and appropriateness of protection much of the lead in directing the debate has come from organisations which represent the views of plant breeders, including those mentioned above involved in the creation of plant variety rights and, most recently, the International Seed Federation (ISF), which now embodies two of the most important organisations involved in the promotion of the needs of plant breeders, ASSINSEL and FIS.[88]

The background against which any evaluation of the rights must take place is the science.

## V. DEFINING THE SCIENCE

As mentioned in the Introduction, man has cultivated plants for his own purposes for thousands of years and the practice of 'plant breeding' obviously pre-dates the developments in genetic science which have taken place over the last century and a half. This connection with plants can be seen in the constant developments in plant uses across the centuries,[89] many of which still form the basis of modern-day medicines (and alternative treatments) or were the precursors of plants now routinely grown around the world for agricultural or ornamental purposes. However, the sciences of botany and chemistry (both of which form the main basis of modern plant research activities) were not formally recognised as scientific disciplines until the 18th century and it was not until the end of the 19th century (following the work of scientific explorers such as Gregor Mendel and Thomas Huxley) that those engaged in plant research were able to exert greater controls over the outcomes of plant reproduction.

[88] According to the organisation's website its mission is to represent the interests of its members including promoting 'the establishment and protection of intellectual property' which lies within 'plant varieties, plant biotechnology seed technology and related subjects'.

[89] This is evidenced by the library holdings of eminent academic institutions such as the Royal Society in London, which provide a vast array of documentation, including hieroglyphics, which relate to plant-related research activities which took place within civilisations such as Ancient Egypt. Documentation relating to plant husbandry as a *science* can be found from the 16th century onwards.

From these developments in the latter half of the 19th century, it took only a few short years for plant breeding itself to become a recognised scientific field, and—with the appearance of new improved varieties on the market[90]—a new industry was born. The value of this new industry lay in being able to produce new and improved crops for use in agriculture (which should not merely be taken to mean for the benefit of farmers and end consumer, but also for the middlemen who transformed plant material into commodities such as beer and flour through malting and milling), and diversity of plants for the delectation of gardeners. This was a crucial moment for the farming community as well, for up until this new discipline emerged, where clearly distinguishable varieties could be produced, the only mode of differentiating between seed on sale was by trade name. The fact that there was only limited variation meant, therefore, that the material being sold (albeit under different names) could be, and indeed often was, the same.

As will be seen later, the work on plants quickly led to a recognition that plants had industrial potential and, therefore, should be protected.[91] As already mentioned, with impressive prescience, Article 1(3) of the Paris Convention recognised the commercial potential of plant when it stated that:

> Industrial property shall be understood in the broadest sense and shall apply not only to industry and commerce proper, but likewise to *agricultural* and extractive industries and to all *manufactured or natural* products, for example, wines, *grain, tobacco leaf, fruit*, cattle,[92] minerals, mineral waters, beer, *flowers* and *flour* [emphasis added].

However, as we know, this did not mean that the results of plant research were immediately protectable. Instead, the fact that the new science allowed only a certain degree of control meant that the resulting plants could not meet the

---

[90] An illustration of how quickly these improvements became publicly available can be seen in an anecdote told by Professor ET Jones (Director of the Welsh Plant Breeding Station during the 1950s). He recollected how, as a boy growing up in the 1890s on a relatively remote Welsh farm, he would eagerly await the arrival of publications such as *The Farmer* and *Stockbreeder* and Garton's *Annual Catalogue*, which would provide details of new cereal varieties. He would then compare the new improved varieties with those his father grew and together they would decide on the next season's crop.

[91] An example of this recognition within intellectual property circles can be seen in many of the articles published in the 1980s, for example those by Beier, Crespi and Straus which appeared in journals such as the *IIC* and *EIPR*, and also in the subject matter of international conferences: see, eg, the conference proceedings of the *WIPO Symposium on the Protection of Biotechnological Inventions* (Ithaca, NY, 1987), and EPO, *Biotechnology and Industrial Property Law* (Munich, 1988).

[92] The reference to 'cattle' belies the argument, often presented from the 1980s onwards, that the industrial property system was not intended to protect animals. For a further discussion of this see Llewelyn, 'From GATT to GATT: Intellectual Property Rights and Genetics Fifty Years after Crick and Watson, Part I' (2003–4) *Bio/Science L Rev* 107. It is interesting to note that despite the wording of Art 1(3) there is no reference to protecting living, or natural, material under the Paris Convention in the World Intellectual Property Organisation's *Introduction to Intellectual Property: Theory and Practice*, above n 63.

criteria for protection.[93] This problem remained until the latter half of the 20th century when more fundamental changes to the nature of plant breeding took place.

Up until the 1950s, the main forms of plant breeding techniques had been those which used hybridisation, such as crossing—with the actual method used to achieve the cross often depending on the plant's own method of reproduction.[94] These techniques (which are still used widely today) require the breeder to appreciate the breeding value of variants within existing varieties, and whilst by the 1950s it was possible to force particular results, or mutations, through external techniques, these were still at their initial stages. This does not mean that this war the only plant research related to plant breeding; extraction techniques involving isolating plant properties were also in evidence from the late 19th century, as demonstrated by Bayer's synthesising of salicylic acid from willow bark thus producing 'Aspirin'. Indeed, the World Health Organisation has estimated that 25 per cent of modern medicines are derived from plant material[95]—and this fact, together with the increased interests in naturally derived medical products, has meant increased interest in innovating in this area.

In simple terms, the art of the traditional breeder is to select two parents the characteristics of each of which would be desirable in a single plant, cross the two parents in the hope that the progeny will express those desired characteristics, identify the resulting plants which best exhibit the desired traits and recross these to reinforce the trait and then replicate the results via seed or cuttings and so on. What appears relatively simple can take many years to achieve (bearing in mind the number of possible genetic combinations at any one stage of the plant breeding process). It is generally accepted that the time taken to develop a new variety, that is one which can be placed on the market with the surety that the desired characteristics are present, is between 10 and 15 years.[96] The original skill came from being able to make judgements about value of any given plant as either a parent, or as a desired progeny, based on an *external* evaluation of the plant—in other words, a breeder's best tools are his eyes. Whilst advances in genetic science have enabled breeders to make use of more invasive means of controlling characteristics (which have meant the development of additional skills) it remains the case that it is still the plant as a whole which needs to be understood and appreciated if a particular end result is to be achieved. In addition, maximising the potential of the plant variety being bred not only means taking into account the genetic components of the plant itself in isolation, but also requires an understanding of a host of external conditions, including an environmental evaluation. Many of these external factors have to be detailed in

[93] As will be seen, the problem over securing industrial property protection was not only encountered by plant breeders but also proved problematic for those working in chemistry.

[94] For example, some species reproduce by seed, others by tubers, others by the use of cuttings and grafting.

[95] www.who.int/mediacentre/factsheets/fs134/en/.

[96] As will be discussed below, the use of modern biotechnological techniques does little to decrease the amount of time necessary to develop a new variety.

any application for plant variety rights as they have a direct bearing on the two-year trialling period which precedes a grant of rights (a description of such external factors not normally being requisite for the grant of a patent).

It is for these reasons that the plant variety rights system focuses on an evaluation of the phenotype (that is, those externally observable properties of the plant such as leaf shape and colour) as opposed to genotype (the assessment of the internal genetic make-up of the plant).[97] It is worth mentioning at this juncture that the emphasis on the phenotypic qualities of the variety goes to the heart of the rationale for plant variety rights and serves to explain what some regard as the limitations of that right which justify the use of patent protection (this will be discussed in more detail in chapters 3 and 4).

The ways in which the industry itself evolved differed across Europe. In the UK, before the 1960s, plant breeding was predominantly publicly funded with only a few private sector companies operating, The reverse was true in France and Germany, each of which had thriving private sector companies, but only limited public investment in the research. As will be shown in the next chapter, both of these countries had a firm policy of providing protection for plant breeders. The scale of operations was also manifestly different. The Engholm Committee[98] commented in 1960 on the French situation that '[t]here is nothing in the United Kingdom comparable in size to these private establishments . . . State breeding . . . plays an important role [but] it is secondary to the private breeder in providing growers with improved new varieties.'[99] The Committee also made a comparable point about the German plant breeding industry.[100] Without wishing to make too glib a point, in some respects the situation in the UK mirrored that of many modern-day developing countries where it is equally true to state that most plant breeding activity takes place within the public and not the private sector. As the results of the EU funded project into attitudes towards plant property rights discussed in chapter 8 will show, the situation has since reversed and the majority of plant breeders now operate within the private sector.

For many of those supporting such research it is fundamental that the results of that research work remain freely available for use by others. The dilemma facing the UK, and arguably that also facing many developing countries, was how to compete within the emerging European market in light of the proliferation of French and German breeders, whilst at the same time not undermining the research work on its own primarily publicly funded plant breeding community. The way in which it, and other European countries, resolved this is discussed in the next chapter.

The 1950s saw greater inroads made into understanding the genetic workings of life forms, the most obvious being Crick and Watson's identification of the

---

[97] The relevance of the phenotype/genotype distinction will be discussed in more detail in ch 3.

[98] The committee set up in the 1950s by the UK government to look into the question whether it was necessary to provide protection for plant varieties: see above n 49.

[99] The Engholm Report, above n 49, p 48.

[100] *Ibid*, p 53.

structure of DNA in 1953. That DNA was the key to understanding the building blocks of life was not new. In 1943 Schrodinger had suggested that genes were the information carriers, and in 1944 a US Government team had said that it believed that DNA was the unit of heredity. What Crick and Watson provided was that critical insight into how DNA was structured thereby enabling scientists to construct and reconstruct living material with greater control and certainty of result than had previously been possible.[101] As Watson himself has remarked, in the 50 years since their discovery:

> DNA has moved from being an esoteric molecule only of interest to a handful of specialists to being the heart of a technology that is transforming many aspects of the way we live.[102]. . . Contained in the molecule's graceful curves was the key to molecular biology, a new science whose progress over the subsequent fifty years has been astounding. Not only has it yielded a stunning array of insights into fundamental biological processes, but it is not having an even more profound impact on medicine, on agriculture, and on the law.[103]

In terms of the impact on plant breeding, the new technologies provided plant breeders with increasingly diverse methods of researching on and with plants which they could use alongside the Mendelian plant breeding techniques of crossing and selection. Scientists developed a whole range of techniques which included making more effective use of hybrid breeding (which, together with crossing and selection, dominated plant breeding until the 1970s) cell and tissue culture, DNA diagnostics and recombinant DNA techniques, sequencing and cloning. Most recent are the more invasive intra-genetic techniques now associated with the terms 'genetic engineering' and 'biotechnology'. Arguably the most significant effect of the deconstruction of DNA has been its impact on human genetics. The first map of a human chromosome appeared in 1999, the first draft of the human genome in 2000, and in 2003 (exactly 50 years after Crick and Watson's identification of DNA), the map of the human genome was finally published.[104]

Whilst this book will not address the highly complex and controversial area of human genetics,[105] it is worth noting that in 2000, following the publication of the first draft of the human genome, there were calls at the highest levels to ensure that information resulting from the project remain freely available for use by scientists. For example, in the same week as the draft was published, US President Bill Clinton and UK Prime Minister Tony Blair issued a joint press

---

[101] For an insight into both the work of Crick and Watson and also the modern genetic evolution which resulted see Watson, *The Double Helix* (Weidenfield & Nicolson, 1968) and Watson, *DNA: The Secret of Life* (Arrow Books, 2004).

[102] See above, Watson 2004, p x.

[103] See above, Watson 2004 p xx.

[104] Dennis and Gallagher (eds), *The Human Genome* (Nature Palgrave, 2001).

[105] For a view on the various legal and political manoeuvrings which surrounded, and continue to surround, the human genome project see Sulston and Ferry, *The Common Thread: A Story of Science, Politics, Ethics and the Human Genome* (Bantam Press, 2002).

statement that it was a desired objective to ensure that patents were only granted over true inventions involving genetic material and should not be granted over basic genetic information. A week later Sir Aaron Klug and Bruce Alberts (President of the Royal Society, UK, and President of the US National Academy of Sciences, respectively) published another joint statement saying that it was 'critical that the benefits to the public be at least reasonably commensurate' to the reward the inventor obtains via a patent, and that the grant of patents 'to any portion [of the human genome] should be regarded as extraordinary, and should occur only when new inventions are understood to confer benefits of comparable significance for humankind.'[106] These views have since been mirrored in other fora. For example, in 2001 the UK House of Lords Select Committee on Science and Technology recommended, in its Fourth Report, that:

> [whilst] patenting in the field of genetics is, in principle, no different from that in other fields . . . the government should press, both within Europe and more widely, for patent rights over genes to continue to be granted only where a significant gene function has been established, and to ensure that the patent should cover only that function and direct extensions of it. Possible but not yet envisaged and speculative uses of a gene should not be patentable . . . . For the future, we recommend that the Government should monitor closely patenting practices in the field of genetics and take steps as necessary to ensure a proper balance is maintained between protecting inventor's interests, facilitating commercial development of ideas and allowing research to flourish.[107]

As will be seen later, these calls mirror those made by plant scientists and politicians in the 1950s with regard to the provision of private property rights over plants.

These modern scientific techniques (which include the ability to use, store and maintain genotypes) enable quick production of new breeding material such as haploids and clones, and through the use of molecular markers, breeders can fast-track selection thereby cutting down the amount of time spent on field trials. During the days of cross-breeding and selection, the field trials would have been the primary way in which breeders would identify the traits they wanted and discover which plants of those they had grown carried them, and the old photographs of breeders in the early part of the 20th century would have shown

---

[106] Alberts and Klug, 'The Human Genome Must be Freely Available to All Humankind' (2000) 404 *Nature* 326.

[107] House of Lords Select Committee on Science and Technology, '4th Report on Human Genetic Databases: Challenges and Opportunities', paras 80.29, 80.30 and 80.31. The Report can be found at www.parliament.the-stationery-office.co.uk/pa/ld/ldsctech.htm. The UK responded to these concerns by commissioning two independent reports, one on behalf of the Department of Health on managing intellectual property rights within the healthcare sector, and the other by the Department of Trade and Industry on current law and practice regarding patents for genetic sequences. The Department of Health's report was published in 2003 and the Department of Trade and Industry report in 2004.

them as much in the field physically evaluating through sight and feel as in the laboratory looking at the material under a microscope. The new genetics means that the breeder can now introduce the new desired characteristics by working within the genetic structure of the plant itself thereby ensuring greater and more targeted genetic variation. In addition, the developing art of genomics means that breeders are able to understand the entirety of the plant genome, giving them a greater ability to directly influence the result.[108] It is important to realise, however, that whilst the modern science of genetics has done much to assist the plant breeder, and render the processes and individual types of genetic information identified as part of modern genetics highly important both in commercial and scientific terms, most of those engaged in using this material do so with the objective of producing new varieties. It is also important to recognise that, notwithstanding the publicity given to the outputs of modern breeding techniques, traditional breeding continues to produce major improvements to plant material. Because of this, the art of genetic engineering does not, as yet, provide a mechanism for bypassing the processes for producing, or accelerating the delivery of, a variety which, irrespective of whether it is protectable, would be able to secure a place in the market. Obviously there are a significant number of companies who are solely engaged in utilising plant genetic material *per se* and are not in the business of producing varieties. These are more concerned with being able to produce plants or plant products with particular genetic characteristics regardless of whether the plants so engineered can be defined as a variety or not (and if patent protection is sought then, within Europe at least, it will be an active objective not to produce a variety). But as the results of the PIP survey detailed in chapter 8 will show, these companies, whilst clearly of importance (not least because many of these are multi-national companies), do not make up the majority of extant plant breeders who are engaged in the production of plant varieties.

Understanding the goals to which breeders aspire is important when assessing how to best protect their interests. In agricultural breeding these goals can be said, in summary, to include developing new varieties which achieve one or more of the following: increased yield; better agronomic traits; greater control over breeding methods and thereby outcomes; resistance to pests, disease or certain herbicides/pesticides better nutritional/fodder/processing qualities; use of natural resources such as nitrogen fixation as well as removing environmental barriers to growth (whether naturally occurring or man-induced).[109]

---

[108] For example, a Dutch research team has developed a transformation method which ensures that plants resulting from a cross-pollinating and vegetative propagated crop (such as potato and cassava) are marker free. This will help alleviate those concerns relating to the use of antibiotic- or herbicide-resistant genes in plant transformation. See www.nature.com/cgi-taf/DynaPage.taf?file=/nbt/journal/v21/n3/full/nbt0303-227.html

[109] The UK's Horticulture Research International is using plants which survive despite the land being contaminated by harmful chemicals (and specifically the radioactive substance, caesium), with a view to producing plants which can grow in contaminated land but still be safe to eat. See www.hri.ac.uk

Traditional breeding can take between 10 and 15 years to develop a variety which can both have the desired trait *and* continue to express that trait through subsequent generations.[110] In ornamental breeding this means that there is greater diversity in size, colour, shape and smell making, the products more appealing in the market place.[111]

There is also intense interest in using biotechnology in the production of medicinal products involving plant material, especially those which will enable greater access to beneficial plant properties previously only available within indigenous communities.[112] For medicinal usage it is maximising the therapeutic properties of a particular plant either by utilising its own natural properties in the most advantageous manner or by combining its properties with those of another plant (or, in an era of increased cross-over of genetic information between species, of another life form) or by making the plant a factory for producing a drug, edible vaccines or other medicinal products which do not naturally occur within that plant. Of particular interest is the use of plants to produce greater quantities of vitamins and minerals, for use in diagnosis and for therapeutic purposes, mass pharming to produce greater quantities of valuable proteins for replacement purposes, and as producers of antibodies. An example of such work can be found at the Institu fur Pflanzengenetik und Kulturpflanzenschung in Germany.[113] It has produced genetically engineered plants (using transgenic potato and tobacco plants) which can produce the human papillomavirus. These plants can then be used to develop vaccines for cervical cancer. There are other uses being made of plants which demonstrate the breadth of potential to be tapped as a result of modern plant research. The Danish biotechnology company, Aresa Biodetection, has produced a plant which changes colour if planted in soil which contains explosives. This means that these plants could be used to detect landmines.[114] These are merely two examples of the range of research work being undertaken in respect of plants; other work includes the use of plants to produce new forms of fuels (for example, by harnessing the energy residing within plant carbohydrates as opposed to simply burning the plants), and the development of alternatives to metals (for the use in the manufacture of items such as car panels). The one thing which all the research has in common is the goal of placing new plant material (whether

---

[110] The fact of engaging in a lengthy breeding programme is no guarantee of success, with possibly as few as only 10% of any research results making it through all the various scientific and regulatory processes. See Lange, *Intellectual Property Protection for Plant Varieties: From a Plant Breeder's View*, Paper given at a conference on Intellectual Property Protection for Plant Innovation (Frankfurt, 2004) (see www.forum-institut.de).

[111] As an example of the significance of this industry, in 2000 the Flower Council of the Netherlands stated that the number of rose varieties had increased 1000% in the decade between 1990 and 2000.

[112] See, eg, the work of scientists at Kew Gardens who are actively engaged in identifying the molecular characteristics of traditional herbal medicines such as sage and lovage.

[113] See Biemelt, 'Human Papillomavirus Type Virus 16 Virus-like Particles in Transgenic Plants' (2003) 77(17) *Journal of Virology* (September 2003), also available at http/jvi.asm.org.

[114] See www.aresa.dk.

in the form of crop varieties or vaccines) into the market place. However, the inroads into plant genetic research are having the effect of blurring the boundaries between plant research activities and the plant products produced as a result of that research. This in turn has implications for the rights available to protect them, especially in respect of establishing clear blue water distinctions between types of protectable material and the role of any public interest provisions (which might be invoked differently according to the type of material and/or the uses to which it is put). There are other applications to which plant material can be put which are also regarded as potentially lucrative. These include applications within the so-called 'alternatives to conventional medicines' industry (such as aromatherapy oils, vitamins and herbal remedies) as well as within the lifestyle industries, such as clothing and cosmetics, where there is also growing interest in the use of naturally derived products.

The perceived economic importance of these plant innovations led to renewed calls within Europe (and at the international level) for intellectual property protection to reflect the changing nature of plant research.[115] In particular, the debate has centred on whether existing provision, which differentiates between types of material, meets the needs of the modern bioscience industry or if it needs further revision, for example by an extension of patent protection. (The perception held by some is that the plant variety rights system is better suited to the old-fashioned type of plant breeding work whilst patent protection is more appropriate for the results of modern plant genetic work.) As was pointed out by the editor of *FloraCulture* in February 2004, 'Strong breeders' rights laws encourage product innovation . . . If you are located in a country with weak laws you are at a disadvantage competing in the world market.'[116] It can be seen, therefore, that a key objective in providing protection is to encourage breeders to continue with their breeding programmes in the hope that once the programme is complete the resulting variety will be protected from copying once placed into market.

This increased ability to understand and make full use of both genotypic and phenotypic aspects of plant material highlights the differences in protectable subject matter—and indicates why there has been a progressive move towards the patenting of plant material. For reasons discussed below and later in chapter 3, the development of a separate system of protection for plant material was specifically directed towards the protection of plant *varieties*. The reasons for this were both that there were concerns that the patent system was not a suitable method of protecting plant material (and that protection of any kind should be over only the most obviously commercially important types of plant material, namely varieties) and also that, until recently, it was not thought possible to

---

[115] The relevance of intellectual property protection to this work can be seen in studies such as Butler and Marion, *Impacts of Patent Protection in the US Seed Industry and Public Plant Breeding* (North Central Regional Research Bulletin No 304, University of Wisconsin, 1985); Diez, 'The Impact of Plant Variety Rights on Research ' (2002) 27 *Food Policy* 171.

[116] Editorial, *FloraCulture*, February 2004.

show that plant material could meet the granting criteria for a patent. The types of modern biotechnology outlined above, which can be shown to be novel, inventive and of industrial use, fall within the sphere of patent protection as they are not plant varieties. Thus, breeders involved in this type of research will be looking to claim patent rights over genes, genetic constructs, promoters, molecular markers, plasmids, vectors and the like, as well as over processes (such as cloning, regeneration and so on) which make use of this genetic material.

Whilst it would be easy to say that modern genetics enables breeders to place new plant varieties into the market place, the reality is that whilst it might accelerate the availability of plant genes or sequences what it does not do is to speed up the actual breeding process, for those genes/sequences still need to be incorporated into a coherent and stable plant grouping which will still take a number of years to achieve. One of the problems facing those assessing the value of plant intellectual property is that the identification and appraised function of genes for use in plants in general can take place at a far earlier stage than the ability to bring a plant variety into being, thus making patent protection appear a more immediately attractive form of protection than a plant variety right.[117]

A further issue which needs to be borne in mind goes to the heart of the difference between patent protection and plant variety rights. In respect of the determination of the best protection, a plant breeder has two separate, and potentially conflicting, positions to consider. On the one hand the breeder wants the best protection possible for the results of his plant breeding work (the main considerations here being the effectiveness of the right, and the speed and cost of acquisition and defending the right). On the other hand the breeder wants to have access to the widest source possible of plant material for use in breeding programmes, such access including being able to use plant material which is the 'intellectual property' of a third party.[118] As will be discussed throughout this book, the plant variety rights system tries to provide a balance between these two potentially competing needs whilst the patent system appears to be more orientated to protecting individual interests.

There is also the economic factor to bear in mind.[119] In recent years an increasing number of patents have been granted over inventions involving living material.[120] The reasons for this are straightforward. The bioscience industry

[117] See Morandini and Salamini, 'Plant Biotechnology and Breeding: Allied for Years to Come in Trends' (2003) 8(2) *Plant Science* 70.

[118] This position was restated at a symposium held jointly by WIPO and UPOV in 2002 on the co-existence of patents and plant breeders' rights in the promotion of biotechnological developments.

[119] For a further discussion of the economic value of plant material see Pardey, Koo and Nottenburg, *Creating, Protecting and Using Crop Biotechnologies Worldwide in an Era of Intellectual Property*, Proceedings of the WIPO–UPOV Symposium on Intellectual Property Rights in Plant Biotechnology (October 2003). There is particular reference to the US markets.

[120] See Wegner, *Patent Law in Biotechnology, Chemicals and Pharmaceuticals* (Stockton Press, 1992); Domeij, *Pharmaceutical Patents in Europe* (Kluwer Law International, 2000); Grubb, *Patents for Chemical, Pharmaceuticals and Biotechnology* (OUP, 1999). For the first full evaluations of the policy and practice see Beier, Crespi and Straus, *Biotechnology and Patent Protection: An*

needs to protect the results of expensive research and development from unauthorised copying and marketing. The promise of patent protection for the results of biotechnological research is a key factor in ensuring ongoing investment and there is an acute need for certainty that such protection will be forthcoming once the research has been completed.

It is hardly surprising that those involved in bioscience research should be demanding this certainty of protection in all global markets. The economic position of these companies, both actual and potential, is such that there is an economic imperative to ensure the availability of intellectual property protection. Patent offices have responded to this need by recognising the value of the 'inventions' being claimed and, provided the applicant can demonstrate a novel technical effect, then patents have been granted notwithstanding the fact that in some the technical effect is similar or identical to one already occurring in nature.[121] At this point an important distinction needs to be made between the way in which genetic information is perceived in science and at law. The notions of novelty and inventiveness (which will be discussed in greater detail later) are *legal* notions, and the ways in which they are interpreted and applied have to be understood in this context.

This pressure to permit patent protection for inventions which involve biological material has meant that the exclusions from protection have come under increasingly close scrutiny. This scrutiny has been undertaken at all levels from governmental to academic. It is intended to assess whether the restrictions on patentable subject matter present a barrier to the development of the biotechnology industry which should be removed, or whether they represent an appropriate safeguard preventing an extension of monopoly rights to inappropriate subject matter.

## VI. KEY POLICY MAKERS

Given the increased economic value of plants, it is unsurprising that there are a number of different organisations and groups which seek to represent the diverse interests of those engaged in research with (and subsequent commercialisation of) plant material. Unsurprisingly, each of these seeks to influence the direction in which the rights develop and many play a key role in determining policy and practice at the national and international level. At the apogee of policy making stand the World Intellectual Property Organisation, the Office of the International Union for the Protection of New Plant Varieties and the World

*International Review* (OECD, 1985); Crespi, *Patenting in the Biological Sciences* (John Wiley & Sons, 1988).

[121] The EU Directive on the Legal Protection of Biotechnological Inventions specifically states that biological material 'which is isolated from its natural environment or produced by means of a technical process may be the subject of an invention [and patentable] even if it previously occurred in nature' (Art 3(2)).

Trade Organisation. But such policy initiatives as are presented by these organ-isations are invariably informed (with differing degrees of influence) by groups such as the International Seed Federation, the International Chamber of Commerce (ICC), the OECD, societies representing interests in seed (such as traders and testers) and in ornamental plant varieties (such as CIOPORA), UN organisations concerned with food and agricultural matters (such as the FAO), groups concerned about access to genetic resources (for example Greenpeace and the Worldwide Fund for Nature), commissions responsible for overseeing sustainable development, environmental programme co-ordinators, groups involved in food technology, agri-food industry associations, organisations rep-resenting bioscience (such as the European Association for Bioindustries) as well as those charged with conservation and research involving specific crops. This latter group includes the Consultative Group on International Agricultural Research (CGIAR), the International Maize and Wheat Improvement Center (CIMMYT), the International Plant Genetic Resources Institute (IPGRI) and International Rice Research Institute (IRRI). A glance at any of the web-sites of these organisations will see position papers devoted to the relationship between patents and plant variety rights as well as to the more specific issues of access to plant resources, determining the application of new principles (such as the extension of protection to essentially derived varieties within plant variety rights) and the farm saved seed provision.

Many of these groups can trace their origins back to the 19th century and early 20th century, with the emergence of not only the new science of plant breeding but also the modern form of industrial property rights following the introduction of the Paris Convention.[122] Because of both their longevity and their closeness with the subject involved (whether the science or the law) these groups can carry great influence, and their role in shaping the law should not be underestimated. It would be impossible for this text to outline the various posi-tions taken by all these organisations but where deemed relevant such references will be made. However, when evaluating the positions taken by these groups it should be remembered that such is the nature of the subject under discussion that these references have to be read in the context of ongoing discussion and evolution and that these discussions will inevitably vary according to the inter-ests of the group concerned.

In addition, consideration has to be given to the influence of those charged with administering the rights themselves, such as the European Patent Office and the Community Plant Variety Office, as well as the courts which review the

---

[122] Examples of these plant breeding organisations include the International Commission for Horticultural Congresses which (although it was not formally set up until 1923) had its origins in the first International Horticultural Congress held in Brussels in 1864 (this became the International Society for Horticultural Science in 1959); FIS, 1924; ASSINSEL, 1938; the International Association of Horticultural Producers (AIPH), 1948; and more recently CIOPORA, 1961. On the patent side, examples include the AIPPI, which was established in 1897, and the ICC, which has a long history of supporting closer links between trade and intellectual property provision, in 1919.

rights once granted. Whilst these ostensibly do not direct policy, a consequence of the decisions they make, over what can be protected and the extent of the protection granted, is to influence the way in which the rights are seen and indicate possible routes forward as to how the rights can, or should, develop.

Before moving to the detail of the rights themselves, it is worth making some general comments about the use of other forms of protection, the use of intellectual property rights in practice, and other legal devises intended to control the protection or exploitation of plant material.

## VII. USE OF OTHER INTELLECTUAL PROPERTY RIGHTS

As can be seen in the results of the EU plant intellectual property (PIP) project,[123] plant researchers will inevitably use a range of different methods for protecting their plant material and not all will seek patent or plant variety rights protection (although these are the most frequently used). The most common other means of protecting material are via trade secrecy[124] and trademarks[125]— the latter being of most importance following the expiration of a patent or plant variety right.[126] This is reiterated by the International Association of Horticultural Producers, which in a statement issued in September 2003, said that where breeders face problems with the plant variety rights system they will 'find additional solutions like the use of trademarks to limit the selling and trade of a variety and try to monopolize the trade in the propagating material'.[127] This latter comment highlights the fact that increasingly owners of genetic information are using other forms of intellectual property protection or, as responses to the PIP project indicate, they are turning to non-intellectual property forms of protection and are using ordinary contracts, in the form of licences, as a primary means of protection.

One of the reasons for this is that contract terms are agreed between the parties to that contract. A breeder can therefore denote the exact terms upon which his plant material is to be used by the other party to the agreement. As the President of CIOPORA acknowledges, '[w]hen you have something really

---

[123] www.shef.ac.uk/uni/projects/pip.

[124] Many breeders seek to protect the parental lines via the use of trade secrecy and, if one US case is an indicator, it would seem that there is no conflict between obtaining plant variety protection and keeping parental lines from which the variety was developed secret. This applies even where it is necessary to return to the parental lines in order to grow the protected variety (*Advanta USA Inc v Pioneeer HiBred International Inc* W. D. Wis No 04–C–238–S 27 October 2004).

[125] For more information about alternative methods see Janis, 'Supplemental Forms of Intellectual Property Protection for Plants' (2004) 6 *Minnesota Journal of Law, Science and Technology* 305.

[126] Hamrick cites the example of the rose 'Sonia'. The plant variety rights over this rose have now expired, but it retains its successful place in the market, and the breeder retains rights over it (and therefore royalties) through the use of the registered trademark 'Sonia': Hamrick, *The State of Breeder's Rights* (FloraCulture, 2004).

[127] AIPH Statement, September 2003, at www.aiph.org.

special, you can demand that the grower follows certain rules . . . the breeder decides what the restrictions are and the grower will decide if he/she can live with them by signing the agreement'.[128] The extent to which the breeder can control every aspect of the use of the protected variety remains an issue. In the same special plant breeders' rights issue of *FloraCulture*, reference is made to a Hortifair which took place in Amsterdam. A number of important horticultural breeders stated that they would only sell to an identified group of growers in order to prevent abuses of protected material (critically for horticultural breeders, the plant variety rights system does not protect the end product, the flower), and the question has been asked 'Can breeders force growers to accept all kinds of marketing and harvest conditions dictated by the breeders? . . . Can he regulate the whole vertical chain from breeding to consumption?'[129] In fact such practices are common in food production, with many food producers using contracts to control all aspects of the production of their produce from the growing (including what is grown and who grows it), the time and manner of harvesting, packing and packaging as well as the selling of their products. It is probably only logical for breeders also to move in this direction if there is a fear that the quality or quantity of the protected product is moving outside their control. A further attractive aspect of contract law is that there is no requirement to take account of any defined exclusions or limitations to that right. Aside from any general sale of goods requirements (such as having the right to sell and quality of product) the only requirement imposed at law is that the terms used must be reasonable.

There are problems with just using a contract as a form of protection. These include the fact that contracts do not actually confer any right of ownership on the person licensing out their 'intellectual property'. Also should a person who is not a party to the agreement make use of the property concerned, the only redress the 'owner' of that property has will be via the criminal law and an action in theft. This will require proof that the property concerned is his. Finally each contract has to be individually agreed.

## VIII. INTELLECTUAL PROPERTY IN PRACTICE

Before moving to a discussion of the specific forms of protection available in Europe, it is important to comment on the use of these rights in practice.

Firstly, whilst lawyers and legal academics tend to focus on the polar areas of grant and litigation, rights holders are not often concerned with the finer points of legal discourse: what they are concerned with is ensuring they have a right which is secure in both the market place and the courtroom. For the holders of the right, the main area of attention lies in the middle ground—the use of the right post-grant and pre-litigation.

---

[128] Maarten Leune, quoted in *The State of Breeder's Right* (FloraCulture, 2004).
[129] Kras, *Breeders Rights* (FloraCulture, 2004).

Once a right has been granted, the systems of protection generally bow out, leaving the rights holder free to deal in the information protected by the right. With certain limited exceptions, most notably in plant variety rights, there are few constraints on the rights holder as to how he deals in the information. He may choose to exploit the material by himself, or he may licence it either exclusively or non-exclusively. The terms of any licence agreement are not governed by intellectual property laws but by the laws common to commerce which provide the parties to the agreement with a significant amount of freedom to dictate the terms of that agreement, and in order to help breeders and growers agree the terms of the licence, a number of organisations provide models or checklists of good practice.[130]

Clearly the rights holder will be in a more powerful position where the protected material possesses a unique quality and those seeking to acquire limited rights to use it are unable to acquire that quality from any other product. Equally, if the rights holder is not in a position to exploit by himself, perhaps because of limited capital or manufacturing capacity he may wish to attract an established company in order to realise the market potential of the protected product. In such instances, it is possible to envisage the established company as having the negotiating edge. More common is that it is mutually advantageous to both parties to enter into the agreement, and the terms of that agreement will reflect the mutual benefit.

The role of mutual benefit carries on even where a rights holder suspects a competitor of infringing his patent or plant variety right. It would be misleading to say that all infringing actions automatically end up in court. The truth is that it is only the most extreme cases which will be litigated. Suspicion of infringement could lead the rights holder to any number of actions. He could ignore it. This is not as strange an option as might be first thought. Choosing to take action will inevitably involve a cost of some kind, even if only in terms of time and energy invested in it. The infringing activity might be minimal and the cost of following it up more than that of letting it continue. In such an instance, as with all choices facing the rights holder, it will be a cost/benefit exercise to see which course is more beneficial or harmful to his company. A second reason for letting the infringement lie is because the term of the right might be about to expire. In such circumstances it may be easier to turn a blind eye. It would be rare for any lawyer to sanction no action, unless the right granted was particularly vulnerable and likely to be revoked if the case went to court, what is more likely is that the alleged perpetrator would be asked to cease and desist, and if the infringing activity continues the rights holder may suggest a licence (again the issue of mutual benefit arises) before taking it to the extreme conclusion of pursuing a legal action.

---

[130] For example, see the checklist for breeders and growers drawn up by the International Association of Horticultural Producers at www.aiph.org.

Of course there will be extreme instances where a rights holder might decide not only to threaten legal action from the moment he/she thinks an infringement has taken place but actively to pursue the alleged infringer through the courts. The decision to do this will depend on the image the rights holder wishes to present, it is not necessarily to its benefit to be perceived as overly litigious, financial considerations and also the security of the right granted will be taken into account. If you have a strong right, that is one which will stand up to intense legal scrutiny, then it is easier to contemplate legal action than if you have a right which might not survive scrutiny as to the validity of grant. The reason why this latter issue is important is that it is, usual for the individual or company accused of infringement to counter the accusation by claiming that the patent (or plant variety right, although this is more rare as there are very few cases involving plant variety rights) is invalid and so the court will be required to look at whether it does meet the granting requirements. As a footnote to this issue, it is worth noting that, at the time of writing, not one case in the UK which has involved an alleged infringement of a patented biotechnological invention has upheld the validity of the patent.

The corollary of this is that when cases do occur they are usually not reflective of the general situation. However, because it is the cases which are reported, are prominent this can give rise to some misconceptions, for example, that there is constant and aggressive litigation. It is true that intellectual property litigation is a growing area but it should not cloud the fact that in practice pragmatism plays a very strong part in the day-to-day use of plant intellectual property rights and going to court is not always the most pragmatic choice. It is also worth noting that any decision to pursue an infringer necessarily will take time and it can be many years, before the action is resolved. This means that few, if any, cases actually deal with current technology and there is not only a time lag involved but a technological one as well. For example, inventor A is granted a patent in 1985 over a technical effect which is ground-breakingly novel at the time of grant. In 1988 company B infringes inventor A's patent. Between 1988 and 1993 the two unsuccessfully attempt to resolve the matter through non-litigious means. Eventually, in 1993, inventor A takes company B to court. Company B counters the claim of infringement by arguing that the patent is invalid. The final court case is heard in 1995. The court in making its decision in 1995 will be basing its assessment of whether the patent was properly granted on the information provided in 1985. It is extremely likely that during the ten years since the patent was granted, other inventors will have continued to make advances in the technology. Notwithstanding this, the decision of the court could be used to determine the validity of other patents notwithstanding that in comparison this decision is now 'old science'. This can create an aura of uncertainty and legally astute scientists will always keep one eye on relevant cases to assess the likely impact on their work. In the case of multi-nationals this is usually done by in-house legal teams. It is not so easy for the independent scientist to keep up to date.

The uncertainty which the time and science lags could create is, however, mitigated by the second point to be made about patent case law. In the main each decision is only relevant to that particular case. A patent which is invalidated because it lacks novelty only invalidates that patent: it will not invalidate other patents in the same technological area. The court may provide a general definition of what it believes constitutes the threshold for protection and (depending on the usefulness of these definitions as well as the status of the court from which they came) these could be used in subsequent cases to decide if the technology involved in a subsequent case meets the granting criteria. As each case will involve different inventive concepts and constructs, such definitions are subject to the interpretive whims of any subsequent judges hearing these other cases.

A third factor is that it is not always possible to identify how many patents over plant inventions exist. The reason for this is because a patent may be granted over a single gene which has been engineered to code for a particular characteristic. The engineered gene may be used in a plant, but the patentee does not have to state that in the application. All that he needs to do is to identify his new technical concept and outline what it can be used for—in this instance to code for a particular characteristic. He is under no obligation to identify where that coded characteristic might be used. The fact, therefore, that a patent over a biotechnological invention does not specifically refer to plants or plant material does not mean that that patent may not have relevance for someone working in the plant sciences.

Fourthly, caution needs to be exercised when looking at any figures which are produced which claim to show the number of patents in any given area of technology. Unfortunately many of these claims tend to elide the number of applications made with the number of patents granted. The two have to be distinguished. Notwithstanding the general presumption of protectability, not all applications are granted. The reasons for this are numerous and include the obvious, inability to meet the granting criteria, through to non-legal matters such as a change in the viability of a particular research programme or a takeover of the company concerned which involves a change in research direction and focus. These attrition rates have to be taken into account when looking at numbers of applications and grants. It is only those rights actually granted which have any impact on access to and use of the protected material. This also applies to plant variety rights, but with slightly less emphasis as there tends not to be the same level of protest at the use of this system of protection. An added complicating factor is the fluctuating status of the companies themselves. Every week seems to bring a merger or take-over which makes it very difficult to track the extent of either rights granted or the number held by competing companies.

Fifthly, there is also the issue of the divergence in legal structures to be noted, with most of Europe adhering to the civil (Roman/codified) law tradition whilst the UK remains common law based. In addition, those member states with a civil law tradition do not necessarily operate the same system(s) of protection, and these differences also need to be noted. The result of this is that court structures, the role of precedence and even the nature of the action (inquisitional versus accusatorial) differs, and these differences will also be found in the various national approaches to legal policy and practice. Such differences need to be borne in mind when assessing how the law will operate in any given jurisdiction.[131]

A further factor to bear in mind is the extent of litigation. Although published reports of cases involving intellectual property rights appear to be peppered with patent law decisions, most patent holders would prefer not to act aggressively against an alleged infringer. They are, however, more prone to bringing an action than plant variety rights holders.[132] This means that there are few cases from the plant variety rights system upon which to pin firm conclusions about the operation of the law in practice.[133] In addition, this does mean that any new provisions (such as essential derivation, the actual basis of which has yet to be determined with reference constantly made to the need for case law on the subject) take on a more daunting appearance to the breeders than might be the case with regard to the inclusion of a new provision within patent law. In respect of plant variety rights, there are comparatively few cases as, firstly, most national systems rely upon arbitration between the rights holder and the alleged infringer and secondly, remedies have tended to be sought through recourse to tribunals rather than the courts. This potentially could be problematic for breeders where the proper interpretation and application of the revised rights are acknowledged to be dependent upon decisions made by a court, for example in determining an essentially derived variety or the nature of the relationship between the differing notions of research exemption in the two key systems of protection. This is a matter which we will return to later.

Finally, it is important to remember that the granting of either a patent or a plant variety right does not provide an automatic right to exploit the protected material, and producers of plant material need to be aware of this.

---

[131] For example, a patent granted in the UK might not be granted in Germany even though the technology is the same. Equally an action for infringement of a UK plant variety right might be successfully litigated in the UK, but a similar action based on a French plant variety right might not succeed in a French court. However, there are also many points of similarity (especially in terms of outcome).

[132] Gurry, 'Plant Biotechnology Developments in the International Framework', above n 64, provided a global figure of 4.37 million patents in force around the world in 1999 as compared to 50,000 plant variety rights. Obviously not all of these have been or will be litigated.

[133] This reluctance to resort to litigation has been present since the rights were first adopted. An example of this can be found in the UK. The Plant Variety and Seeds Act 1964 established the Plant Variety and Seeds Tribunal. It was estimated that the Tribunal would be required to hear between five and ten cases per annum in its first ten years. The reality proved different and by the early 1970s the Minister for Agriculture was sending letters to the expert panellists (drawn from diverse areas of plant breeding) to apologise for the fact that the Tribunal had only sat once. Since then the Tribunal has sat on a number of occasions but not to the extent of the anticipated ten cases per year. Unsurprisingly the equivalent panel set up under the Community Regulation Plant Variety Rights is being called upon to sit more frequently, but the number of cases is considerably fewer than in patent law.

## Sourcing and Exploiting Plants

As this book is primarily concerned with the legal protection of plant material we shall not be discussing in detail any of the other regulatory mechanisms which apply to plant material—most notably those relating to access and exploitation. However, a few general points are worth making.

## Sourcing Plants

Many of the modern-day concerns over access to plant genetic resources relate to a global awareness of the need to protect and conserve genetic material. Before looking at the ways in which these concerns have manifested themselves in international treaties it is worth bearing in mind that many of the major food crops grown in Europe are not indigenous to Europe. Instead the plants have been brought into Europe and, via plant breeding, adapted to exist here. For example, maize has its origins in Central America, and wheat and barley in the Middle East. The fact that there has been a tradition of moving plant material from territory to territory underlines one of the main problems in allocating rights over access to plant material to individual countries and this needs to be taken into consideration when assessing the actual value of the developments designed to protect not only genetic diversity but also the interests of those communities where the plant material is found.

The result of concerns that the world's genetic resources were being depleted was the introduction of a number of international agreements designed to protect biodiversity, and plant material in particular. The most important of these are the Convention on Biological Diversity (CBD)[134] and the International Treaty on Plant Genetic Resources (ITPGR).[135]

## The Convention on Biological Diversity

The CBD operates on the basis of recognising member states' sovereignty over their genetic resources. This provides member states with a right to control their genetic resources. The key obligation is often seen to be Article 8(j), which shows that a 'proprietary' interest vests in the genetic resources themselves; member states should:

---

[134] The CBD applies to plants and animals; it does not apply to human genetic material: Second Conference of the Parties (COP) to the CBD.

[135] See Correa, *Access to Plant Genetic Resources and Intellectual Property Rights*, Paper prepared for the Food and Agricultural Organization of the United Nations, Background Study Paper No 8, 1999.

respect, preserve and maintain knowledge, innovations and practice of indigenous and local communities embodying traditional lifestyles relevant for the conservation and sustainable use of biological diversity and promote their wider application with the approval and involvement of the holders of such knowledge, innovations and practices and encourage the equitable sharing of the benefits arising from the utilisation of such knowledge, innovations and practice . . .

Whilst there is no explicit statement as to the use of *intellectual property rights* as the mechanisms by which to protect the 'knowledge, innovations and practice', the CBD does recognise the importance of intellectual property rights (Article 16) and it does not contain any provision precluding the provision of a private right over genetic resources.

The fact that the CBD does not contain any explicit statement with regard to IPRs should not imply that it has no relevance in determining the availability and scope of such rights. It is clear from on-going activities that many see the CBD as providing the appropriate framework *within* which any intellectual property system should be developed—that is, where genetic resources, of the kind outlined in Article 8j, are concerned, any rights over such resources should be developed in line with the principles of respect, preservation, maintenance, conservation, sustainable use, approval, involvement and equitable sharing of benefits. It is against the background of the CBD, therefore, that proposed forms of protection are being set.

Secondly, the question of access to, and the protection of, traditional knowledge is attracting attention at the highest levels. In addition to the extensive activity which is ongoing via the *ad hoc* working group on access and benefit sharing as part of the Conference of the Parties (COP) meeting of the CBD, the World Trade Organisation, the World Health Organisation, and the World Intellectual Property Organisation[136] are all looking at the question of how most appropriately to protect traditional knowledge. A number of non-governmental organisations such as the International Chamber of Commerce (ICC), and apolitical government committees,[137] have also been looking at this issue. In many instances these organisations are working together in an attempt to achieve consensus.[138] It is reassuring to note that each group recognises the unique value attaching to traditional knowledge, and it is clear from the deliberations that there is general agreement that countries should be allowed to look

---

[136] The WIPO General Assembly has set up the WIPO Intergovernmental Committee on Intellectual Property and Genetic Resources, Traditional Knowledge and Folklore, which has as its mandate the provision of a forum within which member states can discuss intellectual property issues arising in the context of access to genetic resources and benefit sharing—it is currently engaged upon a work programme which includes the provision of a definition of traditional knowledge.

[137] The Commission is made up of experts from around the world and takes a global approach to the issue of genetic resources (the term being used in its broadest sense) and intellectual property laws.

[138] A very good example of this can be seen in the CBD Conference of the Parties (COP) working group meetings on Access and Benefit Sharing (ABS). These meetings are being undertaken in conjunction with the WIPO, which admits that it is inappropriate an organ to decide on ABS as it is purely concerned with the intellectual property issues.

outside the existing forms of intellectual property protection in providing protection for traditional knowledge falling outside the ambit of conventional intellectual property rights.[139] However, there is no consensus within any of these groups as to the form any non-conventional right might take. These differences notwithstanding it is nonetheless important to bear in mind that each of these organisations does recognise the unique quality of traditional knowledge as this provides support for any action taken at the local level. It is equally important that they also recognise that one system does not necessarily fit all.

Whilst the CBD has had a considerable impact on approaches to bio-IPR provision in developing countries it has had little influence on European provision. The final version of the EC Directive pays some lip-service to its existence in that member states are enjoined in Recital 55 to 'give particular weight' to aspects of the CBD, and recognition is made of the need for further work to appreciate the relationship between the TRIPs Agreement and the CBD particularly in respect of technology transfer, conservation, sustainable use and benefit sharing. What the Directive does not do is to make these formal requirements.[140]

Initially, the main point of potential conflict lay in the relationship between the CBD and the TRIPs Agreement, the former seeking to ensure that a) rights are not granted over material which 'belongs' to a local community and b) rights which are granted do not have the effect of eroding the gene pool through an emphasis on genetic uniformity.[141] In so doing the convention places great emphasis on conserving biological diversity, requiring prior informed consent before accessing or using genetic material and ensuring the fair and equitable sharing of any benefits arising out of the utilisation of genetic resources (Article 8j[142]). In contrast, the

[139] There is less clear agreement where that material falls within the ambit of conventional IPRs, for example in the form of material which can be regarded as an invention which is novel, involves an inventive step and is capable of industrial application. The parties to the discussions do not concur as to whether member states of the WTO must protect this material using the conventional form of intellectual property right, of if they are entitled to use a new form of right because of the special nature of the information being protected.

[140] A remaining question is the legal status of the recitals—do they carry the same legal weight as the Articles which follow or are they merely indicators of how member states could, but not should, apply their dependent legislation? European commentators appear divided in this matter, see Beyleveld, 'Why Recital 26 of the EC Directive on the Legal Protection of Biotechnological Inventions should be Implemented in National Law' [2000] 1 *IPQ* 1. Interestingly the revised Implementing Rules of the EPC which adopt the provisions of the Directive for the purposes of supplementary protection (discussed in ch 5) make it clear that the Recitals must be taken into account.

[141] In plant variety rights this concern is focused on the requirement that the variety be uniform and stable, and in patent law on the requirement that any plant material covered by the patent must conform to the description provided within the patent specification.

[142] Art 8j states that member states should 'respect, preserve and maintain knowledge, innovations and practice of indigenous and local communities embodying traditional lifestyles relevant for the conservation and sustainable use of biological diversity and promote their wider application with the approval and involvement of the holders of such knowledge, innovations and practices and encourage the equitable sharing of the benefits arising from the utilization of such knowledge, innovations and practice.' This is generally held to mean prior informed consent from the Community must be acquired before either accessing or using genetic material, that the source of that material be disclosed and finally, that any benefit arising out of that use be subject to benefit sharing with the local community.

objective of TRIPs is to standardise the provision of private property rights, such rights requiring no more than evidence of inventorship and having no overarching obligation to compensate any third parties.

The main problem with the two agreements was that many developed countries refused to accept that the CBD should have any role to play in determining the type and extent of intellectual property protection over genetic material. Many took the view that if there was conflict between the two, then the TRIPs Agreement should prevail, for whilst the CBD was well meaning it was of no real legal importance—at least not for developed countries with their pre-existing practice of providing unfettered private property rights over genetic material. It was not until developing countries cited the CBD as a basis for challenging the extent of the obligation imposed under TRIPs and refused to move from that position with significant political consequences that its role as a determining factor in intellectual property protection was accepted. As a result of having to find ways of working with the agreements it would now seem that they can be mutually supportive and, when used together, can nurture stewardship and the development of genetic innovations. Indeed, this mutuality can be seen in the fact that both the CBD and ITPGR recognise the importance of intellectual property rights (Article 16), and neither includes any provision preventing the grant of a private right over genetic resources. One question being looked at by the WIPO and TRIPs Council is whether, where genetic resources of the kind outlined in Article 8j of CBD are involved any rights should be developed in line with the principles of respect, preservation, maintenance, conservation, sustainable use, approval, involvement and equitable sharing of benefits?[143]

A further factor to bear in mind when formulating intellectual property provision came in 2003 with the International Treaty on Plant Genetic Resources for Food Agriculture.[144]

### The International Treaty on Plant Genetic Resources

The ITPGR, which came into force in July 2003, seeks both to highlight conservation (and on-farm conservation in particular) and to ensure easy and fair access to plant genetic resources. In particular it will permit all researchers using plant

---

[143] An example of how this could be realised in practice is Dutfield and Posey's proposal for a new intellectual property right in the form of a *Traditional Resource Right* (TRR). The TRR takes the form of a framework of rights which 'reflect the diversity of contexts where *sui generis* systems are required'. The term *Traditional Resource Right* is intended to build on existing intellectual property right principles, in the sense of utilising the concepts of protection and reward/compensation, 'while recognising that traditional resources—both tangible and intangible—are also covered under a number of international agreements' and these 'can be used to form the basis for a *sui generis* right.' TRRs will protect both tangible and non-tangible local assets of all kinds (including 'plants, animals and other material objects that may have sacred, ceremonial, heritage, or aesthetic qualities') on the basis that they are of value to the local community. The rights can be used to protect, compensate and conserve. See Dutfield, *Intellectual Property Rights, Trade and Biodiversity* (Earthscan, 2000).

[144] For further information on the Treaty see www.fao.org.

material (whether in the public or private sector) to have equivalent access to the 35 food and 29 forage crops covered by the Treaty through the use of standard terms of access. The Treaty began life as an International Undertaking set up and administered by the UN's FAO in 1983. In this original guise it was a non-legally binding international agreement. Both this and the subsequent Treaty are predicated on the understanding that plant genetic resources are fundamentally the common heritage of mankind, and that any use made of these plants should be on the basis of international co-operation rather than individual monopolisation.

To a considerable extent the objectives of the Treaty are the same as those underpinning the CBD and the two are regarded as closely linked. Indeed, Article 1 of the Treaty expressly states that the objectives of the Treaty, to conserve, ensure sustainable use and foster a fair and equitable sharing of the benefits arising out of use of plant genetic resources, shall be 'in harmony with the Convention on Biological Diversity.' The primary difference between the CBD and ITPGR is that the former primarily seeks to protect and conserve *in situ* genetic material, whereas the latter also seeks to conserve plant material removed from its natural environment primarily for agricultural and food use. In particular, it supports the various collection agencies which have been established to collect and preserve germ plasm and seed. As a result, it is likely that the objectives of the Treaty will be achieved through maximising the close links with the CBD. Because of this the issues relating to the relationship between the TRIPs Agreement and the Treaty are similar to the ones arising in respect of the TRIPs Agreement and the CBD.

As with the CBD there is an express acceptance that intellectual property rights may be used to protect plant genetic resources, indeed FAO Resolution 4/89 expressly stated that plant variety rights were not incompatible with the provisions of the undertaking, although it is worth noting that at the time this resolution was passed it was the 1978 UPOV Act which was in force. The main point of deviation is that Article 12(3)(d) expressly prohibits the granting of intellectual property rights over plant genetic resources 'their genetic parts or components, *in the form received*'. This does not preclude protection over plant material, but merely over material in the form in which it was received under the Treaty. This would appear to mean that where the genetic material has been altered in some manner, whether by tradition or modern biotechnology, then the prohibition will not apply and intellectual property rights may be sought. All that the Treaty states on this matter is that access to genetic resources shall be 'consistent with the adequate and effective protection of intellectual property rights and relevant international agreements' (Articles 12(3)(f) and 13(2)(b)(iii)). The Treaty does not, however, direct the form or effect of that protection.

One of the key developments produced by the Treaty is the introduction of 'Farmers' Rights' (Article 9).[145] This is a right based on the recognition of the contribution made by farmers to preserving biodiversity. This recognition gives rise to rights arising out of 'the past, present and future contribution of farmers in conserving, improving and making available plant genetic resources. The right gives to the cultivators or husbandry of traditional plant material protection over the results of their cultivation work. However it is still uncertain as to how this right would be framed and applied in practice nor is it known if these rights would comply with the notion of an 'effective *sui generis* right' for the purposes of Article 27(3)(b) of TRIPs (discussed in more detail in the next chapter).[146] The Treaty also applies to certain customary uses by farmers and the right of communities to protect their traditional knowledge. The extent to which the former is affected by the TRIPs Agreement will be discussed in more detail in the next chapter—the discussion of the latter falls outside the scope of this book.

Whilst both the CBD and ITPGR are recognised as important international agreements by the European Union (and member states within that Union), neither the CBD nor the ITPGR has had a major role in shaping European plant protection laws. For the most part they have been seen as mechanisms appropriate to the needs of diversity rich countries but not for economically poor countries who have been unable to negotiate equally in respect of the use of indigenous genetic material. Europe does not see itself either as a diversity rich entity or as the weaker party to any bargaining to be made over European 'plant property'. Central to this is the tradition, as discussed above, of granting private property rights over plant material and the established norms upon which such grants are made. The CBD and ITPGR are therefore seen as relevant but only from the perspective of any operations within developing countries, their provisions otherwise being of negligible relevance to European practice. This can be clearly seen in respect of a requirement to disclosure the origin of any claimed genetic material and an indication that consent to use the material claimed has been obtained from the relevant authority in accordance with the provisions of the CBD.

In respect of disclosure of origin, the plant variety rights system does require that the *geographic* origin is provided in the application.[147] However, this is a very bare requirement in that there is no apparent requirement to specify the exact region. There is no equivalent mandate in patent law although the European Directive does state in Recital 27 that where an invention

> is based on biological material of plant or animal origin or if it uses such material, the patent application should, *where appropriate*, include information on the geographical origin of such material, if known; . . . *this is without prejudice to the processing of*

---

[145] The proposed 'farmer's right' should not be confused with the farmer's privilege under plant variety law. For further details see Girsberger and A Martin, *Biodiversity and the Concept of Farmers' Rights in International Law: Factual Background and Legal Analysis* (Peter Lang Publishing, 1999).

[146] At the same Swiss meeting in June 1997 a discussion of the phrasing of the so-called 'farmer's right' was discussed with little success. It was noted that whilst the concept of such a right was very attractive its formulation and application in practice would be difficult to provide.

[147] Art 50(1)(g) of the Regulation on Community Plant Variety Rights.

*patent applications or the validity of rights arising out of granted patents.* [emphasis added].

It can be seen from the wording of Recital 27 that the requirement that the patent application discloses the geographical origin of the plant's or animal's genetic material merely has to be adhered to if it is appropriate (undefined) and that if no such disclosure is forthcoming this will not affect the decision to grant. It appears to be a discretionary requirement which, in the absence of effect on the grant of the patent, has no teeth to encourage adherence.

Neither the patent system nor plant variety rights require any evidence that prior informed consent has been obtained to use the plant material which is the subject of the application. Whilst the CPVR makes no mention of prior informed consent, the Directive does make reference to this in Recital 55, and states the need to take Articles 3 and 8(j) and the second sentences of both Article 16(2) and Article 16(5) into account.

The main reason why this is not thought to be a necessary requirement is mainly to do with the potential impact on breeders being able to secure rights. Both the acquisition of appropriate consent and disclosure of precise country of origin is generally thought too impractical especially where there is more than one possible source for the material, (is one consent sufficient or should all be obtained?), and potentially more than one competent authority. A 'compromise' appears to have been reached that a breeder is required to stipulate from where the material was obtained in an acknowledgement that his source may not be the initial source (that is, the host country of that material), but might be another breeder or plant collection. In respect of demonstrating prior informed consent this again is seen as impractical. Given the nature of plant material to be located in more than one country or community this difficulty in identifying the competent authority is again felt to place too great a burden on the breeder. The compromise again is that where possible a breeder should indicate that the material used has been used with consent, but that this is not a condition for grant or grounds for revocation. It is possible that the national laws of any given European country may place greater emphasis on the provisions of the CBD and Treaty, and it will be necessary for any plant researchers seeking to bring in externally sourced plant material to familiarise themselves with the appropriate national frameworks. It is not proposed to discuss these issues any further here.[148]

## Exploiting Plants

The second point relating to the use of plant material is connected with the capacity to exploit the material protected by the intellectual property right. The

---

[148] For a full discussion of these issues see Dutfield, *Intellectual Property Rights: Trade and Biodiversity*, above n 143.

marketing of a plant variety, whether it is protected by a variety right or not, can take place only if the variety has been approved for marketing[149] and included on the National List of approved varieties for marketing within the EU member state concerned. All member states of the European Union are legally required to produce National Lists of varieties which are eligible for certification and marketing within their territory. The European Commission also provides Common Catalogues (for agricultural and vegetable species) from these lists (entry being dependent on the variety concerned having gained inclusion on the National Lists in one or more member states).[150]

There is no requirement that a variety must also be the subject of a plant variety right, but the usual practice is to seek both the right and registration on the National List—one of the reasons for this is that part of the requirements for inclusion on the National Lists is the demonstration that the variety is distinct, uniform and stable, these being the same requirements for plant variety protection) and as a result the tests for inclusion on the list are usually conducted at the same time as the tests for variety protection. It is important to note that the two are, however, legally totally separate and the requirements for one are not pre- or co-requisites for the other. Where the variety concerned is an agricultural crop then it must be shown to have a Value for Cultivation and Use (VCU). A variety will be deemed to meet the VCU requirement if it can be shown to provide a demonstrable benefit either for cultivation or for other use when compared to other varieties. The VCU requirement, generally, does not apply to varieties of a) vegetables, b) grasses (where these are not intended to be used as fodder), c) any variety which has already been placed on the National List of another member state of the EU, or d) any variety which is merely a component of another variety. In contrast to the plant variety right, which is time barred, registration on the National List remains in effect for as long as the holder of the registration pays the renewal fees.

Where the plant material concerned is genetically modified, then its uses have to comply with European Council Directive 2001/18/EC on the deliberate release into the environment of genetically modified organisms, and any national legislation relating to the use of genetically modified material. In addition, where the material concerned takes the form of food or a food stuff then it has to comply with Council Regulation (EC) 258/97 concerning novel foods and novel food ingredients and national regulation. The variety must also have an

---

[149] For example, the EU has a number of regulations, introduced via Directives, in place which apply to the marketing of certain specified types of seed. These include the marketing of beet seed (Directive 2002/54/EC), fodder plant and cereal seed (Directive 66/401/EEC, amended by Directive 2001/64/EC), seed potatoes (Directive 2002/56/EC) and the seed of oil and fibre plants (Directive 2002/57/EC).

[150] See Council Directive 2002/53/EC of 13 June 2002 on the Common Catalogue of varieties of Agricultural Plant Species (as amended), Council Directive 2002/55/EC of 13 June 2002 on the Marketing of Seeds (as amended), and Council Directives 2003/90/EC and 2003/91/EC of 6 October 2003 setting out implementing measures for the purposes of Art 7 of Council Directive 2002/53/EC as regards the characteristics to be covered as a minimum by the examination and the minimum conditions for examining certain varieties of agricultural plant species.

approved name,[151] and someone must be identified as responsible for maintaining the quality of the variety registered. There are more stringent regulations relating to medical and pharmaceutical products. At the international level, the Cartagena Protocol on Biosafety which governs trade in genetically engineered organisms also needs to be taken into account.

At this stage it might be appropriate to say a few words about genetically modified (GM) crops and the European position on the commercial selling of GM crops. Whilst there remain some very real concerns over the use of the technology, the European Commission, in September 2004, authorised the first genetically modified seeds for commercial use across the EU under the new Directive. In addition, whilst GM crops are not widely commercialised in the EU, approval has been given for their inclusion in the EU Common Catalogue of Varieties of Agricultural Plant Species,[152] and a total of 17 genetically modified maize varieties have been added to the list as well as a strain of genetically modified oilseed rape. In addition, some of the newly associated member states who joined the EU in 2004 already commercially sell GM crops, and other member states permit the sowing of GM crops, for example Spain. There is also evidence that other countries are utilising the new technology, for example there are reports that a new strain of genetically modified grapevine which is resistant to Fanleaf disease, may soon be planted in France.

Further evidence of likely importance of GM crops can be seen in the comments made in 2003 by a group of private sector companies, Agricultural Biotechnology in Europe (ABE), which disseminates information on crop biotechnology. It stated that farmers were beginning to recognise that there could be real economic value in growing genetically modified crops. In justifying this claim the ABE referred to corn farmers in Spain which, it said, had experienced an increase of 800 kilos per hectare for BT corn in comparison with the yield per hectare for the conventionally bred crop.[153] At the global level the International Service for the Acquisition of Agri-biotech Applications (ISAAA) has estimated that the global sales of GM crops have risen from $4.7 billion to $5.25 billion and between 1996–2005 are likely to continue rising to $5.5 billion by 2006.[154] In the country-by-country analysis Europe figures only in a peripheral manner, with Spain's use of BT maize being said to have increased by 6 per cent in 2003 (Romania also apparently recording a significant increase). Notwithstanding the debates in Europe, ISAAA does not expect this upwards trend to reverse and it expresses cautious optimism that farmers will continue to move over to using genetically modified crops. Whilst obviously these views have to be treated with caution and set against the public resistance to GM crops and GM food products, as well as the withdrawal of some plant bioscience

---

[151]  This ensures compliance with Council Regulation (EC) 930/2000.

[152]  In its most recent guise this was established by Council Directive 2002/53/EC of 13 June 2002 on the Common Catalogue of Varieties of Agricultural Plant Species.

[153]  See www.ABEurope.info.

[154]  See www.isaaa.org.

research from Europe, the indications are that there is value in GM crop production (whether for use in Europe or elsewhere) and therefore in acquiring
rights over crops so produced.

Both the breeders and the European Commission are at the fore in trying to
realise this value. In its paper outlining the intellectual property needs of the
modern plant breeder, the ISF identifies various tensions including obtaining an

> acceptable return on research investment, prerequisite to encouraging further research
> efforts, essential to meet the challenges mankind has to face in the coming years, ie,
> feeding an increasing population whilst preserving the planet. These challenges cannot
> be met without further development of new knowledge, technologies and the more
> effective use of a broader base of genetic resources. All of these endeavours require
> substantial, long term and high risk investments.

In 2003, the European Commission called upon its members to take 'urgent and
decisive action' in the life sciences. In 2004 the Commission instigated a
European plant biotechnology strategy which is intended to set down the long-
term vision. The strategy has been developed in consultation with the farming
community, researchers and consumers, as well as the bioscience industry itself.
One of the primary focuses of the strategy is to develop public understanding of
biotechnology, making Europeans more open to using the results of this technology. The strategy is solely directed to the food and agricultural plant biotechnologies.[155] Whilst the vision paper does not seek to address the matter of the
provision of equivalent plant property rights within each member state of the
EU, it does recognise that the work undertaken by the Commission to put in
place appropriate frameworks to regulate, in particular, biotechnology needs to
be translated into action at the national level. The paper specifically mentions
the general lack of implementation of the Directive, citing as a fear that without
this common provision the technology will be produced, and imported in from,
elsewhere.[156]

More specifically, in terms of intellectual property protection, the
Commission, in April 2004, published a report on European biotechnology and
reported, with considerable disappointment, that (at that time) only seven
member states had implemented the patent Directive (discussed in chapter 7),
that eight member states had yet to implement the EU Directive 2001/18 on
GMOs, and there were still far fewer than the hoped-for 15 per cent of SMEs
engaging in the EU's research framework programme. In 2004 the European
Academies Science Advisory Council (EASAC) added its voice to the concerns
by saying that the lack of coherence was having a detrimental effect on the
use of valuable new plant products by farmers. Clearly this is a matter which

---

[155] For further details see www.epsoweb.org/catalog/TP/index.htm. EPSO is the European Plant
Science Organisation, both it and EuropaBio (the association of European bio industries) were
involved in drafting the strategy.

[156] http://europa.eu.int./comm/biotehnology/introduction_en.html.

exercises the Commission, and one which is likely to be the subject of further, possibly more intensive, attention.

A final point on exploitation is that there is a perception that patent holders are much more aggressive in protecting their interests in the patented materials than plant variety rights holders. To an extent this is correct, not least because the cost of acquisition and enforcement tends to be far higher for patents than for plant variety rights, but it needs to be looked at in the context of general practice. Most patent holders do not acquire rights with a view to litigation but rather to secure a market position in order to maximise the economic potential of the invention (not least in order to recoup the research investment). To this end there is great emphasis on establishing licensing agreements on an exclusive or non-exclusive basis. For the most part this is uncontroversial and regarded as being to the mutual benefit of both licensor and licensee. There is an expectation therefore that the holder of a patent will want to disseminate the novel technical effect protected by the patent as widely as possible using the most effective, and valuable way of so doing. A licence relating to intellectual property is treated in the same way as any other commercial agreement or contract and subject to the overarching maxim of sanctity of contract, which means that the courts are loath to interfere with an agreement entered into by the two parties unless there is good cause to do so. In respect of a licence, there is an expectation that the patent holder will set reasonable terms relating to price and use, any concern that the terms are not reasonable being dealt with either by the granting office if faced with an application for a compulsory licence or through invoking competition law.[157] However, the fact that the terms set may not be to the liking of the person seeking the licence does not in itself mean that the terms are unreasonable and the patent holder will be forced to change them. The basic premise is that the patent holder is free to use or exploit the patented technology as he thinks fit—if that means not entering into a licence with any other party then, provided that the patent holder can show that he is working the invention (that is, making it available to the market concerned) then he will be left alone to do so. It is only in rare instances that the licence agreement is unnecessarily onerous and a potential abuse of the monopoly, and unfortunately it is these which tend to be held up as exemplars of common practices within the patent system. Whilst onerous licensing agreements may occur, these are not usually in the interests of the patent holder. More commonly, the patent holder and the recipient of the patented technology agree terms which benefit both—for example, that a university patented technology may be freely used within an

---

[157] The European Court of Justice has confirmed that plant variety rights are subject to the European Community's competition law: see *Nungesser v EC Commission* [1982] ECR 2015. For a discussion of this case see Harding, '*Nungesser and Eisle v Commission*: Plant Breeders' Rights before the European Court' [1983] 3 *EIPR* 57; Harding, 'Commission Decision on Breeders' Rights in Relation to Roses: Hard Line on Restriction of Breeders' Rights Maintained Case Comment' [1986] 9 *EIPR* 284; and Cornish, *Intellectual Property*, above n 32, para 7.34. More generally see Anderman, *EC Competition Law and Intellectual Property* (OUP, 1998).

essentially commercial research programme but that the results of that research work will be shared between the patent holder and the research institute. In this respect, the protected material is used as a carrot to bring new researchers to the licensing negotiating table rather than that the patent is used as a stick to prevent access to that material. The issue of licensing will be picked up again later. In maximising the licensing potential of a protected plant variety, most breeders rely upon the services of agencies, such as the British Society of Plant Breeders. These license, collect and distribute certified seed royalties (often set by the breeder) as well as farm saved seed payments.

### Extending the Period of Patent Protection

One final matter needs to be taken into consideration, and that is the fact that whilst patent protection generally lasts for up to 20 years it is possible, in respect of certain types of inventions, to obtain supplementary protection which extends that term. In the past such protection has been primarily available for pharmaceutical products which require regulatory approval before they can be launched onto the market. The seeking of this approval invariably takes place after the patent has been granted and has the effect of eating into the patent term. To compensate for this it is possible to seek a supplementary protection certificate which extends the patent term up to a maximum of five years.[158] In recognition of the fact that there are some plant products the use of which is also subject to regulatory approval, the EU introduced an equivalent system in 1996.[159]

In order to obtain a supplementary certificate, there must first be a patent in force, and the request has to made within 6 months of the regulatory approval being granted. If the certificate is granted then it will not extend beyond the subject matter for which the patent was originally issued. The duration of the certificate will depend on the time taken to obtain the approval. It is not intended to discuss these conditions further. One question which does arise is whether such certificates comply with the TRIPs Agreement. It would appear that such certificates would not be in violation of TRIPs as Article 33 states that 'the term of protection available *shall not end before* the expiration of a period of twenty years from the filing date' (emphasis added). The use of the words 'shall not end before' indicates that it is permissible to have a term of protection which ends after the expiration of the 20-year period from filing. Article 1 also states that members may 'implement more extensive protection than is required by this Agreement, provided that such protection does not contravene the provisions of this Agreement.'

---

[158] Regulation No 1768/92 concerning the creation of a supplementary protection certificate for medicinal products.

[159] Regulation No 1610/96 concerning the creation of a supplementary protection certificate for plant protection products.

The effect of Regulation No 1610/96 is to require the relevant offices within all EU member states (the national patent offices) to extend the term of an extant patent where 'the period that elapses between the filing of an application for a patent . . . and authorization to place the . . . plant protection product on the market makes the period of effective protection under the patent insufficient to cover the investment put into the research and to generate the resources needed to maintain a high level of research.'[160] Plant protection products are defined as 'active substances and preparations containing one or more active substances, put up in the form in which they are supplied to the user', such products being intended to:

(a) protect plants or plant products against all harmful organisms or prevent the action of such organisms, in so far as such substances or preparations are not otherwise defined below; (b) influence the life processes of plants, other than as a nutrient (eg, plant growth regulators[161]); (c) preserve plant products, in so far as such substances or products are not subject to special Council or Commission provision on preservatives; (d) destroy undesirable plants; or (e) destroy parts of plants, check or prevent undesirable growth of plants. [Article 1] (a)–(e).

Importantly for those seeking patent rights over plant-related products, substances are defined as 'chemical elements and their compounds, as they occur naturally or by manufacture' and active substances means 'substances or micro-organisms including viruses', and as has already been discussed, these terms have a very flexible meaning in patent law, with plant, animal and human genes being regarded as micro-organisms, and no finite distinction between a micro-organism and a plant. The only caveat is that the substances or micro-organisms must have a 'general or specific action against harmful organisms' or 'on plants, parts of plants or plant products'.

When taken with the first set of definitions it can be seen that the substances, which have general or specific action, are taken to form the plant protection product—eg, a product which can be used to protect plants. This product can protect plants against harmful organisms, influence the life processes (this term not being defined) of plants provided that its influence is not as a nutrient, or serve to preserve plant products, such as food, provided that these products which serve to preserve are not themselves subject to any specific Council or Commission regulation regarding their use. Substances comprising the plant protection product can include chemical compounds and micro-organisms (which, according to patent law practice, will also mean plant genes).

Substances which take the form of the plant protection products may have one of two functions. The first is to protect against harmful organisms such as pests. The second itself has two aspects to it. The first is to influence the life

---

[160] Recital 5.
[161] Although it is not clear if the plant growth regulator is given as an example of protectable or non-protectable material.

processes of plants (defined as 'live plants and live parts of plants, including fresh fruit and seed'). The specific reference to the fruit or seeds of the plant indicates that the use does not have to be an external one only and it is possible that the plant protection product could take the form of an internal genetic one such as terminator technology. The second is to preserve plant products. Plant products are stated to be 'products in an unprocessed state or having only undergone simple preparation such as milling, drying or pressing.' The provision relates to material derived from the plant but not to the plant itself. There is a question whether, for example, a patent granted over a particular crop plant, for example, wheat, could have its term extended where the patent claimed not only the wheat but also the flour milled from it. It would seem from the Recitals that this could be the case.

Recitals 1–4 state that:

> Whereas research into plant protection products contributes to the continuing improvement in the production and procurement of plentiful food of good quality at affordable prices; whereas plant protection research contributes to the continuing improvement in crop production; whereas plant protection products, especially those that are the result of long, costly research, will continue to be developed in the Community and in Europe if they are covered by favourable rules that provide for sufficient protection to encourage such research; whereas the competitiveness of the plant protection sector, buy the vary nature of the industry, requires a level of protection for innovation which is equivalent to that granted to medicinal products.

The function of Regulation No 1610/96 is thereby clearly set out, to ensure that those mechanisms produced can secure the 'production and procurement of plentiful food of good quality' and 'continue to improve crop production', the only qualification to the availability of the protection being that:

> a fair balance should also be struck with regard to the determination of the transitional arrangements; whereas such arrangements should enable the Community plant protection industry to catch up to some extent with its main competitors, while making sure that the arrangements do not compromise the achievement of other legitimate objectives concerning the agricultural policy and environment protection policy pursued at both the national and Community level. [Recital 15]

Interestingly, this balance only appears to be required in respect of the transitional arrangements.

The types of plant products most directly affected by the Regulation are the agrochemical equivalents of pharmaceutical products which are intended to be applied *to* plant material. It is unlikely that it will have any effect on plant breeding as such unless a breeder is engaged in the production of a coherent range of products intended to interact with each other. In such an instance, the fact of the supplementary protection certificate (SPC) could be important particularly when looked at in the context of the protection afforded under plant variety rights and that under patent law. Patents protect for up to 20 years; plant variety rights for up to 30 years in the case of trees and vines, and 25 years for all other species. The possibility of extending the patent term to co-exist with the plant variety right term could be attractive to breeders seeking to develop plant products in tandem with new plant varieties.

## IX. CONCLUSION

In summary therefore, the following factors need to be taken into account when evaluating European plant property provision.

It is difficult to provide hard and fast definitions as to what is *European* plant protection policy and practice. Consideration therefore needs to be given to diversities across Europe, both at the pan-European level (as a result of implementation of overarching legislation such as the EPC and the UPOV Conventions) as well as at the national level (for example, the variation in plant variety rights provision with a range of national differences in national adoption of the UPOV Acts), and policy and practice regarding matters such as essentially derived varieties and farm saved seed. In understanding these differences it is critical to bear in mind that decisions relating to legislative change (for example, in respect of upgrading national plant variety rights provision or implementing the EC Directive) are *political* decisions. The lack of any such upgrade or implementation should *not* be taken to necessarily mean a rejection of the rights themselves (although the legislative provision may reflect local concerns over the type and scope of protection); instead the political situation may be such that it has not been opportune, or space has not been found in a legislative programme, to address issues relating to plant protection. At the broader level it must also be noted that there is considerable bleed-through from international developments, with decisions being taken at the European level based either on evolving international obligations or as a result of practices elsewhere which are regarded as sufficiently important to warrant attention at the European level (both of these factors will be dealt with in more detail in the next chapter).

Although the term 'plant property rights' is used throughout this book as short-hand to describe the rights available over plant material, it is important to bear in mind that the modern emphasis on molecular research means that it is not always possible to draw clear distinctions between material specific to plants and that which is applicable to all life-forms. This has two effects. The first is that where a right is granted over genetic material, but the term 'plant' is not used to describe the material protected, this does not mean that the right granted will not affect those engaged in plant research. Users of any product or process which involves genetic material need to be aware of the possible existence, and therefore the effect, of any rights granted over that material. It would be impossible for this book to discuss all rights which have been granted over genetic material. The focus therefore will be on those which are specified to be plant related and which highlight specific issues relating to plant research. Secondly, the erosion of the genetic boundaries makes it increasingly difficult to draw clear lines between protectable and non-protectable material. A key example of this is the fact that the TRIPs Agreement allows legislators to distinguish between micro-organisms, plants and plant varieties. As will be discussed in the next chapter, this implies that there is a clear blue water distinction between the three types of genetic material; however, the scientific, and legal, reality is that such clear distinctions are not easy to draw in practice.

Plants are now being used for a range of different purposes from farming to modern pharma. When plant property rights were first mooted the primary commercial production was in the areas of agriculture and horticulture. Modern plant science, however, encompasses multiple (not necessarily plant-related) uses of individual components of plants as well as whole plants. Not all of these diverse research results have yet been achieved or commercialised. Notwithstanding this, they all need to be borne in mind when assessing the suitability of the protection provided. For example, plant breeders have developed crops which can produce vaccines for TB, diabetes and HIV. Whilst the results of the new pharming programmes are not expected to be generally available for a number of years (the expectation is that field trials will begin in 2006, with human trials beginning around 2010), their development nonetheless raises questions of the appropriateness of the protection provided for producer and recipient alike. The most obvious consequence of this multiplicity of uses is to make plant research highly attractive to the private as well as the public sector. However, it also means that the science cannot be regarded as static but rather in a state of constant evolution. Because of this, the law has to either evolve (in terms of a substantive revision) in order to either include or exclude, or it has to be capable of flexible interpretation enabling an appropriate response to the evolutions in science.

Because of the changes in the science, it is less accurate to regard the rights granted over plant material (and varieties in particular) as single-sector specific. As will be shown, the plant variety rights system was primarily introduced to protect plant breeders, and agricultural plant breeders in particular, with the result that the right is often referred to as a breeders' right. The evolution of plant research has meant that it is now difficult to refer to all those who engage in plant research as plant 'breeders' in the traditional sense of those who use conventional plant breeding techniques to achieve a desired outcome. This has two effects. The first is that there is now a greater diversity in types of plant innovators, from nurserymen through to multi-nationals. It is widely acknowledged that whilst there still are many independent plant innovators, whose sole work is in the area of plant science, there are others, usually falling within the category of multi-national, for which plant research is but one part of a pluralist bioscience research portfolio. The second is that the modern approach to plant property provision reflects the view that the rights exist to protect valuable research *results* rather than the interests of a particular, discreet, group of scientists. This issue is an important one, for many of the principles which underpin the plant variety rights system were introduced to protect the interests of plant breeders as both producers and users of new plant varieties. As will be discussed below, the specific sector focus, which underpinned the introduction of plant variety rights, can be contrasted with the non-sector specific nature of patent protection. This is an important distinction, as the rationales which support the patent and plant variety rights systems are very different, particularly with respect to the role the public interest exclusions/limitations play within each right. Fundamental to understanding the relevance of these distinctions is the question whether plant variety rights should be treated as part of the industrial (or intellectual) property law family.

Other, external, considerations also help explain the way in which the rights have evolved generally speaking, these relate to the way in which intellectual property law operates in practice. In addition to the obvious legal constraints relating to authorisation to use and market, consideration must also be given to the 'soft-law' principles 'governing' the sourcing and exploitation of plant material.

Finally, it must be remembered that this is a constantly evolving area of law. All we can do in this book is to provide a snapshot of the legal environment at a set moment in time. The law (policy and practice) will inevitably change; however, notwithstanding any changes, we would argue that the above factors will remain relevant in determining both the shape of that change and its implications for plant breeders.

At the heart of these considerations lies the question whether the rights provided serve the function for which they were introduced—namely to protect the interests of those engaged in plant research.

As can be seen, the growth in international commercial value of plant products and the deconstruction of genetic inheritance following Crick and Watson's identification of the structure of DNA in 1953 has meant that developments in the form and scope of plant intellectual property became increasingly rapid. One of the consequences of this was the emergence of private sector plant breeding and the growing awareness that this could only achieve long-term security if the results of their time- and money-intensive research programmes were protected thereby enabling them either to exploit the protected material themselves or to license others to exploit on their behalf. By 1998, in Europe at least, all aspects of plant material from genes to species were legally recognised as capable of being private property, and at the start of the 21st century, the presumption, in most of the developed world, is that protecting plant material via intellectual property rights is not only possible but desirable. This extensive provision of protection has been achieved through, on the one hand, the introduction of national and Community plant variety rights and, on the other, the evolution of patent law (via the jurisprudence of the European Patent Office and the introduction of the Directive).

These developments have taken place in an environment of intense scrutiny, but, as will be discussed later, much of the attention now has been diverted to other areas of biotechnological research and development, most specifically human genetic research. As a result, the plant protection systems have been increasingly relegated to the sidelines of both legal and political discussion. This is to be regretted and an absence of awareness and debate of the effects, actual or potential, of the new plant protection regimes within the broader policy context could result in undesirable consequences.

Europe is, if not at the actual centre of global plant breeding, then very close to its heart. Many of the most dramatic evolutions in plant genetics have taken place, and continue to take place, in Europe. The result of this is that there is a long tradition of plant breeding activity within both the public and private sectors, and the facilitation of this activity is regarded as core to the economies of many EU member states. Because of this it is relevant to assess the framework of protection relating to plant intellectual property provision and determine whether, the developments in the framework of protection made available, this protection serves the needs of European plant breeders thereby ensuring both their own, and the breeding programmes', long-term survival.[162]

Often the issue is not one of whether the legislation achieves the objective but whether it is being used to achieve objectives not envisaged at the time of introduction. The question then is whether the law should be used to achieve this secondary aim or if this extension of scope goes beyond a proper application, amounting to an inappropriate use. These are difficult questions, for it is not always clear whether the original stated aim of a piece of legislation means that the legislation is confined to that aim even where the later development is not one which could have been foreseen by the legislators—in such circumstances the usual reaction is to seek the intention of the legislators.[163]

A second question arises where a law was introduced to achieve a particular result and then revised to take account of developments, and that revision serves

---

[162] In discussing European provision, attention will focus on the current legislation. However, it is relevant to note that discussions are also taking place with regard to the introduction of a European patent (Proposal for a Council Regulation on the Community Patent, COM (2000) 412 final). It is not proposed that this should replace the existing patent systems, but rather consolidate the position of the EPO (in the form of the EPC) and harmonise procedural practices at the post-grant stages. In addition to this, the EU is considering joining the EPC as a member in order to ensure parity of policy and action. In the long term, the agenda would appear to be to bring the EPC within the auspices of the EU and therefore subject to EU legislation.

[163] One of the problems facing common law jurisdictions (such as the UK) is that these legal systems are more bound by the letter of the law rather than the spirit. Civil law jurisdictions, such as those of most European countries, operate on the reverse principle. The arguments supporting the former approach include ensuring predictability and certainty within the flexible confines of the language used; support for the latter includes not being bound by previous decisions and not letting the language used stand in the way of achieving the result desired. These differences in approach are very important when looking at decisions relating to the adoption of European legislation. English lawyers will invariably be more concerned with the words used, whereas the Continental lawyers will focus more on gauging what the legislation wishes to achieve. The former again could be viewed as too linguistically-centric but at least has the benefit of ensuring that the law is what it says it is; the latter might provide for more justice, but can lead to alternative arguments as to what is the objective of the law and how it can best be implemented. The problems these approaches can cause will be discussed in more detail in ch 6.

to remove, in part or in apparent entirety, the law from one or all of its original purposes.

In respect of plant property rights, the importance and relevance of the rationale supporting both the introduction and the form of the rights is as pertinent now as when the rights were introduced. As can be seen, whilst recent developments in plant property protection have been driven by global commercial imperatives, many of which are grounded in patent law rhetoric, the foundations for a fully pluralist approach to protecting plant material are firmly rooted in European scientific and legal thinking. Before looking at the evolution of European plant property provision, it is necessary to set this alongside the evolution of protection elsewhere and most notably within the US and under the TRIPs Agreement.

# 2

# Plant Protection Rights: International Influences[1]

## I. INTRODUCTION

ALL LEGAL SYSTEMS are influenced, whether officially or not, by developments which take place elsewhere. This is certainly true of modern European plant protection. Central, therefore, to an understanding of the modern form of European protection is an understanding of these other influences. Of particular relevance is the international framework. As already outlined in chapter 1, both the Paris and UPOV Conventions are inseparable from the origins of European plant protection, and these will be discussed later as part of the chronology of European provision. This chapter will focus on the two primary, non-European, influences which have helped shape attitudes towards, and the substantive revision of, European plant protection. These two influences are the TRIPs Agreement and the law of the United States of America.

Both the TRIPs Agreement and the development of protection in the US reflect decisions taken by a wide range of policy makers. Central to these has been the work of the WIPO and in particular that of its Committee of Experts on Biotechnological Inventions and Industrial Property. The work of the Committee, which builds on that begun in the 1950s,[2] has continued throughout subsequent decades. In 1985 this Committee was charged with assessing the pros and cons of using industrial property protection to protect biotechnological inventions (including 'genetic inventions') at both the national and international levels. This was not new work for the WIPO, as its involvement in the protection of living material can be traced back to the early 1970s and, in addition to its policy statements on the issue of protecting inventions involving living material, has resulted in legislative activity such as the introduction of the Budapest Treaty on the Deposit of Micro-organisms in 1977.[3] In 1987 the

---

[1] The following is only a general overview and should not be taken as definitive statements on either the US or the TRIPs Agreement—the objective is to highlight those issues which may affect/influence European practice.

[2] This will be discussed in more detail in chs 3 and 5.

[3] Budapest Treaty on the International Recognition of the Deposit of Micro-organisms for the Purposes of Patent Procedures 1977. The function of this Treaty, which will not be discussed further

Committee of Experts submitted an *Analysis of Certain Basic Issues in Industrial Property Protection of Biotechnological Inventions*.[4] In summary, the Committee supported the use of industrial patent rights to protect biotechno-logical inventions but with certain caveats. As this work was closely inter-connected with that of the European Commission and its subsequent decision to introduce a Directive on the Legal Protection of Biotechnological Inventions, the views of the Committee will be discussed in more detail in chapter 7. Its relevance here is to demonstrate that the developments in the US and, through the WTO, within TRIPs which were directed towards providing patent protec-tion for biotechnological inventions were not isolated, or contradictory, events.

In looking at this provision consideration should also be given to the CBD and the ITPGR (discussed in chapter 1), as both of these are providing reference points for complying with the TRIPs obligation to protect plant varieties—although both of these are currently at the periphery of influence for European provision.

As will be seen later in this chapter, the TRIPs Agreement is now the primary driving force in determining international intellectual property policy. However, whilst it can be argued that the international standardisation which lies behind the Agreement means that its provisions should be approached on a bias-free basis, there are those who argue that the Agreement cannot be read as an objective document. Instead, it is argued that the Agreement is over-laden with US policy and practice and that the starting point for determining compli-ance (including compliance within Europe) is whether provision equates to US provision, any deviation therefrom only being permitted in limited circum-stances.[5] There are three other reasons for looking at US practice. The first is due to the current lack of case law on the TRIPs Agreement. This means that whilst it is possible to argue that European jurisprudence *might* provide an indi-cator of good practice for the operation of the TRIPs provisions in practice, so too can it be argued might US jurisprudence. The second reason is that the US has been the most vocal in calling for the TRIPs provisions to be given the strongest possible reading thereby providing the greatest protection for the

---

in this book, is to allow the deposit of a micro-organism within a recognised depository to comply with all or part of the disclosure requirement in patent law. A number of conditions apply, includ-ing an inability to describe the micro-organism sufficiently within the specification itself.

[4] WIPO Doc BIOT/CE/11/2, and this was discussed by the WIPO in WIPO Doc.BIOTE/CE/III/31.

[5] Indeed, much of the resistance within developing countries to the TRIPs obligation is based on the perceived close association between the operation of the Agreement and US practice and policy. It would be wrong however, to imply that the US patent system has not itself had to change as a result of the introduction of the TRIPs Agreement. Most notably, it now provides protection for up to 20 years whereas previously protection lasted only for up to 17 years. Given the perception that the US system favours the patent holder, it might seem odd to relate that the revision upwards was strongly opposed by US patent lawyers. It is unsurprising, therefore, that any other attempts to har-monise by bringing the US into line with practices elsewhere were not so successful (eg, a move from first to invent to first to file). The politically sensitive nature of the negotiations leading up to the final TRIPs text cannot be underestimated.

patent holder. The third reason is that the European Commission, whilst paying lip service to the need to compete with other strong economies world-wide (most notably Japan), tends to look at developments in US patent law when assessing its own future direction although, as will be seen, perhaps caution ought to be exercised where those practices have evolved in response to previously inadequate plant variety provision which arguably has not been the case in Europe.

For these reasons, a broad-brush outline of the development of US plant protection law, with its emphasis on strong unfettered rights, is useful before looking at the obligations set down in TRIPs.

## II. AN OVERVIEW[6] OF US PLANT PROTECTION[7]

Article 1(8) of the US Constitution states that 'Congress shall have power . . . to promote the progress of science and useful arts, by securing for limited times to authors and inventors the exclusive right to their respective writings and discoveries.'[8] In respect of patent law, Title 35 of the United States Code (USC) Section 101 states that 'whoever invents or discovers any new and useful process, machine, manufacture, composition of matter, or any new and useful improvement thereof, may obtain a patent therefore.'[9]

Today, this is interpreted to permit the grant of ordinary patent protection over not only inventions involving plants but any genetic material up to, but for ethical reasons excluding, human beings, but this has not always been the case.

---

[6] This is a very basic overview of the US system, and should not be taken as either a comprehensive or a definitive statement on the law. Unsurprisingly, there is a considerable body of literature on this subject which it is impossible to make full reference to. Examples of thinking through the 1980s (the period of most influence in terms of shaping European policy) include Williams, 'Securing Protection for Plant Varieties in the USA' (1981) 8 *EIPR* 222; Casey and Moss, 'Intellectual Property Rights and Biotechnology' (1987) 27(4) *IDEA* 251; Duffey, 'The Marvellous Gifts of Biotech: Will They be Nourished or Stifled by our International Patent Laws?' in Proceedings of a joint WIPO/Cornell University Symposium on the Protection of Biotechnological Inventions (Ithaca, NY, 1987); van Horn, 'Recent Developments in the Patenting of Biotechnology in the United States' in Proceedings of a joint WIPO/Cornell University Symposium on the Protection of Biotechnological Inventions (Ithaca, NY, 1987); Hoffmaster, 'The Ethics of Patenting Higher Life Forms' (1988) 4(1) *Intellectual Property Journal* 1; and Armitage, 'The Emerging US Law for the Protection of Biotechnology Research Results' [1989] 2 *EIPR* 47.

[7] For more information see www.uspto.gov. In looking at US provision it is important to bear in mind that there are a number of procedural differences, most notably those relating to first to invent (as opposed to the first to file principle which operates in Europe) and the existence of a 12-month grace period which allows an inventor to make his invention public without breaking novelty. We will not be discussing these any further. For an excellent evaluation of US provision, see Janis and Kesan, 'US Plant Variety Protection' (2002) 39 *Houston Law Review* 727. For a comparison between the US and Europe see van Overwalle, 'Patent Protection for Plants: A Comparison of American and European Approaches' (1999) 39(2) *IDEA* 143.

[8] The patent laws have undergone a number of revisions over the years, the most significant being a general revision in 1952 (in effect from 1 January 1953) and the introduction of the American Inventors Protection Act of 1999 (AIPA). In looking at the US provision, it is worth noting that it joined the Paris Convention in 1887.

[9] US patent law does not contain any specific exclusions.

Until the 1980s the US operated a far more restrictive approach to what could be regarded as a manufacture than was the case in Europe.[10] As will be seen in chapter 5, whilst European patent law was also concerned with the protection of manufactures, this notion was given a more liberal interpretation by granting offices and it could include inventions involving material drawn from nature. In the US, however, there was a strict adherence to the principle that most inventions involving living material were 'products of nature' and, irrespective of the level of intervention by man, therefore could not be regarded as inventions (or manufactures) by man.[11] This did not mean that all material which had some form of life force was excluded from protection. Inventions involving lower order life forms, such as yeast,[12] were patentable but where the alleged invention took the form of a higher life form then the granting office was less likely to regard it as a manufacture by man. There were, however, two key legislative exceptions to this principle, and both related to the protection of plants. These were the Plant Patent Act 1930 (PPA) and the Plant Variety Protection Act 1970 (PVPA).

### The Plant Patent Act 1930[13]

The Plant Patent Act 1930[14] (which was one of the first pieces of plant protection legislation) provides protection for asexually[15] reproducing plant varieties. Section 161 of 35 USC states that:

> Whoever invents or discovers[16] and asexually reproduces any distinct and new variety of plant, including cultivated sports, mutants, hybrids, and newly found seedlings, other than a tuber propagated plant or a plant found in an uncultivated state, may

---

[10] For example, *Funk Bros Seed Co v Kalo Inoculant* 333 US 127; 130 USPQ 280 (1947), 281; and *Parker v Flook* 437 US 584; 198 USPQ 193 (1978). Echoing the experience within Europe, the first calls for legislation to be enacted came in 1906. These were rejected, as were subsequent proposals put forward in 1907, 1908 and 1910.

[11] This principle was specifically applied to plants in *re Latimer* [1889] *Dec Comm Pat* 123.

[12] For example, the patent was granted to Louis Pasteur in 1873, US Patent 141,072.

[13] In common with utility patents the rights are administered by the United States Patent and Trademark Office. For an historical analysis see C Fowler, 'The Plant Patent Act of 1930: A Sociological History of Its Creation' (2000) 82(9) *Journal of the Patent and Trademark Office Society* 621.

[14] 35 USC §161–64. For more on the history of the Plant Patent Act 1930 and the way it operates in practice see Bent *et al*, *Intellectual Property Rights in Biotechnology Worldwide* (Macmillan, 1987) and Dutfield, *Industrial Property Rights and the Life Science Industries* (Ashgate Publishing, 2003) 181 ff.

[15] The restriction to asexually reproducing varieties was introduced because this is 'the only way a breeder can be sure he has produced a plant identical in every respect to the patent', *Yoder Bros Ltd v Florida Plant Corp* 193 USPQ 264 (1976).

[16] Notwithstanding the wording used, mere discovery does not entitle an applicant to obtain a right. Instead, he has to prove that he has cultivated the discovered material and produced a variety. This mirrors the language of the ordinary US patent law which also refers to whosoever 'invents or discovers', however, the same caveat, a demonstration of expenditure of effort in producing the novel, inventive, result product is also necessary there.

obtain a patent therefore, subject to the conditions and requirements of title. The provision of this title to patents for inventions shall apply to patents for plants, except as otherwise provided.

The right, once granted, lasts for up to 20 years from the date of filing.

The Act clearly indicates that an applicant has to show not only that he has produced a distinct and new variety but also that he has complied with the general 'conditions and requirements' for patent protection. This means that, in addition to the new requirement of distinctness set down in Section 161, the general requirements of novelty, non-obviousness and utility have to be met. These general requirements will be discussed in more detail in the section on utility patent protection below. An applicant has to produce a specification within which must be included a detailed description of the plant and specifically the characteristics which distinguish the variety from other varieties using standard botanical terms, an identification of the parentage (or origin) of the variety and, in particular, the mode of asexual reproduction must be described. Applicants are also required to provide the Latin name of the genus and species. If there are any special qualities about the variety (for example, if it was cultivated from naturally occurring material) then the features which demonstrate the cultivation have to be described. The Act states that material of the variety, such as its flowers, should not be submitted as part of the application unless specifically requested.

In keeping with general notion that products of nature cannot be the subject of a patent, the PPA stipulates that the only plants protectable under it are those which asexually reproduce. This means that the breeder does not rely on the variety itself to self-replicate. Instead, direct action has to be taken to reproduce the variety using such techniques as grafting, the taking of root cuttings, use of bulbs, and tissue culture. Protection is not available for plants which reproduce via seeds, tubers which are not asexually reproduced[17] or plants found in nature.

The right, once granted, prevents others from asexually reproducing or selling the protected variety. The object is to prevent the replication of exact copies of the protected variety. As a result, any sport or mutant of the protected variety is unlikely to be regarded as an exact copy and would fall outside the scope of protection. Indeed, if a variety is produced from that sport or mutation this could itself be the subject of a separate plant patent. Protection also extends only to the variety and not to any other aspects or uses of it. As a result, the patent is confined to a single claim—the variety. This is in contrast with ordinary patents where the patent applicant can make an array of claims relating to the novel technical effect—these claims defining the territory protected by the patent. Further underlining the concerns which existed over providing protection for genetic material (no matter how commercially important), in 1995 the US Court of Appeals for the Federal Circuit in Washington, DC held that the scope of

---

[17] The USPTO's website cites the examples of the Irish potato and Jerusalem artichoke.

protection accorded by a plant patent should be narrowly construed.[18] In *Imazio Nursery, Inc v Dania Greenhouses*, the Court said that the holder of a plant patent has to prove that the alleged infringing variety was actually derived asexually from the protected variety. In making this judgment the Federal Circuit held that 'only a single plant, ie, [asexual] reproduction from one original specimen . . . is protected by a plant patent' and, hence, that 'the term "variety" in section 161 . . . cannot be read as affording plant patent protection to a range of plants, as asserted by [the plaintiff] Imazio.' In 1998, 35 USC §163 was amended to includes 'the right to exclude others from asexually reproducing the plant, and from using, offering for sale, or selling the plant so reproduced, or any of its parts, throughout the United States, or from importing the plant so reproduced, or any parts thereof, into the United States.'[19]

Originally, certain key food crops were specifically excluded from protection under the PPA on the grounds that their production was to the benefit of all society and not merely for the economic interests of the few. This has meant that the PPA has been mainly used to protect fruits and ornamentals.

As already stated, the provisions of the PPA have to be read in conjunction with those which relate to the provision of ordinary patent protection and no concessions are given under these (which relate to the usual threshold for protection involving novelty, non-obviousness and utility). However, a concession to the nature of the material can be seen in the disclosure requirement. Section 162 simply states that: 'No patent shall be declared invalid for non-compliance with section 112 of this title [disclosure] if the description is as complete as is reasonably possible.' Some form of disclosure is still required, but the use of the term 'reasonably' indicates that the USPTO has discretion when deciding if this is sufficient for a grant to take place. The key element is whether or not the disclosure will enable a third party to understand what is protected by the plant patent. This is a question of fact in each instance.

Whilst clearly some breeders benefited from the introduction of the PPA, its limitations meant that many breeders, most notably in the agricultural sector, were unable to acquire protection for their commercially important varieties. Even those whose work was not excluded from protection had difficulties in meeting the threshold for protection. As a result, even though the right remains on the statute book, it is not one which is greatly used. The limited nature of the right meant that plant breeders sought to secure greater protection but these attempts had only limited success. It was not until 1970, following the introduction of the UPOV Convention, that breeders managed to convince the government that there was merit in breeders having stronger rights. The result was a right, ostensibly in line with the principles of the UPOV Convention, which ensured that sexually reproducible plant varieties were afforded protection.

---

[18] 69 F 3d 1560; 36 USPQ 2d 1673 (CAFC, 1995).
[19] Plant Patent Amendments Act 1998.

### The Plant Variety Protection Act 1970[20]

The Plant Variety Protection Act 1970, which was adopted to introduce a UPOV form of protection,[21] opened up protection to sexually reproducing (or what in the US are called seed reproduced) crop varieties which are new, distinct, uniform and stable. However, as with the PPA, this did not mean that all varieties which could meet the criteria for protection were accorded protection. Intense lobbying from certain food producers, fearful that a grant of rights would increase the cost of accessing commercially valuable crops, meant that a number of key species (including tomatoes, peppers and carrots) were originally excluded from protection, as were fungi, bacteria and tuber-propagated and uncultivated plants. In 1980 the law was amended, and carrots, celery, cucumbers, okra, peppers, and tomatoes were added to the list of protectable varieties. In 1994, these were joined by tuber-propagated plant varieties and F1 hybrids.

As per other plant variety rights providers, the US system does require some degree of actual evaluation of the plant material, but in contrast to the European model, this is not a criterion for grant. In the US the applicant is required to provide information about the origin and breeding history of the variety, a statement as to distinctness (usually via a written comparison between the applied-for variety and a variety regarded as most similar), and a statement as to ownership. The examiners then make their determination based on that information. The breeder will include a sample of the seed of the variety, but this will not as a rule be formally examined unless there is a query (usually from a third party) about the ability of the variety to meet the granting criteria. For many this means that the US plant variety protection system is, to all intents and purposes, simply a right by registration.

One of the reasons why the US system is regarded as weaker than that provided by other UPOV member states is because acquisition by registration is generally regarded as providing inferior protection to that acquired following formal examination. The right is regarded as more vulnerable to challenge.

---

[20] USC 2402 §7. The US ratified the 1978 UPOV Convention and became a member in 1981. In 1994 the PVPA was amended to bring provision in line with the 1991 UPOV Convention. In common with other plant variety rights providers, the US system is administered by the US Department of Agriculture. For further information see www.ams.usda.gov/science/pvpo/pvp.htm.

[21] Despite the existence of Art 2(1) of the 1961 UPOV (the dual protection prohibition discussed in chs 1 and 3 (more detail later)), the US was able to join UPOV despite providing both specific plant patents and plant variety rights because the UPOV Union a) agreed that it would be extremely unlikely that both forms could be used to protect the varieties from the same species and b) revised the Convention to permit those countries which already provided *both* to continue to do so. The US did make some concessions to joining UPOV, most notably making revisions to the PPA to bring it into line with certain provisions within UPOV. These revisions took the form of including a nomenclature requirement, provision of samples of seed to the granting office, and changes to the experimental use provision. The situation involving the US can be contrasted with the position of some European countries in the 1950s pre-ratification which provided one form of protection but not both. The choice for them was whether to retain their existing provision or sign up to the UPOV type of right. All chose the latter option.

In keeping with the UPOV obligation, novelty is assessed on the basis of prior commercial availability, and the variety must be given a name (these will be discussed in more detail in the next chapter). The right granted permits the holder to prevent the sale, marketing, offering for sale, conditioning, stocking, reproducing, importing or exporting of the protected variety. In addition, the holder can prevent the repeated use of the protected variety for the production of other varieties, most notably hybrids. The right lasts for 25 years for trees and vines and 20 years for all other varieties.

The public interest concerns which overshadowed the drafting of the legislation meant that broad limitations to the right were permitted. As in Europe these primarily relate to a farmer's right to retain seed from a harvest for resowing in subsequent years—the so-called 'farm saved seed' exemption—and the right to use protected material freely in commercial breeding programmes. In respect of the former, the original exemption was so wide that it also allowed farmers to sell retained seed to other farmers. Unsurprisingly, farmers made good use of this provision, and breeders saw key revenue lines disappear as a result. In 1994, and following the revision of the UPOV Convention in 1991, an amendment was made to the PVPA which restricted the farmers' exemption. Farmers are still allowed to save protected seeds for use on their own farms, but they cannot sell that seed (even if harvested from their own crop) to other farmers. The breeders' exemption has also been restricted in that breeders cannot obtain protection for new varieties which are essentially derived from a protected variety.[22]

Obviously, both the PPA and the PVPA are not without some merit, but, as will be seen, the protection conferred under either looks limited when compared to the protection granted by an ordinary utility patent. Many American breeders regarded (and indeed still regard) the rights (especially plant variety rights) as having minor value.[23] In 1985 the Senate Agriculture Commission asked the US Department of Agriculture to investigate the economic impact of the PVPA. The resulting report[24] (which provides one of the first evaluations of the PVPA), was based on the views of various State agricultural experiment stations as well

---

[22] The notion of an 'essentially derived' variety will be discussed in later chapters.

[23] An example of the extent to which specifically devised plant protection rights are dismissed by those engaged in US plant breeding can be seen in a response given to the authors in 1999 by a global leader in plant science to an invitation to join, as a partner, the EU-funded Plant Intellectual Property project. In refusing the invitation, the company stated that 'plant variety rights are irrelevant to our business.' In 2004 it was noted that the US Plant Variety Protection Office receives approximately 300 applications each year (in contrast to the thousands of patent applications made to the USPTO) of which 75% are for agricultural crops, 18% for vegetable crops, 6% for tuber crops and 1% for ornamentals. For more information about the US system see Strachan, Erbisch and Maredia (eds), *Plant Variety Protection in the USA in Intellectual Property Rights in Agricultural Biotechnology*, 2nd edn (CABI Publishing, 2004).

[24] Butler and Marion, *The Impact of Patent Protection on the US Seed Industry and Public Plant Breeding* (North Central Regional Research Publication) 304. The report provides a great deal of interesting information, including information on market shares, seed distribution and acreage harvested as well as which companies owned the most patents over which varieties.

as those of the people responsible for agricultural policy making. Although the study is now 20 years old, it still has some relevance, as it both indicates concerns which are ongoing but also identifies some more fundamental concerns (such as the balance between public and private sector research) which perhaps have been overlooked in the push to provide strong protection and yet which have resonances in the potential impact of rights on many of those still engaged in plant research. To date this is the most authoritative survey on the impact of the PVPA (although there are other studies which touch on the subject) and for that reason its findings remain relevant 20 years on and indicate why there was support for patenting plant varieties.

The findings were carefully qualified by the authors noting that it was difficult to draw an absolute causal link between the economic growth (or otherwise) and the provision of intellectual property protection (this is a common problem facing any attempt to assess the econometric value of intellectual property rights, especially patents). They also noted that because it can take between 10 and 15 years for a variety to be produced it was difficult to determine, in 1985, whether the PVPA had been effective or not, as the results of many plant breeding programmes which had begun in the 1970s were only just being presented to the Plant Variety Protection Office. Finally there was insufficient data available to assess what the impact of the rights had been on matters such as genetic diversity (the assessment of which the study had also been charged with). The problems with gaining data aside, the authors were able to make the following conclusions.[25]

Impact on the Development of new Varieties

The authors found that whilst the rights had proved useful to private breeders engaged in producing soybeans and wheat, they appeared to have been of negligible value to breeders of other agricultural crops. There was an increase in R&D post 1970, with more firms engaging in plant breeding work, but there was a lack of development of open pollinated varieties other than soybeans and wheat, and the authors were clearly reluctant to say that the growth in private plant breeding firms was due to the introduction of the PVPA. Unsurprisingly, it would seem that much of the pressure for ordinary patent protection came from the private sector. In contrast, there was evidence that the PVPA had had a significant impact on public plant breeding with its emphasis on basic research. The authors noted that there had been a considerable growth in mergers between the private and public sectors but the availability of plant variety protection was seen as only a minimal incentive to such mergers. The primary incentive was the wealth of information and expertise within the public sector which could be utilised in partnership with the private sector. Without these mergers, it was felt that it would be some private (rather than public) firms

---

[25] *Ibid*, pp 1–3.

which would cease to exist. The authors clearly felt that the public sector was of immense value and that any wholesale shift towards private sector plant breeding needed to be monitored.

Impact on Diversity and Access to Protected Material

As noted earlier, the authors felt unable to draw any conclusions as to whether the PVPA was having a positive or negative impact on genetic diversity. However, they did note that the flow of protected plant material from the private to the public sector had slowed down, whereas the flow had increased in the opposite direction due to the aggressive searching by private companies for new plant material upon which to base a plant variety.[26] Unsurprisingly, they also discovered that the use of publicly available plant varieties was greater than that of privately owned and controlled varieties. The PVPA also appeared to be having an impact on which new, and protected, varieties were being adopted by farmers.

Marketing and other Costs

No evidence had been found that the existence of plant variety protection certificates had an anti-competitive effect preventing the use of open pollinated varieties in the seed markets. As the authors noted, this is probably because at that time publicly available plant varieties still dominated the market place and therefore there were only a limited number of varieties being commercialised which were the subject of a monopoly right. Notwithstanding this apparent lack of an impact on competition in the market place, the price of seeds had risen and the PVPA could be seen to have directly contributed to this (advertising costs had also risen and the same connection was made to the PVPA).

The final conclusion of the report is both the most illuminating with hindsight and also the most poignant when applied in a European context. In what is in effect a plea, the authors said that whilst there was 'no evidence that the PVPA has triggered massive investments in R&D . . . there is also little evidence of substantial public costs from PVPA . . . Thus the evidence . . . indicates the Act has resulted in modest private and public benefits at modest public and private costs.' They continued '[i]f a reasonable balance is maintained between the private and public sectors in the breeding of most crops, [then] the present balance of benefits and costs should continue.' The poignancy in this statement lies in its resonances for those traditionally engaged in plant research and also for the type of inventor who makes most use of the patent system. In terms of the US experience, the evolution of universities as private sector companies protecting and exploiting intellectual property to its maximum value shows how that balance between public and private sectors has not been realised in practice.

---

[26] This is something which many developing countries are also increasingly noting.

Inevitably, this pressure to treat all research as of commercial value,[27] and therefore protectable by a patent, has come from industry the interests of which are overseen by trade departments within governments. These departments have not necessarily had the interests of agriculture, or of those engaged in publicly funded plant research, in mind.

It is not known what impact the report had, as references to it rarely appear in discussions of American provision. A possible reason for this was that because the report was primarily directed towards the impact of an Act administered by the Department of Agriculture and the impact of that Act on *agricultural* breeding, it was not seen as being relevant outside that very narrow sphere of activity. It is very unlikely that it played any part in the more famous development in plant protection which took place the same year, namely the decision in *re Hibberd* (discussed below).

Further evidence that the PVPA continues to attract little usage can be shown by a simple comparison with the use of the Community plant variety rights system (which is generally held to be a more robust system than that provided under the PVPA) during its first decade.

Between 1971 and 2002, approximately 5,200 US plant variety protection certificates were issued.[28] In contrast, in the eight years since Regulation (EC) No 2100/94 came into force, approximately 8,500 Community plant variety rights have been granted.[29] It is difficult to argue that European plant breeding is more extensive than in the US, it is simply that the US breeders are not using the PVPA because it is felt to be inadequate for their purposes but, unlike in Europe, also because they have an alternative source of protection.

Therefore, whilst the US might seem to have the widest protection with the three forms of right, the reality is that the limited nature of the PPA and PVPA (and in particular the lack of robustness in examination of the PVPA) explains why it has responded positively to the calls for protection under ordinary patent law. Where the two rights do have value is in protecting pre-existing but uncultivated plant varieties (these being unlikely to meet the novelty threshold in utility patent law) or varieties the production of which is obvious.

The modest impact of both the PPA and PVPA led plant innovators to call for equivalent protection to all other areas of technology, and in particular, for a rethinking of what could be regarded as a manufacture by man for the purposes of applying 35 USC 101. Of particular importance are two cases which, within a bare five years, changed the face of US plant protection—these were *Chakrabarty* and *Hibberd*.

---

[27] This is also happening in Europe.

[28] See Strachan (an official from US Plant Variety Protection Office) *et al*, above n 23, p 86.

[29] Kieweit, *Relation Between PVP and Patents on Biotechnology* (UPOV, 2003).

## *Chakrabarty*[30] and *Hibberd*[31]

As already mentioned, 35 USC 101 states that: 'whoever invents or discovers any new and useful process, machine, manufacture, composition of matter, or any new and useful improvement thereof, may obtain a patent therefore.' Pre-1980, the product of nature doctrine meant that this provision was interpreted to exclude any 'invention' involving living material, as it was not invented by man. It was not until 1980, and the landmark decision in *Chakrabarty*, that this entrenched approach was exploded.[32]

In *Chakrabarty* the US Supreme Court held that Dr Chakrabarty's combination of plasmids to create a new pseudonomas (which was designed to eat oil) fell within the definition of 'manufacture' set down in 35 USC 101. In the now celebrated words of the Court, the concept of a manufacture included 'anything under the sun that is made by man.' In so stating the Supreme Court rejected the arguments of the US Patent Office that the only protection for living material was that provided by the PPA or PVPA. It also rejected the argument that the draftsmen of Section 101 had not intended it to be used to protect animate material. In its view, a proper interpretation of Section 101 could not be dependent on a lack of Congressional foresight as this would be 'the very antithesis of the Constitutional and Congressional purpose of stimulating the creation of new technologies.' The Court concluded by saying that 'the relevant distinction [is] not between living and inanimate things, but between the products of nature, whether living or not, and human made inventions.' The Court decided that Chakrabarty's combination of plasmids would be unlikely to occur in nature. As it only came about through the manipulation by Dr Chakrabarty, it was not a product of nature but a manufacture by man. With this, the 'product of nature' doctrine was effectively abolished.[33] In light of more recent decisions (which have removed the doctrine), it is interesting to note that under the doctrine, notwithstanding the extent of human intervention or degree of genetic material used, anything produced using that material was deemed to be a product of nature. In a virtual reversal of that position, the current thinking, in both US and European patent law, seems to be that no matter the extent of genetic material used the fact of human intervention is sufficient to produce an invention.

Shortly after the decision in *Chakrabarty*, the USPTO announced that applications involving plants would be accepted by the Office. However, this did not

---

[30]  447 US 303 (1980).

[31]  227 USPQ 443 (1985).

[32]  The case drew considerable media attention. See, eg, the report in the *International Herald Tribune*, 'US Ruling May Hasten Patent-seeking by Biologists', 18 June 1980; and in *Newsweek*, 'The Right to Patent Life', 30 June 1980, p 49.

[33]  A UK patent for the same bacterium had been granted to Dr Chakrabarty in 1976. Whilst the decision in *Chakrabarty* attracted much attention, and has tended to be referred to as the key decision in removing internal barriers to patenting living material, it was not an isolated event but was one of many patent applications pushing at the 'product of nature' doctrine.

mean that the patentable status of plant material had been established. The decision in *Chakrabarty* reopened the question of whether, given the obligation undertaken in joining UPOV, it was permissible for utility patents, as opposed to specific plant patents, to be granted over plant varieties. This issue came to a head in the case of *Hibberd* in 1985.

The patent application in *Hibberd* concerned a maize plant which contained an increased level of trytophan, an amino acid. A cell line from a maize plant had been engineered to produce whole plants which would, in turn, produce seeds with the elevated levels of trytophan. Initially the application was rejected, as the patent examiner felt that the existence of both the PPA and PVPA precluded protection under the utility patent system. He also argued that the act of joining UPOV in the early 1970s had had the implicit effect of negating any potential application of Section 101 to plants. The decision was reversed by an internal appeal to the USPTO's Board of Patent Appeals and Interferences.

In a unanimous decision the Board held that the claims to the seeds, plants and tissue cultures were permissible subject matter under Section 101. In reaching this decision the Board looked at the backgrounds to both the PPA and PVPA. It could find nothing to suggest that either was introduced to pre-empt the use of utility patent protection. As the state of scientific knowledge had developed to the point where it was possible for plant innovators to demonstrate that their plant material the threshold for patent protection it was appropriate to allow these innovators to benefit from utility patent protection.

Having decided that plant material did fall within Section 101, the Board addressed the question of whether accession to the UPOV Convention, as well as the existence of the PPA, precluded using Section 101 to protect plant material. It is this part of the decision which is the most interesting. The Board found that accession to UPOV did not limit the application of Section 101, as the Senate had not ratified the Convention. The status of UPOV was, in the view of the Board, merely that of a Presidential executive agreement which, constitutionally, could not pre-empt statutes in the event of a conflict.[34] In basing its decision on what was essentially a procedural point, the Board failed to note that in fact there was no conflict between the provisions of the UPOV Convention and the provision of patent protection under Section 101. As mentioned in chapter 1, the prohibition in Article 2(1) applies only to patents which accord with the provisions of UPOV and, therefore, it does not preclude the use of ordinary patent protection. However, there would have been a problem with providing rights under both the PPA and PVPA, as both of these could be seen to accord with UPOV.

Even though the conclusion was reached in 1985 that there was no conflict between the types of provision available in the US, it was not until 2001 that this was given judicial approval when the Supreme Court held in *JEM Ag Supply Inc*

---

[34] Above n 31.

*v Pioneer HiBred*[35] that the PPA, PVPA and Section 101 were not exclusive of each other and that it was possible to grant cumulative protection over material of the same plant variety (in this instance the case concerned 17 patents granted over corn seed).

There is a very important difference between the cases of *Chakrabarty* and *Hibberd*. The former concerned a genetically engineered bacterium, the latter plant material which had been produced using ordinary plant breeding methods. All that Hibberd and his colleagues had done was to choose plants with increased trytophan and repeatedly cross these until all plants produced contained the increased amino acid. It would be easy to think that the application of the ordinary utility patent law would arise only in situations where the plant had been produced by biotechnological methods and that clear blue water distinctions can be drawn between the protectable subject matter of the PPA, PVPA and utility patent law. The current US position is, therefore, that patent protection is available over both transgenic[36] and traditionally bred plant varieties,[37] and the same types of claims are being made in respect of each. Kock[38] points out that claims can be made over the plant, the progeny (F1), breeding methods, plant parts, pollen tissue culture, transgenic plants derived therefrom, and plants with the same physiological and morphological characteristics. As will be seen in chapter 5, in the discussion of the European Patent Convention, European practice is moving in the same direction.

A bare two years after *Hibberd*, and following a statement made by the Supreme Court in respect of a patent application for a non-genetically engineered oyster,[39] the USPTO published a policy document stating that patents could be granted over genetically engineered animals. In 1988, less than a decade after the decision in *Chakrabarty*, the USPTO granted a patent to Harvard University over a genetically engineered mouse (the so-called 'Harvard Oncomouse' patent). Since then the granting of patents over living material, including inventions involving human genetic material (but excluding human being themselves), has become routine. This does not mean that the practice has been without its problems.

---

[35] 534 US 124 (2001). This case raises many issues relating to the relationship between patent law and plant variety rights (including the relationship between the two research exemptions) which it is not possible to explore in any detail in a text on European provision. See Janis and Kesan (who identify and discuss a number of issues which remain following the decision of the Court), 'Intellectual Property Protection for Plant Innovation: Unresolved Issues After *JEM v Pioneer HiBred*' (2002) 20 *Nature Biotechnology* 1161.

[36] For example, US Patent 6,054,158 granted to Novartis over a genetically modified glyphosate resistant soybean.

[37] For example, US Patent 6,222,101 granted to Pioneer HiBred over canola which has been traditionally bred to have low levels of erucic acid. Interestingly, in respect of the Pioneer HiBred patent the USPTO held that the non-obvious quality of the variety lay in the fact that the combination of phenotypical features was 'unpredictable'. This interpretation of non-obviousness has yet to be tested in the courts.

[38] 'Intellectual Property Protection for Plant Innovation' Paper given at a conference on Intellectual Property Protection for Plant Innovation, Frankfurt, 2004. See www.forum-institut.de.

[39] *Re Allen* (1987) 33 *BNA's Patent, Trademark and Copyright Journal* 638, 664.

As discussed in chapter 1, following the publication of the human genome, then US President Bill Clinton and UK Prime Miniter Tony Blair issued a joint press statement stating that patents should be granted only over true inventions involving genetic material and not over basic genetic information. This view has found support within the scientific community as exemplified by the views expressed also in 2001 by the then Presidents of the Royal Society in the UK, and the US National Academy of Sciences.[40] Most of the more controversial cases in the US have involved human genetic material and what became regarded as the race to patent basic genetic sequences, often without disclosing an actual utility for the sequences described. As will be seen below, the concerns which were levelled at the practice of the USPTO were such that it had to bring in new guidelines for examiners[41] to ensure that the Clinton/Blair mandate that patent should not be granted over basic genetic information was realised in practice. But the practice of the USPTO has been criticised in respect of the policy regarding the patenting of plant material, not least the granting of patents to whole swathes of material such as the patent granted to Agrecetus over all genetically engineered cotton,[42] and rights granted WR Grace & Co over neem[43] and tumeric.[44] As the focus of this chapter is on the influence of US policy on the TRIPs obligation, and therefore its influence on European policy and practice, it is not proposed to discuss the extremely extensive US case law further. However, it is worth noting that many of the controversial patents granted over inventions involving living material have been subsequently invalidated—the question which this raises is why, given later revocation, did the USPTO make the grant in the first place? The explanation lies in the presumption of patentability which is at the heart of the US Patent Act.[45]

---

[40] As stated in ch 1, both held that it is 'critical that the benefits to the public be at least reasonably commensurate' to the reward the inventor obtains via a patent, and that the grant of patents 'to any portion [of the human genome] should be regarded as extraordinary, and should occur only when new inventions are understood to confer benefits of comparable significance for humankind.' Alberts and Klug, 'The Human Genome Must be Freely Available to All Humankind' (2000) 404 *Nature* 326. This concern was restated by the UK Royal Society in 2003 in its report *Keeping Science Open: The Effects of Intellectual Property Policy on the Conduct of Science* (The Royal Society, 2003).

[41] Discussed below.

[42] US Patent 5,159,135 1992. This was subsequently invalidated for lacking novelty.

[43] US Patents 4,556,562 and 5,124,349, both of which are still in force in the US.

[44] For a more detailed discussion of these see Dutfield, *Intellectual Property Rights, Trade and Biodiversity* (Earthscan, 2000).

[45] The US patent system is not the only one operating upon a presumption of patentability; the same is true of most European countries and of the EPO as well. The difference lies in the fact that European patent laws contain specific categories of excluded material whilst the US system does not. One of the problems facing European provision is the tension caused by having both a presumption of patentability and categories of excluded material—the former having the effect of reducing the applicability of the latter. The result is that the value of the categories of excluded material becomes questionable. Not all granting offices are blind to the concerns which have been raised about the presumption of patentability. In its most recent quinquennial review published in March 2001 the UK Patent Office recommended that consideration should be given to looking at the presumption although no statement on this matter has yet been made: 'Quinquennial Review of the Patent Office', January 2001, p 22, §10, para 12.

The American view of protectability is especially important as the US patent system a) has granted the most patents over bio-inventions and b) contains few limitations on the rights granted and has virtually no exclusions from protection.[46]

## Utility[47] Patent Protection

As with the patent laws available elsewhere, the grant of a patent within the US provides a right to exclude others from making, using, offering for sale, or selling the invention throughout the territory of grant (the US) or importing the invention into that territory (the US). The emphasis throughout the various official statements on patent law is the protection of the commercial interests in the protected material, and the fact that US patent law does not exclude any subject matter from protection underlines the encompassing nature of this protection. The right is enforceable only within the US.

Two things need noting about the language used in Section 101, which sets down the general statement on patentability. The first relates to the reference to discoveries as patentable subject matter and the second to the use of the word 'may'.[48]

Section 101 specifically mentions discovering new and useful processes, manufactures etc., and Section 100(a), the definitions section, reiterates the use of the word 'discovery' by stating that 'the term "invention" means invention or discovery.' However, this does not mean that discoveries *per se* are patentable.

The position is that the thing discovered is patentable *provided* that the applicant demonstrates that it is novel, non-obvious and has utility. In doing so the applicant will have to show that he has done more than merely discover the 'invention' claimed. He has to have done something with it which no one has either thought of or achieved before. As will be seen, this produces an equivalent position to that in Europe which, whilst specifically excluding protection

---

[46]  It is because of this strength of protection, together with the political power wielded by the US, that the TRIPs obligation is predicated on the presumption of patentability, and exclusions to that presumption are couched in optional rather than mandatory terms. For those countries, eg those within the EPO, which maintain categories of excluded material but which also operate a presumption of patentability, this means that any exclusions or limitations are given a restrictive application. The premise is clearly inclusion not exclusion. This is one of the reasons why the concept of 'invention' is not defined.

[47]  Whilst it is acceptable to refer to US patent law simply as US patent law without including the word utility, it is also commonplace to stress the function of patent law to protect useful inventions—implicit within this emphasis on the useful nature of the inventions protected as opposed to their novelty or inventiveness lies a clear commercial imperative.

[48]  There are other key elements in US patent law which should be noted but will not be discussed further as they do not have an impact on either the operation or development of European law (although they are important to a plant researcher seeking rights in the US). These relate to the US system using a first to invent principle as opposed to first to file (which is the situation in Europe), and the availability of a 12-month grace period prior to filing during which the inventor can make known his invention.

for discoveries,[49] qualifies the exclusion so that it applies only to the excluded material *as such*[50] and not to any uses made of that material. That means that a claim which relates *only* to the discovered material in its discovered form and which does not demonstrate any inventive activity by the applicant will fall within the exclusion. An application for a novel and inventive use made of that material, however, might be deemed to fall outside the exclusion and could be patentable. This will be discussed in more detail in chapter 5.

The second issue, which is more important for present purposes, regarding the wording of Section 101 relates to the use of the word 'may'. This can be interpreted in two ways.

The first is that an applicant *might* be entitled to a patent—this interpretation carries with it an element of doubt or discretion as to whether the patent will be granted. In many respects this reflects European practice where the existence of the exclusions to patentability permits the refusal of an application even where the granting criteria have been met.

The second interpretation is that a patent *will* be granted provided the granting criteria are met—there being no doubt as to entitlement to protection. The fact that there are no exclusions to patentable subject matter within the US patent law together with the practice of the USPTO indicates that this interpretation is the one employed for American patent law purposes. In addition, patent examiners are explicitly instructed to accept the claims made within the application, with the proviso that if they do not, then they have to provide scientific evidence as to why the claims have not been accepted.[51]

The USPTO's guidelines to examiners state:

An applicant *is* entitled to a patent to the subject matter claimed unless the statutory requirements are not met . . . . When the USPTO denies a patent, the Office must set forth at least a *prima facie* case as to why an applicant has not met the statutory requirements . . . . A patent examiner *must* accept a utility asserted by an applicant unless the Office has evidence or sound scientific reasoning to rebut the assertion. [emphasis added]

When this is taken together with the statement made in 35 USC 102 that: '[a] person *shall be entitled* to a patent . . . .' (emphasis added), the presumption becomes evident.[52]

---

[49] Art 52(a) EPC.

[50] Art 52(3) EPC.

[51] See Federal Register, vol 66(4), 5 January 2001, 1093, which sets out the USPTO examining policy in respect of biotechnological inventions.

[52] Interestingly, a patent holder can rely on a second presumption once the patent has been granted. §182 states that a patent is presumed to have been validly granted—the burden of proof regarding the validity of the patent therefore lying, not with the patentee, but with another. This carries a number of implications which it is not proposed to discuss here. For an examination of these issues see Llewelyn, 'Schrodinger's Cat: An Observation on Modern Patent Law' in Drahos, *Death of a Patent System* (LawText Publishing, 2004) 11.

Because there are no specific categories of excluded material within US patent law, the primary determinant of whether an invention is patentable or not is whether it meets the granting criteria of novelty, non-obviousness[53] and utility.[54] It is not intended to detail the highly complex nature of either the granting process or the granting criteria under US patent law as this is beyond the scope of this study.[55] Instead, the concepts will be discussed in general terms in order to underline the overarching presumption of patentability which underpins not only the US system but also the TRIPs obligation.[56]

### The Granting Criteria

Although it is not proposed to go into the US policy and practice in any great detail it is worth making a number of general points.

The first is that, in contrast to the European model which (as chapter 5 will show) has a single standard for deciding novelty,[57] the US operates a two-tiered system for assessing novelty. On the first tier is the requirement that the invention must not have been known or the subject of a publication in the US prior to 12 months before the patent application was filed. On the second tier is the requirement that the invention must not have been the subject of a publication (including patent applications and disclosure on the internet) anywhere outside the US prior to 12 months before the application is filed.[58] The issue of *knowledge* about or *use* of the invention outside the US does not apply to this second tier. This means that an application which concerns material which is known and used *outside* the US, but which is not known or used in the US, will not lack novelty for a US patent grant unless that knowledge has been reduced to documented form. This US-centric notion of what is novel has been the subject of extensive criticism from those concerned about biopiracy,[59] in particular where patent applications have been made concerning traditional medicines.

---

[53] Which is generally held to be equivalent to the European notion of inventive step, and indeed Art 27(1) of the TRIPs Agreement uses the term 'inventive step', which in turn is equated to non-obviousness in a footnote to the Agreement.

[54] This corresponds to the European notion of 'industrial applicability' although the two concepts can be contrasted. See Llewelyn, 'Industrial Applicability/Utility and Genetic Engineering: Current Practices in Europe and the United States' (1994) 11 *EIPR* 473.

[55] Whilst the US policy and practice might be persuasive it is important to bear in mind that the TRIPs Agreement does not stipulate how the granting requirements are to be interpreted and applied in practice.

[56] Art 27(1).

[57] This being decided on the basis of whether the invention, in that form, was previously available anywhere in the world—as mentioned previously, 'available' is given a broad meaning to include use as well as reduction to printed form.

[58] The inventor has a 12-month grace period pre-filing during which s/he can use/sell the invention in the US and/or obtain a foreign patent and/or disclose the invention through publication. The UPOV system also contains a grace period. This is in contrast to European patent law which operates purely on a first to file basis, any prior enabling disclosure serving to defeat the novelty of the invention being claimed.

[59] For a range of views on this see Dutfield, *Intellectual Property Rights, Trade and Biodiversity* (Earthscan, 2000); Shiva, *BioPiracy: The Plunder of Nature and Knowledge* (Green Books, 1998);

The USPTO has granted a number of patents over medicines which have been used for generations by communities outside the US, the justification for the grant being that as the use was neither known, nor took place, in the US, nor had the use of the medicines by the local community been reduced to print, the 'invention' was new. These patents have been challenged in the courts with variable success. Again it is outside the remit of this book to discuss issues relating to the US practice regarding patent applications concerning traditional medicines or knowledge.

The non-obviousness requirement[60] is shown through an assessment of a) the scope and content of the prior art, b) the type and extent of the differences between that prior art and the invention in question and c) whether the differences would have been reached by a person of ordinary skill working in that area. In respect of biotechnology, concerns have been raised over a) the extent to which inventiveness can be shown by using computers to identify new gene sequences and b) demonstrating non-obviousness when there are only a limited number of possible research avenues. A problem facing all granting offices in the early years was the lack of any thorough understanding of the science itself. This meant that it was difficult to know what was obvious to try and what was not. As the knowledge has developed (both within the scientific and legal communities) so too has grown an understanding of what is inventive and what is not. In the US this has resulted in Section 103 being amended to take account of, in particular, biotechnological processes.[61] As has also been realised in Europe, whilst there is great potential for genetic innovations there are only a relatively few applications which can be said to be inventive or non-obvious to try. The dilemma facing policy makers in both jurisdictions is the extent to which a growth in knowledge (with the concomitant reduction in what is non-obvious to try) should defeat a patent application, especially where the invention concerned has an obvious commercial value.[62]

Whilst the practice of the USPTO in respect of novelty and non-obviousness caused some concern during the 1980s and 1990s it was the third of the granting criteria, utility, which seemed to give rise to most concern (within Europe at least). The requirement is that the invention must be capable of being put to some useful purpose. The question which has arisen is the extent to which this useful purpose must be identified as an actual as opposed to speculative purpose within the specification.

---

Correa, *Intellectual Property Rights, The WTO and Developing Countries* (Zed Books, 2000); and the chapters on plant protection by Heath, Mo, Donavanik, Llewelyn and Sherman, in Heath and Kamperman Sanders, (eds), *Industrial Property in the Bio-medical Age* (Kluwer Law International, 2003).

[60] 35 USC 103.

[61] §103 (b)(1) and (3).

[62] This will be returned to in ch 7, where it will be shown that recent statements issued by the European Commission appear to place a greater emphasis on protecting the commercial value as opposed to inventive activity.

As the policy of permitting patent grants to be made over inventions involving living material became more established it became clear that a significant number of patent applications were being made which included claims to *speculative* uses of the genetic material with only minimal evidence within the specification itself that these uses had been achieved by the applicant. In the eyes of many (including pro-patent supporters) this had the effect of claiming not just basic genetic material but potentially all uses which could be made of that material.

The presumption of patentability (outlined earlier) meant that many of these applications succeeded.[63] However, the result was that this practice rapidly began to bring the patent system, both in the US and abroad, into disrepute as companies acquired overly broad monopolies which placed the ownership of key genetic material into the hands of the few. This drew criticism both from pressure groups opposed to the granting of patents over genetic material and from those engaged in bioscience research. The concerns for the latter group was that this practice meant that not only was basic genetic material being patented (with the obvious effect on their own ability to use and innovate) but, possibly more importantly, that any patents granted were likely to be less secure (on the grounds that when challenged the holder would be less able to show non-obviousness and utility), thereby making the patent more vulnerable to litigation.

In order to regain both public and industrial confidence, the USPTO, in January 2001, revised its guidelines for examination.[64] These now require that at least one of the applications claimed must be *specific, substantial and credible*. This means that where an applicant is claiming a number of different utilities then only one needs to be shown to be specific, substantial and credible. The requirement that the function, or utility, must be specific, substantial and credible has now been adopted by the European Patent Office[65] and also by some European national granting offices.[66]

---

[63] With the notable exception of Craig Venter's attempts in the early to mid 1990s to patent whole swathes of human gene sequences—these applications being thrown out for lack of utility. See Llewelyn, 'Industrial Applicability/Utility and Genetic Engineering: Current Practices in Europe and the United States', above n 54.

[64] Above n 51. This also addresses some of the commonly asked questions about the patentability of biological material, eg how naturally occurring material can be regarded as novel.

[65] The equivalent guidelines for the European Patent Office state in 4.6 that . . .

it is required that the description of a European patent application should, where this is not self-evidence, indicate the way in which the invention is capable of exploitation in industry. In relation to sequences and partial sequences of genes this general requirement is given specific form in that the industrial application of a sequence or partial sequence of a gene must be disclosed in the patent application. A mere nucleic acid sequence without indication of a function is not a patentable invention . . . In cases where a sequence or partial sequence of a gene is used to produce a protein or part of a protein, it is necessary to specify which protein or part of a protein is produced and what function this protein or part of a protein performs. Alternatively, when a nucleotide sequence is not used to produce a protein or part of a protein, the function to be indicated could be that the sequence exhibits a certain transcription promoter activity.

[66] www.patent.gov.uk. A question has been raised in the UK as to whether, in the absence of specific reference to 'specific, substantial and credible' within the domestic legislation, this is a correct

An explanation of how this operates in practice was given by a USPTO official in 2002.[67] Utility is to be demonstrated via a 'real world' use. Any uses which require further research, for example, are not 'real world' uses. Equally a 'throw away' utility (that is a use which is not realisable or realistic) or a utility which is not sufficiently specific will fail to meet the threshold. The example given was of a claim to 'the use of transgenic mice for snake food'. The claim, as phrased, is neither specific (as any type of mouse, and not only transgenic mice, could serve as snake food) nor is it substantial (it is commercially unrealistic, not 'real world', as a transgenic mouse would cost far more than a non-transgenic mouse). Where the claim to the transgenic mouse specifically identified the generation of a particular protein profile which was specifically directed to enhancing animal food then the test for specific and substantial utility would probably be met. With regard to the utility being credible it was indicated that there is a presumption that the use stated is a credible one *unless* 'the logic underlying the asserted use is seriously flawed or the facts upon which the assertion is based are inconsistent with the logic underlying the assertion.'

Interestingly, the fact that the USPTO[68] requires that an application relating to a biotechnological invention must demonstrate specific, substantial and credible utility might be regarded by some as a violation of the TRIPs obligation. As will be seen below, Article 27(1) of the Agreement requires that 'patents shall be available and patent rights enjoyable *without discrimination* as to . . . *the field of technology*' (emphasis added). The requirement that the utility be specific, substantial and credible applies only to biotechnological inventions and therefore could be taken to be a discrimination of the field of technology. This issue will be discussed further in respect of developments within Europe.

The presumption of patentability, which underlines the interpretation of the granting criteria, also goes to an understanding of Article 27(1) of TRIPs.

Exclusions/Limitations to Protection

Whilst the substantive law does not contain any explicit categories of excluded material this does not mean that there are no constraints on patentability. The utility requirement is generally taken to include a public policy and morality element. This means that patents will not be granted over inventions which are regarded as 'injurious to the well-being, good policy, or good morals of society'.[69] An example of this approach can be seen in the statement issued in 1998 by the USPTO saying that an invention relating to part-human/part-animal

---

interpretation of the industrial application requirement. This will ultimately be a matter for the courts to determine.

[67] Karen Handa, Office of Legislative and International Affairs within the USPTO, in a paper given at a conference in Thailand in September 2002. See Conference Materials for Bislaw, 2002, National Center for Genetic Engineering and Biotechnology.

[68] This practice is now followed by the EPO and some national offices (eg, the UK Patent Office).

[69] *Lowell v Lewis* 15 Fed Cas 1018 (CCD Mass, 1817).

inventions would be unlikely to be patentable; however, the Office stopped short of saying such inventions would be *automatically* unpatentable.[70] On the basis of the explicit statement any other invention involving genetic material would seem to be patentable.

This restrictive approach to excluding material goes to an understanding of Article 27(2) and (3) of TRIPs.

The same lack of statutory curbs on the scope of protection can also been seen in the limitations to the right.

The US patent system only has a very limited research or experimental use exemption. Use purely for research purposes, or private use which has no commercial component to it, is generally allowed. However, once that use has a commercial basis then it is not permitted unless with the authorisation of the patent holder. There is one exception to this. In a nod to the importance of encouraging the production of generic equivalents once a drug has come off patent, the US adopted, in 1994, the Drug Price Competition and Patent Term Restoration Act (the Hatch-Waxman Act).[71] This permits both the production of generic equivalents to a patented drug and the use of these generic equivalents in securing regulatory approval necessary before a licence will be granted by the Federal Drugs Agency (FDA). If this exemption were not permitted, then it would mean that the holder of a patent was, in effect, being granted an extension over the patented drug as there would be an inevitable time delay between the drug coming off patent, the generic producer obtaining the necessary approvals and the generic equivalent coming onto market. The gap would enable the now ex-patent holder to continue to monopolise the market place. This exemption does not apply to the experimental use of any other type of protected material; crucially it does not apply to any plant material or to any extract not used in the type of invention covered by the Hatch-Waxman exemption. In common with the European patent system this means that it does not permit the use of patented plant material (including plant varieties) in commercial breeding programmes.

One of the most crucial questions is the extent to which public bodies (for example, universities or publicly funded research organisations such as research units within publicly funded healthcare providers) may use patented material freely in research programmes. As will be discussed later, in Europe there are a number of different ways in which the research exemption is approached. Some companies will police the use of their patented technology meticulously, others will turn a blind eye to the use of their patented technology within a publicly funded research programme, becoming concerned only once that use results in

---

[70] USPTO Press Release, 'Facts on Patenting Life Forms Having a Relationship to Humans', 2 April 1998.

[71] §271(e)(1). This reversed the decision in *Roche Products Inc v Bolar Pharmaceutical Co Inc* (1984) 221 USPQ 157 (CD) (Cal) 182 in which the court rejected a defence of experimental use (relating to the production of a generic equivalent and the use thereof in trials for marketing approval) as the use was based on a commercial interest.

a potentially commercial outcome, at which time they will often secure an agreement with the researcher to enable both to benefit from the new invention's commercial potential. Other patent holders will actively seek to enter into partnerships with public bodies in order to maximise the innovative potential of the information protected. As will be seen, there is such flexibility in Europe that it is difficult to draw hard and fast lines between what is experimental and commercial use. There is, however, a growing recognition that the increasing value placed by universities on *their* intellectual property could mean that any leniency granted to them by patent holders should be tempered in light of the increased commercial output. In this respect there could be a call for a move closer to the US model where universities are not immune from the full force of patent law.

The full impact of this was brought home in the case of *Madey v Duke University*.[72] In this case the Court of Appeals of the Federal Circuit held that the experimental use defence only exists in a 'very narrow and strictly limited' form. The only permitted acts are those which are 'solely for amusement, to satisfy idle curiosity, or for strictly philosophical inquiry . . . the profit or non-profit status of the user is not determinative.' The defence, 'if available at all,' must be established by the alleged infringer, and the accusing party need not establish as part of its initial claim that use was not experimental. Clearly not even universities can rely on the research exemption, as these are now regarded as commercial entities capable of competing with the top flight in commercial research and development. As will be seen in chapter 6 the situation is slightly different, although by no means clearer, in Europe.

The US patent system also does not provide for any form of farmers' exemption. Any farmers wishing to retain seed from one year to the next, therefore, can do so only upon payment of a further royalty, otherwise they face an action for infringement. As will be seen, the EPC is silent on this matter. However, the Directive has introduced a form of farm saved seed provision into national patent law. There is variation at the national level regarding the use of this provision as this depends both on whether a particular member state of the EU has introduced the Directive into its national law and also on the level at which that national provision has chosen to recompense the breeder.

Both the research exemption and the right to retain seed from one year to the next go to the interpretation and application of Article 30 of TRIPs.

US patent law does not contain any statutory provision relating to compulsory licensing. The rationale behind this lack appears to be that as a patent holder has already overcome a number of hurdles, including succeeding in a research endeavour where his competitors have not and acquiring a patent over his research outputs, he should not be required to license out to others (usually his competitors) who have not been able to succeed in that area themselves. This does not mean that there are no external curbs on what the patent holder can do

---

[72] *John MJ Madey v Duke University* No 01–1587 (Fed Cir, 2002).

with his patent. US law seeks to avoid any anti-competitive or abusive uses of the patent via the common law doctrine of patent misuse and anti-trust—laws which operate at both the state and Federal levels.[73] Both of these can be used to prevent an abuse of a market position, for example by tying in the use of patented technology (which has no other equivalent in the market place) with a non-patented service (which is available elsewhere) in a licence agreement. Patent misuse can be used as a defence to infringement whilst the anti-trust laws can serve as a cause of action in their own right. In many respects the anti-trust laws are more effective than compulsory licensing provisions because, as Grubb points out, 'the anti-trust laws are so broadly drafted it is perhaps inevitable that they should be seen as constituting a general principle, to which the patent law forms a strictly limited exception.'[74] In addition, a finding in anti-trust law against the patent holder can be used to invalidate a patent, whereas if a patentee is found to have misused his patent it merely serves to curtail that particular misusing activity. Where these differ from the compulsory licensing provisions common in Europe is that neither has the effect of compelling a patent holder to grant a licence to a person seeking to legitimately use the patented technology. This placing of abuses of position outside the patent system itself is in keeping with the TRIPs Agreement. Article 8(2) of TRIPs specifically states that appropriate measures may be needed to 'prevent the abuse of intellectual property rights by rights holders or the resort to practices which unreasonably restrain trade or adversely affect the international transfer of technology.' The only qualification to this is that such measures must be 'consistent with the provisions of this Agreement.' It also mirrors the development of competition law practices elsewhere.

This difference in circumscribing the rights of the patent holder goes to an understanding of Article 31 of TRIPs.

Under the US system it is possible to obtain a number of different configurations of protection, for example a utility patent and a plant variety protection certificate for sexually produced plants, or a utility patent and a plant patent for asexually produced plants. In deciding which rights to seek, however, the benefits and pitfalls which relate to each right need to be taken into account—for example, although utility patent protection may provide the strongest protection it is more difficult to demonstrate the threshold for protection; equally whilst it might be easier to secure a plant variety rights certificate the right might not be as secure once granted and its limited nature might permit the production of competitively close equivalents.

Critical to understanding the US provision is the fact that it seeks to protect the investment interests of those engaged in bioscience research and the value in the rights primarily is seen, to lie in its market-orientated approach to granting and protecting rights. As can be seen the US legal environment is generally very favourable to plant innovators seeking protection. However, reservations can

---

[73] 15 USC 1–7 (also known as the Sherman Act) 1890.
[74] Grubb, *Patents for Chemical, Pharmaceuticals and Biotechnology* (OUP, 1999) p 427.

be raised relating to its real appropriateness given the emphasis on protecting the interests of the patent holder when there may be other interests (such as those of the research user) which also need to be considered. At the heart of these concerns lies the fact that the presumption of protectability and patentability overarches all patent policy and practice and, as will be seen, the US is not alone in taking this approach. These presumptions pervades both national and international patent law with the result that (at a policy level) it can appear unarguable that patent protection both must and should be available for all types of inventions. In one sense this is unproblematic provided that there is agreement as to what patent law is supposed to achieve and the threshold is set in order to achieve that objective.[75]

There are a number of broad concerns relating to the US system. These are that:

a) despite the introduction of the 'specific, substantial and credible' element to the utility requirement, there remains the perception that the system still allows patents to be granted over both basic genetic information where no real 'invention' can be discerned and 'inventions' the claims to which are of exceptional breadth;[76]

b) it is predominantly concerned with the commercial value of the invention protected and does not take account of broader social (or research) concerns in deciding what can or should be protected—'market forces' being the order of the day;

c) it encourages genetic piracy, particularly through its US-centric notion of novelty;

d) it does not take account of traditional knowledge; and

e) over favours the bioscience industry—although, in terms of comparing the policy and practice with that of other users of the patent system, this view has to be tempered by the fact that the bioscience industry now has the additional, overt, hurdle to jump of showing that its inventions are 'specific, substantial and credible'. This does not apply to inventions in any other area of technology.

The US approach to interpreting a manufacture by man can be contrasted with that of Canada, where problems have been encountered in both introducing plant variety protection and also in using the ordinary patent system to protect plant material. More recently the Canadian Supreme Court has revoked the patent granted over the Harvard Oncomouse, on the grounds that higher life forms cannot be regarded as manufactures for the purposes of Canadian patent law.[77] This

---

[75] A cause for concern, which can only serve as a footnote for consideration in this work, is where certain types of products fall outside the scope of protectability due to an inability to meet the threshold for protection. Such issues have been debated within the context of introducing petty patent, or second-tier protection for inventions which cannot meet the novelty and/or inventive step requirements.

[76] For example in July 2004, Microsoft was granted a patent over the human body as a computer. This is despite not making public the precise use to which this 'invention' will be put. The suspicion is that Microsoft itself does not know and this gives rise to an allegation of speculative patenting where no actual invention can be shown.

[77] *Harvard College v Canada Commissioner of Patents* [2002] SCC 76.

does not mean that no inventions based on living material are patentable in Canada; instead, a sliding scale of protectability exists as is evident in a decision of the Canadian Supreme Court in 2004.[78] Whilst in that case the Court held that plant genes and modified plant cells were patentable it affirmed that anything of a higher order, for example varieties, were not patentable. In common with other patent systems (and as outlined in chapter 1) this does not mean that higher order life forms are not affected by the grant of a patent. The Court went on to say that through a purposive construction of the patent, any use (for example, unauthorised growing) of plants (including varieties) which contain the patented material (modified plant cells) will constitute use of the patented material and can be an infringing activity. In respect of plant varieties this position is equivalent to the European one.

One of the great debates in intellectual property law is the extent to which commercial reasons should drive the provision of protection—and nowhere is this more acute than in respect of providing protection for 'inventions' concerning living material. As will be seen in the discussion of the 1883 Paris Convention on the Protection of Industrial Property in chapters 3 and 5, these issues are not new, but they have taken on an added resonance as a result of both modern biotechnology and the introduction of TRIPs.

As the next section will discuss, the TRIPs Agreement, with its explicit emphasis on protecting trade value, is predicated on the twin presumptions of protectability and patentability. The result is that any exclusions or limitations are given only a limited application. This poses a dilemma for those jurisdictions which maintain a legal distinction between both protectable and non-protectable material and permit limits on the scope of the right granted. They have to find an acceptable balance between meeting their obligations under TRIPs (strong property rights to protecting trade interests) and the safeguarding of other public interest considerations (such as the retention of a genuine territory of non-protectable subject matter and ensuring appropriate access to protected material).

The tone and effect of the TRIPs Agreement also marks the first real shift from a development of plant property principles based on European thinking (for whilst 20th century plant intellectual property initiatives were not confined to Europe, it was the European response to those initiatives which dominated legal developments until the mid-1990s) to ones based on an international (and predominantly transatlantic) perspective of what those rights should be.

---

[78] *Monsanto Canada Inc v Schmeiser* [2004] SCC 34. The Court was split 5:4 on this decision, with the dissenters holding that the patent claims should be restricted to the essential elements only and construed to encompass 'unpatentable plants'. However, they agreed that, in this instance, as Monsanto did not claim to have protection over the plants, but merely the use of the essential element contained within them, the patent was valid. Some might view this as *de facto* patent protection over whole plants. This case will be discussed in more detail in ch 9.

### III. AN OVERVIEW OF THE TRIPS AGREEMENT[79]

The Agreement on Trade Related Aspects of Intellectual Property Rights was signed in 1994 and came into force in 1995. It is one of the agreements for which the WTO[80] has responsibility. Whilst the TRIPs Agreement is arguably the single most significant legal instrument in intellectual property law history it does not seek to reinvent the general concepts which have underpinned intellectual property rights since the late 19th century. Instead, it builds on existing international conventions, including the Paris Convention, with a primary objective to set in place *minimum* standards of protection and enforcement in all member states. The significance of the TRIPs Agreement lies not merely in the standardisation it requires but also in the role the WTO now plays in ensuring that these precepts are adhered to. This makes the new global intellectual property order more forceful than under previous international agreements.

The decision to bring intellectual property rights formally within the international trade regime was based on the recognition that it was increasingly difficult to disentangle the trade value of goods from the intellectual property protection attached to those goods. Much of the impetus for the inclusion of intellectual property in the Uruguay Round of the General Agreement of Trade and Tariffs (GATT, which preceded the WTO) came from the US. Many of the intellectual property principles enshrined in TRIPs can, therefore, be directly traced to the intellectual property norms in operation in the US. It is not proposed to discuss the TRIPs Agreement in full nor to discuss those other trading incentives used to promote global and local interests. It is important to note, however, that the TRIPs Agreement does not operate in a vacuum but needs to be read subject to notions of global governance and other refinements of the world order. It also must be looked at in the context of other trading devices (for example, bilateral agreements and national trade legislation (such as the US's Special 301[81] which allows the US, unilaterally, to take action against imports from any country which does not provide effective intellectual property protection)).

For present purposes, the focus will be on those principles and provisions set down in the Agreement which relate to plant protection. The object is to assess

---

[79] As with the discussion of US plant property provision, the TRIPs Agreement is only discussed in broad outline form. The analysis of what the provisions mean in practice will be assessed later when looking at the implications of European provision. For a more detailed discussion of the TRIPs Agreement see www.wto.org Beier and Schricker, 'From GATT to TRIPs' (1996) 18 *IIC Studies*; Blakeney, *Trade Related Aspects of Intellectual Property Rights: A Concise Guide to the TRIPs Agreement* (Sweet & Maxwell, 1996); and Gervais, *The TRIPs Agreement Drafting History and Analysis*, 2nd edn (Sweet & Maxwell, 2003).

[80] The WTO currently has 147 members including all EU member states, and, crucially for the discussion relating to European provision, the European Union is a member in its own right.

[81] This is a provision of the Omnibus Trade and Competitiveness Act 1988.

the obligation both in the context of the Agreement itself and against the backdrop of other international agreements relating to plant material, most notably the UPOV Convention and, to a lesser extent, the Convention on Biological Diversity and the International Treaty on Plant Genetic Resources.[82]

## The Objectives of the Agreement

The Preamble to the Agreement states that its object is to:

> reduce distortions and impediments to international trade, and taking into account the need to promote effective and adequate protection of intellectual property rights, and to ensure that measures and procedures to enforce intellectual property rights do not themselves become barriers to legitimate trade.

The primary obligation imposed by membership of TRIPs is, therefore, the removal of any distortions or impediments contained in national intellectual property laws which might adversely affect international trade. Specifically, members are required to promote 'effective and adequate' intellectual property rights provided these rights do not themselves become barriers to trade.

The TRIPs Agreement also sets down some basic principles against which the substantive provisions have to be set. These can be found in Articles 1–8.[83] The most relevant of these to plant property protection are Articles 1, 7 and 8.[84]

Article 1 enables member states to provide more extensive protection than that set out in the Agreement—'*provided that such protection does not contravene the provisions*' of the Agreement. This allows a member state to provide additional protection to that mandated in the Agreement and underlines the obligation that member states are not permitted to provide *less* than the protection set out in the Agreement. Where such additional protection is provided it must also not distort or impede international trade. What is not clear is the extent to which Article 1 could be used to limit the range of protectable subject matter—for example by allowing a member state to adopt a locally restrictive concept of novel material or what may constitute a plant for its own national plant protection purposes. This question will be returned to later in this chapter.

Article 7 sets down the presumption that the protection and enforcement of the rights will promote technological innovation and contribute to technology

---

[82] Notwithstanding the fact that there is no mention in the TRIPs Agreement of any of these, they are clearly important to understanding the manner and form of plant protection currently available.

[83] It is not clear if the general principles set down in Arts 1–8 overarch all other provisions (and can be used to trump any onerous provision) or if they have only secondary status and merely serve as a backdrop to the main obligation which is to give effect to the main provisions. This is an issue of particular import for those countries wishing to limit their patent protection provision in the interests of public health or in order to protect the environment.

[84] The other basic principles mainly relate to same treatment as nationals, relevant international conventions and exhaustion of rights.

transfer. To this end there must be a balance between providing rights which are to the advantage of the producers and ensuring that these rights are used '*in a manner conducive to social and economic welfare.*' The issue here is whether, if one regards the development of plants for both agricultural and medicinal purposes as being for social and economic welfare, member states can limit the provision mandated by the TRIPs obligation in instances where it is felt that an inappropriate balance has been struck.[85] This is particularly pertinent with regard to research use and compulsory licensing. These issues will be addressed here and also in chapter 9.

Article 8 adds the notion of public interest to the equation by enabling member states to adopt any necessary measure to protect 'public health and nutrition and to promote the public interest in sectors of vital importance to their socioeconomic and technological development, provided that such measures are consistent with the provisions of this Agreement.' Article 8(2) of TRIPs also permits the use of appropriate measures to 'prevent the abuse of intellectual property rights by rights holders or the resort to practices which unreasonably restrain trade or adversely affect the international transfer of technology.' The only qualification to this is that such measures must be 'consistent with the provisions of this Agreement'. No definition is provided of either 'necessary' or 'appropriate'.

The lack of any definitions within the Agreement is not necessarily a negative, for definitions, by their very nature, are limited by the definition provided and their absence provides member states with an opportunity to negotiate with the WTO the proper scope of these provisions. In addition, the language of the TRIPs Agreement does not preclude member states from adopting definitions at the local level. As will be seen later in this chapter there may be some merit in encouraging member states to do so, providing that the implications for attracting foreign companies to invest in research and technology transfer as well as ensuring compliance with the TRIPs obligation are fully understood.[86]

To date the only statement on the application of Articles 7 and 8, in a bioscience context, has come in relation to their use in reconciling the TRIPs Agreement with the CBD. Paragraph 19 of the Doha Statement of 2001[87] specifically states that the Council's work should be guided by Article 7 and Article 8.[88] The use of these Articles and plant related inventions remains unclear.

---

[85] This need to balance the interests of the rights holder against those of society in general has resonances within the substantive provisions of European patent law which requires national courts to construe patent claims in a way which balances providing a fair position (degree of protection) for the patentee with a reasonable degree of certainty for third parties.

[86] The TRIPs Council (which has responsibility for overseeing the operation of the TRIPs Agreement and includes a representative from each member state of the WTO) favours a minimal use of definitions and has expressly stated so in respect of Art 27(3)(b) discussed below: IP/C/W/369, 8 August 2002.

[87] www.wto.org.

[88] For a further discussion see Correa, 'Intellectual Property after Doha: Can Developing Countries Move Forward Their Agenda on Biodiversity and Traditional Knowledge' (2004) 9(2) *Technology Policy Briefs* 8.

Aside from the possible relevance of these sections with regard to European provision, a further reason for taking note of these provisions is their possible value to developing countries[89] as a basis for adopting a more restrictive approach to the provision of patent protection for genetic information. European breeders seeking to acquire protection abroad therefore need to be aware that even though an objective behind the TRIPs Agreement was to produce a level playing field of protection, there remains scope for national idiosyncrasies.

The main section of the TRIPs Agreement for the purposes of the plant intellectual property is Section V.


## Section V

Section V contains the provisions relating to patent protection, and at the core of the obligation is Article 27 and in particular Article 27(1). According to Gervais, this section proved the most difficult to draft not only because of differences between 'North and South' but also because of concerns between 'North and North'.[90]

Article 27(1) requires that members must allow patent protection for inventions from all fields of technology provided the inventions are novel, involve an inventive step and are capable of industrial application.

It is clear from the language used within Article 27(1) that two presumptions operate. The first is that protection must be available for all types of inventions and the second that the intended form of that protection shall be the patent.[91] Understanding the presumptions inherent in Article 27(1) is critical to understanding the TRIPs obligation. Article 27(1) establishes the primary obligation. Any deviations or limitations to that obligation therefore have to be read subject to the overarching requirement to provide patent protection and, by extension, to protect the interests of the patent holder.

In common with national patent laws, the TRIPs Agreement contains no definition of 'invention',[92] which again underlines the emphasis on inclusion not exclusion. The requirement is that anything which bears the qualities of novelty, inventive step and capacity for industrial application is patentable. The

---

[89] Neither the TRIPs Agreement nor the overarching GATT provides a definition of a developing country. The reason for this is that the term has a variety of meanings and it also carries connotations which some countries find undesirable. As a result it is left to countries to determine whether or not they wish to define themselves as developing or least developed (this latter term being defined by the United Nations on the basis of per capita income, size of population, quality-of-life index and the economy). For a further discussion see Matsushita, Schoenbaum and Mavroidis, *The World Trade Organization: Law, Practice and Policy* (Oxford International Law Library, 2003) ch 15.

[90] Gervais, *The TRIPs Agreement Drafting History and Analysis*, above n 79, p 147.

[91] Since 1998, the same presumption can now be found in European patent law with respect to biotechnological inventions. Art 1(1) of the EU Directive requires that '[m]ember states *shall* protect biotechnological inventions under national patent law'.

[92] Nor does it make any reference to the patentable status, or otherwise, of 'discoveries'.

Agreement does not further define the criteria, which is not surprising given the subtle, and sometimes not so subtle, differences which exist at the national level, for example, the two-tier novelty requirement in US patent law as opposed to the single, absolute, novelty requirement which operates in Europe.

The general principle is, therefore, that any invention involving genetic material must be regarded as patentable provided it meets the threshold for protection. If a patent is granted then the patent holder has the right to prevent anyone else from making, using, offering for sale, selling or importing a) the product, b) a patented process, and c) any product directly produced using the patented process (Article 28). The patent term shall be not longer than 20 years from the date of filing (Article 29).[93]

Unsurprisingly, perhaps, any suggestion during the drafting of the Agreement that Article 27(1) alone should define the obligation was opposed by those countries which permit certain types of inventions to be excluded. The decision was taken, therefore, to permit certain optional[94] exclusions.

The strictness of the requirement in Article 27(1) that protection must be provided for all types of inventions is, therefore, mitigated by paragraphs (2) and (3). These two paragraphs permit member states, if they so wish, the following three exclusions:

a) inventions, the commercial exploitation of which might be contrary to ordre public or morality (Article 27(2)); and/or
b) diagnostic, therapeutic and surgical methods for the treatment of human or animals (Article 27(3)(a)); and/or
c) plants and animals; however, patent protection must be available for micro-organisms, and protection, either by a patent and/or a *sui generis* right, must be provided for plant varieties (Article 27(3)(b)).

In the view of some commentators on the Agreement Article 27(1) is the *primary* obligation and any deviation from, or exception to, the requirement that patent protection be available for *all* types of inventions should be minimal and applied restrictively. This view is certainly supported by the practice within the US and Europe.

The main focus for this book will be Article 27(3)(b). However, that does not mean that the other exclusions, and Article 27(2) in particular, are not relevant. In addition, the Agreement also contains some limitations to the right granted. As with much of Article 27(2), and unlike the obligation in Article 27(3)(b), these are not plant-specific. It is therefore proposed to look at these general provisions before looking at the specific obligation regarding the protection of plant material.

---

[93] This was a highly controversial provision from the perspective of the US as it had previously permitted protection only for a period up to 17 years.

[94] Making these compulsory would have resulted in requiring the US to change its patent law. In turn, not permitting the exclusions would have required a revision of the EPC.

### Non-plant Specific Exclusions/Limitations

These apply to all inventions irrespective of content, and their relevance to plant material has, therefore, to be read into the provisions as opposed to being explicitly stated.

Article 27(2) The Morality Exclusion

Article 27(2) states that:

> Members may exclude from patentability inventions, the prevention within their territory of the commercial exploitation of which is necessary to protect ordre public or morality, including to protect human, animal or plant life or health or to avoid serious prejudice to the environment, provided that such exclusion is not made purely because the exploitation is contrary to law.[95]

As can be seen, the provision provides member states with a degree of flexibility enabling them to restrict patent protection on the grounds that promoting the invention by commercial use could cause harm to plant life or to the environment. Many patent laws contain a specific exclusion of inventions which are contrary to morality; however, there is little jurisprudence on this matter and it is unclear as to which types of inventions (or commercial exploitation) would in practice be regarded as contrary to morality. The specific problems encountered in applying this provision will be discussed in chapters 5, 6 and 7 when looking at the European practice. However, three general, and one specific, points can be made here.[96]

The first is that it is the exploitation of the invention which must be contrary to morality and not the invention itself. This means that, irrespective of the content of the invention, or its manner of manufacture, it is not the invention, itself which must be thought immoral. Rather it is the use made of the invention and specifically the commercial use, which must be contrary to morality. In some respects this can be seen to imbue the invention, in the absence of commercial use, with a value-free status. As will be discussed later, a concern here is that this means that such potential unethical matters as the use of unethical research practices in producing the invention (for example, the method used to obtain the genetic material) are irrelevant to a determination of 'contrary to morality'. When set against Article 27(1) it can be seen that the issue of whether it is morally acceptable to grant patents over inventions involving genetic material is not open for discussion under TRIPs. However, what member states can determine for their own patent practice purposes is where commercial use is made of inventions involving genetic material, of whatever order, for example important

---

[95] Whilst this does not have any equivalent in US patent law, it does reflect the position within Europe. Both the EPC and the EU Directive contain specific exclusions of any invention where the exploitation of that invention would be contrary to morality.

[96] These will be discussed in the specific context of European provision in ch 5.

new drugs or key agricultural crops, and it is thought that that use is likely to have an adverse effect on, for example, public health, then they can prohibit the grant of a patent.

The second general point is that whilst the provision says that member states may exclude such inventions from patentability (implying that this is an issue for determination at grant) the reality is that the value of the provision lies in providing grounds for opposing a patent already granted. The reason for this lies in the need to show that the commercial use of the invention will be so detrimental as to affect public health or the environment. As patents are granted only over novel material (which generally means that the invention is untested in the market place[97]) granting offices will be required to second guess what would be the moral consequences of any use made of the technology. As patent specifications do not require the applicant to specify how they plan to commercialise the technology, patent offices will inevitably find it difficult to prove that the use made will be contrary to morality.[98] In the absence of such an assessment, and given the presumption which operates, it will only be blatantly immoral inventions which will be excluded at the time of grant. It could be argued that applicants should be required to state to what uses the invention could be put, but again this would not solve any perceived problems with the morality provision. Firstly, it is unlikely that patent applicants will draft the specification in such a way as to indicate that the commercial exploitation of the invention would be contrary to morality. Secondly, a patent only gives the holder the right to stop others from making or using the invention in a way which encroaches upon the patent holder's commercial interests in the invention. It would not stop, for example, a person who has legitimately acquired the patented invention from using that technology for a harmful purpose, for example, stockpiling a patented drug which has been approved as a powerful sedative, and legitimately acquired upon prescription, to use to kill an elderly relative. In contrast, the assessment of the moral consequences to which patented technology might be put become clear once that technology is brought into general use. The problem of determining when the evaluation can or should take place becomes more acute when looking at very new types of technology the consequences of even one single use of which might be thought to be potentially extremely harmful and yet until such use is made of the material it is impossible to say if the use will be harmful or not. As will be seen in chapter 5, the approach of the EPO in such circumstances is, in the absence of actual evidence that harm will result, to permit the patent.

The language of Article 27(2) does permit the option to exclude specific categories of material (for example, key agricultural crops) on the grounds that any commercial use (where that use is controlled by a patent holder) could harm public health because the cost of purchasing the crop might be higher than for

---

[97] The extent to which this applies will depend on whether the notion of absolute novelty is in operation or if, on the basis of the US two-tier system, the use of the material takes place in the US or has been reduced to published form elsewhere.

[98] As will be seen, this is a problem which has been encountered by the EPO.

other crops in order to reflect the price paid for the patent right held over it. Where access to vital agricultural crops is truly a matter of life or death then it might be possible to argue that availability has to be on the broadest basis possible. The problem with this approach is that a) it presumes that the technology for which patent protection is being sought will be made available despite the absence of the patent (and the inventor is likely to have little incentive to do so), b) it is likely also to deter other inventors from bringing their technology into a territory where no (or relatively little) protection exists and c) it means that a single standard is being used for an entire group of inventions not all of which might merit its application. This problem of encouraging investment and technology transfer whilst balancing access to the material protected is something which continues to be the subject of heated debate. It is not proposed to discuss this further here. For the purposes of this book, the issue is the actual effectiveness of the exclusion in light of the presumption of patentability and the problems with determining abusive use in the absence of any evidence as to actual use.

The final general point is that the Article clearly states that neither developing nor using a particular invention which is illegal shall be a barrier to securing protection over that invention. Thus, in Europe, a plant biotechnology firm can develop genetically modified plants and obtain a patent over these plants irrespective of the fact that the commercial planting of such crops is currently prohibited. For patent law, at least, legality and morality are not the same thing.

The fourth, specifically plant-related, point is that a member state is specifically entitled to withhold patent protection for inventions which could harm plant life or which could seriously prejudice the environment. This could be used to prevent the patenting of plants the genetic modification of which (whether by biotechnological or traditional breeding processes) risks upsetting the plant environment into which they are placed.

It would appear that the application of Article 27(2) is a matter for determination at the local level. Certainly statements from, and the policy and practice of, both the EPO and the European Commission indicate that they believe that the issue of morality is one which they are free to decide and that they are not constrained by any overarching WTO doctrine as to what constitutes exploitation contrary to morality. This means that member states are free to decide this matter for themselves, although it is possible that the WTO might not accept the local practice.

The next issue is the extent to which member states may limit the scope of the right conferred.

## Article 30 Restricting the Right

Article 30 states that a member:

> may provide limited exceptions to the exclusive rights conferred by a patent, provided that such exceptions do not unreasonably conflict with a normal exploitation of the

patent and do not unreasonably prejudice the reasonable interests of the patent owner, taking into account the legitimate interests of third parties.

This provision dispels one popular myth about the TRIPs Agreement, namely that it prevents member states from restricting the rights granted. Instead, it is clear from the wording of Article 30 that it is up to each member state to decide which restrictions it wishes to impose on the right granted, the only constraints on this right being the proviso that member states must balance the interests of the patent holder with those of third parties. It is this provision which, it is generally agreed, allows the research and farm saved seed exemptions.[99]

As was mentioned in chapter 1, a number of countries (although not the US) permit the unfettered use of patented material for research purposes provided that there is no commercial purpose to that use. However, there are variations within national systems as to the extent to which the exemption applies.

As will be discussed in chapters 7 and 9, some organisations representing the interests of plant breeders have called for an equivalent research exemption to that used in plant variety rights to be included within patent law—for example, the right both to use protected material in a commercial breeding programme and to commercialise the results of that research without restriction. These calls bring into question where the appropriate balance between the interests of the holder and third parties should lie. For breeders, used to the plant variety rights provision, the ability both freely to use protected material in commercial breeding programmes and to commercialise the results of that research is seen as fundamental to the general survival of plant breeding programmes (and as such this right is protected on the basis of public interest). However, patent holders are used to being able to prevent nearly all commercial uses of their protected material and, as will be seen in chapter 7, within Europe this principle has been specifically extended to allow protection to extend into any end product developed using the patented technology. A breeders' exemption of the kind found in plant variety rights would probably not be regarded as providing an appropriate balance between protecting the interests of inventors and those of breeders who might use that technology in an important breeding programme. It will be for those charged with overseeing national provision to decide where the proper balance will lie.

In terms of the use of the provision to permit farmers to save seed, the general presumption appears to be encapsulated by a statement made by the European Commission in a communiqué to the WTO in 2002. The communiqué said that the role of the farm saved seed provision could be very different from that:

where farming has become a commercial and quasi-industrial activity . . . for the least developed or developing countries, where all or part of the farming activity is performed on very small farms at subsistence level or where commercial activities of farmers are of limited geographical scope. In these situations, a Member may well

---

[99] Both of which are key features of both the European patent and plant variety rights systems.

create, in its national law, a broader farmers' exemption for the benefit of subsistence farmers, or of small farmers who customarily reuse seed because they lack access to or financial resources for new seed every growing season. This allows them to save, replant, exchange, share and resell seed (to other small farmers), provided they do not use the denomination of the variety or the related trade mark. In any event, the breeder must remain the only one entitled to derive commercial benefit from the new variety. Another option could be to exempt exchanges of seed that take place within the same community or with neighbours, and between farming communities. However, farmers with significant commercial interests should be subject to more stringent rules

as is the case within Europe.[100]

As Article 30 applies only to patents it has virtually no effect on the limitations included in the plant variety rights system. There is one possible exception to this, and that is where the other system of protection contains provisions which reduce the exclusive right granted under a patent. It is unlikely that the research exemption in plant variety rights would have this effect, as it is recognised that it does not apply to patented plant material. There is however, a possible problem with the European situation regarding farm saved seed. The EU has included matching farm saved seed provisions in both the Directive and the Regulation, the latter specifically directing the practice in respect of the former. Whilst the farm saved provision in both only permits a limited derogation, nonetheless a derogation exists which arguably prejudices the legitimate interests of the patent holder to have the same full, unfettered, right to control access to his patented technology as that enjoyed by other patent holders.[101] As previously stated, the EU position on this matter has not yet been challenged, but that should not mean that it is necessarily a secure position.

The final general provision relates to compulsory licensing and government use.

### Article 31 Compulsory Licensing and Government/Crown Use[102]

This is the longest provision within Section V, and concerns other unauthorised use (that is use unauthorised by the patent holder) of the patented technology. The Article will not be set out as a whole (it comprises twelve subparagraphs to the main paragraph and three further sub-subparagraphs); instead, its general principles will be stated.

In very general terms, the provision recognises that the law of a member state may permit an unauthorised use of patented technology either by the

---

[100] Communication from the European Communities and their member states on the Review of Art 27(3)(b) of the TRIPs Agreement, and the relationship between the TRIPs Agreement and the Convention on Biological Diversity (CBD) and the protection of traditional knowledge and folklore IP/C/W/383 17 October 2002, paras 87 and 88.

[101] The EPC does not contain any such derogation but that is because it is primarily concerned with the granting of patents and not with the use made post grant.

[102] These concepts exist within Europe and are most likely to have relevance when looking at any interaction of plant variety and patent rights.

government itself (government use) or by a third party authorised by the government[103] *if* the following conditions are met:

each authorisation (or licence) must be assessed on its own merits (no general policy relating to a specific type of technology may be invoked) (paragraph a);

the person seeking authorisation must first have unsuccessfully tried to get authorisation from the patent holder (although this requirement can be waived at times of national emergency, in cases of public non-commercial use or where the patent holder is behaving in an anti-competitive manner) (paragraphs b and k);

the scope and duration of the authorisation shall be limited to the purposes for which it was given and that use shall be on the basis of the payment of an equitable remuneration to the patent holder (this can be the subject of judicial review if there is disagreement as to its level) and shall be non-exclusive and non-assignable (paragraphs c, d, e, and h)

the primary use must be to supply the local market (in other words either the patent holder has not realised the full market potential of the patented technology in the territory of grant or his activities in that territory amount to anti-competitive behaviour—in respect of the latter, if this is shown to be the case then the restriction to the local market does not apply) (paragraphs f and k);

if the circumstances for which it was granted cease to exist the authorisation can be revoked and the validity of the authorisation can be subject to judicial review where a particular practice is held to be anti-competitive (paragraphs i and j);

and finally, where a second patent holder seeks to exploit his patent (the second patent), but such exploitation would involve infringing a patent held by another (the first patent), authorisation may be granted provided the holder of the second patent can show that the technological effect claimed in that second patent represents an important technical advance of considerable economic significance when compared to the technology contained in the first patent. If this can be shown then the holder of the first patent will be entitled to a cross-licence to use the invention claimed in the second patent. Finally the holder of the second patent will not be able to assign the right to use the technology covered in the first patent unless he also assigns the second patent as well. As will be discussed below, this has significance for both European patent and plant variety rights provision (paragraph l).

The scope of Article 31 has been discussed extensively in recent years, most notably with regard to its use to ensure access to key medical treatments within the developing world. It is not proposed to rehearse those discussions in detail here, although some mention will be made of them as they are of relevance to a plant bioscientist using plant material to produce a new vaccine or drug.

A number of general points need to be unpicked which go to understanding the impact of this Article on European protection.

---

[103] As most patent offices are government offices, it is probably safe to say that they are able to grant compulsory licences on behalf of the government. Indeed, even where the office is privately controlled (as was mooted in respect of the UK office in the 1990s) this does not mean that it cannot grant licences, as Art 31 opens with the statement '[w]here the *law . . . allows* for other use' and then merely refers to *who* may secure the licence, not who may grant it.

The first is that Article 31 does not prevent the grant of a compulsory licence to non-governmental bodies or individuals—all that it does it set out the framework within which any decision to licence must be located.

The second is that a compulsory licence can be granted in situations other than national emergencies. The perception left by the *South Africa* case, discussed below, is that they will be granted only in cases of national emergencies relating to public health. All that the national emergency reference does is to state that when a national emergency does occur there is no requirement to show that the consent of the patent holder has been previously sought and unreasonably refused. In all other circumstances, the person seeking the licence has to show that action was taken to obtain a licence from the patent holder.

The third is that most of the principles outlined in Article 31 already exist in national patent laws and there is little which is actually new. In terms of comparison with European practices the main point of note is that Article 31 makes no mention of any time barrier to the acquisition of a compulsory licence. Many countries in Europe stipulate within their patent law that a compulsory licence will be granted only after a fixed period has elapsed—generally speaking this period is 3 years. This ensures that the patent holder has a period of time in which to exploit the invention without his ability to control the use of the patented technology being fettered by an imposed licence. The ability to mandate a time period only after the expiry of which will a compulsory licence be granted appears to be permitted by virtue of Article 1 of TRIPs. This allows a country to provide more extensive protection than is provided for in the Agreement. As a moratorium on the granting of a compulsory licence until after a set period has elapsed goes beyond the right granted to the patent holder in the Agreement, it is likely to be deemed a provision of more extensive protection. As the only constraint on the provision of the more extensive protection is that it must not contravene the provisions of the Agreement (and these are predominantly to protect the interests of the rights holder) then this would appear not to be excluded on these grounds.

The fourth point is that, with one exception, Article 31 does not affect *sui generis* plant variety rights. The exception is contained in paragraph l, and this has had a direct impact on European plant variety rights as will be seen in chapter 4.

The final point is that whilst many developed countries contain a provision permitting patent offices to grant licences in circumstances where a third party has unsuccessfully sought to obtain one from the patent holder, the provision is rarely, if ever, invoked. The reason for this appears to lie in the thinking that, once granted, the rights of the patent holder should not be fettered unless exceptional circumstances occur. As the right is a private right, the patent holder should be free to choose with whom he enters into an agreement and it is not for patent offices to impose such a relationship upon him. The value in having such a provision is that where a patent holder behaves in a manner which could give rise to the grant of a compulsory licence, the threat of one being granted can be sufficient to bring him to the negotiating table and agree an appropriate licence with the third party. One of the problems with this carrot and stick approach is that where the patent concerned is over technology which cannot be sourced elsewhere, and the patent holder has adopted an aggressive policy with regard to the exploitation of the patent, then it can be difficult to draw the patent holder to the negotiating table. In such circumstances, the absence of any real teeth to the compulsory licensing provision, by way of actual use, might call into question the actual value of the provision. For most patent holders, the compulsory licensing provision will have only limited application.

Article 31 has attracted a great deal of attention—probably more than any other Article within the TRIPs Agreement including Article 27(3)(b). One of the reasons for this was the high-profile action brought against the South African government in 2001 by a number of pharmaceutical companies. The catalyst for the action was the enactment of a new Medicines and Related Substances Act which permitted both the revoking of any patent which was regarded as making access to medicines too expensive and also the cheap importation of generic copies of drugs which were under patent in South Africa—in particular, this was to encourage access to anti-retrovirals to combat HIV/AIDS. As a result a number of generic manufacturers, and the Indian company Cipla in particular, began to import into South Africa generic copies of drugs which were under patent thereby undercutting the pharmaceutical companies. An action was immediately brought by a number of major pharmaceutical companies (all based in the US and Europe) claiming that this was in violation of Article 31. Following a very public discussion of the matter, the pharmaceutical companies withdrew the action.[104] An agreement was reached between the South African government and the companies under which the companies would make the drugs more cheaply available. The *quid pro quo* for this was a revision of the offending provision within the Medicines and Related Substances Act.

Following the withdrawal of the action, a debate ensued as to the extent to which Article 31 could be relied upon to ensure the availability of essential medicines, the impetus for these discussions coming primarily from African countries. In November 2001 the TRIPs Council issued what has become known as the Doha Statement. The statement acknowledges that members should be able to take measures to protect public health, and that each member has the right to grant compulsory licences and the freedom to determine the grounds upon which such licences should be granted.[105] The Doha Statement is primarily aimed at enabling developing countries to have access to medicines, and it is not clear to what extent developed countries will be able to rely on the 'public health' exemption within their own territory given their sophisticated pharmaceutical base. Indeed, within Europe the matter is being dealt with solely in the

---

[104] A similar action was also brought in Brazil.

[105] The full text can be found at www.wto.org/english/thewto_e/minist_e/min01_e/mindecl_trips_e.htm.

context of developing countries and access to pharmaceutical products.[106] Interestingly, in 2004, Cipla itself secured patent protection in South Africa over its combination drug, Triomune. Whether this patent will be challenged by those companies who hold the patents on the constituent drugs which make up the combination drug, or if the patent itself will have an adverse effect on the cost of access to the drug, remains to be seen.

In terms of the limited application of the compulsory licensing provision (the limitation being most apparent when looked at in the context of the existing use of compulsory licensing in Europe) the question which is posed by Article 31 is the extent to which the rights of the patent holder can, if at all, be fettered. The fact that the language of the Article gives rise to only a limited restriction on the right does not mean that member states cannot curb any abuses of rights granted. However, such measures generally lie outside the patent system in anti-trust or competition laws. Indeed, Article 8(2) of TRIPs specifically states that appropriate measures may be needed to 'prevent the abuse of intellectual property rights by rights holders or the resort to practices which unreasonably restrain trade or adversely affect the international transfer of technology.' The only qualification to this is that such measures must be 'consistent with the provisions of this Agreement.'

It is probably safe to assert that the applications of Articles 30 and 31 are unlikely to extend beyond those which are currently permitted within patent law, and any broader application is likely to be politically sensitive as major companies seek to protect their intellectual property.[107] In so far as the discussions over Article 31 have relevance to the plant research sector, this will lie in the pharmaceutical or healthcare applications made of plant material. Nothing in any of the discussions has related to restrictions on the rights granted to patent holders on the grounds of agricultural need. This means that it might be only those breeders who are engaged in the development of plant products vital to the protection of public health (apparently restricted to medicinal products) which are likely to be affected by the Doha Statement and only then in respect of use within a developing country context. For any other uses of medicinal

---

[106] Proposal for a Regulation of the European Parliament and of the Council on compulsory licensing of patents relating to the manufacture of pharmaceutical products for export to countries with public health problems, COM(2004)737. Whilst the main provisions of the Regulation do not confine those who can request a licence to import products under compulsory licence to developing countries it is clear that it will be difficult for developed countries to rely on the Regulation, as it cannot be used by any WTO member which has made a declaration to the WTO that it will not act as an importing country, and the EU has made such a declaration. In addition, Recital 5 states that '[t]his regulation is intended to be part of the wider European and international action to address public health problems faced by least developed and other developing countries . . .' and Recital 4 states that products manufactured in the EU for export under compulsory licence are not for re-import into the EU.

[107] An example of this can be seen in the statement of the UK government in 2001 in its report from the UK Pharmaceutical Industry Competitiveness Task Force (PICTF), available at www.doh.gov.uk/ pictf/pictf.pdf. This report, which had a foreword by Tony Blair, committed itself to the protection of strong patent rights and refused to entertain any broader application of the restrictions on the rights granted.

plant products within a developed country context, or any other use of plant material at all (whether in a developing or developed country) then it is likely the ordinary national rules on compulsory licensing would appear to apply,[108] as will be discussed further in chapter 9.

These are the general provisions setting out the obligation to protect and the limitations to that right. For plant researchers, however, the key provision is that which governs protection for plant material, Article 27(3)(b). As will be seen, this provision appears to carry a very simple statement but in practice it raises a myriad of issues.

The main provision governing plant protection is Article 27(3)(b) and this will be the focus for the remainder of this chapter.

## Article 27(3)(b)

Article 27(3)(b) states that members may exclude from patentability:

> plants and animals other than micro-organisms, and essentially biological processes for the production of plants and animals other than non-biological and microbiological processes. However, Members shall provide for the protection of plant varieties either by patents or by an effective *sui generis* system or by any combination thereof. The provisions of this subparagraph shall be reviewed four years after the date of entry into force of the WTO Agreement.

Member states may, therefore, exclude plants and animals[109] from patent protection but patent protection must be provided for micro-organisms and microbiological processes. Protection must also be provided for plant varieties, but member states are given the option of the form of protection, having the choice of patents, *sui generis* protection or a combination of the two.

Before looking at what must be protected under Article 27(3)(b), a basic issue needs to be discussed—why, in contrast to any other type of 'invention', is there a specific requirement to protect micro-organisms and plant varieties?

The requirement to protect micro-organisms underlines the significance placed on the use of these within the pharmaceutical industry and also the economic importance of companies engaged in this research.[110] It is commonly stated that the production of one single drug can cost millions, if not billions, of

---

[108] Although it should be noted that the OECD is currently looking at developing guidelines on good practice relating to the general licensing of inventions involving genetic material. It was not clear at the time of writing as to the extent to which these would apply to all genetic inventions (including agriculture) or if they would be restricted to pharmaceuticals.

[109] There is no express reference to the patentability or otherwise of human genetic material.

[110] See, eg, the discussion in Grubb, *Patents for Chemical, Pharmaceuticals and Biotechnology* (OUP, 1999). The protection of other material commonly used in the pharmaceutical industry, such as chemical compounds, falls under the umbrella obligation set out in Art 27(1). These are not generally regarded as having any 'life form' connotations and their status as patentable subject matter is therefore unambiguous provided the granting criteria can be met.

dollars and yet copying the results of this investment-intensive research can cost only pennies—this is the main reason justifying protection.[111] The importance of micro-organisms in the work of the pharmaceutical industry is one of the reasons (if not *the* reason) why the term 'micro-organism' has been given a more open interpretation within patent law than appears to exist within science.

In terms of plant variety protection, Article 27(3)(b) simply reflects a) the economic importance of encouraging innovation in plant breeding and b) the resulting intellectual property expectations of most developed countries, namely that either patent or a *sui generis* system of protection will be available for plant varieties.[112] It is then up to the member states to decide how, if at all, it will protect any intellectual property interests vesting in other forms of plant material. In looking at this obligation it is important to bear in mind that for many countries (and this includes all European member states) the TRIPs Agreement does not set down new standards of protectable subject matter but instead simply reflects the existing intellectual property law practices of many of its member states. In this, the Agreement is merely harking back to the original statement within the Paris Convention that plant material *per se* can be regarded as industrial property—the fact that member states have the option not to treat it as such indicates that there is no requirement that they *must* treat it as such.

For example, whilst the US and Europe both permit patents over plants and plant material, other developed countries (including, as noted earlier, Canada), permit patent protection only for the component parts of a plant (for example, genes[113]) but not for the plant itself. However, all three jurisdictions provide protection for plant varieties under either the patent system (US) or a UPOV-based plant variety rights system (Europe and Canada). Given this variation it would have been hard to dictate that life forms higher than a micro-organism *had* to be patented.[114] As most developed countries protect varieties (whether by patent or by plant variety right), but differ over the protection of other forms of

---

[111] It is perhaps worth noting that these figures invariably come from the pharmaceutical industry itself. The impression given is that each drug is produced on its own and therefore is wholly independent of either any other research into the production of another drug or improvement of any other drug already on the market. The economic reality is less straightforward and it may be that the production of a particular drug itself incurred only minimal costs, but that might be on the back of costly production which took place earlier in the research programme which related to the development of a number of potential drugs, of which the minimal expense drug proved the most efficient. In addition, the references to drug production costs must be placed in the context of how much companies spend on other activities such as advertising. This is not to suggest that patent protection may not be deserved, but rather to underline that the rationale for seeking protection might lie in the need to support a panoply of activities rather than simply to reward/recompense the production of one specific drug.

[112] This is affirmed by the TRIPs Secretariat, which reinforces the notion that plant breeders are entitled to protection in the same way as scientists working in other areas of technology: IP/C/W/369 8 August 2002.

[113] As will be discussed below, there are two ways to look at the patentable status of plant genes. On the one hand, many patent systems treat them as micro-organisms, and therefore member states are required to provide protection for them. On the other, there is an argument that they could be treated as 'plants' and therefore optionally excluded.

[114] Nowhere in the Agreement is the status of human genetic material mentioned.

by plant material the distinction between the obligation to protect varieties and the option to protect other plant material, becomes clear. There are, of course, problems with mapping this minimum standard onto the policies and practices of countries with no previous tradition of providing private property rights over plant material, particularly where those countries have not had the luxury of debating the issues over a number of years (nearly a hundred in the case of Europe and the US), but it is outside the remit of this book to delve further into these problems.

The benefits of having protection are that it encourages investment (especially from the private sector), it encourages the development of better varieties (especially agricultural crops) and it facilitates access to the new technology through licensing and technology transfer. The concerns raised are that it has implications for access to seeds (particularly with regard to use in further breeding programmes), possible erosion of traditional varieties and a reduction of biodiversity. In addition, there are worries about the granting of excessively broad patents and the impact of both patents and plant variety rights on traditional knowledge. The balance between ensuring benefits arise without endangering access or diversity will be dealt with in chapters 9 and 10.

The two main issues which this section will address are:

a) what must be protected, (and in particular the distinction, if any, between micro-organisms, plants and plant varieties); and
b) what is an acceptable or 'effective' *sui generis* right (as the UPOV Convention will be discussed in the next chapter, specific reference here will be made to any options existing under other international treaties such as the Convention on Biological Diversity and the International Treaty on Plant Genetic Resources).

Protectable Subject Matter

Article 27(3)(b) appears to establish clear lines of protectability:

(i)    plants, animals and essentially biological processes for the production of plants and animals which may be excluded from patent protection;
(ii)   inventions concerning micro-organisms, non-biological and microbiological processes for which patent protection must be available;

and:

(iii)  plant varieties for which protection must be provided, whether by patent and/or effective *sui generis* right.

The language of Article 27(3)(b) implies that each of these groups is distinguishable from the others. It also implies that there is clear blue water between the groups, for example between micro-organisms and plants and between plants and plant varieties, and that these distinctions are readily identifiable and commonly accepted in practice. The ability to distinguish between that which must be protected and that which may be excluded is vital when determining the scope of the obligation contained in Article 27(3)(b).

The relevance of Article 27(3)(b) to the European provision lies in the fact that it not only articulates modern European practice—micro-organisms, plants, non-biological and microbiological processes being patentable, with plant varieties protected by *sui generis* rights based on the UPOV Convention—but it also shows how granting practices in respect of micro-organisms have made it very difficult in practice to exclude plants from patent protection (even if there was a desire so to do in Europe).[115]

As micro-organisms have been patentable in Europe since the 19th century, it might be thought that there is no need to discuss the impact of Article 27(3)(b) on European practices. However, it is relevant to look at the law surrounding the patenting of micro-organisms because this demonstrates the way in which legal and scientific concepts can differ. It also helps to understand the very open-textured way in which European patent offices interpret notions of protectable subject matter, as will be discussed in chapters 5 and 6.

A second reason for looking, albeit briefly, at the patent law and micro-organisms is to demonstrate how apparent distinctions between patentable and non-patentable material can be rendered virtually meaningless in practice (often by virtue of incremental developments in case law).

The final reason is that patent practice appears to indicate that where there is any latitude over the precise meaning of any word or term then this is invariably exploited to include the material rather than exclude it—this again emphasises the presumption of patentability.

### Plants and Micro-organisms[116]

The TRIPs Agreement does not provide a definition of 'micro-organism'.[117] Whilst it can be argued that, in keeping with the absence of definitions in the rest of the Agreement, there is no need to try and define this term, the fact that the Agreement permits member states to draw a distinction between a plant and a micro-organism indicates that it is possible to provide definitions for the two. In order to do so reference needs to be made to other sources. The first port of call is Article 31(1) of the 1969 Vienna Convention on the Law of Treaties which governs interpretation.

---

[115] To a large extent this will purely be an academic exercise, but it might have relevance for any country seeking to limit its categories of patentable subject matter and assist in understanding why, if such limitations are put in place, they might be challenged by countries which operate on an inclusion not exclusion.

[116] This argument was first put forward by the authors in Llewelyn and Adcock, 'Micro-organisms, Definitions and Options Under TRIPs' (2000–01) 3 *Bioscience Law Review* 91.

[117] Interestingly, there is no definition even within the Budapest Treaty on the International Recognition of the Deposit of Micro-organisms for the Purposes of Patent Procedure.

Article 31(1) states that the general rule of interpretation is that a treaty 'shall be interpreted in good faith in accordance with the ordinary meaning to be given to the terms of the treaty in their context and in light of its object and purpose.' In order to try and ascertain the ordinary meaning it is necessary, therefore, to look at the meanings given to the term both in science and at law. Immediately a problem arises because any examination of the scientific literature shows that there is no agreed scientific definition.

Generally speaking, the defining property of a micro-organism is that each individual is of microscopic size. It is likely that it was the microscopic dimensions of these organisms which led to researchers separating them from the plant and animal kingdoms. However, equally important to their classification is their morphology, activity, diversity, flexibility of metabolism, ecological distribution, and even their manipulation in the laboratory. The multiplicity of organisms which can fall into these different groups means that the term 'micro-organism' includes organisms which differ widely from one another in form, life cycle and mode of life. As a result there is no single definition for a 'micro-organism'. The various definitions available, and these are too numerous to elaborate here, indicate great diversity of thought. For example, 'micro-organism' has been defined as 'an organism not visible to the naked eye, eg, bacterium or virus,'[118] 'any organism, such as a virus, of microscopic size,'[119] 'a micro-organism is an organism that can be seen only under a microscope, usually, an ordinary light microscope . . . and include bacteria, mycoplasm, yeasts, single-celled algae and protozoa. Multicellular organisms are normally not included, nor fungi apart from yeasts. Viruses are also not automatically included; many scientists do not classify them as organisms as they depend on cells to multiply',[120] 'viruses are included though they are non-cellular particles which are not capable of independent life and can proliferate only in living cells'[121] 'a microscopic organism consisting of a single cell or cell cluster, including the viruses'[122] and 'microscopic life-forms including microscopic fungi, Protista, prokaryotes and viruses'.[123]

On this basis, the term 'micro-organism' may, according to the definition used, include or exclude any of the following: the bacteria, cyanobacteria, archaeabacteria, algae, protozoa, slime moulds, fungi, bacteriophages, plasmids and viruses.

As with any area of science, the characterisation of micro-organisms has developed as the ability to study them has improved. Improvements in light microscopy, followed by the development of confocal and electron microscopy, have not only aided the discovery of new micro-organisms but also the ability to

---

[118] The *Penguin English Dictionary*.

[119] *Collins English Dictionary*.

[120] Institute of Science, UK.

[121] Hawler and Linton, *Micro-organisms: Function, Form and Environment* (Arnold Publishers, 1981).

[122] Madigan, Martinko and Parker, *Biology of Micro-organisms* (Prentice Hall Publishers, 2000).

[123] Heritage, Evans and Killington, *Introduction to Microbiology* (CUP, 1997).

describe them as well. This has resulted in the term 'micro-organism', as used by scientists, becoming widely used but nonetheless ill-defined. Equally, the scientific understanding of what is a 'micro-organism' is continually evolving, with a variety of definitions which encompass an ever-widening range of diverse organisms.

In addition, and relevant again for the purposes of applying the Article 27(3(b) exclusion, the division between plants, animals and micro-orgasms is not a strict one, with significant overlap between the kingdoms. Many organisms have properties which mean that they cannot be readily characterised into a particular kingdom. There are many examples, of which green algae is fairly typical. Green algae have many properties in common with members of the plant kingdom, for example, they contain photosynthetic pigments and are autotrophic, and yet many are microscopic and unicellular and can thus also be considered to be micro-organisms. Furthermore, fungi are frequently included in the term 'micro-organism' and yet many fungi are too large to be considered microscopic.

The kingdom of plants, animals and micro-organisms can be separated into eukaryotes and prokaryotes. Eukaryotes include, at the highest level, animals and plants. At the lower level of classification, they include euglena, protoxoa, fungi and microalgae. Prokaryotes include at the lower level eubacteria and archaebacteria. Straddling both at the level between, on the one side, animals and plants and, on the other, euglena, eubacteria and archaebacteria are micro-organisms. This delineates the genetic division of all organisms and their common ancestry and, in light of modern science, serves to demonstrate that the definition of 'micro-organism' is evolving and not static.

It is therefore, clear that the term 'micro-organism' can have a variety of definitions which may or may not be exhaustive.

In the context of Article 27(3)(b), therefore, it may be possible to define a micro-organism as biological material which is neither a plant nor an animal, but as the above discussion outlines, it is not so easy to draw that distinction in practice—and this is made even more difficult when the jurisprudence of the patent system is brought into the equation. (In European patent law the term 'micro-organism' is given a very broad legal definition and held to encompass bacteria, fungi, viruses and, crucially, human, animal and plant cells.) At law the term 'micro-organism' clearly encompasses more than the common scientific definition of unicellular living organisms capable of independent existence. The inclusion of plant cells and fungi (amongst other non-traditional forms of 'micro-organisms') serves to further blur the line between that which must be protected and that which can be excluded as it begs the question: when is a plant cell a plant? This is an issue of increasing importance for those who prefer clear boundaries between included and excluded material, given the ability of scientists to generate whole plants from just one cell.

The notions of what is a plant and what is an animal have rarely been addressed within the patent systems of developed countries—the reason being that plants and animals are not expressly referred to as included or excluded within the text of patent laws, the exclusions being applied to plant and animal *varieties per se*. As will be seen in chapters 6 and 7, this practice is followed by the EPO and endorsed by the European Commission.

Many developing countries are concerned about the potential blurring between a plant and a micro-organism, as they feel that the compulsory protection of the latter will give rise to *de facto* protection for the former.[124] One way round the problem such cloudiness poses for those seeking to rely on the exclusion of plants but compelled to provide protection for micro-organisms, is to provide a definition of a micro-organism. However, this is likely to meet with resistance, not least from the European Commission. In 2002 the Commission stated that it would be difficult to provide a definition '[f]irstly, because it would be extremely difficult to agree on precise definitions in that context, and, secondly, because it is questionable whether more precise definitions are really necessary, given that they would reduce the flexibility of WTO Members.'[125] Possibly within a developed country context, with a sophisticated patent system, this view is the correct one and it might be appropriate to leave the issue of defining the subject matter to those involved in seeking and opposing patent protection. However, the provision of such a definition might aid developing countries anxious to move cautiously on the pathway to protecting living material.[126] Possibly surprisingly, given the relative acceptability of providing protection for plant varieties, a similar problem could be said to arise in respect of the second obligation in Article 27(3)(b), the protection of plant varieties.

The Protection of Plant Varieties

Article 27(3)(b) mandates that member states must provide protection for plant varieties, but, in contrast to the obligation to patent micro-organisms, member states are given a choice as to the form that protection can take. Protection can be via patent protection or by a *sui generis* right or by a combination of the two. As with micro-organisms, TRIPs fails to provide any definition as to what is a plant variety, with the impression that this is a recognised concept with a single meaning common to both science and law. In addition, notwithstanding that Article 27(3)(b) provides member states with a measure of choice as to the form of protection they adopt over plant varieties, there is a question over the extent to which that choice is real in practice.

As will be discussed in chapters two to eight, most developed countries have interpreted this exclusion (where it exists) as applying to any plant grouping which is capable of being protected by a plant variety right which accords with

---

[124] See 'The Integrating Intellectual Property Rights and Development Policy Report of the UK Commission on Intellectual Property Rights' at www.iprcommission.org/graphic/documents/final_report.htm.

[125] IP/C/W/383, 17 October 2002.

[126] See Llewelyn and Adcock, 'Definitions and Options Under TRIPs', above n 116, and also the report of the UK Commission on Intellectual Property Rights 2002, which supported this proposal.

UPOV. On this basis any plant material which is not capable of being protectable under UPOV is not regarded as a variety and therefore is potentially patentable.[127] The capacity for protection under the UPOV system is, therefore, the decisive factor—if the grouping is recognised as a plant variety under UPOV then the exclusion kicks in, if it is not then the exclusion does not apply. This approach is flawed for one simple reason—the UPOV system recognises *two* types of variety.

### The UPOV Definition

The first thing to note about the UPOV definition of a plant variety is that the definition has varied over the years.[128] The 1961 Act defined protectable material as '. . . any cultivar, clone, line, stock or hybrid which is capable of cultivation and which satisfies the provisions of sub-paragraphs (1)(c) and (1)(d) of Article 6' (Article 2(2)).[129] The 1991 Act, however, does not confine its definition to specific types of plant material but refers to characteristics a protectable variety should have. Article 1 defines a variety as:

> a plant grouping which grouping, irrespective of whether the conditions for a grant of a plant variety right are fully met, can be defined by the expression of characteristics that results from a given genotype or combination of genotypes, distinguished from any other plant grouping by the expression of at least one of the said characteristics, and considered as a unit with regard to its suitability for being propagated unchanged.

In contrast to both the 1961 and 1991 Acts, the 1978 Act does not contain any definition.[130]

The reason for removing the definition from the 1978 Act was that it was thought that there was sufficient common consensus as to what was a variety to render the provision of a definition of variety superfluous. It was also thought that if an attempt was made to revise the definition in light of the scientific developments in plant breeding which had occurred post-1961 then it would be too difficult to do so in language which would not ultimately prove too narrow and, therefore, exclusionary. The only guidance which the 1978 Act provides as to protectable varieties is the statement that 'Each member state of the Union may limit the application of this Convention within a genus or species

---

[127] See *Novartis/Transgenic Plant* [1999] EPOR 123, decision of the Enlarged Board of Appeal; *Novartis/Transgenic Plant* [2000] EPOR 303; Art 4(2) Directive EC/44/98; and also Recs 29–32 of the Directive.

[128] As will be discussed in the next chapter, it is still relevant to discuss all three versions of the UPOV Convention as not all member states of the UPOV Union have revised their national plant variety rights laws to take account of later versions of the Convention. This means that within Europe, for example, the national laws of some member states are based on the 1961 Act, some on the 1978 Act and others on the 1991 Act.

[129] Art 6 contained the substantive granting provisions, distinctness, uniformity and stability.

[130] The reason why it is relevant to take both the 1978 and 1991 definitions into account will be explained below.

to varieties with a particular manner of reproduction or multiplication' (Article 2(2)).

The 1991 Act brought back the definition because it was thought necessary to establish clear blue water between material which could be the subject of a patent, for example the genetic components of a plant, and groupings of plants (which may comprise those components) which collectively can be shown to be distinct, uniform and stable.[131] However, the reintroduction of a definition into the text of the 1991 UPOV Act does not necessarily mean that there is now no ambiguity as to that which is capable of being protected by a plant variety right and that which is protectable by patent.

The language of Article 1 of the 1991 Act clearly indicates that there is more than one type of plant variety—plant varieties which can meet the conditions for grant of a plant variety right and varieties which cannot meet the granting criteria. The reason why UPOV recognises two types of plant variety has been explained by the WIPO[132]:

> In framing a definition in 1991, it was thought that there should be a clear distinction between the definition of 'variety' and a variety which meets the technical criteria of Article 7 [distinctness], 8 [uniformity], and 9 [stability] of the 1991 Act of the Convention so as to be a protectable variety. This is to ensure that a variety with a level of uniformity which is unacceptable for the purposes of a grant of rights may still exist as a 'variety' and be taken into account, for example, for the purposes of common knowledge and distinctness under Article 7.

The value in having the definition therefore lies in enabling granting offices to take into account plant groupings which do not 'fully' meet the requirements for a grant of a plant variety right when assessing if another plant grouping is protectable.

There appears to be a discrepancy between the practice of patent offices (which use the capacity for protection under UPOV as the benchmark for determining if a plant grouping is a variety or not) and the UPOV system (reflected also in the Community Regulation) which distinguishes between protectable and non-protectable varieties. The question which this poses is whether patent offices should interpret any exclusion of plant varieties as applying to those varieties which are not protectable under UPOV? For example, should they be bound also to use the definition provided in the International Treaty on Plant Genetic Resources, Article 2 of which defines a plant variety as 'a plant grouping, within a single botanical taxon of the lowest known rank, defined by the reproducible expression of its distinguishing and other genetic characteristics.' This clearly is not a variety capable of being protected under UPOV as there is no requirement that the replication has to take place in a uniform or stable manner and therefore such a plant grouping may not be recognised as a variety

---

[131] UPOV CAJ/XX111/2.
[132] *Introduction to Intellectual Property Theory and Practice* (World Intellectual Property Organisation, Kluwer Law International, 1997) p 462.

for the purposes of Article 1 of the 1991 Act. This is an issue which has yet to be fully explored and it will be discussed further in chapters 5, 6 and 7, when looking at the practice of the EPO and at the provisions of the EU Directive.

There is one other issue which needs to be addressed when looking at Article 27(3)(b), namely the distinction between that which is *protectable* under either a patent or a plant variety right and that which is *protected* as a result of the right being granted (this issue has already been raised in chapter 1).

Under plant variety rights a breeder can make an application only in respect of a plant grouping the plants of which collectively demonstrate common characteristics in a distinct, uniform and stable manner. He cannot apply for a right over a single gene or trait. However, the right, once granted, permits the breeder to control the use of those elements (the variety constituents) within the plant which give rise to both the characteristics and the capacity to distinguish in a uniform and stable manner. The right permits the holder to protect the internal genetic components of the variety as well as the variety itself even though these elements may not be the subject of a plant variety application.

In patent law, a plant application may not include a claim to a plant variety, but it may claim plant genetic material which could be used to affect the characteristics or traits of a variety. Once the patent is granted (and this is now explicitly stated within the EU Directive) it is held to extend to any material into which the patented invention has been placed (provided that it performs the function for which the patent was granted). The effect of this is to give the patent holder rights over the externalisation of his patented technology, including a variety, even though he is not permitted to claim a variety specifically within the patent itself. This will be discussed in more detail later.

The clear blue water distinction between that which can be protected under patent law and that which is protectable under plant variety rights is, therefore, less obvious than an initial observation would indicate. Instead, there seems to be considerable common ground between that which can be protected under patent law and material protectable under plant variety rights and vice versa. The overlap becomes more apparent when looked at in the context of the argument surrounding the patentability of micro-organisms set out above.

There is one final provision in patent law (and particularly within European patent law) which needs to be taken into account—and that is the impact of process patents on the exclusion of plant varieties.

The TRIPs Agreement expressly states that where a patent has been granted over a process then anything directly produced by that process also may not be used, offered for sale, sold or imported.[133] The exclusion of plant varieties means that the patent holder cannot claim a patent for a plant variety. However, where the patent relates to a process and that process is directly used to produce a plant variety then the patent granted over the process extends to the plant variety directly produced.

---

[133] Art 28(2).

If it is possible to define what is protectable and what may be excluded then what form of protection must be provided, and in particular what constitutes a *sui generis* form of protection?

An Effective *Sui Generis* Right

The language of Article 27(3)(b) permits three possible methods of complying:

1) member states can provide patent protection and/or *sui generis* protection which accords with UPOV (even though UPOV is not specified as the *sui generis* right[134]). This is the approach taken in the US—where patents are available over all plant material, including plant varieties, with breeders also able to apply for plant variety rights if they so wish—and in Europe, where plant varieties are expressly excluded from patent protection but protectable under UPOV style plant variety rights;

or

2) member states can exclude plant varieties from patent protection in favour of protection via a sui generis system which conforms to neither patent law nor UPOV. Examples of this include the Thai Plant Variety Protection Act 1999 and the Indian Protection of Plant Varieties and Farmers' Rights Act 2001.[135] The only constraining factor in such provision is that the countries have to demonstrate that it is 'effective'. The issue of whether the rights enacted are 'effective' or not is not simply an issue for the WTO: for example, the ISF admonished the Indian government for the 2001 Act on the basis that it would not provide effective protection for plant breeders;

or

3) member states can provide both patent protection and a non-UPOV *sui generis* right. To date no country appears to have taken this approach and therefore it is not proposed to discuss this option in any further detail.

Given that UPOV is a proven system of protection, and the fact that it has slowly gained membership from around the world, it might seem odd that it was not specified as the preferred, if not sole, alternative, to patent protection.[136]

---

[134] This is in contrast to the Paris and Berne Conventions which are specifically named. The TRIPs Agreement appears to be stating that a right over plant varieties must be provided, but as the form of that right is not prescribed it could be argued that it need not be an intellectual property right. This reading makes sense if, as the discussion in ch 1 indicated, there is a question mark over whether plant variety rights are intellectual property rights. However, even if the *sui generis* right provided is not an intellectual property right, the TRIPs Agreement will still have an element of control over it, as it will have to be shown to be 'effective'.

[135] Although some of the provisions of the latter may be superseded by the proposed new Patent Law which may curtail the ability of farmers to retain seed from one year to the next.

[136] There are rumours that even those engaged in the debates were unclear as to what the provision was supposed to mandate, with some participants viewing the term *sui generis* as meaning a UPOV system, regarding it as providing members with the option of developing a new system of

The reason why there is no specific reference to UPOV is because of the hostility many developing countries felt at having to provide either patents or UPOV protection—both of which are regarded as Western legal constructs with inappropriate emphases on protection and commercialisation which favour foreign breeders rather than fostering local innovation. This refusal to agree to the developed countries' notions of suitable mechanisms, together with the existing diversity between developed countries (most notably between the US and Europe) caused some problems for the draftsmen.

The first problem was that the draftsmen had to find a form of wording which reflected the strong but diverse protection practices of the US and Europe.

Secondly, they had to take account of the anti-protection views expressed by some developing countries (resulting in part from the predominantly public sector nature of plant research).[137] These views were not directed solely against patent protection but extended to plant variety rights, which many regarded in the same way as patents as being anti-communitarian and developed country-centric. The revision of UPOV in 1991, making the right closer to a patent right, has served to only reinforce these views. A compromise had to be reached which would provide the security of plant variety protection wanted by developed countries and, at the same time, allay the concerns of developing countries. The security of protection was ensured by making the obligation to provide protection for plant varieties mandatory. The allaying of fears over perceived 'bio-colonialism' was more difficult.[138] A solution was presented by the UPOV Union.

The UPOV Council agreed that, despite enacting a new Act in 1991, they would hold open the previous, 1978, Act for signature by new member states until the new Act came into force (which was in April 1998).[139] The 1978 Act,

---

protection which could be based on aspects of UPOV, but also include elements from other sources, such as the CBD.

[137] These were not new views but can be traced back to the 1980s when it was first mooted that there should be an increased use of plant breeders' rights. This was demonstrated in the views expressed, eg, at a meeting of the FAO Commission on Plant Genetic Resources in 1987.

[138] The extent of these views varied from looking at alternative ways of protecting plant varieties through to a wholesale refusal to introduce any form of protection.

[139] Art 37(1) UPOV 1991. Although the 1978 Act is now technically closed this does not mean no new member states can sign up to it. It would appear that, provided some official indication had been given pre-April 1998 that a country wished to join UPOV on the basis of the 1978 Act, then it may still do so notwithstanding the coming into force of the 1991 Act. Examples of this include India. In 2001 it introduced the Protection of Plant Varieties and Farmers' Rights Act, which combines aspects of UPOV and the CBD. In 2002, the Indian government decided to accede to the UPOV Union on the basis of the 1978 Act. On the basis of a decision taken by an Extraordinary Meeting of the UPOV Council in 1997, which agreed that where a country had sought advice as to the conformity of its local plant variety provision before the first anniversary of the coming into force of the 1991 Act (ie pre 1999), then that country should be permitted to join the 1978 Act. This permitted Bolivia, Brazil, China, India, Kenya, Nicaragua, Panama and Zimbabwe to accede to the 1978 Act (with India, Nicaragua and Zimbabwe being given an extension of time in which to introduce appropriate legislation). See www.upov.int/documents/c/33/c-33-18(e).pdf. The specific situation concerning plant variety protection in India is discussed in Adcock, 'Farmers' Right or Privilege?' (2001–01) 3 *Bioscience Law Review* 90.

however, would remain closed to existing members, who were now obliged to introduce the 1991 Act into national law. As will be discussed in chapter 3, the 1978 Act contains certain key differences to the 1991 Act; most notably it contains the dual protection prohibition, it explicitly permits farmers to save seed for use in subsequent years, it has no notion of 'essentially derived varieties' and it does not require member states, upon accession, to provide protection for varieties for all species and genera.[140] The expectation was, and is, that once new members had joined the UPOV Union, via the 1978 Act, they would quickly move to a ratification of the 1991 Act.

Given that two versions of the UPOV Convention would be in force at the same time it is easy to understand why, if UPOV were the only *sui generis* system, no mention is made of the Convention. Any reference would either have simply stipulated a right in accordance with UPOV, but that would have raised questions over which version of UPOV applied, or it would have had to specifically mention both the 1978 and 1991 Acts, which would have made the wording cumbersome. However, irrespective of the problems which might have been encountered in trying to find the right wording if UPOV, in either or both 1978 and 1991 guises, was the only *sui generis* system, then it still would have been expected that a form of words would have been found to make this clear. The fact that it does not indicates that Article 27(3)(b) was possibly intended to permit another right altogether.

If this latter reading is correct (and possible alternative methods of protection are outlined below) this does not mean that the UPOV Convention has no relevance when determining compliance with Article 27(3)(b). Many, including representatives from the WTO, regard the UPOV Conventions (and the 1991 Act in particular) as the preferred, and already accepted, 'effective' form of protection[141]—any deviation from this having to be proved to be 'effective' by the country introducing it. As Heitz has stated:

> whilst the TRIPs Agreement leaves ample discretion to the WTO members in theory, there is in practice a strong commitment, on the part of those members, to abide by established legal systems. Any new plant variety protection system that would be out of line, compared with the UPOV system, and would create 'distortions and impediments to international trade' is likely to attract criticism, if not retaliatory measures. On the other hand, the UPOV Convention—including the 1991 Act—offers enough discretion to States so that they can design their national protection system to fit national circumstances.

---

[140] In respect of this later facet of the 1978 Act, it can be questioned whether limiting the number of varieties which can be protected under the national right fully complies with the TRIPs obligation, as Art 17(3)(b) requires member states to provide protection for varieties. There is no indication that is intended to be qualified in any way.

[141] See Otten, 'Proceedings of the WIPO–UPOV Symposium on Intellectual Property Rights in Plant Biotechnology', October 2003.

And whilst there is no actual requirement that this has to be via UPOV, there are

> objective reasons to join the Union, in particular in terms of: (a) credibility—and practical effectiveness—of the national protection system, (b) ability to share in and benefit from the combined experience of member States, and (c) ability to contribute to the worldwide promotion of plant breeding and to the evolution of the plant variety protection system.[142]

Where a country has chosen not to look to the patent or UPOV routes then member states have a significant degree of control over the form of that right—arguably more than is permitted in respect of the obligation to provide patent protection. For example, member states are not confined to the use of any existing substantive requirements determining protectability. Article 27(1) requires that patents are granted only over inventions which are novel, involve an inventive step and are capable of industrial application. In contrast, the threshold for protection for the *sui generis* system is not prescribed. This means that when formulating the right it is possible to seek guidance and/or inspiration from other international agreements including those not wholly concerned with intellectual property protection.

It is clear that whilst the obligation to protect plant varieties is closed in the sense that protection must be provided, it is nonetheless open in that member states retain a degree of flexibility as to the form that protection should take. There is scope for both imaginative interpretation and application. The question which remains is whether the alternative form of right other than the proven UPOV or patent-type rights, would be accepted as an 'effective' *sui generis* right? Central to this question is the issue of what is meant by 'effective'? Does this mean the right has to comply with the TRIPs Agreement and provide the same type of protection as those rights specifically identified within the Agreement or is it purely a matter of what the local jurisdiction within which the right will operate thinks is 'effective'? A question which goes to the heart of this is whether the *sui generis* right has to be an intellectual property right.

For some, that the right should be an intellectual property right would appear to be a given. The Legal Adviser to the FAO's Commission on Genetic Resources for Food and Agriculture has commented that:

> it is possible to infer, from the general context of the TRIPs Agreement, some of the minimum requirements of the sui generis system, namely: (i) it should be, at least in the broad sense, a system to protect intellectual property rights; (ii) it should be applicable, in principle, to all traded plant varieties; (iii) it should be effective, that is, enforceable; (iv) it should be non-discriminatory as regards the country of origin of the applicant (principle of national treatment); and (v) it should accord the most-favored-nation treatment.[143]

---

[142] www.upov.int. The Preamble to the Agreement states that this is a key function of the Agreement.

[143] Fourth Extraordinary Session, United Nation's Food and Agriculture Organisation's (FAO) Commission on Genetic Resources for Food and Agriculture, December 1997.

However, others such as the European Commission stopped short of defining the right as such;[144] instead, the right, and those elements within it which would render it 'effective' (some of which mirror the requirements identified by the FAO), is couched in more general terms. The Commission has said that member states should be free to introduce protection appropriate to their own national situation, taking into account any agricultural objectives or the needs of key groups such as farmers. In producing this new protection, the law should contain the following: a definition of a plant variety; a defined threshold for protection, with novelty being an essential condition; a definition of the right granted, and in particular what acts, carried out by third parties, can be prevented by the right holder, and also the duration of the right, plus any excluded acts (such as the experimental use and farm saved seed exemptions). In this there are clear resonances with the considerations which led up to the introduction of the first version of the UPOV Convention (which, as mentioned in chapter 1, did not confer an *intellectual* property right over the protected material). In addition, the right should include general TRIPs requirements relating to national treatment and most favoured nation. Finally, there must be a clear process for acquiring the right and a proper administrative system must be put in place, with an organisation established to oversee the grant of rights with proper enforcement procedures in place. However, the Commission does not expressly state that the new law should contain any of the other general principles, such as those contained in Articles 7 and 8. However, the fact that there is a specific reference to the agricultural[145] objectives of the country concerned, together with the needs of groups such as farmers, indicates that these principles can be used to guide the form of right provided. This is also the position of the TRIPs Council.

Unsurprisingly, the TRIPs Council is aware of the dissatisfaction with Article 27(3)(b) in its current form and, as part of its review of the Article,[146] it is looking at various ways it could revise the provision, taking into account the panoply of views as to what plant material, if any, should be covered by the Agreement. It is looking at the exceptions to patentability (although this is not necessarily with a view to expanding them but might take the form of rendering patentable all inventions involving plants), clarifying (or defining) the differences between

---

[144] *Review of Art 27(3)(b) of the TRIPs Agreement, and the Relationship between the TRIPs Agreement and the Convention on Biological Diversity (CBD) and the Protection of Traditional Knowledge and Folklore, 'A Concept Paper'* IP/C/W/383, 17 October 2002.

[145] It is the relationship between agriculture, plant breeding and the protection of plant varieties which lies at the heart of the Art 27(3)(b) obligation and this has been the primary basis for introducing and revising plant variety rights. Given this emphasis it is easy to forget that plant variety rights can be used to protect a range of other types of plant innovations which are not agriculturally related. There is scant debate on the likely impact developments based on agricultural considerations will have on breeders' ability to protect.

[146] As required by the last sentence of Art 27(3)(b). The fact that this review is ongoing, notwithstanding that the intention was that it should have been completed early in the new century, indicates the extent of dissension which continues to exist over whether member states should be compelled to provide protection for plant varieties.

plants, animals and micro-organisms, amending or clarifying Article 27(3)(b) to prohibit the patenting of all life forms, more specifically plants and animals, micro-organisms and all other living organisms and their parts, including genes as well as natural processes that produce plants, animals and other living organisms. The Council may also look at prohibiting the patenting of inventions based on traditional knowledge or those that violate the CBD. To date, however, these are only possible options and the existing obligation to comply with the provisions of Article 27(3)(b) remains the same. As part of this review the WTO sent a questionnaire to member states to try and determine the level of protection available. The results of this survey (which elicited 37 replies) indicate that the majority do not exclude patents for entire plants; however, they do exclude varieties. Most allow claims which are not restricted to a specific variety and to groups of plants defined by reference to a single shared characteristic. In addition, all bar two provide *sui generis* protection for plant varieties and are members of the 1991 Act UPOV.[147]

Because of these concerns the TRIPs Council has actively sought to calm fears. One aspect of the Doha declaration in 2001 (which is mainly heralded for its statement on access to drugs for public healthcare purposes) which is often overlooked is paragraph 19. This states that the TRIPs Council should look at the relationship between the TRIPs Agreement and the CBD and in so doing it specifically states that the Council's work should be guided by Article 7 and Article 8 of TRIPs.[148] This mirrors the activity of the UPOV Union, which also is addressing the relationship between the UPOV Acts, the CBD and the ITPGR.[149]

In addition, the TRIPs Council is also looking at whether the TRIPs Agreement should be amended to require patent applicants to disclose the source of the traditional knowledge or genetic material. In so doing it is also trying to determine the kind of approval which might be needed before this material can be used in an invention, and ways in which any benefits which arise out of these inventions can be shared with the community which provided the information or material. It is clear, therefore, that the issue of plant protection remains a live one and that alternative, non-traditional methods of protecting plant material have not been ruled out by the WTO.

The European Commission has strongly supported these initiatives. Its discussion papers, submitted to the TRIPs Council, indicate the EC's 'willingness to commit to this process in a spirit of openness, with the aim of finding ways of interpreting and implementing the TRIPs Agreement in a way to support the objectives of the CBD' and that 'the intellectual property rights system plays a practical part in promoting the benefits from access to genetic resources and

---

[147] Summary Note on responses to Illustrative List of Questions on Art 27(3)(b), IP/C/W/273/Rev.1, discussed at www.upov.org.

[148] It is noteworthy that the CBD does not relate to human genetic material and the comments of the TRIPs Council about the relevance of Arts 7 and 8 therefore do not extend to inventions derived from or containing human genetic material.

[149] See www.upov.org/en/documents and www.upov.org/en/news/2004/ipgri_press.pdf.

TK.'[150] In the minds of the EU there is an inextricable link between having access to the material, the acquisition of rights over any material produced using the accessed plants and enabling benefit sharing. The view is that the provision of an intellectual property right is essential in order to ensure that the material, accessed, developed and protected, is beneficially shared. Whilst some may baulk at this notion, there is nothing in either the CBD or the TRIPs Agreement which prevents the sharing of any benefits arising from intellectual property protection over inventions incorporating genetic resources or the protection of traditional knowledge. This, whilst providing a nod to the provisions of the CBD, does not require either patent nor plant variety rights applicants to indicate the source of genetic material. Although it recognises it as a principle which should be supported where possible:

> [a]t national level, sound regulation (through legislation or administrative or policy measures) on access and benefit-sharing (ABS) under the CBD is essential to guarantee legal security for all parties involved and to protect the rights of providers of genetic resources. Further details can be settled through contractual arrangements. Legislation/policy measures and contracts are complementary instruments for ensuring fair implementation of the CBD. Further synergies between the implementation of these agreements can be worked out at international level by ensuring policy coherence in all forums which deal with issues relevant to the interplay between TRIPS, the CBD and the FAO International Treaty on Plant Genetic Resources for Food and Agriculture. In this respect the Bonn Guidelines on Access to Genetic Resources and Benefit-sharing adopted at the 6th Conference of the Parties in The Hague on 19 April 2002[151] are an important evolution.

However, the Commission stops short of making this principle a substantive requirement stating that:

> the information to be provided by patent applicants should be limited to information on the geographic origin of genetic resources or TK used in the invention, while such a disclosure requirement should not act, *de facto* or *de jure*, as an additional formal or substantial patentability criterion. Legal consequences to the non-respect of the requirement should lie outside the ambit of patent law.[152]

However, notwithstanding this stated position, the Commission is actively looking to see if it should make disclosure a formal part of the application process in both patent and plant variety rights. These proposals are not supported within either European patent or plant variety rights circles primarily due to the burden they would place on the breeder and the feasibility of being

---

[150] COM (2003) 821 final.

[151] These primarily relate to the standardisation of the terms and form of the agreement to be reached between researcher and supplier, eg ways and means of implementing the principles of prior informed consent and mutually agreed terms and material transfer agreement.

[152] This is reflected in the Preamble to the EU Directive, which also states that it is good practice to provide this information but not a requirement for the securing of patent protection.

able, in all circumstances, to provide the necessary information to adequately disclose and demonstrate informed consent.[153]

The final comment on the TRIPs Agreement is that it is essential when looking at its influence and impact to remember that it is an Agreement the basis for which is *trade*-related issues. It is *only* concerned with those aspects of intellectual property law which relate to trade—and in this context the Agreement is predicated on a need, fostered by commercial interests, to provide protection for anything which has a trade value, which in the modern market era really does mean anything. It is not concerned with any underlying theoretical rationale for the granting of such rights nor does it seek either to acknowledge or to address any other issues which might result from following a solely trade-related approach to intellectual property provision. The result is that intellectual property rights have acquired an aura of inviolability, that is the right to the right cannot be challenged and the overarching interests of the rights holder trump any other interests which might arise in respect of the protected material, any problems with the application and protection of the rights granted being solely the insular responsibility of those involved in granting and protecting, the overarching tenet being that the system itself will ultimately resolve any problems. This issue will not be addressed further in this text, but it is worth bearing in mind that such an autocratic and insulated approach to both the justification of a state-sanctioned private property right, and to the right so granted, brings with it questions of proper public accountability.

IV. CONCLUSION

Many of the perceived problems with the TRIPs Agreement have come from the fact that many see it as merely an extension of US patent law policy and practice, and that any application or interpretation of the TRIPs principles will be set against the 'gold standard' that is US patent law.[154] Whilst recently the WTO has taken steps (such as through the TRIPs review) to distance itself from any such overt connection, there is nonetheless the view that the overly protectionist approach favoured by the US will be taken as the norm and any divergences from this, for example through the use of the public interest exclusions and limitations, will meet with opposition from the US with the resulting threat of WTO action.

The TRIPs Agreement did not establish the principle that plant material can and should be protected by an intellectual property right. What it does do is to

---

[153] The issue of access to knowledge (traditional or not) has also been taken up by the WIPO, which has engaged in extensive discussions with interested parties. These, however, fall outside the ambit of this book.

[154] For a discussion of the highly influential nature of US intellectual property law on the final text of the TRIPs Agreement see Bently and Sherman, *Intellectual Property Law*, 2nd edn, (OUP, 2004) 5.

require member states at least to provide protection for plant varieties, and at most to provide patent protection for all forms of plant material without restriction. The obligation is not all-encompassing. Member states do retain a right to exclude 'plants' from any form of protection via Article 27(3)(b). However, this has to be read subject to the caveat that, as micro-organisms must be protected by patent law and the term 'micro-organism' is broadly defined in patent law, it might be difficult in practice to distinguish between the excluded material and that which must be protected. This is not a problem facing European provision, as this has embraced the full protectionist approach providing plant variety rights for varieties and patents for all other aspects of plant material. This was not, however, always the case. Whilst it would be easy to attribute the moves to provide greater protection which occurred during the late 1980s and throughout the 1990s to the introduction of TRIPs, in reality the drive to provide protection began in the 19th century. The Paris Convention of 1883 established the principle that living material could be the subject of an industrial property right. However, due to the problems inherent in applying the traditional notions of what can and should be protected, this single premise was achieved using two separate routes—firstly, by the introduction of a *sui generis* system of protection for plant varieties (which has led to near pan-European provision), and secondly, by disentangling the patent system from conventional notions of technical manufacture thereby paving the way for the protection of inventions involving plant material. The next five chapters will discuss the evolution of European plant protection as well as its current provision.

# 3

# *The Emergence of European Plant Protection: The Route to UPOV*[1]

## I. INTRODUCTION

AS MENTIONED IN chapter 1, the system of protection set up under the International Convention for the Protection of New Plant Varieties (UPOV) was introduced to solve a specific problem, namely how to protect the socially, and commercially, important results of *agricultural* plant breeding—these results predominantly taking the form of crop varieties. UPOV was not intended to provide a general solution to the problem of how to protect those plant-related products identified within the Paris Convention as industrial property which many member states were having problems with mapping onto their existing industrial property (and predominantly patent) provision.

In order to understand why the decision was taken to introduce a *sui generis* system, it is necessary first to outline briefly the attempts made by some European countries in the 19th and early 20th centuries to provide protection for plant-related inventions (not all such attempts differentiating between types of plant research output). In endeavouring to understand these attempts, it is necessary to remember that it was not until developments in molecular biology that the majority of breeders were able to utilise techniques other than the traditional Mendelian ones. This gave rise to two considerations.

The first was that once these developments in genetics took place, and it was easier to regard the results of such work as having been engineered, then the promise of industrial property protection became a reality. The proper addressing of this issue had grave scientific as well as social consequences, and the question of how to appropriately respond became of political as well as scientific importance.

The second was that agricultural breeding remained (and to a large extent remains) inextricably linked to many of the traditional breeding practices. This is because there is a need not merely to change the genetic make-up of a plant

---

[1] For a more concentrated discussion of the changing face of the plant variety rights system see Llewelyn, 'From "Outmoded Impediment" to "Global Player": The Evolution of Plant Variety Rights in Intellectual Property in the New Millennium' in Vaver and Bently (eds), *Essays in Honour of William R Cornish* (CUP, 2004), 137.

(which can now be achieved in the laboratory using molecular techniques), but because the breeder wishes to ensure that the results of that engineering work will breed true across groupings of plants and through successive generations of those plants. This can only be achieved through an understanding of the hereditary behaviour of that species.

Returning again to one of the themes outlined in chapter 1, one of the main reasons why the discussions in the 1950s, which led to UPOV, placed the emphasis on protecting the results of agricultural plant breeding was because there was a strong body of opinion that this work should not be treated as industrial property protectable by the type of right envisaged by the Paris Convention. This view was based on the belief that, whilst the Paris Convention established the principle that plant products (in the guise of grain, flowers and flour) could be industrial property, the application of the principle did not, and should not, extend to the plants which produced these products. The reasons behind this view related to capacity to meet the criteria for protection as well as the need to protect the public interest which vested in the production of new crop varieties.[2] However, this position was not immediately clear in the years following the introduction of the Paris Convention, and a number of attempts were made to bring plant material in general within either the scope of existing patent laws or via the introduction of a specific new right. As will be seen in the next section, the heavy reliance placed by plant breeders on the Mendelian principle of controlling heredity through external observation (which has only recently been overtaken by developments in molecular biology), together with the emphasis on fostering publicly funded agricultural plant breeding (despite the development of private sector horticultural and ornamental breeding), and the very conventional notion of what could be an invention for the purposes of patent law, meant that these attempts met with only limited practical effect.

## II. EUROPEAN PLANT PROPERTY PROTECTION IN THE EARLY 20TH CENTURY[3]

Many of the first formal calls for protection to be accorded over plant material can be traced back to the same period as the Paris Convention was adopted, for example in 1883 an unsuccessful attempt was made in France to introduce a

---

[2] This interpretation was provided to the Engholm Committee, 'Plant Breeders' Rights Report of the Committee on Transactions in Seeds' (Cmnd 1092, HMSO, 1960). As part of its review the Committee conducted an exhaustive assessment of the various options available to it, including introducing a right under the Paris Convention. The Committee sought the views of a wide range of experts both from within the UK and in Europe and garnered an extensive correspondence on the subject. The detail relating to the Paris Convention did not make it into the final report but was made available to interested parties (private papers of Professor ET Jones, who was an adviser to the Committee).

[3] Further discussion of these attempts can be found in ch 5, in the context of the development of European patent law.

specialist plant protection law.[4] Following this vain attempt, French pro-protection lobbyists waited another 20 years before making a second bid. In 1904 the Congress of the Pomological Society of France proposed introducing protection for plant products. Once again the proposal was not adopted. A third unsuccessful attempt was made in 1911. The problem with each of these attempts was that, notwithstanding the principle set down in the Paris Convention, it was not accepted that the results of plant breeding work *could* be regarded as the proper subject matter for the grant of a private property right.[5] In 1914, breeders in Germany also attempted to secure protection, again with little success.[6] It was not until the 1920s that attitudes began to change.[7] By 1922, it had been recognised, in France, that plants could be protected by a private property right, and in Germany, the Supreme Court allowed a patent to be granted over a breeding process.[8] By 1932, the concept of 'invention' within German patent law had been held to include plants.[9] Other European countries swiftly followed suit,[10] but there was no consistency in practice.

Some countries, such as The Netherlands, merely introduced a limited right for the breeder to control trade in the seed of their variety. Others (such as the UK) provided no protection at all. However, there were some countries, most notably Germany in 1934, which both enacted specific plant protection legislation whilst also permitting, in theory at least, patent protection.[11] The reasons for this are unclear, but would seem to have been a result of the existing policy of allowing micro-organisms and other products of nature to be

[4] Law of 14 November 1883, Recueil Officiel des lois et disposition d'administration publique des Etats Pontificaux.

[5] For a discussion of these attempts see Laclaviere, 'The Convention of Paris of 2 December 1961 for the Protection of New Varieties of Plants and the International Union for the Protection of New Varieties of Plants' [1965] *Industrial Property* 224.

[6] Decision of 12 June 1914, 1914 Bl F PMZ 257 C, discussed in Bent *et al, Intellectual Property Rights in Biotechnology Worldwide* (Macmillan, 1987).

[7] The first recorded specific plant protection, in the form of a breeder's right, was introduced by the Czech government in 1921 but there is little published information about this right.

[8] Decision of 24 June 1922, 1922 Bl F PMZ, 6, also discussed in Bent *et al, Intellectual Property Rights in Biotechnology Worldwide* (Macmillan, 1987) 43. Although the patent related to a process for breeding bacterium, the judgment indicated that protection should not be confined to such lower order inventions.

[9] Decision of 19 September 1932, GRUR 1932 1114. This practice was not approved by the now Federal Republic of Germany Supreme Court until 1969, with the decision in *Rote Taube*, see n 45 below. This case involved a patent, application for a method of breeding doves. The court upheld the patent with the proviso that the method claimed must be easily repeatable by others skilled in the art.

[10] For example, the Netherlands adopted a *Breeding and Material Seed Ordinance* in 1941, Austria introduced a *Plant Cultivation Law* in 1946, and Germany adopted a *Law on the Protection of Varieties and the Seeds of Cultivated Plants* in 1953. In 1951, following decisions of the Italian courts in 1948 and 1950 (Appeals no 1147 and no 1329) Italy began issuing patents for plants—although it did not enact specific protection for plant varieties until 1974. France also revised its law in 1933 (Law of 27 January 1933).

[11] As Bent *et al* outline, in Germany it was possible to acquire protection for plant varieties as well as for plant products and technical processes. In the view of the Patent Office an invention was not excluded from protection merely because it made use of living material. Bent *et al* provide a useful rehearsal of Germany provision between 1922 and the 1950s which it is not proposed to detail here—*Intellectual Property Rights in Biotechnology Worldwide* (Macmillan, 1987) 43–47.

patented.[12] The fact that plants had been stated to be patentable did not mean, however, that they were necessarily patentable in practice. An example of the problems which breeders (and their lawyers) faced in practice can be found in the experiences of Dr Freda Wuesthoff, a German patent lawyer working during the 1930s and 1940s who was one of the most influential proponents of plant protection within Germany.[13]

In an article, published after her death in 1956, she described the problems breeders had encountered in trying to obtain patent protection for plants in both Germany and the UK.[14] She refers to the example of Dr Baur, a scientist who, in 1919, had tried to patent a plant in Germany. The application, for a sweet lupin, was rejected because the plant was already publicly known and therefore it did not comply with the novelty requirement. The case drew the attention of patent lawyers and academics to the problems faced by those seeking to protect the results of plant research. In particular, attention was drawn to the notion of 'invention' within German patent law, which meant that whilst there was the theoretical possibility of protection in practice the actual number of patents granted under the Act was small. When set against the mode of breeding this is hardly surprising, for it was the era of the essentially biological process.

Dr Wuesthoff looked to see if a similar result would occur in other countries, and in 1936, she and a group of other patent lawyers sought to acquire a patent in the UK for an oil lupin. The application was rejected, as was an appeal against that decision, on the basis that 'there was no manner of manufacture which would entitle the applicants to the grant of a patent.'[15] This view was later upheld in *NV Phillips Gloeilampenfabriken*.[16] The real value in both these decisions lies in that in neither was it actually stated that plants were not patentable. Indeed, Dr Wuesthoff refers to an application made to the UK office which had been concerned with 'the breeding of poplars and more specifically with a method of producing rapidly growing hybrid trees.'[17] One of the claims was specifically directed to 'the hybrid tree produced and propagated according to any of the previous claims.' However, hers is the sole reference made to such an application and she does not indicate whether the patent was granted. If such an application existed then it would seem that the fact that a claim was directed to plant material was not an automatic bar to applications of this kind being made and, by extension, potentially grantable. However, in the absence of corroborating information, one must be very careful before stating that this was actually the position in the UK.

---

[12]  It is interesting to note that, at this time, private sector research was much more in evidence in France and Germany than in the UK.

[13]  The involvement of the Wuesthoff family in plant property rights continues today: see Wuesthoff *et al*, *Sortenschutz-gesetz* (VCH, 1990).

[14]  Wuesthoff, 'Patenting of Plants' [1956–58] *Industrial Property Quarterly* 12.

[15]  *Ibid*, p 26. The language here has resonances with that used much later by the Canadian Supreme Court in *Harvard College v Canada (Commissioner of Patents)* [2002] SCC 76.

[16]  (1954) 71 RPC 192.

[17]  Patent Application No 458,388.

Dr Wuesthoff's experience serves to demonstrate that whilst there might have been diversity in legislative responses to the demands for protection, most countries held out the promise of protection (either by specifically legislating for it or by theoretically giving a more expansive reading to their existing patent law). However, in practice, the notion of a manufacture and the level of inventiveness required to secure such rights were too technical for breeders to be able to fulfil, and this was common across Europe.

A backdrop to these initiatives was the changing political nature of plant breeding. The period from 1918 onwards saw agriculture grow into a key economic industry. In the UK, for example, during the Second World War certain sectors of agriculture were regarded as protected occupations, and intense effort went into the provision of agricultural produce which could not only feed a nation at war but also that nation at peace. As will be seen in chapter 5, there was no political or legal will in the 1950s to provide patent protection for plant varieties and it was decided that a more appropriate response to the demands of the plant breeders would be the introduction of a new form of right specifically designed to protect animate material.[18] The result was the International Convention for the Protection of New Plant Varieties. It is useful, before looking at the diplomatic efforts, to outline the provision, within some European countries, which was in place during the 1950s—the time when the discussions surrounding the introduction of a possible *sui generis* system took place.

## III. PLANT PROPERTY PROVISION IN THE 1950S

### France

In France, there was no statutory protection for breeders, but they were able to claim rights over their varieties through the twin use of trade mark law and government-approved voluntary licences which enabled breeders to claim royalties for seed purchased—but these were not State granted rights. The *quid pro quo* for this arrangement was that breeders of agricultural crops were not able to sell their seed unless they had obtained government approval, and the variety was placed on the Official Catalogue of Varieties. The requirements for entry onto the Catalogue were that the variety had to be shown to be distinct, uniform, stable and of cultural value, the determination of each of the above being undertaken during growing trials conducted by the French National Institute for Agricultural Research (INRA). If successful, the 'right' lasted initially for 10 years with an option to renew for further periods of five years. For ornamentals the situation was slightly different in that patent protection could be acquired (this being due to the method of reproduction); there was only a requirement

---

[18] Not all countries seeking to provide protection post 1961 did so via UPOV. In the old Soviet Union, for example, under Order No 729 of the USSR, plant varieties, as well as farm animals, poultry and fur-bearing animals, were treated as inventions and protectable by an inventor's certificate.

that novelty be shown and the right lasted for 17 years. To assist French breeders with arranging licensing and collecting royalties, a specific body, the CGLV, was established (this later became SICASOV).

## Germany[19]

In Germany, the Seed Law of 1953 specifically provided protection for plant breeders (although not for ornamental breeders). The protection extended to varieties which could be shown to be distinct, stable and of agricultural or horticultural value. As with the French system, protection was only granted following growing trials and entry onto the Official Register of Varieties. A Federal Plant Variety Office was set up to oversee the granting of rights. The right lasted initially for up to 12 years, but a breeder could apply for an extension for a second period up to a further 12 years. Austria had a similar system in place via the Plant Cultivation Law 1949.

## The Netherlands

In the Netherlands, the Plant Breeding and Seed Material Order of 1941 provided protection for plant breeders who produced new and uniform varieties (unlike France and Germany there was no requirement that the variety had to have any value), and agricultural varieties had to be entered onto the Official List before they could be marketed. The testing was carried out by the State Institute for Research on Varieties of Field Crops (IVRO) and by the Institute for Horticultural Plant Breeding. Agricultural varieties were protected for a period of up to 17 years, whilst horticultural and ornamental plant varieties were protected for up to 25 years with an option to apply for further extensions of 10 years.

Elsewhere, in Italy, limited patent protection for plants was available,[20] but this was little used.[21] Sweden had no formal system of protection in place, but the mechanisms used to control seed had the effect of giving the breeder certain rights over the production and sale of 'original' varieties, provided that these had been included on the List of Original Varieties.[22] The conditions for inclusion were that the variety should be novel and have value. Spain provided a specific form of protection but only for those varieties which were accepted onto its

---

[19] For a discussion of the scope and use made of these rights see Kunhardt, '25 Years of Plant Breeders' Rights in the FRG FIS/ASSINSEL Congress' [1978] *SAFA* 18.

[20] This can be seen in Appeal No 1147, 1948 and Appeal No 1329, 1950, which indicated that plant varieties could be regarded as 'technical results and patentable'.

[21] See Mangini, 'The Protection of Plant Varieties in Italy and the UPOV Convention' (1987) 6 *Patent World* 25.

[22] See Oredsson, 'Biological Inventions and Swedish Patent Legislation' (1950) 50 *UPOV* 42; and in [1985] *NIR* 238.

Official Register. Other countries (for example, Belgium and Denmark) simply permitted breeders to enter into licensing arrangements with end users of plant varieties, but this was primarily a contractual right allowing the breeder to deal with the variety did not bestow any property rights in or over the material itself. Others, such as the UK, provided no protection at all but were actively looking at the provision of protection. The discussions which took place there provide a useful glimpse of the types of issues which governments across Europe were having.[23]

## The United Kingdom

The UK was rather late in comparison with some of its European counterparts when it came to assessing how best to protect plant material. To all intents and purposes, the evolution of British plant protection can be set alongside the discussions leading up to the introduction of both the EPC and UPOV. Before these discussion, began there appeared to be neither patent nor any other form of protection available for plant material. 1920 had seen the introduction of a Seed Act, but this provided no rights for the breeder but rather, in contrast, provided that any new variety became public property as soon as its seed was placed on the market. For the UK the discussions really began in the 1950s post the international activity. In 1954 the government commissioned a working group to study the legislative practices of other countries and look at the possibility of introducing protection in the UK. The report took six years to complete and was published only a year before UPOV was introduced. Because work in the UK was taking place in parallel with the drafting of the 1961 UPOV Act it is unsurprising that the Plant Varieties and Seeds Act 1964 was virtually identical.

The Report of the Committee on Transactions in Seeds, known as the Engholm Report after its chairman, provides an invaluable insight into the thinking surrounding plant protection in the 1950s. The Committee had a very broad expert base and included plant breeders (from both the public and private sectors) and advisors from the patent office (many of whom were also involved in the discussions leading up to the introduction of the UPOV Convention). Following an extensive investigation into provision elsewhere in Europe, the Committee recommended that a national plant breeders' rights scheme should be introduced which would provide the kind of incentive necessary to encourage growth in the private sector as well as facilitating competition from the public sector. The main issue facing the Committee was the best means of providing this incentive. A careful evaluation was made of the patent system and it was decided that whilst the Committee was happy to recognise that the results of plant research could constitute inventions they were not convinced that patent

---

[23] That these discussions mirrored those taking place in other European countries is likely, as those involved in debating UK provision were also involved in discussing the need for some form of pan-European provision, and therefore it is probable that the same issues arose in both contexts.

protection would provide appropriate protection.[24] The Committee was particularly concerned that plant inventions could not meet the granting criteria and, possibly the fatal blow for obtaining patent protection, that it was not possible to describe the plant invention in such a way which would enable both the person reading it to know precisely the plant material covered by the patent and any person reading the patent specification to reproduce it: '[i]t is the variety itself which is important and not the method by which it was bred . . . a written description of the variety is often not precise enough to identify the variety conclusively.'[25]

The Committee also looked at the question of whether it would be in the public interest to permit patent protection over plant varieties (and it is interesting to note that the sole focus of attention for the Committee was varieties and not single plants or parts of plants). They decided that only a limited right should be granted as that would mean that protected varieties would remain as freely available to the public as possible whilst providing a modicum of protection for the breeder. The Committee also drew a distinction between types of plant material and proposed that only reproductive material, such as seeds and cuttings, should be protected but consumable aspects, such as grain, should be excluded from protection. This view raises a nice point of comparison between the views of the Committee and the text of Article 1(3) of the Paris Convention.

Article 1(3) specifically states that grain should be regarded as industrial property capable of having an industrial property right granted over it. As will be discussed below, the resulting plant variety protection, at that time, did exclude harvested or derived material (although revisions to the Convention have changed this somewhat)—what the Committee probably did not envisage was that such material, if excluded from plant breeders' protection, would end up being the subject of an ordinary patent grant.

It was against this locally devised background that the discussions leading up to the UPOV Convention took place.

### IV.  THE HISTORY OF UPOV[26]

Central to the development of the UPOV Convention was the involvement of the plant breeding organisations which had come into being during the 1930s and 1940s. ASSINSEL, which was founded in 1936, played a central role in promoting the need for rights and its then President, Ernst Tourneur, travelled extensively around Europe to garner support. He came to the UK in 1949 and

---

[24] Interestingly, notwithstanding the principle set down in the Paris Convention, the Committee did not distinguish between plant varieties and other results of plant research.

[25] Report of Engholm Committee, 'Plant Breeders' Rights Report of the Committee on Transactions in Seeds' (Cmnd 1092, HMSO, 1960), para 77.

[26] For more detail see UPOV, 'History, Development and Main Provisions of the UPOV Convention' (1987) 7(8) *Industrial Property* 320.

his speech to the Seed Trade Organisation and National Association of Corn and Agricultural Merchants sparked the debate in the UK, although the proposal did not always find support.[27] However, despite the apparent strength of feeling of those who were unconvinced of the need to protect plant research, as the movement towards protection grew, so these views became increasingly in the minority. It is clear that the development of the right would not have occurred had it not been for the widespread commitment of the breeding community. As will be shown, this involvement of the end users of the system remains a central motif within the system.

By the mid-1940s there was such a groundswell of opinion supporting protection for plant varieties that in 1947 ASSINSEL felt able to approach the AIPPI. It obtained an assurance from them that the issue of plant protection would form part of the agenda to be discussed at the AIPPI Vienna Congress in 1952. However, whilst the issue was raised at the Vienna Congress, and a recommendation passed that protection should be available, there was no indication given as to the form that protection should take. Laclaviere, writing in 1965,[28] said that one of the problems was the phrasing of the recommendation—it said that new varieties of plants (and this is the first indication that the right being sought would relate only to plant varieties) should be protected by way of a patent 'or by an equivalent right.' According to Laclaviere, plant breeders had, at that stage, 'placed all their hopes on acquiring patent protection' and the provision of an equivalent right was not seen as meeting their needs. Central to the decision to develop specific plant property protection was the need, as recognised by the OECD in 1954,[29] to coalesce protection across all of Europe.

Following the Vienna Congress, ASSINSEL debated the issue both at its Paris meeting of 21 November 1955, and at its Congress in Semmering in 1956. It was at the conclusion of the 1956 Congress that ASSINSEL made a request to the

---

[27] For example, in 1952 Sir George Stapleton, founder of the Welsh Plant Breeding Station (one of the world's leading public centres of plant breeding research), wrote to the then director, Professor ET Jones (generally regarded as the father of the modern oat variety), saying that: '. . . no breeder ever has had or ever can have any sort of monopoly of his product.' Professor Jones replied with equal caution:

> I am fully aware that a breeder has no monopoly of his products except that he might exercise some form of copyright restriction should he feel that this might be a wise thing to do, but scientific work should have no restrictions, and copyright should preferably only be used in order to ensure that the public generally gets the benefit of receiving an article in the form in which it is intended by its producer.

Adding significance to this remark is that Professor Jones was one of the experts called upon to discuss the form and scope of plant varieties during the discussions held in the 1950s and early 1960s and he also was one of the original members of the Plant Varieties and Seeds Tribunal set up following the enactment of the UK Plant Varieties and Seeds Act 1964. Clearly he was sufficiently reassured by the form of the right introduced that, notwithstanding the concerns expressed in 1952, he was prepared to support the right introduced in the 1960s.

[28] See Laclaviere, 'The Convention of Paris of 2 December 1961 for the Protection of New Varieties of Plants and the International Union for the Protection of New Varieties of Plants', above n 5.

[29] See the proceedings of the Conference on Development of Seed Production and Seed Trade (Stockholm, OEEC Project number 214, 1954).

French government for the organisation of an international convention for the protection of the rights of plant breeders—this resulted in a Diplomatic Conference in 1957, the subject of which was the protection of new plant varieties. Involved in these discussions were the AIPPI, CIOPORA and FIS.

Twelve European countries participated in the 1957 ASSINSEL Conference Austria, Belgium, Denmark, France, the Federal Republic of Germany, Holland, Italy, Norway, Spain, Sweden, Switzerland and the UK. As can be seen from this list, it was quintessentially a European affair. The national delegations were joined by representatives from intergovernmental organisations including the International Bureau for the Protection of Intellectual Property Law (BIRPI), the UN's FAO and the Organisation for European Economic Co-operation (OEEC).[30]

The conference delegates were faced with two problems: the first was to achieve harmonisation of provision and the second to decide between revising the patent laws of participating countries or creating an independent plant breeders' rights convention.

It was finally decided that, for reasons of perception, but also because of the scant use made of patent protection where that possibility existed, it would be more appropriate to provide a specifically designed *sui generis* right. In particular, it was felt that:

a)  plant material could not meet the patent law notion of novelty;
b)  plant breeding programmes could rarely be shown to be inventive;
c)  whilst the results of plant breeding were undoubtedly of industrial application, it would not be in the public interest to allow plant breeders to have an over-extensive monopoly; and
d)  it would be difficult for plant material to meet the disclosure (teaching) requirement—namely that a person skilled in the art can reproduce the invention merely by following the information contained in the specification. Even where a full description is given as to how the plant material was produced, it does not guarantee that following the same route will give rise to an identical result (that is, the plant material could mutate or sport).

The first session of the Diplomatic Conference took place on 7 May 1957 and led to the adoption of the Final Act providing for a second conference following further preparatory work. A Special Committee of Experts was created to look at whether the Convention which they were charged with preparing should be a special Agreement within the framework of the Paris Union of 1883 which resulted from the Paris Convention for the Protection of Industrial Property, or if it should constitute a separate convention. As the Convention was primarily

---

[30] In 1954 the OEEC published a paper which recognised the need to provide breeders with appropriate protection for their research work. The paper did not say what the OEEC thought that form of protection should be: *Seed Production, Testing and Distribution in European Countries* (OEEC Technical Assistance, Mission No 106, January 1954).

seen as providing protection for the results of agricultural plant breeding which, it was felt, should not be the subject of an industrial property right, the experts decided upon the latter option, subject to the reservation that those states which so desired could apply either this new Convention or the Paris Convention. That the UPOV Convention was intended to provide protection which could stand alongside those rights defined under the Paris Convention is clear from the text of the 1961 Act, within which several references to the Paris Convention are made. There are no such specific references to the Paris Convention in either the 1978 or 1991 Acts. This should not be taken to indicate that the subsequent Acts are intended to distance the right from the Paris Convention family of industrial property rights, but rather shows that it was necessary when drafting the 1961 Act to give a nod at least to the importance of the Paris Convention.

The second conference took place in November 1961 and added to the ranks of the delegates were representatives from the European Economic Community (EEC) and ASSINSEL. Amongst the participants were some of the leading scientists of the time, including Dirk Boringer, Jean Bustarret, Bernard Laclaviere, Ernst Tourneur and Rene Royon.[31] The conference produced a draft text which was then opened for discussion. Only one country, the UK, provided any comments, 25 in total, of which 16 were adopted. None of these were sub-stantive changes but related to semantic issues such as the designation of the Head of the Union (from Chairman to President) and the order of the official languages (from French, English and German to English, French and German).

On 2 December 1961, the 41 Articles of the Convention were adopted and the International Convention for the Protection of New Varieties of Plants came into being. The Convention was signed first by Belgium, France, the Federal Republic of Germany, Holland and Italy. In 1962, on 26 November, Denmark and the UK signed, with Sweden following suit on 30 November. The first instrument of ratification was deposited in 1965 by the UK, the second in 1967 by the Netherlands, and the Convention entered into force on 10 August 1968 after ratification by the Federal Republic of Germany and began functioning, in Paris, on 26 November 1968 when the first meeting of the Council took place.

As a point of reference it is also worth noting other activities affecting agri-culture which took place at approximately the same time as the introduction of the new right. Early in the 1960s the Common Agricultural Policy was adopted, and in order to control the quality of seeds produced and used within the new European Community, a number of regulatory Directives were issued. In order to provide an effective counter to overly strict Community measures, the seed community introduced various trade organisations including COMESCO (Seed Trade 1961), ASSOPOMAC (Potato Breeders 1964), AMUFOC (Forage

---

[31] Even though he recently stood down as Secretary General of CIOPORA (which he founded in 1961), M Royon has continued to play a major part in the development of plant intellectual prop-erty rights and was a major contributor to the EU Plant Intellectual Property (PIP) project discussed in ch 8.

Seed Production 1970) and finally COMMASSO (Plant Breeders 1977). In 2000 these consolidated to create the European Seed Association (ESA). The function of ESA is to represent 'the totality of the European seed industry active in research, breeding, production and marketing of seeds.'[32] These organisations grew out of a need to curb any overly restrictive legislation emanating from the Community and, initially at least, their focus was on the regulations adopted which controlled seeds placed in the market place. Increasingly, however, the areas of interest have extended to include plant property rights.

As mentioned, it was decided, quite early on, that the patent route was not the appropriate one to take. Whilst the development of European patent policy and practice will be discussed in more detail in chapters 5 and 6, it is useful to outline here how that activity ran in parallel with that relating to plant variety protection.

**Excluding Patent Protection?**

In 1950, the Council of Europe's Committee of Experts on Patents, which was charged with overseeing the harmonisation of European patent provision,[33] gave unanimous support for the introduction of a uniform system of protection specifically for plant inventions. However, because of the developments taking place which led to the introduction of UPOV (and bearing in mind that many of the representatives participated in both sets of discussions), the Council decided that it would be 'inexpedient to impose a common solution [within Europe] . . . for the patentability of plant varieties' until the discussions surrounding the possible international convention had been concluded. On this basis it is not surprising that the Council awaited the outcome of those meetings before making a statement on the patentability of plant material within a *European* context. It was not until 1960 that the Council issued its next statement, which stated that the decision to introduce a *sui generis* form of protection indicated that this form of protection was a) more suitable for the protection of plant varieties and b) provided evidence that any attempt to harmonise national provision relating to the patentability of plant varieties would be too great an obstacle to overcome. The work of the Council became, in its first incarnation, the Strasbourg Convention on the Unification of Certain Points of Substantive Patent Law, which evolved into the European Patent Convention in 1973.[34]

---

[32] www.euroseeds.org.

[33] This work eventually gave rise to the European Patent Convention.

[34] It is worth noting that the discussions which took place in respect of both patent law and a *sui generis* system occurred at a time of other developments in intellectual property law. It was during the 1950s that three of the major intellectual property conventions were either introduced, as in the case of the Universal Copyright Convention of 1952, or preparatory work was begun, as in the case of the Rome Convention on the Protection of Performers, Producers of Phonograms and Broadcasting Organisations, The Berne Copyright Convention had only recently been revised, in 1948, and would be revised again in 1967. All of these indicate dynamic activity across all

As discussed in chapter 1, one of the most common myths surrounding the UPOV Convention is that it prohibits the grant of a patent over a plant variety—the so-called 'dual protection prohibition' which was contained in Article 2(1) of both the 1961 and 1978 UPOV Acts.[35] As was explained, this interpretation was due to a misunderstanding of the actual meaning of Article 2(1). This misunderstanding was the cause of most of the criticism for the plant variety rights system during the 1980s and led to its removal from the text of the 1991 Act.

Over the years this provision has been taken to mean that dual protection could not be sought using both ordinary patent law and a right under the UPOV Convention. This interpretation was given additional weight by the specific exclusion of plant varieties in the European Patent Convention. Because of this perception, many commentators on the plant variety rights system thought that the obligation imposed by UPOV, and reiterated by an equivalent bar in European and national patent law, rendered the plant variety rights system, in both form and intent, an 'impediment'.[36]

Article 2(1) was not intended to prevent member states from providing both patents and plant variety rights, but rather to prevent a member state from using the *sui generis* right and patent protection where both accorded to the provisions of UPOV. Ordinary patent protection was not prohibited. UPOV itself has made it clear that whilst Article 2(1) did ban dual protection, it applied only where both the patent and plant variety protection accorded with the provisions of UPOV—in other words, the patent grant depending on the variety being distinct, uniform and stable, the right granted applying only to the reproductive material of the variety and being subject to the research and farm saved seed derogations.[37] The prohibition did not apply to situations where the member state provided ordinary patent protection which was not in accordance with UPOV. The Convention permitted each member state to choose how to protect

aspects of intellectual property, and this context is important when looking at the initiatives to introduce specific plant protection. It is difficult to say whether the moves to introduce an international convention for plant varieties was a by-product of the activities in other areas of intellectual property or whether it merely coincided with this activity.

[35] As mentioned in ch 1, this says that

member states may recognise the right of the breeder provided for in this Convention by the grant either of a special title of protection or of a patent . . . a member State of the Union whose national law admits of protection under both these forms may provide only one of them for one and the same botanical genus or species.

The use of the present tense denotes the fact that there remain some countries within Europe which are still signatories to these two Acts and have not brought their national provision into line with the 1991 Act. They can continue to rely on the prohibition

[36] This is epitomised by the views expressed by Cornish, *Intellectual Property: Patents Copyright Trade Marks and Allied Rights*, 2nd edn (Sweet & Maxwell, 1989), but can also be seen in the numerous publications on the subject produced during the 1980s by other eminent patent law commentators such as Beier, Crespi and Straus.

[37] Greengrass, 'The 1991 Act of the UPOV Convention' (1991) 12 *EIPR* 467. See also Greengrass, 'UPOV and the Protection of Plant Breeders—Past Developments, Future Perspective' (1989) 20 *IIC* 622.

a particular genera or species. The choice made, however, did not affect the ability of member states also to provide protection for that same genera or species under its ordinary patent law. This explains the ability of the US to join UPOV despite the fact that it provided protection using patents and plant variety rights, and it had to amend its plant patent provisions before acceding to the Convention.[38] The decision to do this was one of the first taken by both the meetings leading up to the UPOV Convention and the new European patent regime. That this flexibility lay behind the dual protection prohibition can be seen in the deliberations of the Special Committee of Experts charged with assessing whether plants should be protected by a special Agreement or as part of the Paris Union.

Underlining this choice, it should be remembered that the Committee of Experts had explicitly said that states which so desired in framing their plant variety rights laws could do so under the auspices of either the new Convention or the Paris Convention. What the Committee did not do was to say that member states could only apply either the new Convention or their ordinary patent laws but not both. If the choice was to introduce a right under the Paris Convention then the expectation seems to have been that, whilst the right would have had to be called a 'patent' (the list of rights covered by the Paris Convention being exhaustive) the form of the right would contain those features now connected with a UPOV right (the DUS criteria and so on). The result was the express prohibition (in Article 2(1)) of dual protection where *both* accorded with UPOV law.

A further reason why the perception arose that it was the dual protection prohibition which stood between the grant of a patent over a plant variety was the way in which the equivalent provision was introduced in patent law.[39]

As originally constructed, European patent law did not prohibit the granting of a patent over a plant variety. Article 2 of the Strasbourg Convention (which evolved into the European Patent Convention in 1973) simply stated that: '. . . the Contracting States *shall not be bound* to provide for the grant of patents in respect of pharmaceutical or food products, or of new plants or animals' (emphasis added). The opportunity therefore existed under both UPOV and the Strasbourg Conventions for members to develop their patent law to include plant varieties if they so wished.

However, as will be seen in chapter 5, whilst the 1960s (and indeed 1970s) saw more countries open up their patent laws to permit the protection of pharmaceutical products, not all chose to embrace the possibilities of using patent protection for other innovations based on living, or naturally occurring, material. When looking at the policy approaches, a distinction can be drawn between the approach taken towards the protection of, on the one hand, pharmaceutical

---

[38] See Llewelyn and Cook, 'Debate' in *Plant Variety Rights: An Outmoded Impediment? A Seminar Report* (London, Intellectual Property Institute, 1998).

[39] This will be discussed further in ch 5.

products, foodstuffs and agricultural/horticultural processes and, on the other, plant and animal varieties. In respect of the first former group, the option to exclude was merely transitional. This meant that member states must, within 10 years of joining the Convention, provide patent protection. In order to ensure that the new requirement did not 'interfere with the traditional agricultural and horticultural cross-breeding methods'[40] without hindering protection for the new pharma-technical processes, the Convention permitted members to exclude essentially biological processes but required protection for microbiological processes and the products thereof (as with the exclusion of plant varieties, the precise ambit of this exclusion caused some confusion).

The optional nature of Article 2 of Strasbourg is critical to understanding the problem. Because there was no mandate to provide, or exclude, protection, views across Europe continued, and in some areas continue, to differ over whether patent protection should be available for pharmaceutical products and foodstuffs (including those which involved the use of lower order biological material, such as micro-organisms and microbiological products[41]) and plants. The debates which took place during the 1980s over the extent of the exclusion and the relationship between the patent law and plant variety rights are testament to this.[42]

Whilst Armitage and Davis argue that Article 2 permitted only a temporary right to reserve patent protection for certain categories of invention, and the underlying intention was that this right to reserve would mutate into a permanent exclusion,[43] as other commentators demonstrate,[44] the immediate response

---

[40]  Armitage and Davis, *Patents and Morality in Perspective* (CLIP, 1994) 15.

[41]  See Grubb, *Patents for Chemical, Pharmaceuticals and Biotechnology* (OUP, 1999), chs 4 and 13.

[42]  It is not proposed to rehearse these arguments here. A selection of these pieces includes Adler, 'Can Patents Co-exist with Breeders' Rights? Developments in US and International Biotechnology' (1986) 17 *IIC* 195; Berland, 'Breeders' Rights and Patenting Life Forms' (1986) 322 *Nature* 785; British Association of Plant Breeders, *Interaction between Patents and Breeders' Rights* (Plant Royalty Bureau, August 1986); Crespi, 'Biotechnology Patents: A Case of Special Pleading?' [1985] 7 *EIPR* 190; Huni and Buss, 'Patent Protection in the Field of Genetic Engineering' [1982] *Industrial Property* 356; Lange, *The Nature of Plant Breeders' Rights (Plant Variety Protection Law) and their Demarcation from Patentable Inventions* (Industrial Property Symposium, Geneva, 1984); Llewelyn, 'The Problems of Patenting Plants in Europe' [1987] *Patent World* 16; Llewelyn, 'Future Prospects for Plant Breeders' Rights within the European Community' [1989] 9 *EIPR* 303; 'National Council for Agricultural Research Plant Breeders' Rights and Patent Rights in the Relation to Plant Genetic Engineering' (The Hague, 1985); Neumeier Sortenschutz und/oder Patentschutz fur Pflanzenzuchtungen (Carl Haymanns Verlag KG, 1990); Royon, *The Interface of Patent Law and Plant Breeders' Rights: The Possible Extension of Existing Legal Systems*, Paper presented at the EPO (February 1988); Straus, 'Patent Protection for New Varieties of Plants, Produced by Genetic Engineering—Should Double Protection be Prohibited?' (1984) 15 *IIC* 426; Straus, *Industrial Property Protection of Biotechnological Inventions: Analysis of Certain Basic Issues* (WIPO IPD/2867, 1 July 1985); Straus, 'The Relationship between Plant Variety Protection and Patent Protection for Biotechnological Inventions' (1987) 18 *IIC* 723; UPOV, *Industrial Patents and Plant Breeders' Rights—Their Proper Field and Possibilities for their Demarcation* (Plant Variety Protection No 44, June 1985).

[43]  Armitage and Davis, *Patents and Morality in Perspective* (CLIP, 1994) 11.

[44]  Above n 42.

to that temporary right differed extensively. As will be seen in chapter 5, even those countries which did attempt to keep their patent law options open, found problems in putting this policy into practice.[45] The way in which the EPC was introduced created further problems which became apparent only in the 1970s.

The first was that plant and animal varieties were grouped together in Article 53(b) for equal treatment and yet the two could, and can, easily be distinguished. The former were not regarded as unprotectable *per se* as plant variety rights could be sought, and yet, in the absence of any equivalent animal breeders' rights system, the latter clearly were unprotectable. For some, putting the two together indicated that the spirit of the exclusion went beyond the material actually specified and was intended to reflect a more fundamental principle, namely that plant and animal material in general was not patentable. Given that the Convention was introduced at a time when patent protection was not being sought for either plant or animal material, and the status of the exclusion within patent law had not been extensively analysed, it becomes more understandable.

The second problem with the wording of Article 53(b) was the lack of a direct reference to the plant variety rights system. It might have been thought that if the Article were to be given the restrictive application, which the EPO later stated it was intended to have, and only apply to those varieties capable of protection under plant variety rights then it would have stated as much within the Article itself. The fact that it does not do so provides a further reason why the Article was taken by some not to be confined to varieties which were protectable elsewhere, but rather that the text was shorthand for plant material *per se* (the same point can be made about Article 27(3)(b) of TRIPs).

The misunderstanding over both Articles explains much of the hostility to the plant variety rights system which emerged in the 1980s and 1990s. However, whilst the accusation has been levelled that the dual protection prohibition was a primary cause for the absence of a proper extension of patent law, it should be noted that the reality was that it was the patent system itself which stood, and continues to stand, in the way of extending patent protection to plant material.[46]

Because it was recognised that there were misconceptions as to the interpretation and application of the prohibition, UPOV voted to remove the dual

---

[45] For example, Germany had a very progressive approach to the protection of inventions concerning living material. The first German patent grant over a plant took place in 1932 (Decision of 19 September 1932, GRUR 1932, 1114). In 1968 it removed the barriers to the patentability of pharmaceutical products. However, it was not until 1969 that the Supreme Court confirmed that inventions involving living material could be patented: *Rote Taube*, 27 March 1969, reported [1970] 1 *IIC* 136. The case concerned a patent granted over an animal breeding process. In language reminiscent of the US Supreme Court's statement in 1980 that 'anything under the sun' could be patented (*Chakrabarty*, 447 US 303 (1980)), the Federal Supreme Court said that 'the intent of the Patent Act itself not only permits but compels taking into account the latest state of scientific knowledge to interpret the concept of invention . . .' However, despite recognising the principle of protectability, the Court's strict adherence to the traditional application of the granting criteria had the effect of rendering many forms of biological innovations 'banished from the paradise of patent protection': Beier and Straus, 'Genetic Engineering and Industrial Property' (1987) 11 *Industrial Property* 447.

[46] See Cook, *Plant Variety Rights: An Outmoded Impediment?*, above n 38.

protection prohibition from the 1991 text. This means that member states may now provide either or both forms of protection which, in turn, leads to greater accord between the 1991 UPOV Act and Article 27(3)(b) of TRIPs, as this will enable member states to make use of the cumulative aspect of the obligation.[47] The only barrier, or impediment, to protecting plant varieties under patent law is the exclusions contained within the patent law. This is certainly the case within the European Union—although it should be stressed that the option, such as it is, operates at only the national, and not community, level. The reason for this is that the Community Regulation does contain a dual protection prohibition which specifically relates to the provision of Community patent protection. This will be discussed in more detail in chapter 4.

## V. THE UPOV CONVENTION[48]

The UPOV Convention has been revised three times since 1961, with two substantive revisions taking place in 1978 and 1991.[49] As explained in chapters 1 and 2, all three versions remain relevant for a discussion of European provision.[50] In particular, the 1978 and 1991 Acts remain relevant for they both form a reference point for determining an 'effective *sui generis* right' under Article 27(3)(b) of TRIPs.

The result is that there are, in effect, four differing levels of plant variety rights of provision in operation in Europe. The first is the 1991 UPOV Act, which sets down some minimum standards for protection. The second is the Community Plant Variety Right which, although based on (and compliant with) the 1991 Act, expands upon its provision in certain key areas (such as farm saved seed). The third is the 1978 Act, to which a number of EU member states are still signatories, and the fourth (and arguably of least importance) is the 1961 Act. In addition, two member states, Greece[51] and Luxembourg, are neither signatories of UPOV nor do they have any national system of plant variety rights.[52]

Rather than looking at each of the Acts in turn (which would give rise to unnecessary repetition) we will focus on the communalities and variations

---

[47] 'Members shall provide for the protection of plant varieties either by patents or by an effective *sui generis* system *or by any combination thereof*' (emphasis added).

[48] Under Art 37(1), the 1978 Act remained open for new member states to join until the 1991 Act came into force, which was in April 1998. As discussed in the previous chapter, provided that a country had indicated that it wished to accede to the 1978 Act before the deadline in 1999, it would be able to introduce a right according to the 1978 Act even where the deadline has passed.

[49] The other revision, in 1972, related primarily to the system of contributions.

[50] The precise nature of the national provision is set out in ch 8.

[51] Greece is in discussions with UPOV with a view to introducing a national plant variety rights system.

[52] This does not mean that plant variety rights are unenforceable within either territory. As members of the EU, any right granted under the Community Regulation can be both infringed, and therefore litigated, in either Luxemburg or Greece.

between the three using the generic term 'the Convention' where the Acts are the same. The objective is to demonstrate how the right has evolved over time to take account of the changing scientific, industrial and political climate.

### The Three Acts: Political Pressures for Change

Laclaviere, writing in 1969, said that the ultimate objective of the Convention was to promote the creation of new plant varieties which were more useful or better adapted to human needs and provide a contribution to the 'material betterment of mankind's future.'[53] One of the fundamental axioms underlying the original Convention was the desire to stimulate agriculture as well as to safeguard the 'moral and material'[54] interests of the plant breeders. It is worth placing these initial principles, based as they were on fostering agriculture, against the evolution in plant research outlined in chapter 1 and in particular against the changes which have happened in terms of the types of plant varieties (and material) being produced and requiring protection.

Such literature as exists on the subject indicates that the right operated successfully during the 1960s and 1970s,[55] and whilst the Convention was revised twice in 1972 and 1978, these revisions were limited, with many of the substantive provisions of the 1961 Act remaining unchanged.[56] During this time, it should be remembered that the full potential of modern plant genetics was only just becoming known but there were few realised results.

The 1980s changed all this and plant scientists began to produce wholly new plant constructs, some of which fell into the category of protectable subject matter under UPOV, but others clearly fell outside the notion of a 'variety'. The market for these new plant products developed equally rapidly, and the nature of the rights which could be secured over them became an issue for intense scrutiny. In particular, it was felt that the 1961 and 1978 Acts were tailored to the needs of a specific group of plant breeders (those engaged in agricultural

---

[53] Laclaviere (1969) 8 *Industrial Property* 155. See also 'Report of International Conference for the Protection of New Plant Products' [1961] *Industrial Property Quarterly* 104; 'Report of International Conference for the Protection of New Plant Products' [1962] *Industrial Property Quarterly* 5; Laclaviere, 'The Convention of Paris of 2 December 1961 for the Protection of New Varieties of Plants and the International Union for the Protection of New Varieties of Plants' [1965] *Industrial Property* 224.

[54] *Ibid.*

[55] In addition, the fact that there was pressure from US breeders for a similar system underlines the importance given to the right.

[56] The objective behind the 1978 revision was to allow member states greater flexibility in interpreting the provisions of the Act. To achieve this (and reminiscent of the activity in the 1950s), a committee of experts was set up in 1975, and a revised text was adopted at a diplomatic conference in October 1978. As will be seen below, the main changes involved removing the definition of a variety and expanding the number of plant species which a member state had to provide protection for. For a full discussion of the rationale lying behind the 1978 revision see *Note on the Diplomatic Conference on the Revision of the International Conference for the Protection of New Varieties of Plants, 9–23 October 1978* (UPOV, Newsletter No 16, March 1979) 6.

plant breeding) and that it was time that the interests of other breeders should be given more obvious equal weight. This was notwithstanding the fact that whilst the Preambles to both Acts specifically refer to agricultural crops they also make it clear that these are not the only or even the main types of plant varieties to be covered by the right. However, the perception was that UPOV was not interested in the protection of non-agricultural plant varieties. Even though the UPOV Convention had only recently been revised, there was considerable pressure for further action to be taken. The recognition that plant-related products possibly required greater protection than the law currently provided can be seen in discussions which took place in organisations such as the WIPO, AIPPI and OECD. Studies were undertaken to assess if the existing provision was effective and appropriate and also to identify if there was any political will to extend patent protection to a greater range of inventions involving biological material. The impact of these on patent law will be discussed in more detail in chapters 5 and 7.[57] This interest extended to the academic literature, and (as shown in the previous chapters and again in the next) academic commentators also weighed in with their views as to how properly and effectively to protect this increasingly important economic sector.

At the national level many European countries put decisions relating to protection on hold whilst these discussions were ongoing. An example of this can be seen in the UK government's White Paper on Intellectual Property and Innovation published in 1986.[58] Whilst this stated that there were signs of a change in attitude towards plant variety rights, it did not elaborate what those changes were. However, the White Paper did say that:

[t]he interface between patents and plant breeders' rights, particularly in relation to developments in biotechnology, is being considered within international fora such as the International Union for the Protection of New Varieties of Plants (UPOV) and the WIPO. It will only be when these discussions have progressed that the Government will be in a position to consider whether amendment of UK patent law is necessary.[59]

This fence-sitting could have been due to the fact that both the UK patent office and the UK plant variety rights office were playing key roles at the European Commission in the discussions surrounding the proposed introduction of the Community Regulation and the Directive.[60] A reluctance to commit to one view

---

[57] There is extensive documentation, which was produced during this period, which it would be impossible to mention here. The best sources for this information are the WIPO and UPOV newsletters dating from the late 1970s through the 1980s, which provide extensive detail of the discussions which took place. Many of those who had been instrumental in setting up the UPOV system, such as Dirk Boringer and Rene Royon, also contributed to the discussion.

[58] Cmd 9712, HMSO.

[59] Surprisingly the White Paper made no mention of either the EPC or the discussions which would result in the TRIPs Agreement despite the latter being only eight years away.

[60] Interestingly the representatives from various interest groups from the US were also present at many of the discussions over the Directive on the Legal Protection of Biotechnological Inventions both to observe and to explain the US experience.

or the other whilst these discussions were ongoing is therefore understandable. Such discussions as did take place tended to be low key in nature.

In contrast, other countries, and Germany in particular, saw interested parties taking a more proactive role, with conferences being held in order to inform the thinking of the government. At a conference held in Munich in January 1987, ministers from the German government, as well as the heads of the EPO and German patent office (both of which are based in Munich) heard calls to open up the patent system for the protection of all forms of plant material. These views, which prevailed at the conference, were then widely reported in both the German legal literature and those abroad. A similar conference held in Cambridge in September 1989, which urged caution over the patenting of plant material, did not receive the same coverage.

At the international level, there also appeared to be a growing consensus that plant breeders should be given the choice as to which form of protection to acquire. However, as will be seen below, the European Community favoured a more cautious approach. One thing was clear and that is that whilst there was general agreement within Europe that the UPOV Convention had served the purpose for which it had been introduced, it was no longer, in either its 1961 or 1978 guises, necessarily the only mode of protection for the results of the new plant genetic research. Whilst there was no overt call for the demise of the system there were clear signs that many felt that it had, at best, outlived any general usefulness in fostering plant research and, at worst, was hampering the use of patent protection. The WIPO, following on from an extensive two-year examination of plant property provision, deemed the UPOV system to be 'weak'[61] and concluded that it would be possible for general patent law principles to be applied to most, if not all, results of plant research.

As already mentioned in chapter 1, in a prescient passage written in 1989, Cornish[62] stated that '[e]nough can be seen to suggest . . . that the existing regime for plant variety protection (under an international convention which precludes patent protection from its territory[63]) is rapidly becoming an outmoded impediment to a logical framework of protection' and this view reflected a mood[64] in European patent circles that the exclusion, which many national patent laws contain, was an anachronism.[65] There was also a strong feeling that

[61] Report of the Committee of Experts on Biotechnology and Intellectual Property, (WIPO, 1988).

[62] Cornish, *Intellectual Property: Patents Copyright Trade Marks and Allied Rights*, 2nd edn (Sweet & Maxwell, 1989).

[63] Another indication of the lack of understanding of the Art 2(1) prohibition.

[64] Beier, Crespi and Straus, *Biotechnology and Patent Protection: An International Review* (OECD, 1985). Bent *et al* called it a 'bifurcation' of variety protection rights 'to the detriment' of patent protection for plants (*Intellectual Property Rights in Biotechnology Worldwide* (Macmillan, 1987)) whilst Straus called it 'a sacrifice on the altar of European patent law unification': 'Genetic Engineering and Industrial Property' (1986) 11 *Industrial Property* 454.

[65] See, eg, Crespi (one of the main architects of the EU Directive), 'Innovation in Plant Biotechnology: The Legal Options' (1986) 9 *EIPR* 262 in which he stated that '[t]he chief obstacle in Europe to the patenting of plants lies in the specific exclusion of plant varieties from patent protection.' He goes on to say that the UPOV system is appropriate for the results of traditional breeding

the more appropriate protection (especially in the modern plant biotechnology era) was the patent system.[66]

In light of these views, Cornish cautioned those then engaged in a revision of UPOV[67] 'to consider whether the regime has a viable future.'[68]

Opinions such as these appeared to contain thinly veiled criticisms of plant variety rights in general, and the so-called 'dual protection prohibition', contained in Article 2(1) of the 1978 UPOV Convention Act, in particular. As Cornish correctly pointed out, by the late 1980s there was a growing recognition of the economic potential of the plant bioscience industry. This recognition meant that the question of how to protect new plant innovations took on a far higher legal and political profile than had previously been the case (with the discussions on patentability attracting wide attention whilst those involving plant variety rights were comparatively low key).

More overtly strident in its criticism of the UPOV system was the International Chamber of Commerce.[69] This stated, in 1987, that it could see:

> no good reason . . . why plants or their propagating material should be treated any differently to micro-organisms or any other living or non-living subject matter . . . . While plant variety protection under UPOV continues to fulfil a valuable need [to protect material which cannot meet the threshold for protection] . . . it is . . . inherently less suitable to stimulate the desired research and progress in the field of plant biotechnology and variety development. In particular, UPOV plant variety protection provides neither the necessary degree of exclusivity to stimulate the heavy research investment required, nor the necessary element of early public description and disclosure to aid further research, that are both inherent in the patent system.[70]

The paper goes on to say that the UPOV system (in its then current 1978 guise) had limited value but 'while the system can and should be improved its existence must not be allowed to form a barrier to the patenting of true inventions (which meet all the normal requirements of patentability) in the area of plant biotechnology and *variety* development'[71] (emphasis added). Because of the limitations to the breeders' right (such as permitting material to be used for research pur-

---

(p 263) but that for 'the products of micro propagation/tissue culture techniques . . . plant variety protection would be inadequate' (p 266).

[66] See, for example, the views expressed by the International Chamber of Commerce (ICC) in a position paper published in 1987 in which it stated that 'the patent system offers the best prospect of protecting inventions in biotechnology and thereby stimulating research and accelerating progress' (1978) 18(2) *IIC* 223.

[67] Cornish, *Intellectual Property: Patents Copyright Trade Marks and Allied Rights*, 2nd edn (Sweet & Maxwell, 1989) and above n 42.

[68] *Ibid*, p 37.

[69] As this is a highly influential organisation which can effect change in practice it is worth rehearsing their views on the UPOV system.

[70] Above n 66, p 226.

[71] *Ibid*, p 235.

poses and protection only extending to the propagating material) the ICC felt that:

> there should be no special restrictions on patent protection in the field of plant biotechnology . . . [and] it sees no persuasive reason why both patent protection and plant variety protection should not be available in appropriate cases or why the inventor should not be free to choose whether he wants one or both types of protection.[72]

In terms of suggesting substantive improvements to the UPOV system, the ICC proposed that protection should be extended to cover end products as well as the propagating material, and that protection should be available for all varieties.[73] As will be seen in the discussion of the 1991 Act, these suggestions were amongst those adopted. The WIPO also called for action, arguing that the 'present system of international protection of intellectual property will survive only if it can demonstrate its flexibility and its ability to respond quickly enough to the needs of new developments.'[74] As the WIPO has always maintained that the patent system is the best means of protecting scientific research results (including plant-related inventions) then it is likely that the flexibility called for was with respect to determining the threshold for protection and the role, if any, of the exclusions to protection. In the specific context then it would seem that the flexibility of response necessary to meet the demands of the new science (for greater protection) were thought best met from within the patent system. As to whether the reference to international systems of intellectual property protection was intended to include the UPOV system can be doubted, given that the WIPO does not appear to recognise the system as a form of intellectual property right.

Whilst no one suggested that the UPOV system had ceased to have any value, it is clear from the arguments presented (and this can also be seen in chapter 7 when looking at the discussions leading up to the Directive) that the expectation was that a change in the law, together with the move away from traditional breeding practices, would mean that increasingly fewer varieties would be protected under the UPOV system. If the predications about the science were correct then the decrease in traditionally bred varieties would commensurately

---

[72] Above n 66, p 236.

[73] *Ibid*, p 237. It is worth noting that, following the revision of UPOV, debates over the proper implementation of Art 27(3)(b) and introduction of the EU Directive, the ICC has been silent on the matter of the patenting on plant varieties although it has been a key (and invaluable) player in seeking to reconcile the TRIPs Agreement with other international treaties, and the Convention on Biological Diversity in particular.

[74] Schafers, the Deputy Director General, WIPO, 'Legal Protection of Industrial Property in the New Technological Fields—Trends and Influence on Economic Cooperation, Paper presented at an International Symposium on Protection of Industrial Property and Promotion of Economic Cooperation, June 1987.

result in a decrease in UPOV variety rights—possibly to the point where the system itself did cease to have any real value. It would seem that an anticipated outcome of the removal of the bar to patent protection would be the inevitable demise of plant variety rights. As will be seen in chapter 7, the thinking of many patent protagonists during the 1970s and 1980s was that the right only survived in the absence of any choice, and once that choice was provided then the patent system would prevail and plant variety rights would fall into disuse. The last 10 years, in particular, have given the lie to this expectation. Not only does the exclusion in patent law remain (whilst the dual protection prohibition has been removed), but the place of plant variety rights within the global industrial property family, for developed as well as developing countries, has been both affirmed and secured through the debates surrounding Article 27(3)(b) of TRIPs. In achieving this, the plant variety rights system has removed its own internal 'impediments' to the patenting of plant varieties whilst, in contrast, the hoped-for radical rethink of the patent law exclusions has failed to materialise. This has been achieved by the substantial reinventing of the plant variety rights system within the 1991 UPOV Act, bringing the right closer to a patent-type right.[75]

It was against the backdrop of dissatisfaction over provision that the most significant revision of the UPOV to date took place. It is not proposed to rehearse the discussions which led up to the revision in 1991, not least because a) many of the concerns raised remain (and we will be returning to these in chapters 4 and 9), but also because b) in terms of European provision, there was near uniform consensus between parties (and across breeding sectors) that the right needed to be strengthened if European breeders were to continue to invest time and resources into new breeding programmes and also to compete effectively with each other at home and with breeders from abroad. As Ardley[76] recollects, there was an expectation that because of the extensive discussions which had been taking place within UPOV and collectively with the WIPO (and other organisations) the revision process would be relatively straightforward. Needless to say, as with any process of revision, it was not quite as straightforward as this, with particular sticking points proving to be the definitions section and the perceived impact of the new provisions on essentially derived varieties and farm saved seed. Suffice to state that there was general support, from within Europe, for the revision, although there were concerns over the impact of

---

[75] For a more detailed discussion of the thinking behind the changes see Greengrass, 'The 1991 Act of the UPOV Convention' and 'UPOV and the Protection of Plant Breeders—Past Developments, Future Perspective', above n 37; and Ardley, 'The 1991 UPOV Convention: Ten Years On' in the *Proceedings of the Conference on Plant Intellectual Property within Europe and the Wider Global Community* (Sheffield Academic Press, 2002) 73.

[76] Formerly the Deputy Controller of the UK Plant Variety Rights Office and a central figure in both the revision of the 1991 Act and the introduction of the Community Regulation on Plant Variety Rights: *ibid*.

certain of the new provisions (especially the extension of protection and restrictions to the farm saved seed provision). A significant difference between the discussions which preceded the 1991 revision and those which took place in the 1950s and 1970s is that the 1991 debate was international in a way that neither previous debate had been. The discussions in the 1950s were almost wholly European in form, and whilst the Convention was not intended to attract membership solely from within Europe, by the time the 1978 Act came into being there were only a couple of non-European member states (these being Israel and South Africa). In contrast, by the time of the discussions leading up to the 1991 Act Australia, Japan, and the US had become members with others (such as Argentina, Canada, and New Zealand) joining shortly afterwards. Clearly at that time there was no longer just the issue of whether to provide protection, but more importantly how to respond to the requirement in Article 27(3)(b) that protection for varieties must be provided. Throughout all the debates leading to the 1991 Act, one theme is obvious—to make the plant variety rights system more attractive to breeders. In order to do this, as will be seen in the comparison of the three UPOV Acts which follows, the decision was taken to bring the rights closer to a patent-type right. As the previous chapter explained, the fact that this made the system *less* appealing to many developing countries led to the decision to keep the 1978 Act open for ratification for a period. Following the revision in 1991, the criticisms lessened—although there are still some who would like to see the system fade away.[77]

Probably the most important consequence of the introduction of the 1991 Act, at least from the European perspective, has been its use as the model for the Community Plant Variety Right. As will be seen in the next chapter, the Community Regulation has used the options provided in the UPOV Act to set down a clear framework of protection. It will also become clear that there has been a significant move away from the effect and extent of rights originally established under the 1961 Act.

In discussing the evolution of the right it is proposed to identify the general themes and set out how these vary between the three main Acts.[78]

---

[77] See Llewelyn and Cook, above n 38; and Straus, *Patenting of Life-forms—The European Experience in Perspectives in Intellectual Property: Trade, Competition and Sustainable Development* in Cottier and Mavroidis (eds), vol 3 (World Trade Forum, University of Michigan Press, 2002) 341.

[78] The Convention was also revised in 1972, but these revisions were procedural in nature and related to such matters as the majority needed for decisions of the Council.

## The Three Acts: Commonalities and Variations

### The purpose of the Conventions

As already mentioned, the Preambles to both the 1961 and 1978 Acts recognise the importance of providing protection for all types of new plant varieties. They also specify that the rights granted are necessary to safeguard the interests of the plant breeder, with the proviso that 'special problems' can arise in respect of protecting these interests and that the exercise of the rights may be curbed in order to protect the wider public interest.[79] The language of the Preambles indicates a recognition that these problems might differ between member states and therefore it merely mandates that it is 'highly desirable' that any problems with the effect of the rights granted should be resolved 'in accordance with uniform and clearly defined principles' which provide a framework within which the member states can find a suitable resolution. In contrast, the 1991 Act does not contain a Preamble. Instead the UPOV Office has produced a Mission Statement which states that the object of the UPOV Union is '[t]o provide and promote an effective system of plant variety protection, with the aim of encouraging the development of new varieties of plants, for the benefit of society.'

The Mission Statement underlines the fact that there is now no need to spell out the justification for the right nor is the right to be seen as primarily of value to one particular sector of plant breeding but rather that the right is both applicable and relevant to all sectors of plant breeding (and indeed to all varieties howsoever grown, whether by the use of traditional Mendelian, or modern molecular, breeding techniques). A further point of contrast is that the Mission Statement does not contain any specific reference to the need to take account of the public interest in determining what rights the breeder should have. Given the changes which the 1991 Act has made to the rights granted to the breeder, the lack of an overt reference to the need to protect the public interest might indicate that the primary objective of the Convention is now to provide 'effective protection', the benefit to society coming through the provision of protection rather than through any overarching notions of limiting the rights granted. However, it is also possible to read into the reference to the provision of an effective system which encourages the development of plant varieties for the benefit of society a clear public interest element, not least as it is unlikely that anything which prevented the development of new varieties (for example, through an overly protectionist approach to the provision of protection) would be regarded as benefiting society.

The key elements to both the Preambles and to the Mission Statement would seem to be the expressed juxtaposition of the function of the right to provide

---

[79] It is these which provide the basis for the breeders' exemption, the farm saved seed provision and approach to compulsory licensing.

protection with the need to benefit society. It is this which underpins the robust use of the limitations to the right granted within plant variety rights.

Protectable Varieties

The concerns about an over-monopolisation of plant material are apparent in the 1961 Act. Article 4 stated that a member state 'may' apply the Convention to all plant varieties but it merely required that protection must be progressively provided for varieties falling within a list of 13 genera appended to the Convention.[80] The requirement was that once the Convention came into force at the national level, member states were required to provide protection for at least five of the genera contained on the list; within the next three years a further two genera had to be included; four genera within six years; and all on the list within eight years. Member states were not precluded from protecting other species and genera in addition to those on the list. The obligation to expand the number protected to include those on the list remained irrespective of the number of other, non-specified, genera and species which were protected. The contents of the list reflected that fact that the pressure to introduce the right had primarily come from the agricultural plant breeding sector.

By 1978 the requirement to protect five genera or species upon entry into force was retained but the number to be progressively protected increased, and the list of 'have to' protect species was removed. Under the 1978 Act members had progressively to provide protection for an additional 10 genera within three years, 18 genera within six years, and 24 genera within eight years.

By 1991, the element of national determination as to which species would be protectable was deemed to be outdated, and Article 4 now stipulates that *all* genera must be protectable within five years of joining the new Act. This is one of the provisions in the new Act which is most problematic for developing countries.

Defining Variety

As discussed in the previous chapter, Article 2(2) of the 1961 UPOV Act defined a plant variety as '. . . any cultivar, clone, line, stock or hybrid which is capable of cultivation and which satisfies the provisions of sub-paragraphs (1)(c) and (1)(d) of Article 6.' Article 6 contained the substantive granting provisions: distinctness, uniformity and stability. This definition was clearly not considered to be binding, as some signatories to the 1961 Act used alternative language.[81]

---

[80] The 13 species on the list were wheat, barley, oats or rice, maize, potatoes, peas, beans, lucerne, red clover, ryegrass, lettuce, apples, and roses or carnations.

[81] For example, s 38(1) of the UK Plant Variety and Seeds Act 1964 defined a variety as any 'clone, line, hybrid or genetic variant,' thus clearly showing continued disparity.

When the UPOV Convention was revised in 1978, the definition was deleted. The reason for this was the belief that there was sufficient common consensus as to what was a variety to render the provision of a definition of variety superfluous. It was also thought that if an attempt were made to revise the definition in light of the scientific developments in plant breeding which had occurred post-1961 then it would be too difficult to do so in language which would not ultimately prove narrow and, therefore, exclusionary. Interestingly, the only guidance provided in the 1978 Act as to what is protected takes the form of indicating what member states may exclude from protection—the revised Article 2(2) of the 1978 Act read: 'Each member State of the Union may limit the application of this Convention within a genus or species to varieties with a particular manner of reproduction or multiplication.' This removal of a definition was not mirrored by equivalent amendments to existing national laws.

In the discussions leading up to the 1991 UPOV Act it was proposed that a definition should be reintroduced. The reason for this was that a definition was seen as necessary in order to establish clear blue water between the rights available to a breeder for the genetic components of a variety (these being potentially patentable), and rights which the breeder could claim over a grouping which collectively, and in a uniform and stable fashion, comprised the genetic components. As with Article 2(2) of the 1961 Act, the definition of variety is intended to be read in conjunction with the application of the substantive granting criteria.[82]

Article 1(iv) states that the term 'variety' means a plant grouping within a single botanical taxon of the lowest known rank, which grouping, irrespective of whether the conditions for the grant of a breeder's right are fully met, can be:

— defined by the expression of the characteristics resulting from a given genotype or combination of genotypes,
— distinguished from any other plant grouping by the expression of at least one of the said characteristics, and
— considered as a unit with regard to its suitability for being propagated unchanged.

In terms of satisfaction with the definition chosen, there has been some acknowledgement from those involved in the drafting that the provision of a definition which would correspond in all its various language guises was problematic. This is a problem facing any European piece of legislation where there is a requirement that the final text be agreed in a number of different languages. The view seems to be that, in so far as it was possible, the definition contained in Article 1 is 'the best definition of plant variety.'[83]

However, as discussed previously, the reintroduction of a definition into UPOV does not necessarily mean that there is now no ambiguity as to what is

---

[82] UPOV CAJ/XX111/2.
[83] Ardley, 'The 1991 UPOV Convention: Ten Years On', above n 75, p 7.

capable of being protected by a plant variety right and what is protectable by a patent. Instead, the reference in Article 1 of the 1991 Act to two types of plant variety, those which can meet the granting criteria and those which cannot, instils a degree of ambiguity into the Convention. For the purposes of plant variety protection, this ambiguity does not appear to be significant—either the plant grouping concerned is capable of being shown to be distinct, uniform or stable (discussed below), or it is not. However (as will be discussed in the next two chapters), the fact that the UPOV Convention (and the Community Plant Variety Rights Regulation) specifically mentions two types of plant variety does bring into question the way in which the plant variety rights definition is used for the purposes of identifying what is excluded from European patent protection.

Protection of Discoveries

Each of the various UPOV Acts has recognised that whoever has bred, or discovered and developed a variety should be entitled to protection (provided the granting criteria are met). On the face of it, this is a clear distinction between that which is patentable (discoveries being specifically excluded from patent protection) and that which can be the subject matter of a plant variety right. However, in terms of protecting the investment (time and financial) in producing a product usable by others in roughly the same form as that over which the protection was granted, the two notions are closer together than might first appear. Protection is not available over mere discoveries but will be granted only if the breeder can show that the collective plants of the applied-for variety breed in a distinct, uniform and stable manner. This will invariably require intervention (or development) by the breeder. In addition, the breeder will have to show that the distinct characteristics of the variety can breed in a uniform and stable manner, and it is this latter ability which will usually require direct input by the breeder, making the protection of wholly naturally occurring varieties which breed true across an entire plant grouping year after year a rarity. The rationale for including discoveries within the Convention is that, as discoveries, are a valuable source of genetic variation for the production of varieties the system would be failing in its objective to maximise research using a diversity of genetic sources if they were excluded. Indeed, as Heitz has said 'their exclusion might act as a disincentive to the search for and exploitation of mutations and variations.'[84] Because of the emphasis on the development (or domestication) of plant variety in order to secure protection, the UPOV system is not concerned with protecting most indigenous plant groupings—and this is one of the reasons for many developing, and genetically rich, countries seeking to protect their local plant life through a combination of UPOV-styled protection which can extend to plants found in the wild.[85]

---

[84] Heitz, *Intellectual Property Rights and Plant Variety* (Protection paper given in 2001): see www.upov.int.
[85] An example of this can be seen in the Thai plant variety rights law.

The emphasis is, therefore, on showing that the discovered or bred variety as cultivated by the breeder is capable of meeting the threshold for protection.

The Granting Criteria[86]

Protection extends to plant groupings which are distinct, uniform and stable (DUS) following repeated reproduction (each of these three elements will be looked at further below). Both the 1978 and the 1991 Acts also require that the variety must be shown to be commercially novel in the sense that it must not have been offered for sale prior to the right being applied for (this is not the same as novelty in patent law). Article 5 of the 1991 Act also makes it clear that no further or different conditions should be placed on the breeder.[87] This has been used to defend decisions not to require breeders to produce information or material relating to their variety for use by third parties for the purposes of pursuing a related breeding programme.

The DUS Criteria[88]

*Distinctness*

Distinctness means that the essential characteristics of the variety must be distinct from other varieties within the same genus or species. Distinctness is assessed according to whether the variety is clearly distinguishable from any other variety whose existence is a matter of common knowledge. The evaluation of distinctness is based on whether the physiological characteristics of that plant grouping, when taken as a whole, render the collective sufficiently distinct from other varieties within the same species.

The question of whether or not a variety is a matter of common knowledge is decided by reference to a number of different factors, including whether it is already being cultivated or marketed, whether it has been entered onto an official register of varieties and whether there is precise information about it placed in a collection or publication. The 1961 Act states that where a variety has been marketed in the territory for which the right is being sought and that marketing has taken place with the agreement of the breeder, then that variety will be deemed a matter of common knowledge. This is qualified in that where the country concerned permits a grace period of one year for marketing, then provided the marketing takes place within that 12-month period the variety will not be deemed to be a matter of common knowledge. Equally, the variety must not have been marketed in any other state for a period longer than six years in the

---

[86] The concepts outlined here also apply to the Community Plant Variety Rights system.

[87] This can be contrasted with the TRIPs Agreement, as Art 1 states that 'Members may, but shall not be obliged to, implement in their law more extensive protection than is required by this Agreement.'

[88] There will be further discussion of these concepts in the next chapter, with examples of their application in practice in the context of the operation of the Council Regulation on Community Plant Variety Rights.

case of vines, forest trees, fruit trees and ornamental trees, and four years in the case of all other plants. Again, the marketing must have been undertaken with the agreement of the breeder. The 1961 Act does state that the use of the variety in trials which do not involve offering for sale or marketing and any other factor through which the variety has become a matter of common knowledge where that activity does not involve offering for sale or marketing will not affect the ability of the breeder to acquire rights (Article 6).

The 1978 Act additionally includes the requirement that the characteristics which define and distinguish a variety 'must be capable of precise recognition and description' (Article 6(1)(a)). Interestingly, the 1991 Act is less specific on both the issue of common knowledge and the requirement for precise recognition and description than either the 1961 or 1978 Acts.

Article 7 of the 1991 Act simply states that the variety must be clearly distinguishable from other varieties the existence of which is a matter of common knowledge at the time of filing. It does not further define what constitutes common knowledge other than to state that the filing of an application for a breeder's right or for entry onto an official register will be deemed to render the variety a matter of common knowledge 'provided that the application leads to the granting of a breeder's right or to the entering of the said variety in the official register . . .' It is important to note that this requirement goes to the nature of the distinctive quality of the plant variety and not to whether it is novel or not. The use of the phrase 'in particular' would seem to indicate that other factors, not defined in the Act, may also be taken into account which could include those contained in Article 6 of both the 1978 and 1961 Acts, as well as others not previously identified.

The notion of 'common knowledge' can be contrasted with the patent law requirement that the invention must not have been disclosed prior to the patent application being filed. In practice, and this is discussed in more detail in chapter 5, the requirement in patent law is that the technical effect being claimed must not previously have been known *in the context of the application to which that technical effect is now put.* This is a much more difficult standard to meet than the common knowledge requirement.

A problem with the common knowledge requirement is that there is no comprehensive database nor collection of plant material which can be used to measure whether a claimed variety is a matter of common knowledge or not. The ISF has suggested that the problems encountered in trying to determine common knowledge as a result of the increasing numbers of applications being made and granted around the world could be alleviated if a world-wide database were set up which contained a phenotypic description of varieties held to be in common knowledge. The suggestion is that whilst the database should be restricted to those phenotypic characteristics indicated in the UPOV Guidelines, it should not be confined only to UPOV-referenced varieties. This reinforces the fact that there are recognisable plant groupings which can be called varieties other than those which meet the granting criteria.

Returning to the main criterion, the key element to proving distinctness is that a clear visible distance can be shown between the collective phenotypic characterisation of the claimed variety and its closest neighbouring varieties within the same species. One of the questions facing granting offices is the extent to which modern DNA technology should be used to determine whether a variety is distinct or not.

As will be seen, the view of the breeding organisations appears to be that they would, for the present, resist the use of this technology for this particular purpose (although they would support its use to determine whether a variety is essentially derived or not).[89] The reason given is that it would be technically and financially too consuming and would serve to remove the focus from the phenotypic aspects of the variety, which is what the UPOV system was designed to protect, to more minuscule aspects. The effect of relying on a determination of internal markers would be both to reduce the distance between varieties and arguably to reduce the effect of the breeders' right, as one genetic change could be argued to place a DNA distance between two otherwise equivalent varieties (which are not alleged to be connected by any form of essential derivation).[90] There are some concerns, however, that such an absolute stance could mean that valuable traits are not regarded as protectable as they have no phenotypic expression. Amongst those who work in some areas of plant breeding, for example with ornamental and medicinal plants, there is a view that greater use should be made of new technologies to determine both grant and scope.[91] For these reasons the possibility of using DNA technology in the future has not been ruled out. To this end UPOV has set up a Working Party on Biochemical and Molecular Techniques, the remit of which is to see if such techniques could be used to aid determining whether the DUS criteria have been met. In addition, the ISF, noting that different species may require different assessment methods, has recommended that the determination of the minimum distance between varieties and use of molecular technologies should be addressed on a species by species basis. In addition, some suggestions have been made by the ISF as to how to classify further the characteristics which are assessed in order to determine DUS; in so doing the ISF is underlining that it is the phenotype which is the proper focus for assessment and not the genotype.

The ISF has suggested that to the list of standard phenotypic characteristics which the UPOV Office produces should be added any other phenotypic characteristic, provided that it a) meets the general requirements for a characteristic (is the result of a given genotype or combination of genotypes), b) is sufficiently consistent and repeatable in a specific environment, c) demonstrates sufficient

[89] For example see the European Seed Association Position Paper on 'The Possible Use of Molecular Markers for DUS Testing' (ESA_03.0022.6).

[90] Drawing parallels with another area of intellectual property law, the notion of single feature alteration has long been a matter for debate within copyright, and the notion that a single altered configuration could be held to give rise to an original work as opposed to being found to be a substantial copy has long been regarded as problematic within the computing software industry.

[91] See the comments made at the PIP workshop, at www.shef.ac.uk/uni/projects/pip.

variation to enable distinctness to be established, and is itself capable of precise definition and recognition, and d) fulfils the uniformity and stability requirements following repeated reproduction or multiplication. In addition, these extra characteristics must have been used by at least one UPOV signatory and been submitted to UPOV for approval. The ISF sees these characteristics as being predominantly physiological and falling within the general groups of yield, sugar content, resistance to pest or disease, and tolerance to herbicides. ISF advises that these additional characteristics should not be regarded as exhaustive and also that their usage should be on a crop-by-crop basis.

It also suggests including 'additional convincing evidence'—such as the use of protein characteristics—but these are not to be used for populations or synthetic varieties of cross-pollinating species. If these are permitted they should only be used with the permission of the applicant, if all the other characteristics fail to establish clear distinctness, and if a test procedure for this characteristic has been agreed by the applicant and the authority concerned. The ISF suggests that these protein characteristics should only be used to determine distinctness if used in combination with both the current and suggested characteristics.

The ISF remains of the opinion that whilst breeders must embrace new technologies the use of such technologies should be on the basis that they solve more problems than they produce. At present 'DUS testing should continue to be based on phenotypic characteristics [and] it is preferable . . . that D, U and S can be recognized in normal growing conditions.' The ISF is opposed to the use of DNA markers for DUS testing because a) these are not yet predictive of many of the phenotypic characteristics due to a lack of genetic linkage information, not to mention the complex way in which genetics control the phenotypic traits, b) if these markers were used to determine distinctness then they could also be used to determine uniformity and stability which could give rise to both financial and technical problems, c) their use would not recognise the extent of existing variability within a variety which avoids narrow genetic diversity and could serve to emphasise cosmetic or non-valuable characteristics and d) it could serve to decrease the minimum distance between varieties and jeopardise the value of the right granted.

Noting the work of the UPOV Office's Working Party on Biochemical and Molecular Techniques, the ISF indicates cautious support and suggests that it should focus on defining minimum distances, look at the impact on uniformity and stability and also assess the practical difference between the concepts of distinctness and essential derivation if both are assessed using molecular markers. As these are issues which as yet have no resolution, the ISF believes that the use of DNA markers would reduce and not increase the value of the breeder's right.

The ISF also looked at what it considers to be the special case for disease resistance. As this is proving to be increasingly important in terms of breeding outcomes, the ISF supports the use of DNA technology to determine distinctness, provided that it meets the general conditions outlined above. In addition, the breeder should define the resistance(s) and identify the genus, species and, if possible, the pathogens concerned. If the resistance applies to a number of races then the specific race should also be identified. The resistance should be evaluated by a standardised method which should be made known through a known publication and added to the guidelines relating to the testing for that species. Where the characteristic relates to a different level of resistance then this will only be sufficient for distinctness purposes if the levels of expression can be clearly established and the test results are both consistent and technically reliable. The same level of enthusiasm is not evident in the views of the ESA.

Whilst UPOV and the ISF clearly are open to the possibility of using DNA technology as a means of assessing the minimum distance between varieties, the ESA considers 'the actual system of DUS testing based on phenotypic assessment [to be] the most appropriate way to deal with differences.'[92] It considers the use of molecular markers to be inappropriate because:

a) there is insufficient information about genetic linkage and therefore DNA marker profiles would not be predictable 'for most phenotypic characteristics'; also phenotypic traits are subject to 'relatively complex genetic control';
b) the use of such markers could result in a decrease of distance between varieties and would therefore 'jeopardise the value' of the rights; and
c) the markers would have to be used to test uniformity and stability as well as distinctness and there could be consequences (unspecified by the ESA) in using the markers for that purpose.

The ESA fully supports the setting up of a UPOV database on phenotypic characteristics and it does not wholly rule out a role for molecular markers in the future but it sees their value as predictors of traditional characteristics and, in particular, where the characteristic is one which cannot be 'consistently observed in the field or require[s] additional special arrangements,' such as the determination of disease resistance. As will be seen later, all three, UPOV, the ISF and the ESA, support the uses of DNA techniques in the determination of essential derivation.

Another problem facing granting offices is the sheer scale of information available relating to plant material, and the need for granting offices to be able to access this in order to make a proper determination as to whether a variety is distinct or not. One of the constant calls made is for granting offices to exchange information with each other to help in an increasingly complex area.

### Uniformity/Homogeneity

This is the requirement that the variety must breed true through subsequent reproduction or propagation. Both the 1961 and 1978 Acts define the requirement as being that the variety 'must be sufficiently homogenous.' The 1991 Act

---

[92] ESA Position Paper, 'The Possible Use of Molecular Markers for DUS Testing' (2003).

rewords the requirement and states that a 'variety shall be deemed to be uniform if, subject to the variation that may be expected from the particular features of its propagation, it is sufficiently uniform in its relevant characteristics' (Article 8). In practice, the change in terminology makes little difference other than the change in the requirement from the variety 'must be' homogenous, which indicates an obligation on the part of the applicant, to 'shall be deemed' uniform, which indicates an obligation on the part of the examiner. Under the previous law, the breeder had to prove that the plant variety has a certain quality, whereas with the 1991 Act the granting office had to accept that the variety will be uniform. This emphasises the move towards the presumption of protectability.

The rules established by UPOV relate to all types of varieties, including vegetatively propagated varieties, truly self-pollinated varieties, mainly self-pollinated varieties, cross-pollinating varieties and hybrid varieties. In producing these guidelines, UPOV is primarily concerned that the variation should be as limited as possible and in so doing they take into account the way in which that variety breeds, and the occurrence of 'off-types' (that is, the non-uniform plants within a plant grouping). The emphasis is on ensuring that distinctness can be shown across the whole grouping, that an accurate description of the grouping as a whole can be made and to ensure stability.

## Stability

The final requirement common to each of the Acts is that the characteristics which distinguish the plant grouping from other groupings through uniform reproduction also reproduce in a stable manner. As with the uniformity and distinctness requirements, this has to occur both within an extant plant grouping as well as through subsequent generations. As with the other criteria, the language has changed slightly in the 1991 Act. Both the 1961 and 1978 Acts refer to the requirement that the 'variety must be stable in its essential characteristics . . . it must remain true to its description after repeated reproduction or propagation or, where the breeder has defined a particular cycle of reproduction of multiplication, at the end of each cycle.' The 1991 Act merely states that the 'variety shall be deemed stable if its relevant characteristics remain unchanged after repeated propagation or, in the case of a particular cycle of propagation, at the end of each such cycle.' Again there is new emphasis on what must be accepted as constituting a stable variety, there is also the change from a requirement that it must remain true in its 'essential characteristics' to remaining true in its 'relevant characteristics' (Article 9). As the requirement is that those characteristics which are essential or relevant for determining whether the variety is distinct or not, as well as those which are required to breed in a uniform as well as true manner, the change in wording is unlikely to mean any shift in either policy or practice.

## The Practical Assessment

The right is granted following a minimum of two years of trialling, undertaken by the granting office, during which time the plant material is assessed for the DUS criteria against control varieties from within the same species. This can be contrasted with the patent system, where the examination of the invention pre-grant consists of a paper exercise.

In order for granting offices to examine varieties in a coherent and consistent manner they have to ensure that they are, in so far as it is possible, operating to the same standard. Because of this, and due to the practical dimension inherent in the granting of a right, it has been necessary to establish working practices which share the burden of both examination and administration.

The first of these practices is that offices are encouraged to examine varieties using an agreed measure as to what is distinctness, uniformity and stability. As species differ in respect of the communal characteristics, this means that different measures have to be used for different species. There is a need, therefore, to produce highly technical data relevant to each species against which any new variety can be compared. This might seem to be a very onerous expectation for each country to meet (especially those with low levels of technical expertise in respect of a particular species). In practice, provision of this information is not much of a problem because, in order to ensure consistency, the UPOV Office compiles and disseminates this data to member states by way of very detailed guidelines. These documents, which are extensive, consist of written technical information about a species as well as drawings and photographs[93] and are constantly being updated. Whilst the use of the guidelines is not binding, most member states do use them as the basis of decision making—and if any national variation on the guidelines is applied this is usually fed back to the UPOV Office and, if appropriate, included in the next update of that guideline.

Secondly, as there is a requirement that reproductive material of the protected variety can be recalled at any time during the period of protection for retesting, member states have to build and maintain live collections of plant material. This both is very expensive and could result in a duplication of held material across member states. An amendment to the 1961 Act therefore requested member states to collaborate where appropriate.

---

[93] An example of this pre-1991 was UPOV Guidelines TG/20/7 relating to oats. These required the breeder to provide three kilograms of seed each year and that the seed should have 99% purity. The seed must not have undergone any chemical treatment, and the testing should be undertaken at two different testing stations. In order to assess distinctness and stability, no fewer than 20 plants should be examined. To assess homogeneity (or uniformity) 100 plants had to be examined. As uniformity relates to the plant grouping as a whole, the entire plot had to be assessed and the breeder was permitted only five aberrant plants out of 2,000. If the plot indicated a higher level of reduced homogeneity, seed could be harvested from the plot and sown again the following year. This was then compared with seed supplied by the breeder. When assessing distinctness, the characteristics of oats could be divided up into stem, primary grain, grain and seasonal type (eg, winter or spring oats). This information can be supplemented by national granting offices' own data.

The third is that granting offices need to be able to call upon the expertise of scientists knowledgeable about any given particular species. It is their job to compare the applied-for variety against the technical information. This can provide problems where a country has, for example, plant breeding expertise in oats but not in rice. An expert in the former is probably not going to be able to make a exact determination as to DUS in respect of the latter. Again, where that technical expertise is available elsewhere this can be called upon.

Finally, there must be appropriate terrain within which to grow the applied-for variety. Most varieties are bred with specific soil conditions in mind and not every country has the necessary local conditions. This has lead to further bilateral co-operation between granting offices with agreements being drawn up which permit the testing of a variety outside the territory where the grant will take effect if the appropriate growing conditions lie outside that territory.[94]

The DUS criteria are therefore, assessed a) by reference to a written description provided by the applicant and b) through a practical examination of the material itself. Once a right has been granted then a breeder may be required at any point in the duration of the right to provide reproductive material of the variety in order to prove that it is still breeding the distinct characteristics in a stable and uniform manner.

As previously mentioned, whilst none of the UPOV Acts contain specific details as to how to determine the DUS of a variety, this does not mean that the UPOV Office is not concerned with how these requirements are put into practice within member states. The UPOV Office provides, by way of a 'General Introduction to the Examination of Distinctness, Uniformity and Stability and the Development of Harmonized Descriptions of New Varieties of Plants',[95] general guidance designed to assist national offices in making consistent determinations. In addition, the Office produces more detailed Guidelines for the Conduct of Tests for Distinctness, Uniformity and Stability[96] which relate to specific species—the latter having been produced with the assistance of experts in the field and approved by the relevant plant breeding organisation prior to adoption.[97] One of the reasons for having both the General Introduction *and* the specific test guidelines is that not all species have guidelines. Where a variety for which no guidelines exist is submitted for examination, the granting office is directed to the General Introduction.[98] A further way in which the UPOV Office seeks to ensure consistency is by encouraging national granting offices to liaise with each other and share practices and procedures and, where possible

---

[94] Issues of collaboration will not be discussed further—for more information on co-operation in examination see www.upov.org/en/documents/c/37/c_37_5.pdf._.

[95] TG/1/3.

[96] TGP/2, List of Test Guidelines Adopted by UPOV.

[97] There will be further discussion of this in ch 5 when looking at the Community Plant Variety Rights Regulation and the operation of the Community Office.

[98] Ch 9 of the General Introduction, Conduct for testing DUS in the Absence of Test Guidelines.

establish harmonisation (such an event being notified to UPOV).[99] In the event that there is neither prior practice nor an existing test guideline for a variety, then UPOV urges the member state concerned to develop its own testing procedures.[100]

For the ISF, the DUS criteria, as set down in UPOV, 'guarantee the quality and the pertinence of the Breeder's Right,' and national and international authorities must ensure scientific rigour in the application of these principles as this 'is essential to ensure the reproducibility of the results obtained and the consistency of the observations made by different competent authorities on the same characteristics.' The ISF also gives total support for the UPOV guidelines on the conducting of the DUS tests, and it encourages the use of these guidelines in order to achieve harmonisation.

The fourth requirement is that the variety must be new.

### New

It is important when looking at this requirement to note that this is not a novelty requirement in the absolute sense understood in patent law.[101] Instead, the requirement is that the variety must be commercially new.

The concept that the variety must be new varied under the 1961 and 1978 Acts. The 1961 Act consistently refers to the 'new plant variety'; however, 'novelty' was not itself defined anywhere in the Convention. From the context within which the term was used, it would seem that novelty was to be found by reference to the extent of any marketing of the variety occurring prior to filing. The issue was whether the breeder had marketed the variety, or given permission for the variety to be marketed, in the territory within which protection was sought, for a period longer than one year, or four years in territories other than the one in which protection was being sought. If the offering for sale or marketing of the variety had taken place before the permitted periods then the variety would not be novel. No other guidance on novelty was given.

Under the 1978 Act the references to the '*new* plant variety' were removed and the text now simply refers to the 'variety'. This does not mean, however, that the novelty requirement has been removed. Whilst there is no specific requirement that the variety must be new, the implicit requirement is that it must, in a very limited sense, be relatively novel. This can be seen from the grace periods permitted. The 1978 Act retains the one-year grace period for marketing within

---

[99] TGP/5, Experience and Cooperation in DUS Testing.

[100] TGP/7, Development of Test Guidelines.

[101] Generally, this requires that the subject matter of the application should not have been known in that form anywhere in the world prior to the date of filing. The notion of novelty does have some significant national variances, eg in the US there are two notions of novelty: the first requires that the invention must not have been published or used in the US prior to filing in the US (a one-year grace period also exists); the second states that the invention must not have been published anywhere in the world prior to filing in the US. This means that where an invention has been used elsewhere in the world (eg as a form of traditional medicine) but not reduced to printed form then, provided it has also not been used or published in the US, it may be patented.

the territory for which protection is sought, and also the longer grace period for marketing in all other territories. However, with regard to the latter grace period, a distinction is drawn as to the type of plant material concerned—the marketing of vines, forest trees, fruit trees and ornamental trees (including their rootstocks) was permitted for a period up to six years before the novelty of the material ceased to exist. The previous four-year period is retained for all other plant varieties. In contrast to the 1961 Act, the 1978 Act provides further detail as to what activities with the plant variety do not affect the quality of novelty. Article 6(1)(ii) states that neither trials involving the variety (provided these are not related to the sale or offering for sale of the variety), nor any other means by which the variety has become a matter of common knowledge (provided this does not take the form of selling or offering for sale), will affect the rights of the breeder.

The 1991 Act does not refine to any great extent the concept of novelty as set down in the 1978 Act. What it does do (in common with the other granting criteria) is to stipulate clearly that novelty is a requirement upon which a grant of rights depends. Article 6 of the 1991 Act serves to separate out several elements necessary in order to establish novelty and it reiterates the requirement that the breeder must not have consented to the selling, or otherwise disposing of, the variety to others—the 1991 Act adds the caveat that the selling or otherwise disposing of must not have been undertaken for the purposes of *exploiting* the variety. It is clearer than ever that it is commercial novelty which is at issue.

The 1991 Act makes no substantive change made to the 1978 grace period, and the breeder retains the right to sell or dispose of the variety for a period of not more than 12 months prior to the filing of an application in the territory[102] for which the right is being sought; or within six years of application for trees and vines or four years of application for all other plants in territories other than the one in which the right is being sought.

The only significant addition made by the 1991 Act relates to varieties which previously were protected under a national system of plant variety rights. This takes into account the requirement under the 1991 Act that *all* varieties must be protected, with no sliding scale as to how many must be protected at any given time. Where a party is considering an application relating to a previously unprotected variety and that variety, is considered of 'recent creation' but has previously been offered for sale or otherwise disposed of for a period longer than that permitted in paragraph 1, then the party *may* still choose to provide protection for that variety.

As with the DUS criteria, the novelty requirement applies to all plant varieties howsoever created. There is an issue, however, as to whether hybrid parental

---

[102] Territory is given a broader meaning than simply the physical territory of a particular country. The key element is identifying the nature of the contracting party. Where the contracting party to the Convention is a country then the Act applies to that territory. Where the contracting party is an intergovernmental organisation, such as the EU, the territory to which the contracting party can apply the Convention is that of the EU.

lines which have previously been produced or sold can be regarded as novel.

The question which has been raised is whether the seed of a hybrid variety produced is equivalent to the harvested material of the parental lines—the seed of the variety and the harvested material of the parental lines being genetically the same thing. The nub of the issue is whether the sale of the seed of the hybrid variety defeats novelty for parental lines which produced the variety, and vice versa. As novelty requires that the propagating material of the variety applied for must not previously have been sold or otherwise exploited, then the seed of the hybrid variety cannot be held to be new, as it has been previously exploited in the form of the harvested material of the parental lines.[103] The ISF does not agree with this interpretation but argues that neither parental line will in itself give rise to the hybrid and that the hybrid therefore can be taken to be a variety as defined under UPOV.[104] This issue has not been resolved one way or the other for, as the President of the Community Plant Variety Office has recognised, the fact that some of the delegates at the 1991 Conference leading up to the 1991 UPOV Act thought that the use of a hybrid defeated novelty for its parental lines, and these same delegates agreed the text of Article 6(1), indicates that they read Article 6(1) as having this effect. The result is that different practices exist at the national levels. Within Europe, for example, the French, German and British laws all treat the disposal of hybrid material as disposal of the parental lines and therefore the parental lines cannot themselves be regarded as novel. The position is slightly less emphatic under the Community Regulation, as will be seen in the next chapter. It is worth noting that many breeders choose not to seek intellectual property rights over parental lines, as the value of these lines lies in their scarcity in the market place. For this reason, breeders prefer to protect by keeping the lines secret.

Aside from serving to recognise the importance of placing plant varieties in the market place as quickly as possible, the limited nature of the novelty requirement means that breeders are given a greater opportunity for acquiring plant variety rights in a number of different countries. This is important not only for the continued survival of the system of protection itself but also because if the novelty requirement was as strict as that within patent law, breeders would not merely be given no opportunity to test the market viability of the new plant variety in as many countries as possible, but there would be no opportunity to assess if the physical conditions were appropriate for that plant material.

It might be useful to unpick the novelty requirement. Breeder A has bred two different plant varieties, a variety of oats and a variety of apple. He markets both varieties in country X. Provided that he has not marketed both varieties for a period of longer than 12 months in country X, he will be able to seek plant

---

[103] This view was put forward by a US representative at the Diplomatic Conference of March 1991, and supported by other delegates at meetings of the UPOV Council's Legal and Administrative Committee in 2001 and 2002.

[104] See 'The ASSINSEL Position Paper', adopted May 2000, www.worldseed.org.

variety rights for both within country X. But internal marketing is not the only factor for consideration. The granting office will also take into account his marketing activities in other countries, and he will have to show, in addition to complying with the one-year grace period requirement in the country of application, that in respect of the oat variety he had not marketed it in any other country for a period longer than four years. In respect of the variety of apple, then in addition to showing that he has not marketed or offered the variety for sale in the country of application for a period longer than 12 months, he must also show that he has not marketed the variety in any other country for a period longer than 6 years.

If breeder A has no existent market in country X, but has sold his oat variety in country Y for five years or his variety of apple in country Z for seven years then, notwithstanding that he has no market in country X (and would seem to fall within the local grace period), he will not be able to acquire rights in country X as he will not be compliant with the extra-territorial grace periods. It does not appear to be a requirement that the territory other than that of the country of application itself needs to be a member of UPOV.

Denomination[105]

The final, often undiscussed, requirement is that the breeder must attach a name or denomination to the variety, and the registration of this name must take place at the same time as the issuance of the plant variety right. The function of this requirement is to enable the variety to be identified and to ensure that there is no confusion in the market place as to which plant material is being sold. The inclusion of this requirement is again based on public interest. As plant varieties are invariably sold according to name and the qualities accorded to the variety invariably also attach to that name, it is regarded as critical that the breeder only uses an approved denomination.

Article 13 of the 1961 Act stipulated that such denomination must not consist only of figures, it must not mislead or confuse as to the characteristics, value or identity of either the variety or the breeder and, in particular, it must differ from any other denomination used for a variety from the same or closely related species. Where a denomination was refused the breeder was given an opportunity to submit an alternative. There were a number of other qualifications which applied. The first is that where a breeder had an existing trade mark (which may not necessarily be used in relation to a plant variety) he could not use that trade mark for the plant variety unless he renounced his rights to that trade mark other than those rights which related to its use in connection with the plant variety. Where a breeder is applying for variety rights in a number of different

---

[105] One of the very few academic discussions of this requirement was provided in the mid-1980s by Piatti and Jouffray, 'Plant Variety Names in National and International Law Parts 1 and 2' [1985] *EIPR* 283; [1985] *EIPR* 311. Whilst this does not apply to the 1991 UPOV Act many of the points made by the authors are still relevant.

countries he had to submit the same denomination in each state, and the state concerned was required to register it unless it was deemed unsuitable for that country. Anyone who then offered for sale or marketed the variety, even if s/he was not the breeder, was required to use the denomination in connection with that variety, and this obligation remained even after the expiry of the variety right. Once a right had been issued over a variety with a specific denomination, then that denomination could not be used for any other variety of the same species or closely related species. And in an extension of the right, the Act went on to say that the name or one confusingly similar could not be registered under trade mark law for identical or similar products. Where it was the same product then a breeder might acquire a trade mark over the name. This did not affect the rights of those with a prior right to use the name.

Both the 1978 and 1991 Acts make two subtle changes to the requirement. The first is that the requirement that the denomination must not consist entirely of figures is qualified in that it will be permitted to acquire a figures-only denomination where that is the established practice for designating varieties. The second, and most significant, revision is that both lessen the constraints of the ability of the breeder to use an existing registered trade mark in respect of the variety concerned. Both Acts permit the association of an existing trade mark (or trade name or other similar identifier) with the variety, provided that the denomination is clearly identified. This does not mean that an existing trade mark may be used to denominate the variety (although this is not expressly denied) but means that a breeder may, in addition to the use of the denomination also use his trade mark in connection with the variety, provided that the denomination, separate from the trade mark, is itself easily recognisable. This gives the breeder additional protection and both permits him to reinforce an existing trade mark through association with a new variety and also supports the variety concerned through association with a known trade mark. Not everyone is happy with the way in which the requirement operates in practice. It has been pointed out that 'it is difficult to know for sure that a plant is protected if you only know the trade name.'[106] Hamrick goes on to say that whilst 'sometimes the proposed denomination is also the trade name . . . this can be rejected by the plant breeders' rights office if it is too close to an existing denomination' and that 'some breeders use codenames as the denomination for breeder's rights registration and a different name to market the variety.' This is an issue which organisations representing plant breeders are addressing.

Scope of Right Granted

Both Article 5 of the 1961 and of the 1978 Act, state that the authorisation of the breeder was needed 'for the production, *for the purposes of commercial marketing*, of the reproductive or vegetative propagating material, as such of the

---

[106] Hamrick, *The State of Breeder's Rights* (FloraCulture, 2004).

new variety, and for the offering for sale or marketing of such material.' The right, therefore, was to prohibit others from *commercially* using the protected material, the notion of what is commercial being limited to the act of selling or marketing in the sense of holding the material out as being available for sale. The right to use the material non-commercially, that is not to sell it, was not affected.

Article 14(1) of the 1991 Act, which sets out the scope of the right granted, does not restrict the right of the breeder merely to the commercial marketing of the protected variety, but covers most uses of the variety from production and conditioning, to offering for sale, selling, exporting and importing, and including the stocking of a protected variety for any of those purposes.

Both the 1978 and 1991 Acts allow a party to extend protection 'in particular to the marketed product', to provide additional protection for ornamentals. In addition, Article 14(2) specifically extends the right set out in Article 14(1) to harvested material (which includes entire plants and parts of plants) where this has been obtained through the unauthorised use of propagating material of the protected variety. Any use of this material will require the authorisation of the breeder unless 'the breeder has had reasonable opportunity to exercise his right in relation to the said propagating material' and thereby exhausted his rights over it. This right is subject to Articles 15 (exemptions from the right) and 16 (exhaustion of rights). This broadens considerably the protection afforded by a UPOV right.

The 1991 Act further provides an option, within Article 14(3), allowing parties to extend protection to material derived from the protected variety. As will be seen in the next chapter, the Community Regulation does include such a provision, but at the time of writing it remains unclear as to how, and to which types of material, this provision will apply. At the national level, this option has not been exercised by any party.[107] In addition, the 1991 Act permits parties to include acts in addition to those outlined in Article 14(1); however, where this occurs, attention has to be given to both the exemptions to the right and the exhaustion of the breeder's right.

As will be discussed further below, the 1991 Act now specifically deals with the derogations from the right as opposed to the practice under the 1961 and 1978 Acts where the ability to use protected material without authorisation was by inference rather than express sanction. A further example of the change to the scope of the right granted produced by the 1991 Act is that whilst the use of the variety as an initial source of variation for the purpose of creating new varieties is not an infringement of the right and this principle remains core to the UPOV system, it has been refined to take account of 'essentially derived' new varieties. This will be discussed further below.

---

[107] This was introduced primarily at the behest of the French perfume industry: see Ardley, above n 75.

Duration

Once granted, the rights lasted under the 1961 Act for not less than 18 years for vines, forest trees, fruit trees and ornamental trees (including rootstocks), and 15 years for all others. The use of language here is interesting in that the Act mandates the minimum period of protection not the maximum. Article 8(3) enabled parties to adopt a period longer than that set down in Article 8(1) in order to take account of external regulations relating to the production or marketing of the variety. Although not specified as such, these could be seen to refer to those external controls which are required to assess the market worthiness of the variety which might serve to decrease the actual length of protection available to the breeder.

Under the 1978 Act, the duration of protection is the same as that under the 1961 Act, but whilst the text reiterates that protection should not be less than either 15 or 18 years according to the plant material concerned, it does not contain an equivalent statement to that in Article 8(3) of the 1961 Act relating to the ability of parties to expand the duration of protection provided. The implication therefore is that the set duration is the stated term, although the fact that the requirement is to protect for not less than that period does not preclude an extended duration.

The 1991 Act changes the position. It now specifies that the right shall be granted for a fixed period which is not less than 30 years for trees (with the removal of the specific reference to forest, fruit and ornamental trees) and vines, and 25 years for all others.

Territoriality of Grant

The right is a local right—there is no such thing as a UPOV right granted and enforceable by the UPOV Office. Instead, the rights are local rights granted by national offices which have effect within that jurisdiction. The only pan-jurisdictional plant variety right is that provided under the Council Regulation on Community Plant Variety Rights, which provides a right enforceable in all EU member states. The one thing these national rights have in common is their adherence to the UPOV provisions.

Cancellation or Voidance of the Right

A breeder will bring to an end the period of protection by failing to provide the necessary information, documentation or material (such as the seed or reproductive material of the protected variety) which verifies that the variety as protected remains distinct, uniform and stable, if they fail to pay the necessary fees to keep the right in force, or if, in the absence of providing a suitable denomination, no alternative suitable denomination is proposed.

Derogations/Limitations to the Right[108]

The UPOV system contains two central derogations to the right. The function of these is to ensure that there is a proper balance between protecting the interests of the breeders and those of end users. The first limitation allows other breeders the right to use protected varieties in commercial breeding programmes. The second permits farmers to retain seed from one year to the next without having to pay an additional royalty. Both of these have undergone extensive revision in the most recent UPOV Act in order to take account of the changes to both the nature of plant breeding as well as the end use. As will be seen, the general principle of free access and use both remains. However, the 1991 UPOV Act extends the rights of a breeder to varieties which are essentially derived from their protected varieties, and it permits parties (which so wish) to curb the scope of the farm saved seed provision.

The Research/Breeder's Exemption

Arguably the more important derogation is the breeder's exemption. This permits breeders to use protected material for research purposes even where there is a defined commercial objective to that research. Where the research leads to a new variety then the breeder of that new variety can claim rights over it without having to obtain permission from the first breeder. This exemption is regarded as particularly beneficial to small to medium-sized enterprises because it means that any barriers to engaging in plant breeding are fairly low. In particular, it will allow a breeder to 'build on the value of foreign-bred varieties [a vital new source of biological diversity], and produce locally adapted varieties which are an improvement on both foreign bred and existing local varieties.'[109]

The three Acts are in accord with regard to the underlying principle, although they vary in the language used.

Article 5(3) of both the 1961 and 1978 Acts states that the authorisation of the breeder is not required for the use of the protected variety 'either for the utilization of the new variety as an initial source of variation for the purposes of creating other new varieties or for the marketing of such varieties.' The Article goes on to say that authorisation will be necessary where the protected variety has to be repeatedly used for the commercial production of the other variety. In this qualification to the exemption can be seen the emergence of what has become the essentially derived variety provision discussed further below.

---

[108] It is also relevant to note that the UPOV Convention merely sets out certain acts which a breeder is permitted to do, and parties may, in addition, adopt other measures which restrict access to protected material, such as those being developed under the CBD and International Treaty on Plant Genetic Resources.

[109] Jördens, *Plant Biotechnology Developments in the International Framework*, proceedings of the WIPO–UPOV Symposium on Intellectual Property Rights in Plant Biotechnology, October 2003.

The 1991 Act provides more detail, and Article 15 sets out those research acts for which the authorisation of the breeder is not required. Article 15(1) contains the compulsory exceptions and these all relate to research use.[110]

Article 15(1) states that three types of activity will not require authorisation:

(i)  acts done privately and for non-commercial purposes;
(ii)  acts done for experimental purposes; and
(iii)  acts for the purpose of breeding other varieties

In respect of this latter right the breeder of the new variety is permitted to produce, market, offer for sale, sell import and export the variety. This right to use for commercial breeding purposes is however circumscribed by the need to show that the resulting variety does not fall within the EDV provisions in Article 14(5).[111]

The first two qualifications to the rights are common to a raft of intellectual property rights, including many patent law systems which also permit the unrestricted use of patented material for private, non-commercial use and experimental purposes.[112] There is no equivalent provision to Article 15(1)(iii). The question which concerns breeders is whether the patent law provision would permit the free use of patented technology within a commercial breeding programme (which may take up to 15 years to complete) or if the breeder will have to pay an agreed royalty for that use, as there is clear commercial intent.

The change to the previous position can be found in the last sentence of Article 15(1)(iii) and the circumscription of the right where the breeding programme results in the production of an essentially derived or dependent variety. As will be seen in chapters 8 and 9, for breeders it is the relationship between the breeders' exemption and the EDV provision (contained in Article 14(5)(a)(i)) which causes most concern.

Essentially Derived and Dependent Varieties

Article 14(5)(a) states that the rights granted under Article 14(1)[113] shall also apply in relation to:

---

[110] Art 15(2) contains the provision which can be applied to farm saved seed.

[111] Notwithstanding the apparently clear language of both the 1978 and 1991 Acts, there apparently has remained some confusion over the nature of both exemptions and, in 2004, the UPOV Office issued a clarifying statement. This stated that Art 15(1)(iii) is to be read as meaning that authorisation of the breeder is not needed where protected material is being used for the purpose of breeding other varieties, nor for the marketing of any resulting varieties. Where the 1978 Act is concerned, this exemption does not apply where the repeated use of the variety is necessary for the commercial production of another variety (Art 5(3)), and the 1991 Act extends this further to any essentially derived varieties: see www.upov.int.

[112] While the EPC (Art 69 and Protocol) specifies that the scope of the right is determined by the terms of the claims, the acts constituting infringement are found in the CPC (Arts 25–28), the exceptions being specified in Art 27.

[113] This sets out the scope of the right, which primarily relates to production, conditioning, offering for sale, selling, exporting and importing, and stocking a protected variety for any of these purposes.

(i)    varieties which are essentially derived from the protected variety, where the pro-
        tected variety is not itself an essentially derived variety,
(ii)   varieties which are not clearly distinguishable in accordance with Article 7[114]
        from the protected variety and
(iii)  varieties production whose requires the repeated use of the protected variety.

Generally speaking, there is little concern over either (ii) or (iii). These basically
extend the right of the breeder of an initial variety to any variety bred using it
where that second 'variety' cannot be distinguished from it (using the principles
enshrined in Article 7) or where the reproduction of the second variety is contingent upon the continued use of the initial variety. The critical (and new) provision) is that within subparagraph (i), the extension of rights to material which
is essentially derived from the initial variety.

The objective lying behind the provision is to prevent breeders 'freewheeling'
on the back of research work undertaken by others and stop what is in effect a
'substantial copy'[115] of the initial variety being marketed as something different.
As Koller has stated, this:

> principle . . . is taken from patent law and takes into account the fact that new tech-
> niques will make it easier to change a variety, resulting in a distinctive and protectable
> variety while keeping the necessary characteristics which are important for its eco-
> nomic exploitation. This regulation should limit the consequences of breeders' privi-
> lege where . . . a breeder takes economic possession of the breeding success of another
> breeder with small expenditure.[116]

The nature of the right is such that it is for the breeder of the initial variety to
identify that an EDV might exist and to take any necessary action against the
breeder of the EDV.

The provision was introduced to solve three problem areas. The first relates to
an increase in the number of varieties being produced, the distinctiveness of

---

[114]  This sets out the distinctness criterion.

[115]  The notion of 'substantial copying' is not new in intellectual property law. As will be seen
below, the modern use of the purposive construction in patent law has the effect of extending the
rights of the patent holder to material which is not wholly identical to the patented invention but
which, nonetheless, achieves the same technical function. In copyright, protection extends to material which has the effect of expressing the same creative concept but is not an exact copy. In both
patent law and copyright, as now in plant variety rights, it is impossible to define what is a substantial copy, and the issue of when a copy is a non-infringing work is the subject of intensive disagreement amongst many academics and practitioners.

[116]  'Plant Breeders' Rights: An Effective Legal Protection of Plant Varieties', *Proceedings of the
Conference on Plant Intellectual Property within Europe and the Wider Global Community*
(Sheffield Academic Press, 2002) 81, 85. In this, Koller is drawing on the notion of technical 'equivalence' (subject to the sensitivities mentioned in ch 3 over using this term), which is often used in
patent law to determine whether, where two ostensibly different inventions do the same thing, the
second invention is based on a new way of looking at the same problem or if it is an obvious variant. Whether the obvious variant is captured by the first patent will depend on the extent to which
the two correspond in fact and the scope of claims deployed—but if it is an obvious variant then
even if the initial patent does not apply, no second patent can be secured.

which is purely cosmetic—in other words, there is no genetic distinctiveness between the initial and second varieties. The second is that genetic distances between varieties are becoming increasing small and both breeders and granting offices are finding that varieties are being presented as 'distinct' which are in fact very close to varieties already protected (this is proving to be particularly problematic in respect of ornamentals and fruit trees). The third reason is the increased use of genetic engineering. Modern biotechnology means that a breeder can, for example, make single gene changes to a plant whilst leaving the remainder of the plant unchanged. The result is a variety which is in effect a clone with only a single gene differentiation and yet this is being presented as sufficiently different to the unaltered plant to warrant protection. Article 14 marks a difference between the 1978 and 1991 Acts. Under the 1978 Act, the breeder of any new variety is free to exploit that variety commercially irrespective of the genetic distance or proximity of the two varieties. In contrast, the 1991 Act (and CPVR) curbs this freedom and states that the right to commercialise may be exercised only if the variety concerned is not essentially derived.

Article 14(5)(b) provides a definition of an essentially derived variety. It states that a variety shall be deemed to be essentially derived from the initial variety when:

(i) it is predominantly derived from the initial variety, or from a variety that is itself predominantly derived from the initial variety, while retaining the expression of the essential characteristics that result from the genotype or combination of genotypes of the initial variety,

(ii) it is clearly distinguishable from the initial variety and

(iii) except for the differences which result from the act of derivation, it conforms to the initial variety in the expression of the essential characteristics that result from the genotype or combination of genotypes of the initial variety.

It is clear from the wording used that a number of conditions must apply before the provision will operate:

a) the initial variety must itself be the subject of a plant variety right.
b) the derivation must have only involved that single initial variety.

All the elements must be shown. If one of them is missing then essential derivation will not have been proved.

Finally, paragraph (c) indicates the methods of derivation which may given rise to an essentially derived variety. These include the selection of a natural or induced mutant (or of a somaclonal variant), the selection of a variant individual from plants of the initial variety, backcrossing, or transformation by genetic engineering. This is not an exhaustive list. As can be seen, this is not merely a phenotypic matter but is one which can involve an appraisal of the genotype.

The critical issue is whether the two varieties are essentially the same or if they are sufficiently distinct from each other. In terms of the relationship between the EDV provision and distinctness, it is clear that these are separate concepts. As the ISF has explained, the notion of distinctness is determined by reference to a clear *difference* between the expressed characteristics of the applied-for variety and those the existence of which was a matter of common knowledge at the time of application. This issue is one which goes to *grant* and is a matter for determination by the granting office. In contrast, essential derivation depends on demonstrating *conformity* between the two varieties and *relates* to the scope of protection granted over the initial protected variety. It is, therefore, a matter to be proved by the holder of the variety right over the initial variety. These quintessential differences between the two concepts further underline, in the mind of the ISF, the reason why for the former the focus should be on evaluating the phenotype whilst in respect of the latter inclusion of an assessment of genotype might be appropriate.

That this should be the chronology is obvious once the effect of the timings is taken into account. When a variety has been deemed to be distinct etc then it is published in the official gazette of the granting office concerned. In the absence of prior published material about the variety concerned a breeder might expect the granting office to inform him that there is a suspicion that a variety is essentially derived or otherwise identification prior to an application for a breeders' right would be impossible.

There are a number of problems with this provision which relate to concerns over the definition of essential derivation, the impact on breeding programmes, and the remaining possibility that the small changes could still be regarded as providing a sufficient distance between one variety and another. As the secretary of the Dutch Plant Variety Rights Board has pointed out, this could mean that, in horticultural/ornamental terms, a variety which expresses a colour mutation which is different to that expressed by the initial variety cannot be regarded as either retaining or conforming to the essential characteristics of the initial variety and probably would fall outside the provision.[117] The question which is being asked is whether the notions of retention and conformity are to be interpreted literally. As with the novelty requirements, various organisations have sought to provide clarification on this.

The determination of whether a variety is an EDV falls to the breeder of the initial variety. It is not a matter for the granting office. There are a number of reasons why the granting offices are not responsibility for determining EDV.

The first is that granting offices are concerned with issuing rights not policing them. Acts of infringement (which the creation and use of an EDV would be) are matters to be dealt with through the courts. On this basis, EDVs should be treated no differently (the rights granted are, after all, private rights). It is far better for the breeders themselves to agree industry-specific notions of what would be an EDV and use this within the courts than to rely on a definition

---

[117] In Dutch terms this is important as the language of the Dutch plant variety rights legislation conforms wholly to the language used in the 1991 Act.

imposed by an administrative body. To this end, as we will see below, both plant breeders and organisations representing the plant breeding industry have taken a very proactive approach to developing their own definitions.[118]

The second is that whilst obviously granting offices are well placed to make determinations as to distinctness they are less able a) to determine the level and quality of the essential characteristics of one variety against another and b) to balance the competing interests of two or more breeders.

Finally, if they did undertake this task it would inevitably have the effect of raising the cost of using the granting offices. As the majority of users of the system are unlikely to rely on the EDV provision it would mean that the many would pay for a service utilised by only the few.

Determining Essential Derivation

A number of different organisations and individuals have been involved in trying to define the parameters for deciding if a variety is an EDV or not. The following is based on comments made by Joel Guiard (one of the principle architects of the 1991 Convention).[119]

Firstly, the EDV has to itself be distinct. If it is not distinct from the original variety then it is the original variety and falls within the scope of the right granted over the initial variety, and the breeder of the EDV cannot claim any rights in the variety. This raises the question of the quality or degree of distinctiveness.

Secondly, the EDV must have been developed from *a* non-EDV initial variety and not be the result of any crossing/selection involving the initial variety plus another. This requirement is important as it serves to avoid an ever-decreasing gene pool such as is likely to result from an inverse cascade effect where the concept of an EDV is held to include an EDV derived from an EDV which itself is derived from an EDV, and so on. What is interesting is that the principle clearly relates to an EDV which is derived from an initial variety and not varie*ties*. In other words the EDV has to be the result of breeding from within the plant grouping making up one variety and not the result of any breeding using more than one variety. This is important for the third criterion.

Once the proximity of characteristics has been proved the next issue is to assess whether the predominant derivation is *from* the initial variety. This requires that the *genotype* of the EDV must essentially conform to the initial variety—essentially this means that it is the same variety *but for* the characteristic which gives the EDV its distinctive quality. ASSINSEL suggested that this could be shown using either or both phenotypic characteristics or by

---

[118] The ISF, for example, has been extremely active and is actively seeking to provide guidelines as to possible thresholds prompting the use of the EDV provision. The species they have been working on include tomato, rye grass, lettuce, oilseed rape and maize.

[119] See *Plant Intellectual Property in Europe and the Wider Global Community* (Sheffield Academic Press, 2002).

identifying what it called reliable molecular markers. The objective would be to show that a conformity threshold has been met—this conformity threshold having a parallel function to the minimum distance used to determine distinctness, the difference between the two being that the latter is intended to demonstrate divergence and the former convergence.

Finally the EDV must be predominantly derived from the protected variety, which means that there must be a clear phenotypical link between the initial variety and the EDV which inextricably connects the EDV to the initial variety and to no other. All these elements have to be shown.[120]

Article 14 provides a non-exhaustive list of some of the types of breeding practices which might give rise to an EDV but, as Guiard states, too much emphasis should not be placed on the *way* in which the EDV has been produced. He provides an example:

> when you consider . . . making a cross between two varieties and then two back crosses afterwards; the average of the genome of the varieties we can be obtained are statistically 75%. But when we observe the progeny, we could have a variety which can be very close to the initial variety, but then others could be far removed from the initial variety. The method itself is not enough to declare that the variety is an EDV.

That said, he recognises that 'some methods make it easier to get an EDV in comparison to others.'

Further factors which need to be borne in mind are: a) that there is no proscribed threshold for determining when a variety is an EDV (for example, exactly how much must the genotype of the EDV mirror that of the initial variety, 100 per cent, 99 per cent, 80 per cent or 50 per cent?), and b) whether the transmission of a single, but trait-important, gene would be sufficient to create an EDV.

It is recognised that it would be impossible to have a single standard applicable to all species. Instead, a standard of derivation will have to be decided upon on a species-by-species basis. Such an approach would again correspond to the principle of permitting distinctness to be proved if the variety can be shown to

---

[120] Not all parties to UPOV have implemented identical requirements. The Australian Plant Breeder's Rights Act 1994, for example, requires that the variety, in addition to being predominantly derived and retaining the essential characteristics of the initial variety, must not exhibit any 'important' features which can serve to differentiate it from the initial variety. In this the Australian system is apparently unique. According to the Standing Committee on Agriculture and Resource Managements within the Department of Agriculture, Fisheries and Forestry, 'important' probably denotes 'significant changes that affect performance, value or place in the market.' The Act also goes further than the minimum requirements set down in Art 14 of UPOV (which is permitted by the language used in the 1991 UPOV Act), and therefore both national European plant variety rights laws and the Community Regulation, as it mandates that such characteristics as 'heritable traits . . . that contribute to the principal features, performance or value of the variety' are essential characteristics (s 3(1)); that the important (non-cosmetic) differences must be demonstrated (by the holder of the right over the initial variety) if EDV is to be proved and finally that the Plant Breeders' Rights Office should make the (preliminary) decision regarding determining if an EDV exists.

be distinct within certain parameters of genetic variation within the plant grouping concerned. The degree of variation permitted is determined by UPOV and national granting offices, taking into account the characteristics of the differing species. It would be strange if the same sensibility to genetic variation within a given species was not also taken into account when deciding essential derivation.

The balance which has to be struck in defining an EDV lies between protecting breeders against an increased proliferation of varieties which are effectively the same as varieties they have spent time and effort developing and making breeders unnecessarily cautious over pursuing a breeding programme where the research focuses on utilising a variation within one initial variety.

There is also the issue of the burden of proof placed onto the holder of variety rights over the initial variety. Some feel that this could be too great to discharge, and the ISF has recommended that where a breeder has provided reasonable evidence (by way of demonstrating strong phenotypic similarity, or only minor variations in inherited characteristics or a strong genetic similarity[121]) that a variety is essentially derived then a reversal of the burden should take place. If this occurs then it will be up to the second breeder to prove that his variety is not essentially derived. In making the determination, it is clear that, in contrast to the determination of compliance with the granting criteria, there is an expectation that DNA technology will be used to determine genetic equivalence.

The introduction of this provision has met with strong approval from within the plant breeding community as it is thought to have 'the potential to drastically decrease the risk of plagiarism' since it is not seen as detrimentally affecting the breeders' exception. Breeders remain free to use protected plant varieties within breeding programmes. The effect of the introduction of the EDV provisions, however, places an additional responsibility onto the shoulders of a breeder who uses a single variety as the initial source of genetic information in the breeding of a second variety, and indeed, in 2003 at its Bangalore meeting the ISF stated that even though there are not yet any universally agreed rules on what is an EDV, 'the concept has already greatly contributed to avoid infringement, breeders being more careful in their breeding programmes.' This underlines that it is the responsibility of a breeder to make sure that what is produced at the end of the breeding programme is a variety which is sufficiently distant from the initial variety to fall outside the concept of an EDV, 'the aim . . . was to say that the breeder had to consider the EDV question before delivering the variety or during the breeding programme.' In contrast to determining grant, which is decided by the granting office, the issue of whether a variety is essentially derived or not is something to be proved by the breeder who is claiming that an EDV has been created using his protected variety.

---

[121] The language used by the ISF is that only one of these should be shown before the reversal takes place.

Indeed, this principle now forms a cornerstone of the ISF, which states that its goals include 'striving for a strict interpretation of the exceptions to the breeder's right; a strong, practical and enforceable [essentially derived variety] system, a better protection of parental lines that have not been sold, exploited or otherwise disposed of, and ratification of the 1991 Act by all UPOV Members.'[122] The Convention contains no statement on whether the provision applies retrospectively to rights granted before the Act came into force. The ISF has recommended that any variety rights granted before a member state has implemented the 1991 UPOV Act should be treated as independent and not subject to the new stricture. There has been no official comment on this suggestion.

In order to try and actively engage with the concepts, organisations, such as ISF, and companies, such as Group Limagrain, have sought to provide their own clarification on essentially derived varieties.

In 2002 the ISF agreed a Code of Conduct for establishing essential derivation and in June 2005 it published further principles relating to situations where the derivation is from an as yet unprotected variety and introduced a Regulation for the Arbitration of Disputes concerning Essential Derivation (RED).[123] However, the main interest rests in the Code.

The Code consists of a threshold (seven for the squared Euclidean distance between pairs, using 60 plants per variety, with a five primer combination, and a testing protocol provided by the ISF) and four principles. These are that:

— In the case of any doubt, the breeder of the initial variety should have the squared Euclidean distance between the two varieties measured and where the distance is less than seven the ISF should be asked to arbitrate, which may result in a reversal of the burden of proof. If this happens then the breeder of the alleged EDV will be required to show that his variety is not the result of work involving essential derivation from the initial variety. In making their assessment the arbiters may also seek to check that the initial variety is not itself essentially derived.

— The Code only applies to varieties which are commercialised or registered after the Code comes into force, but clearly those varieties which are the subject of breeding programmes but not yet commercialised at the time the Code comes into force will be caught by it.

— The threshold may be refined to take account of molecular data, and to facilitate this, the Code will regarded as in transition for a period of five years

---

[122] www.worldseed.org.

[123] *Ibid*. The use of the Regulation is not mandatory but it does go a long way to helping to determine if an EDV situation has arisen. For example, it establishes that the burden of proof is reversed (the rights holder must demonstrate essential derivation) but that where the genetic conformity meets the threshold for EDV then the breeders of the 'putative EDV has to prove that it is not essentially derived', and it establishes that both phenotypic and molecular information needs to be supplied. The ISF is also in the process of producing specific EDV guidelines for individual species such as lettuce, and policies on EDV plus the Regulation on Arbitration, are intended to be used in conjunction with these.

(until 2007). During this transitional period any company which adheres to the Code must not claim any dependency rights over any EDVs which are commercialised or registered for the first time during the first two years of the life of the Code. When this occurs those companies concerned must also agree that the EDV involved will be compulsorily licensed from the owner of the initial variety for a royalty of 50 per cent, provided that this results from normal commercial practices and the EDV (over which dependency rights cannot be claimed) is commercialised or registered for the first time during the subsequent three years.

— Finally, after this period of five years, a review will take place of the threshold and any necessary revisions will be made. Following this assessment the Code will come into full force and the owner of the EDV will be able to exercise his full rights as set down in the national laws.

This Code has in general been welcomed by plant breeders and it has been used as a foundation for other proposals. For example, in a statement issued in September 2003, Group Limagrain prefaced its comments on EDVs with a statement in bold that it had 'unreserved support for the principle of essentially derived variety' and also that it has a 'constant commitment at [the] professional level for the implementation of the concept of essential derivation.' In seeking to achieve a professional consensus Group Limagrain is 'collaborating with other seed companies to find fair solutions that stress priority for a free acceptance and adoption of this legal concept by the profession, rather than implementation imposed by the courts.' It is in this spirit that Group Limagrain put forward its ideas of how the concept *could* be defined—in so doing it draws upon the ISF Code.

Group Limagrain has proposed a species-by-species approach with the following common elements:

— the use of 'proven and reliable technical and statistical methods' to determine genetic similarity;
— that within any given species comprehensive knowledge must be available about all commercially available genetic variants;
— that the application of the EDV provision must evolve and not remain a static notion as that would 'maintain a status quo that is the result of past practices and technical possibilities' rather than recognising modern advancements; and
— that the application of the concept must take into account 'the need for competition between the various entities involved in the field of agriculture' (and it can be presumed, by extension, to apply to pharma as well).

Finally Group Limagrain says that when making the determination there must be a recognition of the 'priority to be given to professional expertise when resolving differences' and that 'it should be the breeders themselves that solve any differences.'

The focal point for putting these principles into practice has been a paper produced by ASSINSEL (before it merged with FIS to create the ISF) and at present these proposals provide the benchmark against which the current discussion is taking place.[124]

ASSINSEL suggests the use of distance co-efficients which measure the genetic proximity or otherwise of material. At the time of publishing its paper, ASSINSEL had only been working on distances established by molecular markers, but it reported that it would also be possible to establish a distance co-efficients using phenotypic markers as well. However, there were concerns that these would not prove as suitable as using genotypic markers as these could be swayed or obscured by reasons such as environmental factors, and expense. The implications of these principles have been studied by the various ASSINSEL section groups (which are defined according to species). Each group recognised that the determination of the appropriate threshold and construction of the distance coefficient will vary according to the species concerned, so there can be no single standard.

In making a proposal as to how to apply the provision, ASSINSEL suggested that there should be two thresholds: the first determines that a variety is not essentially derived, the second determines that it is. The way the two operate is that if one threshold is met then this indicates that the other cannot be met. As it is likely that the determination of whether a variety is an EDV will not always be clear cut, ASSINSEL suggests building a gap between the two thresholds. This will indicate that in certain instances a variety may fall between the two and be neither clearly derived nor clearly non-derived. As a result of this, three zones are produced.

The first zone, where the variety is not essentially derived, is the green zone. If the work of the second breeder falls into this zone then he is free both to pursue the research and to exploit the resulting variety.

The third zone is the red zone. This is where the variety is clearly an EDV and whilst the breeder may freely pursue his breeding programme he may not exploit the resulting variety unless permitted to do so by the owner of the initial variety.

The second zone is the orange or amber zone. If there is any doubt as to whether the variety falls into the first or third zones then it will be considered within the orange zone. It is in respect of the orange zone that negotiations and arbitration will need to take place. As ASSINSEL recognises, such an apparently simple way of demarcating between types of variety is not so straightforward in practice as agreement has yet to be reached on defining the thresholds for zones one and three, and it is recognised that ultimately the validity of any threshold set will be a matter for the courts to decide.

---

[124] The position paper can be found on the ISF website at www.worldseed.org/Position_papers/ derive.htm.

In terms of the impact of the EDV provision on breeding practices, ASSINSEL was of the view that these should be regarded positively as the provision will focus the breeder's attention more closely on matters such as:

— the choice of parents and any legal barriers to use;
— the type of breeding method used (the use of traditional methods based solely on backcrossing, etc, being more likely to give rise to an EDV than uses of modern gene technologies), although ASSINSEL was very careful to reiterate the key role that traditional breeding methods have and will continue to have in plant breeding programmes. The organisation is merely highlighting the fact that these methods used alone could cause problems;
— the need to produce technical information not only in respect of the specific variety in question but also to help define the thresholds to be used. This would enable the breeders to have a good knowledge of the phenotypic, molecular and physiological variability of those varieties already on the market as well as providing a profile of this genetic material, its breeding history and any documentation relating to access.

Breeders are also to be encouraged to use breeding notebooks outlining the details of specific breeding programmes. This will provide information as to parental lines and breeding methods. These can be seen as equivalent to the laboratory notebooks frequently cited as indicators of good practice and used, especially in the US, to support a subsequent patent application.

The joint position reached by the Code and proposals such as those from ASSINSEL and Group Limagrain indicates that it is likely that a common, albeit very general, position is achievable. However, these are still frameworks and it remains to be seen if they can work in practice.

One thing does appear clear and that is that the evolution of the concept of EDV will be a gradual one and in all likelihood it will be determined on a case-by-case basis, possibly within a framework of a species standard.

It is interesting to note that nearly all official statements on EDV have taken a determinedly positive approach to the provision, seeing it as strengthening the rights of the breeder. Such faith in the ability of the system to achieve mutuality in practice is probably not misguided. One of the singular successes of the plant variety rights system has been its ability to balance the interests of the various parties affected by the grant of a variety right with only minimal recourse to litigation. This facet of the system is apparent in all European member states which use it and can be contrasted with the patent system, where litigation is often the name of the game. However, not all share this positive approach. As will be seen in chapter 8, many breeders are wary of the possible impact of the EDV provision on their breeding programmes. Whilst the official commentators are sensitive to these concerns their approach has tended towards achieving a co-operative resolution rather than unpicking the concerns themselves. The ISF, for example, recommends to its members that in the event that a dispute arises they should first try to find redress using the Federation's conciliation or arbitration procedures.[125] Concerns, however, do remain and this will need to be borne in mind in ensuring that the provision works as intended.

The second derogation relates to the practice of permitting farmers to retain seed from one harvest to the next for the purpose of resowing—a practice which, as the ISF notes, is as old as agriculture itself.[126]

Farm Saved Seed (or Farmers' Privilege)

The introduction of a specific right to retain harvested material for this purpose was seen as a key component in the original UPOV Convention. Its purpose was to aid the acceptance of plant protection within the farming community— the idea being that it would serve as a *quid pro quo* for growing the new plant crops. There was a fear, voiced by some policy makers in the 1950s, that farmers might be reluctant to grow new crops because of a loyalty to tried and tested varieties and that the plant property protection system should not introduce a further disincentive by requiring all further uses of the reproductive material of the plant to be subject to an additional royalty. Initially, therefore, it was decided to limit the breeder's right to commercial marketing—thereby giving rise to the twin rights, or a right to use for further breeding and the right to retain seed from one year to the next for the purpose of resowing. As will be discussed below, the removal of the reference to *commercial marketing* has broadened the scope of the right granted, with the effect of reducing the scope of permitted acts.

As mentioned above, Article 5 of both the 1961 and 1978 Acts restricted the right of the breeder to the use of the reproductive or vegetative propagating material for 'commercial marketing'. The right, by third parties such as farmers, to use the material non-commercially was not affected. This meant that farmers were free to retain harvested material from one year to the next for the purposes of sowing a new crop—this practice was commonly known as the farm-saved seed provision, or (denoting the way the provision increasingly became viewed by breeders), farmers' privilege.

The permissibility of this practice reflected the recognition that the plant variety rights system had to tread a fine line between encouraging the development of new agricultural crops whilst not alienating the farming community by presenting them with a right which encroached on their ability to use material, freely bought, for their own purposes. However, notwithstanding its central place within the UPOV system, breeders (within Europe and the US) found themselves becoming hostile to the 'privilege', as suspicions grew that farmers were retaining larger than necessary amounts of the harvested material in order to sow greater areas of land—thereby denying the breeder a further return on

---

[125] Set up under the ISF's Conciliation and Arbitration Procedure Rules.
[126] *Ibid.*

their research investment. In the absence of any internal controls on this practice, and breeders did make attempts to stem the practice by the use, for example, of hybrids bred to be sterile, they increasingly began to call for the provision
to be removed.[127]

As can be seen the 'privilege' did not exist as a specific exception to the rights
of the breeder in either the 1961 or 1978 Act; rather, it was permitted because
the right was limited to commercial marketing. The 1991 Act, in contrast,
specifically grasps this particularly contentious issue and whilst the premise is
retained, parties are given an option to restrict the practice if they wish. It is the
first UPOV Act to include a specific reference to farm saved seed.

As mentioned previously, Article 14 of the 1991 Act does not restrict the right
of the breeder to the commercial marketing of the protected variety, but gives
the breeder rights over most uses of the variety including production, conditioning, offering for sale, selling, exporting and importing. This broadens
considerably the protection provided by a UPOV-type right. However, noting
the need to protect other societal interests, the 1991 Act does not eliminate the
possibility of permitting farmers to retain harvested material from one year to
the next.

Article 15 contains the exceptions to the right. Paragraph 2 of Article 15
contains an optional exclusion. It permits member states to 'within reasonable
limits' and 'safeguarding the legitimate interests of the breeder' to 'restrict the
breeder's right . . . in order to permit farmers to use for propagating purposes,
on their own holdings, the protected variety' or a variety covered by the EDV
provisions. Aside from the requirement that the legitimate interests of the
breeder must be protected (and therefore any possibility of the restriction being
used in a way which is tantamount to an abuse must be removed) this is the same
exemption as existed under the 1961 and 1978 Acts, albeit now in expressed
form. There are a number of elements to this ability to use.

Firstly, the limitation must be reasonable. This is generally taken to mean that
there must only be reasonable use by the farmer in terms of quantity retained,
acreage sown, and return, if any to the breeder. Secondly, and defining what is
reasonable, the Article states that the use must be on the farmer's own holdings,
and indicates that it must not be a commercial use.

In addition (and this is stressed by organisations such as the ISF), this provision has to be read subject to two overriding considerations. The first is that the
option must be exercised within reasonable limits and the second is that such

---

[127] Some evidence of the impact which this practice was having on plant breeding activity can be
found in 'The Report of the UK's House of Lords Select Committee on the European Communities
on Patent Protection for Biotechnological Inventions' (HL Paper, 1994) 28. The evidence provided
by the British Society of Plant Breeders indicates (following a survey of a number of breeders) that
investment was decreasing, staffing numbers were being reduced, research work transferred to other
jurisdictions and some breeding programmes stopped altogether. The evidence also cited a small
survey of 500 farmers which found that over half (261) used farm saved seed. Of this half, 61%
retained over 50% of their crops for re-sowing, with nearly 60 farmers using 90%–100% of farm
saved seed.

use, reasonably limited, must safeguard the legitimate interests of the breeders. Any limitations, no matter how reasonable for the farmer, which do not safeguard the legitimate interests of the breeder, will not comply with Article 15. As will be seen in chapter 4, the Community Regulation has attempted to set down the boundaries within which the right to retain is permitted to operate. This provision has been adopted in part by the European Community.

In many respects the right which is given to the farmer is tantamount to a compulsory licence imposed on the breeder. In the past, where the farmer was freely able to retain the seed, this was a licence to use without compensation and, as will be seen, in those systems, such as the European model, which have reinvented the concepts in recent years, the introduction of a mandatory remuneration in respect of further sowing means that the right bears the hallmarks of a licence.

One further effect of the 1991 revision is to make it clear that the practice of farm saved seed is to be given a narrow application and that the optional exception 'should not be read . . . to open the possibility of extending the practice . . . to sectors of agriculture or horticultural production in which such a privilege is not a common practice on the territory of the contracted party concerned.'[128]

One of the misconceptions about the 1991 Act is that it removes the right to retain seed from one year to the next in its entirety and that therefore over-zealous rights holders will be able to control access to vital crop material and hold farmers, particularly those in developing countries, hostage via extortion-ate fees. The reality is that the provision applies only if the plant variety rights system of the country concerned does not include this optional provision. It is also important to remember that plant variety rights are essentially territorial. A right granted in country A which has adopted Article 15(2) does not mean that a farmer in country B which has not adopted Article 15(2) has to pay a new fee in successive years even where the plant breeder holds rights in both countries. The matter would obviously be different if the farmer were based in country A—then he would be required to pay the additional fee. National rights granted under the UPOV Convention, and under national patent law, do not extend beyond the territory of grant. This does not mean that access to material protected in one country for the purposes of use in another country might not be conditional upon further payment, but this would be an issue for determination within the contract agreeing access, and a matter for negotiation between the parties; it does not arise because the rights over that material have extra-territoriality effect.

The decision whether or not to permit farm saved seed is not imposed by UPOV (as was the case under the old UPOV Acts), but rather it now permits member states to choose how they best wish to balance the protection of the interests of the farmers and the breeders. The ability to restrict the right of farmers to retain seed was 'designed for economies where farming has become

---

[128] Proceedings of the Diplomatic Conference of 1991; see www.upov.int.

a commercial and *quasi*-industrial activity performed by a small minority of the population and where plant breeding has become an industrial plant breeder's activity.'[129] The intention is to provide member states with the opportunity to balance the local interests, access to new crops and medicinal varieties as well as environmental factors, against the interests of the breeder.

This practice can be contrasted with that permitted under the patent system. As will be shown later, the patent system permits only minimal derogations from the right granted and the right to retain seed from one year to the next is not generally one of these (an exception to this can be found in the Directive and will be discussed in chapter 7). This extends the right to permit farmers to reproductively use and reuse certain specific patented material and applies to both animal and plant material. In respect of the latter, the touchstone for the Directive is the determination of the practice as set down in the Community Regulation. However, as will be shown, whilst the exemption is contained within the Community Regulation, it has been significantly curtailed when compared with the practice pre-1994, the date upon which Regulation (EC) No 2100/94 came into force. As a result, the scope of the right, within Europe at least, can be said to have moved closer to a patent type right than previously was the case.

Other Limitations: Compulsory Licensing[130]

All three Acts allow further restrictions on the free exercise of the right, but these are subject to two conditions. The first is that the restriction must be for

---

[129] Communication from the European Communities and their member states on the Review of Art 27(3)(b) of the TRIPs Agreement, and the Relationship between the TRIPs Agreement and the Convention on Biological Diversity (CBD) and the Protection of Traditional Knowledge and Folklore, IP/C/W/383, 17 October 2002, para 87.

[130] The importance given to the compulsory licensing provision can be seen in the comments of the UK Engholm Committee, 'Plant Breeders' Rights Report of the Committee on Transactions in Seeds' (Cmnd 1092, HMSO, 1960). Whilst reiterating the need for breeders to control the issuing of licences for the reproduction and sale of their protected varieties, the Committee did not think that it would be

> wise to rely solely on this . . . We therefore recommend that the rights . . . should be exercised within the framework of a system of compulsory licences. The guiding principle we would like to see adopted is that all competent growers and sellers should have an opportunity to produce or trade in a protected variety on reasonable terms. With this limitation on the breeder's freedom of action, the system of exclusive rights which we recommend for plant varieties would be potentially less restrictive, so far as the public is concerned, than either the patent or copyright systems. We are satisfied that this is right in view of the vital importance of making new plant varieties widely available on reasonable terms. (paras 187–89)

In recognition of the importance of some species of plant, the Committee recommended that the availability of a compulsory licence should be deferred for a period no longer than five years post grant. They indicated that they felt this could apply to roses but not to self-fertilising crops such as wheat and oats. The Committee also suggests that factors to be taken into account should include opportunity to build up sufficient stock to meet the market and the nature of the market concerned (eg, is it such that a breeder might have difficulty earning an adequate reward if only royalties were available?). Critically the Committee stated that 'it would not be necessary, under this system, for

reasons of public interest. The second is that where such an additional restriction is placed on the free exercise of the right then the member state concerned must take all measures necessary to ensure that the breeder receives 'equitable remuneration'. Neither the 1961 Act nor the 1978 Act specifies the type of act envisaged, but the 1991 Act specifically relates to the restriction permitting a third party to carry out acts for which the breeder's authorisation is needed.

Article 17 of the 1991 Act states that:

(1) [Public Interest] Except where expressly provided in the Convention, no Contracting Party may restrict the free exercise of a breeder's right for reasons other than of public interest.
(2) [Equitable remuneration] When any such restriction has the effect of authorizing a third party to perform any act for which the breeder's authorization is required, the Contracting party concerned shall take all measures necessary to ensure that the breeder receives an equitable remuneration.

As will be seen in the next chapter, the Community Regulation contains a different provision.

None of the Acts specify what form the equitable remuneration should take. This is a matter for individual member states to determine and this is likely to be determined on the basis of what would be commensurate with the degree of interference to the right which the further restriction provides. An example can be seen in the Community Regulation, which specifically states that where a farmer retains seed from one year to the next then, provided that the variety concerned does not fall within a specified list, the farmer has to pay an equitable remuneration to the breeder. The matter of that remuneration has been predominantly left up to member states to determine.

A critical issue, which returns us to the rationale for the right, is the extent to which public interest plays a part in deciding whether a right should be restricted (by way of exemption or compulsory licence) or not.

### Enforcing the Right

The UPOV Office is not responsible for either granting rights or overseeing any matters relating to enforcement, licensing[131] or litigation. However, the 1991 Act does require that each member states shall 'adopt all measures necessary for the implementation of this Convention' and in particular it must provide 'appropriate legal remedies for the effective enforcement of breeders' rights'

an applicant . . . to show that the holder of the rights in a variety had abused them. On the contrary, the onus would tend to fall on the person holding the rights to show why the authority should not order the issue of a compulsory licence to the applicant.' In this the Committee was seeking to provide a similar situation to that which existed under the 1949 Patents Act.

[131] Help in negotiating an appropriate licensing deal can be obtained from organisations which both represent the interests of plant breeders in general (eg the British Society of Plant Breeders) or from bodies representing the interests of a specific group of breeders (eg the International Association of Horticultural Producers (AIPH)).

(Article 30(1)(i)). The UPOV Office does not, however, have any control over what these measures can or should be. At the Community level there is a degree of additional control, as the European Community has adopted a Directive which sets down the standards for enforcement of intellectual property rights and this includes plant variety rights. This will be discussed in chapter 4.

As the issue of enforcement is, in the main, a purely national matter, any issues relating to infringement will be dealt with by the appropriate body (in some jurisdictions this takes the form of a tribunal, appeals from which can be made via the usual court system, whilst others permit direct recourse to litigation through the courts). In terms of determining if an infringement has taken place, then this is a question of fact which requires a comparison of the protected plant material with the alleged infringing material. Where the issue does not involve essential derivation, then this is mainly a matter of phenotypic observation (and in this the issue of determining infringement can be seen to be close to that employed in copyright, where a direct comparison between the protected material and alleged copy is made). If the case does involve essential derivation, then the courts will be able to employ further genetic techniques, and the matter becomes one of technical equivalence (which is closer to the test employed in patent law). As chapter 1 explained, precisely how each member state decides matters of infringement is down to local jurisprudence although with the advent of greater Community controls, there is likely to be an increasingly important role for the European Court of Justice.

Membership of the Union

Pre-1991, membership was seen in terms of individual States acceding to and implementing the provision of the Convention. In contrast, Article 1 of the 1991 Act makes it clear that accession is also open to intergovernmental organisations and in June 2005 the European Community became the first such organisation to become a member of the UPOV Union (another group which may become a member is the African Intellectual Property Organisation).[132]

By the end of 2004, the UPOV Union comprised 58 member states, the most recent recruit to the 1991 Act being Austria.[133] It is important when looking at these figures to note that not all member states are signatories to the most recent UPOV Act. Thirty-one are signatories to UPOV 1991, 25 to the 1978 Act and two to the 1961 Act. A further 18 member states and organisations (which range from Iceland to Equatorial Guinea) have begun procedures for becoming members and another 46 are in contact with UPOV with a view to possibly becoming members (this group includes Greece).[134]

---

[132] UPOV Press Release No 65, 29 June 2005.

[133] July 2004.

[134] For a full list of these see www.upov.int. When looking at these figures, it is worth remembering that the recent growth in membership is due, in part, to the obligation set down within the TRIPs Agreement.

The lack of convergence over which Act is in force can give an impression of disharmony, for example within Europe, the Council Regulation on Community Plant Variety Rights implements the 1991 UPOV Act, whereas some member states of the European Union have either yet to adopt national plant variety rights (Greece) or still adhere to the 1961 or 1978 Acts. This does not necessarily mean that there is a problem with the provision of plant property rights *per se*, but rather that there might be other external considerations which need to be addressed before legislative action can take place. For example, is there a sufficiently strong local plant breeding base to warrant introducing national protection or are imports of plant produce being affected by the lack of protection or the lack of the right calibre of protection? Central amongst these considerations are issues relating to the impact of plant property rights on the users of the protected material and in particular on farmers. It is worth again reinforcing the point that no law operates in isolation and that whilst a particular right might be approved by those who professedly will benefit from it, there are others who regard the right as a barrier to more appropriate protection—most notably, patent protection. Their interests, especially where each side has a significant political profile, need to be balanced.

## VI. GENERAL CONCERNS OVER THE CONVENTION

The next chapter will look at how the provisions of the 1991 UPOV Act have been applied within a European context. However, there are some general concerns about the Convention which it is worth mentioning here.[135]

As has been reiterated throughout this chapter (and in chapter 1), the Convention was primarily introduced as a response to demands from agricultural plant breeders wanting equivalent protection to that provided for other scientists. Whilst the right which resulted was not intended to be solely directed to protecting the interests of the agricultural plant breeding sector, many of its provisions are seen as being more applicable to the traditional breeding results from that area and as less appropriate for other branches of plant breeding. Examples of this include the emphasis on varieties and protecting the reproductive material (and, in particular, sexually reproducing varieties). The focus on agricultural plant breeding is further underlined by the fact that nearly all the systems of protection in operation in Europe are administered by government offices charged with overseeing agricultural matters. Clearly the 1991 Act has attempted to broaden the ambit of the right by extending protection to the constituent elements of the variety and to derived material but, as was mentioned in chapter 1, the focus remains the protection of a *variety* and this is not necessarily the primary end-point for all plant research. Indeed, for those

---

[135] These concerns have been around for some time: see, for example, Royon, 'The Limited Scope of Breeders' Rights under the International Convention for the Protection of New Varieties of Plants Opinion' (1980) 5 *EIPR* 139.

engaged in producing end products, the concern is that not only is protection limited under the UPOV system, but the difficulties inherent in securing patent protection mean that there is less protection available for them.

Whilst for those entering new pharma-plant breeding, the issue of protection is a new one, for others (especially those working within the ornamental breeding sector[136]) the belief that UPOV fails to meet their needs can be traced back to the 1950s. For these breeders, notwithstanding the changes brought about by the revision of the Convention in 1991, there remain 'deficiencies . . . which need to be remedied.'[137] These deficiencies range from concerns over the cost and time involved in obtaining a right, that there remains non-conformity of provision between parties (even between signatories to the 1991 Act), that the notion of 'distinctness' is still too broadly defined and will permit cosmetic breeding around, and that there remain inconsistencies between parties with respect to which species are protected (which, in the view of CIOPORA and the Community Plant Variety Office, constitutes a breach of Article 27(3)(b) of TRIPs). There are also concerns that the protection granted is still directed to protecting the reproductive material of the variety as opposed to the variety itself, that certain notions such as what a breeder must do before his rights are exhausted are not defined and therefore remain ambiguous, that the notion of an 'effective' *sui generis* system for the purposes of Article 27(3)(b) of TRIPs is one which contains a right equivalent to a patent, and that there should be greater parity between the research exemptions in both plant variety rights and patent law. The essential derivation principle should be more clearly stated, and it is felt that some countries (although not within Europe) are using Article 15 in order to permit the unfettered reproduction of non-agricultural plant varieties (and that the principle of farm-saved seed was not intended to be used for this purpose), and that infringement procedures should be more compliant with TRIPs. In respect of a number of the points made, the approach taken will clearly depend on whether the plant variety right is to be treated as an industrial property right or not.[138] The fact that these concerns remain should not be taken as indicating that the UPOV Convention is ripe for yet further revision. There is, as yet, very little political will to introduce a fourth Act and in light of the current environment (where there remains unease in many new UPOV member states over the strength of protection provided under the 1991 Act) any attempts to begin such a process will inevitably result in an opening of a 'Pandora's box, with all the risks involved.'[139] It is expected therefore that the current, albeit uneasy, position is likely to remain for the foreseeable future.

[136] Such as CIOPORA.

[137] CIOPORA Green Paper on Plant Variety Protection, November 2002. The views of CIOPORA have not changed since then.

[138] For example, in respect of the last point, the enforcement procedures should comply with TRIPs. The relevant provision of the Agreement, Art 41, only applies to *any act of infringement of intellectual property rights covered by this Agreement.* Clearly its application will depend on whether a) plant variety rights are a form of intellectual property right and b) the reference to a *sui generis* system indicates a right covered by the Agreement.

[139] Kieweit, *Evolution of the Legal Environment of Plant Breeders' Rights* (May 2004), at www.upov.int.

## VII. CONCLUSION

Whilst there may be some who question the value of the UPOV system even they would have to acknowledge that the Convention continues to have considerable influence and, notwithstanding the increasing availability of patent protection, attracts wide usage. Those cynical about a continued need for a specific form of protection for plant varieties might argue that this is due to the lack of any viable alternative. It is true that whilst UPOV continues to grow in membership and the number of rights granted has increased,[140] it is in many respects a child of its time and area. It developed out of the needs of European agricultural plant breeders in the post-war industrialisation of plant breeding. At that time the right was constrained for the reason that most of this plant breeding activity was undertaken by publicly funded bodies. The rights were seen as critical to underpinning this public research work and it was intended that they would encourage institutions to maximise both income generation and dissemination of their research results. As the private sector has become increasingly involved to the extent that it now dominates the European plant breeding scene the rights have slowly shifted emphasis and are no less limited in scope and application. As this book will discuss, there is an issue as to whether the shift in provision, when taken with developments in patent practice and policy, serves to benefit European plant breeders.[141] However, there remain issues as to whether the evolved European model is necessarily or automatically the best system for developing countries in the 21st century—not only are their plant breeding sectors closer to those which existed in post-war Europe but also the nature of their agricultural communities differ as do their economic climates. Whatever the merits of plant intellectual property rights in Europe, care has to be taken when using the European experience as a measure of how countries should respond to their TRIPs obligation.

Back in the 1950s it was agreed that patents were not appropriate and a new form of protection best suited to the needs of plant breeders was required. The resulting UPOV Convention was constructed with the needs of plant breeders in mind and, as will be discussed later, it operates very much on the basis of involvement by plant breeders. However, it would be strange, to say the least, if those involved in setting up and administering the UPOV system, who supported the need for a *sui generis* system, rejected the notion that a new form of *sui generis* right might now be necessary to take account of the different social and industrial needs of non-European/developed country plant breeders. As Mr Justice Laddie[142] said at a meeting of the UK's Commission on Intellectual Property Rights in March 2002, it would be wrong to think that one system can

---

[140] The most recent figures provided by UPOV indicate that in 2002 there were 51,106 titles of right in force across all UPOV member states: www.upov.org.

[141] One interesting development has been a renewed commitment by some government agencies to public plant breeding undertaken for the broader communal good as opposed to private self-interest. See, eg, the statement, in 2004, from the British Biological Sciences Research Council (BBSRC) that there was an increasing need to foster public sector plant breeding.

[142] One of Europe's leading intellectual property law judges.

or should fit all. However, whilst there may be problems with the system which exists, attempts to introduce new rights, or significantly to revise the existing ones (with all the political ramifications involved), might only serve to make the position worse rather than better.

The plant breeding community has generally given an enthusiastic welcome to the changes brought about through both the revision of the UPOV and the introduction of the Community Regulation. However, there are some aspects which remain of concern, most notably the definition of essential derivation, the relationship between plant variety rights and patents, and the protection of certain elements of plants critical to value but difficult to define. These issues will be discussed further later. One additional factor needs to be taken into account and that is the precise nature of the interaction between the various international conventions and treaties on intellectual property and plant variety protection and in particular the extent to which one can dictate the operation of fundamental principles under another (an example of this is the right to use protected material freely for research purposes under UPOV and the restricted notion of research use within patent law).

One final consideration needs to be mentioned and that is the fact that with regard to the UPOV Convention, there has been continued revision of the provisions governing plant variety protection. The UPOV Convention has been revised three times since its inception in 1961, with each revision looking at the nature of the protectable material and the obligation imposed on parties as well as at the scope of the right granted. In contrast, prior to the decision to adopt the EU Directive, any changes in patent practice were achieved on a case-by-case basis. Substantively, therefore, European patent law has remained essentially static since the introduction of the EPC in 1973. There are a variety of different reasons which can be given for this and it is not intended to discuss these further other than to say, firstly, any revision at the national level would have had to be such that it did not interfere with the obligation entered into under the EPC,[143] and secondly, if revisions were undertaken in respect of one specific type of material then arguably they would have to take place with regard to other categories of protectable material. Until recently it was thought that the operation of the various patent offices, and the emphasis on interpreting within the confines of the provisions provided, could be undertaken sufficiently flexibly to ensure all inventions meriting protection were protected—however, recently it has become clear that there are categories of 'invention' which are failing to be protected and which, for various reasons, usually to do with economic value, are now deemed sufficiently important to warrant individual action within the patent system. Biotechnological inventions make up one of these categories, the other most notable category being computer-implemented inventions. The next chapter will look at the way in which the Council Regulation on Community Plant Variety Rights has built upon the UPOV principles.

---

[143] The problem this caused with respect to the drafting and desired effect of Directive 44/98 will be discussed in more detail in ch 4.

# 4

# The Council Regulation on Community Plant Variety Rights

## I. INTRODUCTION

FOLLOWING THE INTRODUCTION of the UPOV Convention in 1961 the majority of European countries introduced national plant variety laws. Since 1994, it has also been possible to acquire a Community right under the auspices of the Council Regulation (EC) on Community Plant Variety Rights.[1] Although the EU did not become a member of UPOV until 11 years after the introduction of the Regulation, the Regulation is modelled on, and intended to comply with, the 1991 UPOV Act.[2] In order to ensure that the Regulation did in fact conform with 1991 Act, in 1997 the European Commission sought an opinion from the UPOV Council and confirmation of conformity was given at a meeting of the Council in April 1997. The fact that the EU has only just become a member of UPOV is significant when looking at the emphasis given to its various international obligations, and in particular the relationship between the obligation under TRIPs and that under UPOV.

In contrast to the EU Directive there is very little documentation available which either details the background to the proposal for a Community Plant Variety Rights Regulation or critiques the resulting text.[3] There are a number of possible reasons for this.

---

[1] No 2100/94. This is the Basic Regulation. It has been revised on a number of occasions subsequently, although none of the amendments affect the substantive provision: Council Regulation (EC) no 2506/95, implemented by Regulation (EC) No 1239/95, amended by Regulation (EC) No 2506/95, *Exercise of enabling power* (Art 19, §2), Regulation (EC) No 2470/96, amended by Regulation (EC) No 1650/2003, amended by Regulation (EC) No 873/2004.

[2] As mentioned in the previous chapter, the EU became a party to UPOV in June 2005.

[3] The main official sources of information from the European Commission are two articles by Dieter Obst, who had responsibility for overseeing the introduction of the Community scheme, and papers presented at conferences in, eg, Paris and Cambridge, by officials from various national plant variety rights granting offices (most notably John Ardley of the UK Plant Variety Rights Office, who has played a pivotal role not only in the introduction and operation of the Community system but also in the revision of the UPOV Convention in 1991), as well as position (or, opinion) papers published by plant breeding companies such as the Dutch company, Zaadunie (eg, the paper presented by Urselmann on the *Proposed draft on an EEC Plant Breeders' Rights Scheme—A Critical Appraisal* presented in Paris 1989, and the work of the UK company ICI (Seeds)). For information on the preparatory work behind the Regulation, see Commission of the EuropeanCommunities, *The Draft*

The first is that the discussions for a Community Regulation took place at the same time as the drafting of the 1991 UPOV Act. As one of the functions of the Community Regulation was to correspond to the new UPOV Act, it is probable that the talks which took place in respect of the substantive UPOV revisions were deemed also to apply to the Community Regulation.

The second possible reason is that the plant variety rights system, in Europe at least, was, and is, uncontroversial and of interest to only a specialist few. The matter of introducing Community-wide protection therefore attracted only minimal attention.

The third possible reason is that the discussions surrounding the Directive attracted attention from some of Europe's leading patent lawyers, eager to be involved in the evolution of its provisions. As mentioned in the previous chapter (and reiterated in chapter 7) there was such dissatisfaction within patent law circles towards both the plant variety rights system and the exclusion of plant varieties from within patent law that there was an expectation that the results of the discussions would be a wholesale freeing up of the patent system to protect all forms of living material with no exclusions. As mentioned in the previous chapter, the corollary of this expectation was to be the demise of the plant variety rights system. If a system of protection is expected to wither and die in the face of competition from another system of protection, it is understandable that those who favoured patents over plant variety rights should show no interest in any proposals to develop plant variety rights, as these developments would be thought to have only limited use, such use itself being short-lived. As will be seen in chapter 6, this expectation did not take account of either political or scientific sensitivities towards the removal of the exclusion nor of the ability of the plant variety rights system to reinvent itself. As nearly all the academic, and most of the professional, attention was focused on the Directive, those engaged in drafting the Regulation were comparatively free to develop the system away from the glare of academic and public attention.

The reasons lying behind the introduction of the Community system were also three-fold.

The first was that membership of UPOV simply ensured that *national* provision was in line with the Convention. As already noted above, at the time that the proposal for a Regulation was introduced not all Community members had national plant variety rights and of those that had, not all were signatory to the same UPOV Act (a situation which remains today).

The second reason was that national rights are restricted to the country of grant and not available, or enforceable, at the Community-wide level. This led the Commission to decide to improve the situation by creating EC-wide

*Council Regulation on Community Breeders' Rights* (2376/IV/88–en); D Obst, *Developments in the Field of a 'European Community Plant Breeders' Rights'* (Scheme Utrecht, 1986); D Obst, *EEC Ruling in the Field of Plant Breeders' Rights* (EEC 2349/VI/88 en); and Ardley, *Proposed EC Plant Breeders' Rights Scheme—An Overview*, Paper presented in Paris, October 1989.

protection 'based on the simple idea of treating the whole Community for the purposes of plant breeders' rights as if it were a single Country.'[4]

The final reason was that, under both the 1961 and 1978 UPOV Acts, members could decide which varieties were protectable within their territory. This meant that there were discrepancies between the national lists of protectable plant material—for example, in 1986 (a time when the impetus for a Community Regulation was growing apace), broccoli could be the subject of a plant variety right in Germany but not in the UK, whilst a primrose could be protected under UK plant variety rights law, but not in Germany. The concern which this engendered was that these differences could result in a barrier to trade in varieties. As is well rehearsed elsewhere, the Commission has as its mission the removal of any perceived or actual barriers to trade.

The decision to introduce a Community Breeders' Rights[5] scheme was made in 1978 at the time of the third revision of UPOV. By 1986 it had been decided that the 1978 revision of UPOV was not sufficient for the changing needs of European plant breeders and that there needed to be both activity at the international level to secure a further revision of the UPOV Convention and, consequent on that activity, action at the Community level.

Notwithstanding the close connection between the Community right and the revision of the UPOV Convention, the first text of the Regulation (which was published in 1988) was unwieldy and to the uninitiated often confusing.[6] Two examples demonstrate this. The first draft of Article 5(2) defined the protected material as:

> any group of botanical individuals of a botanical species or sub-species which can be defined on the basis of the characteristics of the common, genetically determined expressions of the characteristics of its individuals and thus distinguishable from other groups of live botanical individuals of the same botanical species or sub-species.

As will be seen, a far less cumbersome definition than this was eventually included within the Regulation.

The second example relate to the first draft of Article 7 which required that a variety must be distinct from other varieties the existence of which is common knowledge at the time the application was made. In the first text one of the definitions given to the concept of 'common knowledge' was 'notoriously cultivated'. This highly ambiguous phrase (which conjures up visions of cucumbers or other 'botanic individuals' being prominently displayed on the front page of tabloid newspapers rather than the presumed meaning, which is prevalent advertising in trade papers and availability to the public) was, thankfully, removed from the final version. As will be seen, as the discussions leading to the

---

[4] Obst, 1986 M035/8, 2.

[5] The name change came in the 1980s although the reasons why are unclear—it could be because of the changing nature of plant breeding discussed in ch 1.

[6] The Draft Council Regulation on Community Breeders' Rights, 2376/IV/88 en.

1991 UPOV revision reached consensus on these matters, so too did the language of the Community Regulation.

In addition, as the Obst[7] papers explain, the original intention was to provide protection not only for varieties but also for new breeding processes. As will be seen, this was not included in the final text. The reasons for this exclusion are not clear but probably lie in an inability to overcome the unease felt in a) extending the right to include processes (which would be a move away from UPOV) and b) granting private property rights over traditional breeding methods (patent protection being theoretically available for non-traditional, molecular, breeding processes[8]). There may also have been some concern over clearly distinguishing between that which could be protected by a patent (non-essentially biological processes) and that protected by a variety right.

In terms of the right to be provided, the initial proposals said that it would not be restricted to the reproductive material but would also apply to 'individuals of the variety.' This later became 'variety constituents' within the final text of the Regulation (this concept is discussed below). The private use of the protected material without the consent of the breeders for research and the farm saved seed provision would continue to be permitted, but the option under the 1991 Act would be taken up and 'limits defined in such a way as to exclude certain undesirable extensions.'

Obst provides some useful comments on the proposed relationship between the Regulation and patent protection. He makes it clear that the Regulation and Directive were intended to work together in order to ensure total protection for life-forms within the EEC and also to ensure that such protection as is contained within each system will not overlap or impinge upon the rights provided by the other. However, he admitted that whilst '[b]oth initiatives have their respective merits and scopes and will in future coexist . . . it cannot be denied that there are some fields where the two instruments would overlap. It is obvious that a clear and proper delineation has to be made . . .' As will be seen from the discussions in chapter 7, this commitment to a mutual co-existence was not as evident in the drafting of the Directive and there remains a question mark over whether that 'proper delineation' has occurred in practice.

## II. THE OBJECTIVES OF THE REGULATION

The Recitals to the Regulation make it clear that the function of the Community right is multi-fold. It is intended:

— to stimulate the breeding and development of new varieties, and be available for all botanical genera and species;

---

[7] Above n 3.

[8] Art 53(b) of the EPC simply excludes 'essentially biological processes for the production of plants.' As will be discussed later, an intervention in that process could be capable of rendering it non-essential and therefore potentially patentable.

— to ensure that, where possible, a common definition of 'plant variety' should exist which applies to both patent and plant variety rights laws;

— to conform to the internationally recognised rule of free access to protected material for breeding purposes;

— to recognise that certain restrictions should be placed on the rights for reasons of public interest;

— to recognise that there is a need for farmers to obtain authorisation for the use of protected material for certain purposes; and

— to permit compulsory licensing in certain circumstances.

Article 1 further states that the right is to be 'the sole and exclusive form of Community intellectual property rights.' Articles 2 and 3 state that the Community right shall have uniform effect (Article 3), and that the Regulation shall be without prejudice to the national property laws of member states (Article 2). Article 4 establishes the Community Plant Variety Rights Office (CPVO), which is situated in Angers.[9]

The Regulation permits breeders to obtain, upon making a single application, plant variety protection 'with uniform, and direct effect in the entire Community'—that is, all 25 EU member states.[10] The scheme was not envisaged as replacing national provision, but rather as an 'additional option' for the breeder. However, choice is limited to deciding between EU-wide protection or national protection; a breeder cannot acquire both. If a national right is sought then it is enforceable only within the territory of the country granting the right. If a Community right is sought then the right is enforceable in *all* member states of the European Union. The rationale for keeping the two tiers of protection (national or European Union-wide) rested on the understanding that for some species or crops there might be a limited territoriality within which the plant variety could flourish and consequently only a limited market which the breeder might wish to exploit. There would be little point in providing a breeder with only the option of acquiring European-wide rights if the variety could only be viably commercialised in one or two countries. In addition it was envisaged that the right would not merely be available to member states of the EU, but that other 'geographically close' countries with whom Community countries trade in plant material should be able to benefit from the scheme. This was important for European countries which were not EU member states but which nonetheless had close, often formal, trade links with the EU.

Because it is meant to establish a Community-wide system the Regulation does not directly affect grants made under the national plant variety rights laws

---

[9] The Offices comprises an Administrative Council, a Management Team (including the President), a Technical Unit, a Finance and Administration Unit, a Legal Unit (and the general service units relating to Personnel and IT) and the Board of Appeal.

[10] In this the Community Plant Variety Rights Regulation achieves something which the patent system currently does not. As mentioned in ch 1, there are proposals for a EU patent which would permit Community-wide protection.

of member states. It is recognised that there may be differences between member states (the Preamble to the Regulation states that 'the content . . . [of national plant variety rights regimes] is not uniform') but the function of the Regulation is to resolve any inconsistencies at a Community rather than national level. This means that, unlike in respect of the obligation imposed by the Directive, there is no requirement for member states to amend their national laws to take account of the provisions of the Regulation.[11] However, there is indirect pressure from those involved in the system for member states to offer the same (1991 UPOV Act) level of protection. The main effect of the Regulation on member states is to require national courts to recognise and enforce a right granted under the Regulation, but this role is primarily directed towards matters of infringement. Issues relating to the validity of grant (and also nullity and cancellation) are dealt with by the CPVO. As far as any member state is concerned they *must* treat the right as having been validly granted. If there is any doubt over the validity of grant then this must be referred to the CPVO. Again a distinction can be drawn with the patent system, where (notwithstanding that the grant may have been made by an overarching body such as the European Patent Office) local courts will often look to the validity of grant. The reason for the difference is that a patent granted under the EPC is treated *as if* it were a national grant. The courts are therefore able to look to the validity of grant. However, the Community plant variety right remains a *Community* right, the validity of which is a Community matter.

Because of the close correlation between the Regulation and the 1991 UPOV Act it is not proposed to go through each and every provision (for example by setting out that which relates to distinctness), as that would mean reiterating much of what has already been said in chapter 3. Instead, this chapter will concentrate on the operation of the system, with specific reference to those provisions which build upon UPOV. For a more detailed guide to the Regulation it is advised that the Community Plant Variety Office[12] be contacted or reference made to the only existing detailed commentary on the operation of the Regulation, by van der Kooij.[13] As the Regulation has only been in force for a relatively short space of time, since 1994, there is, to date, only minimal case law, and again, as with any piece of European Union legislation, the final determinant will be the European Court of Justice.

---

[11] Art 105. For those matters relating to civil law claims, infringement and jurisdiction see Part Six of the Regulation.

[12] www.cpvo.eu.int.

[13] van der Kooij, *Introduction to the EC Regulation on Plant Variety Protection* (Kluwer Law International, 1997).

## III. THE REGULATION[14]

### Obtaining a Community Right

The Application Process[15]

In order to obtain a right, a breeder has to file an application which can be to the CPVO direct or via a national office which then passes the application on to the CPVO. The breeder is required to submit a sample of the variety and this is then subjected to a technical examination. The examination process can last from one to six years depending on how long it takes to assess if the variety is distinct, uniform and stable following repeated reproduction. The longer terms tend to apply to certain species of trees. The breeder is also required to provide a denomination for the variety and this will be examined by the Office. Once the technical and administrative procedures have been satisfactorily completed then a grant will be made. A key difference between the examination processes for plant variety rights and patents is that in order for a plant variety right to be maintained, that is in order to justify the continuation of the right, the right holder must submit material of the variety to the Office whenever requested in order to ensure the 'continuing existence unaltered of the variety.'

The Granting Process[16]

A 'variety' is defined in Article 5(2) and this mirrors the definition provided in Article 5 of the 1991 UPOV Act. Article 6 reiterates the UPOV requirements that the plant grouping must be demonstrated to be distinct, uniform, stable and new. These requirements are further defined in Articles 7–10 and whilst these are essentially identical in form and application to the UPOV provisions there are unique features.

---

[14] The Regulation has seven parts. The 1st contains the General Principles; the 2nd, the Substantive Law; the 3rd contains the provisions relating to the Community Plant Variety Office; the 4th part refers to Proceedings before the Office; the 5th to Impact on Other Laws; the 6th to Civil Law Claims, Infringements and Jurisdiction; and the 7th to the Budget, Financial Control and Community Implementing Rules.

[15] Council Regulation (EC) No 1239/95 of 31 May 1995 establishing implementing rules for the application of Council Regulation (EC) No 2100/94 as regards proceedings before the Community Plant Variety Office (OJ L 121 of 1 June 1995, p 37), amended by Regulation (EC) No 448/96 (OJ L 62 of 13 March 1996, p 3).

[16] Further underlining the relationship between the Regulation and UPOV in October 2004 the UPOV Office and CPVO signed a Memorandum of Understanding stating that they will cooperate in the development and maintenance of web-based plant variety databases with a view to maximising information available to users: www.upov.int.

Distinctness

Article 7 states that a variety

> shall be deemed to be distinct if it is clearly distinguishable *by reference to the expression of the characteristics that result from a particular genotype or combination of genotypes*, from any other variety whose existence is a matter of common knowledge on the date of application . . . (emphasis added).

Article 7 differs from the wording of Article 7 of the 1991 UPOV Act in that distinctness is to be determined by reference to the *expression* of the characteristics exhibited by the applied-for variety. The UPOV provision, in contrast, merely refers to the need to show that the variety is 'clearly distinguishable'. As mentioned previously, assessing whether a variety is distinct or not is primarily a phenotypic rather than genotypic evaluation. Obviously, the two provisions will have the same effect if the expression of the characteristics is an external, observable, expression. However, whilst the language used in the UPOV Article does not exclude the possibility of an internal (genetic) evaluation of distinctness, the reference to 'clearly distinguishable' (in the context of the trialling) implies a degree of visibility which tends to steer towards the external rather than internal. In contrast, the Regulation, with its emphasis on the expression of characteristics, more clearly permits either an internal or external expression to be sufficient for the purposes of distinctness. This could be important where the characteristic which distinguishes the variety from other varieties is not externally observable (for example, through use as a producer of antibiotics).

A further difference lies is defining 'common knowledge'. Article 7 states that distinctness is assessed according to whether the variety is clearly distinguishable from other varieties which are a matter of common knowledge at the date of application. As already mentioned in chapter 3, the UPOV concept specifies that 'common knowledge' is to be determined by reference to whether the other variety was the subject of a plant variety right or entered in an official register of the Community or any State. In one of the very few cases on the Regulation, *Comtesse Louise Erody*,[17] the Board of Appeal of the CPVO said a variety which had been offered for sale by the nursery from which it came, together with its supply to, and maintenance by, the Botanical Garden in Heidelberg, to which there was public access, meant that it was a variety of common knowledge. This extends the notion beyond that within UPOV.

---

[17] Case A–23/2002. The case also concerned the matter of whether the variety had been given a proper name in accordance with the denomination provisions. The Board ruled that, as the variety was a matter of common knowledge, and therefore no rights could be acquired over it, it was not necessary to address the question of whether the name was correct or not.

## Uniformity

Article 8 also differs slightly. It states that a variety shall be deemed uniform if

> subject to the variation that may be expected from the particular features of its prop-
> agation [which relates to the manner used to replicate it], it is sufficiently uniform in
> *the expression of those characteristics which are included in the examination for
> distinctness* as well as any others used for the variety description.

Again, this would appear to indicate a variety can be deemed to be uniform if
there is an internal conformity (possibly without a commensurate external uniformity, as might be the case if a new pharma variety was produced, the method
of propagation being genetic engineering with an accepted end result being the
provision of internal characteristics in common). Article 8 of UPOV simply
states that a variety will be uniform if 'subject to the variation that may be
expected from the particular features of its propagation, it is sufficiently uniform in its relevant characteristics.'

## Stability

Article 9 states that a variety will be deemed stable

> if the expression of the characteristics which are included in the examination for dis-
> tinctness as well as any others used for the variety description, remain unchanged after
> repeated propagation or, in the case of a particular cycle of propagation, at the end of
> each such cycle.

Again this includes the possibility of both an internal, not externally visual, stability as well as the more common external stability of distinctness across a
grouping and through generations. Article 9 of the UPOV Convention simply
states that a variety will 'be stable if its relevant characteristics remain
unchanged after repeated propagation or, in the case of a particular cycle of
propagation, at the end of each such cycle.'

In order to assess if these DUS criteria are present the Regulation requires that
a technical examination of the variety takes place.

## The Technical Examination[18]

The Office does not itself conduct any of the technical examinations; instead,
these are conducted by appropriate official bodies across the EU. In order to
help these bodies in their decision making, the Technical Unit of the Office has
produced a number of Technical Protocols which can be used alongside the
UPOV Technical Guideline to determine whether a grant should be made. The
Protocols are for use by those organisations deemed competent by the CPVO
Administrative Council to carry out the technical examination of distinctness,
uniformity and stability.

---

[18] Arts 55–57.

The Protocols consists of four Protocol groupings which cover 1) agricultural crops, 2) vegetables, 3) ornamentals, and 4) fruit. Each Protocol contains a specific set of guidance for particular species within that grouping. In agricultural crops, the species are barley, durum wheat, maize, oats, oilseed rape, pea, potato, rye, sunflower, sugarbeet components, triticale and wheat. In the vegetable grouping, the species are asparagus, Brussels sprouts, cabbage, carrot, cauliflower, corn salad, cucumber and gherkin, endive, French bean, leek, lettuce, melon, pea, pepper, radish, spinach, sprouting broccoli, calabrese, and tomato. In ornamentals the species are alstroemeria, anthurinum, bouvardia, calibrachoa, carnation, celosia, elator begonia, exacum, freesia, fuchsia, gerbera, guzmania, gladiolus l, hydrangea, kalanchoe, lily, ling (scots heather), new guinea impatiens, osteospermum, zonal pelargonium or ivy-leaved pelargonium and hybrids, petunia, phalaenopsis, rose, schlumbergera, spathiphyllum, statica, tulip, weeping fig, weigela, and zantedeochia. The fruit group contains actinindia, apple, cherry, European plum, grapevine, Japanese plum, peach/nectarine, raspberry and strawberry. Each of these sub-groupings, in turn, has it own Protocol which outlines the requirements to be met before the variety is held to be DUS.

Using wheat as an example, the Protocol for wheat states that it adheres to the technical procedures agreed under UPOV documents TG/1/3 and TG/3/11 (the UPOV technical guidelines which apply to wheat). The Protocol sets out the procedure for submitting the seed (or other material) of the variety, indicating quantity, whether any prior chemical treatment is permitted (not in the case of wheat) and identification requirements, for example, the labelling of the seed, information about the breeder, and so on. It then sets out the basis for the examination, namely the determination of the DUS character of the variety, indicating that this will be done by a direct comparison with other varieties of the same kind within that species and that varietal material is retained in a collection in order to facilitate conducting the comparison. The Protocol then moves on to more species specific matters such as grouping wheat varieties into four categories within which characteristics are known not to vary, or to vary only slightly, within a variety and so an assessment of these will be precise enough to determine if the DUS criteria are met. The four categories are 1) the pith of the straw in cross-section, 2) the presence of awns or scurs, 3) the colour of the ears of wheat, and 4) the seasonal type of the variety. These will be assessed over two growing cycles and each test will involve about 2000 plants. Where a seasonal type is involved then this assessment should be carried out on about 500 plants. For ear type the test should be carried out on not less than 200 ears. Where the variety is a hybrid then the parent lines have to be included in the test and an assessment made on about 200 plants. The observations on individual plants for the purposes of assessing distinctness should involve 20 plants or parts of 20 plants. A breeder can indicate if there is a special characteristic which will aid the determination of distinctness. The Protocol then outlines the standards for deciding DUS. For distinctness the two main methods of assessment involve evaluating the qualitative and quantitative characteristics. In respect of the former this is achieved by showing that the expression of the characteristics of the variety are not the same when assessed against the characteristics of the control varieties. In respect of the latter this is achieved by evaluating where, on a range of expression, that particular expression falls and this may either be measured or visually observed.

Uniformity is determined by a visual observation (which underlines the view that a breeder's main tools are his eyes) and involves a check for 'off-types'—that is, the number of plants which do not demonstrate the distinctive characteristic(s) (for example, for wheat the number of 'off-types' should not exceed three in one hundred). Assessing this can be done by using either type A or type B characteristics. Type A characteristics are assessed by checking for 'off-type' incidence in 20 plants—if more than three are observed then the variety is not uniform. If between one and three plants are 'off type' then an additional 80 plants will be observed. If the characteristics fall into the Office's type B group, then a sample of 2000 plants is needed. Off-types here must number no more than five in the 2000. For hybrids the extent of permitted off-types is no more than 27 in 200.

The main body of each Protocol sets out in detail those species-specific characteristics which will be used to assess DUS and it also indicates which characteristics are regarded as falling into types A or B. Characteristics include growth habit, frequency of recurled flag leaf, time of ear emergence, glaucisity of sheath, leaf and ear, length of stem ears and so on, shape of ear, colour of ear, hairiness of the convex surface, shoulder shape and width of the lower glume, and colour of grain. Annex 1 then sets out the explanation for and methods to be employed in assessing these characteristics. These include determining sample size, level of measurement and degree of visual observation for each of the characteristics outlined in the main body of the Protocol, indicating such factors as where the variety is grown (greenhouse or field, temperature, level of light and so on), and providing diagrammatic guidance for visual observations of characteristics such as thickness of straw, shape of ear, hairiness of convex surface, and shoulder width of lower glume. It then sets out the decimal code for the growth stage, with 00 being dry seed, through 11 (first leaf unfurled), 20 (main shoot), up to 91 (where the caryopsis is difficult to divide) to 99 and the loss of secondary dormancy. Also indicated is the period when it is optimal for harvesting. Annex 2 of the Protocol outlines the use of electrophoresis, prefacing its inclusion with the reminder that many UPOV parties do not like using this method as the sole determinant of distinctness and that it should only be used to complement the use of morphological or physiological methods. These are highly technical calculations and it is not proposed to outline them here. Finally Annex 3 of the Protocol contains a technical questionnaire which has to be completed by an applicant for Community plant variety rights and this is again specifically tailored to an application involving wheat.

Equally detailed Protocols exist for each of the sub-groupings within the four main groupings this means 72 Protocols in total, each of which is consistently being updated to take account of new developments within a species.[19]

Provided that there is no evidence of any lack of uniformity, the variety will also be deemed to be stable.

## Novelty

Article 10 sets down the requirements for the newness or novelty of the variety. Article 10(1) states that 'a variety shall be deemed to be new, if at the date of application . . . variety constituents or harvested material of the variety have not been sold or otherwise disposed of to others, by or with the consent of the breeder . . . for the purposes of exploiting the variety.' The Article goes on to provide the breeder with a grace period in that the variety must not have been sold or disposed of earlier than one year within the territory of the Community or earlier than four years (or six years in the case of trees and vines) outside the territory of the Community.[20] This simply requires that the plant variety has not been on the market for more than one year prior to the application being filed. As already noted, this provides the breeder with a grace period of one year within which he can market the variety before filing the variety right application. However, if he has marketed for a period longer than one year before filing he will be deemed to have lost commercial novelty.

The Regulation defines 'disposal' further. Paragraph 2 states that disposing of the variety constituents either for statutory purposes (for example to secure a plant variety right) or to others in order to produce, reproduce, multiply, condition or store the constituents is not a disposal within paragraph 1 unless this is for the purpose of using repeatedly to producing a hybrid and disposing of the constituents or harvested material of the hybrid. Equally, where the variety constituents or harvested material have been produced as a result of experimental purposes (under Article 15(b)) or for the purpose of breeding, or discovering and developing other varieties (under Article 15(c)), then disposal of these will not be regarded as a disposal under paragraph 1. In addition, the Regulation also permits disposal where this was due to or as a consequence of displaying the variety at an official, or officially recognised, exhibition.

The first sentence of Article 10(2) defines 'otherwise disposed of'. It states that where the 'disposal of variety constituents to an official body for statutory purposes, or to others on the basis of a contractual or other legal relationship is *solely* for production, reproduction, multiplication, conditioning or storage'[21]

---

[19]   The fact that the CPVO has established its own set of protocols does not mean that each member state automatically has to follow them; rather they remain free to introduce their own standards, the only caveat being that these clearly should not countermand or undermine either the UPOV or CPVO provisions. Equally, the procedural elements may differ, an example of this is the recent consultation undertaken by the UK Department for the Environment, Food and Rural Affairs as to whether applicants for protection over ornamental species should be required to provide a DUS report as part of their application.

[20]   For the purposes of comparison with patent law it is worth noting that European patent law does not operate a grace period, although a 12-month grace period does exist in US patent law.

[21]   Emphasis added.

then this is not disposal for the purposes of breaking novelty. As the requirement is that the disposal has to be *solely* for the purposes outlined above, there is an inference that such use must not be commercial in nature, or in other words that it is not use 'for the purposes of exploiting the variety.'

This appears unproblematic. However, an issue does arise when identifying which aspects of the applied-for plant variety must have been previously disposed of in order to defeat novelty. Critical to this determination is the fact that the language of the Regulation here differs from that set down in the 1991 UPOV Act.

Article 6(1) of the 1991 UPOV Act requires that the 'propagating or harvested material' of the variety must not have been sold within the stated grace period. The Regulation, however, refers to the 'variety constituents or harvested material.' It would seem that the difference in language is intended to provide a solution to the problem, identified at the UPOV level and discussed in the previous chapter, as to whether parent lines, which have been used to produce a hybrid, can be regarded as novel where that hybrid, or material harvested from it, has been previously exploited. The reason why this is an issue is due to the nature of a hybrid.

Hybrids are bred using two in-bred parent lines, and recourse to the parent lines is necessary in order to produce the hybrid repeatedly. Agreement on how to treat parental lines could not be found at the UPOV level with, as mentioned previously, ASSINSEL maintaining that their use to produce the hybrid parental lines could be treated as novel, and others, most notably the US, maintaining that they could not. The second sentence of Article 10(2) of the Regulation is intended to provide some clarification on the matter.

It states that where the variety constituents have been made available in order to be 'repeatedly used in the production of a hybrid variety and if there is disposal of variety constituents of the harvested material of the hybrid variety' then this will defeat novelty for those variety constituents (for example, parental lines). As the President of the CPVO has explained 'if a breeder "disposes" parental lines to a third party, without handing over the right of ownership to them, for the production of hybrids and basic or harvested material of those hybrids are sold, this disposal of material prejudices the novelty of the parental lines.'[22] The result is, for Community plant variety rights purposes (but not necessarily in respect of national granting practices), such use will be deemed to be novelty-defeating providing that, not only are the components of the hybrids disposed of, but also that the breeder relinquishes physical control of the parental lines. The President regards this as a 'middle way' between the position adopted by ASSINSEL and that of member states such as France and Germany.[23]

---

[22] Kieweit, *Plant Variety Rights in a Community Context* (2002): www.UPOV.org.
[23] *Ibid.*

There is a question, as yet unanswered, as to whether this complies with UPOV or if Article 10(2) provides an exception to it—the latter being predicated on the basis that protection of parental lines even where they have been repeatedly used to produce a hybrid is permitted under UPOV, but not under the CPVR. In the view of the President of the CPVO, there is nothing within Article 10(2) which contradicts Article 6 of the 1991 UPOV Act, and, therefore, Article 10(2) should be taken as an expansion, and not a contraction, of the principle.

Article 10(3) also reinforces the right to use protected material for research and breeding purposes.

Article 11 states that the person who is entitled to the right is whoever bred, or discovered and developed, the variety. Where there has been more than one person involved, then all may claim a joint title and where the breeding has been undertaken in the course of employment then the national employment laws will apply. As will be seen below there is a close relationship between this provision and those relating to distinctness (and the issue of in what context must a variety previously have been a matter of common knowledge) and novelty. Article 12 establishes that either a natural or legal person can be entitled to a plant variety right; the only requirement is that they must be domiciled or have their headquarters based in the European Union. Where the individual or organisation is based in another UPOV member state then they can also claim Community rights provided they can show that they have an agent who is domiciled within the EU.

In 2003 the Board of Appeal held that a person claiming to be the breeder of a variety of canna could not be regarded as such if the variety had not been bred by him.[24] In this case all that the alleged breeder had done was to take home some rhizomes from a garden and propagated from them. Whilst the Regulation does not provide a definition of 'discovered', the 1991 UPOV Act does provide some definition.[25] It states that the concept of discovery is activity which involves 'selection within natural variation' and recognises that identifying a new characteristic in a mutant or through an assessment of variants within an existing variety is important but this is only a potential source for improvement; the key to gaining a right over the plant material is to demonstrate that this potential has been realised through the actions of the breeder. In the case before the Board there was no evidence that the defendant had exerted even the most minimal degree of effort to bring about the variety—all that had happened was that he had been shown the variety and was given material of that variety which he then replicated. This did not give him any rights in or over the variety itself. Interestingly, the Board referred to a South African decision involving the same case.[26] In that decision the court held that 'developing a market is not the same as developing a plant.' This point, which was not echoed in the comments of the CPVO Board, could be relevant when looking at situations where a 'breeder'

---

[24] Case A–1/2004.
[25] UPOV Document C (Extr) /19/2, rev August 2002.
[26] Case No 515/2002.

purports to claim rights over a variety which is new to the European Community market but which is considered part of the public domain in a developing country.

As mentioned in chapter 1, one of the key differences between the plant variety rights system and patent law is that there is no requirement that the breeder must have engaged in 'inventive activity'. This was underlined in a decision in 2003, where the CPVO Board of Appeal stated that 'the concept of breeding . . . does not necessarily imply inventing something totally new, but includes the planting, selection and growing on of pre-existing material and its development into a finished variety.'[27]

Scope of the Right Granted

Article 13 is the first of the substantive provisions which expands upon the 1991 UPOV Act.

Article 13(2) sets out the rights held by the holder of a Community plant variety right. These are that the rights holder controls the production, reproduction, conditioning for sale, offering for sale, selling, exportation from the Community or importation into the Community and stocking of the variety constituents or harvested material of the protected variety. As can be seen, the rights granted under the Regulation are identical to those contained within Article 14 of the 1991 UPOV Act and they extend to the constituent parts of a variety, the variety itself and material harvested from that variety (rights in respect of this latter category are, however, subject to Article 14 and the farm-saved seed provisions, discussed below).

The first main point of divergence from the UPOV Convention would appear to be the use of the terms 'variety constituents' and 'harvested material' in Article 13(2). Article 14(1) of the 1991 Act simply refers to the rights of the holder over 'the propagating material' of the protected variety. Article 14(1), however, has to be read in conjunction with Article 14(2), which allows the right granted over the variety to extend to harvested material, this term being taken to include entire plants and parts of plants, which could be taken as a different way of saying 'variety constituents'. This will be discussed further later as it brings into question both how far the right should be allowed to extend and also the ability to differentiate clearly between material protected by a plant variety right and that protectable under patent law. It is in paragraphs 4, 5 and 8 that Article 13 really expands upon UPOV.

Article 13(4) states that the protection set out in paragraph 2 may be extended to material/products produced from material of the protected variety. This adopts the option set down in Article 14(3) of the 1991 Act. This is subject to conditions which mainly relate to obtaining these products through unauthorised use. To date this provision has not been invoked, but if it were then it could

---

[27] Case A–17/2002 *Sakata Seed Corp v SVS Holland BV.*

be used to protect essential oils for use in perfumes[28] or medicinal/herbal products.[29] Van der Kooij makes the point that the language used in Article 13(4) is rather unclear and that for full compliance with the equivalent Article in UPOV (Article 14(3)) it should have read 'products obtained directly from *harvested* material of the protected variety.'[30]

Article 13(5) states that protection under Article 13(2) extends to any varieties which are 'essentially derived' from the protected variety and sets down the conditions necessary for determining whether a variety is essentially derived or not.

Article 13(8) introduces a new factor for consideration by breeders, namely that specific attention is drawn to the fact that the actual use of the protected material may be dependent upon other, external factors, such as the protection of public morality, public health and the protection of the environment. The Article makes its clear that the grant of a right is not dependent on the external factors being present but rather it serves to merely draw the breeder's attention to the fact that such factors may exist. Their application, however, is a matter for other bodies. This can be contrasted with the equivalent provision in patent law, where the grant itself is dependent on showing that the invention is not contrary to morality, and so on.

Article 14 relates to farm saved seed and takes up the option provided in Article 15(2) of the 1991 Act to 'restrict the breeder's right . . . to permit farmers to use for propagating purposes, on their own holdings, the product of the harvest which they have obtained by planting, on their own holdings,' but also takes into account the need to safeguard 'the legitimate interests of the breeder.' In introducing this provision, the Regulation has adopted a unique, tiered system of entitlement. This entails both the provision of a royalty to the breeder and unencumbered use by the farmer, both elements being dependent on certain factors (discussed in more detail below).

Article 15 limits the right granted in respect of private, experimental or commercial breeding use (discussed in more detail below).

Article 16 covers exhaustion of rights—such rights having been deemed to come to an end when the breeder placed the protected material into the market—the principle of exhaustion being held not to apply where the material so placed is further used as propagating material (unless this propagation was the purpose for which the material was placed into the market) nor to the export of variety constituents into a third country where no rights are available. Where the export is for consumption purposes then the ordinary rules on exhaustion apply. This will be discussed further below.

---

[28] See Ardley, 'The 1991 UPOV Convention: Ten Years On' in *Proceedings of the Conference on Plant Intellectual Property within Europe and the Wider Global Community* (Sheffield, Academic Press, 2002) 74.
[29] For a further discussion of this see Llewelyn, 'European Plant Intellectual Property' in Johnson and Franz (eds), *Breeding Research on Aromatic and Medicinal Plants* (Haworth Press, 2002) 389.
[30] van der Kooij, above n 13, p 32.

Articles 17 and 18 relate to variety denomination, and as this requirement is the same as that under UPOV, it will not be discussed further.

The right lasts for up to 30 years for trees, potatoes and vines and 25 years for all other varieties. The rights granted do not extend to preventing the use of the protected variety for private purposes nor, more critically, does the right prevent the use of the protected variety for breeding purposes.[31] There is a right to appeal both a grant and a refusal to grant, but both of these are subject to time limitations.[32] Once a right has been granted the holder may protect it via the national courts (which, as already mentioned, are required to treat the right as valid[33]). Article 94(1) also sets out the basic principle that a rights holder has a right to reasonable remuneration where there has been an infringement of his right, even where the infringer used the protected variety in good faith. The simple requirement is that the person using the protected variety must not have been entitled to do so (Article 94(1)(a)). However, the extent to which the infringer is liable will depend on the type of use and its effect. Where infringement has been intentional or the result of negligence then the rights holder is able to claim more in the way of damages than if the use was innocent.

A number of key issues arise out the Regulation which have a relevance at both the internal and external levels. These are:

— a sole and exclusive industrial property right
— protectable and protected material—cumulative protection?
— protection of products directly produced
— essentially derived, approximate and dependent varieties
— morality
— farm saved seed
— exempted activities
— the compulsory exploitation right
— exhaustion of Rights
— who is a breeder?

Some of these issues have also been raised by the breeders and organisations representing them (in particular, the notions of essential derivation, research use and the compulsory exploitation right).

---

[31] Art 19.
[32] Art 67.
[33] Arts 94 and 105.

## IV.  KEY ISSUES

### Sole and Exclusive Right

Article 1 of the Regulation states that the protection provided under it shall be the 'sole and exclusive form of Community industrial property for plant varieties.' Two important points need to be made in respect of Article 1.

The first is that this is the first time that the right (in any of its guises, UPOV or national) has been formally stated to be an industrial property right. This is an important development for it both sends the clear signal that this is a right on a par with the patent system, but also means that the right could be taken to be subject to the same overarching considerations. In particular, this could be taken to mean that protecting the interests of the holder is paramount and the right should not be unfettered other than *in extremis*. This, of course, could have considerable significance for the restrictions to the right (such as the breeders' exemption and compulsory licensing) which were introduced to serve a defined public interest role. An interesting question (and one which falls outside the scope of this book) could be asked as to whether the specific use of the term 'industrial property' could be taken to prevent a future introduction of an *intellectual* property right for plants based on copyright law.[34] As a point of contrast, the EU Directive makes no mention of the provision of an 'industrial property' right but rather confines its references to 'patent law'.

The second relates to the reference to the right as the sole and exclusive form of industrial property protection for plant varieties. This appears to say that no other form of industrial property protection is permitted for plant varieties other than protection under the Regulation. This clearly sits easily with the patent practice (adopted by the European Patent Office in its 1999 decision in *Novartis*,[35] and reiterated in the EU Directive) of confining the exclusion from patent protection to varieties as defined within the plant variety rights system. However, the effect of the reference may not be as simple to describe as this and it has to be read in the context of what follows next in the Regulation.

Article 1 states that the right is to be the sole form of Community protection. Article 3 states that the Regulation 'shall be without prejudice to the right of member states to grant national property rights for plant varieties.' This is important because without this caveat the Regulation would effectively prohibit the use of existing national plant variety rights systems and that was not the intention of the Commission.[36] The implication of Article 1 would therefore

---

[34] Such a notion is not inconceivable although it is unlikely. In the seminal text, Laddie *et al*, *The Modern Law of Copyright and Designs*, 3rd edn, vol 2 (2000) ch 38, the notion of using copyright law to protect molecules is examined with a predominantly favourable outcome (albeit more theoretical than practical).

[35] [1999] EPOR 303. This is described in detail in ch 6.

[36] Even if the Regulation was intended to operate as the sole industrial property right at both the national and Community levels for plant varieties, an argument could be made that national

seem to be that it excludes the provision of another form of industrial property protection.[37] As it is unlikely that the Regulation is forestalling the introduction of a new system of variety protection, this must mean that it is excluding the possibility of an existing form of industrial property right being extended to include varieties. As it is also unlikely that this is intended to refer to the copyright system (which, although mooted by some as a possible form of protection for scientific results,[38] has not been mooted as a method of protecting varieties), this means that the prohibition relates to the provision of patent protection. However, when looked at closely, the language used within the Regulation does not in fact prohibit the use of patent protection.

Article 1 refers to the Regulation as providing the 'sole and exclusive form of *Community* industrial property rights.' This means that it prohibits the provision of another industrial property right where that right is also a *Community* right—that is, a right introduced using Community legislation with Community-wide application granted by a Community Office. If this is the correct reading to be given to the reference to Community right, then it does not preclude the use of either national patent laws to protect plant varieties (even where those national rights are prescribed by Community legislation, for they remain national not Community rights), nor would it prevent the acquisition of a European patent granted by the EPO, as this also does not result in the provision of a Community right. As will be discussed in chapter 5, the EPC is not an instrument of the EU (it stands alone and is wholly autonomous). It does not provide a European right (in the form of a right enforceable across all of its member states), but rather produces a bundle of national patents enforceable in those countries designated in the patent application. It does not provide a Community industrial property right.

The only Community legislation which might be affected by the prohibition in Article 1 is the proposed EU patent.[39] The proposal is for the introduction of a system which will permit a single application to give rise to a right which is enforceable in all EU member states—a Community right. The effect of Article 1 would mean that even if there were a political will to include plant varieties as patentable subject matter (for example, as part of the proposed EU patent) then the draftsmen would not be able to do so as the grant of a patent would be the grant of a Community right.

This reading of Article 1 is supported by both Article 3 (which simply refers to the ability of member states to 'grant national property rights', but does not state that the national property right granted has to be a plant variety right) and

provision is normally not in the form of an industrial property right, but rather as an agricultural right and as such existing national provision is unlikely to fall foul of the Art 1 prohibition of other forms of industrial property protection.

[37] Other than a national plant variety rights system, even where that system is regarded as an industrial property right.

[38] See Laddie *et al*, above n 34, ch 38.

[39] Above ch 1, n 162.

Article 92, which precludes the granting of both a national and a Community right.

## Article 92—Cumulative Protection?

As already noted, the Regulation was drafted to ensure compatibility between Community provision and the protection accorded under the 1991 UPOV Act. The correlation between the 1991 Act and the Regulation is not absolute, however. The 1991 Act is silent on the matter of patent and/or plant variety protection whilst the Regulation appears to both anticipate the availability of both but equally rejects the possibility of cumulative protection at the EU level.

As Article 1 refers only to the provision of a *Community* right (and not to a national property right, industrial or otherwise) it is possible to argue that the Regulation would not prohibit member states from protecting plant varieties under another national system of protection, for example patent law. This reading is supported by Article 92 of the Regulation.

Article 92, which is entitled 'Cumulative Protection Prohibited', states that:

1) Any variety which is the subject matter of a Community plant variety right shall not be the subject of a national plant variety right *or any patent* for that variety. Any rights granted contrary to the first sentence shall be ineffective.
2) Where the holder has been granted a right as referred to in paragraph 1 for the same variety prior to grant of the Community plant variety right, he shall be unable to invoke the rights conferred by such protection for the variety for as long as the Community plant variety right remains effective. (emphasis added)

Article 92 clearly refers to the possibility of acquiring either a patent or a plant variety right over a particular plant variety. Its effect is to prevent any other national right being obtained (or retained), whether in the form of a patent or a national plant variety right, over a variety for which Community protection has also been secured. If Article 92 was not intended to be taken to refer to the possibility of both a patent and a plant variety right being available then why specifically prohibit cumulative protection under both systems? The prohibition on cumulative protection only makes sense if both forms of protection can or could be accumulated.

When taken in the context of the Article 1 prohibition, the position under the Regulation appears clear. The only form of Community protection for a plant variety is that provided under the Regulation. This does not prevent the provision of national patent or plant variety rights protection but where that protection is available then, depending on when that right was granted, the Regulation will have one of two effects. If the right was granted after the Community right, then the national right *shall be ineffective* (Article 92(1)). If, however, the national right was granted before the Community right then the holder loses his right to invoke the national right *for as long as the Community plant variety right remains effective.* In theory this permits the national right to lie dormant for such time as the Community right is in force. In practice, however, it would be very unlikely, for reasons of cost, that the national right would be kept alive (unless there was a question over the commercial viability of the protected variety at the Community level) and the effect would be that the national right would probably be allowed to lapse.[40]

Obviously there are some countries around the world which do permit the grant of either a patent or a plant variety right or both; the US is the obvious example, but the Regulation is not intended to apply to these countries. It is specifically intended to 'create a Community regime which . . . allows for the grant of a industrial property rights valid throughout the Community.'[41] Article 92 can only be read, therefore, as anticipating the situation where it is possible to obtain a valid national patent over a plant variety within the European Community.[42]

The issue of dual protection also arises when looking at the material protected by a plant variety right.

### Protectable/Protected Material

In terms of what is protected, the matter of how to define a 'plant variety' has been discussed earlier and it is not proposed to rehearse those arguments again here. It is, however, worth noting that whilst much play has been made of what is a 'plant variety' for the purposes of determining what is capable of being protected by a plant variety right, the Regulation extends the debate by referring to broader notions of plant material which are also covered by the right.

Article 13 of the Regulation makes it clear that the right extends both to the variety constituents and to any harvested material (the latter extension being subject to the provisions of Article 14[43]). The Regulation does not define 'variety constituents'; however, a leading commentator on the Regulation takes the

---

[40] A nice question does arise: if a member state did provide patent protection for varieties and a breeder first secured national patent protection and then Community protection for a variety, and he could keep the patent 'alive' (through paying renewal fees) but did not enforce the patent right (on the grounds that this would be contrary to Art 92), could a competitor request a compulsory license for that variety on the basis that there was not a proper working of the patented variety— even if there was a full commercialisation of the variety as protected by the Community right? This is extremely unlikely to occur in practice because of the cost of maintaining both the patent and Community right, but it is nonetheless of academic interest.

[41] Preamble to the Regulation.

[42] On the basis of the example set by the plant variety rights system it might have been thought that the draftsmen of the patent Directive would have taken advantage of the opening offered by the Regulation and also allowed for the possibility of patenting plant varieties. However, as will be discussed in ch 7, it is clear from the text of EC Directive 98/44 that the concern to ensure parity between the EPC and the Directive took precedence over any wish to align the Directive and Regulation. The text of the Directive therefore reiterates the exclusion on patenting plant varieties contained within Art 53(b) EPC.

[43] The 'farm saved seed' provision.

view that the fact that the Regulation contains the terms 'variety constituent', 'propagating material' and 'components' and uses them 'inconsistently' throughout the Regulation indicates that there is some interchangeability. For van der Kooij, this indicates that the intended meaning lying behind one (to ensure protection extends protection beyond the grouping as a whole) can encompass all three.[44] In the absence of a clear definition for each it is hard not to agree. On this basis it follows that the terms are intended to refer to those elements of a plant which are capable of reproducing the distinct, uniform and stable plants which, collectively, form the variety. This means that 'if a single plant cell were capable of producing an entire plant, a grouping of such plant cells would be treated in the Regulation as "variety constituents"'[45] and therefore be protected by a right granted under the Regulation. If this is an accurate interpretation of the term then there could be a conflict between the patent system and plant variety rights, as clearly the granting of a patent over a single plant cell capable of producing an entire plant could be regarded as the granting of a patent over variety constituent which is protected by a grant of a plant variety right. The issue here is whether the notion of what is protect*able* under plant variety rights—plant groupings which are distinct, uniform and stable—is the *only* concept against which the patent law exclusion is to be tested and not that which is actually protect*ed* under plant variety rights, namely the constituent elements of the distinct, uniform and stable plant variety?

Whilst there may not be any concern in principle over cumulative protection (for example, the same information is often concurrently protected by patents, copyright and trademarks), that there has been such an emphasis on the disparate nature of the subject matter protected by a patent and that under a plant variety right means that a justifiable concern can be raised. It would seem that there is the possibility of both rights being used to protect the same material, in respect of the patent, the right over the plant gene being actively sought as the subject matter of the patent, and in respect of plant variety rights, the plant gene being protected as a result of the grant of rights over a distinct, uniform and stable plant grouping. A question which remains is whether, if van der Kooij is correct in his interpretation of the term 'variety constituent' (and it would appear consistent with the thinking behind both Grubb's understanding of the term 'micro-organism' discussed in chapter 2, as well as a scientific understanding of what is a variety constituent[46]), the fact that both a patent and a plant variety right can protect a particular plant gene means that dual protection is, in reality available under both systems. This, in turn, is subject to a number of important questions.

---

[44] It is not clear why this change has been made, but it could be because it was recognised that the term 'propagating material' carried overtones of traditional plant breeding and did not reflect the more modern practices.

[45] van der Kooij, above n 13.

[46] And indeed, as will be seen in ch 7, the rationale behind Art 12 of the EU Directive in respect of compulsory cross licences.

The first is whether the issue of dual protection applies only to the seeking of rights as opposed to the subject matter of the right once granted. Is it only prohibited to seek both patent and plant variety rights for the same material? If that is the case then Article 92 will not apply, as clearly it is not possible to seek plant variety rights over a plant gene. However, if the issue is one of ensuring that the same subject matter is not protected under both systems, then that which is protect*able* becomes secondary to that which is protect*ed*. The Regulation clearly extends protection beyond the grouping to those constituent parts, the genes, which provide the grouping with its distinct, uniform and stable characteristics. There is, therefore, an obvious overlap between that which is protected by a patent and that under plant variety rights. The only difference being that under patent law, plant genes are both protect*able* (in that protection can be sought for a gene) and protect*ed* (as a plant gene), whereas under plant variety rights only plant groupings (which are distinct, uniform and stable), are protect*able* whilst the constituent parts of the plant grouping (which can include the plant genes) are protect*ed*.

This bring us to a deeper question which is whether there is a conceptual difference between a variety and the constituent elements which make it up or can the two be regarded as synonymous? On the one hand, it is difficult to separate the grouping itself from the elements which give it the distinct, uniform and stable characteristics requisite for the grant of the right to be made. On the other, there would seem to be an obvious distinction in that one is a grouping of complete individuals which express the requisite characteristics whilst the other is merely one source or factor giving rise to those characteristics. The Regulation is one conferring plant *variety* rights, not plant material rights. However, it does enable protection to be obtained over those elements making up the material. This implies a degree of confusion as to what the right protects and what in practice is protected.

This is potentially an important issue not least for the application of Article 92, which refers to dual protection for plant varieties. If this concept is purely taken as referring to plant groupings when taken collectively (in other words, plant groupings for which protection may be sought) then dual protection for the constituent parts will not be prohibited. However, Article 92 also states that 'any rights granted contrary' to the prohibition will be ineffective, which appears to be a post-grant issue. As the above argument makes clear, the effect of a grant of plant variety rights is to protect more than just the variety. If the prohibition applies to that which is actually protected then dual protection for plant genes (at the national and EPC levels), where these are capable of giving rise to whole plants which may form a variety, will be prohibited. The use of 'variety' within Article 92 would appear to indicate that it is an additional right over the plant grouping which is not permitted. This would mean that a breeder could acquire both a patent and a plant variety right which in effect protects the same material. Some might find this to be too monopolistic. However, if the latter reading is given to the prohibition then this could have quite serious implications for existing patent law policy and practice in cases where a breeder holds a national or EPC patent over a gene which is later incorporated into a variety protected by a Community right.

It is likely that, for pragmatic reasons, Article 92 will be simply taken to refer to cumulative protection over a variety as such and not to the acquisition of any national rights over the constituent parts of the variety. However, the language of the Regulation, when taken in the context of what the right serves to do overall, does remain open to this additional interpretation.

There are issues which also arise in respect of the extension of protection to other material.

## Extension of Protected Material

### Protection of Products Directly Produced

Article 13(4) permits the rights granted under the Regulation[47] to extend in 'specific cases' to 'products obtained directly from the material of the protected variety' (Article 13(4)). However, at the time of writing no decision to implement this provision in practice has been taken. If it were to be utilised then it could provide protection for such derivatives of plants as essential oils (used in the perfume and aromatherapy industries) and medicines (for example, herbal remedies and vaccines)[48] where the use is unauthorised and the breeder has not had a reasonable opportunity to exercise his rights over the variety from which the material has been derived. It is widely assumed that this provision was incorporated at the behest of the perfume industry, but the fact that it has yet to be put to use indicates that there is both legal and scientific sensitivity to extending protection to derived products. In raising this it is important to draw a distinction between other varieties which are essentially derived from a protected plant and distinct products, such as oil, which have been derived from those plants, as the function of plant variety rights has always been to protect the variety as bred by the breeder, no more and no less. As the discussion of the Paris Convention in chapter 3 (and revisited in chapter 5) has shown, products derived from plants have been thought to be protectable by an industrial property right in the form of a patent. However, it is possible that the Regulation, which is overtly stated to contain an industrial property right, is now intended to serve as an industrial property right in the tradition of the Paris Convention suitable to protect those plant-related products described in Article 1(2) as industrial property. Whatever the intention behind the extension of protection, the fact remains that the provision has yet to be invoked and there is little indication that this will happen in

---

[47] To produce, reproduce, condition for sale, offer for sale, sell (or otherwise market), export from the Community or import into the Community and stock the variety constituents or harvested material of the protected variety—Art 13(2).

[48] For example, crops bred to produce vaccines for tuberculosis and malaria.

the foreseeable future, leaving such material ripe for patent protection (if the threshold for protection can be met).[49] If the provision is invoked in the future then it could have great significance for the new vaccine crops (and the new pharming industry in general) in a way in which the plant variety rights system has not had to date. The extension of protection would mean that a single grant could protect the plant genes (as variety constituents), the variety itself and the product (vaccine) directly produced—which might make the system more attractive than having to combine patent and plant variety protection. Of particular relevance here would be the impact of any decision to use the plant variety rights system's overarching public interest provisions, especially as the pharmaceutical industry is more used to the patent system.

At present, the extension of protection under either Article 92 or Article 13(4) is hypothetical, and it is the other, actual, extensions of the right granted which have caused the most concern to the plant breeding community. It is these, together with changes to the public interest derogations/limitations, which reflect the move closer to a patent-type right.

**Essentially Derived, Approximate and Dependent Varieties**

As discussed in the last chapter, in a move away from the previous Conventions, the 1991 UPOV Act allows parties to extend the protection conferred by a variety right to essentially derived varieties and to varieties which are either approximate to or dependent upon a protected variety. Again it is relevant to note that this change, which has been adopted via the Regulation, does not appear in earlier UPOV Acts and that a number of national laws of the EU are still based on these earlier Acts. However, this does not mean that these countries can ignore the Community provision.

Essential Derived Varieties

Article 13(6) defines an essentially derived variety. It states that a variety is essentially derived if: a) it is predominantly derived from the initial variety or if it has been derived from another variety which is predominantly derived from the initial variety; b) it is distinct in accordance with the provision relating to distinctness (Article 7); and c) notwithstanding that it accords with the requirement under Article 7, it nonetheless conforms to the initial variety in its essential characteristics. This generally corresponds to the definition used within Article 15 of the 1991 UPOV Act, although there is a difference in that Article 13 does not make any specific reference to the derived variety having to retain the expression of the essential characteristics that result from the genotype or combination of genotypes of the initial variety nor that it should conform to the

---

[49] See Llewelyn, above n 29.

initial variety in the expression of the essential characteristics that result from the genotype or combination of genotypes of the initial variety.

As with the UPOV provision, it is clear from the wording used that a number of conditions must apply before the provision will operate. The breeder must be able to show that his protected variety is not itself an essentially derived variety and that whilst the claimed EDV appears distinct from his initial variety it nonetheless conforms to the initial variety in its essential characteristics. Some indication as to how this might be determined in practice has been given in the previous chapter. In terms of a general policy, the critical element appears to be that the EDV must be shown to have retained the essential characteristics of the initial variety. The Regulation, however, does not make retention of those essential characteristics a requirement. Instead, Article 13(6) merely requires that it must be shown that the alleged EDV was predominantly derived from the initial variety and conforms in its essential characteristics to that initial variety. Here it is the genotypic elements of the plant as opposed to phenotypic which are regarded as crucial to establishing essential derivation.

The effect of Article 13(6) is to require that the holder of a plant variety right over the initial variety has to give his approval for any commercial use of a plant variety bred using his protected variety where that is deemed to have been essentially derived from his initial variety. The lack of a more precise definition as to what is an essentially derived variety has caused problems. As mentioned in the previous chapter there have been concerns that very minimal changes, such as a colour mutation, could be sufficient to allow what is in effect an EDV, to fall outside the provision and that there needs to be greater clarification as to what this provision will mean in practice.

The burden of establishing if an EDV has been created lies with the breeder of the initial variety. As this is, therefore, a matter which goes to infringement (and is not a formal issue for granting offices to concern themselves with) the question of how to define the concept is being left to plant breeders and other relevant organisations to determine. Notwithstanding the fact that they have not been formally required to be involved in the discussions over the application of the essential derivation provision, both the UPOV Office and Community Plant Variety Office are engaged in ongoing discussions to resolve any concerns plant breeders have. The most recent discussion took place at the UPOV Office in September 2002.[50] As will be seen, the lack of a more precise definition is enabling the development of an agreed framework for determining 'essential derivation' which is more flexible and evolutionary than arguably a hard and fast definition contained within either the UPOV Convention or the Regulation would have been.

A further reason for the lack of a definition is that this is a matter to be established once a right has been granted, and therefore goes to the issue of infringing uses, which is a matter for the courts to decide. It is because this is a

---

[50] Details of the discussion can be found at the UPOV website, www.upov.int.

matter which goes to infringement that all EU member states will be bound to decide matters relating to EDV. As mentioned earlier, all member states of the EU are required to enforce a right granted under the Regulation. This means that even in those countries which do not have an essentially derived provision within their national law (for example, because their law is based on the 1978 UPOV Act) then notwithstanding this the local court will still be required to make a determination as to whether the alleged EDV is essentially derived or not.

To date the only recorded judgment is a provisional one delivered by the Civil Court of the Hague in 2002.[51] The case concerned three varieties from the species *gypsophila*. Two of the varieties, 'Blancanieves' and 'Summer Snow', were owned by a Dutch-based plant breeder, and both varieties were the subject of Community plant variety rights. The third, named 'Dangypmini', was owned by a breeder based in Israel and it too was the subject of a Community plant variety right. It was claimed that both 'Blancanieves' and 'Summer Snow' were essentially derived from 'Dangypmini'. Two DNA tests had been carried out on 'Blancanieves' and it was claimed that these tests proved that 'Blancanieves' was 'a mutant' of 'Dangypmini'. The Dutch-based breeder brought that case before the Civil Court. In its provisional judgment the court held that, as no DNA tests had been presented in respect of 'Summer Snow', there was no evidence to show that it was a mutant of 'Dangypmini' and therefore 'it is assumed that all actions of Party B with respect to "Summer Snow" are wrongful.' In respect of 'Blanacanieves', the court said that the question was whether 'the harvested material of that variety resembles the original variety as far as the expression of the characteristics resulting from the variety "Dangypmini" are concerned.' The court noted that:

apart from differences in the genotypes of the two varieties, the phenotype of 'Blancanieves' differs from that of 'Dangypmini' on several points according to the test results presented . . . the Court qualifies these characteristics as essential characteristics, resulting from the genetic material of 'Blancanieves' which are not present in 'Dangymini'. Party B has not persuaded the Court that these essential differences are related to the act of derivation . . . . [c]onsequently it is assumed, provisionally, that it is not probable that 'Blancanieves' is a mutant of 'Dangypmini' [and therefore it is not] covered by the scope of the breeders' right granted to the breeder of 'Dangypmini'.

Unfortunately the court does not provide any further detail for its reasoning.[52]

---

[51] *UPOV Gazette No 94*, December 2002, 7.

[52] The effect of the introduction of the EDV provisions is to place an additional responsibility onto the shoulders of a breeder who uses a single variety as the initial source of genetic information in the breeding of a second variety, and indeed in 2003 at its Bangalore meeting, the ISF stated that even though there are not yet any universally agreed rules on what is an essentially derived variety 'the concept has already greatly contributed to avoid infringement, breeders being more careful in their breeding programmes.' This underlines that it is the responsibility of a breeder to

Approximate Varieties

Article 13(5)(b) extends the rights granted to the breeder to varieties which approximate to the initial variety. This is to prevent breeders abusing the research provision (discussed below) which permits the free use of protected varieties for further breeding programmes but does not give the holder of the right over the protected variety any rights over any resulting variety. The function of the provision is to ensure that breeders do more than make mere cosmetic changes to an existing protected variety. The object is to prevent breeders from claiming that such cosmetic changes render their variety distinct (and therefore a new variety which can itself be protected by a variety right) and allowing them to market that variety in direct competition to the originating variety from which it is not, other than in purely superficial aspects, any different or distinct (Article 13(5)(b)). The problem is determining the degree of development necessary in order to show that the two varieties are not essentially the same. In many respects, this equates to the old-style minimum distance requirement which required a breeder, in order to establish distinctiveness, to show that there was a distance between the characteristics of his variety and those of other varieties within the same genus or species.

Dependent Varieties

Article 13(5)(c) prevents breeders from producing varieties the repeated reproduction or multiplication of which can only be achieved through continual use of another breeder's variety or varieties. In other words, a variety bred using another breeder's protected variety must be free-standing by the end of the breeding programme. Its continued existence must not be dependent on the continued use of the parent varieties. The rationale behind this function is to encourage developments or improvements in plant production which demonstrate a move away from existing plant varieties. The development of a plant variety which remains dependent on the parent varieties is not an improvement on those varieties.

As will be seen there is a direct correlation between the extension of protection to essentially derived, approximate and dependent varieties and the right to use protected material freely in research. As will be seen in chapters 8 and 9, the main concerns about these provisions lie in their potential impact on research. In terms of their value to the breeder holding the right over the initial variety, then these provisions have been generally welcomed by breeders as strengthening the right granted.

---

make sure that what is produced at the end of the breeding programme is a variety which is sufficiently distant from the initial variety to fall outside the concept of an EDV, 'the aim . . . was to say that the breeder had to consider the EDV question before delivering the variety or during the breeding programme.' www.worldseed.org.

The extension of protection to essentially derived varieties as well as to those which approximate to the protected variety and those dependent on the initial variety for continued production have resonances with the patent system. Under patent law, careful wording of the claims, together with the purposive approach[53] taken to construing the claims, will ensure that the patent extends to anything which, in technical terms, is essentially the same as, or approximates to, the invention claimed. It is also possible to draw an analogy between the extension of protection to dependent varieties and the extension of patent rights to products produced using a patented process. In the instance of a dependent variety, obviously a process is not being used but rather a protected product, but as in the case where the use of the patented process gives rise to a right over a product produced using that process, one can see a similar thinking in the plant variety rights where no process claims are permitted, but the use of a protected product (the variety) can give rise to the production of a second product (the dependent variety). As a result, where the repeated use of a protected variety is necessary for the production of another variety, it is accepted that the inventive acumen of the initial variety breeder, which is so necessary to the production of the second variety, should be rewarded over that of the second breeder who has been unable to develop a manner of producing the second variety without repeated recourse to the protected variety.

## Morality

Article 13(8) states that the exercise of a Community plant variety right may not

> . . . violate any provisions adopted on the grounds of public morality, public policy or public scrutiny, the protection of health and life of humans, animals or plants, the protection of the environment, the protection of industrial or commercial property, or the safeguarding of competition, of trade or of agricultural production.

The first thing to note is that, unlike in patent law, the issue of whether a plant variety, or use made of that variety, is immoral is not relevant for the purpose of either securing or of retaining a plant variety right. All it relates to is the exercise of the protected variety post-grant. This means that a breeder has to be aware of other possible constraints which will affect his ability to exploit, or otherwise use, the protected variety. Neither the determination of what these might be, nor their relevance for the purposes of granting a variety right, is seen as a matter for the plant variety rights system, but is rather a matter for other external regulation which might control the use of the protected plant variety.[54]

---

[53] As will be discussed in ch 6, the purposive approach means that the claims will be read against what the patentee intended to claim as opposed to a strict literal interpretation of what has been claimed.

[54] Examples of these include the European Council Directive 2001/18/EC on the deliberate release into the environment of genetically modified organisms, and Council Regulation (EC) 258/97 concerning novel foods and novel food ingredients.

In terms of the relationship between this provision and the UPOV Convention, it can be seen that Article 17(1) of the latter simply states that '. . . no Contracting Party may restrict the free exercise of a breeders' right unless such use would not be in the public interest.' There is no definition of 'public interest' but it would be logical to infer that any use which could cause harm to the environment or to human or animal life would fall within the concept of not being in the public interest. What the Regulation has done is to go further than UPOV and link the concepts of public interest and morality.

There is a lesson to be learnt for the patent system from this approach to morality for, as will be discussed in the next set of chapters, the requirement in the EPC that morality should form part of the pre-grant process has caused many problems. Both Article 27(2) of TRIPs (the language of which is mirrored in Article 13(8)) and Article 13(8) of the Regulation provide routes by which issues relating to morality can be or are removed from the framework of intellectual property protection. The option provided within TRIPs and the example provided by the Regulation might have offered a more sensible approach to the issue of morality. As will be seen in chapter 7 even where there was an opportunity for a non-EPC form of words to be used within EU patent law this was not taken.

It is not proposed to discuss Article 13(8) any further.

### Farm Saved Seed/Agricultural Exemption[55]

Another significant development following the revision of the UPOV Convention in 1991 is the limitation given to the right of farmers to retain reproductive material of the protected variety from one year to the next for the purpose of resowing. This is often called either farmers', or the 'farm saved seed', privilege. In contrast to the 1978 UPOV Act, which provided an explicit farmer's use exemption, Article 15(2) of the 1991 UPOV Act merely states that parties may, *if they wish*, restrict the right granted—it is an optional exclusion.

Article 15(2) states that:

> a Contracting Party may, within reasonable limits and subject to the safeguarding of the legitimate interests of the breeder, restrict the breeder's right in relation to any variety in order to permit farmers to use for propagating purposes, on their own holdings, the product of the harvest which they have obtained by planting, on their own holdings, the protected variety or a variety covered by Article 14(5)(a)(i) or (ii).[56]

Article 14 of the Regulation[57] makes full use of this option and provides a unique tiered system under which a breeder can claim royalties over the retention of harvested material of the protected variety for resowing by the farmer.

---

[55] This is the term used by the Community Office.

[56] This covers essentially derived or approximate varieties but Art 15(2) does not apply to dependent varieties.

[57] As implemented by the implementing rules on the agricultural exemption to Community plant variety rights provided for in Art 14 of the Basic Regulation: Commission Regulation (EC) No

In apparent keeping with past practice, paragraph 1 states that farmers may retain harvested material from one year to the next for the purposes of resowing in subsequent years however, paragraph 2 circumscribes this right. Article 14(2) permits this use only in respect of certain, listed, categories of *agricultural* species. Varieties of any plant species not identified in this list, for example decoratives or crops bred for pharma, are not subject to the exemption, and a full royalty has to be paid for any subsequent use.

Inclusion on the list does not mean, however, that farmers may *freely* use any material from plant species identified on that list. Paragraph 3 makes it clear that the subsequent use of the specified plant species is itself subject to a payment, the concession given is that the payment must be an equitable remuneration *sensibly lower* than that originally paid.

The only farmers who do not have to pay any additional royalty are farmers who fall within the EU definition of a small farmer according to Council Regulation (EEC) No 1765/92. Small farmers are defined as farmers who do not grow plants on an area bigger than that needed to produce 92 tonnes of cereals.

Under the Regulation there is, therefore, a three-tiered structure relating to the right to resow harvested material.

The first tier comprises those plant varieties which may not be resown without a second full payment being made to the plant breeder; these varieties are all those which do not appear on the list making up the second tier. This is the one area where the Regulation can be seen not to be variety-neutral. Article 14 of the Regulation applies only to agricultural plant varieties; all other varieties are not subject to the farm saved seed provision. This means that any rights over varieties from species not on the list would be automatically infringed if, for example, a nurseryman kept back seed, or other reproductive material, from one year to the next for the purpose of growing further plants.

The second tier applies to varieties within certain designated species. These may be resown but only upon the payment of an equitable remuneration sensibly lower than that originally paid (that original price still being payable on those varieties not falling within the list).

The final, third, tier consists of those farmers who fall within the EU classification of a small farmer. This is defined as a farmer who does not grow more than 92 tonnes of cereals on his farm. Only this group of farmers are exempt from paying any further royalties.[58]

The reason for the change in practice is, as mentioned in the previous chapter, a simple recognition of the value lost to plant breeders through the previous

1768/95 of 24 July 1995, implementing rules on the agricultural exemption provided for in Art 14(3) of Council Regulation (EC) No 2100/94 on Community plant variety rights, amended by Commission Regulation (EC) No 2605/98. As might be expected, a number of organisations have published position papers commenting upon the revised 'farm saved seed' provision. These include the ISF (www.worldseed.org) and the European Seed Association.

[58] This classification can be criticised on the grounds that it relates only to the productivity of the farmer; those farmers who grow less than the equivalent of 92 tonnes of material, but who have the land capacity to grow more will not be caught by the exception.

practice of total exemption from subsequent payment. The level of payment has been negotiated by the relevant plant breeding authorities in conjunction with farmers' unions. The level of payment required varies both across countries and within any territory across varieties. It would have been too difficult (not least for political reasons) to either impose or secure a common royalty level across the whole of Europe. As on example of this variation, in Germany payment of a royalty is required if more than 46 per cent of farm saved seed is used, in the UK it is 30 per cent, in France 35 per cent, in Portugal 75 per cent and in Spain 88 per cent.[59] To date breeders do not appear to have experienced any problems with this variation.

It might have been thought that the curbing of the farmers 'right' to retain seed from one year to the next without having to pay any additional sum to the breeder would have been controversial. In practice, with few exceptions,[60] the implementation of a new form of farm-saved seed provision has been relatively free from contention. One of the reasons for this is the close working relations which have developed over the years between farming organisations, the representatives of the plant breeding community, seed collection agencies, royalty collection societies and plant variety rights offices. Central to this is a collective acceptance that there have been abuses of the farm-saved seed provision and a need for additional support for the plant breeding community. It would, however, be incorrect to imply that there have been no problems with this provision. In particular, the issue of how much the equitable remuneration should be has been heatedly debated and where the relevant organisations have been unable to agree a figure then the Commission has imposed the figure of 50 per cent of the original sum.[61]

In respect of justifying this (albeit minimal) restriction on the right held by a breeder, the European Commission has relied upon Article 27(3)(b) of the TRIPS Agreement.[62] What is interesting about this is that Article 27(3)(b) makes no mention of any right to restrict the rights granted under the *sui generis* system. This would seem to indicate that either the *sui generis* system should not contain any limitations to the right, which seems an unrealistic presumption, or that the *sui generis* system can contain limitations but these do not necessarily need to correspond to those which apply in patent law—in other words that the limitations can be externally sourced. The fact that the Commission makes this

---

[59] http//www.grain.org/seedling/seed.

[60] Most notably, those jurisdictions with a politically strong farming community.

[61] Commission Regulation (EC) No 1768/95 implementing rules on the agricultural exemption provided for in Art 14(3) of Council Regulation (EC) No 2100/94 on Community plant variety rights, as amended by Commission Regulation (EC) No 2605/98, specifically Art 1, which adds a new paragraph to Art 5 of Reg 1768/95. Para 5 now reads 'where . . . an agreement . . . does not apply, the remuneration to be paid shall be 50% of the amounts charged for the licensed production of propagating material.'

[62] Review of Art 27(3)(b) of the TRIPs Agreement, and the relationship between the TRIPs Agreement and the Convention on Biological Diversity (CBD) and the Protection of Traditional Knowledge and Folklore, IP/C/W/38317, October 2002, para 86.

reference to TRIPs indicates the uncertainty over not only whether the Agreement does apply to the *sui generis* system but also which provisions apply if it does. If all the provisions apply then it might have been expected that the reference would have been to Article 30. However, this appears to apply only to patents—and indeed, as will be seen in chapter 7, the Commission makes direct reference to Article 30 of TRIPs when justifying the equivalent farm saved seed provision within the EU Directive. However, even though the Agreement does not appear to apply to limitations to the *sui generis* right, nonetheless the Commission still felt it necessary to find support for its actions in respect of plant variety protection and therefore hooks the farm saved seed provision onto Article 27(3)(b). It might be wondered why the Commission did not simply state that the farm saved seed provision corresponds to that which is permitted under the 1991 UPOV Act, the provisions of this Convention not appearing to either conflict with, or be controlled by, the provisions of the TRIPs Agreement. But this might lie in the fact that at that time the EU was a member of TRIPs but not UPOV.

To date there appears to have been little in the way of backlash against either plant breeders or the plant variety rights system from within the farming community. However, it should be stressed that the full impact of the curbs on the right, not to mention any problems which might appear over policing the right, has yet to be felt. As will be noted in the responses of the plant breeders to this provision, the breeders themselves do have some concerns, but these primarily relate to the setting up of collection agencies (the monitoring of the practice is the responsibility of the rights holder: Article 14(3) (5th indent) of Regulation 2100/94) and the determination of the equitable remuneration.

### Exempted Activities

Whilst there are curbs on the rights of farmers to retain seeds there are no equivalent restrictions on the ability of other plant breeders to use protected material in commercial breeding programmes. Article 15(a)–(c) stipulates that the rights granted under the Regulation do not extend to prevent: (a) acts done privately or for non-commercial purposes; (b) acts done for experimental purposes; or (c) acts done for breeding or discovering and developing other varieties. The language of Article 15(c) differs slightly from that used in the 1991 UPOV Act most notably by its use of the term 'discovering or developing' and by the reference to 'other varieties'.

In respect of the former, Article 15 of the 1991 Act states that acts done privately and for non-commercial purposes, acts done for experimental purposes and acts done for the purpose of breeding other varieties do not require the authorisation of the breeder. No mention is made of discovering or developing new varieties using material from a protected variety. Article 15(c) of the Regulation appears to be broader in that it permits use not only for the purposes of *breeding* but also for *discovering* and *developing* new varieties. However, the term 'for the purpose of breeding' is equally broad and it is likely, in the absence of any discernible difference between breeding, discovering and developing a new variety, that this term also includes the two additional acts specified in Article 15(c) of the Regulation.

With regard to the use of 'other' when referring to the variety so bred, discovered or developed it is not clear if the resulting variety has to comply with the definition of a variety which is capable of attracting protection under the Regulation or if it can be a variety regardless of capacity to attract plant variety protection. If it is the former which is envisaged then this means that the breeding, development and discovering must take the form of the production of a variety which is new, distinct, uniform and stable. This clearly would indicate a level of activity involving the protected variety which gives rise to the separately protectable new variety. If it is the latter, then it would indicate that the variety produced might merely be something which the 'breeder' has stumbled upon, but which is not yet, or indeed may never be, capable of demonstrating the level of distinctness, uniformity or stability necessary to attract protection. As the Regulation recognises the existence of the two forms of variety it is likely that the production of a variety which will comply with the granting criteria of the Regulation is a pre-requisite to a breeder relying on Article 15(c).

The research or breeders' exemption is regarded as fundamental to the plant variety rights system and its place within the system rarely challenged. As will be seen in chapter 9, the problem which has arisen recently is the relationship between the research exemption in plant variety rights and that which exists in patent law where use for commercial research purposes is prohibited.

Article 15(d) and (e) also set out some further exceptions to the right. Article 15(d) emphasises that the right does not extend over plant varieties other than the protected variety. Therefore the right does not extend to a variety resulting from a breeding programme unless the resulting variety falls within the definition of an essentially derived variety in Article 13(5) nor does it extend to any variety or material of the protected variety if that material is protected by a property right (such as a patent) which does not contain an equivalent provision to Article 13(5). Article 15(e) also states that the rights granted do not extend to acts which would violate Articles 13(8) (morality) or 14 (farm-saved seed) or 29 (compulsory exploitation right).

### Article 29, Compulsory Licences (Exploitation)

In keeping with most other intellectual property rights, the Regulation does not permit the rights holder to be the final arbiter of who has access to the protected material. Instead, and to ensure that the rights holder does not act in an undesirably anti-competitive manner, Article 29 of the Regulation contains a compulsory exploitation right. However, this will be granted 'only on the grounds of public interest' (Article 29(1)). As will be discussed later, Article 29 has recently been revised to bring the language of the Regulation in line with Article 31 of TRIPs. Part of the revision has been to change the title of the provision from Compulsory Exploitation Right to Compulsory Licence. The effect is to imply a closer correlation between the provision and its equivalents in patent law. This is an unfortunate name change for the original title was closer to what the provision was intended to achieve. Because of the exempted acts there is no need for traditional breeders to seek a licence in order to use protected plant varieties for private, non-commercial or further breeding purposes. For these, the most likely reason for seeking a licence would be to use the protected material itself as itself (or in a sufficiently corresponding form—for example as an EDV or dependent variety) in a commercially exploitative context. However, the exempted acts may not permit the use of the protected variety in non-breeding but commercially directed research (this will depend on how the notions of production and reproduction are interpreted), and the change in title will underline that in such a context it will be possible to seek a licence if the holder of the variety right is acting unreasonably.

As discussed in chapter 1, the plant variety rights system has very strong public interest overtones (arguably more than under the patent system where the individual rights of the patent holder are paramount). Both the 1961 and 1978 Acts, in particular, specifically recognise that the exercise of the rights may be curbed in order to protect the wider public interest. This has been achieved through the research exemption, the farm-saved seed provision and the use of the compulsory licence/exploitation[63] right. This adherence to the public interest has been predicated on the belief that the interests of the breeders must be looked at alongside wider societal interests, with the latter being used to constrain the former if necessary. This same internal reference to 'public interest' is not found within patent law.

Whilst the plant variety rights system was seen as either a *quasi-industrial/intellectual* property right or an agricultural right, then the intellectual property presumption that the public interest was first and foremost protected by the granting of rights over material which met the approved threshold for protection did not have much of an impact. However, the emergence of the European plant variety rights system as an industrial property right, the EU's adherence to the TRIPs Agreement, action at the EU level on the patenting of living material and the patentisation of variety protection have all served to change the balance. This could mean that it will be increasingly difficult to rely on the public interest aspects of the Regulation to curb over-monopolisation

---

[63] The original text of the Regulation was unique in that it referred to a compulsory exploitation right as opposed to the more usual 'compulsory licence' which is used in patent law. This difference in terminology was probably due to the fact that as breeders have a right to use protected material in commercial research programme the only other circumstance when they might need to have access to a protected variety is in order to exploit it in the market place. In contrast in patent law, as there is no right to use protected material in commercial breeding programmes, a licence could be sought for commercial research purposes only, even where there is no evidence that that work will result in an actual exploitable product.

of plant material if these measures conflict with the interests of the rights holder.

Providing further evidence of the way in which European plant variety protection is going is the fact that in 2003 it was recognised that the different approaches to the provision of a compulsory licence contained within the Regulation and Directive could cause problems a) with the correlation between the Regulation and the Directive and b) with EU compliance with Article 31(l) of the TRIPs Agreement. As discussed in chapter 2, Article 31(l) states that where a licence is needed in order to work a second patent, such working being an infringing act without a licence, then the applicant for the licence has to show that the invention protected by the second patent involves an important technical advance of considerable economic importance in relation to the invention contained in the first patent. Where such a licence is granted, the owner of the first patent will be entitled to a cross-licence on reasonable terms. This will allow him to use the invention protected by the second patent. The compulsory licence can only be assigned if accompanied by an assignment of the second patent. The reason why this is relevant in this context is that licences are likely to be sought over protected plant varieties into which a patented invention has been placed.

As will be seen in chapter 7, the EU Directive uses near-identical language to Article 31(l) and stipulates that the deciding factor is whether the technology in which the patented invention has been used represents a significant technical progress of considerable economic importance. In contrast, the original text of Article 29 of the Regulation said that the grant of a compulsory exploitation licence was dependent on the public interest. Unsurprisingly, given the breeders' exemption, no mention was made of the need to provide a cross-licence where the person seeking the compulsory licence has a variety which the other may wish to use nor whether, in such a circumstance, there would be a need to show that the other variety represents a significant technical progress. Even where a compulsory exploitation right was sought to use an essentially derived variety, there was no equivalent right granted to the person seeking to exploit the essentially derived variety (who would most likely be the person who bred it) to have a cross-licence entitling them to exploit the initial variety. The sole emphasis in the Regulation was on whether the public interest would be served by granting such a licence. Because of this there appeared to be an element of imbalance between the Regulation and the Directive.

As the EU is a member of TRIPs, but was not, at the time of the revision, a member of UPOV, the primary obligation was to align its legislation, including the Regulation and Directive, with TRIPs. There was, at that time, no equivalent mandate to comply with UPOV. For this reason Article 29 was amended in 2004 to bring it into line with the language of both Article 31 and the Directive.[64] There is a question as to whether this revision complies with the UPOV obligation.

---

[64] Council Regulation No 873/2004 amending Regulation (EC) No 2100/94 on Community Plant Variety Rights came into force on 29 April 2004.

The decision to revise is an interesting one not least because the Preamble to the Regulation states: 'Whereas it is indispensable to examine whether and to what extent the conditions for the protection accorded in other industrial property systems, such as patents, should be adapted or otherwise modified for consistency with the Community plant variety rights system.'[65]

Notwithstanding that this would indicate that the later law (the Directive) should be adapted to comply with the earlier law (the Regulation), TRIPs clearly was taken to trump both the principle and the practice.

The effect of the amendment is to retitle the compulsory exploitation right a 'compulsory licence' and to align the concept in Community plant variety rights with that contained in the Directive. Article 29(5)(a) contains the new provision. In summary it states that a non-exclusive compulsory licence shall be granted to the holder of a patent over a biotechnological invention provided that the patentee demonstrates that a) they have unsuccessfully sought a licence from the plant variety rights holder and b) the invention covered by the patent constitutes a significant technical progress of considerable economic interest when compared to the protected variety. Such a licence will be subject to the payment of a reasonable royalty and limited to the territory of the Community where the patent is in force (for example, in the UK only if it is a UK patent, or in those territories designated if the patent is granted under the EPC).

Where a breeder of a new variety wishes to either acquire rights over that variety or exploit it and that breeder holds a non-exclusive licence to use patented technology in order to develop the variety, then a non-exclusive cross-licence, on reasonable terms, shall also be granted to the patent holder to exploit that plant variety.

When the discussions were held as to the possible impact of such a change, a view frequently expressed was that it could have the effect of undermining the public interest basis for the grant of the licence. It is reassuring for those who were concerned about this that the revised Article 29 begins with the same statement made in the original Article 29(1) that a compulsory licence will only be granted on the grounds of public interest and this is reiterated in Article 29(2). The question posed by the new language used in Article 29(1) is whether the public interest element has to be shown in all the circumstances covered by the Article or whether it merely applies to the granting of a licence over protected plant varieties but does not apply in the other two instances described in Article 29(5)(a) which relate to the granting of a compulsory licence or compulsory cross-licence to a patent holder.

In addition, Article 41 of the Commission Regulation (EC) No 1768/95 states that public interest is to be assessed on the basis of i) the protection of life or health of humans, animals and plants, ii) the need to supply the market with material offering specific features or iii) the need to maintain the incentive for continued breeding of new varieties. These provisions could be crucial when

---

[65] There is no equivalent statement within the Directive.

assessing the extent to which the limitations to the right can be used to curb an over-zealous approach to protecting the rights granted. This is important not least because of the fact that the freedom to use protected plant material in breeding programmes has always been a resolute part of the plant variety rights system. The notion that the future of breeding programmes could be compromised by licence fees which are subject to the negotiating skills of the parties involved has always been an anathema to plant breeders, although the romantic element of such a statement should be circumscribed by saying that probably many plant breeders would welcome being able to claim additional royalties for the use of protected varieties within breeding programmes. However, this self-interest is two-sided and there is a keen awareness that the right to claim royalties carries with it the concomitant right of others to claim royalties from them.

Arguably there is a type of curb on the research practices of breeders in that the essentially derived provisions mean that breeders could a) have more control over the results of breeding programmes undertaken by others and b) find that their own breeding programmes will be more carefully directed to ensure that their end results do not fall within the Article 13(5) extension of protected subject matter.

Whatever the role of the public interest, a compulsory licence shall be granted only if the office has been satisfied that certain conditions have been met, and it will decide the terms of that licence—these could include time limitations, appropriate royalties, and obligations imposed on the holder. The Article also provides for a one-year appraisal of the operation of the licence at which time any of the parties could seek to have it cancelled or amended. The sole determinant here will be whether there has been a change in circumstances meriting such alteration. It will be possible to acquire a compulsory licence over an essentially derived variety but again only where it is in the public interest to do so. The Article concludes by making it plain that the matter of the grant of a compulsory licence in respect of a Community plant variety right is the concern of the Community Office and not member states. Any party (including someone not party to the licence) has the right, after one year, to seek for the licence to be cancelled or amended, provided that they can show that in the intervening 12 months the circumstances which led to the granting of the licence have changed.

## Exhaustion of Rights

Article 16 states that where the holder of a Community plant variety right has placed his variety in any place in the Community (this basically means placing it for sale within the Community) then he is deemed to have exhausted his rights over both the variety and the material of that variety. This is subject to the necessary caveat that his rights are not exhausted if a) the use of the variety involves further propagation, unless the breeder intended this to be the use when placing the variety into the Community or b) the use involves the exporting of the variety into a third country which does not provide protection for plant varieties of the genus or species to which the variety belongs unless the material exported is intended for final consumptive purposes. What is interesting about this latter provision is that no mention is made of the *equivalence* of the protection provided by the third country. Nor does it identify if, for the purposes of the Regulation, the Community as a whole is taken to be one country which has equivalence of protection by virtue of the Community Regulation or if it is a number of differing countries any one of which could be the third country the national laws of which may not provide protection for the particular genus or species (for example, those member states of the EU which are signatories to the 1978 Act, which does not require protection to be provided for all genera and species, in contrast to the 1991 UPOV Act, and the Community Regulation, which do).

### Who is a breeder?

One problem facing the Community Office is determining whether an applicant has the right to claim a variety as his own. The lack of an absolute novelty requirement means that there is the potential for applicants to 'pass off' a variety as their own. Within the context of breeding within the Community this is probably unlikely to happen, as breeders have a greater awareness of each other's breeding activities as well as access to the register of applications (administered by the Community Plant Variety Office). The problem is more likely to arise where the claimed variety has been sourced from outside the EU. It is possible for a European breeder, or seed marketer, to identify a variety which is known and used in, for example, Thailand, but not known or used in the EU. The applicant could bring that variety to Europe and seek Community rights over it. Obviously the grant would not affect the ability of the original users of that variety to continue to use it freely within their own jurisdiction but they would not be able to exploit that variety within the territory of grant—for example, the EU. Situations could arise where non-EU based users of the variety, who have used that variety for generations, could be required to obtain a licence from the holder of the Community right in the event that they wish to market the variety within the EU.

Article 11 states that the person who is entitled to protection is the person who 'bred, or *discovered and developed* the variety' (emphasis added). The reference to two apparently distinct types of activity which can attract protection raises a question as to what an applicant has to show he has achieved in order to secure protection. 'Bred' appears self-explanatory and implies breeding activity. Less certain is the reference to 'discovered' and, more crucially, 'developed'. The fact that the first type of activity indicates an active, breeding role in producing the plant grouping which is a distinct, uniform and stable variety, would seem to suggest that the latter activity, does not. In theory, therefore, developing a variety could mean simply doing that which is necessary to bring the discovered variety to the European market. On this basis, protection is secured by showing that the discovered variety is distinct, uniform and stable. What does not appear necessary is that the discoverer/developer has to show that, through breeding activity, he was responsible for producing the distinct, uniform and stable characteristics which distinguish the plant grouping from others within the same species—such an applicant could be a seed merchant. Protection is, therefore, conferred for the act of bringing a commercially new variety to the Community market place. This is underlined by Article 7.

Article 7 requires the variety to be distinct, the distinctive quality of the variety being determined by reference to other varieties which are a matter of 'common knowledge' at the time of application. The standard of 'common knowledge' is a very low one. It merely requires that the variety must have been the subject of a grant of a plant variety right whether within the Community or in any other state or must have been lodged with any intergovernmental organization which has the relevant competence (Article 7(2)(a)). The nature of the international organisation is not detailed but one would imagine that it is intended to take account of such organisations as the International Plant Genetic Resources Institute (IPGRI) and the Consultative Group on International Agricultural Research (CGIAR). Where the plant variety has not been entered onto a public register, or it has not been exhibited (such as in the *Comtesse Louise Erody* case[66]), it would seem that it falls outside the notion of being a matter of common knowledge. In some respects, this is analogous to the US concept of novelty, which regards inventions not previously used within the US as patentable, provided that the subject matter of that invention has not been published elsewhere in the world. The question of *use* elsewhere other than within the US is redundant. The same would appear true of the Community Regulation. Exacerbating the potential problem is the fact that the novelty requirement within the Regulation relates *only* to the placing of the variety within the Community market *by the breeder* (Article 10(1)). The only safeguard would appear to be the final sentence of Article 7, which states that '[t]he implementing rules pursuant to Article 114 may specify further cases as examples which shall be deemed to be a matter of common knowledge.'

On one level the position under the Regulation appears reasonable. A key objective of the Regulation is to foster the development of new varieties for sale within the Community. If an individual has invested in bringing a previously unavailable variety to a European market then they deserve protection; however, this situation does appear unfair where that variety has been known and used outside the European Community. In such an instance it would seem that, notwithstanding the prior knowledge and use, this might not be sufficient to defeat an application for a grant of rights within the Community. This is one of the clearest examples of the plant variety rights system being primarily about

[66] Above n 17.

protecting a market interest. In this respect, and if one agrees with the justification for the grant of an intellectual property right lying in protecting more than a commercial interest, then one has difficulty in seeing how the holder of the variety right in this situation deserves the protection. If one subscribes to the notion that such rights are merely commercial tools then the situation under the Regulation appears fair: after all, the prior users have not sought to exploit the European market potential of the variety themselves. In this respect, the plant variety rights system appears more monopolistic and commerce-driven than the patent system, which requires absolute novelty.

As noted in chapter 3, there is no current formal obligation for a breeder to disclose the geographical origin of the variety (although this may be a matter which also goes to the issue of common knowledge within distinctness) nor to provide evidence that prior informed consent has been given if the variety has been sourced from an indigenous population. In respect of the former, the President of the CPVO has said that the issue of disclosure does go to the assessment of who is the breeder but he is reluctant to make disclosure of geographical origin a formal requirement within the system.[67] He cites, approvingly, the statement made by the ISF in 2003 that this should be an administrative matter only, which, if not complied with, should not result in the invalidation of any grant made (the same principle is also held to apply to the notion of prior informed consent). Clearly whilst for many the concept of disclosure remains a key issue, for those charged with administering the system the logistical problems in requiring sufficient disclosure would make it inexpedient to make the requirement compulsory. According to Kieweit, the Commission is not happy with this approach and there are ongoing discussions to see if a more formal requirement should be included within the Regulation.

### Acquisition, Appeals, and Enforcement[68]

Figures produced by the CPVO in 2003 indicate the success of the system.[69] In 1996, 1385 applications were received by the Office. By 2003 this figure had nearly doubled to 2521. Figures for 2003 also indicate a further 13.4 per cent increase. Of these applications the majority have been for ornamentals (61 per cent in the period 1995–2003), agricultural species (22.7 per cent), vegetables (10.5 per cent), fruits (5.6 per cent) and 0.2 per cent for what the CPVO describes

[67] Kieweit, *Evolution of the Legal Environment of Plant Breeders' Rights* (May 2004), www.upov.int.

[68] Commission Regulation (EC) No 1238/95 of 31 May 1995 establishing implementing rules for the application of Council Regulation (EC) No 2100/94 as regards the fees payable to the Community Plant Variety Office (OJ L 121 of 1 June 1995, p 37).

[69] Figures provided by the CPVO in February 2004. For a more detailed evaluation see Kieweit, *Principles, Procedures and Recent Developments in Respect of the Community Plant Variety System*, Paper given at the 2004 International Conference on Intellectual Property Protection for Plant Innovation (Frankfurt, February 2004): see www.forum-institut.de.

as miscellaneous species. The difference in numbers between the ornamental applications and applications in respect of other species is not surprising given the ease with which it is possible to copy most ornamental varieties—it also shows that the textual changes contained within the Regulation (with a greater emphasis on the various aspects making up the variety as opposed to merely the grouping itself) makes the right more attractive to ornamental breeders. Also related to this was the fact that in the period from April 1995 to July 2003 the largest number of applications filed[70] came from the Netherlands[71] (which has the highest incidence of ornamental plant breeders), followed by Germany,[72] France,[73] Denmark[74] and the UK.[75] In 2003 the President of the Office stated that the number of Community plant variety rights *in force* was approximately 8500.[76] This has been held to reflect that fact that 'the breeding industry . . . is still able to create a constant stream of new varieties . . . with traits such as higher yield [or] more effective resistance against pests or diseases.' More importantly for the patent/plant variety rights debate it can be taken as an indicator that 'although other industrial property rights are available . . . the UPOV type is still considered by breeders as an adequate instrument to protect . . . new varieties of plants.'[77]

In appraising these figures, and in particular when comparing them to the figures produced by the European Patent Office in respect of applications for biotechnological innovations, it is important to bear in mind the size of the industry concerned and the fact that the right relates to a single type of subject matter. Figures produced by the EPO relating to the period 1996/2000 indicate that there was a 239 per cent increase in applications (from 1030 to 3497) from EU member states for inventions from what the EPO defines as the biotechnology sector. Genetic engineering, which is treated separately, saw a 306 per cent increase (from 651 to 2645) over the same period. The information from the EPO does not break these figures down further to indicate plant-specific applications. The number of applications to the CPVO compares most favourably. As with the various national systems, there have been very few legal cases brought under the Regulation, with the result that only parts of the Regulation have been tested. As for the national systems, this lack of litigation may be taken as evidence of success although some lawyers might not agree.

The current cost of a Community plant variety right is:

Application fee 900 euros.

---

[70] Figures provided by van Wijk in 'The WIPO/UPOV Symposium on Intellectual Property Rights in Plant Biotechnology' (October 2003), www.upov.org.
[71] 6322 applications.
[72] 2753 applications.
[73] 2455 applications.
[74] 1016 applications.
[75] 947 applications.
[76] Kieweit, *Relation between PVP and Patents on Biotechnology* (November 2003). For the preceding years the UPOV Office puts the figures as 5,868 in 2000; 6,843 in 2001; and 7,798 in 2002.
[77] *Ibid.*

Thereafter examination fees differ according to whether the variety falls within one of four groups.

Group A (Crops) = 1020–1100 euros;
Group B (Vegetables) = 1050–1200 euros;
Group C (Ornamentals) = 1105–1200 euros;
Group D (Fruit) = 1050 euros.

These figures do not include renewal fees (200 euros per variety per year), fees for taking over rights, or lawyers' fees. It is worth noting that in 1999 these fees were reduced in order to bring them more in line with the expectations of the plant breeders. Of key importance when looking at the cost of acquisition in comparison with that for patent protection is that, generally speaking, it is not necessary to use the services of a third party, such as a patent agent. As third party costs are not curbed this means that they may charge whatever is the appropriate rate for the service provided. The absence of third party involvement at the acquisition stage means that there are no hidden output costs at this point. As the right will be litigated at the national level, it is not possible to state what the cost of policing and enforcing the right will be, as this will necessarily be subject to the local court costs and consequential costs incurred through use of the relevant legal professional.

Appeals

Since the Regulation came into force in 1995, and the first rights granted in 1996, there have been (at the time of writing) 58 appeals lodged at the Community Office, of which 23 have been heard by the Board of Appeal.[78] Any appeal from decisions of the Board can be made to the European Court of Justice (ECJ).

To date, the main decisions of the CPVO have related to the notion of 'breeding' (which is determined by the production of a finished variety which is distinct, uniform and stable), establishing 'common knowledge' (including the 'commercialisation of the propagating . . . material of the variety,' the existence of living plant material in publicly accessible plant collections (*Comtesse Louise Erody*[79]) and the notion of 'discovery' (this concept, for the purposes of bestowing plant variety rights, necessitating a minimum of activity by the person who claims to be the discoverer. In one case decided by the Office,[80] a person to whom a variety had been shown could not claim to be a discoverer simply because they subsequently propagated that variety. To date only one case has come before the ECJ. The case of *Schulin*[81] dealt with an administrative point raised by Article 14(3), indent 6 of the Regulation. This states that a farmer must provide information to the holder of a right on their request. In this

---

[78] See www.cpvo.fr/en/droit/BOA.htm.
[79] Above n 17.
[80] *Ibid.*
[81] Case C–305/00 *Schulin v Saatgut-Treuhandelverwaltungsgesellschaft mbh.*

instance the court held that the requirement for a farmer to provide relevant information to the holder of a right does not apply 'where there is no indication that the farmer has used or will use' the protected variety for further propagating purposes on his farm. According to Keitwiet, this means that life for the plant breeder who wants to collect farm saved seed royalties will not be made easier as a result of this decision, the problem being that it is difficult for the breeder to keep track of all the diverse users of their protected material.

Enforcement

As stated above, the Regulation is not concerned with enforcement, but with grant. However this does not mean that EU member states are free to decide how to enforce the rights as granted. In 2004, the European Community adopted a Directive which sets down the standards for enforcement of intellectual property rights.[82] Although this Directive does not make any specific reference to plant variety rights, Article 1 clearly says that the term 'intellectual property' 'includes industrial property rights.' As the Regulation is concerned with the provision of Community industrial property rights over plant varieties, the rights contained within it clearly come within the 2004 Directive.[83] The effect of the enforcement Directive (which also applies to rights mentioned under the patent Directive) is to ensure parity of enforcement procedures and measures. However, despite drawing these practices together, the Directive cannot prescribe either how these are to be treated by the courts or what the outcome of any court action can or should be. National differences will therefore remain. In addition, it is important to monitor international obligations (especially those under the CBD and ITPGR outlined in chapter 2) which are increasingly relevant at the local EU level and therefore may have a formal impact on protection policies and practices in the future.

## V. CONCLUSION

As the last two chapters have shown, whilst it took nearly 80 years from the time plant material was recognised as industrial property (in the Paris Convention) for a form of protection to be introduced for one type of plant material (the variety), once the decision had been taken to introduce the right, there appears to have been consensus that the right adopted fulfils the needs of the majority of plant breeders.

---

[82] Directive 2004/48/EC of the European Parliament and of the Council of 29 April 2004 on the Enforcement of Intellectual Property Rights.

[83] Indeed, even though the Directive refers to such international treaties as the Paris Convention and does not mention UPOV, the references are in open terms indicating that they are not exhaustive lists.

The adoption of a new Act of the UPOV Convention together with the introduction of the Community Plant Variety Rights Regulation has increased the scope of protectable plant varieties and the strength of the right granted. These changes have been relatively uncontroversial and in general, as the results of the PIP survey indicate, they have been welcomed by most plant breeders. This can be seen in the number of plant variety applications and grants which are being made—as well as in the range of material which forms the subject matter of these applications and grants. However, a number of concerns remain and these include the lack of parity of protection at the national level, and the precise impact of some of the new provisions on plant breeding activity and practice (particularly those which challenge the traditional plant variety rights notions of serving a broader interest than that of individual breeders). These raise both internal questions as to how these provisions will affect the operation, and perception, of the plant variety rights system itself, but also external questions as to effectiveness when looked at in the context of overall plant property provision.

In contrast, the route to the protection most likely to have been envisaged by the draftsmen of the Paris Convention as the means of protecting plant material, the patent system, has been mired in controversy. As the next three chapters will show, whilst the Paris Convention may have established the principle that plant material can be patented, over 100 years later there remain problems with putting this policy into practice. At the heart of the problem lie the twin questions of whether plant-related inventions can meet the threshold for protection and whether, if they can, the patent system should be used to protect them.

The next two chapters will look at the evolution of the European Patent Convention and, in particular, the policy and practice relating to the threshold for protection and applying the exclusions from patentability. Chapter 7 will then look at the patent law policy and practice of the European Community.

# 5

# *The European Patent Convention*[1]—
# *General Practice*

## I. INTRODUCTION

THIS CHAPTER WILL chart the European response to the Paris Convention principle that plant products are industrial property and therefore capable of protection by an industrial property right. It is not proposed to look at the history of the national responses of each European country to the demands for protection coming from the plant breeding industry (not least as this would require some discussion of the changing nature of both territorial boundaries and country designations during the last century), but rather to concentrate on the current systems of European patent provision. Principally this involves an assessment of the European Patent Organisation whose members are signatories of the EPC. In particular, specific attention will be given to the general principles of the EPC and those substantive provisions which apply to all bioscience inventions (and indeed to all inventions) and are not directed to plant-related material. The next chapter will look at the two explicit exclusions of plant varieties and essentially biological processes for the production of plants. It will also raise some post-grant issues (for example, the use of patented material for research purposes and compulsory licensing), but it should be noted that these are matters for national law[2] and are raised in the context of patent practice in general as opposed to the EPC specifically. When looking at the *practice* of the EPO it will be important to bear in mind the fact that this must be looked at in the context of developments elsewhere. In particular, it has to be assessed alongside *policy* decisions of the European Commission. As this chapter and the next will show, the operation of the EPC falls outside the control of the European Union, and therefore the EPO is not required to follow any policy or legislative decisions taken by the EU. However,

---

[1] This chapter will focus on the substantive provisions of the Convention. In respect of more general matters such as filing dates etc, the Convention must be read alongside its international counterparts and, in particular, the Patent Law Treaty 2000, which came into force on 28 April 2005. These will not be discussed further here.

[2] Although these may form part of the promised EU patent: European Patent (Proposal for a Council Regulation on the Community Patent), COM (2000) 412 final.

the fact that the patents laws of nearly all EU member states[3] are based upon the EPC means that in the event that the Commission wishes to get involved in directing national patent practices, the two inevitably become intertwined (although not necessarily in a formal manner).

As may be clear from the discussions in previous chapters, of the two forms of property right discussed in this book, the older is the patent system.[4] The first recognisable patent rights can be traced back to the 13th and 14th centuries (although these bear little similarity to the right we know today). In the main, these first rights were not rewards for innovation in the modern sense, but were rather trading licences granted as a privilege by the head of state to be used as 'safe-conduct passes'[5] securing a right to produce and to sell material new to that trading territory—the innovation lay in making the product publicly available rather than in the conceiving of the thing itself.[6] It was not until the latter half of the 19th century, and the emergence of mass production which enabled both increased distribution of products as well as the technological capacity to copy (the latter also providing the incentive to develop different methods or processes for the production of market-desirable products), that the precursors of modern patent law began to appear. Within Europe, national laws were either introduced, or significant revisions took place, in Austria (1852), Belgium (1854), Denmark (1884), Finland (1898), Germany (1877), Italy (1864), Norway (1885), Portugal (1896), Spain (1820), Sweden (1884), Switzerland (1888) and the UK (1852 and 1883). These changes in patent provision stood alongside both developments within genetics as well as the international consolidation of patent law via the Paris Convention on Industrial Property 1883.[7]

## II. THE PARIS CONVENTION AND
## THE PATENTING OF PLANT MATERIAL

This Convention is arguably the most important international agreement in the field of intellectual property. Even the TRIPs Agreement is predicated on its principles of eligibility, reciprocity and same treatment.[8] As has already been said, the Paris Convention has great significance in relation to the protection of

---

[3] At the time of writing only Malta is not a member of the EPC, but it has been invited to accede to the Convention.

[4] For an discussion of the historical development of patent law see Sherman and Bently, *The Making of Modern Intellectual Property Law* (CUP, 1999). For a discussion of the philosophical justifications see Drahos, *A Philosophy of Intellectual Property* (Dartmouth, 1996).

[5] Phillips and Firth, *Introduction to Intellectual Property Law*, 4th edn (Butterworths, 2001).

[6] There is a possible parallel here with the principle within plant variety rights of granting a right to the discoverer of a variety—as the last chapter indicated, it is possible for a Community right to be granted over a variety which is commercially new to Europe but known outside the EU (although not necessarily a matter of common knowledge).

[7] Not all European countries were originally members of the union which emerged as a result of the Paris Convention. For example, neither Austria nor Germany were original members.

[8] Arts 1, 2 and 3.

plant material. Whilst there is justifiably still some dissension over the form of that protection, it is now clear that the legal basis for regarding plant material as industrial property, the technical essence, as well as physical embodiment, of which can be 'owned', dates back to 1883.

Article 1(3) of the Paris Convention states '[i]ndustrial property shall be understood in the broadest sense and shall not apply only to industry and commerce proper, but likewise to agricultural and extractive industries and to all manufactured or natural products, for example wines, grain, tobacco leaf, fruit, cattle, minerals, beer, flowers and flour.' The Paris Convention does not, however, elaborate as to the form of this protection.

As mentioned in chapter 1, some viewed this reference to agricultural products as indicating a 'conviction that patent protection for agricultural living matter inventions, plants and animals alike, was a desired objective.'[9] In assessing the response to the edict that plant products could be industrial property it should first be remembered, however, that the Paris Convention covers a number of industrial property rights and not only patents. Therefore caution has to be exercised before necessarily attributing to those who drafted the Convention a desire to protect this material through the provision of a patent as that would be to infer into the Convention a conviction which is not necessarily apparent from the text itself. It is unlikely that it was anticipated that either trade marks or industrial design protection were envisaged as the best mode of protection, but it is possible that, given the relative simplicity of the science at the time, the lesser form of patent protection, the utility model, might have been thought appropriate. It is not proposed to outline this form of protection in any detail (not least because there is no common agreement as to the form of utility model protection)—but it is worth noting that the right primarily protects those 'inventions' which cannot meet the threshold required for patent protection. In particular, the right carries with it a lower level of novelty or inventive step which might be thought more apposite to the type of plant breeding activity taking place at the time the Convention came into force. However, the utility model system has not been mooted as a method of protecting plant material (possibly because in the early days it was closely allied to the design right[10]), and most recent attempts to introduce a common European form of the right have specifically excluded biological material from the scope of protectable material.[11]

Whether or not the intention lying behind Article 1(3) of the Paris Convention was to indicate that patent protection was the desired form of protection for living material, the more immediate problem facing those responding to it was matching the material to the requirements for patentability—these being then as now a matter for national interpretation. This required an assessment of

---

[9] Bent *et al*, *Intellectual Property Rights in Biotechnology Worldwide* (Macmillan, 1987) 41.

[10] See Sherman and Bently, *The Making of Modern Intellectual Property Law* (CUP, 1999).

[11] For a discussion of utility models and biological material see Llewelyn, *Utility Model/Second Tier Protection: A Report on the Proposals From the European Commission* (Common Law Institute of Intellectual Property, 1996).

whether the material is novel, inventive, capable of industrial application and sufficiently disclosed. It was difficulties in applying the granting criteria which, arguably more than the concerns over extending the patent monopoly to plant material, led to the introduction of the *sui generis* right.

In Bent *et al*'s view,[12] the problem in realising the objective of the Convention lay with those responsible for overseeing the operation of patent system, namely that there was too rigid an application of the patent law and that if granting offices had been more open-minded about the treatment of living material as inventions then the desired objective would have been achieved far earlier.[13] This view has some merit when looking at the first attempts to provide protection for plant products. Those countries which did try to adopt a more flexible approach to patenting plant-related inventions (France,[14] Germany[15] and Italy,[16] for example) encountered problems in applying this approach in practice (as the experience of Dr Wuesthoff in Germany, discussed in chapter 3, indicates). The patent systems of these latter countries clearly were not seen as impenetrable in either language or strictures but because the notions of a technical manufacture, and required threshold for protection, were geared towards inanimate types of innovation it was difficult to extend these definitions to inventions involving animate material. It was because of these problems that other countries, such as the Netherlands[17] and Austria,[18] introduced more plant-specific legislation. It was this variation in provision which the policy makers in the 1950s were concerned to address.

One final comment on the Paris Convention principle and that is that it is worth recollecting that the WIPO Special Committee of Experts, created in the 1950s to look at the best method of protecting plant material and charged with deciding whether the system of protection for plant material should be a special Agreement within the framework of the Paris Union of 1883 or a separate convention, decided upon the latter option, subject to the reservation that states which so desired could apply either this new Convention or the Paris Convention. This action indicates that those who actually were concerned with introducing protection for plants did not necessarily share the apparent

---

[12] Bent *et al*, *Intellectual Property Rights in Biotechnology Worldwide* (Macmillan, 1987), a view which is shared by a number of pro-patent law commentators.

[13] This is an argument which continues to dog the operation of national patent law, particularly with regard to compliance with the TRIPs obligation. The use of the threshold for protection as the primary arbiter of what can be protected, however, cuts two ways and whilst a more flexible interpretation (such as that which operates at the European level) can permit more research results to be protected, a more restrictive application can deny protection. This is a matter which some countries are actively looking at when deciding how to apply the general principle of the Agreement.

[14] Law of 27 January 1933.

[15] Decision of 19 September 1932, GRUR 1114.

[16] Case law indicates that new plant varieties were regarded as 'industrial results': Appeal No 1147 (1948) and Appeal No 1329 (1950).

[17] Plant Breeding and Seed Material Order (1941).

[18] Plant Cultivation Law (1949).

'conviction' that patent protection was 'a desired objective' for all plant-related material.

As mentioned in chapter 3, because many of the same participants took part in both the discussions leading up to the UPOV and European Patent Conventions, there is a degree of synergy between the two Conventions—the most obvious being the decision to provide a subject-specific form of protection for plant varieties. However, the parallels go beyond this and have more fundamental resonances. Both Conventions were quintessentially European in their derivation and remain so (even though the UPOV Convention now has a more global outlook guided by external considerations). The problem with this is that the old European legal order, from which both the EPC and the UPOV Convention sprung, and the principles upon which they were based (such as the exclusions from patentability) can stand uneasily when placed alongside the more market-orientated emphasis now being given to global intellectual property rights.

## III. THE HISTORY OF THE EPC: THE STRASBOURG CONVENTION[19]

During the 1940s and 1950s, in the context of the discussions which eventually led to the creation of the European Economic Community, it was agreed that there was a need to harmonise European patent practice ensuring both parity of granting criteria and reciprocity of rights. The ideal was to allow patent applicants to make one application, with any resulting patent having the same force in all member states. The problem was achieving this in practice.

The fact that signing up to the Paris Convention required certain commonly accepted principles to be in place at the national level might lead one to imagine that harmonising provision would have been relatively straightforward. However, the extent of national variation was such that it proved more difficult to put these into an agreed format. As will be seen later, the model chosen to resolve these differences itself created a degree of uncertainty and this had a direct effect on perceptions as to what could be protected. The first common position adopted was the Strasbourg Convention on Unification of Certain Points of Substantive Patent Law (the Strasbourg Convention), which was introduced in 1963—this eventually evolved into the EPC.[20]

---

[19] More detailed expositions of the general history of the EPC can be found in Paterson, *European Patent System*, 2nd edn (Sweet & Maxwell, 2001) and, specifically on the exclusions relating to morality and plant and animal varieties, in Armitage and Davis, *Patents and Morality in Perspective* (Common Law Institute of Intellectual Property, 1994). This latter text is a response to Beyleveld and Brownsword, *Mice, Morality and Patents* (Common Law Institute, 1993).

[20] What is interesting about the whole process is that, in many respects, it mirrored what had taken place in the 1880s prior to the introduction of the Paris Convention. There was a clear legislative will to provide protection for the broadest grouping of inventions which can be contrasted with an apparent political will to confine the categories of excluded material. Both Tilton Penrose, 'The Development of the International Convention for the Protection of Industrial Property' (Johns Hopkins University Press, 1951), reproduced in Abbott, Cottier and Gurry (eds), *The International Intellectual Property System: Commentary and Materials, Part One* (Kluwer Law International,

One of the key issues driving the patent law revision was the growth in pharmaceutical and chemical research and development. Ad hoc provision had grown out of the adaptation of the patent system to fit post-World War II developments in pharmaceutical and agricultural chemistry;[21] however, these developments in patent law were by no means uniform across the whole of Europe. With the push for communitarianisation well under way, there was a clear need for consolidation and clarification. It quickly became clear that the need to protect was so acute that legislation would be needed to remove existing restrictions thereby allowing patents for classes of chemicals,[22] chemical and technical interventions in agricultural methods,[23] living matter (such as yeast and later micro-biological material); and chemical and pharmaceutical substances[24] (including claims for these substances *per se*, which were not tied to the method used to produce them[25]). For political reasons, the responsibility for developing a common European patent system was given to the Council of Europe and, as a result, the agreed legal framework developed externally to the European Union.[26]

Notwithstanding these political and economic pressures to achieve consensus, those engaged in formulating that protection recognised that there were member states which were concerned about the extension of patent protection to new groups of material. For this reason, a 'big bang' approach to the introduction of the new system was thought too difficult to achieve. Instead, it was decided to allow member states time to adjust national provision into line with the new system. They were also given an opportunity to exclude some categories of 'inventions' if they so wished—although these options were themselves

1999) 642 and Armitage and Davis certainly ascribed the reluctance to open up the definition of technology or manufacture to political concerns which were not apparently shared by the patent lawyers present.

[21] See Dutfield, *Industrial Property Rights and the Life Science Industries* (Ashgate Publishing, 2003), ch 4; and Cornish, Llewelyn and Adcock, *Intellectual Property Rights (IPRs) and Genetics: A Study into the Impact and Management of Intellectual Property Rights within the Healthcare Sector* (Department of Health, 2003).

[22] This included applications where the inventive act involved the discovery of the practical benefit of one or more members of a class of chemicals and enabled claims to the chemical structure of the whole class. The test which is used here is whether the same benefit could, in some measure, be predicted for the whole class. See White, 'Gene and Compound per se Claims: An Appropriate Reward? Part One' (2002) 31(2) *CIPA Journal* 134; and White, 'Gene and Compound per se Claims: An Appropriate Reward? Part Two' *CIPA Journal* Dec 2005 volume 34 No 12, 751.

[23] As discussed in ch 3, the introduction of the UPOV system of plant variety rights underlines the recognition given to the not inconsiderable scientific investment in agriculture.

[24] For example, in Italy, the patent law excluded any form of pharmaceutical inventions. The country accordingly fostered competition via generic imitations until the exclusion in the law was held unconstitutional in the 1970s. Even so, it took time to reach the same level of patent protection for pharmaceuticals in Italy as in the rest of the EPC states.

[25] This can be seen in the UK Patents Act 1949.

[26] This is an important factor to bear in mind when a) looking at the operation of the European Patent Office and b) understanding the impact of the proposals of the European Commission to reform European patent law.

limited.[27] Although the decision taken to introduce the new patent provision in a staggered form clearly had its political merits, the result was that not only did patent provision continue to differ for many years after the Strasbourg Convention had evolved into the EPC but also that some parties continued to read into the EPC exclusions the same optional element contained in the Strasbourg Convention. It was this perception which, in part, led to the confusion over the availability of protection for plants.

When looking at the policy approaches, a distinction can be drawn between the approach taken towards the protection of, on the one hand, pharmaceutical products, foodstuffs and agricultural/horticultural processes and, on the other, plant and animal varieties. In respect of the former, the option to exclude was merely transitional and member states had, within 10 years of joining the Convention, to provide patent protection. In order to ensure that the new requirement did not 'interfere with the traditional agricultural and horticultural cross-breeding methods'[28] without hindering protection for the new pharma-technical processes, the Convention permitted members to exclude essentially biological processes but required protection for microbiological processes and the products thereof. A further attempt to assuage fears over the monopolisation of basic material was an explicit division between unpatentable discoveries (comprising unutilised information) and patentable inventions (which resulted from the application of inventive insight in order to bring about a novel use of that information).

In contrast to the transitional exclusions, the option to exclude plant and animal varieties could be relied upon permanently. By the time the Strasbourg Convention had morphed into the EPC, the optional exclusion had given way to a mandatory one on the basis that plant varieties, at least, could be protected under the more appropriate UPOV-type system.[29] In addition to these exclusions, and almost as an aside, the Strasbourg Convention draftsmen introduced, via Article 2a, an exclusion of inventions which would be contrary to morality or *ordre public*. The decision to move from the exclusion being permissive to mandatory took place with apparently little discussion and it remains unclear why this took place, other than because of a perception that the variety rights system was the more appropriate form of protection.[30]

As the intention was to harmonise the principles surrounding *patentabilty*, the draftsmen of the Strasbourg Convention did not overly concern themselves with issues of infringement or derogation. These were seen as matter for the national

[27] This can be contrasted with the proposed plant variety rights system, the introduction of which at the national level was thought unlikely to require any radical revision of existing plant variety protection practices.

[28] Armitage and Davis, above n 19, p 15.

[29] See Armitage and Davis, *ibid*, p 11. They described the option as permitting a 'temporary reservation'.

[30] Teschermacher, *The Practice of the European Patent Office Regarding the Grant of Patents for Biotechnological Inventions* (GRUR International, 1987) 285, also published in English in (1988) 19(1) *IIC* 18 (the latter reference will be used).

offices and courts. Most jurisdictions put in place certain curbs on the rights granted, such as a right to use the protected material for purely private or experimental use and the exclusion of certain methods of treatment and surgery. Most of these were introduced using both the Strasbourg/EPC route and other patent law initiatives, most notably via the now defunct Community Patent Convention.

Because of the difficulties encountered in bringing the laws of all member states into line, some of the principles enshrined within the Strasbourg Convention did not actually come into force until the 1980s[31] and the effects are only now being fully felt. This lack of harmony contrasts with the situation under plant variety rights where, initially at least, there was consensus over the form and scope of the right.[32]

### The Strasbourg Convention and Plants

In 1951 the Council of Europe's Committee of Experts on Patents gave unanimous support for the introduction of a uniform system of protection for plant inventions. The matter appeared to be left until 1960 when the Committee again formally looked at the issue of including plant material as patentable subject matter. The fact that there was nearly 10 years between the two meetings should not, however, be taken as indicating a lack of either interest or activity. It should be remembered that the Council of Europe Committee met at the start and conclusion of the discussions leading up to the introduction of an *international* convention and also that many of the participants in the discussions over the UPOV system were also engaged in the discussions surrounding the proposed European patent system. In a report published in 1960 the Committee stated that, due in part to the contemporaneous discussions taking place in Paris which lead to the UPOV Convention 1961, it would be 'inexpedient to impose a common solution . . . for the patentability of plant varieties.' It is not surprising therefore that they awaited the outcome of those meetings before making a statement on the patentability of plant material within a *European* context.

A draft text of the Strasbourg Convention was released in 1961. The key Article relating to the protection of plants was Article 2. This stated: '. . . the Contracting States *shall not be bound* to provide for the grant of patents in respect of pharmaceutical or food products, or of new *plants* or animals' (emphasis added). By the time the Convention was adopted in 1963 this had been revised to read that '. . . the Contracting States *shall not be bound* to provide for the grant of patents in respect of pharmaceutical or food products, or of new plant or animal *varieties*' (emphasis added). When this is read alongside

---

[31] Indeed, some only came into force in the 1990s—for example, Art 69 (which relates to claims construction) only came into full force within the UK in 1998.

[32] Although, as ch 3 indicated and ch 8 will address, the consensus over plant variety rights (at both the European and international levels) has lessened as the right has become closer to that of a patent.

the UPOV 'dual protection prohibition' it can be seen that the combined effect was that parties could chose if they wished to protect plant varieties. If they did wish to do so, a further choice was available to them as to which of the two forms of protection to use. The only constraint was that if the country concerned was a member of the UPOV Union it could not offer both forms of protection for the same genus or species.

It is not clear why there was a change from the 1961 text, excluding plants, to the 1963 text, which excluded plant varieties, but it is probable that the change resulted from the introduction of the UPOV system which solely provides protection for plant varieties. It would be easy to regard the change in text as signalling a general recognition that the exclusion should apply only to plant varieties, with all other types of plant material therefore being potentially patentable. However, it does seem that the previous reference to an exclusion of plants in general did have an impact on the way in which the eventual exclusion was perceived. Whether one agrees that the language of the exclusion was unambiguous or not, one thing does seem evident and that is that, during the 1960s, 1970s and 1980s, confusion reigned as to how the exclusion should be applied in practice (this confusion extending to the practice of the EPO). It is possible to ascribe this confusion to the view that, notwithstanding the actual language used in the eventual Article 53(b), the spirit of the exclusion was thought to be that represented by the language of the 1961 draft, which indicated a more fundamental principle, namely that plants in general, and not only plant varieties, were not patentable. A further factor which gives additional weight to this view was that until the 1990s the exclusion applied not merely for public policy reasons (for example, plants should not be the subject of a private monopoly right) but, more pragmatically, because there was very little in the way of tangible plant innovation results which *could* be patented. As will be discussed below, it was only once the modern plant bioscience industry started to produce products and processes involving plant material that the actual ambit of the exclusion, and its relationship with the plant variety rights system, was tested.

Whatever the spirit of the exclusion (or the intention lying behind its incorporation into patent law), not all viewed the decision to exclude plants and plant varieties in positive terms. Some have called it a 'bifurcation' of variety protection rights 'to the detriment' of patent protection for plants and others 'a sacrifice on the altar of European patent law unification.'[33] These views have been rebuffed as 'smacking of pathos' which overstates the case and misses the fact that a more suitable form of protection for plant varieties had been agreed both at the meetings which led up to the UPOV Convention and at those that preceded the Strasbourg Convention.[34] However, notwithstanding this, both views

---

[33] For example see Bent *et al*, *Intellectual Property Rights in Biotechnology Worldwide* (Macmillan, 1987) 64; and Straus, 'Genetic Engineering and Industrial Property' (1986) 11 *Industrial Property* 454.

[34] Teschermacher, 'The Practice of the European Patent Office Regarding the Grant of Patents for Biotechnological Inventions', above n 30.

have merit and echo the problems encountered by those seeking to coalesce patent protection.

Whilst it may have been agreed that a separate form of protection designed with plant varieties in mind *might* be the more suitable form of protection, this did not mean that this should necessarily be at the expense of patent protection for plant varieties. That some European countries permitted patent protection for varieties, together with the fact that it was not agreed that the provision of protection under one system *should* automatically prohibit protection under the other (and, as discussed in chapters 1 and 3, Article 2(1) of the UPOV Convention did not prevent dual protection of this kind), indicates that there was a degree of flexible thinking during the 1950s as to how the patent system could itself respond. The fact that the decision was taken to exclude plant varieties from patent protection indicates both a recognition that consensus on their patentability would be difficult to achieve *and* as its use became more widespread (and it appeared to be effective), that the system which had evolved specifically to protect varieties was the more appropriate.

A further factor which needs to be taken into account, is that at the time that the Strasbourg Convention was being drafted not all European countries were members of UPOV. Those which were not members might have wished to look at other options for protecting plant innovations. Of course, the fact that the option to exclude plants and plant varieties from patent protection was revised to make such exclusion mandatory could be a further indication that the plant variety rights system was increasingly seen as the more appropriate system. By the time the EPC opened for signature, nearly all those who ratified it had become UPOV.

That confusion reigned over the precise ambit of both the Article 2(1) UPOV dual protection prohibition and the exclusion of plant varieties from patent protection can be seen in the legislation of some European countries. For example, the New Belgium Law of 28 March 1984, Chapter II, Part One, Section 4(1) stated that '. . . the protection granted by this law shall not extend to: vegetable creations of species or of varieties covered by the system of protection established by the law of 20 May 1975 on the protection of vegetable creations.' Article 7 of the New French Law No 84,500 of 27 June 1984 also stated that: '. . . the following may not be protected: b) plant varieties of a kind or of a species coming under the system of protection established by Law No 70–489 of 11 June 1970 on the protection of plant varieties.' Belgium is a signatory to the 1961/72 UPOV Act and France to the 1978 Act. Both of these a) contain the dual protection prohibition (which does not preclude ordinary patent protection for plant varieties) and b) do not require member states to provide plant variety protection for varieties from all genera and species as is the case under the 1991 UPOV Act.

It might be wondered how these countries could provide patent protection for plant varieties given that the laws concerned were introduced *after* the EPC came into force. There are two reasons for this. The first is that the EPC merely states that a *European* patent shall not be granted over plant varieties—it does not prevent the grant of a *national* patent. Secondly, whilst many member states revised their laws to bring them into line with the provisions of the EPC not all did so immediately or using precisely the same language. The clarity which hindsight has provided as to what the legislators intended obviously was not apparent at the time that countries were charged with revising their laws.

It is difficult to state whether the growing number of European countries which joined UPOV in the 1960s reflected a political view that this system was the better form of protection or whether this was due to the growing recognition that the patent system was not suitable and protection under that system would not be forthcoming. Whatever the subsequent views on the value of the exclusion, it was approved not only internally (at the European level) but also externally by the WIPO (which viewed the exclusion as in keeping with the principles established within UPOV).[35] There is significance to both the WIPO statement that Article 53(b) was commensurate with UPOV and the fact that nearly all those who signed up to the EPC were existing members of UPOV. This significance lies in that the policy and practice of the EPO was, from the start (and notwithstanding doubt at the national level), that plant innovations are patentable provided that the invention meets the threshold for protection, does not contravene morality and does not take the form of a plant variety. The problems, insofar as it has experienced any, lie in a) the perception of others outside the EPO that the exclusion of plant varieties is an expansive exclusion covering more than just plant varieties, b) agreeing an internal definition of plant variety against which claims to plant groupings can be assessed and c) matching the material to the threshold for protection. These will be discussed in more detail below and in chapter 6.

## IV. THE EUROPEAN PATENT CONVENTION[36]

The EPC came into force in 1973 under the auspices of the Council of Europe and with it the European Patent Organisation came into being.[37] The European Patent Office (EPO) oversees the administration of the system. This is a fully

---

[35] Minutes of the Working Party 1, BR/135 71, November 1971, para 98.

[36] For more detail about both the substantive provisions and the operation of the system in practice see www.epo.org.

[37] As of 1 March 2006, there were 31 the EPC: Austria, Belgium, Bulgaria*, Cyprus, the Czech Republic, Denmark, Estonia, Finland, France, Germany, Greece, Hungary, Iceland*, Ireland, Italy, Latvia, Liechtenstein*, Lithuania, Luxembourg, Monaco*, the Netherlands, Poland, Portugal, Romania*, Slovakia, Slovenia, Spain, Sweden, Switzerland*, Turkey* and the UK (those countries marked with an asterisk are not member states of the EU). As with EU member states there is concern in the non-EU member states of the EPC over the use of the patent system to protect living material. This is especially the case within Switzerland, as the creation, in 2004, of a coalition comprising farmers, researchers, consumers and ecologists demonstrates. The coalition is opposing proposed changes to the Swiss patent law which would facilitate the patenting of plants and animals. The patenting of plants is central to their objections.

autonomous entity with its own internal review, appeal and accountability mechanisms. It is not an office of the European Union and, therefore, it is not directly affected by decisions of the European Commission, European Parliament or the European Court of Justice. However, as will be seen in chapter 7, there is great similarity between the practice which has evolved at the EPO and the policy direction taken by the European Commission.

The fact that the EPC is not an instrument of the EU does not mean that it can be treated as wholly separate from the EU. EU member states form the core of the European Patent Organisation and, despite the general lack of formal convergence, there has been in recent years concerted action to find common ground between EU and EPO policy and practice.

In evaluating the role the EPC has played in the protection of plant material, it is worth bearing in mind the following three factors.

Whilst the EPC may have come into force in 1973, it has taken time for its jurisprudence to evolve. Its policy and practice relating to bioscience innovations did not emerge fully formed but has taken time to develop and only now is becoming settled.

The science itself was not fully understood by those involved in research and development. Unsurprisingly, as a result this meant that in the early days, the examiners were themselves not necessarily versed in the science but instead often came from other disciplines such as chemistry. As Crespi succinctly put it in 1981:

> there is a great comprehensibility gap between the genetic manipulation workers and professional advisers . . . the patent lawyer coming to terms with these problems has a two fold task, first to understand the technology, and secondly to do what he can about the state of patent law and its application to biological material.[38]

As knowledge about the subject grew, and both examiners and patent lawyers became increasingly drawn from the field of molecular biology, so too increased the ability of lawyers and granting offices alike to more fully understand the applications being placed before them.

Finally, the invention which is protected may not be confined to plants as such but the claims may relate to a range of different applications involving that material (not all of which necessarily need be animate). This does not mean that the invention (or the principles which apply to the protection granted over it) does not apply to those engaging in plant research. Equally, the invention may involve material common to a cross-section of life-forms (for example, a protein found in both plants and animals) and the patent will need to be read in light of the range of possible affected material. A consequence of this is that it is impossible to state the number of *plant*-related applications which are made or rights granted.

---

[38] Crespi, 'Biotechnology and Patents: Past and Future' [1981] *EIPR* 134. This view was echoed by Teschermacher (then Head of Legal Services at the EPO) in 1987, above n 30, p 19.

Before looking at the specific practice of the EPO regarding plant innovations it is worth explaining the nature of the relationship between the EPC and the patent laws of its signatory states.

## The EPC and National European Patent Laws

The introduction of the EPC had two effects. The first was to establish its own procedures for the granting of a European patent. The second was to attempt to bring national patent practices into a degree of conformity.

In respect of the first, the procedures set down in the EPC build on those set down in the Paris Convention and are intended to remove any overly mechanistic or rigid application of patent law. The objective was to open up the patent system to a diverse range of new products and processes. At the core of this move was the recognition that whilst these products and processes had little technically in common they all had commercial potential. Because of the diverse nature of research results it was felt inappropriate to maintain the closed notion of what could be an invention. Instead, it was agreed that the determining factor should be the ability to meet the threshold for protection rather to match a prescribed idea of invention. For the reasons outlined above, the only restriction on the acquisition of a right comes in the form of the exceptions. As the Convention is concerned with the grant and scope of the rights provided under it, it does not address matters such as research use or licensing. These remain matters for national patent laws. The Convention does provide direction as to how the claims within a patent should be interpreted,[39] but again the precise application of these principles is a matter for the national courts.

When applying, the inventor can decide in which of the EPC signatory states he wishes the patent to have force. He can choose only one or two countries (although this is probably not cost effective and he would be better advised to secure national patents from the national patent offices) or all of them. Once granted the effect is to create a bundle of patent rights which can be enforced in those countries designated. Each right can be enforced in exactly the same way as if they had been granted by the national patent offices. The main difference is that any opposition to the *grant* of the patent will be made using the EPO procedures. In contrast, any litigation relating to *infringement* will be dealt with by the local courts of the country where the infringing activity took place, provided that it is one of the countries designated in the patent. If a country is not designated then the patent has no force in that country. For example, if a European patent designates France and Belgium but not the UK, the patent holder can control the uses of the patented technology in France and Belgium but he has no right (under patent law) to prevent any uses of that technology within the UK. As per any national patent, the duration of a patent granted under the

---

[39] Art 69 and its Protocol.

Convention is up to 20 years (subject to any national system of supplementary protection—this is discussed in the next chapter).

In order to try and ensure parity of protection between itself and national patent laws, the second effect of the EPC was to try to harmonise this national provision. However, it has only been able to do so at the conceptual level by directing the form of the substantive provision (such as the requirements of novelty, inventive step and industrial applicability). The nature of the European Patent Organisation is such that the EPO cannot compel national patent offices (or courts) to interpret or apply these substantive provisions in a particular way. Instead, it is left to national granting offices (and courts) to decide upon appropriate local practice. As Straus and Moufang noted in 1989 any further harmonisation has been achieved on a 'largely voluntary, unilateral, uncoordinated basis' as member states of the EPC are 'not obliged to automatically align their national patents laws with the EPC.'[40]

In terms of the protection of inventions involving living material, as will be discussed below, the EPO now fully recognises that these inventions can be the subject of a patent grant (although this was not always the case). However, not all of its member states have been prepared to adopt an equivalent practice at the local level. It was for this reason that the European Commission (which does have the power to direct national policy and practice) introduced the Directive on the Legal Protection of Biotechnological Inventions.

**The Application Process at the EPO**

As per general patenting practice, a patent will be granted only if the applicant can show that the invention concerned is novel, involves an inventive step, and is capable of industrial application,[41] and it is sufficiently disclosed. In order to do this the applicant must submit a patent specification (which takes the form of a written document usually drafted by a patent agent). The specification outlines:

(a) what was known previously;
(b) how the invention builds upon this prior knowledge in a novel and inventive manner (the problem/solution approach is used) which identifies a function(s) for the material; and
(c) the claims which define the boundaries of protection.

The first concept which must be understood is that the notions of novelty, inventiveness and industrial applicability are *legal* notions. The standard for each requirement is therefore what it means *at law* and these legal definitions are left

---

[40] Straus and Moufang, *Legal Aspects of Acquiring, Holding and Utilizing Patents with Reference to the Activities of the International Centre for Genetic Engineering and Biotechnology (ICGEB)*, ICGEB/Prep.Comm/14/3/Add.1 (1989).
[41] Art 52.

to the patent lawyers primarily to provide.[42] The determination of a patentable invention is made by reference to these criteria and not, initially, by reference to the subject matter of the invention itself. An external reference is made only if there is a question mark over whether the material claimed is not an invention[43] or is an invention which, for public policy reasons, is excluded. In the latter case, even then the notion of whether the material is an invention or not is not at issue; the question is whether the material falls within external reference points (such as the UPOV definition of a plant variety) which are used when exercising the exclusion. The broader concept of whether it is an invention *per se* remains internally referenced. The invention must also not fall within the categories of excluded material.

The EPC recognises three categories of material:

i)   non-inventions (which includes discoveries);[44]
ii)  inventions (which are patentable because they meet the threshold for protection);

and

iii) inventions which may meet the threshold for protection but which, for reasons of public interest, are deemed not to be patentable.

For plant innovations the relevant categories are the exclusion of discoveries,[45] inventions the publication or exploitation of which would be contrary to morality,[46] plant varieties, and essentially biological processes for the production of plants and animals. However, patent protection must be available for microbiological processes and the products thereof.[47] As will be discussed further below the categories of excluded material are given a restrictive interpretation; for example, a discovery is simply held to be material for which no novel or inventive use (or application) has been demonstrated. In common with both the TRIPs Agreement and the US position, the EPC is predicated upon a presumption of patentability. As already stated, the Convention does not contain any definition of an 'invention' but rather relies upon the threshold for protection to determine protectable subject matters. This means that plant innovations are, for the most part, treated in exactly the same way as any other type of 'invention', whether involving animate material or not, in that there is a presumption that protection should be accorded. This is most evident in the way in which

---

[42] An example of this was given in ch 2 when looking at the different definitions given to 'microorganism' by law and science.
[43] Typically these include artistic works, mental acts etc.
[44] There are other groupings regarded as non-inventions but these are not relevant for the purposes of this book.
[45] Art 52(2)(a).
[46] Art 53(a).
[47] Art 53(b).

terms such as 'micro-organism' (discussed in the next chapter) have been applied. The flashpoints arise when the presumption of inclusion not exclusion is set alongside the exclusions.

It is impossible to go through the entire history of EPO patent practice relating to inventions involving material of natural extraction or which involve naturally occurring elements. The reason for this is that this line of jurisprudence did not, in the main, evolve independently of that relating to other types of inventions, most notably chemical inventions. Instead, the jurisprudence grew incrementally out of the existing notions not of what could be protected (in terms of subject matter), but of the ability to meet the threshold for protection.[48] In terms of application to bioscience inventions this means that the modern thinking relating to genes evolved out of the policy and practice relating to chemicals and micro-organisms. With regard to innovations involving material of a higher order, then it can be seen that the thinking which became established in respect of chemical inventions was extended first to plants and this then in turn was extended to apply to animal and, latterly, human genetic material. The reason for this unformed and incremental extension lies in the lack of a definition of an 'invention'. In deciding whether or not to make a grant, all that the Office is concerned with is whether the application concerns material which a) meets the criteria for grant and b) is not excluded.

The next chapter will look specifically at the exclusions contained within Article 53(b) and, in particular, at the way in which the application of these provisions has been refined and the notion of protectable plant innovations has evolved. Before so doing it is necessary to outline the EPO's practice with regard to genetic inventions in general. This is essentially a matter of stating its practice with regard to the interpretation and application of the granting criteria. In so doing, we are going to make a slight leap forward and rather than giving a history of the granting criteria and other provisions, we will merely outline what these say and what the problems are in applying these provisions, and then outline the current plant patenting practice of the EPO. In respect of the latter this will require reference to the EU Directive. As will be seen later, the Directive clearly establishes that inventions (whether products or processes) involving biological material can be patented. In 1999 the EPO Council agreed to adopt the Directive for the purpose of supplementary interpretation via new Implementing

---

[48] For a more detailed evaluation see Dutfield, *Industrial Property Rights and the Life Science Industries* (Ashgate Publishing, 2003); Domeij, *Pharmaceutical Patents in Europe* (Kluwer Law International, 2000); Grubb, *Patents for Chemicals, Pharmaceuticals and Biotechnology* (OUP, 1999); Beier, Crespi and Straus, *Biotechnology and Patent Protection: An International Review* (OECD, 1985); and Crespi, *Patenting in the Biological Sciences* (John Wiley & Sons, 1982).

[49] 'Decision of the Administrative Council 16 June 1999 to Amend the Implementing Rules of the European Patent Convention' [1999] *Official Journal of the European Patent Office (OJ EPO)* 437; [1999] *OJ EPO* 573, rule 23(b)(1). For European patent applications and patents concerning biotechnological inventions, the relevant provisions of the Convention shall be applied and interpreted in accordance with the provisions of this chapter. Directive 98/44/EC of 6 July 1998 on the legal protection of biotechnological inventions shall be used as a supplementary means of interpretation. Only those provisions which relate to plant innovation will be discussed here.

Rules.[49] What this means is that the Directive now serves as a reference point for deciding practice at the EPO. For the purpose of setting out the EPO position, we will merely make reference to the new EPO rules and postpone discussion of the background to these (and the Directive itself) to chapter 7.

## The EPC and the Patentability of Biotechnological Inventions

In the 1980s the EPO was faced with the problem of how to respond to the increased use of microbiology to perform new tasks and also form the basis of new products in both pharmaceutical and agricultural research. In terms of the latter there was intense interest is using the emerging technologies to develop increased yields, encourage nitrogen fixation, and produce agro-chemicals. The problem facing the patent world was how to handle applications relating to these inventions given the understandable dearth of jurisprudence on the matter.

## General Principles of Patentability

Article 52(1) of the EPC simply states that: 'European patents shall be granted for any inventions which are susceptible of industrial application, which are new and which involve an inventive step.' Paragraph (2) then states that for the purposes of the Convention certain types of information shall not be regarded as an invention; the list includes discoveries. No further definition of an invention is given. The principle of protection has been extended to nucleic acids, proteins and gene sequences, and higher life forms such as whole plants and animals have been patented. In addition, those technologies which lie at the interface between two different scientific disciplines (for example, bioinformatics which intersects bioscience and information technology) are also securing protection.

There are two problems with this practice for those who disagree with the patenting of inventions involving genetic material. The first is that there is a view that inventions involving living material cannot be patented, as genetic material is quintessentially a discovery. Secondly, even if it can be described as an invention, there are concerns that such inventions lack the capacity to be patented as they cannot meet the threshold for protection.

Discoveries

The issue here is whether inventions involving living material should be regarded as unpatentable on the grounds that any naturally occurring element of the invention is not an invention by man. Furthermore, where the living material is being used to produce the same effect as is produced in nature, albeit within a controlled (non-natural) environment, then should this use merely be deemed a utilisation of a discovery and not an invention by man.

Pre-1999, patent lawyers had to explain why, in patent law terms, this material could be regarded as an invention. The key element was the demonstration of an action by man which made that previously unutilised material (for example; material which only functioned in its natural environment) accessible through his developmental actions, the view taken by patent lawyers being that the unutilised natural form of the material is often not suitable for sustained and repeated use as is required under patent law.[50] In this *legal* sense a discovery is simply latent information for which a use has yet to be found. Once a novel and inventive use has been found for the discovered material then this may be patentable. There remains a concern that this is a form of legal sleight of hand and that this treatment of material discovered in nature as inventions for patent law purposes merely on the basis of whether a legal threshold has been met means that natural elements are patented. That this has been held to extend to inventions involving the modification of plant genes can be seen as far back as 1989 and the grant of a patent (subsequently amended) to Mycogen Plant Sciences.[51]

It is worth bearing in mind when looking at this interpretation, that a discovery is rarely in itself and of itself useful—it is the purpose to which it is put which can be meritorious. The level at which the meritoriousness is set should be sufficiently stringent to ensure that basic information common not to mankind but to a raft of likely innovative developments should not be claimed as part of any one of these but should be freely available to ensure the development of all. The EPO remains convinced of the appropriateness of this interpretation and application of the invention/discovery distinction. Indeed, this position is also generally accepted by those involved in protecting plant varieties. Speaking as to the UPOV position on this matter, Heitz has said that '[t]he identification of a gene existing in nature is not an invention, but a discovery. The gene, in its isolated form, can be an invention,'[52] and UPOV has no problem with the gene, as utilised, being patentable. It is worth also noting that few breeders questioned as part of the PIP study (discussed in chapter 8) had a problem with the definition which is used; quite possibly this was because the plant variety rights system itself permits a right to be granted over discoveries. However, despite these views there has remained some confusion on the precise application of the distinction and one of the functions of the new Implementing Rules was to clarify (and explain) the practice of the EPO.

The Rules refer to the qualities which a biotechnological invention should have to attract the grant of a patent. Rule 23(b) of the Rules (which contains the definitions) states that biotechnological inventions are those 'inventions which concern a product consisting of or containing biological material or a process by means of which biological material is produced, processed or used.' The Rule further defines 'biological material' as any 'material containing genetic

[50] See Teschermacher, above n 30, p 24.

[51] Mycogen, 'Plant Sciences/Modifying Plant Cells' [1997] *OJ EPO* 408 (T0694/92).

[52] Heitz, *Intellectual Property Rights and Plant Variety* (Protection paper given in 2001): see www.upov.int.

information and capable of reproducing itself or being reproduced in a biological system and includes products consisting of or containing biological material or a process by means of which biological material is produced, processed or used.'

This means, subject to the exclusions outlined in Rule 23(d) below, any material of the kind outlined in Rule 23(b) is potentially patentable. In keeping with the overall objective of the Convention, the Rules make it clear that the key requirement for protection is capacity to meet the threshold for protection.

The Granting Criteria

Each of these requirements must be demonstrated in the patent specification, which also must allow a person skilled in the art to reproduce the invention simply by reference to the specification. In contrast to plant variety rights, each application is subject to a paper examination only; there is no physical examination of the invention. The requirement is that the applicant must show that the invention is novel, involves an inventive step, is capable of industrial application and has been sufficiently disclosed.

It is important to remember that the principles being described have not necessarily developed as a result of patent applications involving plant material. In many instances what has occurred is the establishment of a principle which has then been applied to genetic material. It is also important to note that, aside from the specific exclusion of plant varieties, there is no specific provision relating to plant material within the EPC. Plant inventions are, therefore, not considered to be any different from other types of inventions, they are not singled out for special treatment (other than having the patent applications examined by examiners with a background in plant genetics), nor are they regarded as requiring any special application of the general principles of patent law. Because of the generalist nature of the system, a particular principle may have been established in a case involving material far removed from a case to which the principle ultimately is extended. This is not an argument for ignoring or rejecting the principle being applied. In terms of the application of the granting criteria to any invention involving living material, one of the most important cases in recent years is the *ICOS* patent decision in 2001.[53] The patent concerned genomic DNA encoding the V28 protein and, whilst the specification did not relate in any way to plants, the decision is as relevant for any application involving plant material as it is for applications involving proteins. This patent, which was granted, was revoked by the Opposition Division on the grounds that although the patent had not been granted over a mere discovery, it nonetheless did not relate to a patentable invention as the patent holder had failed to demonstrate an inventive step or any industrial application and sufficiently to disclose the invention. Leave was given to the patent holder to appeal, but this was not pursued. The substantive aspects of the decision will be discussed under the

[53] Patent no 94 903 271.8–2106/0630405/, 22 August 2001.

relevant headings below. It should be noted that the *ICOS* case is exceptional in that the patent was revoked on nearly all the substantive grounds used to justify grant.

### Novelty

Article 54(1) of the EPC states that a patent will only be granted over an invention which is novel. Novelty is assessed by reference to whether the material being claimed previously formed part of the state of the art. The European concept is an absolute notion, with the state of the art being taken to comprise everything made available to the public by means of a written or oral disclosure, by use or in any other way, before the date of filing the application. In the past, questions were raised as to whether inventions involving living material (and particularly those which involved material sourced from a natural host) could be regarded as patentable. The view was not dissimilar to that found in the US in the 'product of nature doctrine.' As the growth in bioscience patenting indicates, this was not a problem which exercised the granting office for long.

The explanation why inventions involving living material can be regarded as novel lies in the fact that novelty is a quantitative concept.[54] This means that the subject matter of the patent application must not replicate anything which is already available *in that form*. The nature of the requirement is such that the issue is not whether the application involves material which has an existing equivalent, but whether the two manifestations of that information are, in form, the same. On this basis, producing something which appears to be the same as something already in existence, but which is technically different, can result in a patentable invention. The issue is simply one of whether a person working in that area of science would have thought of replicating the existing material in that way.[55] An example of such an invention could be the use of synthetic chemical constructs to mimic the naturally occurring properties of a plant. Whilst the properties produce the same effect, they have not been achieved in the same way. Provided that no one else has been able to achieve this effect in the same technical way, the synthetic version could be patentable—the issue is whether it was inventive to think of producing a copy in this way.

The novelty in any given invention lies in determining whether it was previously available in the form being claimed in the patent application. Two distinct, but interrelated, elements have to be shown. The first is whether the information was available. The second is whether the information already available discloses the invention being claimed in a manner which will enable a

---

[54] This is very clearly explained in Bently and Sherman, *Intellectual Property Law*, 2nd edn (OUP, 2004) 443.

[55] There is also the issue of whether the existing material is itself under patent, in which case the claims of that patent might extend to other technical realisations which achieve the same effect. This is essentially a matter of claims construction, which will be discussed in the next chapter.

person, not necessarily skilled in the art, to comprehend the inventive concept being claimed as the novel feature of the invention.

The first element is whether the public previously had access to the inventive concept being claimed—the fact that the information utilised in the invention might already exist, for example as a gene within an indigenous plant, is not usually sufficient to deem it to have been available in the patent law sense, the reason being that the gene within the plant is not directly accessible—indeed, outside the scientific community it is unlikely the gene itself will be known; there might be knowledge that plants contain genes, but not specific knowledge of that gene. Equally, knowledge of the general construction of a plant does not mean that there is general access to the constituent parts of the plant in the sense of the general public being able to separate genes from their host environment. Obviously if the gene has previously been isolated then it is known in that isolated form; the question then is whether the form being claimed in the patent is sufficiently different from that already known to hold that the invention involving that gene is novel.

The second element is whether the invention was actually available in the form claimed in the patent application. A plant gene *in situ* is unlikely to be regarded as available as it could not be accessed. Once that gene has been isolated then, provided no one else has isolated that gene, the inventor will be able to show that the plant gene is now available (accessible) in a form (isolated from its original source) in which it was not previously available. Where a gene has already been isolated by another scientist, the question for the patent examiners is whether the patent applicant can show that the gene as used in the form described in the patent application was not known before. The issue as to whether there is merit in either the isolation or the application to which the isolated gene is put is determined by the inventive step and industrial application criteria.

The same test applies to any construct using genetic material—was that genetic material, the technical essence of which is being claimed, known in that form before the patent application was filed? The key is not whether the genetic material *per se* was previously available, but whether someone having access to that genetic material would have sufficient access to its technical construction to understand what the inventor is claiming as their novel invention. The deconstruction of the genetic material in order to describe the foundation upon which an application of that genetic material has been built can form the novel feature of such patent applications. Plants surround us, and in this strict sense nearly all forms of plant material are in the public domain. But it is extremely unlikely that the public noting a particular plant will be able to understand its precise genetic make-up or recognise the effects of a plant breeding programme merely by looking at the plant. More information needs to be provided. It is the provision of this information which can render the information about the plant novel. However, merely making this information known does not of itself make the plant material patentable.

This distinction has been challenged on the grounds that the fact that the use of the information might be novel and inventive should not be sufficient to render the basic information so used as novel and inventive and therefore itself covered by the patent, whereas that information should remain unprotected as simply a discovery created by natural forces notwithstanding the intervention by the 'inventor'. Another objection to the discovery/invention distinction used in patent law is that often patents will be granted where all that has occurred is the ability to replicate that which previously was produced by nature alone. The issue here is whether the decision to replicate a natural effect can be regarded as inventive. It is not proposed to discuss these criticisms further, but it is worth repeating that, in the absence of any political will, or other influential statement for example from the WIPO, the definitions given to these terms will be those determined by the granting offices. In such circumstances, which include a recognition of the presumption of patentability, it is unsurprising that the definitions which have been adopted should be ones which favour an inclusionary approach.

In *Howard Florey/Relaxin*[56] the EPO held that the isolation of a human protein which had not previously been in the public domain, together with the use made of that protein once isolated, was patentable. Similarly in *ICOS*[57] (which was decided after the Implementing Rules were amended), the Opposition Division of the EPO stated that, whilst the claimed V28 gene and protein 'exists as a segment of the human genome and thus it is a part of nature, the purified and isolated nucleic acid having that sequence does not exist in nature and thus, cannot be discovered. The purified and isolated polynucleotide encoding V28 protein is, *de facto* not a discovery' and, therefore, novel.

The Implementing Rules provide some guidance on novelty and biotechnological inventions. Rule 23(c) establishes both that patent protection shall be available for biotechnological inventions and that such inventions will be taken to include biological material which is isolated from its natural environment or produced by means of a technical process even if it previously occurred in nature. This means that any naturally occurring plant material which is used in the production of a novel and inventive result could be patented even if the information previously occurred in nature. In many respects this merely reaffirms the existing situation in patent law. It is rare for any material to be wholly new in origin but in respect of chemical patents, in particular, the basic material usually consists of that which already existed. The fact of its previous existence has not been a bar to patentability the barrier is whether the use of that information is both new and not obvious to anyone else skilled in that area.

The second of the granting criteria is inventive step.

### Inventive Step

'An invention shall be considered as involving an inventive step if, having regard to the state of the art, it is not obvious to a person skilled in the art' (Article 56). The Implementing Rules do not include any statement on inventive step.

Because the requirement is that the inventive conceit must not have been 'obvious to a person skilled in the art,' this criterion is often also referred to as non-obviousness (which is the term used in the US). Inventive step is commonly regarded as the most difficult of the criteria to demonstrate, as it calls for evidence that what the inventor did would not have been obvious to anyone else working in that area. Unlike novelty, which is a quantitative matter, inventive step is essentially a qualitative matter. At the very general level, many offices, such as the European Patent Office, operate a variety of different notions of inventive step including the so-called 'Problem and Solution' approach. This involves a determination of whether the inventor has demonstrated that the invention, as described in the specification, provides a solution to the problem of getting from the prior art to the new technical effect. The application is examined a) to identify the prior art, b) to identify the technical problem—using the invention as described and the prior art, and c) to assess whether a skilled person in the art, using the prior art, would have arrived at the same solution. In other words would it have been obvious to the person skilled in the relevant art to produce the invention which solves the problem. This is essentially a question of fact.

The difficulty with identifying inventive step is that what the patent applicant might have done might not have been particularly inventive in the sense of a prolonged intellectual investigation of a particular problem. Instead, they might have stumbled upon a simple explanation as to how to achieve a particular result, or indeed something they think might achieve a number of particular results. In such circumstances the intellectual endeavour could be said to come from unravelling how that 'breakthrough' in understanding can be applied in a consistent manner and defined as a single inventive construct (albeit one which might have a variety of diverse applications, not all of which are identifiable at the point of invention.) In addition, where an application relates to the use of a known technique in a new context then the question is whether a person skilled in the art would have thought that there was a reasonable expectation of success. In a case which came before the Technical Board of Appeal (TBA) in 2000,[58] an appeal made by Monsanto against a revocation of a patent for a method of effecting somatic changes in plants was rejected on the grounds that the patentee had not shown that a skilled person would have thought there were any obstacles to carrying out the experiments in plants. The decision of the TBA indicates that the fact that a particular research avenue is known to others working in the area is not necessarily a defeating factor *if* the patentee can show that by taking that route he has achieved something which others skilled in the art did not think had a reasonable expectation of success, or, in other words, the patentee found a solution to the problem which others skilled in the art thought existed in trying to follow that particular route. In the context of the patent before it, the Board held that whilst Monsanto had put forward various

---

[58] *Monsanto/Somatic Changes* [2003] EPOR 327.

arguments as to why others may have been pessimistic about the likelihood of success in using an anti-sense strategy (proven to be successful in bacterial and mammalian cell systems) in plants, it had not provided any evidence that the pessimism alleged (which related to general inexperience in genetic engineering at the time the inventive activity took place) would have created 'a prejudice' or constituted 'a real obstacle to carrying out anti-sense experiments in plants' for those skilled in the art. Clearly there is a need to show more than just doing that which others have not yet done. The Board did say that where a new field of technology is involved then generally the lower the expectation of success, but it said that the 'absence of a factor' alleged to be an obstacle (such as the lack of general knowledge) 'should not be taken as an indication that the invention could not be achieved.'[59]

Another problem with the concept is that it is always applied with the benefit of hindsight, and therefore what might not have been obvious at the time of 'invention' might be thought blindingly obvious once the explanation is provided. Phillips and Firth use the elegant example of a crossword puzzle—the solution to a cryptic clue might elude the keenest of minds, but frequently once the solution is provided it appears self-evident.[60] A problem for the courts is that often a case is heard many years after the invention was made—once again the level of understanding at the time of the action should not be used to determine that existing at the time of invention. Examiners, and courts hearing patent cases, have to put explanatory information post-invention out of their minds—the relevant point in time for their consideration is the period leading up to the development of the invention claimed—what was known then, not what is known now. This can be difficult, for the evolution of any given invention might be protracted with much being discovered by others working in the field which circles around the production of the invention being claimed without actually producing it. Equally, as indicated above, the solution to the technical problem might result from stumbling across the novel conceit. Determining what was known to be possible, what was thought to be possible and being able to develop something which makes it possible is not an easy task.

A further challenge to the criterion arises where the problem is commonly known and a solution identified but realising that solution rests on taking a commercial decision to invest in realising the solution. Is the taking of that decision to fund the research an inventive step? The practice of the EPO appears to suggest that it would be. Whilst this might seem to fly in the face of the notion that a patent serves to reward inventive activity, in practice it is not such a difficult approach to understand. As the depth and extent of knowledge about a given subject area increases, the capacity to innovate within that area (in a way which is not obvious to any others skilled in the art) correspondingly decreases. If encouragement is to be given to continued research and development then

---

[59] [2003] *EPOR* 327.
[60] Phillips and Firth, *Introduction to Intellectual Property Law*, above n 5, p 51.

alternative reasons for granting protection have to be found—one of which might rest on the investment risk inherent in bringing a particular product to market. Where the invention concerned is of a traditional type then the granting of rights may be justified on the basis that it is possible for competitors to invent around the application by developing an alternative product which produces a corresponding result (the only caveat being whether this falls within the claims of the initial patent). That said, where the subject matter concerned is of a highly sensitive nature then granting rights to those who have the financial where-withal to invest in research might not be seen as appropriate or in the public interest. Such, it is argued, is the case with genetic material. The fact that often it is not possible to invent around the patented territory as it is unique, and the development of any corresponding invention will therefore fall within the scope of the patent, means that there is less acceptance of a commercially orien-tated policy towards applying the inventive step criterion than in respect of any other type of invention. Central to the disquiet such a policy would create is the US experience outlined in chapter 2.[61]

The most problematic aspect of the requirement concerns inventions at the cut-ting edge of technology, such as much of modern plant science. The test is whether a person skilled in the art would have thought to take that particular inventive step forward. In an area of technology where there are a *minimal* num-ber of persons skilled in the art but those who are have *maximum* understanding of the possible breakthroughs to be achieved, demonstrating that such a person, albeit in hypothetical form, would not have thought of pursuing the line of enquiry leading up to the novel inventive construct can prove insurmountable.

In *ICOS*,[62] the Opposition Division held that the important factor was 'the degree of characterisation of the disclosed V28 protein in comparison with the state of the art.' In this particular instance, whilst the invention did provide a solution to a particular problem (namely the provision of a nucleotide sequence which could encode an additional 7TM protein which can be predicted to func-tion as a receptor), it was not thought to be a particularly inventive solution. Documents submitted to the Division provided evidence that the solution being claimed by ICOS had previously been predicted and therefore achieving this solution using methods already well-known was not inventive: 'the Opposition Division takes the view that these kinds of choices [deciding which process to use to identify the protein] fall within the routine procedure followed by the skilled persons.' Equally, the claims which were dependent upon the sequence thus identified were not considered inventive either.

Once the level of obviousness in patent law is understood it become clearer as to why the results of traditional plant breeding, together with the processes used to achieve these, were not regarded as patentable. With the advent of the modern intra-genetic technologies it becomes more possible to show a

---

[61] For a discussion of this practice see Llewelyn, 'Industrial Applicability/Utility and Genetic Engineering: Current Practices in Europe and the United States' (1994) 11 *EIPR* 473.
[62] Above n 57.

patent-compliant notion of not being obvious, although the highly competitive aspect of all areas of biotechnology can mean that more than one company can be racing to achieve the same result. As the knowledge of the potential uses of plant material increases, the degree to which those uses can be said to be unobvious correspondingly decreases. However, the results of this research might have great commercial potential. The issue which has yet to be fully thrashed out within any patent system is whether the commercial value of a particular result could be sufficient justification to outweigh any deficiencies in complying with the inventive step requirement.

Great concern has been expressed in a number of quarters as to what could be termed the rather arbitrary manner in which this requirement has been determined by granting offices. The result has been, in Europe at least, that patent offices, including the European Patent Office, have tightened up their practices, meaning that in future it is less likely that patents will be granted over minor developments.[63]

The reasons lying behind this tightening up indicate an increased readiness of granting offices to respond to both commercial and social concerns about their practices. A key reason for this change is that the science has now moved on to the point where sufficient is understood about the mechanics of genetics to know what is inventive and what is merely day-to-day plodding research. In the past, patent offices were placed in the position where insufficient information was known either by their examiners or by the experts called upon to make an educated evaluation of the inventiveness exhibited in any given invention. The problem with this approach was that it sat alongside the presumption of patentability and there was a tendency to err on the side of the patent applicant and, in the absence of any contrary evidence, to grant the patent. The fact that there was little external evidence of any kind upon which to make any educated decision about the inventiveness of a particular invention should perhaps have led offices to hold fire on granting patents. The justification for this approach was that if there was an issue over the inventiveness of an invention then this could be brought before the courts, which would be better placed to make a determination. The reason why the court will be able to make a fuller assessment of the inventive quality attaching to the invention is the fact that the granting Office will have had before it only the application and any information which is in the public domain. In contrast, a court is likely to have access to information about any contemporary work of competitors which may have been undisclosed at the time that the patent concerned was being examined. This information is unlikely to have been known at the time of application (for reasons of trade secrecy and the need to protect the competitor's intellectual property, actual or prospective); however, it may be disclosed in the event that the competitor wishes either to oppose the grant made or to defend an allegation of infringement.

---

[63] An example of this can be seen in the UK Patent Office Guidelines for Examination of Biotechnological Invention, which state that the advancements in science mean that even where there might be a *de facto* invention, *de jure* it might not be patentable: www.patent.gov.uk.

Given the presumption of patentability and the strong commercial imperatives to foster the new biosciences, the decision to go ahead with granting patents in the expectation that the issue of an appropriate level of inventive step would be left to the courts is understandable, for it is at the stage of litigation that the full range of information about a given research area is likely to become known. However, this does mean that the certainty over the grant made, and predictions over the patentable status of research in a given area, is reduced until such time as the court makes its decision. Even when the decision is made this does not resolve the problem about the general level of inventiveness required, as the decision will only relate to that particular patent, and does not go to the practice of the granting office. In order to avoid any allegations that its practice was giving rise to more uncertainty than certainty through operating too low a level of inventive step (rendering a patent grant vulnerable to challenge via the courts), the granting offices, needing to retain trust, had to revise their policy, and it is now unlikely that patents will be granted over minor developments. This view is shared by many patent practitioners, including Andrew Sheard (whose views carry great weight as he is one of the authors of an authoritative text on the EU Directive), who stated at a meeting of the UK Human Genetics Commission in March 2002, and at a conference on Law and Genetics held in November 2002, that in his view the concerns expressed over a proliferation of gene patents will not be realised, as the majority of the applications will fail for a lack of inventiveness.

Patent offices now place greater emphasis on the standard requirement of inventive step (non-obviousness) as the requirement which will do most to retain genetic patenting within acceptable bounds. With the growth of bioinformatic techniques to achieve automated comparison of gene functions between different species, it becomes increasingly hard to characterise the work as anything other than routine. Indeed, on 18 May 2004 the Opposition Division revoked one of the patents[64] held by Myriad genetics over the BRCA genes (these are genes which code for breast cancer).[65] Whilst the case involved human genetic material, it nonetheless has significance for all other biotechnological patents in that the reason given for revocation was that the 'patent did not meet the requirements of the EPC, in particular as regards inventive step (level of invention).'[66] In January 2005, the Opposition Division also agreed to maintain, in a revised form, two other patents held on the breast and ovarian cancer susceptibility gene by Myriad (and others),[67] as the claims were held to relate to a diagnostic method (which is also an excluded category under the Convention). At the time of writing the full reasoning for the decisions had not been published.

[64] EP 699754, granted 2001.

[65] The opposition was brought by the Institut Curie, with, amongst others the Hopitaux de Paris, Institut Gustav Roussy, the Belgian Society for Human Genetics and the Associazione Angela Serra per la Ricerca sul Cancro.

[66] EPO Press Release, 18 May 2004.

[67] EP 705902 and EP785216.

It is relevant therefore to be aware that inventive step is probably the most evolutionary of three granting criteria and the most difficult to sum up. It is important to recognise, however, that there is a multiplicity of ways to decide inventiveness. In particular, the degree of knowledge and ingenuity held by this hypothetical person skilled in the art serves to highlight national differences—for example, in the UK the person skilled in the art has no imagination, whereas in Germany the same notional person is taken to exhibit some ingenuity.

The third substantive requirement is industrial application.

## Capable of Industrial Application

Article 57 states that an 'invention is considered as susceptible of industrial application if it can be made or used in any kind of industry, including agriculture—this does not include methods of human treatment.' In the past, the industrial application criterion has been regarded as the easiest of the substantive requirements to demonstrate. All that it requires is for the application to show that the invention is in a finished form (and does not require any further research to complete the inventive concept being claimed) and that it is capable of being used within an industrial (essentially commercial) context, this latter element being necessary to ensure that the protected invention is capable of dissemination thereby providing a public interest *quid pro quo* for the grant. For the most part this has been a relatively uncontroversial provision however, concerns about its application have been raised in respect of bioscience inventions.

The Implementing Rules state in Rule 23(3) that 'the industrial application of a sequence or partial sequence must be disclosed in the patent application as filed.' As this is contained in Rule 23(e), which specifically relates to the patentability of the human body, it is unclear whether this requirement applies to all bioscience inventions or only those involving human genetic material. In the UK the same concept has been introduced on a 'pan-bio-science' basis;[68] however, as the Directive also places the requirement into its Article relating to human genetic material (Article 5(3)) it is possible that other national laws may do the same.

The reason for the emphasis on an actual disclosure of function was because of concerns that patents were being applied for, and granted over, 'inventions' which identified particular genes or gene partial fragments, but the application (and later specification) did not disclose any industrial application or function for that material—for example. it did not disclose that the 'inventor' had accomplished a use for them. Many of these patents were granted, although strictly speaking they were over discoveries rather than inventions, and it was quickly realised that the enthusiasm of granting offices had to be curtailed.

---

[68] Examination Guidelines for Patent Applications relating to Biotechnological Invention in the UK Patent Office, above n 63, para 42.

The main research project affected was the Human Genome Project. What was happening was that some companies sought to patent commercially important results before an application had been identified. This practice was particularly prevalent in the US, where patents were frequently granted for gene fragments the full sequence and function of which were unknown. This attracted a raft of criticism from all quarters and, as mentioned in chapter 2, in 2001 the United States Patent and Trade Mark Office issued new guidelines requiring the patent specification to demonstrate a utility that is specific, substantial and credible, rather than merely speculative. The provision is still somewhat weak, since the utility need only be theoretically possible and only one actual function needs to be demonstrated whilst the applicant can also claim a number of speculative functions as well.

The revised Implementing Rules do not make any reference to the need for the function to be specific, substantial or credible, but subsequent case law of the EPO indicates that it has adopted this principle. The Opposition Division, in revoking the *ICOS* patent, stated that as the patent specification simply stated potential uses for the V28 protein as a receptor, this did not equate to disclosure of a function which was 'specific, substantial and credible.' Nor, in the absence of any disclosure of the therapeutic uses to which the invention could be put, could it be seen 'why it would be useful to produce said protein on a large scale in industry.'

As already mentioned, some national granting offices, such as the UK office, have, through specific revisions to their examination guidelines, adopted much the same standard. The UKPO Guidelines refer to the need for different approaches to claims for sequences within genes and within proteins. What is not tackled by these general rules is the question whether use-limited claims alone should be allowed when one function for a gene, protein or receptor has been discovered and then a second function is separately discovered.

The last of the substantive requirements is that the patent application must fully disclose the invention.

Sufficiency of Disclosure

The disclosure requirement is fundamental to the justification of the patent.[69] It serves two functions. The disclosure must be such that it enables a person skilled in the art a) to understand the novel technical effect being claimed (and therefore know the extent of territory claimed) and b) to reproduce that novel technical effect. This can be achieved by a written description, drawing, inclusion of diagrams or any combination. In addition, the issue of disclosure, and the extent of the same, goes to the heart of the novelty requirement, as only that which has been made public can be taken into consideration when assessing the novelty of

---

[69] Art 83 of the EPC states that the patent application must disclose the invention in a manner sufficiently clear and complete to enable the invention to be carried out by a person skilled in the art.

any subsequent material. If the sole source of any prior information, or art, is a patent then the extent to which that prior patent discloses the inventive concept claimed in a later patent will determine the novelty of that later invention.

Two useful examples of the disclosure requirement in practice are the *ICOS* and *Pioneer/oilseed brassica* cases.

In *ICOS* the Opposition Division held the patent to fall for a lack of sufficiency of disclosure on the following grounds. First, there was insufficient information about the specific nature of the ligands involved, meaning that a person skilled in the art was likely to have to test millions of candidate compounds to try and identify the appropriate ligand for V28. Secondly, the disclosure of the amino acid sequence of the V28 protein and the prediction of a function as receptor together with the method for identifying the ligand was not sufficient to disclose the claimed receptor protein. Thirdly, the claim for an antibody substance specific for V28 protein could not be sustained, as there was no disclosure of an antibody substance which had this capacity to recognise V28. Finally the claim to an *in vitro* method which relied on the use of either an agonist or antagonist of V28 was not thought to have been sufficiently disclosed, as the specification merely referred to antibodies and not antagonists. The Opposition Division was not prepared to accept the patentee's argument that antibodies were a 'well-known class of antagonists' in the absence of any specific disclosure in the specification of the type of antibody which could act as the antagonist.

In *Pioneer/oilseed brassica*,[70] the Examining Division refused to grant a patent over a *brassica* plant which contained a homozygous fertility restorer gene and had a low glucosinolate content. The Division thought that the prior art, which took the form of a document which disclosed using the crossing of oilseed plants in order to break the known link between restorer genes and high glucosinate levels, disclosed the invention claimed by Pioneer. The Technical Board of Appeal upheld an appeal by Pioneer that the prior documentation did not disclose the homozygosity of the restorer gene nor the low glucosinolate content in a single *brassica* plant. In addition, the document which was alleged to form the prior art was not an enabling disclosure as no deposit of any seeds or markers had been made. This fact also went to the extent of the prior disclosure as the Board held that the results outlined in the document were due to a 'fortuitous' event which, in the absence of the seeds or markers, meant that repeating the results would be difficult and the content of the document 'cannot be considered for judging the novelty of the subject matter of the . . . present application.'[71] The Board referred the application back to the Division for reconsideration. (The application concerned a conventional breeding programme, involving crossing and selection. The patentability of the results from such programmes will be discussed in the next chapter.)

---

[70] [2004] *EPOR* 421.
[71] *Ibid*, p 426.

The issue of whether an invention has been sufficiently disclosed is usually tested only once the patent has been granted and a competitor attempts to replicate the inventive concept. In disclosing the invention, a balance often has to be struck between, on the one hand, ensuring that the patent covers minor variations to the invention and, on the other, not claiming more than the inventor has actually achieved. The issue of breadth of claims, claiming whole swathes of uses of the 'invention', is very controversial and one which we will return to later.

The ability to meet the threshold for protection does not guarantee that a patent will be granted; an assessment also has to be made as to whether the invention described in the patent application falls within any of the categories of excluded material.

Excluded Material

When looking at the categories of excluded material, it is important to bear in mind that the subject matter concerned in these categories is not excluded because it is not an invention. Notwithstanding its ability to meet the threshold for protection, it is excluded from protection because it is not in the public interest to permit patent protection over these types of inventions.

The relevant provision for plant innovations is Article 53 of the EPC. This excludes three main types of inventions: inventions the publication or exploitation of which would be contrary to morality plant varieties;[72] and essentially biological processes for the production of plants (the last two on this list will be discussed in the next chapter).

**Article 53(a) Morality**

Article 53(a) states that European patents shall not be granted respect of 'inventions the publication or exploitation of which would be contrary to "ordre public" or morality, provided that the exploitation shall not be deemed to be so contrary merely because it is prohibited by law or regulation in some or all of the Contracting States.'

There are five key elements to Article 53(a). These are that the

(1) publication,

or

(2) exploitation

of the invention must not be contrary to

(3) morality

---

[72] And animal varieties.

or

(4) *ordre public*;

it is irrelevant for the purposes of applying Article 53(a), whether the exploitation (and, by inference, publication) is

(5) prohibited by law in one or all member states of the EPC. In other words the fact that something is illegal does not make it immoral.

The Guidelines to the EPC provide some assistance on how this provision is to be interpreted in practice. Part C IV3 of the Guidelines to the EPC states that the exclusion in Article 53(a) is intended to cover those inventions 'likely to induce riot or public disorder' or which would lead to 'criminal or other generally offensive behaviour.' It cites as 'obvious examples . . . letter bombs and anti-personnel mines.' The most important part of the guidance then follows when it states that 'this provision is likely to be invoked only in rare and extreme cases.' Once this is understood then the application of the provision in practice becomes easier to understand. In addition, the Guidelines state that the benchmark for deciding if an invention falls within the provision is whether the public would find it 'abhorrent'. In terms of the application of the provision to biotechnology, paragraph 3.3b refers the examiners to the amended Rule 23, which excludes protection for processes for cloning human beings; processes for modifying the germ line genetic identity of human beings; uses of human embryos for industrial or commercial purposes; and processes for modifying the genetic identity of animals which are likely to cause them suffering without any substantial medical benefit to man or animal, and also animals resulting from such processes. Rule 23(e) then contains some specific statement on the patentability of the human body and its elements.[73] As can be seen none of these relates to plant material, and any exclusion of plant material (for example on the grounds of harm to the environment) would have to fall within the general principle in Article 53(a).

This means that an invention involving plant material will be excluded only if it is likely to induce riot or public disorder or would lead to criminal or other generally offensive behaviour which the public would find abhorrent. As this is to be used only in rare and extreme cases, it is difficult to see how this can be applied to plant innovations other than where there is clear evidence that the invention concerned would cause serious harm to public health or the environment. As will be seen when discussing some of the cases below, this is very difficult to do in practice.

---

[73] An example of this operating in practice can be found in Patent No 0695351, 22 February 2000 (the so-called Edinburgh University patent granted over the cloning process which produced Dolly the Sheep) which claimed the results of the cloning processes including humans. This was amended in 2002, on the basis that this claim violated Rule 23(e): EPO Press Release, 24 July 2002.

Publication or Exploitation

The notions of publication and exploitation have not really been addressed by any of the Boards of Appeal of the EPO. Suffice to state that it appears from the cases brought before the Boards that these terms refer to the use to be made of the patented technology. 'Publication' seems to refer to placing the material into the public domain (as opposed to merely publishing in a print sense of the term) and 'exploitation' to making use of the technology. When looking at the EU, one point of important comparison arises and that is that the EU Directive uses different wording and refers to the 'commercial exploitation' (Article 6(1)) of the invention with no reference to 'publication'. This could give rise to an inconsistency between the operation of the two exclusions, as publication could include use in an unethical research programme whereas it is unclear whether this would be covered by the term 'commercial exploitation'. This will be discussed in more detail in chapter 7.

In the cases which have been brought, the primary focus of attention has been defining morality or *ordre public*.

Morality or *Ordre Public*[74]

The *Plant Genetic Systems*[75] (PGS) case (discussed further in the next chapter) provides a useful guide to the distinction between *ordre public* and morality in respect of plant innovations.

The Technical Board of Appeal stated that:

the concept of 'ordre public' covers the protection of public security and the physical integrity of individuals as part of society. This concept encompasses also the protection of the environment. Accordingly, under Article 53(a) EPC, inventions the exploitation of which is likely to breach public peace or social order . . . or seriously to prejudice the environment are to be excluded from patentability as being contrary to 'ordre public'.

In respect of morality the Board stated that the concept

is related to the belief that some behaviour is right and acceptable whereas other behaviour is wrong, this belief being founded on the totality of the accepted norms which are deeply rooted in a particular culture. For the purposes of the EPC the culture in question is the culture inherent in European society and civilisation. Accordingly, under Article 53(a), inventions the exploitation of which is *not* in conformity with the conventionally-accepted standards of conduct pertaining to this culture are to be excluded from patentability as being contrary to morality.[76]

---

[74] By and large the cases referred to below were decided before the new Implementing Rules were adopted. However, there does not appear to be any inconsistency between the Rules and the prior practice.

[75] 'Plant Genetic Systems/Glutamine Synthesise Inhibitors' [1995] *EPOR* 357, 366, para 5.

[76] *Ibid*, para 6.

In making these statements the Board acknowledged that the draftsmen of the Convention had recognised that there was no European definition of either morality or *ordre public* and that the assessment of each would be a matter of interpretation. Despite drawing this distinction between the two concepts it is common for the Board to elide the two in its decisions and it can be difficult to determine which is being applied. This was certainly the case in *Plant Genetic Systems,* where the opposition, which was based on a claim that genetically modified plants would be harmful if released into the environment, was discussed in the context of both *ordre public* and morality.

The PGS case concerned a patent granted over plants (including seeds) which had been developed to be resistant to a particular group of herbicides. Greenpeace lodged an opposition based on both parts of Article 53—the exclusion on grounds of morality and that relating to plant varieties (discussed later). The opposition under Article 53(a) was that the plants claimed would, if used, prove contrary to both *ordre public* and morality as they could cause harm to the environment, and a number of publications were cited in which it had been asserted that there was a possibility that genetically engineered plants could turn into weeds. Greenpeace also relied upon two studies, undertaken in Sweden and Switzerland, to indicate that the public was against the patenting of genetically engineered plants. The Technical Board of Appeal dismissed the argument.

The Board held that there was no actual evidence that the plants would cause the harm alleged and therefore the granting of the patent over them was not contrary to *ordre public*. The Board said that, in its view, plant breeding involving biotechnological methods was no more morally doubtful than traditional plant breeding, both being geared towards the same result, the changing of the genetic properties of plants, albeit by different methods. The Board accepted that there was concern over biotechnology and that where the use of the invention concerned was directed to a misuse or a destructive use then Article 53(a) would clearly apply. However, in the specific instance before it there was no evidence that Plant Genetic Systems was proposing that the plants claimed would be misused or used for destructive purposes. As no misuse had been shown, the invention could not be said to contravene any conventionally accepted standard of conduct of European culture and therefore was not contrary to morality.

The Board also dismissed the evidence provided by the two studies in Sweden and Switzerland. It held that these were not sufficient to indicate a common consensus across Europe regarding the patentable status of plant material, as the veracity of the information contained in the results of surveys and opinion polls could fluctuate according to multifarious circumstances including the type of questions asked and the size and group of sample asked.

In making its determination, the Board accepted that it stood 'at the crossroads between science and public policy' but it did not accept that this position was an isolated one. Instead, it stood alongside other authorities, particularly those concerned with the regulation of new technologies. The contention that the technology underpinning the plants claimed by Plant Genetic Systems would seriously prejudice the environment 'presupposes that the threat to the environment be sufficiently substantiated at the time the decision to revoke the patent is taken by the EPO.' The evidence provided by Greenpeace did not provide this substantiation. The EPO did not consider that it should fill any gaps left by inadequate regulation by denying a patent on the speculative basis that an invention might cause harm.

This case is often used to demonstrate the problems opponents face when trying to establish a possible moral outcome which would prove detrimental, and the fact that it would seem that in order for Greenpeace to have any chance of successfully opposing the patent they would have had to permit the very thing they were seeking to avoid in order to prove that their argument had merit. What is not often discussed is what this case says about the differential in the requisite levels of evidence required from each party. Greenpeace lost because it failed to demonstrate that there was a real or actual detriment which would result from the use of the protected plant material. Plant Genetic Systems however, succeeded purely by showing that there was a likelihood of benefit—they did not have to show that this benefit *would* result. It is clear that speculative benefit is sufficient for the EPO to uphold a patent, but speculative harm is insufficient to either reject or revoke one. As the invention is not subject to any further scrutiny by the granting office once a grant has been made, unless at the EPO an opposition is lodged by a third party, the extent to which the speculative benefit is realised post-grant is never actually tested by those who have overseen the grant and who have taken the application on trust as being for that which will provide a benefit and not a harm.

Other cases useful to understanding how the general provision applies in practice include *Harvard/Oncomouse*[77] and *Relaxin*.[78]

The *Oncomouse* case concerned a patent which had been granted over a mouse genetically engineered to develop cancerous tumours. Hearing an internal appeal from its Examining Division, the Technical Board of Appeal of the European Patent Office decided that the proper interpretation of the provision lay in the use of a straight utilitarian approach. The simple question asked was whether the potential benefit to mankind outweighed any disbenefits in the form of suffering to the animals, and the answer was, yes. The decision, which provoked a storm of controversy[79] (not least because of the way in which it placed the interests of the animal kingdom below those of mankind), made it clear that a patent will be refused granted for reasons of morality only if the invention was abhorrent and, notwithstanding that abhorrence the *only use* to which it would

---

[77] [1990] *OJ EPO* 476; [1992] *OJ EPO* 589. The Oncomouse patent has been the subject of constant oppositions and appeals since the patent was first granted. These appear to have come to a conclusion in 2004 when the Technical Board of Appeal confirmed that the patent was to be restricted to mice alone—the original patent having claimed 'non-human mammalian animals' [2005] *EPOR* 271. The judgment discusses Art 53(a) in considerable detail but with specific application to animal inventions.

[78] [1995] *EPOR* 541.

[79] For example, see Beyleveld and Brownsword, *Mice, Morality and Patents*, above n 19; and Armitage and Davis, *Patents and Morality in Perspective*, above n 19.

be put would be to cause harm, the clear indication being that where an invention could be used for both beneficial and harmful purposes then the potential benefit would outweigh the possible harm and the patent would be granted. Even if there were a requirement to state the 'moral' purposes to which an invention is going to be put (which there is not) no patent applicant is going to indicate in the application that the use to which the invention will be put is purely a harmful one. This means that either the invention must be so clearly in itself and of itself immoral for an examiner to reject the application or, in the absence of this, and once a patent is granted, it will be for opponents of that patent to indicate the offensive nature of the use to which the invention could be put—the difficulty which this presents in practice will be discussed further below.

The *Howard Florey/Relaxin* case is useful as it addressed the matter of morality and genes or gene components. The patent was for a protein which had been isolated from pregnant women. The Technical Board of Appeal held that DNA is merely a chemical and as such could not be deemed 'life', therefore the opposition that the patent was for an immoral invention as it sought to patent on life did not contravene morality.[80]

Recent cases indicate that the EPO is taking a broader approach to defining morality. As yet these cases have not involved plant genetic material, but have concentrated on the more delicate subject of the patentability of human stem cells. In 2002, the Opposition Division heard an opposition to the patent granted to Edinburgh University over a patent relating to 'animal transgenic stem cells'. The question before the Division was whether the term 'animal' included humans for if it did then the invention could fall foul of Rule 23(e) of the Implementing Rules. In this instance the Division held that the term did extend to include human material, and the invention was, therefore, held to claim human stem cells. The next question for the Division was whether this amounted to a use of an embryo for industrial or commercial purposes. Stem cells are currently obtained though the development of an embryo from which the cells are harvested before the embryo is destroyed.[81] The Division had to decide if this constituted an industrial or commercial use of the embryo. It decided that it did on the basis that the human body was already excluded under Rule 23(d)—if Rule 23(c) was held to merely restate Rule 23(e) then this would make Rule 23(d) effectively redundant. It had, therefore, to perform a separate function and this was to exclude those parts of the embryo which might be used for research purposes. It has been pointed out that this approach sits uncomfortably alongside the more circumspect approach to applying the provision which is evident in cases such as *PGS*.[82]

---

[80] There were other grounds to the opposition, namely that the patent enslaved pregnant women and was contrary to human dignity. The opposition failed on these as well.

[81] Most countries which permit stem cell research require that the embryos are destroyed within 14 days of creation.

[82] Laurie, *Embryonic Stem Cell Patents: The European Experience*, Paper presented at the Conference on Bioethical Issues of Intellectual Property Rights (Tokyo, 2004), see www.ipgenethics.org. See also Laurie, 'Patenting Stem Cells of Human Origin' [2004] *EIPR* 59.

In 2004 the Examining Division looked at a patent application from the Wisconsin Alumni Research Foundation (WARF) relating to 'primate embryonic stem cells'. The Division held that all of the claims could be extended to include human embryonic stem cells and these were invalid under Rule 23(d). Key to the decision was the fact that embryos had to be used in order to produce the stem cells and it held that it was impossible to separate the end product from the method used to produce it. As Laurie put it, the Division chose to use a holistic approach to interpreting the claims.

It is not clear if a similar approach would be applied to plant innovations, but it is probably unlikely because the EPO does not have an equivalent rule relating to plants to that in Implementing Rule 23, which appears only to apply to human genetic material. Rather it is constrained merely to use the text of Article 53(a) in conjunction with existing precedent. In addition, there is a difference in the degree of moral concerns about inventions involving human genetic material and those involving plants, the former bearing overtones of the instrumentalisation of human beings, which many find abhorrent in a way which does not apply to uses made of plant material.

The issue of how to define and apply morality is a difficult one for the Office. It is primarily concerned with the granting of patents over inventions which meet an agreed, technical, threshold for protection and arguably it should not be concerned with more nebulous concepts such as defining morality. However, unlike the plant variety rights system, which clearly places this issue outside the purview of those administering the rights, by virtue of Article 53(a) the EPO is required to make such a determination, and the unease with which it undertakes this obligation is palpable.

Prohibited by Law or Regulation

The exclusion on moral grounds states quite clearly that an invention should not be excluded simply on the grounds that it is prohibited by law or regulation. Illegality and immorality are separate. However, notwithstanding this wording a recent decision by the Opposition Division of the EPO appears to indicate that where an invention has not been prohibited by *regulation* then this fact alone can be used so that the invention does not fall within Article 53(a).

In *Leland Stanford/Modified Animal*[83] an opposition was lodged against a patent which had been granted over a mouse which had been implanted with human tissue for use in the development of anti-AIDS remedies. One of the grounds for the opposition was that the invention posed an ecological risk in the possible generation of new pathological viruses. The Opposition Division dismissed the case saying that whilst the use of human foetal cells might appear distasteful the medical benefits were undisputed and not opposed by any regulatory authority. More significantly the Division said that the hypothetical

[83] [2002] *EPOR* 2.

ecological risk was not a reason for refusing a patent under Article 53(a) and that 'the EPO is not vested with the task of monitoring and assessing such risk, which instead falls to the appropriate regulatory authorities.' The implication from this is that the responsibility for regulating sensitive areas of technology should lie elsewhere and it is not for the EPO to directly concern itself with such matters. This approach raises certain questions.

Article 53(a) states that the exclusion does not operate *merely* because the publication or exploitation of the invention is prohibited by law or regulation. The exclusion does not, however, state that the provision operates in isolation from the legal or regulatory frameworks. Indeed, the mere fact that the invention is prohibited is not on its own sufficient to deem the publication or exploitation contrary to morality or *ordre public*. It would seem that there has to be something else which acts *in addition* to the legal or regulatory prohibition which triggers the exclusion. What is not clear, however, is if the legal or regulatory prohibition can itself serve as an initial trigger for the operation of Article 53(a), and once triggered, other moral objections to the patent being granted can be raised or if the moral concerns have first to be raised and these concerns imbued with weight by the fact of the legal or regulatory prohibition. In *Leland Stanford* the inference is that if the external regulatory authorities had assessed this virus as a risk, then the EPO *might* have applied the Article 53(a) exclusion. As there was no external regulatory prohibition, the EPO was not prepared to look further at whether the invention was contrary to morality or not. This would seem to suggest that whilst the legal or regulatory status of the invention does not in itself trigger the exclusion where moral concerns have been raised which could give rise to an exclusion under Article 53(a), a decision as to whether the exclusion applies or not could depend on whether the invention is subject to external regulation—in the *Leland Stanford* case the lack of any such prohibition being sufficient to allow the EPO to reject an application for revocation under Article 53(a).

It is questionable whether the EPO approach is a correct one, as it could be argued that whereas the illegality of an invention is not to be taken into account when determining if that invention is contrary to morality then equally the fact that it is legal or not excluded on regulatory grounds should also not be taken into account when establishing that the invention is not contrary to morality.[84] Either the legal/regulatory status is relevant for *both* purposes or it is relevant for neither. As before, the taint of the presumption of patentability is tangible. It is also perceptible, and arguably more so, in respect of the application and

---

[84] One of the few times when the EPO has directly referred to the ethical nature of a particular *type* of invention was in *Georgetown University/Pericardial Access (T35/99)* [2001] *EPOR* 169 in which it was stated, when discussing the exclusion of methods of treatment, that there are two types of treatment, that which gives a 'priority to maintaining life or health' and 'those procedures whose end result is the death of living beings . . . These "lethal" procedures, in accordance with their definition, involve sacrificing life, and are therefore subject to ethical considerations (see Art 53(a)).' This statement provides perhaps a key to the thinking of the EPO and its view on the 'ethical' nature of the job it seeks to do.

interpretation of the other categories of excluded material such as discoveries and plant varieties.

It is not proposed to discuss the theoretical underpinnings of these concepts further but it should be noted that there are some fundamental philosophical questions which can be asked about the definitions given to these concepts as well as about the application of these concepts in practice.[85] The belief that an invention should not be patented because it is contrary to morality must be one of the most obvious legal exclusions to have.[86] As this would appear to be fundamental, it might be thought that the exclusion would be at the heart of the system, and the presumption operating that any immoral invention would be excluded from grant, with the onus on the patent applicant to demonstrate that the invention will benefit rather than harm society. However, the overarching presumption of patentability, together with the apparent presumption in favour of accepting the argument for protection presented by the patent applicant unless scientific evidence can be presented for not making the grant, means that the issue of morality only arises a) where there is such an obvious moral repugnance to the invention concerned that the examiner, through reading mere technical detail, can identify this or b) where an opposition is lodged by a third party. In addition, the fact that the Patent Office would seem to accept that a putative benefit is enough to outweigh any harm alleged by an opponent would appear to indicate that the provision will apply only where the sole application for the invention concerned is a harmful one. Looking at the cases outlined above, it would seem that the exclusion will only operate in the most extreme of cases. In terms of its application to plant material, it appears unlikely that the provision will have much relevance, for, as the *PGS* case demonstrates, if it is not clear from the face of the patent specification that an invention will cause harm, then an opponent must provide unequivocal evidence that it does (merely alleging that it *may* cause harm seems not to be enough). It is doubtful that an applicant will include a claim which stipulates an overtly environmentally harmful application for the invention. It is equally doubtful that an opponent will be able to show at the time of application (and given the nature of the novelty requirement this will invariably be pre-grant) that the invention is, in itself and of itself, harmful. The fact that the invention may be capable of being put to harmful uses

---

[85] For example, see Beyleveld, Brownsword and Llewelyn, 'The Morality Clauses of the Directive on the Legal Protection of Biotechnological Inventions: Conflict, Compromise and the Patent Community' in Goldberg and Lonbay (eds), *Pharmaceutical Medicine, Biotechnology and European Law* (CUP, 2000) 157.

[86] Indeed, it can be argued that so fundamental is this notion that there is no need for the exclusion to be directly stated but rather that there should be an overarching presumption that patents are granted only over morally appropriate inventions; for a discussion of this see Llewelyn, Beyleveld and Kinderlerer (eds), *Commentary, including Alternative Text, on the Report of the Legal Affairs Committee of the European Commission on the Proposal for a Directive on the Legal Protection of Biotechnological Inventions* (Sheffield Institute for Biotechnological Law and Ethics (SIBLE), 1997) available from the author. It should be said that there are those who practise patent law who, whilst not necessarily countering that morality is a relevant issue, argue that this is matter for more proper authorities, for example, Government, than patent offices.

is also not an issue for the Patent Office but rather seen as a matter for external regulation.

## V. CONCLUSION

With the benefit of hindsight it would be easy to say that provision of protection under the EPC is relatively straightforward—anything which was capable of meeting the threshold for protection was protectable unless the invention fell within one of the categories of excluded material (narrowly construed). However, it has taken time for the Office to develop this jurisprudence and whilst it has evolved there have been some who have queried whether such an expansive approach to patenting is appropriate, especially within the biological sciences. Of particular concern are the legal definitions given to the discovery/ invention distinction, novelty and inventive step, as well as the commercial emphasis now apparently underpinning the industrial application criterion. The concerns are that the legal constructs bear little relation to their scientific counterparts and that legal semantics are being used to achieve results acceptable to an applicant (at the point of grant) but not necessarily to a scientific community as a whole. In addition, the emphasis on grant means that there are those who feel that the operation of the EPC is less rigorous than it should be, with the benefit of any doubt going to the applicant—the effect of this is to make grants less secure and more vulnerable to challenge. Such criticisms have to be looked at in the context of an Office which is, to a large extent, the victim of its own success. Applications to the Office increase yearly and there is intense pressure placed on the Office to grant rights quickly. It can be difficult both to achieve a swift grant and to ensure that a full, detailed, and exhaustive examination takes place for each invention, particularly given the global information era and also the rapidly changing nature of most areas of modern science. This should not serve to remove any obligation on the Office to maintain the highest standard of examination, but the fact that it might not necessarily always achieve this has to be assessed in the context of the rapid developments in science, and the subject expertise of its examiners as well as the political pressures to provide quick and appropriate protection to those who generate new products for the market place.

In respect of genetic inventions, the jurisprudence of the European Patent Office permits patent protection to be granted over a range of different genetic material including micro-organisms (broadly defined to include cells, proteins and enzymes) as well as higher order life-forms (such as the animals produced using the Roslin Institute's method of cloning). In addition, protection can be accorded to the various techniques used to produce these. In terms of plant-related invention, the practice is that anything can be patented provided that it meets the threshold for protection (including sufficiency of disclosure—often forgotten outside the patent world as a key requisite for protection) and is not excluded. As the discussion on morality shows, the onus for showing that an invention is *not* patentable lies with opponents to the grant and whilst the Office has had occasion to raise internal queries over whether a grant should be made it is only in exceptional cases that this has served to defeat either an application or a grant. The apparent simplicity of the policy which the Office now applies to genetic material (unless it is specifically excluded it is included) belies initial uncertainty as to the precise ambit of the exclusionary provisions. To an extent, the discussions over the role of Article 53(a) articulate this uncertainty; however, this provision has had only minimal application in respect of plant material and irrelevance is unlikely to change. Of far greater importance is Article 53(b). As the problems encountered in applying this provision go a long way to explaining the perceived relationship between patents and plant variety rights, a full discussion of this Article will form the basis of the next chapter.

# 6

# *The European Convention—the Article 53(b) Exclusions and Post-grant Issues*

## I. INTRODUCTION

A S THE LAST chapter has indicated, the current practice and policy of the EPO is to give a broad interpretation to the notion of what can be novel, inventive and of industrial application. In contrast it gives a narrow interpretation to the categories of excluded material. Whilst some commentators state that this approach was the one always intended,[1] the practice of both the Office and national granting offices, in the early days of the EPC at least, belies this. Nowhere is this uncertainty over what the Convention was intended to protect more apparent than in the application of Article 53(b).

## II. ARTICLE 53(B)

Article 53(b) states that 'European patents shall not be granted in respect of: 'Plant or animal varieties[2] or essentially biological process for the production of plants or animals; this provision does not apply to microbiological processes or the products thereof.'

For the purposes of modern-day application, Rule 23 of the new Implementing Rules provides further clarification on the scope of this provision. Rule 23(b) states that a plant variety is a

> single botanical taxon of the lowest known rank, which grouping, irrespective of whether the conditions for the grant of a plant variety right are fully met, can be (a) defined by the expression of the characteristics that results from a given genotype or combination of genotypes, (b) distinguished from any other plant grouping by the expression of at least one of the said characteristics, and (c) considered as a unit with regard to its suitability for being propagated unchanged.

---

[1] See Armitage and Davis, *Patents and Morality in Perspective* (Common Law Institute of Intellectual Property, 1994).

[2] Which will not be discussed here.

As can be seen, this mirrors the definition provided in Article 1(iv) of the 1991 UPOV Act.

Rule 23(c) further states that a microbiological (or other technical) process is patentable, as is any product obtained by means of such a process provided that this product does not take the form of a plant variety. Crucially, Rule 23(c) states that where the technical feasibility of the invention is not confined to a particular plant variety (that is, where what is being claimed is not a plant variety as defined in Rule 23(b)) then the exclusion does not apply.

On the face of it, the position under Article 53(b) appears clear.

A patent will not be granted over a plant variety which accords to the UPOV definition of a variety even where the variety has been produced by a microbiological process. Nor will a patent be granted over an essentially biological process for the production of plants.

The exclusion does not, however, apply to plants produced by an essentially biological process. As will be seen, these are patentable (provided that the threshold for protection has been met). Nor does the exclusion apply where the claims are not confined to a plant variety.

However, as was shown in chapter 2, the fact that apparently specific terms have been used does not necessarily indicate that those terms have either a precise or an agreed meaning. In particular, it should be noted that there is no universal definition of what is a plant or a plant variety, and this is exemplified by the continuing discussions over whether fungi are plants or micro-organisms. Equally there is no consensus over what is an essentially biological process.

As with Article 27(3)(b) of TRIPs, the language of Article 53(b) is open to various interpretations and the EPO has at times struggled both internally to agree what the exclusion covers and externally to convince others that its approach is the correct one. As will be shown, the overarching presumptions of protectability and patentability have meant that the exclusion is given a restrictive rather than expansive interpretation.

As stated earlier, the EPO now avers a policy of granting patents over inventions involving plant genetic material,[3] but putting this policy into practice was not as simple as the policy itself might indicate.

### The Article 53(b) Exclusion Generally.

For our purposes, Article 53(b) contains two exclusions: the exclusion of plant varieties and the exclusion of essentially biological processes for the production of plants.

There are four key questions which need to be addressed.

1) whether the exclusion of plant varieties applies to *all* plant material of an order higher than a micro-organism;

---

[3] Mycogen, 'Plant Sciences/Modifying Plant Cells' [1997] *OJ EPO* 408 (T0694/92).

2) whether the exception to the exclusion applies to varieties which have been produced using a micro-biological process;
3) whether the exception to the exclusion applies to plants (other than a variety) which have been produced using a micro-biological process;

and

4) whether plants which have been produced using an essentially biological process are patentable.

Each of these will be addressed in turn.

In order to assess the EPO's practice on the exclusion of plant varieties it is first necessary to look at its practice in respect of the protection of micro-organisms and distinguish between these, plants and plant varieties.[4]

Micro-organisms

One of the things which was agreed early on was that micro-organisms should not be excluded from protection. As explained in chapter 2, there has long been a recognition that the protection of processes involving micro-organisms is vital to securing investment within the pharmaceutical industry. From the outset, therefore, it was agreed that the protection afforded under the Strasbourg Convention/EPC should be explicitly provided for microbiological processes and the products produced by such processes. One of the earliest questions asked was whether this meant that protection extended to micro-organisms. As Teschermacher said in 1998, with hindsight the answer to the question whether such material might be patentable seems 'self-evident'.[5] However, when the first applications involving micro-organisms were filed, the Office was uncertain how to respond. One of the reasons for this initial hesitancy was the fact that a number of national patent laws of member states explicitly excluded micro-organisms. The Office was therefore unsure whether there was consensus within the European patent community for it to adopt a pro-patenting policy. Following extensive discussions (and against the backdrop of the Supreme Court's decision in *Chakrabarty* in 1980) the EPO decided to act and in 1981 the Guidelines for Examination were revised in order to clarify the position. These were amended to read that 'the propagation of a micro-organism itself is to be construed as a microbiological process and consequently the micro-organism can be protected *per se* as it is a product obtained by a microbiological process.'[6] In addition, the

---

[4] For a discussion of the early cases, see Jaenichen and Schrell, 'The European Patent Office's Recent Decisions on Patenting Plants' [1993] *EIPR* 466.

[5] Teschermacher, *The Practice of the European Patent Office Regarding the Grant of Patents for Biotechnological Inventions* (GRUR International, 1987) 285, also published in English in (1988) 19(1) *IIC* 18.

[6] Ch C–IV, 3.5.

EPO issued a statement that micro-organisms were neither plants nor animals and were therefore suitable subject matter for patent protection.[7] In terms of defining what constituted a micro-organism, the same chapter states that the term included 'plasmids and viruses'. This definition has been expanded upon within the 1999 Implementing Rules. These state that:

> The term 'micro-organism' includes bacteria and other generally unicellular organisms with dimensions beneath the limits of vision which can be propagated and manipulated in a laboratory including plasmids and viruses and unicellular fungi (including yeasts), algae, protozoa and, moreover, human, animal and plant cells.[8]

On the basis of the practice of including rather than excluding material, this means that patents have been granted over processes for producing micro-organisms, the micro-organism as produced by that process, new micro-organisms (irrespective of whether they have been produced by a specific new process), the process which uses a micro-organism to produce a specific end product, for example vaccines, and the product produced by that process.

Irrespective of whether one agrees with this practice, that such a clear statement over what will be regarded as life invention has been made should have put an end to the question of how far the principle of patentability was to extend. However, as can be seen, this definition is clearly intended to be non-exhaustive and the language used underlines the notion of inclusion not exclusion. Whilst this emphasis on inclusion not exclusion might be acceptable to those wishing to extend the limits of patentability, the apparent absence of any control over the extent to which this definition is appropriate adds to the concerns of those who favour a more restrictive approach. That these concerns are justified can be seen in the apparent acceptance of a blurring of the line between protectable and unprotectable material, and in particular between that which a scientist might define as a micro-organism and the definition utilised within patent law. One of Europe's leading patent law specialists, Andrew Grubb[9] has stated that whilst '[m]ost patent laws do not deal specifically with the question of whether or not a new living strain of micro-organism is itself patentable . . . the [UK] Patents Act 1977 and the EPC do not exclude such a possibility.' He goes on to state that '[i]t must be remembered that the term "micro-organism" is interpreted broadly

---

[7] For a discussion of this practice see Teschermacher, 'Patentability of Micro-organisms Per Se' (1982) 13 *IIC* 27; and Cadman, 'The Protection of Micro-organisms under European Patent Law' (1985) 16 *IIC* 311.

[8] For the EPO the stumbling block to granting protection has not been whether micro-organisms should be regarded as patentable subject matter but whether it is possible to disclose the material sufficiently within the patent specification. These concerns have been alleviated to a considerable extent by the evolving practice using the Budapest Treaty on the International Recognition of the deposit of Micro-organisms for the Purposes of Patent Procedures, 1977.

[9] Grubb, *Patents for Chemical, Pharmaceuticals and Biotechnology* (OUP, 1999), 226 and 227.

so as to include not only bacteria and fungi but also viruses and animal and plant cells.'[10]

As stated in chapter 2, at law the term 'micro-organism' encompasses more than the general scientific definition of unicellular living organisms capable of independent existence. Plant, animal and human cells do not fall within the scientific definition but nonetheless they are treated as micro-organisms for the purposes of applying the patent law. This would appear to indicate that there are two, albeit general, definitions in use—that used in science and that in law, with the latter encompassing a broader range of material than the former. Some might regard this as an unacceptable extension of the notion which could cause problem for scientists working to one notion and then finding themselves constrained through a legal system to working to the other. To date, however, there is no evidence that this has happened in practice.

The second reason why Grubb's statement gives cause for concern is because he makes it clear that in patent law it is now accepted practice to use a broad definition of micro-organism in order to ensure that patent protection does extend to plant and animal cells. This approach begs the question: where is the exact point of demarcation between a plant or animal cell (regarded in patent law as a micro-organism and therefore patentable) and a plant and an animal (which may be excluded from protection)? Indeed, what is the status of a plant which is derived from a single plant cell (as is now possible through the use of modern biotechnology). In other words, what precisely can be excluded and what precisely *must* be included? The reason this is highlighted is because, even though European patent law does not distinguish between plants and microorganisms, it serves to explain the way in which scientific notions are given legal definition and, in the context of patent law, to demonstrate how the use of any definitions generally errs on the side of capturing material within the scope of protection with the result that, with the aid of careful claims drafting, that which might appear to be excluded can be included.[11]

Once it had been decided that micro-organisms were patentable *per se* it was a short step to deciding that other life-form inventions were also patentable— the only barrier to protection being the categories of excluded material. In reaching this decision, the EPO had to decide if the exclusion of plant varieties only applied to varieties as such or if it extended to any plants of an order higher than a micro-organism but not taking the form of a variety. At the back of the

---

[10] This approach in mirrored in earlier writings, eg Wegner, 'Patenting Nature's Secrets—Microorganisms' (1976) 7(2) *IIC* 235; Marterer, 'The Patentability of Micro-organisms Per Se' (1976) 18(5) *IIC* 666; Teschermacher, *The Practice of the European Patent Office Regarding the Grant of Patents for Biotechnological Inventions* (GRUR International, 1987) 285, also published in English in (1988) 19(1) *IIC* 18; and Teschermacher, *Patentability of Micro-organisms Per Se*, above n 7.

[11] The prime example of this is the *Novartis* decision at the EPO which permitted the grant of a patent over plants up to and including a species, the application not falling foul of the exclusion of plant varieties as no claims to a variety as such were made in the patent application. This was notwithstanding the fact that the Board of Appeal accepted that the claims might 'encompass' plant varieties—provided the claims were not directed to them then the exclusion did not operate.

minds of those making this decision was the fact that if the exclusion was held to include plants other than in the guise of a variety, then the exclusion from patent protection, and the availability of UPOV-type protection for only plant groupings which were distinct, uniform and stable, would mean that there would be a group of plant-related inventions which would not attract any form of protection.

One of the reasons why this question taxed the EPO at all was the fact that, as the discussion in the previous chapter showed, after the Strasbourg Convention/EPC, some jurisdictions continued (in theory if not in practice) to treat the exclusion of plant varieties as a broad exclusion which permitted the wholesale exclusion of life-form inventions. In this they were taking their lead from the optional exclusion of *plants* contained in Article 2 of the Strasbourg Convention and applying it in a post-EPC environment either because nationally it was not accepted that plants of any order should be patented or because there was a general lack of awareness of the change effected through the transformation of the exclusion from the Article 2 *plants* to the Article 53(b) *plant varieties*. As patent applications relating to plant material began to appear (and given the lead they had taken on the protection of micro-organisms) the EPO decided to take a pro-active approach and adopted an explicit policy based on the view that the exclusion under the first half of Article 53(b) applied only to plant varieties protected under UPOV. The test case for this principle came in the form of an application from Ciba Geigy for a patent over plant seed coated with a chemical to make it resistant to weedkillers.

### Excluding parts of plants, whole plants, plant groupings or varieties?

*Ciba-Geigy* and *Lubrizol*[12]

In *Ciba-Geigy/propagating material* the claim related to 'propagating material, treated with chemical agents, for certain genera of plants.' The application referred to 'cultivated plants' bred from the coated propagating material but it did not seek to claim any individual varieties. An objection was lodged on the grounds that the claims fell within Article 53(b); however, the Technical Board of Appeal did not agree as no individual plant variety had been claimed and the opposition failed.

In an important statement, the Technical Board of Appeal said that plants and plant varieties cannot be treated as being the same thing for the purposes of applying Article 53(b). All that the Article excludes from protection is plant varieties. If the draftsmen had intended *all* plant material to be excluded then Article 53(b) would have been worded to have this effect. The Board provided a definition of a plant variety saying that it was a 'multiplicity of plants which are

---

[12]  Case T–49/83 [1984] *OJ EPO* 112.

largely the same in their characteristics and remain the same within specific tolerances after every propagation or every propagation cycle.' To a large extent this definition mirrors the principle which underpins the UPOV concept of a plant grouping which remains stable and uniform following repeated reproduction.

In this case, the Board felt that the plant material concerned did not fall into this definition as the invention merely related to seed coated with the chemical element. This treatment, with an oxine derivative, did not affect the genetic characteristics of the plant and therefore could not be regarded as an integral part of the plant which would be expected to replicate in a stable and identical manner in subsequent generations. The Board held that as far as it was concerned there was no conflict between that which can be protected under plant variety rights and that under patent law. It was immaterial to them that the reproductive material to which the chemical had been applied was capable of developing into a plant variety. The Board stated that the legislators of the EPC had not intended plant groupings of the kind defined as protectable under the 1961 UPOV Act to be protectable under the EPC. It held, however, that the exclusion applied only to 'plants or their propagating material in the genetically fixed form of the plant variety.' As the claims in the patent concerned related to seeds which had been treated with the oxine derivative, which was not a form of plant breeding which was concerned with genetic alteration, they did not fall within the scope of Article 53(b). A key statement by the Technical Board was that they felt it was acceptable for the exclusion to be 'restricted . . . to cases in which plants are characterised precisely by the genetically determined peculiarities of their natural phenotype.'[13] This restriction of the exclusion to those plants characterised by their phenotype, as opposed to genotype, corresponds to the protectable subject matter under plant variety rights.

Whilst the principle of protection was established within *Ciba Geigy*, the invention related to an external treatment of the seed—its genetic make-up had not been altered in any way. Five years after the decision in *Ciba Geigy*, the EPO made its first grant of a patent for a genetically engineered plant.

In *Lubrizol/hybrid plants*[14] a US company, Lubrizol, was granted a patent which covered both a method for inserting genes into plants, these genes serving to boost the plant's ability to store proteins, and the plants which resulted from the use of this method. In reaching this decision the EPO made it clear that the hybrid plants were patentable as they did not collectively meet the requirements for a grant of a plant variety right.[15] Most critically it held that the plants lacked the requisite stability across the population. Because of this, the EPO held that the patent did not relate to a plant grouping which remained essentially the same through repeated reproduction, and was, therefore, a variety. An issue also arose as to whether the plants had been produced by an essentially biological

---

[13] *Ibid*, para 4.
[14] Case T–320/87 [1990] *OJ EPO* 71.
[15] These elements being distinctness, uniformity and stability.

process (as some crossing and selection had been involved in their production) or whether they were the result of a technical process (because cell culture had also been used). This will be discussed below.

Both *Ciba Geigy* and *Lubrizol* are important cases for they establish the principle that the application of Article 53(b) was restricted to those plant groupings which were capable of protection under the plant variety rights system. This approach was externally endorsed by the Office itself within a key report published in 1987.[16] In this it said that:

> there is no general exclusion for plants in the EPC . . . [the] provision prohibits only the patenting of plants in the genetically fixed form of a variety. This allows protection in cases where the application does not claim a plant in a homogenous and durable form . . . but contains an innovation which refers to a specific property for a whole group of plants eg, a certain resistance for any wheat. Accordingly, the practice of the EPO makes a distinction between plants or certain groups of plant which may be protected and plant varieties which are excluded.

The Report went on to say that this applies not just to single plants but it was 'applicable to a whole family of plants.'[17]

In adopting this approach the EPO did not act in isolation. As can be seen, the practice mirrored, to a considerable extent, the thinking taking place within other organisations, for example, the WIPO.[18] Whilst the WIPO had not, in the mid-1980s, decided that patent protection was necessarily the right form of protection for *all* bioscience inventions, it was generally agreed that, in respect of plants, protection could be best provided by a combined use of patents and plant variety rights, with the former protecting anything not protectable under the latter.[19] This approach was not, however, universally accepted.

---

[16] See, eg, the Report of the EPO on Project No 12.3 (April 1987) within which is outlined its patent practices in respect of 'higher organisms', p 52ff.

[17] *Ibid*, p 53.

[18] The role of the WIPO is interesting for whilst the documentation discusses the relationship between patents and plant variety rights the clear emphasis is on securing patent protection—this is significant in respect of the perception of a) plant variety rights as a member of the intellectual property law family and b) its status *vis à vis* patent protection. This continues to be the view of the WIPO as can be seen in comments made by the Assistant Director General of the WIPO at a Symposium organised by both the WIPO and UPOV in October 2003, when he said that 'plant biotechnology evokes first and foremost the patent system': Gurry, *Plant Biotechnology Developments in the International Framework*, Proceedings of the WIPO–UPOV Symposium on Intellectual Property Rights in Plant Biotechnology (October 2003). This work of the WIPO will be discussed further in the next chapter.

[19] See, eg, the work of the Committee of Experts, BioT/CE/I/2, 'Industrial Property Protection of Biotechnological Inventions'; BioT/CE/I/3, 'Report of the Committee of Experts on Biotechnological Inventions and Industrial Property'; and BioT/CE/II/2, 'Industrial Property Protection of Biotechnological Inventions'. When looking at these papers it is important to remember that the meetings were taking place against the backdrop of a possible demotion of the plant variety rights system, and there was an emphasis, even within the WIPO, on the need for a more extensive use of patent law. For a contemporary critique of these discussions see *Report of the Joint WIPO and Cornell University Symposium on the Protection of Biotechnological Inventions* (New

In 1987, the then Vice-Secretary General of UPOV, Heribert Mast, wrote that limiting the exclusion to varieties *per se* was not very logical as it would result in whole plant species being patented, such species inevitably comprising a number of varieties.[20] In his view, the result would be that whilst a single variety would be excluded from patent protection, a grouping of varieties within one species could be patented simply on the basis that they all exhibited the same inventive feature. He drew an analogy with pigs carrying foot and mouth disease. He said that using this kind of semantic distinction, it would be possible to import pigs carrying the disease if they were merely described as vertebrates and not pigs. The fact that some of the animals within the grouping might also be described as pigs would appear to be a coincidence of little consequence to the person authorising their importation. (As will be discussed later, the Technical Board of Appeal made a similar point about the use of legal semantics in 1999.)

Mast was not alone in voicing concern, although the other voices foresaw a different problem to the one of extending protection to whole families or species of plant. Writing in 1988, Teschermacher (the then Head of the Legal Service of the EPO) indicated that whilst the principle established in *Ciba Geigy* could be confirmed, the matter of what could be protected was not as simple as merely determining what could be protected under plant variety rights.[21] However, having affirmed *Ciba Geigy,* and stating that recombinant DNA sequences and plant cell strains would probably be patentable, he went on to say that '[t]he question of how to treat whole plants or their propagating material . . . is more problematical.'[22] The problem for him was the relationship between the two parts of Article 53(b) and the extent to which the second half of the Article countermanded the first. However, whilst there was a problem in determining the precise nature of the relationship between the two parts in both the decisions, the fact that those charged with administering the practice of the EPO (such as Teschermacher[23]) used the plant variety rights system as the touchstone for operation of the exclusion should not be taken as meaning that there was clarity as to what this meant in practice. In particular, the issue would revolve around two questions, the first being how to define that which is protected under plant variety rights and the second relating to the question of whether the plant variety rights system applies only to varieties conventionally bred, with *all* results of genetic engineering (including varieties) being patentable.

---

York, 1987); and *Prospects for Change and Harmonisation* Report of a Conference on Biotechnology and Industrial Property Law (EPO, 1988).

[20] Mast, *The Relationship between Plant Variety Protection and Patent Protection in the Light of Developments in Biotechnology* (UPOV, Plant Variety Protection No 52, June 1987) 13.

[21] Above n 7, p 18.

[22] *Ibid*, p 31.

[23] And reinforced by those who use the system such as Grubb.

Disquiet was also expressed about the emerging policy of the EPO by many environmental groups; however, their concerns (at that time) were directed more to the patenting of living material *per se* than about the proper application of the Article 53(b) exclusion.[24] In the main, however, these decisions attracted relatively little comment or criticism from within the mainstream intellectual property circles—or indeed from within the plant breeding community. There are a number of reasons for this.

The first is that there was, at that time, relatively little awareness of plant variety rights outside the plant breeding circles. For those reasons outlined in chapter 1, the lack of a need to secure the services of a third party to acquire the rights, and the role of the national tribunals in deciding disputes, meant that there was little recourse to intellectual property practitioners. As a result of this, few patent lawyers knew (or indeed thought) much about either the plant variety rights system or, indeed, the basis for the Article 53(b) exclusion. For those who followed developments within patent law (and this would not have included many plant breeders) the decisions made in both *Ciba Geigy* and *Lubrizol* would, in the context purely of patent law, have sat easily alongside other developments in patent law (for example, those relating to the protection of pharmaceutical products).

Secondly, plant breeders have traditionally not used the patent system as a means of protecting the results of their breeding programmes. Any interest they might have had in developments in private property rights (and, as will be seen in chapter 8, this has been minimal) would have concentrated on plant variety protection. Breeders are unlikely to have either noticed or thought about decisions made by the EPO. Certainly the challenges made to patents granted did not come from plant breeders *per se*, although too much must not be read into this fact as a general lack of awareness of patent law developments could as easily explain this as any assertion that breeders knew but did not object.

As a result, the EPO continued to pursue a policy of actively granting patents over elements of plant material (as, for example, in *Mycogen Plant Science Inc/Modifying Plant Cells*[25]). However, in 1995, the unease expressed by Teschermacher over the relationship between the variety rights system and patent law came to a head in *Plant Genetic Systems/glutamine synthetase inhibitors* (PGS). This case both tested the plant/plant variety distinction and also addressed the question of whether a plant variety produced by a microbiological process was patentable by virtue of the second half of Article 53(b).

---

[24] As stated in ch 1, we are not concerned with the issue of *whether* plants should be the subject of an intellectual property right, but rather with the availability and impact of the rights which *are* available.

[25] EPO 14 2924 Case No TO116/85; Heitz, *Intellectual Property Rights and Plant Variety* (Protection paper given in 2001); see www.upov.int.

*Plant Genetic Systems*[26]

As discussed in the last chapter, the granted patent concerned plants which had been genetically altered to make them resistant to certain herbicides. Greenpeace lodged an opposition based on both parts of Article 53, arguing that a number of the claims made, and Claims 14 and 21 in particular, related to plant varieties.

The case came before the Technical Board of Appeal, which considered both parts of Article 53(b), the exclusion of plant varieties and the exemption of microbiological processes and their products.

In respect of plant varieties, the Board referred to both the *Ciba Geigy* and *Lubrizol* cases and confirmed the definitions used in both, namely that a variety is a 'multiplicity of plants which are largely the same in their characteristics and remain the same within specific tolerances after every propagation or every propagation cycle.'[27] The Board went on to say that:

> the concept of 'plant varieties' under Article 53(b) EPC, first half sentence, refers to any plant grouping within a single botanical taxon of the lowest known rank which, irrespective of whether it would be eligible for protection under the UPOV Convention, is characterised by at least one single transmissible characteristic distinguishing it from other plant groupings and which is sufficiently homogenous and stable in its relevant characteristics . . . a product claim which embraces within its subject matter 'plant varieties' as just defined is not patentable under Article 53(b) EPC, first half-sentence.[28]

The Board then turned its attention to the two main claims alleged to refer to varieties.

Claim 14 of the patent was to:

> plant cells, non-biologically transformed, which possess a heterologous DNA stably integrated into their genome, said heterologous DNA containing a foreign nucleotide sequence encoding a protein having a non-variety specific enzymatic activity capable of neutralizing or inactivating a glutamine synthetase inhibitor under the control of a promoter recognised by the polymerases of said plant cells.

Adopting the practice of the EPO outlined above and underlined within the Guidelines for Examination, the Technical Board did not accept that this was a claim to a plant variety, as plant cells are neither a plant nor a plant variety.

---

[26] Case T–356/93 [1995] *EPOR* 357. For a more detailed discussion of this case see Reid [1995] 8 *EIPR* D–140; Llewelyn, 'Art 53 Revisited: *Greenpeace v Plant Genetic Systems NV*' (1995) 10 *EIPR* 506; Roberts [1996] 3 *EIPR* D–90; Schell, 'Are Plants (Still) Patentable? Plant Genetic Systems (EPO Decision T–356/93)' (1996) 4 *EIPR* 242; Roberts, 'Patenting Plants Around the World' (1996) 10 *EIPR* 531, 534; Reid (1996) 11 *EIPR* D–341.

[27] [1995] *EPOR* 357 at para 21.

[28] *Ibid*, para 23.

Claim 21 related to

> plants, non-biologically transformed, which possess, stably integrated in the genome of its cells, a foreign DNA nucleotide sequence encoding a protein having a non-variety specific enzymatic activity capable of neutralizing or inactivating a glutamine inhibitor under the control of a promoter recognised by the polymerases of said cells.

The Technical Board did agree with Greenpeace that this amounted to a claim over a plant variety. In making this decision, the focus for the Board was the reference to plant which had 'stably integrated' within the foreign DNA nucleotide sequence.

The Technical Board reasoned that as the claim related to genetically modified plants which remained stable in their modified characteristics, it was a claim to a plant variety 'as they [the plants] comply with the definition of the concept of "plant varieties" being distinguishable, uniform and stable in their relevant characteristics.'

The Board went on to state that 'Claim 21 defines plants which, regardless of whether or not they belong to any particular variety, are distinguishable from all other plants by the stated specific characteristic which is transmitted in a stable manner to the progeny.' Whilst Claim 21 defines the distinctive feature common to all plants covered by this claim, the working examples[29] of the patent in suit show that the practical forms of realisation of the invention according to Claim 21 are 'genetically transformed' plant varieties. Consequently, the subject matter of Claim 21 'encompasses genetically transformed plant varieties showing said singly distinctive feature, even though this claim is not drafted in terms of a variety description.'[30]

In arriving at this decision, the Technical Board of Appeal made a specific reference to capacity to attract protection under UPOV and this is one of the earliest, if not the first, mention made of capacity for protection being the benchmark for deciding if the exclusion applied.[31]

There is a major failing with the Technical Board's decision and that is in making their decision as to what constitutes a plant variety for the purposes of plant variety rights the Technical Board of Appeal demonstrated 'a profound misunderstanding of the nature of a UPOV plant variety right.'[32]

The Board based its decision on the fact that the claim was to a single gene which had been stably integrated into the plant. However, evidence of one single stable gene within a grouping of plants is insufficient to warrant these plants

---

[29] The reference to a working example should not be taken to indicate that it is necessary to provide working examples of the patented invention prior to grant, contradicting one of the distinctions between patents and plant variety rights mentioned in ch 1. Instead, and purely for the purposes of the appeal in hand, the patent holder was required to explain how Claim 21 worked in practice. The difference, although subtle, is an important one.

[30] Above n 26, para 40.5.

[31] Above n 26, para 23.

[32] Roberts, 'Patenting Plants Around the World', above n 26, p 535.

being considered as a variety for plant variety rights purposes. As Roberts explained, a plant variety 'is characterised by essentially all of its genes' (ie, its overall phenotype), and not simply by one gene[33] (which goes more to genotype). He goes on to say that a 'plant grouping characterised by a single novel gene is a generic invention . . . [i]t is not a plant variety and cannot be protected as such.' In order for a plant variety to be protected using plant variety rights it is necessary for the grouping *in its entirety* to be stable, not merely for one gene within that grouping to be capable of stable replication as is the case with regard to the claim made in Claim 21. The Technical Board simply had not grasped this basic fact about plant variety rights.

However, the Board did not rule out protection for varieties *per se*. In a key part of its judgment the Board said that if 'the subject matter of this claim [had been] the product of a microbiological process' then the exception to the exclusion would have operated and the claim would be valid by virtue of the second half of Article 53(b).[34] In arriving at this interpretation of the second sentence of Article 53(b) the Technical Board relied upon the *Harvard/Oncomouse* decision. It stated that:

> . . . the second half-sentence restores the general principle of patentability laid down in Article 52(1)[35] EPC for inventions involving microbiological processes and the products thereof. Thus, from this decision [Decision T19/90—the *Harvard/Oncomouse* decision] it follows that animal varieties are patentable if they are the product of a microbiological process within the meaning of Article 53(b) EPC, second half-sentence. In the Board's judgment, this principle applies *mutatis mutandis* to plant varieties.

In this instance as the claimed plants were 'not merely the result of the . . . initial [microbiological] step but also of the subsequent series of relevant agrotechnical and biological steps', which included regenerating and reproducing the plants, the Board held that the impact of the 'process of regenerating a whole plant from plant cells or tissue . . . comprises a series of important events and phases . . . which require the careful selection of the appropriate working conditions, for example, the manipulation of nutrients and growth regulators', as well as the importance of other factors such as fertilisation and germination, should be looked at when determining the successful development of the whole plant. It concluded that 'a whole plant cannot be assimilated to a plant cell or tissue for the sole reason that it has acquired its characterising feature during the initial "microbiological" step of transforming the plant cell or tissue.' Therefore, despite the 'decisive impact' of the initial step on the final plant, the subsequent steps meant that the resulting plants were not the products of a

---

[33] *Ibid.*

[34] As will be seen in the next chapter, this thinking mirrored that which lay behind the first drafts of the EU Directive on the Legal Protection of Bio Inventions.

[35] 'European patents shall be granted for any inventions which are susceptible of industrial application, which are new and which involve an inventive step.'

microbiological process and the Technical Board felt unable to restore the general principle of patentability.

The decision in *PGS* caused a great deal of concern not only among those wishing to see a clear pro-plant patenting policy within the EPO but also among those who wished to see clear blue water between that which is protectable under patent law and that under plant variety rights.

The signals sent by the EPO as a result of the *PGS* case were mixed, to put it mildly. On the one hand, it appeared to reaffirm that plant varieties were not patentable (and in so doing it acknowledged the role the UPOV Convention, which had only been revised four years previously, played in determining that which was excluded under Article 53(b)) and yet it also said that where a variety had been produced by a microbiological process then, irrespective of correspondence with the UPOV definition, it would be patentable. This lack of understanding about the nature of plant variety rights, together with the statement that the exception *only* applies where the plant variety concerned is not the product of a microbiological process, served to cause confusion both as to the exact nature of the relationship between the two rights and as to whether there was in fact the promise of dual protection for biotechnologically created varieties.[36]

That considerable confusion following the *PGS* decision can be seen in the fact that almost immediately the President of the EPO referred the question '[d]oes a claim which relates to plants or animals but wherein specific plant or animal varieties are not individually claimed contravene the prohibition on patenting in Article 53(b) if it embraces plant varieties?' to the Enlarged Board of Appeal. In his opinion both the *Oncomouse* and *Ciba Geigy* cases had indicated that the exclusion applied only to varieties specifically claimed, and that it did not extend to plant material, individual plants, or groupings which encompassed more than one variety. The Enlarged Board, however, did not agree there was a conflict and held the referral to be inadmissible.[37] The next time the Enlarged Board would be called upon to decide the issue of the patentability of plant material it would be faced with the exact same question as well as the additional question of the relationship between the two parts of the exclusion.

The concern which *PGS* engendered (which encompassed lawyers and plant scientists alike) was that it meant that, for the purposes of patent law, any single genetic change (which was stable in its effect) was considered to give rise to a variety. For many this meant that *all* plant genetic innovations fell within the exclusion. The result, whilst satisfactory for those wholly opposed to the granting of patents over plant material, was that there was no protection available for those plant innovators working in areas other than the production of plant varieties.

---

[36] Bearing in mind that the dual protection prohibition had been removed from the 1991 UPOV Act—however, it remained within the 1978 Act, to which some EPC member states still were signatories in 1985.

[37] Case G–3/95 [1996] OJ EPO 169 'inadmissible referral'.

The decision was also worrying because it appeared to indicate that only those plant varieties which had been produced by essentially biological processes were excluded from protection. Not only did this cause concern that there would be a legal apartheid between those varieties which could be patented and those which could not, but that the distinction drawn by the Technical Board between essentially biological and microbiological was unclear and did not pinpoint when a process would be said to be no longer essentially biological.

All agreed that there needed to be a similar fact case to go to the Enlarged Board for final clarification on the actual ambit of the exclusion. It took five years before such a case occurred, during which time the position remained unclear as to which aspects of plant material (or indeed the products of which types of processes) could be protected by a patent. This did not stop applications being made to the EPO, but it did hold up the granting of patents as the Office itself awaited an indication from the authorities within as to what the practice should be.

The case was *Novartis*, and this is probably the most important plant patent case affecting Europe. Not only did this case cement the EPO's practice of patenting plant inventions other than plant varieties, but it also sought to clarify whether the exception to the exclusion applied to plant varieties produced by a microbiological process.

There are two key judgments relating to the *Novartis* patent. The first is that of the Technical Board of Appeal (which was published in October 1997). The second is the judgment of the Enlarged Board of Appeal (the senior Board), which was given in December 1999. The timings of these two judgments are important. In the period between the referral from the Technical Board to the Enlarged Board, the EU Directive had been adopted by the European Parliament, and Rule 23 amended to reflect the provisions of the Directive. Whilst there was no formal statement that the timing of the decision was down to any policy to match EPO practice to the new EU patenting environment, it is tempting to draw the conclusion that it was not coincidental. Certainly the similarity between the thinking at the EPO and that which lay behind the Directive is striking in a way which is not immediately evident in comments made by the EPO following the *PGS* decision. At that time it appeared reluctant to appear guided by any decision taken in Brussels.

The decision in *Novartis* will be discussed in some detail not merely because, notwithstanding the apparent consensus which now exists within the EPO (as evidenced by the synergy between the eventual decision in *Novartis*, the amended Implementing Rules and the EU Directive) it demonstrates that only a few years ago there was diversity of opinion within the EPO as to the application of the exclusion. Before looking at the substantive issues, the appeals structure of the EPO needs to be explained. The appeals process is such that a request has to be made to the Technical Board of Appeal to refer points of substantive law to the Enlarged Board of Appeal for consideration—this is done by way of specific questions which the Technical Board asks the Enlarged Board to consider. In making its referral, the Technical Board of Appeal is able, if it so wishes, to comment on the questions. In *Novartis* the Technical Board of Appeal[38] availed itself of this possibility and made a number of key statements which represent an almost diametrically opposite view to that later expressed by the Enlarged Board.

### Novartis

The case concerned an application for transgenic plants and the method of producing these plants. Of particular interest were claims 19 and 23.
   Claim 19 read:

> A transgenic plant and the seed thereof comprising recombinant DNA sequences encoding
>    (a) one or more lytic peptides, which is not lysozyme, in combination with
>    (b) one or more chitinases; and/or
>    (c) one or more beta–1,3–glucanases in a synergistically effective amount.

Claim 23 read:

> A method of preparing a transgenic plant which is able to synthesis one or more lytic peptides together with one or more chitinases;
> and/or one or more beta–1,3–glucanases in a synergistically effective amount;
> said method comprising the steps of preparing a transgenic plant comprising recombinant DNA sequences encoding one or more lytic peptides, which is not lysozyme, together with one or more chitinases;
> and/or one or more beta–1,2–glucanases.

In 1996[39] the Examining Division (the Division) of the EPO refused to grant a patent on the grounds that the subject matter claimed was excluded as it corresponded to that claimed in the *PGS* case. In making its decision, the Division restated that a claim to genetically engineered plants and seeds was a claim which encompassed varieties, and these varieties (not being the product of a microbiological process) were not patentable. Shortly afterwards, the Technical Board of Appeal (TBA) agreed to refer four questions to the Enlarged Board of Appeal (EBA). Three of the questions related to the interpretation and application of Article 53(b) and the fourth to Article 64(2).[40] Article 64(2) states that where 'the subject matter of the European patent is a process, the protection

---

[38] It is interesting to note that of the members of the Technical Board of Appeal who sat in both the *PGS* and *Novartis* decision only one, Kinkeldy, sat in both. In *PGS* the other members were Galligani and Moser, and in *Novartis* they were Davison-Brunel and Perryman.

[39] Coincidentally, this was the same year that the EBA refused to address the question referred to it by the President of the EPO.

[40] 'If the subject matter of the European patent is a process, the protection conferred by the patent shall extend to the products directly obtained by such process.'

conferred by the patent shall extend to the products directly obtained by such process.' In addition, the Board referred to Article 84, which requires that the claims made must 'define the subject matter for which protection is sought. They shall be clear and concise and be supported by the description.'

The four questions which the TBA sent for referral were as follows.

1) To what extent should instances of the EPO examine an application in respect of whether the claims are allowable in view of the provision of Article 53(b) EPC that patents shall not be granted in respect of plant varieties or essentially biological processes for the production of plants, which provision does not apply to microbiological processes or the products thereof, and how should a claim be interpreted for this purpose?
2) Does a claim which relates to plants but wherein specific plant varieties are not individually claimed *ipso facto* avoid the prohibition on patenting in Article 53(b) EPC even though it embraces plant varieties?
3) Should the provisions of Article 64(2) EPC be taken into account when considering what claims are allowable?
4) Does a plant variety in which each individual plant of that variety contains at least one specific gene introduced into an ancestral plant by recombinant technology fall outside the provision of Article 53(b) that patents should not be granted in respect of plant varieties or essentially biological processes for the production of plants, which provision does not apply to microbiological processes or the products thereof?

First the TBA and then the EBA responses to each question will be summarised in the following section.

The Reference from the TBA[41]

— Question 1—what is the proper interpretation of Article 53(b)?

The TBA argued that there were three elements to this question.

The first related to whether a substantive or formal approach should be taken when interpreting the provisions of the EPC. Novartis had argued for the latter approach on the basis that whilst the scope of Claim 19 could be said to encompass plant varieties the claim itself did not specifically relate to a plant variety. As Article 53(b) only excludes plant varieties which are specifically claimed, on a formal reading of Article 53(b) the claim was valid. The TBA, however, took the view that a claim which could be read as covering two embodiments of the claimed material (eg, plant varieties and non-varieties), would have the effect of allowing any patent granted over one embodiment (non-varieties) to extend to the other (varieties). In its view the claim fell within

---

[41] Referral from the Technical Board of Appeal, *Novartis/Transgenic Plant* [1999] EPOR 123.

the exclusion.[42] In a key passage the TBA said that if a formal (or literal) interpretation were given to the claim then this would have the effect of merely
requiring granting offices to check if the word 'variety' appeared in the claim. If
it did not then the claim would be valid. The view of the TBA was that: 'this
would make examination for conformity with Article 53(b) EPC a very facile
procedure' as it would 'abdicate any responsibility for examining the substance
of the claim and the outcome of any application would depend to the verbal skill
of the patent attorney concerned.'[43] This parallels the comments made by Mast
in 1987.

The TBA did not believe that the draftsmen of the EPC intended Article 53(b)
to have no substantive function. For these reasons, the TBA concluded that the
substantive approach was the correct one—the question which had to be asked
therefore was whether any *potential* embodiment of a claim was a plant variety.[44] If it was then the claim would be invalid under Article 53(b).

The second element lay in the matter of what was an essentially biological
process and whether this concept applied to Claim 23. The Board stated that it
did not consider Claim 23 to be clear and concise in accordance with the requirement under Article 84 and therefore it was not allowable. The Board admitted
that increased understanding of biological processes and the ability to use this
knowledge in 'gene technology' makes distinguishing between an essentially
biological process and that which is microbiological 'problematic'.[45] It outlined
a number of approaches, including that used in the *Lubrizol* case, which
involved ascertaining the degree and impact of any human technical intervention. But as such an approach would require an assessment of whether a claim
was directed to one or other process it was felt that the outcome could be uncertain and still not sufficiently clear or concise.

The third element related to what was meant by microbiological processes
and the products thereof.

The TBA stated that all plant varieties are to be treated as excluded under
Article 53(b) even those which were the products of a microbiological process.
In so doing it appeared to contradict both the decision in *PGS* and also that of
the Examining Division. The reasoning given by the TBA was that genetically
engineered plants are far removed from the original concept of the products of
a microbiological process envisaged when the EPC was being drafted, or in
other words that they had not envisaged that varieties could be the products of
microbiological processes. In reaching this conclusion, the TBA referred to the
*PGS* case. In *PGS* it had been held that the processes used to create the transgenic

---

[42] *Ibid*, para 18.
[43] *Ibid*, para 20.
[44] On the question put by Novartis as to whether the substantive approach would have the effect
of requiring disclaimers to be made in respect of any genes placed into plant varieties the TBA said
that this did not relate to the case in hand and it would not therefore comment on this matter—
p 133.
[45] Above n 41, para 24.

plants did not constitute microbiological processes within the meaning of Article 53(b), as the process concerned took the form of an agrotechnical process of which the microbiological aspect played only a minimal part. However, in reaching this view, the TBA made no mention of another key part of the *PGS* decision.

In *PGS,* it had been stated that the *Oncomouse* judgment decided that the second sentence of Article 53(b) is:

> an exception to patentability provided for by the first half-sentence of this provision. Accordingly, it is held that the second half-sentence restores the general principle of patentability laid down in Article 52(1) EPC for inventions involving microbiological processes and the products thereof. Thus, from this decision it follows that animal varieties are patentable if they are the product of a microbiological process within the meaning of Article 53(b) EPC, second half-sentence.

In the view of the Board 'this principle applies *mutatis mutandis* to plant varieties.' No reason is given at to why the TBA in *Novartis* chose not to refer to this part of the judgment.

Given that the *Novartis* decision came after the decision to remove the dual prohibition provision from UPOV, it might have been thought that those (such as patent granting offices) seeking to extend patent protection to varieties would have leapt at the opportunity presented to secure the principle (which seems to have been first set down in *Oncomouse* and reinforced in *PGS*) that patents could be granted over varieties produced by a microbiological process. As chapter 4 showed, not even the Community Regulation (which was in place and fully operational at the time that the TBA made its reference) would stop such an interpretation, as it only prohibits the grant of both a Community right *and* a national right. It does not prevent opting for the patent over the Community right. It is unclear why there was such reticence to providing an exception to the exclusion for plant varieties other than that (as will be seen below when looking at the comments of the Enlarged Board) there was an absolute conviction that Article 53(b) had not been drafted to allow such an exception and there was no political will to reinterpret in light of the demands of modern bioscience companies. Another reason why the door against patenting plant varieties might have been so firmly shut is because of the proposed EU Directive, the provisions of which would include an exclusion of plant varieties. As will be discussed in the next chapter, one wonders why both the EPC and the draftsmen of the Directive (who included those who railed against the exclusion, including Straus) did not seek to achieve the 'paradise' of patent protection allegedly so cruelly denied to them by the original drafting of the EPC.

Whatever the reasons for so doing the TBA in *Novartis* stated that '. . . a genetically engineered plant variety bear no relation to what was originally meant by the product of a microbiological process . . . whereas it is virtually indistinguishable in type from conventionally produced plant varieties.'[46] However, the Enlarged Board was under no compulsion to accept this reading of Article 53(b).

The TBA made it clear therefore that a formal or literal approach to ascertaining whether a claim was directed to a variety or not was not acceptable, that in addressing this matter it was necessary only to take into account the claimed material. The manner of production was irrelevant as the exclusion applied irrespective of whether the variety had been produced by an essentially biological or microbiological process.

— Question 2—are claims embracing, but not confined to, plant varieties permitted?

In its submission Novartis had raised the 'more than one variety argument', that is where a claim does not refer to an individual variety but can be read as encompassing more than one variety then it does not fall within the Article 53(b) exclusion. Support for this argument was presented as coming from a number of learned sources.[47] In taking this approach, Novartis made a specific reference to the EU Directive (which, as will be seen in the next chapter, expressly states that such claims are permissible[48]).

The TBA dismissed this argument on the grounds that whilst there may be good reasons why a patent applicant would benefit from being able to make such a claim this was not a sufficient justification for overriding the overarching prohibition on plant varieties. The Board added that the idea of refusing a patent over a single variety but permitting a claim in respect of more than one variety did not 'comply with the normal rules of logic.'[49] In its view '[t]o expand the "exception to the exception" of Article 53(b) . . . so far as to hollow out and nullify completely the prohibition on the grant of patents for plant and animal varieties seems to go beyond any legitimate form of interpretation.'[50]

In response to the argument that the Directive was evidence of approval for the 'more than one variety' approach, the TBA stated that: 'treating the . . . Directive as evidence of any agreed subsequent practice under the EPC would appear problematic.' A possible reason for this response was that, at that time, it was still unclear as to whether the Directive would be adopted.

The TBA made it clear that legal semantics were not be used to allow claims to more than one variety and also, notwithstanding that this was to be the case

---

[46] *Ibid*, para 30.

[47] *Ibid*, para 33.

[48] Art 4(2) of the Directive states: 'Inventions which concern plants or animals shall be patentable if the technical feasibility of the invention is not confined to a particular plant or animal.' Recital 31 of the Directive reinforces this premise: 'Whereas a plant grouping which is characterised by a particular gene (and not by its whole genome) is not covered by the protection of new varieties and is therefore not excluded from patentability even if it comprises new varieties of plants.'

[49] Above n 41, para 36.

[50] *Ibid*, para 50.

at the national level (via the Directive), that following this lead would be too uncertain a route for the EPO to take.

— Question 3—to what extent is Article 64(2) relevant?[51]

Article 64(2) states that where a patent has been granted over a process then the patent over that process extends to any product directly produced using that process. The TBA drew a distinction between material which could be the subject of a patent application and that which was protected by the right once granted. It said that Article 64(2) was only relevant for the purposes of determining infringement and not relevant to the determination of whether particular subject matter was suitable for a grant of a patent.[52]

In what might seem to be a contradictory statement, given the comments made in respect of Questions 1 and 2, the TBA stated that it did not see any problem with a court holding that a patent for a process (for example a microbiological process) was infringed where that process had been used to produce plant varieties and those plant varieties had been exploited without the authorisation of the patent holder.[53] This does appear to sit somewhat uncomfortably with the rejections of the arguments that patents cannot be granted which encompass plant varieties even where they are the product of a microbiological process and yet where a patent has been granted over a process then that patent extends to any plant varieties created by using the protected process. The net result is surely that by obtaining a patent over a method of plant breeding (broadly defined) there is equally gained indirect patent protection over plant varieties.

— Question 4—are plant varieties which are the product of a microbiological process patentable?

Staying with the theme of the impact of the new technology, Novartis argued that the exclusion of plant varieties had to be read in light of the developments in biotechnology. Biotechnology had not been envisaged when the Convention was drafted and as such it was not appropriate to apply the exclusion to plant varieties bred as a result of genetic engineering.

The TBA held that this was a matter 'for the legislator'[54] and not for the courts. Given that the 'EPC provides protection for processes which are not essentially biological, and for plants which do not possess the characteristics of plant varieties . . . [t]he legislator might . . . be of the opinion that enough had already been done.'[55] In making this comment, the Board felt that the fact that

---

[51] General issues relating to Art 64(2) are discussed further below.
[52] Above n 41, para 80.
[53] *Ibid*, para 82.
[54] *Ibid*, para 94.
[55] *Ibid*, para 94.

a plant variety had been derived using genetic engineering should not place the producer in a 'privileged position' in relation to the breeders of traditional plant varieties.[56]

The views expressed by the TBA left very little doubt as to what it thought the outcome of the appeal should be. In so doing it also passed some comment on the impact the Directive was felt to have. The Board not only refused to take account of the Directive in its deliberations over the interpretation of Article 53(b) but also clearly stated that the Directive should itself be construed in a narrow manner (with such protection as is available resulting from an application of Article 64(2)) and that the exclusion should apply irrespective of whether the plant variety is the result of a microbiological process or the claim encompasses more than one variety. In each instance, the Board was urging parity of practice between the EPO and the Directive but *along* the lines outlined by the TBA in *Novartis*.

This 'treatment' of the Directive can be contrasted with what the draftsmen of the Directive had been proposing. Whilst the Directive was never intended to do other than correspond in large measure to the language and patenting granting practices of the European Patent Office it was made plain at the outset that there was an intention that the 'indirect effects . . . should be substantial.'[57]

Needless to say, the views of the Board elicited considerable criticism not least because they appear to fly in the face of everything which seemingly had been agreed by the EU group of member states of the EPC.[58] One leading commentator went so far as to say that in his opinion: '. . . the Board's view on the Directive [is] plainly wrong. On the Board's approach both under the EPC and Directive only process claims and product-by-process claims would be allowed . . . . That cannot have been the European Parliament's intention. The Board must be wrong.'[59]

In December 1999 the Enlarged Board gave its decision, overruling nearly all of the arguments presented by the Technical Board.

### The Decision of the Enlarged Board of Appeal[60]

Before looking at the arguments presented it is worth reminding that in the time between making the referral from the TBA to the Enlarged Board, the

---

[56]    *Ibid*, para 92.

[57]    Explanatory Memorandum, p 24.

[58]    Bostyn, 'The Patentability of Genetic Information Carriers' [1999] 11 *IPQ* 14; Nott, 'The Novartis Case in the EPO' [1999] *EIPR* 33; 'Chartered Institute of Patent Agents Backs Plant Patents in Novartis Appeal Case' [1999] *CIPA Journal* 272. In discussing the implications of the TBA's comments, the Chartered Institute extended its comments to Art 53(a) by saying that if the Board were correct and a patent extended to any embodiment which it might encompass then many patents would be invalid on the grounds that they encompassed inventions which could be considered contrary to *ordre public* or morality. The example given is of drugs which can be poisonous if given in the wrong dose—'if the Board's approach is correct, thousands of patents would have to be refused under EPC Art 53(a). This cannot be what the law-makers intended.'

[59]    Nott, above n 58, p 35.

[60]    *Novartis 'Transgenic Plant'* [2000] *EPOR* 303.

Implementing Rules of the EPC had been amended to reflect certain provisions of the EU Directive, including the definition of a 'plant variety'. It is these Rules, and Rule 23 in particular, which now govern the application of Article 53(b).

Rules 23b(4) states that the term

'plant variety' means any plant grouping within a single botanical taxon of the lowest known rank, which grouping, irrespective of whether the conditions for the grant of a plant variety right are fully met, can be: (a) defined by the expression of the characteristics that results from a given genotype or combination of genotypes, (b) distinguished from any other plant grouping by the expression of at least one of the said characteristics, and considered as a unit with regard to its suitability for being propagated unchanged.

In its decision the Enlarged Board confirms that this and Article 5(2) of the Council Regulation on Community Plant Variety Rights are 'identical in substance.'[61]

Rule 23(c) states that 'biotechnological inventions shall also be patentable if they concern . . . (b) plants or animals if the technical feasibility of the invention is not confined to a particular plant or animal variety.'

On this basis, the Board held that Article 53(b) did not, nor was it intended to, exclude anything other than plant varieties which can be protected under plant variety rights.

In arriving at its decision the EBA also took into account the views expressed by the President of the EPO (dismissed by a previous EBA), and submissions from professional groups (such as institutes of patent agents), bioscience companies, environmental organisations (such as Greenpeace) and the Community Plant Variety Office.

The CPVO provided a statement saying that it 'preferred the approach according to which a claim covering, or potentially covering, a plant variety should be rejected' and that this should apply regardless of how the variety had been produced. The CPVO had no problem with claims which related to plant material not in the fixed form of a variety, but felt that 'the exclusion from patentability would be seriously undermined if it could be circumvented simply by formulating claims sufficiently widely to avoid express reference to an individual plant variety.' It also expressed concern that Article 64(2) could provide a back-door route by which varieties which are directly produced by a patentable process would fall within the scope of that patent for that process and that there was a 'conflict between Article 53(b) and Article 64(2).' Because of this conflict there 'was no choice but to take Article 64(2) into account when considering whether a claim was "in respect" of a plant variety.'

The views expressed by the Community Plant Variety Office are particularly relevant in assessing the value of the decision in *Novartis* for, as will be shown, the EBA appears to have paid them scant attention, in contrast to the obvious influence of the EU Directive. In one sense, this is understandable as the EPO

---

[61] *Ibid*, p 313.

had, only a few months earlier, adopted the Directive for the purposes of supplementary interpretation and therefore it could be said to be part of the legislative framework within which the EBA had to operate. In addition, the EPO stands outside the EU and it is not bound to give undue prominence to the views of an organ of that union. However, given the sensitivity of the area under review, and the fact that the Community Office was in a uniquely qualified position to comment on the protection of plant varieties (not to mention any desire for harmonisation between the two systems), it might have been politic to at least have appeared to pay these views more attention. However, to give the views of the Community Office any persuasive quality would have meant a very different result, as arguably the significance of the *Novartis* action lay in ensuring that more rather than less was patentable (with the objective of the EBA being to mitigate the effects of the *PGS* decision). On this basis it is easy to see why any submissions not sanctioning this objective would carry little weight irrespective of their source.

In drawing the line between that which is patentable and that which is excluded the EBA placed great emphasis on the rationale underlying the introduction of the EPC, and in particular they drew on the fact that the Strasbourg Patent Convention (SPC) and subsequent EPC were textually different in respect of the obligation to exclude plant varieties from patent protection.

The EBA saw the open-ended nature of the SPC text as providing a solution to the problem faced by those countries, in the 1960s, which were members of both UPOV and the SPC, and which permitted patent protection for plant varieties. The dual protection prohibition in Article 2(1) of the 1961 UPOV Act meant that member states had to ensure that protection was not available for the same genus or species under both systems. In order for member states to decide for themselves which species and genus were to be protected under which system, the text of the SPC had to provide for the possibility of patent protection for plant varieties. The requirement, in UPOV, for member states to expand plant variety protection to an increasing number of varieties clearly meant that there was the potential for conflict. To mitigate the potential for increased diversity of plant intellectual property provision it was decided to make the exclusion mandatory. In probably the most important part of its decision, the EBA then said that the purpose of Article 53(b) EPC and Article 2 SPC were the same—to exclude from protection only those plant varieties which were protectable under the UPOV Convention. To support this contention the EBA relied on a 'brief remark' in the *travaux préparatoires* which said that Article 53(b) 'simply follows' Article 2 '[a]ccordingly, inventions ineligible for protection under the plant breeders' rights system were intended to be patentable under the EPC provided they fulfilled the other requirements of patentability.'[62]

---

[62] *Ibid*, p 317.

We will now look at the EBA's response to the four questions.

— Question 1—what is the proper interpretation of Article 53(b)?

The EBA chose not to provide a direct answer to the question of how Article 53(b) should be interpreted. Instead, it felt that its answers to the three other questions would encompass this question as well.

— Question 2—are claims embracing, but not confined to, plant varieties permitted?

The EBA looked at the distinction drawn by the TBA between the substantive and literal approaches. The EBA said that the important thing was to assess the underlying invention and therefore it was 'a question not of form but of substance.' If an applicant has made an invention of general applicability then he may claim the invention in the broadest form which complies with the requirements for patentability (that is, it meets the threshold and is sufficiently disclosed). In addressing the concern that such an approach would enable applicants to avoid the exclusion by means of careful claim drafting, the EBA said that any patents granted on this basis would not result from the verbal skill of the patent attorney but would result from the breadth of application of the invention. This does seem to be slightly disingenuous as the breadth of application of any invention is determined by claims drafted. If this is not down to the verbal skill of the patent attorney (this term being taken in its broadest sense to include all those involved in prosecuting a patent application) then it is hard to know what it is due to.

In respect of how far the exclusion extends, the EBA asserted that it was not the intention of the draftsmen of the EPC to ban protection for all types of plant material but rather to ensure that those plant groupings which were protectable under the UPOV Convention were not subject to double protection by being patentable at the same time.[63] This means that a claim which does not refer to plant groupings which are distinct, uniform and stable when considered as a unit would not fall within the exclusion. Nor did the EBA think it appropriate to hold that they should fall within it, as such an extensive exclusion was never intended.

> In summary, according to Article 53(b) a patent is 'in respect of plant varieties' and shall not be granted if the claimed subject matter is directed to plant varieties .... The extent of the exclusion for patents is the obverse of the availability of plant variety rights. The latter are only granted for specific plant varieties and not for technical teachings which can be implemented in an indefinite number of plant varieties.

---

[63] *Ibid*, paras 3.4–3.8.

It was the EBA's view that a plant variety is defined by reference to its genome *as a whole*. Any plant into which a single gene has been inserted in order to introduce a specific characteristic is defined by that single characteristic and is not, therefore, a plant variety. Any grouping of plants which only had that single gene in common equally could not constitute a plant variety, as only one aspect was held in common. As the claim was not directed to a variety or a multiplicity of varieties it did not fall within the scope of the Article 53(b) exclusion.

The result here appears clear—in order for the exclusion of plant varieties in Article 53(b) to apply the claim must be directed to a variety capable of being protected by a plant variety right. Where the general plant material claimed cannot be protected by a plant variety right then it will be patentable.

— Question 3—to what extent is Article 64(2) relevant?

The Technical Board of Appeal, in referring this question to the EBA, asked whether the fact that the application of Article 64(2) could result in a patent being indirectly granted over a plant variety should be taken into consideration when determining the grant of a patent. The Technical Board said that it could 'see no conflict between . . . the plant variety indirectly enjoying patent protection as the direct product of a process under Article 64(2) and . . . the plant variety as such not being patentable under Article 53(b) EPC.'[64] The matter, the TBA felt, was 'purely for the courts considering infringement and the relevant licensing authorities, and . . . not to be taken into account when a patent office considers compliance with the provisions of Articles 52–57.'[65] The EBA concurred with the Technical Board.

The EPO clearly regarded the question as to whether a plant variety produced by a patented process is protected by the patent over that process, as a matter for consideration by the courts at the national level. This is not surprising, as the EPO is primarily concerned with questions of grant, not scope. What is interesting is that, as an effect of Article 64(2) could be to negate Article 53(b), the EBA chose not to echo the comments of the Technical Board and say that this is perhaps a matter for consideration by the legislators. Instead, the EBA was silent on the matter.

— Question 4—are plant varieties which are the product of a microbiological process patentable?

The EBA stated that the term 'microbiological' referred to those processes which involved the use of micro-organisms. Whilst plant cells are treated as micro-organisms for the purposes of the EPC this does not mean that this treatment should be extended to include plants produced using a process involving micro-organisms. 'Such an analogy and formal use of rules of interpretation

---

[64] Above n 41, para 82.
[65] *Ibid*, para 87.

would disregard the purpose of the exclusion . . . [which is to exclude] from patentability subject matter which is eligible for protection under the plant breeders' rights system.' As the plant variety rights system does not distinguish between the manner of production for the purposes of deciding grant, therefore the patent system equally should not do so for the purposes of applying Article 53(b). With that, the EBA effectively closed the door on using the second half of Article 53(b) to circumvent the exclusion of the first half. Because of this there was no need for the EBA to discuss the extent to which a microbiological process has to direct the outcome.

Following both the amendment of the Implementing Rules and the decision in *Novartis* the current EPO practice can be summarised as follows.

Article 53(b) applies only to plant groupings which can be protected under plant variety rights. All other plant material, including plant groupings, other than those protectable under plant variety rights, are patentable. Claims made to plant groupings which encompass plant varieties (such as a plant species) are patentable provided that the claims are not specifically directed to an individual plant variety.

In respect of the second sentence of Article 53(b) and protection conferred by virtue of Article 64(2), the EPO draws a distinction between that which can be claimed and that which is covered by a claim. Irrespective of the manner of production, no claim may be directed to a plant variety as such and the second sentence of Article 53(b) cannot be used to circumvent this. However, Article 64(2) permits a patent over a process to extend to all products directly produced by that process. The precise extent of this provision is a matter for infringement and determining the actual scope of the patent. Whether this permits patent protection to extend to plant varieties produced by a particular process, there-fore, is a matter for national courts. That this is the proper interpretation of Article 53(b) is supported by Armitage and Davis, who were both involved in the drafting of the EPC.[66]

They state that it 'almost goes without saying that there was no intention [at the outset] to exclude new plant forms in general . . . if that had been the case, quite different language would have been used.' As further support of this reading of Article 53(b) they draw attention to the difference in language used in the first sentence of Article 53(b) where the exclusion clearly relates to plant *varieties* and that used in the second sentence where the exclusion relates to essentially biological processes for the production of *plants*. The second sen-tence does not discriminate as to the form of the produced plant material.[67]

There is a problem with the reasoning in *Novartis* and that is that it fails to take notice of the fact that the plant variety rights system draws a distinction between that which is *protectable* under plant variety rights (plant groupings

---

[66] Armitage and Davis, *Patents and Morality in Perspective* (CLIP, 1994).

[67] Although there remains an argument as to whether the exclusion of products produced by an essentially biological process refers to whole plants or to those plant elements with the capacity to develop into whole plants: see ch 1.

which are distinct uniform and stable) and that which is *protected* (variety constituents, propagating material and plant components). The former relates to collectives which demonstrate common characteristics in a distinct, uniform and stable manner. The latter includes those elements within the plant which give rise to both the characteristics and the capacity to distinguish in a uniform and stable manner—this would include plant genes.

As is clear from the *Novartis* decision, under patent law it is only the former, the grouping, which is capable of acquiring plant variety protection, which is used for the purposes of applying the exclusion. Any other plant material is deemed patentable including the constituents making up the plant variety. However, as was shown in the previous chapter (chapter 4) on Community plant variety rights, the protection granted covers the constituent elements of the plant grouping (as well as harvested material and, theoretically, products derived from the protected plant material). Far from the blue water distinction between that which is protectable under plant variety rights (plant groupings which are distinct, uniform and stable) and that which can be patented (all other aspects of the plant including plant genes) there would appear to be conformity as to subject matter, with *both* the patent and plant variety rights systems providing protection for plant genes. The extent of the overlap becomes more apparent when looked at in the context of the argument surrounding the patentability of micro-organisms set out in chapter 1. This pro-patenting practice has been sharply criticised from some plant breeding quarters.[68]

Having determined that only plant varieties are excluded from protection, the next issue is whether the exclusion of essentially biological processes for the production of plants extends to the plants produced by that process.

Patenting Breeding Processes

Article 53(b) excludes essentially biological processes from patent protection. It is generally recognised that the primary function of this is to ensure that normal biological propagating methods (such as crossing and selection) are not patented (although the need for such an exclusion can be questioned as there are only a limited number of such methods and they are very well known which makes it extremely unlikely that any such methods could be shown to be either novel or inventive).

The EPO Guidelines, Chapter IV, Part C, paragraph 3.4 states that the 'question whether a process is "essentially biological" is one of degree depending on the extent to which there is technical intervention by man in the process; if such intervention plays a significant part in determining or controlling the result it is

---

[68] Assinsel, *The Attack on Plant Breeeders' Rights Legislation and the Involvement of the Multi-nationals in Plant Breeding and the World's Seeds Business 1986 and Study of the National Council for Agricultural Research Plant Breeders' Rights and Patent Rights in Relation to Genetic Engineering* (The Hague, 1985).

desired to achieve, the process would not be excluded'. This is then qualified in paragraph 3.5. This says that:

> the exclusion referred to in the preceding paragraph does not apply to microbiological processes or the products thereof. The term 'microbiological process' is to be interpreted as covering not only industrial processes using micro-organisms, but also processes for producing micro-organisms, for example by genetic engineering. The product of a microbiological process may also be patentable *per se*.

The issue of what is an essentially biological process and what is a process which is capable of attracting patent protection is an important one, especially because, as will be seen below, the perception that patents only protect the biotechnological inventions, is incorrect. There is, however, very little internal guidance as to the extent of the intervention necessary in order to turn an essentially biological process into a non-essentially biological one. It is unclear if it is a question of how dominant the intervention by man is or if it is a question of the significance of this intervention on the result achieved. The distinction is important, for any scientist could argue that their intervention was significant whilst the actual impact of that intervention on controlling the outcome, in other words how dominant it is, might be minimal.

In *Lubrizol*[69] it was stated that:

> whether or not a [non-microbiological] process is to be considered as 'essentially biological' within the meaning of Article 53(b) has to be judged on the basis of the essence of the intervention taking into account the totality of human intervention and its impact on the result achieved . . . . Human interference may only mean that the process is not a 'purely biological' process, without contributing anything beyond a trivial level. It is further not a matter simply of whether such intervention is of quantitative or qualitative character.

But this still does not resolve the matter, and the unhappiness at the wording of the phrase can be seen in attempts during the 1980s to have it removed. These calls came from organisations such as the International Chamber of Commerce (which had representatives from multinational companies such as Ciba Geigy, ICI, Sandoz, Solvay and Roussel-Uchaf on its working party). To a considerable extent this issue has been resolved through the EU Directive, as it contains a more complete definition of an essentially biological process.

Because of this lack of any agreed scientific definitions, concepts such as plant variety and essentially biological processes have been left to the granting offices and lawyers to define, which can mean that what at law constitutes a plant, micro-organism, essentially biological process or plant variety may differ from that recognised by scientists. In this there are similarities with the granting criteria which are equally legal rather than scientific constructs.

---

[69] Above n 14.

In recent years there has been an increase in patent applications being filed over inventions which fall more closely within the traditional or classical type of breeding. In May 2003 the EPO announced that it had granted a patent to Monsanto[70] over wheat which produces soft-milling flour. The patent covers not only the flour, which was produced using 'conventional crossing techniques', but also 'the wheat, the flour, and dough obtained from and resulting foodstuffs.' The patent, which has become known as the 'biscuit patent', has attracted great criticism, not least from interested parties in India who claim that the flour was originally developed in India for use in the production of chapattis. Monsanto's counter to this is that whilst some of the genetic material in the wheat does originate from an Indian land race, Nap Hal, this material has been crossed with other plants to develop the particular strain which is the subject of the patent (this original work having been undertaken by Unilever, the wheat division of which had been acquired by Monsanto in 1998). The EPO viewed the development of the new strain as a production of a novel invention and therefore it was patentable. In January 2004 Greenpeace, together with the Indian Research Foundation for Science, Technology and Ecology (RFSTE) and the Bharat Krishak Samaj (BKS), filed an opposition to the patent. The basis for the opposition is that Monsanto is claiming a right over plant material already in the public domain. According to Greenpeace, their investigations had shown that the 'examiners at the EPO knew that the wheat involved is cultivated entirely normally and that it is not an invention, Monsanto employed all kinds of tricks and deception to conceal this fact although the truth is amply clear on proper examination.'[71] The issue which remains is whether the EPC excludes the products of what are essentially biological (or what can be called classical breeding) processes. Clearly, on the basis of the *Novartis* decision, where that product is a plant variety then that variety cannot be claimed; however, the exclusion in the second sentence only applies to essentially biological processes for the production of plants and animals and not to the plants and animals so produced, nor, therefore, to any other material produced by that process.

The *Monsanto* patent indicates that, far from the patent system being used to protect the results of high-tech biotechnical research, it is now being used to protect all aspects of plant breeding including those which do not involve 'genetic manipulation'. This again underlines the fact that it is not the subject matter of the invention which is the primary issue but rather the capacity of that invention to meet the granting criteria. Even where a process would be excluded from protection, this does not mean that the plant material produced by that process would be excluded from patent protection; cases such as *Pioneer/ Oilseed Brassica*[72] clearly indicate that the fact that plants have been produced through natural crossing and selection does not preclude them from patent protection.[73]

---

[70] EP-B–0 445929, see also EPO Press release, 27 January 2004. The patent was later sold and then withdrawn by its new owner.

[71] www.greenpeace.org.

[72] Case T–1026/02 *Pioneer/Oilseed Brassica* [2004] *EPOR* 41.

[73] This concerned an application claiming, amongst other matters, 'a *Brassica* plant comprising

As shown by the decision in *Novartis,* the fact that Article 53(b) serves to exclude plant varieties does not mean that plant varieties may not be 'captured' by a patent.

Article 64(2) of the EPC Products Produced Using a Patented Product[74]

The decision in *Monsanto* clearly shows that, not only does the EPO permit claims to the process for producing new products, but it will also permit claims to be made to anything produced using material covered by the patent. This could have very severe implications for breeders using patented technology belonging to another for the purposes of breeding new plants or developing plant-derived products. This is essentially a matter relating to claims drafting and being able to link the derived material to the inventive activity disclosed. The *Monsanto* patent covers 'the wheat, the flour, and dough obtained from and resulting foodstuffs'. In particular, the claims include 'the manufacture of crisp farinaceous edible products such as biscuits and the like.' This patent has caused some concern, although interestingly not because of the extension of protection to the flour etc, but, as previously discussed, more because it relates to a conventional breeding method; however, the fact that it does extend to material produced by the patented process is important to note. The decision to grant the patent indicates that protection will be available over plants, products harvested from those plants (flowers) and material produced using this material (for example, essential oils) apparently irrespective of whether the end product retains any of the inventive characteristics of the patented technology. It is possible to envisage a situation where a patent will be held to extend to any plant derived material including food products, clothes,[75] and fuels. The question is whether this is an acceptable extension, as it could give a single patent holder an extensive monopoly across a range of market places which some might feel goes beyond the inventive act which produced the initial plant.

a homozygous fertility restorer gene with specific yields and glucosinate contents of less than one of three different limits,' these limits being specified in claims 1, 2 and 3. The Examining Division initially rejected the application for lack of novelty—however, in rejecting the application the Division did not raise the issue of the subject matter of the claims, indicating that such a claim was permitted. The applicant successfully appealed against the decision and the application has been referred back to the Examining Division. In referring the application back, the Technical Board of Appeal focused on the sufficiency of the disclosure of the breeding programme: [2004] *EPOR* 421. The TBA also did not refer to the admissibility, or otherwise, of the subject matter of the application.

[74] According to at least one commentator '*all* of the commonly used methods for generating transgenic plants (eg Agrobacterium, gene guns, etc) are currently under patent' (although not necessarily under European patent): Spillane, *Recent Developments in Biotechnology as they Relate to Plant Genetic Resources for Food and Agriculture* (Commission on Genetic Resources for Food and Agriculture, Background Study Paper Number 9), available at www.fao.org.

[75] An example of this is the new fibre 'Ingeo', which is made from genetically modified corn. The corn was developed by the US company Cargill Dow and it states on the website for the fibre that it is protecting both processes and applications. It is unclear if the Cargill Dow patents extend to products made using the corn, but if the company were seeking European protection then it might be possible (applying *Monsanto*) to include cloth made from its fibres in the patent.

Article 64(2) Products Produced by a Patented Process

The basic principle that the protection conferred by a patent granted over a process extends to any material directly produced using that process is laid down in Article 64(2) of the European Patent Convention. Article 64(2) states that: 'If the subject matter of the European patent is a process, the protection conferred by the patent shall extend to the products directly obtained by such process.'

Issues relating to the scope of protection are matters for determining infringement, and as Article 64(3) goes on to state, '[a]ny infringement of a European patent shall be dealt with by national laws.'

As already mentioned above, the European Patent Office has stated categorically that it sees 'no conflict between . . . the plant variety indirectly enjoying patent protection as the direct product of a process under Article 64(2) and . . . the plant variety as such not being patentable under Article 53(b) EPC.'[76] The matter is 'purely for the courts considering infringement and the relevant licensing authorities, and are not to be taken into account when a patent office considers compliance with the provisions of Articles 52–57.'[77] Both the Technical Board of Appeal, which made these comments, and the Enlarged Board of Appeal, which concurred, are clear on this matter. The position appears to be that a plant variety is not itself capable of attracting patent protection, but where it is the direct product of a patented process then it is capable of falling within the ambit of the protection which that process attracts.

Whilst it is, on the one hand, not surprising that a patent *granting* office should distance itself from the consequences of a grant which is a matter to be determined by the courts, it is, on the other hand, extraordinary that an exclusion which has been reinforced, although arguably diluted, by the decisions of the EPO should be effectively made redundant by the simple fact that it is possible for the identical material, which will be denied protection in its own right, nonetheless to be the subject of protection for another right. If the exclusion is to retain any meaning, and it can be argued that a granting office acting on the twin presumptions of protectability and patentability with the emphasis on inclusion not exclusion is not interested in giving real meaning to any exclusion, then it should be clear that any extension of the scope of protection conferred over either a product or a process does not include extension to material which is specifically stated as not capable of attracting patent protection in its own right.

Another factor which needs to be borne in mind when assessing the meaning of Article 64(2) is that the plant variety caught by the patent is very likely not to have been the result of plant breeding activity by the patent holder—instead, mere use of the patent holder's protected process which results in the produc-

---

[76] Above n 41, para 82.
[77] *Ibid*, para 87.

tion of a plant variety. So the right to control the use of the variety probably will not even go to the person who has made use of the process to produce the new variety.

The EPO clearly regards the question as to whether a plant variety, produced by a patented process, is protected by the patent over that process, as a matter for consideration by the courts at the national level. It is not a matter for the EPO. This in itself gives rise to concern. As has been stated at other junctures throughout this book, the one thing which is constantly being sought is coherence, consistency and comparability across Europe. Leaving the issue of the extent to which a patent over a process is infringed by the use of that process to produce a plant variety to national courts means that there could be some courts which will refuse to permit the right to extend that far, as that would have the *de facto* effect of allowing the patent to cover material for which a patent cannot be sought, and equally there will be other courts which will permit the right to extend that far—as has been stated by an eminent commentator on the issue of the law and biotechnology, it is this practice of excluding under one guise but including under another which some feel brings the patent system into 'disrepute'.[78]

## III. EPO POLICY AND PRACTICE REGARDING GENETIC RESOURCES AND TRADITIONAL KNOWLEDGE

One of the most frequently debated issues is the extent to which patent offices can or should grant patents over inventions which either comprise indigenous plant material or are based on traditional knowledge, such material or knowledge often being brought into Europe from developing countries. The EPO has granted a number of patents which appear to blur the notions of novelty and inventiveness—in other words, these are patents granted over inventions which make use of information arguably already in the public domain or which are directly based on a prior use of that information.[79] It is not proposed to discuss this practice in any detail,[80] but merely to mention that the view of the EPO is that inventions based on this material (which cover the gamut of bioscience from medicinal plants to crop production) are often of great public, and therefore commercial, importance. The absence of patent protection might deprive

---

[78] Comment made by Professor Deryck Beyleveld at a workshop held as part of the PIP project on the implications of Art 64(2).

[79] For example *Neem* EP–B–0 436 257 and *Hoodia* EP–B–0 973 534. On 10 May 2000, the Opposition Division of the EPO revoked a patent granted to the American Department of Agriculture and the company WR Grace in 1995 over a neem tree-derived fungicide on the grounds that the patent lacked novelty because of prior use by Indian farmers. This decision was upheld in March 2005. At the time of writing the full judgment was not available.

[80] For a more detail analysis of the issues involved see Dutfield, *Intellectual Property Rights, Trade and Biodiversity* (Earthscan, 2000); and Dutfield, *Industrial Property Rights and the Life Science Industries* (Ashgate Publishing, 2003).

countries with no prior access to this material of the benefits of this material and it might be argued that companies which invest in discovering the information and in the production of a commercial application which makes the information more widely available should be rewarded. As knowledge of the prior use is frequently not documented it can be difficult for a granting office to discover this use during the examination process and in the absence of any general database which can be easily searched, novelty and inventiveness would appear to be served by the application. The EPO is trying to address the problem and in May 2005 it entered into an agreement with India which would give the EPO access to a digital database containing information about some 136,000 forms of traditional Indian medicine. Of course, such agreements are only possible where there is a database which the EPO can use as a reference tool. It should be noted that many of the patents granted over inventions concerning traditional knowledge have subsequently been revoked.

Of central importance to the debate over whether, and to what extent, patents can be granted over traditional knowledge and indigenous plant material are the CBD and the International Treaty on Plant Genetic Resources discussed in chapter 1. Those charged with overseeing these two international agreements, together with initiatives undertaken by the WIPO and WTO, are striving to find a balance between the different interests.[81]

The EPO has been sharply criticised over its policy and practice and it will be interesting to note if any conservatism is introduced into the granting of patents or if the current prevailing view that any doubt over a grant should be properly addressed through the various opposition mechanisms available will remain. This view clearly underpinned the EPO's statement in respect of the Edinburgh patent that, whilst that part of the patent which claimed human beings produced by cloning process had been granted in error, the fact of the opposition brought demonstrated that 'the opposition procedure, anchored in the EPC, has once again proved its worth as an effective and transparent means of reviewing patents granted by the EPO.'[82]

The right granted by a patent permits the rights holder to prevent most uses (primarily commercial) of the protected invention for a period of up to 20 years,[83] and the right is limited to the countries designated. The objective is to

---

[81] For a further discussion see Heath and Kamperman Sanders (eds), *Industrial Property in the Bio-medical Age* (Kluwer Law International, 2003); and Bragdon, *CGIARS and IPRs*, Conference proceedings of the Conference on Plant Intellectual Property within Europe and Wider Global Community (Sheffield Academic Press, 2001).

[82] EPO Press Release, July 2002.

[83] Whilst the right can last for up to 20 years (with the possibility of supplementary protection for an additional five years for pharmaceutical products where it can be shown the external factors, such as trialling of the product, have whittled the actual market protection of the right to what could be an unacceptably low duration), in practice, the rapid turnover of products within that market means that, for many products (pharmaceuticals being the obvious exception), the period for which that protection is valuable is far less, often between six and ten years. It should be noted that renewal fees become payable three years after grant and that these increase in sum the longer the right is claimed.

provide the patent holder with a protected lead in time to the market. It is important to note that the right is a negative, not a positive right. The grant of a patent does not give the patent holder any right to use the patented material but rather to prevent others from using. The corollary of this is usually that the patent holder is the only one allowed to use the protected material in practice, but this use might be subject to other constraints such as the legality of using or selling the protected material (illegality not being a bar to obtaining patent protection), meeting health and safety requirements or passing the requisite medical trials necessary before launching onto the market. Unlike under the Community plant variety rights system, which specifically draws attention to the fact that the exercise of the right granted may not 'violate any provisions adopted on the grounds of public morality, public policy or public security, the protection of health and life of humans, animals or plants, the protection of the environment, the protection of industrial or commercial property or the safeguarding of competition, of trade or of agricultural production' (Article 13(8)), the patent system does not specifically draw attention to any external restrictions on using the material post-grant. These, however, are critical to understanding the impact of the grant of a patent.

## IV. POST-GRANT ISSUES

Once a patent grant has been made, all issues relating to the *use* of the patented product potentially become a matter for opposition[84] or infringement. The EPC, generally speaking, does not concern itself with such matters (the exception being the provision of guidance on the matter of interpretation by national courts). Notwithstanding the fact that the patent system primarily exists to protect the interests of the patent holder, many patent systems also contain some derogations or limitations to the right granted (as is reflected in Article 30 and 31 of the TRIPs Agreement). These mainly relate to the right to use patented material for research purposes, the granting of compulsory licences and ability of governments to secure the use of the patented technology in the absence of consent from the patent holder. As these are matters relating to the post-grant use of the technology, they do not form part of the EPC, but are primarily matters for individual national patent laws. The one area where the EPC does provide guidance is in respect of the interpretation (or construction) of the claims contained within the patent specification.

---

[84] Opponents to a patent are able to make formal representations to the EPO during the nine months immediately following grant in order to seek a revocation (Arts 99–101). Many national patents laws do not include such a procedure.

## Claims Construction

Article 69 of the EPC allows courts discretion as to whether they rely on the language used to determine the scope of protection or, where appropriate, they can look behind the language to determine the invention protected.[85]

Article 69 states: '(1) The extent of protection conferred by a European patent or a European patent application shall be determined by the *terms* of the claims. Nevertheless, the description and drawings shall be used to *interpret* the claims' (emphasis added).

In order to assist in applying this provision, a Protocol on the Interpretation of Article 69(1) was introduced. This means that the claims are 'to be interpreted as defining a position between those extremes which combines a fair position for the patentee with a reasonable degree of certainty for third parties.' The intention is to achieve a balance between two potentially extreme positions, defining the scope by reference to the strict literal meaning of the wording used in the claims (which was the traditional UK practice) and using the claims as guidelines which simply indicate that which is protected (which was the German practice).

A couple of initial observations can be made about Article 69. The first is that whilst it is clear that the starting point for determining the scope is looking at the claims stated, courts can use the information provided by the patentee (by way of the description of the invention) to decide what it actually claimed. The second is that the French and German texts of the EPC[86] use the terms *teneur* and *inhalt* respectively and both of these have a wider meaning than the English word *claim*. This means that whilst, for an English audience, the reference to what is to be assessed appears clear, if looked at from either the French or

---

[85] The impact of the Art 69 has been different according to the previous practice of each jurisdiction. For example, British patent law is at a key stage in its development, particularly with regard to the question of construction. Over the past 25 years the system has gone through three distinct periods following the adoption of the EPC in 1973 which necessitated a change in national patent law. The UK implemented the EPC in 1977, and the 1977 Act took effect in June 1978, but the full force of that implementation did not take effect until the 1990s. These three periods, which necessarily overlapped, mark three approaches to construction. The first affected patents granted before June 1978. These were to be construed according to the 1949 Patents Act, which required a literal approach to be used. The second period was a transitional period which lasted from June 1978 to 1998, at which date Art 69 came into full effect. During this time there was a degree of uncertainty over the extent to which the Article had to be applied to cases of infringement. The final period began in 1998 when Art 69 became the governing law and the accompanying Protocol the basis for determining its application. It is only recently, therefore, that the full force of Art 69 has been felt; however, that has not prevented the courts from using the Article as the backdrop to the decisions pre-1998. As Cornish states, this means that the time could be ripe for a reconsideration of Art 69 and its Protocol from the British perspective. His view, however, would appear to be that the shackles of over literal interpretation should be shed to make the law more forgiving, and this view is shared by many within the patent profession. In so doing they are embracing a very civil law approach to construction, based on the spirit of the agreement rather than the actual language used.

[86] English, French and German being the official languages of the Convention.

German perspective, then the focus of attention is less obvious and seems to indicate that the courts can look behind the claims stated.

As discussed in chapter 1, the scope of a patent is determined by reference to the claims. It is these which define the territory protected by the patent. As also discussed in chapter 1, there is some discussion as to whether the claims should act as 'fence posts' which set out the outer reaches of the territory claimed or if they should act as 'sign posts' which indicate where the territory claimed can be found.[87] The problem with the former is that if the claims are given too literal a reading then they might not cover all the inventive work undertaken by the patent holder. The concern here is that this would allow competitors to 'piggy-back' on this work and compete unfairly in the market place. The problem with the 'sign-post' approach (which looks to the purpose of the patent to determine what it is intended to cover) is that it might not provide third parties with sufficient information as to what is protected by the patent. To some extent, the approach taken will depend upon the policy adopted at the national granting office and judicial level; however, there has been an attempt to provide a harmonised approach.

The objective of claims interpretation is not to allow competitors to freely use a technical equivalent which is to all intents and purposes the same as the patented invention but which because of the language used in the patent is not actually covered by it. In order to give effect to this middle ground, what is sought is to identify what the patentee intended the patent to cover and to assess whether any third party (skilled in that area) would have realised that the intention was for the patent to cover variants such as the allegedly infringing act. In many respects this is the patent law equivalent to the common law contract principle of the 'officious bystander', this being a hypothetical individual used by the courts to see if both parties to the contract intended a term to be in that contract when in fact no such term is present. If, at the time that the contract was made (or the patent issued), both parties (the patentee and the third party) realised that the terms (claims) were intended to cover variants of the kind which are alleged to infringe then the court will hold them to have been included by implication. The two critical elements are that a) *both* parties must have understood that the claim was intended to cover the variant concerned and b) this understanding should have been obvious at the time the patent was granted. This is intended to give certainty as to extent of protection for the duration of protection.

The potential danger with the purposive approach is that it might overly rely on what the patentee *intended* the patent to cover.[88] Implicit in this is that if the

---

[87] For a clear explanation of the function of registration see Burrell and Handler, 'Making Sense of Trade Mark Law' [2003] 4 *IPQ* 388. Whilst the article concentrates on trade mark registration the authors make some very useful points in their introduction relating to registration in general. One of the issues they discuss is whether patent claims should be treated as fence posts or sign posts.

[88] Although decisions such as that of the UK House of Lords indicate that the language used, as opposed to the intention lying behind, will be the focal point when interpreting the claims: *Kirin-Amgen v Hoechst Marion Roussel* [2005] 1 All ER 667.

patentee could not be shown to have intended the claims to extend beyond a certain point then that territory falls outside the scope of the patent. Where the intention can be shown then the material can be claimed. What is not asked, is what would society accept as a proper territory for protection? That this question is not asked is perfectly understandable. Where a court is determining the territory of a patent then it is doing so because it expects the patent to have been validly granted (unless a third party proves otherwise)—the contribution which society is rewarding has, therefore, been properly assessed and having been so assessed then it is permissible for external factors, such as public interests in permitting the monopoly, to drop out of the equation. What is relevant at the moment of determining scope is ensuring that the patent holder can make full, and best, use of the right as granted. Reliance on determining what the patent holder intended the patent to cover could provide an unpredictable environment for third parties, as it might not be possible to identify whether a patent could be construed in court in such a way to cover their research activity.[89]

Given the extent of genetic research and the likely impact of overly broad patents on those using genetic material in research it could be argued that a patent should be subject to a simple test, namely that claims must be written in clear and ambiguous terms and that where there is any ambiguity or the claim seeks to capture an unreasonable amount of material then it should be construed against the party seeking to rely on it.

There is a particular problem concerning construction which applies to genetics and that is the extent to which a patent should be held to protect variants on the patented invention which could not have been envisaged at the time the patent was sought. The present approach to patent construction focuses on what the patentee intended the patent claims to cover at the time that the patent was granted. If he could not, at that time, have foreseen that a particular variant could later occur, does that mean that the variant automatically falls outside the scope of the patent? In particular, what if the variant adds to the body of knowledge and itself represents an inventive step forward?

This issue is closely related to industrial applicability and inventive step, but it is nonetheless distinct. It is also the most controversial legal-cum-policy issue that is currently outstanding. If the current policy and practice relating to pharmaceutical patenting is analysed it can be seen that there are two policy choices in current patent law. First, there is the rule that the first person to identify one use for a novel thing or substance should be entitled to a patent over all its uses; secondly, the rule that subsequent researchers who add inventive knowledge to an earlier invention can claim a selected thing or substance as such, once again on the basis that a newly uncovered use has been revealed. The controversial

---

[89] A patent taken out by Human Genome Sciences Inc (HGS) provides an excellent example. HGS obtained a patent for a gene as a receptor. Other researchers later identified its use in identifying the entry point for the AIDS virus. The claims were held to be sufficiently broad to allow HGS to claim the use of the gene for AIDS research—put another way, the intention behind the claims was that HGS should capture any use made of the gene it has identified.

aspect is the extent to which the first patentee's claim should 'reach through' to subsequent uses. If this is permitted then it could give rise to a cascade of rights, with all resulting users having to seek licences from the holders of the various rights over the technology. This could give rise to royalty stacking or a thicket of patents making it difficult for the patented technology to be used by third parties in practice. The result is likely to be a royalty stack which could well impede new R&D further down the line. The issue which this raises is whether each of the patentees should be entitled only to a patent for the use discovered by him and not for any improvement on that use not identified in the initial patent.[90]

A further concern is that overly broad patents are being granted to inventions involving genetic material, with claims being made to any and all uses of particular genes. Whilst, strictly speaking, unutilised genes cannot be the subject of a patent, the effect of allowing patents to be granted which claim all uses of that gene is to render the gene itself protected by the patent. In Europe the requirement that the patent must disclose the function or use of the gene before a patent will be granted, together with the requirement in some jurisdictions[91] that the function must be shown to be specific, credible and substantial, and also the existing requirements that the claimed uses must be novel and inventive, are intended to mitigate against any inappropriately broad patents. The general view amongst many users of the patent system is that it will be increasingly more difficult to obtain a patent over genetic material as a result.

In the UK the Nuffield Council on Bioethics published a Discussion Paper on the Ethics of Patenting DNA in 2002 which raised concerns over overly broad monopoly. The view expressed is that many patent systems have been too generous in the scope of rights granted and that this practice, together with the likely decrease in inventive activity as genetic knowledge increases, has encouraged the seeking of broad patents as early as possible. The Council recommended that consideration should be given to 'limiting the scope of product patents that assert rights over naturally occurring DNA sequences to the uses referred to in the patent claims, where the grounds for inventiveness concern the use of the sequence only and not the derivation or elucidation of the sequence itself.' The restriction to the uses referred to in the application presumably means demonstrable, rather than theoretical, uses.

---

[90] Sir John Enderby speaking about the Report of the Royal Society published in the UK in April 2003 said: 'The current intellectual property system needs to be tightened for the sake of both science and society. Researchers should be rewarded for the contribution that they make and the system should provide incentives for carrying out research and development. However some patents are slipping through the net, which give some researchers far greater reward than they actually deserve. This affects all of us. If patents are granted which are too broad in scope, they block other researchers from carrying out related work and so hold up the development of medicines and treatments. This is tremendously bad for science, but the ultimate losers are the patients who wait longer for beneficial drugs to reach their hospitals and pharmacies.'

[91] See, eg, the UK Examination Guidelines for Biotechnological Inventions, November 2003, above ch 5, n 68; and the general practice of the USPTO post US Guidelines on the Examination of Biotechnological Inventions, as published in the 66(4) *Federal Register*, 5 January 2001.

As the next chapter will discuss, the EU published its first report on the Directive on the Legal Protection of Biotechnological Inventions in 2002. This also discussed the issue of scope, but purely in the context of elements isolated from the human body. The Report states that the granting criteria, and in particular the requirement of sufficiency of disclosure and support, should be enough to enable an examiner to reject any application the claims of which are too broad. As already stated, particular consideration needs to be given to the scope of claims relating to inventions involving DNA sequences, proteins derived from those sequences, express sequence tags (ESTs) and single nucleotide polymorphisms (SNPs). It should also be noted that once the Directive comes fully on stream then there will be the added likelihood of cases being heard before the European Court of Justice.

The particular question which this poses is the extent to which the new concept could be at the expense of the reasonable interest of third parties in trying to invent around the patent. The situation raises that classic dilemma in patent law of deciding which instances warrant giving both contributors patents in a final product or procedure. When should it be found that each has made a significant intellectual contribution to that outcome and should therefore have a patent from which a share can be claimed in any exploitation? A balanced answer will only emerge if the same factors as were mentioned previously are given serious attention: the need first to show industrial application, then inventive step in the particular circumstances; there should be a limitation of claims to demonstrated uses unless there really is a general principle uncovered which warrants a claim to all consequent deployments of the principle.

Adding to the complexity is the extent to which something which is technically equivalent to the patented invention but which is not covered by the language used in the specification infringes. In the US the 'Doctrine of Equivalents', whilst controversial, remains a central part of American patent law.[92] A question often asked is the extent to which European patent law should include a corresponding provision to the US 'Doctrine of Equivalents'. This would permit the courts to determine if the alleged infringing item was technically equivalent to the inventive concept described in the patent and therefore did infringe even though it did not fall within the scope of the claims. Many countries (most notably the US, the Netherlands and Germany) favour this approach, but others (the UK, in particular) are reluctant to make this a general principle in patent law as it is felt that this would give rise to too much uncertainty as to what has actually been claimed by the patentee. In the 2000 amendment of the EPC it was proposed that the Protocol should include an 'equivalents' paragraph.[93] Following a lengthy debate it was decided that the Protocol should only be amended to require that 'due account shall be taken of

---

[92] *Festo v Shoketsu Kinzoku* 122 SCT 1831 (2002).

[93] The new paragraph will read: 'For the purpose of determining the extent of protection conferred by a European patent, due account shall be taken of any element which is equivalent to an element specified in the claims.'

any element which is equivalent to an element specified in the claims' when determining the extent of protection.[94] The Conference failed to agree on a definition of 'equivalent' and the amended Protocol is silent on this matter. It also does not state at which date equivalence is to be determined. The revised Convention will come into force only two years after the ratification process has been completed at the national level by 15 of the Contracting States or, if earlier, three months after all Contracting States have ratified and deposited their instrument of ratification. In practice, this may mean closer to 2010 than 2006.

There are a number of issues relating to the way in which patents are interpreted which are too numerous and complex to elaborate upon here. It is worth noting, however, that so far there have been very few plant-related patents which have required judicial interpretation and therefore it is problematic to provide any clear guidance on how the courts are likely to interpret such patents in the event of litigation. It should also be recollected that in the absence of a European patent court this will remain a matter for national courts and there may be variation in practices. One final point needs to be taken into account and that is the fact that membership of the EPC does not necessarily mean that all its provisions have to be complied with immediately upon succession. Where an international obligation has the effect of amending existing national laws then usually member states are provided with a transition period during which they can gradually bring national provision into line. The extent to which the EPC is in full force in any given jurisdiction therefore also needs to be taken into account.

It is important to remember when looking at the EPC that it is primarily concerned with the granting of patents and not with their enforcement. It is for the courts to decide the proper extent of the right granted. As a patent granted under the EPC takes on the form of a national right in those countries designated by the patent applicant, the nature of the right acquired is determined by the national laws of the countries so designated. This means that the same patent can be interpreted differently in different national courts (and will be subject to the judicial views of the judges who sit). The result is that without precision from the outset of grant as to the exact scope and the opportunity for national deliberation and determination the same patent can be held to mean one thing in one member state and another elsewhere.

The devolution of the evaluation of the scope of the right until such time as a court dissects the claims can give rise to uncertainties. For example, the exact extent of the protection conferred by the patent may not be known by either the patentee (who arguably accepts this risk when applying for a patent) or third parties (who do not knowingly accept the risk) until such time as the claims are tested in court. Equally, until a court decides either the validity of a patent as a whole, or any claim within it, neither the holder nor third parties, for example

---

[94] This was the result of the Diplomatic Conference on the revision of the EPC held in Munich between 20 and 29 November 2000.

other researchers, will know the extent to which the patent is secure. Another problem is that there will inevitably be variance between the interpretations given to patent claims at the different national courts (and indeed between the levels of court in any one jurisdiction). One thing is certain and that is that the responsibility for maintaining the right (through the payment of renewal fees, which often increase as the monopoly lasts in order to reflect the fact that the patent holder should pay more the longer he seeks to keep the claimed material under patent) and protecting it (through identifying infringements and instigating either a licence or litigation) lies with the patent holder.

### Derogations/Limitations

One of the most important things which a user of patented material needs to know is the extent to which s/he can use the protected material in research. The patent laws of most EPC countries contain limitations allowing both private, non-commercial use and experimental use (often lumped together as the 'research exemption'[95]).

### Research Exemption

Unlike the situation in the US (discussed in chapter 2), European patent law does permit the free use of patented material in research.[96] The EPC itself makes no mention of any right to use patented material freely for research purposes; however, Article 31(b) of the Community Patent Convention permits acts done for experimental or non-commercial purposes where the act relates to the subject matter of the invention. Whilst the CPC itself is not in force, this principle has been adopted by most member states of the EPC. There is, however, a question as to what constitutes an experimental or non-commercial purpose. The position is not helped by the fact that there are only a handful of cases on research use and none of these relates to plant material. While the evolving European position on the research exemption does give rise to ambiguities, at least it can be said that a more coherent dynamic prevails in Europe than in the US.

In the past, many European countries restricted their research exemption to non-commercial activity (normally to that work conducted within universities and public institutions which did not have industrial backing). The modern patent law in contrast separates out the various aspects to the exception and, on the one hand, exempts use which is private and non-commercial and, on the other hand, exempts experimental use. The general rule of thumb appears to be

---

[95] While the EPC (Art 69 and Protocol) specifies that the scope of the right is determined by the terms of the claims, the acts constituting infringement are found in the CPC (Arts 25–28), the exceptions being specified in Art 27.

[96] There is one area where the situation is at present better in the US than in Europe and that is that there is a specific statutory provision which permits the use of material identical to that protected by a patent by companies producing generic equivalents of patented drugs for the purposes of securing regulatory approval. An equivalent provision has been introduced in Europe.

that if the patented material is being used with a direct commercial objective in mind then it is unlikely to fall within the research exemption.[97] However, recently courts across Europe have shown increased willingness to treat experimental research as exempt from patent liability even where it has a commercial purpose,[98] although it is unlikely that such a liberal approach would extend either to the production of a direct competitor to the patented technology or to the production of a new product which includes the patented invention. Under the experimental use exception it is permissible to conduct research which may modify or improve the invention patented[99]—and in Germany at least, this includes providing further information about the properties of the invention, for instance through clinical trials.[100]

But limits remain, and these relate to the requirement that the experimental or non-commercial use has to relate to the subject matter of the invention. This is generally taken to mean that a third party is able to conduct research on or into the patented material (such as looking for a specific function of a gene or checking that it does what the patent holder claims it does) but not on uses of or with the patented technology (such as placing that gene within a plant variety for the purposes of generating a particular trait within that variety). One major ambiguity about the experimental use exception, as it affects biotechnological patents, concerns how far clinical tests (which involve a pharmaceutical product) can be regarded as experimental, since treatment and the continuing search for further genetic knowledge often enough go hand in hand. It may well be that they can only be treated as exempt where the latter objective is a dominant motive for the tests but the law remains rather uncertain. A number of European countries are looking at the nature and function of the research exemption at present at the local, national, level, but with an eye on possible EU and international changes.[101]

One particular problem facing European plant breeders is the impact of an increased use of patent protection on the ability of breeders to use plant material in commercial breeding programmes. As indicated in both chapters 3 and 4, the principle that protected material should be freely available for use in commercial breeding programmes is enshrined within plant variety rights. However, this is not always the case in patent law. Generally speaking, the research exemption in most patent laws means that a breeder will either need to acquire

[97] See Cornish, 'Experimental Use of Patented Inventions in European Community States' (1998) 29(7) *IIC* 735.
[98] For the UK, see *Monsanto v Stauffer* [1985] RPC 515; for recent confirmation of the new approach in France, *Wellcome Foundation v Parexel International & Flamel*, Tribunal de Grande Instance de Paris, 20 February 2001, *Intellectual Property News*, Issue 17, July 2001.
[99] The exception must also cover experiments to discover whether the invention can be made from its description in the patent specification (essential if the patent is to be challenged).
[100] Two decisions of the German Supreme Court treat clinical trials of pharmaceuticals as falling under the exception: *Klinische Versuche I and II* [1997] RPC 623; [1998] RPC 423.
[101] See, eg, the UK's DTI study, 'Patents for Genetic Sequences: The Competitiveness of UK Law and Practice', www.dti.gov.uk, within which the research exemption was singled out for specific attention.

a licence from a patent holder to use a patented gene or plant in a breeding programme or face an action for infringement.[102] There are a number of concerns which plant breeders have, for example, does use of a plant which contains a patented gene constitute non-commercial use if the object of the research is to produce a plant variety which does not contain that patented gene? Secondly, even if the act of breeding is regarded as exempt (and this is unlikely), when would the exemption, if ever, cease to have effect? Would it continue to protect the breeder of the new commercial product during the period of commercialisation (as per the plant variety rights system), or would it cease to have effect at the moment of commercialisation (and how is this to be determined—is it when the decision to commercialise is made or when the product is offered for sale), or (if a variety is concerned) when the variety is submitted for VCU/DUS trials?

### Compulsory Licensing/Government Use

Most European countries also permit a third party to seek a compulsory licence where it can be shown that the patent holder has unreasonably refused to grant a licence. However, such provisions are rarely, if ever, invoked. The value in the provision appears to be as a means of getting the patent holder to the negotiating table. However, a number of factors need to be taken into account; these include the fact that Article 31 of the TRIPs Agreement now sets down a number of specified conditions which the person seeking the licence has to meet before a compulsory licence will be granted and that the Paris Convention prescribes that a compulsory licence may not be sought before a period of at least three years has elapsed. This latter has significance for the use of the compulsory cross-licensing provision within the EU Directive. An alternative to seeking a compulsory licence would be to invoke competition law.

There is a specific issue relating to compulsory licences where the parties concerned hold both patent and plant variety rights. This situation arises where the rights are governed by the Directive and the Regulation, the individual provisions of which are discussed in chapters 4 and 7 (with the collective position examined further in chapter 9).

Many national patent laws also permit their governments to use patented technology without needing to acquire a licence (compulsory or otherwise). This is usually done either on the basis of needing to protect national security or in order to promote a specific public interest, such as the provision of new drugs. As with the compulsory licensing provision, this also appears only to be used in extremis, with most uses relating to defence. If a government decides to invoke this provision then it usually can only do so if it pays reasonable compensation to the patent holder.

---

[102] Concerns over the impact of this current practice on breeding programmes has meant that one European country, Germany, has attempted to introduce a similar provision to that contained in plant variety rights into its national patent law.

The role the limitations play is an important one, for it is in respect of the application of these that the *type* of subject matter could be relevant. As has already been noted, EPC patent law does not, in the main, differentiate between types of inventions for the purposes of *grant*. A pharmaceutical product will be treated in the same way as an agricultural one. However, there could be a marked difference in the way in which the limitations to the right operate which does depend on the type of material involved. For example, there might be a greater acceptance of the use of the compulsory licensing provisions (and indeed government use) if the plant material concerned is a medicinal plant. Equally the notion of experimental or research use might be given a more flexible inter-pretation to include use of patented medicinal plant products in clinical trials (as is currently the case in some European countries), but continue to be given a restrictive application in respect of use in a commercial agricultural breeding programme. These issues will be discussed in more detail in chapter 9.

Acquisition

One of the main criticisms levelled at the EPC system is the cost and time involved in acquiring a right. The current average cost of a European patent, valid in eight member States and in force for a 10-year period (including trans-lation costs, professional representation fees (but not patent agent fees[103]) and renewal fees of 8,500 euros per year from the fifth to the tenth year) would be 29,800 euros (approx).[104] As might be realised, a patent which is valid in *all* EPC member states will be exponentially more expensive (this is another reason why the European Commission wishes to take action). It can take between three and five years to acquire a patent (for an ordinary, non-controversial invention).

It is very difficult to determine the number of patents granted by the EPO over plant-related inventions. A main reason for this is that the term 'biotechnology' is generally used to cover *all* bioscience-related applications and grants;[105] whilst some applications may specify that the claims relate to a plant, others may not and yet the applications covered by the claims made may extend to plant material. One thing is clear and that is that the number of applications relating to biological material in general has risen.[106] It is also important when looking at the EPO statistics to take note of the fact that a European patent can belong to a non-European individual or company. In terms of European activity, the OECD figures indicate that Denmark makes the most applications,

---

[103] These are wholly subject to market value and will depend on both the expertise of the patent agent hired and the amount which the inventor wishes to pay.

[104] www.epo.org. As can be seen, this figure is significantly more than that for a Community plant variety right.

[105] Both the European Commission's Report (discussed in ch 7) and analyses of European patent-ing activity (such as that undertaken by the OECD) do not differentiate between the subject matter of applications, merely instead using the global terms 'biotechnology' and 'genetic engineering'.

[106] *Ibid,* and for a recent analysis of these figures in the context of global practices see the OECD's 'Compendium of Patent Statistics 2004' at www.oecd.org.

followed by Belgium, the UK, Ireland, the Netherlands, Norway, France, Austria, Sweden, Germany, Spain, Finland and Italy. There is no indication of any activity within Greece or Portugal. Whilst in the immediate term it is likely that the number of grants made will also rise, it is possible that in the longer term the refinements made to the granting criteria (and in particular the notion of an inventive step) may serve to limit the number of patents granted. For those who are concerned about proliferation of patents over genetic material, the possibility of a more measured application of the system will be welcome. However, a more cautious approach has to be tempered with the need to foster the bioscience industry and in this the discussions between the industry, its legal representatives and the granting office as to best practice will continue to play a significant role. As the next chapter will show, the fact that the number of grants is likely to reach a plateau or even fall is not something which the European Commission wishes to see happen.

## V. EPO DEVELOPMENTS IN CONTEXT

There are a number of important factors to bear in mind when assessing the evolution of the practice of the EPO.

1) It was not (and never has been) the function of the EPO to establish *policy*. Its primary role was (and is) to determine whether a patent should be granted over a particular invention. Its function was not to decide whether a particular area of technology could or should be excluded from seeking that protection. Obviously as the jurisprudence evolved, so too did the semblance of a policy, but this policy resulted from the *practice* of the Office rather than through a pre-determined agenda.

That the EPO did not see itself as determining policy is clear from the fact that in many instances the queries as to how to apply the Convention came from the Examining Division and answers to these queries were 'worked out' by the Boards of Appeal, sometimes with inconsistent results.[107] In so far as any policy can be deduced it is simply that the Office is concerned with granting patents, and any exceptions or limitations to this are to be given a restricted application.

In many respects the EPO was, in the early days of gene patenting at least, placed in a complicated position. It would have been aware of policy decisions being taken elsewhere (often after many years of discussion), and the form of these discussions may have provided it with confidence to continue with the evolving practice of granting patents—however, as it was charged with granting

---

[107] For example, in the original *Onco-mouse* decision it was stated that the second half of Art 53(b) (which refers to the patentability of the microbiological processes and the products thereof) meant that an animal variety which had been produced by a microbiological process would not be excluded from protection. The *PGS* decision extended this exception to the exclusion to plant varieties. The decision in *Novartis* made clear that the exception to the exclusion did not extend to plant or animal varieties irrespective of how they were produced.

patents it could not wait until these discussions had been concluded before applying the provisions of the Convention. This meant it had to evolve its practice alongside (but not necessarily in response to) the policy decisions being taken elsewhere. Certainly, at the same time that the EPO was making its first judgments as to patentability, other organisations such as the WIPO and the OECD (as well as the European Commission) were looking at how best to protect the emerging results of bioscience research. In extreme summary, each of these eventually took the position that there was nothing inherently problematic with granting patents over genetic material provided that the threshold for protection had been met.

2) Given the pan-European impact of the EPC, together with the obligations it engendered at the national level, a period of consolidation as to policy and practice was only to be expected. Secondly, the establishment of any firm policy and practice was dependent on patent applications relating to bioscience being filed and examined.

3) The EPC was immediately successful and quickly attracted a large number of applications from all areas of technology.[108] The EPO had (and has) to treat all applications equally and it could not favour one type of application over another either in terms of prioritising examination or the establishment of a subject matter-specific policy (if indeed the EPO was prepared at that time to develop a diversity of practice according to subject matter). Finally, there was a dearth of patent examiners proficient in the biosciences and therefore able properly to determine the novelty and inventiveness of the applications before them.

4) As the policy that it is permissible to grant patents over genetic material has become established and the number of applications has increased, with a commensurate increase in expert examiners, so too has the ability of the EPO to define and defend the role (and interpretation) of the EPC with confidence. Arguably it is because of that confidence in its established practice that the Office felt comfortable with adopting the EU Directive to supplement its own implementing rules.

Finally there was the matter of the relationship between the EPO and the EU. As can be seen, throughout the 1980s and 1990s the EPO took active steps to provide patent protection for a broad range of bio-inventions. If this activity had been the sole arbiter of European patent policy and practice then, given the apolitical nature of the EPO, it is possible that disquiet over the patenting of bio-inventions would have been confined to lobbying for a change in the EPC to enhance the scope of the exclusions or to bringing oppositions at the EPO itself. However, the EPO (whilst influential) could not direct the interpretation or application of national patent laws.[109] For the European Commission, eager

---

[108] It should be borne in mind that not only was the Office having to deal with applications from member states but it was also open to non-European applicants seeking European patent protection.

[109] Decisions of the EPO are not binding on national courts, although they may be highly persuasive.

both to ensure parity of provision and also to avoid the problems encountered by the EPO, this meant the introduction of specific legislation. One of the most interesting things to observe about these developments was the way in which both the EPO and the European Commission viewed the influence of the other.

Up until the time that it formally adopted the Directive for the purposes of supplementary interpretation, the EPO had, whilst maintaining an interest in the discussions (and, indeed, provided a presence for conferences and meetings on the subject), given only a cautious welcome to the EU intiatives. Its official position was that it was in the process of evolving an appropriate jurisprudence and any 'teething' problems encountered in applying patent law to bioscience inventions would be resolved in time. There are any number of hypotheses as to why the EPO adopted this position. The most obvious is that it was mainly concerned with its own operations and on this basis, with the jurisprudence evolving, the EPO did not see any need for any external direction as to how it should apply the provisions of the EPC. Another possible reason is that, given the nature of the EPO there was felt to be the possibility that if the proposals from Brussels were welcomed too enthusiastically then this could undermine the autonomy and independence of the EPO. This reading of the situation gains support from the fact that the EPO consistently maintained that its decisions were not (and would not be) influenced by Brussels—and this can be seen in the judgments of the Boards of Appeal which, pre-1999, refused to do anything other than to refer to the Directive without using it as the basis for any final decision.

The same reluctance to follow in the footsteps of the EPO can be seen in the actions of the European Commission. Certainly at the beginning of the discussions leading up to the introduction of the Directive, the Commission did not feel itself bound to follow either the letter of the EPC nor the practice of the EPO.[110] However, any concern felt by the EPO that the EU might try and influence its practices did appear to be well-founded for, as will be discussed in the next chapter, the Commission made it clear from the outside that at the very least it hoped that the Directive would have an indirect effect on existing international laws in this area.

However, notwithstanding any posturing which each might have taken as to the exact nature of any subsequent responses, the reality was that neither could wholly distance themselves from the activities of the other. All members of the EU are also members of the EPC. As a result of this, the national patent laws of the EU comply, in form if not in interpretation, with the provisions of the EPC. Any attempt to amend significantly these national patent laws by Brussels could have had the effect of rendering EU member states of the EPC non-compliant with their obligations under the EPC unless there was a commensurate revision of the EPC (and during the 1980s there was no political will to revise the

---

[110] For example, one of the first drafts simply stated that all inventions involving biological material were patentable and contained no exclusions from protection.

Convention; indeed, the revision which took place in 2000 made only minimal substantive changes). The effect of this on the actual ability of the EU to shape patent practice will be discussed in the next chapter, but the connection (in form if not principle and informally if not formally) between the two remains evident.

## VI. CONCLUSION

In retrospect it is easy to characterise the plant patenting practices of the EPO as transparent and apparent from the time the Convention came into force. However, the situation at the time was not so clear and the issue of how to protect plant bio-inventions exercised the keenest of minds. A considerable amount of literature was produced by organisations such as the WIPO, as well as eminent academics, which sought to address the questions of a) whether genetic material should be patented and b) the nature of the relationship between the patent and plant variety rights systems.[111] To a considerable extent, debate under the former focused on whether there was an external ethical bar on patenting genetic material of all orders. In respect of the latter, the discussion predominantly focused on the perceived inadequacies in plant variety rights protection and the need to rethink patent law in general to encompass commercially valuable plant-related products and processes. The main criticisms of the practice of the EPO were directed to its practice of granting rights over inventions involving genetic material (and these criticisms encompassed, but were not confined to, plant material), the height (or lack thereof) of the threshold for protection, the scope of protection and its difficulties in interpreting and applying the notion of a plant variety. As we will see in chapter 9, many of these problems continue to resonate in the modern plant protection environment.

Notwithstanding these concerns, the EPO continues to grant patents for plant genes, gene sequences, plants, methods of producing plants (providing these are not wholly essentially biological in form), groupings of plants (provided the claim is not directed to a variety as such—although the claim may encompass a number of varieties), material harvested from the plants and products produced using the harvested material. The only excluded materials are unutilised discoveries, plant varieties (which accord to the UPOV definition) and essentially biological processes for the production of plants (plants produced by an essentially biological process are patentable). It can be seen, therefore, that the patent system can be used to protect a vast range of plant-related inventions, the only restrictions on protection being capacity to meet the threshold for protection and a failure to fall into one of the categories of excluded material.

---

[111] It would be impossible to detail all the discussion, but a glance at any of the leading science journals (*Nature, Science, New Scientist*) or intellectual property law journals eg (*EIPR, IIC*), not to mention the documentation emanating from organisations such as the OECD, the WIPO and UPOV of that time, will indicate the extent and scope of the interest. Many of these have been, or will be, referred to throughout this text.

As is well rehearsed within intellectual property literature, patents are commonly accepted as a vital part of the commercial environment. The right both acts as an incentive to undertake research and ensures the dissemination of the results of that research work. Certainly for those engaged in plant research of a kind which can attract patent protection, it is likely that the increased availability of this form of protection will prove to be of value, especially for those companies which place great store by the acquisition of strong private property rights. However, the fact that the system has operated to the benefit of some sectors (most notably the pharmaceutical industry) does not mean that it is necessarily as suitable for all sectors.

It is clear that the system provides a valuable right for those with the confidence to use it, that confidence coming from knowing the right is secure and there is financial provision to protect it through the courts. However, not all users or potential users have this surety. This lack of certainty is even more acute where the industry concerned is a) operating within a cutting-edge technology (as many plant bioscientists who would be seeking to use the patent system will invariably be—the changes to patent practice in light of biotechnological developments will ensure that low-tech grants will be more difficult to obtain) and b) many of the primary proponents are small to medium-sized enterprises which traditionally have not made use of the patent system for reasons usually thought to be based on the cost and time involved in both acquisition and protecting post-grant.[112] As will be seen, when the right is assessed against the backdrop of the views of the plant breeding industry, this does not necessarily mean that there needs to be a wholesale review of the patent system, but what we do believe is necessary is a recognition that one system does not necessarily fit all and also that the needs of a specifically affected industry might need to take precedence over a perceived inviolability of the system itself.

In terms of the European Patent Organisation (as denoted by membership of the European Patent Convention) then it is likely that the role of the European Patent Office will grow in importance. Not only will it serve as the arbiter for grants under the EPC, but proposals emanating from the European Commission designed to further harmonise European patent practice indicate that if a new European Union patent[113] is introduced then the EPO should oversee the granting of European patents. As the proposals do not purport to affect what is patentable nor the limitations to the right granted, it is not proposed to discuss them any further in this book. It is worth noting, however, that unless there is a radical revolution in the thinking of the EPO with regard to the interpretation and application of the substantive patent law principles it will necessarily build on its existing jurisprudence. The result will be that more patents will be granted

---

[112] For a discussion of this, with a particular emphasis on bioscience needs, see Llewelyn, *Utility Model/Second Tier Protection: A Report on the Proposals From the European Commission* (Common Law Institute of Intellectual Property, 1996).

[113] That is, a patent which is enforceable in every EU member state but which requires only one application to be made.

and that the categories of excluded material could increasingly become redundant in the face of a positivist approach to the presumptions of protectability and patentability.

In preparing itself for this role, the EPC has been the subject of a revision, which began in 2000 with the holding of a Diplomatic Conference in Munich. One objective was to bring the Convention into line with TRIPs and also with the Patent Law Treaty signed in Geneva on 2 June 2000.[114] More importantly, for the purposes of enlarging the role of the EPO, another aim of the Conference was to move some substantive issues from the main text of the Convention to the implementing Regulations, which will allow the Administrative Council to make further amendments without recourse to another Diplomatic Council. These revisions, aside from the one relating to an amendment to the Protocol to Article 69 (referred to earlier), need not concern us further here.

A key feature of the developments at the EPO has been the seeking of a balance between three, possibly competing, factors. The first is demonstrating that policy and practice is receptive to the experiences of other patents systems (especially those which it would regard as being its competitors, such as the US and Japan[115]), the second is that it needs to match the expectations of those who use a multiplicity of different patent systems and finally it has to take account of the specific interests of European inventors and the European research community. In particular, the EPO needs to be sensitive to the fact that the European research base may differ from those within other jurisdictions and this sensitivity has to underpin any decisions (regarding policy or practice) which it takes. This is not always an easy balance to achieve particularly when, as will be discussed in the next chapter, the other key protagonist in European patent policy, the European Union, takes a more trade-orientated (and arguably American) approach to the provision of rights.

As will be seen, the EU emphasis, which is often based on the quantity of protection rather than quality, may shift the focus from ensuring that clear lines of protectability exist (which balance the equal interests of both the inventor and third parties) to a focus on protecting commercial potential. These various political, economic and legal tensions which are circulating within Europe broadly defined, and are based on international as well as local developments, need to be taken into account when assessing the policy and practice of the EPO.

---

[114] This primarily relates to procedural matters or formalities, such as what the Treaty calls 'the recordation of information within the application for filing/priority date purposes'. The Treaty entered into force on 28 April 2005.

[115] In the 1990s the three largest granting offices, the EPO, Japanese Patent Office (JPO) and the USPTO agreed to conduct a comparative trilateral study to look into certain aspect of patent granting practice which could give rise to anomalies between the three and adversely affect the patenting activities of bioscience inventors. Trilateral Project B3b sought to produce a Comparative study on Biotechnology patent practices. The project had a number of themes relating to reach-through claims, patentability of DNA fragments, and the protection of nucleic acid molecule-related inventions whose functions are inferred based on homological study. In addition Project WM3 looked at protein 3-dimensional (3-D) structure claims.

Of most significance is the fact that whilst the emergence of the new TRIPs-order did not create these tensions (they have been in evidence since the proposal was first made to introduce a European patent system), what it has done is to underscore them and, for the first time, formally to render European provision subject to transatlantic influences.

# 7

# The European Directive on the Legal Protection of Biotechnological Inventions[1]

## I. INTRODUCTION

A S NOTED IN the previous two chapters the EPO is an autonomous entity and is not required to implement decisions taken elsewhere. This does not mean, however, that it operates within a vacuum. Specifically, the Office is sensitive to external decisions made by, or which affect, its member states and, in particular, it is alert to developments within the European Union. The relationship between the two has not, however, been either an easy one or one which is straightforward to describe. Until the 1980s, the nature of the relationship seemed primarily academic, with an acknowledgement of the existence of the other made by each but no real attempts made to work together or influence initiatives. This is probably unsurprising given that most members of the European Community were still coming to terms with the impact of membership of the EPC (the transitional provisions meaning that members could stagger implementation with a resulting variation in compliance existing between member states). Given the problems which had been encountered in trying (in the 1970s) to introduce a Community Patent Convention,[2] the European Commission, perhaps wisely, left patent matters predominantly to the local legislators. The emergence of biotechnology, and the realisation of its economic potential, changed all that.

The European Commission, keen to promote the new science actively, sought to provide an appropriate platform not only upon which could European bio-industry flourish but which would also attract companies from abroad to Europe in order to undertake research and development. The provision of strong intellectual property protection was central to achieving this. The

---

[1] *Official Journal of the European Communities*, L 213/13, 30 July 1998.

[2] The intention lying behind this Convention was to provide a single Community patent which would be enforceable in all Community member states. The Convention was never fully implemented (for political reasons) but it nonetheless had had an influence on European patent practices, not least in the use of its research exemption (discussed in the previous chapter).

Commission quickly recognised that there were two problems with relying on the EPO to shape this provision. The first was that the EPO appeared to be slow (and possibly inconsistent) in the evolution of its own practices on the matter of plant patent protection. The second was that, notwithstanding the merits of that practice, the EPO could neither control nor direct national patent practices, and there was great variation in these practices.[3] Without going into detail as to the nature and extent of the national differences, this variation has ranged from uncertainty as to whether inventions involving biological material could meet the granting criteria,[4] inconsistency in provision of patent protection for a new genus of plants where the genus claimed is not a variety,[5] problems over applying the exclusion of varieties, problems over patenting plant cells (as micro-organisms), as well as uncertainty as to the patentable status of individual whole plants (for example if one plant is the first representative of a new variety[6]).

The lack of parity of provision caused great concern to the European Commission. It could see that national protection not only fluctuated across the EU but also that this fluctuation could potentially conflict with a) the practice of the EPO and b) the policy direction being taken by organisations such as the WIPO. Early in the 1980s, and almost before the EPO had had time to define and defend its jurisprudence, the European Commission decided to seize the policy initiative and take legislative action which would compel member states to provide uniform protection. The result of this activity was the Directive.

The first formal activity took place in 1983, when the European Commission submitted to the European Council of Ministers a communication entitled 'Biotechnology in the Community'.[7] This emphasised the increasing importance of biotechnology and the lack, within Europe, of a suitable environment for bio-science research. This lack of a suitable environment, the communication claimed, was directly responsible for a reduction in the ability of the European Community to keep pace in bioscience research with the rest of the world, most notably with US and Japan. Having made it clear that it was not prepared to support this position, the Commission instigated an investigation into the provision of a suitable environment within which to foster European biotech-nological research, an investigation which would be incomplete 'if . . . not accompanied by appropriate intellectual property legislation which offers to

---

[3] For a discussion of the EEC case law in the period leading up to the Commission's decision to act see Vossius, 'Patent Protection for Biological Inventions: Review of Recent Case Law in EEC Countries' (1979) 10 *EIPR* 278.

[4] See, the following discussion which took place in the UK Select Committee on the European Communities, *Patent Protection for Biotechnological Inventions* (House of Lords, March 1994, Session 1993–94, 4th Report, HL Paper) 28.

[5] For example: in Germany a patent was granted in 1986 over a 'Tomoffel' (which was half tomato, half potato) Patent No 2.842.179.6.

[6] This was a question debated by the Dutch National Council for Agricultural Research in 1985 and was one to which they could not find an agreed solution: Study 14dE, National Council for Agricultural Research, *Plant Breeders' Rights and Patent Rights in Relation to Plant Genetic Engineering* (The Hague, 1985).

[7] COM (88) 496.

Community science and industry legal protection indispensable for their protection' on the grounds that 'the absence of a harmonised system of laws [would] be particularly harmful and dangerous to an entity like the European Community.' In 1984 the Commission held a round of meetings with industry and various government officials to sound out whether there was support for any activity. According to Keegan, 'industry entirely supported such an initiative' whereas 'the reaction of the Member States was universally unenthusiastic.'[8] The result was agreement that the Commission should develop a European Community-centric approach to the protection of biotechnological inventions. In scientific terms, whilst it was acknowledged that this work might have to be expanded to take account of scientific developments involving animals and (at the then extremes of research possibilities) human genetic material, the initial main focal point was the protection of plants (including an evaluation of both patents and plant variety rights) and micro-organisms.

At this early stage no decision had been taken as to the form the protection should take and it was decided that, given the existing national legislation (based upon the EPC and UPOV), the task of assessing the type of protection needed should be divided between two directorates-general, DG 3 (Agriculture) and DG 6 (Innovation/Single Market). In June 1985, the Commission made public its intention to formulate measures concerning the protection of biotechnological inventions[9]—this being achieved by the introduction of a Community system of plant variety rights (to be overseen by DG 3, as discussed in chapter 3) and the harmonisation of national patent practices through the introduction of an EU Directive (to be overseen by DG 6).[10]

The first draft of the Directive was published in November 1988, and a revised version followed in September 1989. In 1995 the European Parliament voted to reject the Directive (primarily because it did not take sufficient account of non-technical matters such as morality). In December 1995 a revised version was published and following extensive consultation (including the use of the conciliation process within the European Commission as well as widespread public debate) a second vote was taken by the European Parliament in 1998. This time the Directive was adopted (although the vote was not unanimous).

As will be seen, the original proposals mirrored, to a considerable extent, those which were being suggested elsewhere. In particular, they echoed proposals coming from the OECD and the WIPO. Before looking at the proposals, it is therefore worth looking at outcomes of those other discussions and also again at the relationship between the EU legislation and the existing treaties and conventions (and in particular the EPC).

[8] 'A View from the Commission of the prospects for Change and Harmonisation in Biotechnology', Paper presented by Sandra Keegan (originally charged with drafting the Directive) at the European Patent Office, 1987.

[9] COM (85) 310.

[10] The reasons why the Commission did not, at that time, propose to introduce a Community-wide patent system were a) because the EPC was already in operation and b) because of the problems which had been encountered in attempting to introduce a Community Patent Convention in the 1970s.

## II. THE ROAD TO ADOPTION

**International Influences**

a) Relationship with the OECD and the WIPO

From the outset, the Commission admitted that it was taking its lead from the ongoing work of the OECD[11] and the WIPO.[12] In 1983 the OECD[13] published a report on biotechnology which set out the potential both scientifically and economically of the new bioscience.[14] This report was followed by a second in 1985 which looked specifically at intellectual property rights and biotechnological inventions.[15] Both reports clearly linked the need for strong and effective intellectual property protection with realising the (agricultural and pharmaceutical) potential of biotechnology.

At the same time (and as indicated previously), the WIPO also decided to look into this matter and it set up a Committee of Experts on Biotechnological Inventions and Industrial Property to assess whether there was need for any action. In 1985 the Committee submitted to the WIPO Office an *Analysis of Certain Basic Issues in Industrial Property Protection of Biotechnological Inventions*.[16] Following publication of the report, the Committee of Experts prepared two sets of questionnaires which were sent to all member states to be issued to all interested parties. The responses to these questionnaires formed the basis of 19 'Suggested Solutions' which were considered by the WIPO.[17] One of the functions of these questionnaires was to assess the extent to which there were national differences in provision. The results indicated that there were differences especially in respect of the application of the discovery/invention distinction, definition of micro-organisms and microbiological processes and the application of the exclusion of plant varieties.

It is not proposed to discuss either the OECD reports or the WIPO suggestions in great detail—instead, an outline will be given of their recommendations/solutions.

Both suggested that plants should not be excluded from patentability (and indeed that varieties should not necessarily be regarded as excluded either—but the inclusion of this goes to the fact that the reports were intended for an

---

[11] The OECD takes an active role in the protection of biotechnological inventions and in the provision of patent protection in particular. Its website contains an array of documentation ranging from statistical evaluations of the number and value of patents granted through to consultation documents on the protection of biotechnological inventions. See www.oecd.org.

[12] Keegan, above n 8.

[13] For information about the OECD, go to www.oecd.org.

[14] Bull, Holt and Lilly, *Biotechnology: International Trends and Perspectives* (OECD, 1983).

[15] Beier, Crespi and Straus, *Biotechnology and Patent Protection: An International Review* (OECD, 1985).

[16] WIPO Doc BIOT/CE/2.

[17] WIPO Doc BIOT/CE/II1/2.

international audience including the US which, of course, does not exclude plant varieties from patent protection), that plant products containing patented material should be covered by the patent and that where a patent has been granted over a plant then the right to exploit any variety developed containing the patented material should only be permitted under licence from the patent holder. As will be seen, these general principles can also be found in the subsequent EU legislation. In respect of the two studies, each was agreed that patent protection should be more widely available for biotechnological[18] inventions and that any restrictions to that protection should be minimal.

That the work of the OECD and the WIPO should reach the same conclusions is not surprising. Whilst work in this area was extensive, there were comparatively few experts on whose knowledge the various committees could draw. It is not coincidental, therefore, that the same people should be involved in many of the same discussions (the same, after all, was true of the discussions in the 1950s which preceded the Strasbourg Convention and UPOV). In terms of European practice, of particular significance was the involvement of the leading authority on patent law and biotechnology, Professor Joseph Straus of the Max-Planck Institute, Munich, for he was also consulted by DG 6 in respect of the form and content of the EU Directive.[19] As a result, there was a marked similarity between the conclusions of the 1995 OECD report, the 'Suggested Solutions' offered by the WIPO[20] and the text of the first draft of the Directive. This was acknowledged by the Economic and Social Committee of the European Council[21] who agreed that 'most of the solutions adopted are those suggested by the World Intellectual Property Organisation.' Equally, the draftsmen of the Directive noted the similarity between the draft and the WIPO 'Suggested Solutions', saying that: '. . . the "Suggested Solutions" of the International Bureau of the WIPO form the basis of or are even in part incorporated in the solutions of the proposed Directive.'[22]

The purpose of the OECD report was primarily to indicate those areas where further legislative work was necessary in order to maximise the use of the patent system; the report could not, itself, compel such action. The WIPO, as the chief policy maker in respect of IP, however, could. The dilemma facing the European Commission was whether it could afford to wait until such time as the WIPO had considered all relevant matters and decided upon on a desired solution, or

---

[18] The term 'biotechnological' implies that only those inventions which involve extensive manipulation by man were to be regarded as potentially patentable. As indicated in the previous chapter, inventions involving only minimal intervention are patentable—the use of the term 'biotechnological' merely serves to underline the fact that naturally occurring material is not patentable.

[19] In terms of his work for the OECD see Beier, Crespi and Straus, *Biotechnology and Patent Protection: An International Review* (OECD, 1985). One of his co-authors also has a close connection with the EU Directive. Crespi, a long-time advocate of strong patent rights for bio-inventions, was also consulted as to form and content.

[20] Above n 17.

[21] 'Opinion on the Proposal for a Council Directive on the Legal Protection of Biotechnological Inventions', OJ No C 159 (October 1989).

[22] Above n 9, Explanatory Memorandum.

if it should take matters into its own hands and direct the form of that activity at the European Community level. It decided on the latter, not least because

> . . . the efforts of WIPO in this area will most likely end in no more than a recommen-
> dation addressed to the Member States of WIPO by its Director General. In view of the
> complexity of the issues and the interests involved, it is only realistic to note that such
> a recommendation could result in changes in national legislation, at best, in several
> years. Notwithstanding the well founded and balanced Suggested Solutions, the WIPO
> initiative is unlikely to bring about a prompt, positive and harmonised response at the
> world or even the European level.[23]

As will be seen below, the implicit assumption in this statement that the European Commission would be able to facilitate a 'prompt, positive and harmonised response' proved to be wide of the mark.

b) Relationship with International Treaties/Conventions

With regard to the relationship between the Directive and other existing, internationally agreed, Conventions on intellectual property provision, the Explanatory Memorandum to the original 1988 draft of the Directive stated that it was 'intended to co-exist, and not interfere with the existing international legal network in which the EPC, the UPOV Convention and the Budapest Treaty [on the Deposit of Micro-organisms] are the cornerstones.' This state-ment does not appear in the final version of the Directive but, as will be dis-cussed below, this should not be taken to mean that there was no longer an intention to 'co-exist and not interfere with' the existing legislative framework. Some might wonder why there was no reference to the TRIPs Agreement, but the reason is simple. It would be a further six years before the TRIPs Agreement came into being, and the relationship between the two will be discussed below. Whilst the Commission would have been mindful of the discussions pertaining to the GATT review (and indeed it is a member of the WTO in its own right), it is probable that its view was that until there was confirmed international agree-ment as to the form and content of any new piece of legislation, there was no requirement to comply. This is an important issue for, as raised in chapter 2, the TRIPs Agreement requires member states to ensure that there is no discrimina-tion relating to the field of technology, as to the availability and enjoyment of patent rights granted. The Directive (as will be seen) does not appear to discriminate, in that its function is to clarify the patentable status of biotechno-logical inventions and set out the perimeters of that protection (which concur with those available for other types of inventions). However, the way in which member states implement the Directive could be regarded as discriminatory if

---

[23] Above n 8. Keegan also said in 1987 that the work of the WIPO was likely to take a number of years 'which the Commission does not have to spend if the existing gaps . . . between the Community and the US and Japan are to be closed or, at least, narrowed.'

higher standards are required or the protection provided less than that available for or enjoyed by inventors working in other fields of technology. Examples of this could be the UK's use of the specific, substantial and credible criteria for assessing the industrial applicability requirement, and Germany's restriction to one function claims in respect of inventions involving human genetic material. The permissibility of these will depend on how the courts (and the WTO) decide to judge the relationship between the obligation not to discriminate and the Doha statement by the WTO that the Agreement should be applied in ways commensurate with local needs (and practices), with members permitted to rely on the General Principles.

As might be inferred from the previous chapter, co-existence was particularly necessary in respect of the EPC. All EU national patent laws are based on the EPC and the practices of both local granting offices and courts are influenced both by the substantive provisions (for example, in interpreting claims) as well as, albeit on a persuasive basis, by the practice of the EPO in applying those provisions. As the EPC directs the form of national substantive law, there was little that the draftsmen of the Directive could do in terms of revising that substance—to do otherwise could have placed the EU (and national patent laws of its member states) in direct conflict with the EPC. Instead, the European Commission had to find some way of co-habiting with the EPC whilst at the same time to try (through indirect means, as the EU had no authority over the EPO) and eliminate any of the uncertainties which the practices of the EPO had generated. In order to achieve this, the Commission had to use politically subtle language. The original Explanatory Memorandum makes it clear that the Directive was never intended to do other than correspond in large measure to the language and patent granting practices of the European Patent Organisation—however, it did state that there was an intention that the 'indirect effects . . . should be substantial',[24] although it did not indicate what those effects might be.

### The Objective behind the Directive

The main objective lying behind the Directive was the desire to minimise those aspects of patent law which could obstruct the protection of bioscience inventions and to counter 'any existing gap between Europe and the US and Japan,' with the objective of encouraging 'industrial exploitation'[25] of bioscience research results. At this stage it was envisaged that the 'actual number of problems which need to be resolved will be small' and the focus would be on harmonising granting practices, clarifying the exclusions (especially the exclusion of plant varieties), addressing the scope of protection and looking at deposit and the burden of proof.[26]

[24] Above n 9, Explanatory Memorandum, 24.
[25] *Ibid.*
[26] *Ibid.*

In particular, the Commission was keen to dispel any notion that inventions involving biological material could not attract patent protection. From the outset, therefore, the Directive was predicated on an overarching presumption that 'a subject matter of an invention shall not be considered unpatentable for the reason only that it is comprised of living material' (Article 2 of the 1988 text). Its second function was to address some of the specific problems relating to the patentability of biological material, such as the threshold for protection, and to this end the first draft focused primarily on the provision of technical language which would facilitate the granting of patents. To a considerable extent this was the downfall of the original drafts. The focus on the technical means meant that those aspects of patent law which provided the demarcation between patentable and non-patentable inventions were overlooked. Whilst the Commission might have hoped that its proactive attempts would be widely applauded, this emphasis on the technical aspects of the law meant that the first draft did not receive the reception anticipated. One reason for this was the failure to address the difficult question of the morality provision. The explanation given for this omission was that 'the ethical question was largely deemed unnecessary due to the existence of Article 53(a) EPC.'[27] The context within which this statement was made needs to be understood.

At the time that the Directive was first proposed (the early 1980s), the issue of morality was not seen as particularly relevant a) because most of the published research work related to plants and micro-organisms (and this research was not thought to raise ethical questions) and b) because the morality provision was, for many, a forgotten (and possibly irrelevant) aspect of patent law. However, science rapidly moved apace and scientists became increasingly able to apply their knowledge to higher life forms (as for example in *Onco-mouse*). As inventions involving higher life forms were developed and public attention[28] was drawn to the question of whether it was appropriate to 'own life',[29] it became clear that non-technical matters needed to be addressed within the Directive. This backdrop to the Directive is crucial to understanding not only the pressures placed on those drafting the Directive to take account of the rapid developments in science (and the economic implications of these), but also the need for the draftsmen to be alert to the changing social and political attitudes towards those scientific developments.

The various texts of the Directive will not be discussed in any detail. What is relevant in understanding the implications of the 1998 text is the way in which the 1988 text dealt with the issue of the patentability of plant material (including plant varieties). The reasons for drawing attention to this early draft are

---

[27] Kamstra *et al*, *Patents on Biotechnological Inventions: The EC Directive* (Sweet & Maxwell, 2002) 3.

[28] Ultimately the decision lay with Members of the European Parliament, who were subject to extensive lobbying by those concerned about patent practices (both for and against).

[29] This misleading term, together with 'Frankenstein foods', were probably the two most used terms in the media when referring to the use of patent laws to protect bio-inventions.

firstly, because it provides an indication of attitudes towards plant variety protection within policy making circles in the 1980s, and secondly, because it shows that, notwithstanding any apparent support for the plant variety rights system, the agenda was clearly to make patent law the dominant system of protection. It might seem that in highlighting these views we are drawing undue attention to the more negative aspects of the pro-patenting lobby. This would be the wrong impression to draw, for the debate was predominantly positive in seeking to achieve maximum benefit by clarifying provision—however, the oft-undisclosed aspect of these debates is the attitude towards plant variety provision, and it is this which we feel aids an understanding of the political and legal climate at the time that the Regulation and Directive were being considered.

## The Early Drafts and Plant Varieties

### The 1988 Text

As already mentioned, the Explanatory Memorandum to the 1988 text stated that the Directive was 'intended to co-exist, and not interfere with the existing international legal network in which the EPC, the UPOV Convention and the Budapest Treaty [on the Deposit of Micro-organisms] are the cornerstones.' However, this did not mean that those drafting the Memorandum thought that this existing provision was necessarily appropriate to the needs of the modern plant biotechnologist. Indeed, initially at least, it seems that the Commission was encouraged to use the Directive as an opportunity to re-enter the 'paradise of patent protection' from which plant innovations had been 'banished' as a result of the introduction of the UPOV and Strasbourg Conventions.[30] As there was a general consensus (at the policy and practice levels of the WIPO, OECD and EPO at least) that plant material, other than varieties, was patentable, the perceived barrier to this provision was seen to be the UPOV system, and the draftsmen directed their attention to this. Their objective was clear and that was to downplay any significance which the UPOV system might have had in realising the benefits of plant science and to try and bring plant varieties within the scope of patent protection. In assessing the impact of these proposals it is important to bear in mind the audience to whom the Directive was directed. This would have predominantly been comprised of intellectual property lawyers (the majority of whom would, at that time, have had little experience of the agricultural system of protection enshrined in UPOV) and politicians (who would have had little knowledge of either system, but who would have been likely to at least know of the existence of patent law). Of particular relevance were Articles 3, 12, 13 and 14.

---

[30] Beier and Straus, 'Genetic Engineering and Industrial Property' (1987) 11 *Industrial Property* 447.

The original draft of the Directive made it clear that there were to be minimal exceptions to the general principle that inventions involving living material were patentable. Little attention was therefore given to specific categories of patentable material (such as plant cells or species) and instead focus was directed to addressing the question of what the exclusions actually excluded. Particular attention was paid to the exclusion of plant varieties.

The 1988 Explanatory Memorandum stated that 'the UPOV-type protection [which, at that time took the form of 1978 Act] . . . does not offer appropriate incentives' and as such was 'an insufficient incentive to investments in truly new developments.' Implicit in this criticism was that another, more appropriate, form of protection should be used to protect plant innovations and, given the context of the comment, this appeared to be via patent law. What is not clear from this statement is just how the views expressed in the Explanatory Memorandum could be realised in a way which 'co-existed', and did 'not interfere', with UPOV.

The apparent dismissal of the UPOV system, and protection of plant varieties by a *sui generis* right, was evident elsewhere in the Explanatory Memorandum. The text was peppered with deprecating phrases such as '*certain* positive effects, *in part* experienced with plant breeders' rights . . . *in those areas* of plant agriculture in which *such rights* are *effectively* available . . .'[31] (emphasis added). The most sweeping criticism of the plant variety rights system took the form of a claim that:

> traditional breeding methods, *supported by plant breeders rights*, were not able to prevent the present situation in Community agriculture in which the EEC is unable either to consume or to sell all that it produces. Biotechnological methods for developing new plant products offer genuine promise for producing commercially desirable and therefore saleable agricultural material. (emphasis added)[32]

The clear implication is that the biotechnology industry, and by inference the patent system which would be used to support it, would reduce the unnecessary waste. Then (as now) it is difficult to equate the potential, and indeed for some people the sole purpose, of biotechnology to increase crop and animal production with the ability to regulate the amount that Europe produces and wastes. Clearly in the minds of those drafting the Directive, however, an ability to make these 'commercially desirable and therefore saleable' products went hand in hand with the ability to ensure that production did not outweigh demand.[33] It is difficult to find support for this view. Whilst obviously there was great potential for the results of the new molecular forms of plant breeding to produce highly valuable crops, this did not necessarily mean that such crops would be

---

[31] Para 47.
[32] Para 48.
[33] See Llewelyn, 'Future Prospects for Plant Breeders' Rights within the European Community' (1989) 9 *EIPR* 303.

automatically commercially viable.[34] The Commission did not confine its comments to breeding methods or to the efficacy of the plant variety rights system. They went further and formally proposed that the exclusion of plant varieties within patent law should not be all-encompassing, and in so doing there was an explicit intention to gradually make the exclusion meaningless. The Memorandum stated that a '*destructively applied exclusion*[35] of patentability of plant varieties as such will not harm developments in modern biotechnology and *could be tolerated*' (emphasis added).[36] The way in which the Commission proposed that the exclusion would gradually destruct would be by permitting plant varieties which had been produced by a microbiological process to be patented.[37]

Before looking at the way in which the Commission proposed to achieve this gradual destruction it is interesting to draw a parallel with the comments made by Cornish in 1989 (one year after the first draft of the Directive was published). As previously mentioned, he said that '[e]nough can be seen to suggest . . . that the existing regime for plant variety protection (under an international convention which precludes patent protection from its territory[38]) is rapidly becoming an outmoded impediment to a logical framework of protection.' He argued that the right, which had been introduced to serve a specific purpose in the 1960s, by the 1980s (and together with the Article 53(b) exclusion) imposed 'unwarranted barriers against some of those who invest in biotechnical and agricultural research and wish to have patents for their successful results.'[39] In language similar to that used in the Directive he said that it could be predicted 'that the EPC provision will be progressively pared down by interpretation, on the ground that it imposes unwarranted barriers against some of those who invest in the biotechnical and agricultural research and wish to have patents for their successful results.' If the UPOV system was to continue to exist, he warned, then

[34] Indeed, purported capacity to reduce waste notwithstanding, the draftsmen clearly did not appreciate the extent to which there would be public resistance within Europe to the use of genetically modified crops.
[35] In the sense of an exclusion which eventually destructs (or becomes redundant) through use.
[36] Above n 9, para 47.
[37] Given the previous statement that traditionally bred varieties protected by plant variety rights were not capable of averting wastage, it could be that part of the thinking behind this statement was that microbiological processes would rapidly become the method of choice for production, and therefore an exclusion which only applied to traditionally bred varieties would rapidly sink into disuse. This statement pre-dated the decision by the EPO in *PGS* (which held that the exception to the exclusion could be used to protect plant varieties); however, until 1999 (and the decision in *Novartis*) the EPO had not pronounced on whether this was the correct interpretation of the exclusion. Given the eventual decision in *Novartis* (that the exception could not be used to circumvent an exclusion introduced to apply to all varieties), it would seem that the view of the Commission was premature and, on the basis that the Enlarged Board in *Novartis* relied on the preparatory documentation to the EPC to arrive at their conclusion, indicates an incorrect reading by the Commission of what the exclusion was intended to achieve.
[38] Cornish, *Intellectual Property: Patents Copyright Trade Marks and Allied Rights*, 2nd edn (Sweet & Maxwell, 1989).
[39] *Ibid.*

those engaged in the revision of the Convention 'ought to consider whether the regime has a viable future.'[40]

Cornish was not involved in the drafting of the Directive, but his views would have carried (and continue to carry) great authority—he also moved in the same circles as some of those advising on the Directive. It is possible that his views represented a collective view within the intellectual property intelligentsia that a paring down of the exclusion in Article 53(b) was both necessary and desirable. Certainly his views that the UPOV system was an impediment and that the exclusion of varieties within patent law should, as a result, be progressively pared down to exclude the bare minimum of plant innovations bear a striking similarity to the sentiments being expressed by the OECD and the WIPO, as well as the Commission.

It is hard to reconcile the comments made in the Explanatory Memorandum with the views also expressed that there was no intention to interfere with existing systems of protection. Instead, it is difficult to draw any conclusion other than that there was an underlying agenda to 'interfere' with UPOV, this interference taking the form of a) undermining the protection itself by referring to its unsuitability as an incentive to invest in plant bioscience, b) drawing an explicit causal link between the right and the creation of the various mountains of food products which producers were unable to sell and c) indicating an intention to pare down the exclusion of plant varieties. This latter was achieved by a careful drafting of Articles 3, 12, 13 and 14. As will be seen, this intention to move away from plant variety protection did not meet with the approval of the various Committees the Commission charged with reviewing the proposals made, and in particular, the Economic and Social Committee (ESC).[41]

## Article 3

Article 3 of the original text appeared merely to repeat the language of Article 53(b) EPC, as well as the emerging practice of the EPO.

Paragraph 1 said that:

> micro-organisms, biological classifications other than plant or animal varieties as well as parts of plants and animal varieties other than propagating material thereof of the kind protectable under plant variety protection law shall be considered patentable subject matter. Claims for classifications higher than varieties shall not be affected by any rights granted [presumably referring to rights other than patent rights] in respect of plant and animal varieties.

Paragraph 2 stated that 'notwithstanding the provisions of paragraph 1, plants and plant material shall be considered patentable subject matter unless such

---

[40] Above n 38.
[41] 'Opinion on the Proposal for a Council Directive on the Legal Protection of Biotechnological Inventions', OJ C 159 (October 1989).

material is produced by the non-patentable use of a previously known biotech-nological process.'

The significance of the two paragraphs lay in their relationship with each other.

Article 3(1) appeared to say that the exclusion should apply only to plant varieties and plant propagating material which could be protected by plant vari-ety rights. All other aspects of plants from genes to species would be patentable. As all other plant material would have been patentable the question had to be asked what was the purpose of paragraph 2?

On the face of it, paragraph 2 seemed to provide a qualification to the general principle that plant material could be patented by saying that where that mate-rial had been produced by a known, unpatented, biotechnological process, then patent protection would not be available, irrespective of whether the material itself was capable of meeting the threshold for protection. It is unclear why this qualification to the general principle was included. One possible explanation is that it was in recognition of the fact that where plant material had been produced by a known (or traditional) method then it was more likely that the outcome of using that process would itself be known or foreseeable. It might also have been included in an attempt to assuage concerns that there would be an over-monopolisation of plant material by requiring that the process used to produce the plant material must itself be sufficiently technically advanced to be capable of attracting patent protection (although not necessarily patented).

In respect of the material to be excluded, Article 3(1) simply said that '. . . bio-logical classifications other than plant varieties . . . shall be considered patentable . . .' It did not state that plant varieties were unpatentable. It might be thought tenuous to argue that the absence of a specific statement that plant varieties were excluded meant that they were patentable, given that the corol-lary of saying that biological classifications *other* than plant varieties are patentable is to exclude plant varieties from protection. However, the fact that there was no specific statement that plant varieties were excluded becomes sig-nificant when taken in the context of paragraph 2 and, in particular, the Explanatory Memorandum.

The Explanatory Memorandum stated that plant varieties may 'in certain circumstances' be excluded from patentability, the language used making it clear that the presumption was that unless those 'certain circumstances' arose, varieties *were* patentable. In addition, the statement said that a '*destructively applied exclusion*[42] of patentability of plant varieties as such will not harm developments in modern biotechnology and *could be tolerated*' (emphasis added).[43] This indicated that the exclusion was not intended either a) to apply to all varieties or b) to apply in perpetuity. The narrow application to be given to the exclusion of plant varieties was in further evidence in the Recital to Article 3(2). This said that:

[42] In the sense of an exclusion which eventually destructs (or becomes redundant) through use.
[43] Above n 9, para 47.

the Commission considers that it would be harmful neither to the interests of European industry engaged in biotechnological research nor to the purposes for which the Directive is designed to allow a *certain number* of cases, likely to have applications as plant varieties, which would otherwise have been patentable, to be excluded from patentable subject matter . . . when such plants have been produced by a known biotechnological process. The principle of Article 3(2) is *necessary* to ensure this result.[44] (emphasis added).

The use of the term 'a certain number' shows that not all plant varieties would automatically be regarded as excluded. Whilst Article 3(1) excluded plant varieties, paragraph 2 ensured that plant varieties produced by unknown plant breeding methods would be patentable. These processes, however, would not appear to have themselves been patented or indeed patentable.

Given the commitment made to the UPOV system (both in terms of national implementation and the explicit exclusion within the EPC not to mention the proposal to introduce a Community plant variety rights regime) this does seem to bring into question whether the Commission really was committed to the intention 'to co-exist, and not interfere with the existing international legal network [including] the EPC [and] UPOV Convention.'

There is a further question which can be raised about the language of Article 3(2) and that is what was intended by the requirement that the process not be known. Was the process to be unknown at the time that the Directive came into force (with only those processes previously out in the public domain being regarded as 'previously known') or was it a continuing concept? If the latter, then this seems to have meant that any process used at any time prior or subsequent to the introduction of the Directive must have been, and remain, unknown. This would have been an unrealistic requirement given both the rapid dissemination of information and the limited methods (even using molecular techniques) which could be used to produce plants. If the process itself had to remain unknown at all times then the limitation to the exclusion would have had minimal effect in practice, and the language of the Explanatory Memorandum appears to indicate that this was not the intention.

The refinement of the Article 53(b) exclusion was also evident in the original Article 12.

Article 12

Article 12 stated that

(1) If the subject matter of a patent is a process for the production of living matter or other matter containing genetic information permitting its multiplication in identical or differentiated form, *the rights conferred by the patent shall not only extend to the product initially obtained by the patented process but also to the identical*

---

[44] *Ibid*, para 36.

*or differentiated products of the first or subsequent generations there from,* said products being deemed also directly obtained by the patented process.

(2) *Any extension* of the protection conferred by the patent to a process as indicated in paragraph 1 to a product obtained thereby *shall not be affected by any exclusion of plant* or animal *varieties from patentability.* (emphasis added)

Article 12 makes it clear that a product (for example in the form of a plant variety) produced by a patented process is covered by the patent on that process and also that this protection would extend to any subsequent product as these will be 'deemed' to have also been directly produced by the patented process. It is unclear if the deeming would have meant that a challenge to any allegation of infringement would have succeeded if it was shown that the product was not produced using the process or whether, irrespective of any actual use of the patented process, anything produced could be said to have been capable of being produced by that process would be taken to have been produced by that process. Whatever the intention, the second paragraph makes it clear that plant varieties would have been captured by the patent on the process.

With regard to the exclusion of 'essentially biological processes', Articles 5, 6 and 7 indicated that the extent of intervention necessary in order to render the process patentable was minimal and what was necessary in order for the process to be patented was evidence that the 'human intervention consist in more than selecting an available biological material and letting it perform an inherent biological function under natural conditions.' Whilst this language was also revised in the 1990s, the premise has found its way into patent law, with breeding processes which might have been thought essentially biological in nature being patented.[45]

Article 12 demonstrates that the Directive was intended to permit patent protection for two types of plant varieties. Article 3(2) would have enabled plant varieties produced by an unknown biotechnological process to be patented and Article 12 would have allowed successive generations of plant varieties produced by a patented process to be protected by the patent over that process.

Whatever the views might have been about the availability of patent protection for plant material, the fact is that the UPOV system of protection was available for *all* types of plant variety irrespective of the manner of production. The decision to permit patent protection for plant varieties produced by unknown processes (which presumably was intended to refer to modern biotechnological processes) could only have been intended to eat into plant variety rights. Even if one supported such a reading of the exclusion, it is difficult to see the proposal as having any effect other than to interfere (albeit indirectly by providing an alternative form of protection for varieties produced by a biotechnological process) with UPOV. Concerns over the two Articles were voiced by the influential Economic and Social Committee (ESC) of the European Commission in 1989.

---

[45] See the Monsanto patent, *Monsanto/Somatic Changes* [2003] EPOR 327.

### The ESC and Articles 3 and 12

In respect of Article 3, the ESC said that the provision was 'too general' and it did not reflect the principle enshrined in Article 2(1) of UPOV (the 'dual protection prohibition'). In addition, the Committee thought that Article 12 was inconsistent with Article 3. They asked for the Directive to state clearly that where a variety was capable of protection under plant variety rights then it would not be patentable, irrespective of the means of production. The Committee also requested that the statement that patents could be obtained for classifications higher than a variety should be removed. The first of these requests was adopted (and indeed found reflection in the decision made by the EPO in *Novartis*); however, as will be seen, the second did not find its way into the final text.

### Article 13

Article 13 stated that 'the protection for a product consisting of or containing particular information as an essential characteristic of the invention shall extend to any products in which said genetic information has been incorporated and is of essential importance for its industrial applicability of utility.' The Explanatory Memorandum makes it clear that this Article was intended to apply to plant varieties '[i]f the particular industrial applicability or usefulness of a variety directly results from an invention which has been patented, then such a variety owes its unique characteristics to the effects of the invention and should therefore come within the scope of protection accorded by the patent.'

This inclusion of the variety within the scope of a patent granted would only have occurred if it could have been shown that the patented invention was of 'essential importance' for the variety's industrial applicability or utility. The Memorandum goes on to make it clear that the draftsmen wished to secure an extension of patent protection in order to ensure that a patent owner could control any varieties incorporating patented material. In their view 'to be excluded from patentability does not mean that a variety should be free from the effects of a patent granted in a case where an invention in the field of plants concerned a generic concept which is characterised by new genetic information and which can be realised in a multitude of different varieties.' To do otherwise would have been viewed as 'insufficient' and as such 'patent rights might be legislatively prescribed for any final product whose utility, commercial value or industrial applicability depends on a patented invention. The rule must be legislatively mandated in light of the variety of views on this issue for which existing patent laws provide no solution.'

The effect of this provision (and the adopted text contains an equivalent, although differently worded provision) is to render *any* uses of a variety containing patented material subject to the authorisation of the patent holder, even where that variety is itself the subject of a plant variety right. The language of

Article 13 makes it clear that the rights of the patent holder would supersede all others. The subordination of plant variety rights to patent law could also be found in Article 14, which contained the licensing provisions.

## Article 14

This was one of the longest Articles in the original text and it needs to be seen in full.

Article 14 read:

(1) If the holder of a plant breeders' right or a variety certificate can exploit or exercise his exclusive rights only by infringement of the rights attached to a prior national patent, a non-exclusive licence of right shall be accorded to the breeders' right holder to the extent necessary for the exploitation of such breeders' right where the variety protected represents a *significant technical progress*, upon payment of reasonable royalties having regard to the nature of the patented invention and consistent with giving the proprietor of such patent due reward for the investment leading to and developing the invention.

(2) A licence under paragraph 1 shall not be available prior to expiration of three years from the date of the grant of the patent or four years from the date on which the application for a patent was filed, whichever period last expires.

(3) If a licence according to paragraph 1 has been granted, and if a variety protected by a plant breeders' right or variety certificate can be exploited by the patentee only by infringement of the rights attached to such variety, a non-exclusive licence shall be accorded to the original patentee to the extent necessary for the exploitation of the breeders' right or variety certificate, upon payment of reasonable royalties having regard to the nature of the improvement and consistent with giving the proprietor of the breeders' right due reward for the investment leading to and developing the new variety. (emphasis added)

The objective of this Article was to establish a dependency provision between patents and plant breeders' rights (and there is an equivalent in the final, adopted, text). The Memorandum makes it clear that Article 14 was necessary in order to give effect to 'the public interest in promoting further developments of agricultural inventions through breeding activities and to recognise the interests of the patentee to enjoy his exclusive rights which provide the incentive for engaging in innovatory activities.'

In the 1988 version there was, however, a clear inequity between the burden placed on the plant breeder seeking to acquire a licence to use a patented invention and that placed on the patent holder seeking to use a variety protected by plant breeders' rights.

A breeder would have been able to apply for a licence only if a) he could show that the variety affected by the patent represented a significant technical progress and b) the designated period of time (either three or four years) had elapsed. The Directive was silent on the matter of what could count as 'significant technical progress' and it is unclear what the breeder would have had to show to demonstrate that his variety met this requirement. It is possible that this could have been shown by reference to market-worthiness. However, the fact that this is, usually, assessed at the same time as the breeders' rights are sought (via the value for cultivation and use test necessary for inclusion on the National List) might have meant that it would not have been acceptable for the purposes of meeting a patent law requirement. One of the main concerns with this provision, in addition to the clear inequity, was that it was perfectly possible to foresee a situation where the breeder had spent years developing a new variety only to find that he could not commercialise it because it contained a patented invention and the variety incorporating that invention would not have been considered to demonstrate a significant technical progress. This would have had the effect of also denying the breeder the right to exploit any breeders' right he had acquired over the variety. As will be seen, this is an issue which still dogs the adopted text.

In contrast, a patent holder would have been able to secure a licence over the variety at any time (there being no time bar to application) and without any need to show that his patented technology represented a significant technical progress.

This provision was the one which attracted the most comment from plant breeding circles. It was widely criticised on the grounds that it could potentially undermine any plant variety right held by serving as a curb on that right. The Economic and Social Committee was also concerned about this and refused to accept the proposal on the grounds that they believed paragraph 3 represented 'a serious legal injustice as between the interests of the breeder and of the patentee.'

On the basis of the above it is difficult to marry the original assertion that the Directive would not 'fetter' the UPOV system of rights with the 1988 proposal. If the objective had been to widen the choice for plant breeders then the draft might have been commendable, but it is clear from the Memorandum that a widening of choice was not the goal. The disparaging remarks made about plant breeders' rights make it obvious that a key objective was to discredit plant breeders' rights and to reduce their applicability by stealthy encroachment. The Explanatory Memorandum states that it was 'indispensable to ensure the undisturbed functioning of the patent system in areas clearly allocated for patent protection.' Without any apparent regard for the activity being undertaken at UPOV or within DG 3, DG 6 had no compunction in allocating to itself the role of defining what that material should be. This was a serious misjudgement and by the time that the final text was agreed both the negative references to the plant variety rights system, as well as the attempt to extend patent protection to certain types of plant varieties, had disappeared. However, the principles underpinning Articles 3 (in terms of permitting plant material other than varieties to be patented), 5, 6, 7, 13 and 14 remained.

When the Commission first mooted the possibility of taking Community action to direct the national patent policies and practices, it probably did not realise the extent to which its proposals would be opposed both by Offices of the Community (and their various committees) as well as by key interest groups—including patient groups environmental lobby groups, religious organisations, consumer groups, and, critically for any hope of a smooth passage, Members of the European Parliament (MEPs). Interestingly, those involved in plant research, and traditional plant breeders in particular, were not amongst the more evident opponents, and commentaries from organisations such as ASSIN-SEL and FIS (in their pre-ISF guises) indicate that there was a degree of support for the Commission's initiatives because some plant researchers would be able to secure stronger protection over a wider range of material than was possible under the 1978 UPOV Act.

The problems facing the Commission became obvious almost from the moment that DG 6 published the first draft in November 1988. Criticisms were first raised by those involved in the Commission's own internal review (this included representatives from national patent offices as well as various interest groups), which resulted in the draft being revised in and republished in 1989. The next stage was to obtain approval from the European Parliament. This it gave, but subject to 44 key amendments. The Commission took three years to respond and in 1992 it published its response, accepting 22 of the 44. The next two years saw the Commission, the Council and the Parliament continue to bat back and forth further amendments and in 1994 the Directive was referred to the Conciliation Committee in the hope that it would be able to find a common solution. In January 1994 the Conciliation Committee approved a joint text[46] and finally the Directive could go to the European Parliament for approval.[47] During this time there was intense lobbying by those opposed to the Directive (both on environmental as well as health grounds) and the main targets of this lobbying were the MEPs.

On 1st March 1995[48] the European Parliament rejected the Directive on the grounds that MEPs were unconvinced that the text provided a proper balance between protecting the interests of society and those of the bio-industry. In particular, MEPs had paid close heed to the views expressed by lobby groups that the Directive was in effect a licence to 'patent life' (and in particular that patents were being granted over the basic building blocks of life which, it was argued, should be regarded as the common heritage of all and property of none) and that because the Directive was focused predominantly on technical matters, it

---

[46] C4–0042/95–94/0159(COD), doc PE–CONS 3606/1/1995, 21 February 1995, OJ No C 68, 20 March 95.

[47] For an example of a parallel debate at the national level see Select Committee on the European Communities, *Patent Protection for Biotechnological Inventions* (House of Lords), above n 4. The Committee was presented with evidence from a wide range of individuals and organisations including patent agents, representatives from bio-industry, medical research and the farming community. There was also evidence from the British Society of Plant Breeders, the involvement of which did not mirror the more general omission of plant breeding interests at the discussions within the Commission.

[48] Coincidentally this was the same day that the EPO published its decision in *PGS*.

had not paid sufficient attention to the ethical dimensions of the new technology.

Some thought this rejection would be an end of the matter and that the Directive was too much of a political 'hot potato' to warrant resurrecting. However, nine months later, in December 1995, the Commission published a new draft.[49] Any number of reasons can be given for the decision to revive it. A great deal of effort and time had been invested in the Directive and to 'give up' in 1995 would have seen all that wasted. Of possibly more significance was the concern that was being expressed in many patent law, and bio-industry, circles over the emerging jurisprudence of the EPO. In 1995, not only had the Technical Board of Appeal revoked the patent granted to PGS (thereby causing confusion as to the scope of the exclusion of 'plant varieties'), but there was also still no decision on the *Onco-mouse* application. The dominant concern was that, in light of both the rejection of the Directive and the developments at the EPO, Europe would not be seen to be the favourable environment for bioscience research that the Commission had hoped it would be.[50] The 1995 draft speaks of patent law being 'even more incomplete and uncertain than in 1988, and it is not realistic to hope that this can always be remedied through an unambiguous and equitable interpretation shared by all the courts in all the Member States.'[51] It was for these reasons that the Commission decided the tackle the matter one last time.

## The 1995 Text

The primary concerns which the 1995 text was intended to address were those relating to ethics.[52] The draftsmen tinkered a little with the previous substantive provisions, but not to any great extent, as the general effect was intended to be the same. The Commission did, however, seek to provide greater clarity as to what could be patented and in so doing made it clear that whilst DNA would not be patentable in its natural state, applications involving genes would be patentable provided that the threshold for protection was met.

In contrast to the previous drafts, the background statement to the 1995 draft made only one, limited, reference to the protection of plant material and this was simply to the fact that the new text included an equivalent farm saved seed provision to that contained within the Community Regulation. There were no

---

[49] COM (95) 661 final.

[50] As evidence of the economic need to provide certainty of provision, the Commission said that in the period between the original draft text and 1995 the estimate of the potential value of biotechnology had risen from US$40 billion to US$83.3 billion, and that its own group of independent advisers (the Molitor group) had, in June 1995, urged that a revised Directive be introduced to 'avoid further increasing the gap between the legislative framework for investment in the EU and its main competitor countries': Brussels, June 1995.

[51] Above n 49, p 5.

[52] *Ibid.*

equivalent references to any perceived problems with the plant variety rights system to those in the 1988 text. The reasons for this were the revision of the UPOV Convention in 1991 and introduction, in 1994, of the Community Regulation on Plant Variety Rights, both of which a) provided stronger protection than had been available at the time the 1988 draft was being prepared and b) had won political approval from nearly all member states of the EU. In respect of compliance, the new draft therefore had to show compliance with the EPC and with the other form of Community protection for plant bio-inventions, the Community Regulation. Adding a further layer of interest was the fact that, by 1995, the TRIPs Agreement was firmly in place and the EU (as discussed in chapter 2) had been at the head of those lobbying to retain the right to exclude plant varieties. In light of these events it would have been odd, to put it mildly, if the Commission was then seen to water down these rights through any initiatives which sought to allow the exclusion to gradually destruct.

In terms of protectable subject matter, the 1995 text excluded plant varieties and essentially biological processes for the production of plants. The term 'plant variety' was not further defined. Article 2 defined an essentially biological process as 'any process which, taken as a whole, exists in nature or is not more than a natural plant breeding or animal breeding process.'

Article 7 stated that any use of plant material, other than a variety, and nonessentially biological processes was patentable. Article 2 also defined a microbiological process as any 'process involving or performed upon or resulting in microbiological material; a process consisting of a succession of steps shall be treated as a microbiological process if at least one essential step of the process is microbiological.' The explanation to Article 2 further stated that 'microbiological material, therefore, means any biological material made up of microorganisms or cellular or subcellular biological material derived from plants, animals or the human body.' In addition, the draft made clear that an invention involving biological material would not be regarded as unpatentable if that material had a natural existence. If the construction of the invention involved a technical advance then it might be patentable (Article 8). Articles 10, 11 and 12 stated that the protection conferred by a patent would extend a) to any biological material derived from the patented biological material (or through use of a patented process) provided that it retains the same characteristics, b) to any material in which the patented material had been incorporated where the incorporation resulted in the genetic information being expressed; however, the patent rights would not extend to c) biological material produced by way of multiplication or propagation of the patented biological material where such multiplication or propagation necessarily resulted from the use for which the material was placed in the market. As will be seen, each of these has an equivalent in the final adopted text.

Article 13 introduced the farm saved seed principle, making it clear that the scope of this was to be confined to that permitted under the Community Regulation. This remained unchanged in the adopted text. More significantly, a revised Article 14 removed the imbalance between a variety rights holder and a patentee in respect of acquiring a compulsory cross-licence and put both parties onto an equivalent footing. Both now had to show that they had unsuccessfully sought a licence from the rights holder and both now had to show that the exploitation of the variety or invention would represent a significant technical progress.

The decision to introduce a new text did not mean that the path to adoption was now smooth and a pattern of amendment followed by approval ensued (for example, Parliament approved the new draft in 1997, but on the basis of 66 amendments—the Commission quickly responded and, also in 1997, published a revised text which incorporated 65 of the 66, stating that there now was a common position). As part of this process, the categories of excluded material, and the definitions sections were revised and the principle that only plant material protectable under plant variety rights was to be excluded from patent protection became part of the substantive text. It is perhaps fair to say that whilst there were these revisions to the provisions relating to plant material, the main focus was on those which applied to human genetic material and the ethical issues relating thereto.

In May 1998 the European Parliament accepted this and voted to adopt the Directive without further amendment. This was not a unanimous decision. The Netherlands voted against[53] and both Belgium and Italy abstained. In June 1998 the Directive was formally adopted and member states had until July 2000 to implement its provisions within their national laws.

The vote by the European Parliament should have been an end to the matter, but almost immediately, the Netherlands (supported by Italy and Norway) lodged a challenge to the validity of the Directive at the ECJ.[54] The basis of the challenge was mainly procedural but it also contained arguments a) that the Directive would provide further confusion as its provisions were not sufficiently clear and b) that it violated the fundamental principle of human dignity. The Dutch were not alone in being concerned. As will be seen, there was, and is, considerable unease at the local level across the EU about the implications (and in particular the ethical consequences) of implementing the Directive. As a result, many countries chose not to implement as required but to await the decision of the ECJ. By the deadline of July 2000 only three countries (Denmark,[55] Finland[56] and Ireland[57]) had fully implemented the Directive, with another (the UK[58]) having implemented most of the Directive but reserving implementation of Article 14 (the compulsory cross-licensing provision).

---

[53] This was because the Dutch had just adopted legislation relating to transgenic animals which would conflict with the obligation under the Directive.

[54] *Netherlands v Parliament and Council* [2001] ECR I-7079, para 27.4. See Scott, 'The Dutch Challenge to the Bio-patenting Directive' [1999] 4 *EIPR* 212.

[55] May 2000.

[56] June 2000.

[57] July 2000.

[58] July 2000.

The fact of the challenge did not, however, release member states from their obligation to implement and to reinforce this, the European Court of Justice, in an interim judgment handed down in July 2000, ruled that member states were nonetheless under a continued obligation to implement the Directive. A year later, in June 2001 Advocate General Jacobs delivered his opinion on the case stating that the action should be dismissed[59] and on 9 October 2001 the ECJ delivered its judgment and it also dismissed the action.[60] Both the Advocate General and the ECJ made it clear that the correct procedure had been used and, of more interest, that there was nothing in the Directive which could either cause confusion in terms of patent practice or violate principles relating to human dignity. The Court, in a very short, uninformative, judgment held that that the Directive dealt appropriately with issues relating to morality.[61] It did concede that it was understandable that there should be concern over the patenting of biotechnological inventions but said that this was matter which was best addressed through monitoring patent practices and it should not stand in the way of introducing the Directive. In neither the Advocate General's opinion nor the judgment of the ECJ was there any reference to the protection of plants or consequences of patenting plant material. That there was resistance to the Directive should not have come as a surprise to the Commission, for even as far back as 1987 it had been expected that there would be a 'negative reaction from the Member States.'[62]

By March 2006, 23 EU member states had implemented the Directive (in addition to the four mentioned above and all new member states, these include Austria (2005), Belgium,[63] France (2004), Germany,[64] Greece,[65] the Netherlands (2004), Portugal,[66] Spain[67] and Sweden (2004). As already mentioned in chapter 5, the EPO also implemented the Directive in September 1999 for the purposes of supplementary interpretation. Of the original 15 countries (which were

[59] http://curia.eu.int/jurisp/cgi-bin/.

[60] http://europa.eu.int/jurisp/cgi-bin/form.pl?lang=en. Details about implementation can be found at http://europa.euint/comm/internal_market/indprop/docs/invent/state-of-play-en-pdf.

[61] The ECJ also addressed the question of consent—which was interesting as it had not been specifically asked to so do. The question here was whether Recital 26 required a patent applicant, applying for a patent over an invention involving human genetic material, to obtain consent from the individual from whom the material was obtained. The view of the ECJ was that it did not—this is not a view which is shared by all: see Beyleveld, 'Why Recital 26 of the EC Directive on the Legal Protection of Biotechnological Inventions should be Implemented in National Law' [2000] 1 *IPQ* 1.

[62] Keegan, above n 8.

[63] Act of 28 April 2005, amending the Patent Act 1984, which came into force on 23 May 2005. There is a question mark over whether the implementation is appropriate, as certain provisions, such as those relating to experimental use and compulsory licensing, seem to go beyond what was either intended within the Directive or via membership of TRIPs. This will be discussed later.

[64] December 2004. Serious questions have been raised as to whether the German implementation meets the requirements of the Directive. The concerns include the restriction of claims to a single identified function and a proposal to introduce an equivalent breeders' exemption to that in plant variety rights.

[65] October 2001.

[66] March 2002.

[67] April 2002.

members of the EU at the time that the Directive was adopted) two remain apparently non-compliant (Luxembourg and Italy should implement the Directive during 2006). To try and facilitate implementation, the European Commission, in July 2003, referred the then eight[68] member states which had not implemented the Directive to the European Court of Justice. As will be discussed later, the main focus for those countries which have yet to implement the Directive is Article 5 which relates to the patentability of human genetic material. Perhaps unsurprisingly, there is great political sensitivity about this issue which has not been evident in respect of the protection of plants. This is unfortunate because it is within the plant breeding sector that the full impact of both the new technologies and the rights granted over them are most likely to be felt.

### III. DIRECTIVE 98/44

The objectives lying behind the Directive are outlined in its Recitals. Primarily these are stated to be to further the development of biotechnology for the benefit of the environment (Recital 10), and health, and in particular to assist in combating major epidemics in developing countries and to alleviate hunger (Recital 11). The need for the Directive is reiterated within Recital 9, where it is stated that 'certain concepts in national laws based upon international patent and plant variety conventions have created uncertainty regarding the protection of biotechnological inventions and certain microbiological inventions; whereas harmonization is necessary to clarify the said uncertainty.' The Recitals do not identify the specific 'certain concepts' within national laws which have created the uncertainty, but it is likely that this is intended to refer to an overly expansive interpretation of the exclusion of plant varieties and problems in applying the threshold for protection to inventions involving animate material.

In assessing the Directive, it is important to note that in shaping national provision it does so on the basis of the expectations set down in the TRIPs Agreement.

### The Directive and TRIPs

As the EU is a member of the WTO, it is required to comply with WTO legislation. The text of the Directive, therefore, is predicated upon the notions of patentability contained within the TRIPs Agreement.

Recital 12 makes it clear that the Directive takes as its starting point the expectation set down in Article 27(1) of TRIPs that patent protection should be available for products and processes in all areas of technology. What it does not do is to make any direct stipulations as to whether it is equally bound by those guiding principles set down in TRIPs relating to the ability of member states to

---

[68] At this time the group included Belgium, France, Germany and Italy.

circumscribe the protection granted on the grounds of public health or concerns over the environment. What the Directive does do, in Recital 14, is to state that:

> substantive patent law cannot serve to replace or render superfluous national, European or international law which may impose restrictions or prohibitions or which concerns the monitoring of research and of the use or commercialisation of its results, notably from the point of view of the requirements of public health, safety, environmental protection, animal welfare, the preservation of genetic diversity and compliance with certain ethical standards.[69]

If this is taken to mean that the Directive is bound by external concepts of morality or public interest, then it is possible to see a correlation between this and the general Principles underpinning TRIPs; however, it could be argued that there is a significant difference.

The TRIPs Agreement makes it clear that member states may take into consideration issues relating to public health, the environment, and so on when 'formulating or amending their laws and regulations.' The text of the Directive acknowledges the latter, the formulation or amendment of *regulations*, but does not appear to recognise the former, that members may take these matters into account when formulating or amending their substantive patent *laws*. The Directive appears to be saying that the protection of those factors mentioned in Recital 14 is a matter for external regulation and not for internal control within the patent law itself.

The interest in this distinction could be said to be mainly one of perception. The wording of the Directive is such that it does not appear to accept any need for additional internal constraints on the patenting of biotechnological inventions other than those which already exist by virtue of the provisions of the EPC. The TRIPs Agreement, in contrast, acknowledges that the protection of certain types of material (and the general principles provisions apply to all the forms of intellectual property set out in the Agreement) could be subject to overarching public interest provisions and it leaves it to member states to decide whether, within the confines of the obligation entered into, there is a need to set in place these overarching public interest provisions. In practice, the shift in emphasis is unlikely to make much difference. As with any innovative practices, there is little incentive for inventors to carry on with a particular research programme if, irrespective of the availability of patent protection, the resulting product or process cannot be utilised due to external restraints. Having said that, it would seem that the recent de facto moratorium on the growing of genetically modified crops has not affected the decisions of some plant breeders to carry on with the research leading up to the creation of new types of genetically modified plant material.

---

[69] The Recital is silent on what is meant by 'certain ethical standards', but as the later Recitals, 37–45, discuss the types of ethical issues which should be considered when applying the internal morality provision, it might be that these comprise the certain ethical standards referred to in Recital 14.

Where the principle set down in Recital 14 *could* have an impact is in the operation of those provisions within patent law which are supposed to protect the public interest—for example, excluding material because it violates national concepts of morality, allowing use under the research exemption and compulsory licensing. The language used seems to indicate that the Directive cannot conflict with any external regulation relating to public health or the environment but that it does not necessarily have to take these issues into consideration when applying its own internal provisions. This will be returned to below.

An additional point of comparison is that the Recital 14 recognition of possible external constraints on the use of the patented material mirrors Article 13(8) of the Community Plant Variety Rights Regulation, which equally removes the need to discuss issues of morality or harm to the environment from the point of grant.

In terms of its relationship with the key substantive patent law provisions within TRIPs, the Directive is mainly silent. Clearly the exclusions of inventions contrary to morality and plant varieties mirrored existing European patent practice but, as the original draft showed, there was equivocation over the extent to which these should form part of the new EU legislation. Comparisons between the provisions of Article 27(2) and Article 27(3)(b) will be made below. Of specific significance is that the Directive makes only a minimal nod to either Article 30 or Article 31.

## The Directive as Gold Standard

Despite the initial 'hope' outlined in the 1988 draft that the Directive would effect a more radical approach to patenting all forms of living material the fact that the Directive has to live alongside the practices of the EPO (and it could not undermine either these or any other aspects of the general patent structure) meant that all the Commission could realistically expect to achieve was to establish a gold standard of good practice which would direct national patent provision. In particular, the expectation is that where there remains ambiguity over what can be patented the Directive will provide pan-European clarification. However, notwithstanding this objective, the Directive itself is not wholly clear as to what is patentable and what is not. The reason for this lies in the highly political nature of the background to the final draft.

The Directive, adopted in 1998, sought to try and do too much. Not only did it try to take account of the interests and views of disparate groups of interested parties (including industry, political lobby groups, patient groups, and non-governmental organisations) but it also tried to take account of the various patent law needs of all areas of biotechnology. The fact that each sector has very different patenting interests and needs means that the final text is a hotchpotch of issues, some of which find their way into the Articles of the Directive (these are the provisions which must be implemented) whilst others are contained within the Recitals (which arguably do not need national implementation). As some of the principles set down in the Recitals are arguably as important as those set out in the Articles it is not clear why the Directive has been framed in the way it has—and this causes confusion over what a member state *has* to do in order to implement as opposed to what it is *permitted* to do within the form of that implementation.

A key issue here relates to the status of the Recitals and whether they carry the same full force as the Articles which follow or if they merely serve an illustrative purpose.[70] It is not proposed to discuss the status of the Recitals here, although those relevant to the protection of plants will be discussed later, but it is possible that the status of the principles enshrined in the Recitals could be the subject of future litigation if a member state chooses to ignore this principle and instead provide (or refuse) protection in a manner directly contrary to a Recital but not, apparently, to an Article. An example of this is Recital 32, which states that plant varieties produced using a microbiological process are not patentable. However, the statement is not echoed in any Article. It might be possible that a member state may choose to interpret the substantive exclusion as only applying to traditionally bred varieties (on the basis that Article 4(3) contains an equivalent exception to the exclusion as in Article 53(b) of the EPC). Would the member state be held to be non-compliant?

A further matter relates to the emphasis placed within the Recitals on the benefit to be gained from having patent protection thereby encouraging bioscience innovation. The relationship between the public benefit, the impact of a strong system of patent protection and plant research could come under scrutiny especially where medicinal plants are concerned, and yet these principles do not find their way into the substantive provisions.

The ECJ ruling would appear to indicate that the Recitals are there to provide guidance but do not require compliance. This is in contrast to the Implementing Rules of the EPC, which make it clear that the Recitals to the Directive must be taken into account when applying the Rules.

A follow-on question is the extent to which member states will be allowed to develop national policy which does take account of any specific sectoral interests. As will seen, a couple of countries have chosen to implement the Directive alongside additional provisions which could moderate the strength of the right granted. Whilst any implementing legislation has to be approved by the Commission (and therefore these variants on patent provision appear to have been approved), the fact that some eminent commentators on patent law have queried whether these do constitute appropriate implementation means that there could be a residual question which may only be answered by the ECJ. More generally still, there is a worry that the emphasis on ensuring the availability of protection could mean that the needs of those potentially most negatively affected by the granting of rights could be neglected (in the short-term, at least). Such a group could be the traditional plant breeders who, as will

---

[70] Beyleveld, 'Why Recital 26 of the EC Directive on the Legal Protection of Biotechnological Inventions should be Implemented in National Law' [2000] 1 *IPQ* 1.

be discussed in chapter 8, typically have little experience of, or interest in, the patent system.

## The Substantive Provisions of the Directive[71]

In contrast to the Community Regulation, the Directive has only national, as opposed to Community, application. It does not, therefore, create a Community right. The only similarities between the two are that both relate to private rights which, once granted (by the national patent offices in the case of the Directive or by the Community Plant Variety Office in respect of the Regulation), are enforceable, by the right holder, through the national courts. In addition, they contain certain parallel provisions although the application of these differs between the systems.

As the Directive has only had minimal impact to date (due to both the inconsistency of implementation as well as the inevitable period whilst the principles became established through national practice) it is not yet possible to comment on any impact it may have had. Indeed, it could take many years before it is possible to comment on whether it has achieved its objective. There are two factors which need to be taken into account. The first is that national offices and courts will need to decide on the meaning of each of its provisions for their own purposes (with the inescapable time lag between grant and litigation). Secondly, national practices could themselves be subject to scrutiny by the European Court of Justice. Until the ECJ provides a definitive statement on what is an appropriate implementation and interpretation of the Directive (and this may take place via separate judgments on each of the provisions and in respect of all the varying different types of biotechnological innovation to which the Directive can be applied) then there remains the potential for continued uncertainty at both the local and pan-EU levels.

## Protectable Subject Matter

### General Principles

In keeping with the dictat set down in Article 27(1) of TRIPs,[72] Article 1(1) contains an unambiguous statement that member states *shall* provide patent protection for biotechnological inventions if they did not do so at the time the

---

[71] It is not the intention to discuss every provision of the Directive, but to focus on those relevant from a plant perspective. Other provisions, which relate to matters such as the protection of human genetic material and animals, are discussed extensively elsewhere, most notably in the Report of the Nuffield Council on Bioethics (*The Ethics of Patenting DNA*, July 2002) available at www.nuffield bioethics.org/publications/pp_0000000014.asp; and in Kamstra *et al*, *Special Report Patents on Biotechnological Inventions: The EC Directive*, above n 27.

[72] That patent protection must be available for inventions from all fields of technology.

Directive came into force. Article 1(1), therefore, establishes the general princi-ple that inventions involving biological material are patentable and it requires that '[a]ll member states of the EU [should] provide patent protection for biotechnological inventions.' In so doing, and '*if necessary*' members should 'adjust their national laws to take account of the provisions of the Directive.' All the other provisions (and the exclusions in particular) have to be read against this mandate. In requiring member states to provide protection, the Directive is careful to provide a reminder that the grant of a patent does not give the holder any authority to use the invention in any way they wish, but that this use may be subject to other national laws which restrict or prohibit certain uses, or which control research practices (including the commercialisation of that research), and in particular that these laws or regulations may be used to pro-tect 'public health, the environment, animal welfare, the preservation of genetic diversity' and to comply with 'certain ethical standards' (Recital 14). What is unclear is whether this (and in particular the part relating to ethical standards) can be relied upon by those member states reluctant to compromise their laws relating to bio-ethics (which may prohibit the patenting of any part of the human body[73]) by complying with the requirement in Article 5 that elements of the human body (other than simple elements) may be patentable.

Before looking at the obligation itself, it should be noted that Article 1(1) does not actually require that member states *must* amend their national laws. The requirement is to provide protection 'if necessary' by adjusting national law. If national patent laws and practice already achieved this result, or were capable of so doing, then one could assume that should be sufficient. However, the fact that the Commission has referred *all* non-implementing member states to the ECJ (without apparently having assessed whether their existing provision suf-fices), when taken with the fact that all those which have implemented have done so by amending their national patent laws, indicates that the option not to amend is not an option in practice. It would be interesting to see if any member of the EU (either from the original 15 or including the 10 new members) will try to argue that the objectives of the Directive can be realised through its existing provision—none have done so to date.

Article 3: Biological Material

Article 3(1) states that inventions which meet the usual threshold for protection (novelty, inventive step and industrial application) shall be patentable 'even if they concern a product consisting of or containing biological material or a process by means of which biological material is produced, processed or used.' Article 2 (which contains the definitions) defines biological material as 'any material containing genetic information and capable of reproducing itself or being reproduced in a biological system.' The principle of patentability is there-fore clearly extended to plant material.

---

[73] Such a law existing, eg, in France.

A concern for many is that granting offices will apply a low threshold of novelty, inventive step and industrial application, with the result that patents will be granted over very basic genetic material (as chapters 2, 5 and 6 have indicated, these are accusations which have been levelled at the US and European Patent Offices). There is little within the Directive which serves to alleviate these concerns and its provisions are directed towards ensuring protection is afforded as opposed to presenting potential obstacles to protection. Indeed, as will be seen below in respect of determining the novelty of material isolated from a natural environment or with a natural equivalent, the Directive has actively sought to render key criteria for protection open to greater interpretation. However, the recent practice of the EPO, as well as that of offices within the EU, appears to indicate that instances of grants being made to inventions which stand at the border of the invention/discovery distinction are now few (although some exist) and increasingly far between.[74]

One reason for this concern is the extent to which the applicant has to demonstrate an actual as opposed to speculative use for the applied-for invention. This falls within the scope of the industrial application criterion.[75] The Directive does make a reference to this, but in the context of Article 5 which relates to the patentability of the human body and genetic material isolated from it. Article 5(3) states that '[t]he industrial application of a sequence or a partial sequence of a gene must be disclosed in the patent application.' Recitals 22–25 also refer to this requirement, but again apparently only within the specific context of the patentability of human genetic material. The question is whether the same requirement to disclose the industrial application of a gene sequence isolated applies to sequences isolated from plant, or other, genetic hosts. It would seem odd if this were not the case, but if the provision was intended to have this general effect then one would have expected that it would be contained in Article 3—which contains the general statement relating to the threshold of protection.[76]

There is also the issue as to whether an applicant can claim undisclosed functions in addition to the disclosed function. As will be seen in chapter 9, the German implementing legislation draws a distinction between human genetic material (for which only the disclosed function may be claimed) and other bio-inventions (for which undisclosed functions may also be claimed).[77]

---

[74] Examples of this can be seen in a number of studies, eg the Intellectual Property Research Institute of Australia (IPRIA) survey of the practices of the European, US and Japanese Patent Offices in respect of applications involving genetic material, which showed diversity in method but similarity in outcome; Straus, *Genetic Inventions and Patent Law* (OECD, 2002); and the Report by the UK's Intellectual Property Institute prepared for the Department of Trade and Industry, *A Study into Current UK Law and Practice Regarding Patents for Genetic Sequences*, above ch 6, n 101.

[75] See the Straus and the Intellectual Property Institute publications, above n 74.

[76] §76 of Schedule A2, para 6 of the UK Examination Guidelines for Patent Applications Relating to Biotechnological Inventions in the UK Patent Office revised in 2003 do not appear to confine the requirement to human genetic material: www.patent.gov.uk. However, other jurisdictions may choose to give it the more limited application apparently permitted under the Directive.

[77] This has been criticised by commentators such as Straus who have queried if this constitutes a proper implementation.

Article 3: Isolated or Replicated Material

Another concern was that inventions which involve isolated, or which replicate, material which exists in nature would not be able to meet the novelty requirement. The concern was that if this was taken to be an absolute definition (as is the case for all types of inventions) then protection would only be available to a very limited group of genetic inventions. To avoid this limitation, the Directive states that where the material has been 'isolated from its natural environment or produced by means of a technical process' then this 'may be the subject of an invention even if it previously occurred in nature' (Article 3(2)).

The worry here is that this could lead to a possible erosion of the concept of novelty, and the question arises whether it is correct to hold that isolating biological material, or replicating material which already exists in nature, renders that isolated or replicated material novel. For those unversed in, or sceptical about, patent law it can be difficult to understand the thinking behind the Article. When seeking an explanation it is important to remember that the notion of novelty is a legal and not a scientific one. Whilst scientists might not view isolated or replicated material as novel, if such an interpretation is acceptable for legal purposes then patent lawyers may use it. The only proviso to this is that this has to be accepted either by virtue of implementing the concept via legislation (as is the case here) or through approval by the courts. This does not mean, however, that all isolated or replicated material will automatically be patentable. The isolation or replication will itself have to be novel, inventive, capable of industrial application and not give rise to excluded material. In both instances, the patent granted would not be taken to extend to the material in its natural, unutilised, form.[78] Genetic material presented to a granting office in its wholly natural form will not be patentable and any application rejected on the grounds that it is a discovery. As discussed in chapter 5, a discovery is latent information for which a use has yet to be found. In that unutilised form it would be regarded as a discovery and unpatentable. Once the information has been utilised then provided that this utilisation has not been achieved, in that manner,[79] by anyone else and it is inventive and industrially applicable, then a patent could be secured over it. Recital 34 makes it clear that nothing within the Directive shall 'prejudice [the] concepts of invention and discovery, as developed by national, European or international patent law.'

---

[78] An example of this is the *Howard Florey/Relaxin* case which was discussed in ch 5. The EPO held that the patent extended only to the protein in the form produced by the Howard Florey Institute and it did not extend to the protein as naturally produced by pregnant women.

[79] This is another important factor in patent law—the question is whether the invention has been previously known in that form, where previously known can mean either that it has been actually achieved before or that the possibility has been anticipated by another in a patent claim relating to material involved in the subsequent invention. It is possible that if the reality of the utilisation has not been achieved before but simply anticipated in a existent patent the claims of that patent might include any acts which serve to realise the possibility, in which case the second invention could be claimed by the first patent holder.

Article 4: The Protection of Plant Material

Article 4(1)(a) reiterates the exclusion of plant varieties stating that these 'are not patentable.' The Directive makes it clear that this exclusion is limited and only applies to varieties recognised as such under plant variety rights law.[80] Recital 30 provides further detail and states that 'a variety is defined by its whole genome and therefore possesses individuality and is clearly distinguishable from other varieties.'

That a restrictive application is to be given to the exclusion of plant varieties is clear from Article 4(2). This states that where the technical feasibility of the invention, that is the novel technical effect being claimed, is not confined to a particular plant variety then the invention is patentable. This permits groupings of plant which are 'characterised by a single gene rather than its whole genome and . . . not protectable under plant variety rights [are] not excluded from protection under patent law' (Recital 31). As discussed in the last chapter, this resonates with the decision made by the Enlarged Board of Appeal of the EPO in *Novartis*. As with that decision, the concern engendered by this is that all that could be required to avoid the exclusion is the omission of the words 'plant variety' or any reference to a plant grouping compliant with the UPOV or Community Regulation criteria in order for the application to succeed.

The intention is to remove any doubt over the patentability of plant-related inventions and to provide clarification as to the scope of the exclusion of plant varieties.

In respect of this provision, the main concern is whether the reference in Recital 30 and Article 2(2) to a plant variety being defined according to the plant variety rights system is a reference to those plant varieties *protectable* under plant variety rights or to all types of plant varieties recognised by the plant variety rights system as varieties not all of which are protectable under that system.[81] The question which this poses is whether a plant grouping which is recognised as a variety under plant variety rights but not capable of being protected by a plant variety right would be excluded from patent protection.

It is possible that those charged with interpreting and applying this provision will adopt a default definition, namely, that notwithstanding the wording of Article 5 of the Community Regulation (and its equivalent within the 1991 UPOV Act), the practice will be that the exclusion applies only to those varieties capable of being protected by a plant variety right—that is, those varieties which collectively are distinct, uniform and stable.

If the overarching presumptions are accepted to be those of protectability and patentability then the limitation of the exclusion to only those varieties capable

---

[80] Art 2(3) states that plant varieties are defined according to the Community Plant Variety Rights Regulation.

[81] As was discussed in ch 1, the plant variety rights system recognises two types of plant varieties: those which can meet the DUS criteria and those which cannot. Both groups are specifically referred to in Art 5 of the Community Regulation.

of protection under the plant variety rights system might be justified. However, the Directive (and the case law of the EPO) simply states that the exclusion is to be defined according to the definition of a plant variety within plant variety rights. There is no recognition of the fact that both the UPOV and Community Regulation definitions are two-tiered. It is not clear therefore if the exclusion applies to *both* types of variety or only to those capable of plant variety protection. As discussed previously, there is a question whether there should be a grouping of plants which are recognised as a variety for the purposes of plant variety rights protection but not capable of attracting plant variety protection, but which also are, by dint of being a 'variety', unpatentable. In other words, is it acceptable that there could be a grouping of plants for which no form of protection will be available? Because of the presumption of protectability which operates at all levels of intellectual property law, it is unlikely in the current intellectual property law climate that this will be the interpretation given to the exclusion. However, given that there is a dual definition within plant variety rights it might have been useful to make it clear in the Directive that, for patent law purposes, a variety is a plant grouping capable of protection under plant variety rights. It would also have been useful, if this is indeed the intention behind the exclusion, to have had a formal policy statement to this effect. As it is, the unqualified reference to the plant variety rights definition means that it is possible for the exclusion to be given a more expansive application which will continue to carry with it the now familiar question of what qualities a plant grouping must have to be regarded as a variety.

## Article 4: Essentially Biological/Microbiological Processes

Article 4(1)(b) also excludes from protection 'essentially biological processes' for the production of plants. Paragraph 3 qualifies this exclusion by stating that '[p]aragraph 1(b) shall be without prejudice to the patentability of inventions which concern a microbiological or other technical process or a product obtained by means of such a process.' Article 2 defines both essentially biological and microbiological processes.

Article 2(1)(b) defines a 'microbiological process' as any process involving or performed upon or resulting in microbiological material.

Article 2(2) defines an 'essentially biological process' as a 'process for the production of plants and animals which consists *entirely* of natural phenomena such as crossing or selection' (emphasis added).

The language of Article 2(2) appears to indicate that where a process does not consist entirely of natural phenomena then the products produced by that process will be patentable. There is no further indication (in any other Article or Recital) of the level of technical intervention required nor of the meritoriousness, or otherwise, of that intervention. It would seem that it will be for national patent offices, in the first instance, and the European Court of Justice in the last, to determine the extent of intervention needed before a process is rendered non-essentially biological. It is possible that in deciding this national offices may look to the jurisprudence of the EPO for guidance.

In the *PGS* decision the Technical Board of Appeal held that 'a process for the production of plants comprising at least one essential technical step *which cannot be carried out without human intervention and which has a decisive impact of the final result*' does not fall under the Article 53(b) exclusion of an essentially biological process. This approach, when taken with the statement in *Lubrizol* that the intervention had to go beyond 'a trivial level', is so far the only guide we have as to what is an essentially biological process and the level, and type, of intervention needed to render a process patentable.

One question raised by the language of Article 4(3) is whether the reference to the products of the microbiological processes being patentable could serve to provide an exception to the exclusion of plant varieties in Article 4(1)(a) (as was proposed in the 1988 draft of the Directive). There is no specific reference to this within the substantive provisions but Recital 32 does provide some clarification. This states that where a plant variety has been genetically modified, or is the result of a biotechnological process, 'it will still be excluded from patentability.' Given the apparently questionable status of the Recitals it could be asked as to why either Article 4(3) does not itself specifically state that the inclusion of the products of microbiological (or other technical) processes does not extend to plant varieties, or why, equally, Article 4(1)(a) does not refer to plant varieties 'howsoever bred'.

The extent to which Article 4 can be taken as guaranteeing the exclusion of all plant varieties irrespective of the method of breeding used will depend on whether Recital 32 has any force. If the Recitals are merely indicators of good practice, but not binding as such, then it remains possible for a member state to use Article 4(3) to restrict the application of Article 4(1)(a). It might be thought that this would be unlikely in the current political and legal environment, but it is worth remembering that there was a degree of political will to engineer such an outcome in the original draft of the Directive and also that the EU is, at present, experiencing its biggest political change yet with the entry of 10 new member states, one at least of which permits the patenting of plant varieties.[82]

An example of this lack of clarity at the national level can be found in the UK implementation of the Directive. The Patent Regulations 2000 amend the Patents Act 1977. Schedule A2, section 76A(3)(f) states that patents shall not be

---

[82] Hungarian Law No XXXIII on the Protection of Inventions by Patent. Art 1, which defines patentable subject matter, contains no reference to plant varieties. However, Art 6 states that plant varieties are patentable, and here is a further layer of confusion, as ch XIII, which contains the requirements for patent protection for plant varieties, mirrors in many respects (but not all) the conditions for the grant of a plant variety right. It would seem that in the case of Hungary the option to use a Paris Convention route was taken up. However, the inclusion of plant varieties within the patent law framework, albeit on the basis of compliance with UPOV-style requirements, does further serve to cloud any precise distinction between the two rights.

available for 'any variety of animal or plant or any essentially biological process for the production of animals or plants, *not being a micro-biological or other technical process or the product of such a process*' (emphasis added). No mention is made that the exception to the exclusion does not include plant varieties produced using either a microbiological or other technical process. It could be argued that the use of 'any' before variety indicates any variety howsoever produced, but the use of the phrasing *not being* would appear to mean that the exclusion only applies to those varieties not produced by a microbiological or other technical process. There is nothing else in the amending Regulations which helps clarify this. It is interesting to note that in its 2002 revised Examination Guidelines for Patent Applications relating to Biotechnological Inventions, the UK Patent Office makes a specific reference to the *Novartis* decision and to the exclusion applying irrespective of the manner of production, but it falls short of explicitly stating that this will be the practice of the UK Patent Office. This reference could be taken as meaning either that the *Novartis* decision indicates the general position on the patentability of plant varieties (which the UK Patent Office endorses) or it might merely indicate EPO practice (which can differ from that of the national offices), and the lack of an equivalent statement within the UK law itself taken to mean that the views of the EPO are not necessarily shared by the UKPO.

The Directive does not contain any reference to the protection of micro-organisms.

Article 6: Morality

In keeping with the provisions of the EPC and Article 27(2) of TRIPs, the Directive excludes from patent protection inventions which would be contrary to morality. As the objective of the Directive was not to introduce new legal principles but to provide in essence an indication of good practice it was thought inappropriate to redraft the text of Article 53(a) of the EPC. However, the Directive did achieve two key changes, the first is the provision, within Article 6(2), of a non-exhaustive list of types of genetic research which would automatically be regarded as not protectable under the 'contrary to morality' heading. As these relate to human beings and animals and not to plants, they will not be discussed any further here. The second is that it circumscribed the arena within which the immoral activity is to take place—and this is the only part of the provision which could be relevant for plant innovations.[83] Through the adoption of

---

[83] It would be misleading to state that the draftsmen of the Directive are wholly responsible for the circumscription of the morality provision. Art 27(2) of the TRIPs Agreement, which came into force in 1992, also contains the more restricted version and the Directive makes a reference to this in Recital 36. However, as the European delegation for the TRIPs negotiations played a key role in drafting this provision it is possible to see a correlation between the objectives achieved in TRIPs and the change ensured in Europe.

the Directive by the EPO for the purposes of supplementary interpretation, this circumscription now also applies to Article 53(a).[84]

There is an important distinction between the language of the Directive and that of the EPC (although not Article 27(2) TRIPs).

Article 6(1) of the Directive states that '[i]nventions shall be considered unpatentable where their *commercial* exploitation would be contrary to *ordre public* or morality; however, such exploitation shall not be deemed to be so contrary merely because it is prohibited by law or regulation' (emphasis added).

In contrast, Article 53(a) of the EPC refers to the exclusion of inventions 'the publication or exploitation of which would be contrary to *ordre public* or morality.'

The Directive merely requires that the commercial use must not be contrary to *ordre public* or morality. The EPC, however, refers to publication as well as exploitation, with the latter not even necessarily being commercial in nature. It is possible that the use of unethical research practices or where a patented invention is exploited in a non-commercial manner will fall outside the exclusion within the Directive whilst possibly still providing grounds for challenge at the EPO.

The main text of the Directive does not make any specific reference to morality and the protection of plant material. However, Recital 36 does refer to Article 27(2) of the TRIPs Agreement and includes protecting 'plant life or health' and the avoidance of 'serious prejudice to the environment' as factors to be taken into account when applying the general principle enshrined within Article 6(1). As a counter to morality as a ground for *exclusion*, other Recitals contain references which have 'moral' overtones which member states will be expected to take into account when deciding upon the proper application of the law. These include 'the development of methods of cultivation which are less polluting and more economical in their use of ground' (Recital 10), and taking into account the importance of national, European and international law concerning 'environmental protection [and] the preservation of genetic diversity' (Recital 14).

Of particular relevance to the protection of plant innovations is the requirement, within Recital 55, that '[m]ember states must give particular weight' to various Articles of the Convention on Biological Diversity. These are Article 3, which contains the general principle that

---

[84] Rule 23(b)(1) of the Amended Implementing Rules 'Decision of the Administrative Council 16 June 1999 to Amend the Implementing Rules of the European Patent Convention' [1999] *Official Journal of the European Patent Office (OJ EPO)* 437; [1999] *OJ EPO* 573. In terms of its impact at the EPO, the Directive has a broader application in the EPO than just for biotechnology (eg genetically modified material using new gene technologies). In the recent case *Leland Stanford/Modified Animal* [2002] EPOR 2, the Opposition Division stated that the principle set down in Art 6 of the Directive as adopted by the EPO for the purposes of interpreting Art 53 applied to genetic inventions even where the living material had not been genetically modified. In this instance, the case concerned a mouse implanted with human genetic material for the purposes of developing anti-AIDS remedies.

States have, in accordance with the Charter of the United Nations and the principles of international law, the sovereign right to exploit their own resources pursuant to their own environmental policies, and the responsibility to ensure that activities within their jurisdiction or control do not cause damage to the environment of other States or of areas beyond the limits of national jurisdiction]

Article 8(j) [the requirement to

respect, preserve and maintain knowledge, innovations and practice of indigenous and local communities embodying traditional lifestyles relevant for the conservation and sustainable use of biological diversity and promote their wider application with the approval and involvement of the holders of such knowledge, innovations and practices and encourage the equitable sharing of the benefits arising from the utilisation of such knowledge, innovations and practice];

the second sentence of Article 16(2) and Article 16(5) [which recognise the importance of intellectual property rights] of the [Convention on Biological Diversity (CBD)] when bringing into force the laws, regulations and administrative provisions necessary to comply with this Directive' (Recital 55).

Recital 56 also states that further attention has to be given to the relationship between the TRIPs Agreement and the CBD

in particular on issues relating to technology transfer and conservation and sustainable use of biological diversity and the fair and equitable sharing of benefits arising out of the use of genetic resources including the protection of knowledge, innovations and practices of indigenous and local communities embodying traditional lifestyles relevant for the conservation and sustainable use of biological diversity.

It would seem, therefore, that member states have a clear mandate to take into account environmental concerns if required in applying the provisions of the Directive. However, as a note of caution, and as with other statements made in respect of the Recitals, it remains to be seen as to the actual extent to which member states could, if they wished, rely upon these to restrict the granting of patents.

In order to attempt to sway any unduly unilateral national reaction to concerns over the morality provision, the Commission, via Article 7, has charged its Group on Ethics in Science and New Technologies to evaluate all ethical aspects of biotechnology, although its remit is restricted to evaluating the technology only 'at the level of basic ethical principles.' It is unclear as to the extent to which plant innovations, as opposed to those involving human genetic material, could, in the 21st century, be said to raise basic ethical concerns.

Having set down that which can be the subject matter of a patent, the Directive then turns its attention to the scope of the right granted.

**Scope of Protection**

The Directive is silent on the matter of the proper scope of protection (this being a matter for general patent law). Instead, the focus is on the extension of protection to products which either incorporate patented material or which have been produced using a patented process.

We have seen in chapter 6 that the protection conferred on a patented process extends to any product directly produced using that process. In addition, it is common patent practice for the claims to extend to any material within which the patented invention is placed or utilised. Articles 8 and 9 of the Directive reiterate both these principles and attach them firmly to biological material.

Article 8

Paragraph 1 states that the protection conferred by the patent on biological material which possesses specific characteristics shall extend to any biological material derived from the protected material (by multiplication or propagation) where that derived material (which may be identical or divergent) possesses those same characteristics.

In plant terms this means that a patent granted over a gene which codes for a particular characteristic (for example disease resistance) will extend to any plants in which the patented gene is found. There are two interesting questions which arise.

The first is whether the reference to the derived material *possessing* the same characteristic means that the patented information (for example a gene) merely has to be present in the derived material but not necessarily performing any specific function. For example, a plant may contain a patented gene (coding for a particular colour), but a breeder may wish to use that plant for further breeding purposes based on other genetic factors such as height or foliage shape which are not dependent upon the patented gene. The breeding programme could result in plants in which the patented gene is latent and does not perform the function for which it was patented. Does the presence of the gene mean that these plants are captured by the patent? The wording of Article 8 would appear to indicate that they are. That the Directive is intended to allow a patent to capture even a latent or passive inclusion of the patented technology becomes more evident when Article 8 is read alongside Article 9, discussed below.

The second question is whether this provision can be used to circumvent the exclusion of plant varieties. It states very clearly that the protection conferred will extend to *any* material produced through propagation or multiplication which possesses the characteristics of the invention. There is no specific exclusion of varieties—nor is there any reference within the Recitals to this provision not applying to varieties (as was the case in respect of the Recital 32 qualification to Article 4(3)). On the basis of existing patent practice it is likely that this provision will be taken to include plant varieties, the argument being that the exclusion only applies at the point of grant and, more specifically, to claims made to a plant variety. In contrast, where a patent has been granted over an invention which is patentable (for examplea gene) then the effect of that grant is to provide protection for applications of that invention including uses made within plant varieties. As the issue is not one of grant but of scope, the exclusion of plant varieties does not apply. This once again goes to the issue of what is protected as opposed to what is protectable.

Article 8(2) states that where a patent has been granted over a process, that process enabling the production of biological material possessing specific characteristics, then protection shall extend to any product directly obtained through that process, *and* to any other material derived from that directly obtained material which possesses the same specific characteristics. This builds on Article 64(2) EPC and underlines the fact that not only will protection extend to the first generation of material produced using the patented process, but where that obtained material itself is used to produce further derived material then that material will also be captured by the patent over the initial process. The language of Article 8(2) indicates that the patented process does not itself have to be used to produce the further derived material. The only relevant factor is that the future derived material must have a causal connection to the process by possessing the same specific characteristics as the initial invention produced using the patented process.

This means that where a patented process has been used in order to produce a plant variety with a specific characteristic, and that plant variety is then used in an ordinary breeding programme (which does not involve the patented process) then, notwithstanding the absence of the use of the process, the patent over that process will reach through to any resulting plant material bred using the initial variety, the protection conferred by the patent over the process apparently extending through the generations until such time as the plant material ceases to possess the same characteristics as the plant variety originally produced by the patented process.

Article 9

Article 9 also extends the scope of the right granted. It states that the protection conferred by a patent shall extend to all material (except the human body) in which the genetic material protected by the patent is 'incorporated and in which the genetic information is contained and performs its function.'

As has been shown above, Article 8 appears to say that mere passive inclusion of patented technology within biological material is sufficient for the patent holder to claim the material in which the patented technology has been included. Article 8 can be read as extending protection to passive or latent inclusion because Article 9 specifically states that the patent rights extend to material in which the patented technology *performs its function*. If Article 8(1) was intended to apply to an active as opposed to passive use of the patented technology then there would be no need for Article 9.

The effect of Article 9 is simply to extend the patent to any material within which the patented technology is placed (for example a gene within a plant) where that technology performs the function for which the patent has been granted (for example, coding for, and expressing, a specific characteristic such as colour or resistance).

With both Articles 8 and 9 there appears to be no cut-off point down the generational spectrum at which the patent will cease to have effect. Instead, it will continue to have an impact until such time as either the patented technology ceases to be ascertainable in the subsequent generations or the patent runs out of term.

A question asked by Kamstra *et al* is whether the existing patent law of exhaustion of rights could be used to restrict the extension of protection provided under both Article 8 and 9.[85] The exhaustion of rights doctrine operates where it is thought that the exercise of the right has been such that the holder of the right effectively has exhausted his control over the subject matter of that right, although he will not exhaust his right to replicate that subject matter. Within the EU this is taken to occur when the holder places the patented technology into the EU market place—once he has so done then he cannot control any further sales of the technology, for example from the UK to France. What the patent right will permit him to continue to do is to prevent others from replicating the patented technology in any way which infringes his patent. Kamstra *et al* ask whether a placing of biological material into the EU market place will not render the rights exhausted over that material but also any other material derived from it. This is clearly going to be a matter for the ECJ to determine and at present it remains unclear whether a patent holder who places, for example, his patented genetically modified plant cells into the market can prevent a plant breeder from using and then selling any plant variety breed which incorporates those plant cells.

The Recitals are largely silent on the matter of the extension of protection, other than to say that the holder of a patent should be entitled to prevent the use of material in situations which are equivalent to the production of the patented product itself.

### Derogations to the Right

The Directive, unlike the EPC, specifically permits certain derogations from the right. Interestingly, however, it makes no mention of any right to use protected material for research purposes. This is curious given that such an exemption is

---

[85] Kamstra *et al*, *Patents on Biotechnological Inventions: The EC Directive*, above n 27, para 5.01.

central to plant variety rights and, as will be seen, there have been attempts to correlate the Directive with the Regulation in respect of other derogations to the right. The impression left by this omission is that the strength of the patent is clearly of more value to the Commission than the benefit to be had from having the protected material freely available for use in further breeding programmes. The lack of an explicit reference to research use should not be taken to mean, however, that the Directive has no impact on research practices, for it does.

Articles 8 and 9 mentioned above have clear implications for breeding programmes if the plant material bred contains a patented gene, and as mentioned above, there is an interesting question as to how far the patent right will extend where the patented gene has been used in a breeding programme, but it is not actively expressed in the resulting plant material, or where material has been produced using a patented process. It is also relevant in looking at the ambit of the compulsory cross-licensing provision discussed below. As will be seen in the discussion of research in chapter 9, Germany proposed including a specific derogation to the patent right in respect of research within its proposals for implementing the Directive.

The Directive contains two derogations to the right, both of which are of import to those seeking to use patented plant material.

Article 10

Article 10 qualifies the extension of protection provided under Articles 8 and 9. It states that protection 'shall not extend to material obtained from the first multiplication or propagation of biological material . . . where the multiplication or propagation necessarily results from the application of the material for which it was marketed.' This freedom to replicate or multiply does not extend to any subsequent multiplication or propagation involving the material so obtained.

This appears to indicate that where patented plant material, such as seed or cuttings, has been bought and sown, then the *first* issue of that sowing or replication will not be a violation of the rights of the patent holder. However, it would seem that any further multiplication or replication would constitute an infringing act. This suggests that a flower grower, who has, for example, purchased certified flower seeds or cuttings, can grow plants from the seeds or cuttings, can pick the flowers, but cannot retain any seeds from the plants or make further cuttings for the purpose of further multiplication or propagation nor sell any flowers grown from the second set of plants. Two further factors need to be borne in mind which could, potentially, have serious implications for end users of protected material, for example farmers. The first is the emphasis on the need to show that the *first* multiplication or propagation must *necessarily* result from the application or use of the material, that being the purpose for which it was placed on the market. This implies that any inadvertent second multiplication or propagation could be an infringement—for example where patented material is sown in a field and transfers to a neighbouring field where it replicates itself. The second, closely related to the first, is that it is unclear whether the right to first multiply and restrictions on second use apply only to the person who bought the material or whether they apply to any users irrespective of a commercial connection to the person who brought the material to market.

Unlike the second derogation (which only applies to farmers) the derogation in Article 10 applies to *all* users. In terms of the possible impact on domestic users (that is non-commercial private use of patented genetic material) then it is possible, depending on the defences available within local patent law, for a private individual to rely on the defence of private, non-commercial use against any allegation of infringement. However, any other use, such as unintentional use which does have a commercial result (for example developing a new colour in an ornamental or increased yield in a crop) would seem to fall outside the derogation and this applies irrespective of the occupation of the person using the patented material. This gives rise to two potentially serious implications regarding the application of Article 10.

The first is that the derogation does not extend to the use of the material produced for the purposes of other multiplication or propagation. 'Other propagation or multiplication' would include use on breeding programmes. It would seem therefore that Article 10 could prevent the use of protected material for any research purpose and there is nothing in the Directive to rebut this interpretation. The question which this raises is whether this has to be read in light of any national research exemption, which might permit the use of patented material for non-commercial or experimental purposes, or if it is intended to supplant such an exemption. If the latter, then this could mean that no use other than a first use will be permitted, irrespective of the form of that subsequent use.

The second issue relates to an apparent contradiction between Article 10 and Article 11. As the next section will show, the Directive contains an equivalent farm saved seed provision to that contained within the Community Regulation. As discussed in chapter 4, the derogation in the Regulation is very limited and the only category of farmer who does not have to pay any form of royalty is the small farmer as defined by Council Regulation (EEC) No 1765/92. This defines a small farmer, as one who does not grow plants on an area bigger than that needed to produce 92 tonnes of cereals. The question which Article 10 begs is whether, notwithstanding the exemption of small farmers, they will nonetheless be unable to retain and multiply harvested material because of Article 10.

For some, Article 10 might seem to be an inappropriate constraint on the ability of a *bona fide* purchaser to use the subject of that purchase as they wish. In general patent law terms, there is usually no constraint on post-sale use provided that this use does not conflict with the ability of the patent holder to maximise their economic interest in the patented technology. If the replication or multiplication is such that it prevents the patent holder from being able to control the market then this could be seen as something which the patent holder should be able to prevent. As before, the lack of clarity over this provision means that the full extent of the derogation will become clear only once pronounced upon by the ECJ.

The Recitals are silent on the issue of the extent of the derogation within Article 10. It is possible that Article 10 could constitute a new restraint on the ability to use patented material. The same is not true of the second derogation, which is firmly based on an existing principle enshrined within plant variety rights—the farm saved seed provision.

Article 11

Article 11 states that a farmer may use the produce of any harvest 'for propagation or multiplication on his own farm, the extent and conditions of this derogation corresponding to those under Article 14 of the Regulation (EC) No 2100/94.' As outlined in chapter 4, this right has a limited application (the extent of which is defined according to the three-tier structure), it applies to certain, specified, crops and is dependent upon the payment of a reduced royalty

Article 11(1)[86] explicitly states that the provision corresponds to Article 14 of the Regulation. This permits farmers to use protected material (other than a hybrid or a synthetic variety) for propagating purposes on their own holding; however, this right is limited in that:

1) the farmer can only retain propagating material for this purpose from one of the following categories:

   a) fodder plants (chickpea, milkvetch, yellow lupin, lucerne, field pea, Berseen/Egyptian clover, Persian clover, field bean, common vetch and, in Portugal only, Italian rye-grass);
   b) cereals (oats, barley, rice, canary grass, rye, triticale, wheat, durum wheat, spelt wheat);
   c) potatoes;
   d) oil and fibre plants (swede rape, turnip rape, linseed with the exclusion of flax).

Farmers' privilege does not apply to any other plant varieties. In addition:

2) the farmer must pay an equitable remuneration sensibly lower than the amount originally charged—the common figure across the EU is 50 per cent of the original price.

As discussed in chapter 4, only small farmers, as defined in the Community Regulation are exempt from this obligation.

---

[86] Art 11(2) introduces a corresponding provision relating to the breeding of livestock.

As this provision is intended to operate on the same basis as Article 14 of the Community Regulation, similar issues arise about its operation in practice as were discussed in chapter 4 and therefore it is unnecessary to discuss these further here. There is one patent-specific issue which is worth mentioning and that is that the notion of a right to save seed from one year to the next without having to pay an additional royalty is essentially one rooted in the philosophy of the plant variety rights system. It is, therefore, a novel concept in patent law. This raises the spectre of a number of problems, not least that, normally, patent holders are disassociated from any end user of the patented products. The lack of any prior relationship between patent holders and farmers means that there is the potential for misunderstanding to arise over the actions of each side. For patent holders there could be a further disadvantage in that they do not currently have in place the buffering mechanisms plant variety rights holders have in the form of collection agencies.

### Licensing

The background to the compulsory cross-licensing provision has already been discussed. The version of Article 12 adopted in 1998 goes some way to reducing the imbalance between the rights of the plant variety rights holder and those of the patent holder. However, a number of concerns remain.

The Article, which it should be remembered introduces for the first time compulsory cross-licences between patents and plant variety rights, now requires that where a breeder, or inventor, cannot exploit a protected variety or patented invention, without infringing another party's plant variety right or patent, then both parties can acquire a licence to use the other's protected property provided that the breeder/inventor seeking the licence shows:

a) that they applied unsuccessfully to the holder of the plant variety right/patent,

and

b) that their plant variety or invention constitutes a significant technical progress when compared with the protected plant variety or invention.

Article 12(4) states that each member state shall designate the national authority or authorities responsible for granting the licence. Where the licence for a plant variety can be granted only by the Community Plant Variety Office, then Article 29 of Regulation (EC) No 2100/94 shall apply.[87]

---

[87] This contains the compulsory licensing provision, discussed in ch 5, including the amendment in 2004 relating to the need to show that the applicant has first sought to obtain a licence from the patent holder and that their technology represents a significant technical progress.

Notwithstanding the discussions which surrounded the drafting of Article 12, a number of issues remain unresolved. These include the matter of determining what quality a plant variety or invention must have in order to represent a 'significant technical progress'.

Firstly, the provision does not expand on what is meant by 'significant' nor 'technical' nor 'progress'. It is arguable that these are highly subjective terms, any one of which could be denied by the relevant rights holder refusing to accept that that invention/plant variety concerned represents a significant technical progression when compared with their protected material. Complicating the matter further is the fact that the language used within both Article 12 and the Recitals (52 and 55) makes it clear that the progression envisaged need not be purely scientific in nature, but rather could be economic. These state that either the plant variety or invention concerned must represent 'significant technical progress of considerable economic interest compared to' the plant variety/ invention protected by the plant variety right or patent.

There would appear, therefore, to be two hurdles for the breeder/inventor to jump. The first is that the invention or plant variety must be in itself be a significant technical progress when looked at against the protected invention or plant variety. 'Progress' will be determined on the basis of a technical, scientific, evaluation. The second is that this technical progression must be of 'considerable economic interest'. The question here is: of considerable economic interest to whom? Is it to the public (who may purchase the invention or variety and could include other breeders or researchers), to the holder of the right or to the breeder or inventor seeking the licence? These are issues which remain undecided and which could cause problems for both breeders and inventors wishing to make use of genetically valuable, but protected, varieties or inventions.[88]

There is a further issue and that is the potential time differentials in availability of the licences. Commonly, a compulsory licence is available only once three years have elapsed from the date of grant of a patent. In comparison, there is no general equivalent provision within plant variety rights. Some countries, such as the UK, do permit the relevant government ministers to specify, for each species or group of plants, any period within which a compulsory licence cannot be granted (licences may be granted during the moratorium period, but will not come into effect until it has ceased), but this is not necessarily common or uniform practice.[89] The significance of this lies in being able to protect the economic value of the variety or invention for a designated period. Article 12 (when taken in the context of general patent and plant variety rights law) will appear to permit a patent holder to secure a cross-licence from the moment that a variety right has been granted, whereas a plant breeder will have to wait until three

---

[88] See Ardley, 'The 1991 UPOV Convention: Ten Years On' in *Proceedings of the Conference on Plant Intellectual Property within Europe and the Wider Global Community* (Sheffield Academic Press, 2002) 77.

[89] §17(8) of the Plant Varieties Act 1997.

years have elapsed from patent grant before they can secure an equivalent licence. This will be discussed further in chapter 9.

Inextricably tied up with Article 12 is its potential impact on research. What constraints, if any, will the provision place on plant breeders who wish to use a patented gene for research purposes where there is a defined commercial end in sight (and few plant breeders undertake lengthy research programmes without a defined objective in sight), which means that the research will not be covered by the research exemption in patent law. The breeder might not know if he will be able to claim a compulsory licence giving him a right to exploit any resulting plant variety until such time as the research work is complete, which might be 10 to 15 years after the start of the breeding programme. Until such time as the work is complete and the breeder can demonstrate that the resulting variety does represent significant technical progress, he could be faced with the situation where he either infringes the patent by using the patented gene without permission or he might be subject to a licence fee which, if the gene is a particularly important one, might have stringent terms attached. This provision continues to be the subject of much debate as it is not clear what the requirement that the plant variety or invention must constitute a significant technical progress means.

There could, however, be a benefit to Article 12. Because it is unclear as to what the provision means (either in the abstract or in practice) it might encourage both breeders and inventors to enter into mutually beneficial partnerships, such as those which are already prevalent in many sectors of the pharmaceutical industry. Those who defend the lack of use of the compulsory licensing provisions within patent law often do so on the basis that the fact that the provision exists is usually enough to bring the parties to the negotiating table and encourage the development of these mutually beneficial arrangements.[90]

The last substantive provision of the Directive is Article 13, which permits material not in the public domain, which cannot be described in a patent application, to be deposited in a recognised depository institution. This merely mirrors the existing practice under the Budapest Treaty.

As mentioned earlier, in 2003 the Commission referred eight of the then 15 member states to the ECJ for non-implementation. This underlines the Commission's commitment to fostering biotechnology as one of its key industries for the 21st century. However, before then, the Commission had signalled that it expected member states to endorse its patenting policy, with the result that there would be an increase in the number of patents granted. This came in

---

[90] It is interesting to note that the Directive is silent on the matter of governmental use within patent law, ie is the right of a government to make use of patented material where it is in the public interest so to do. In instances such as this, the patent holder is paid reasonable compensation. Governmental or Crown use is frequently used in the defence industry and less so in respect of healthcare—it is worth bearing in mind that whilst most perceptions of plant breeding relate to agricultural or ornamental breeding, the new pharming industries are booming and the use of plants to develop new medicines increasing, particularly in light of the public's embracing of more naturally derived products.

October 2002, when the Commission published its first report on the impact of the Directive on bioscience.[91]

The degree and type of implementation necessary for compliance with the Directive may also be subject to change as a result of the Commission's changing notions of governance. Increasingly the emphasis is on implementation according to local demands rather than pan-European uniformity. Whether these principles (which have evolved since the Directive was adopted) apply to existing EU obligations remains to be seen, but if they do then the potential for ongoing divergence in practice (which the Directive was intended to remove) will continue.

## IV. THE EUROPEAN COMMISSION'S REPORT ON THE DEVELOPMENT AND IMPLICATIONS OF PATENT LAW IN THE FIELD OF BIOTECHNOLOGY AND GENETIC ENGINEERING

The Report provides an extensive overview of the Directive. In addition to discussing the substantive legal issues arising from the text of the Directive, it provides detail of the action brought by the Dutch government to annul the Directive and the responses of both the Advocate General and the European Court of Justice to that action. It also explains how the Directive sits alongside the European Patent Convention and outlines its relationship with the international agreements such as TRIPs.[92]

It is not proposed to discuss the contents of the Commission's Report in great detail, because it a) mainly restates the text of the Directive and b) does not dwell specifically on issues relating to plant material.

In summary, the Report reiterates the presumption of patentability of inventions involving genetic material and it also identifies the two issues which the Commission intends to investigate via further research. These two issues are:

— the scope to be conferred to patents on sequences or partial sequences of genes isolated from the human body, and
— the patentability of human stem cells and cell lines obtained from them.

Three pages of the 47-page Report are devoted to plants, although there are some general points which apply to genetic material irrespective of source.

---

[91] COM (2002) 545 final. Art 16(c) of the EU Directive on the Legal Protection of Biotechnological Inventions requires the Commission to undertake an evaluation of the provision of patent law over biotechnological inventions every five years. The Report published by the Commission in October 2002 is the first such Report. A second Report was published in 2005, but added little by way of analysis to the 2002 Report: Report from the Commission to the Council and European Parliament, *Development and Implications of Patent Law in the Field of Biotechnology and Genetic Engineering*, COM (2005) 312 final.

[92] The Report states that it is 'incontestable that the [biotech patenting] Directive is fully compatible with the existing treaties,' including the TRIPs Agreement.

**Plant Patents**

The Report indicates that the reason for distinguishing between plants which are patentable and plant varieties which are not lies in 'the means of achieving the product concerned: a plant or animal variety is generally obtained by essentially biological processes (sexual reproduction observable in nature), while transgenic plants and animals are obtained through non-biological processes forming part of genetic engineering.'[93] For the Commission, therefore, the plant variety rights system is seen as being primarily concerned with traditional breeding methods and the development of varieties dependent on the application of those methods. In contrast, the development of plant material using non-traditional methods is seen as falling within the domain of patent law. This view is clearly at odds with the actual practice of the plant variety rights system, which does not discriminate as to method of production.

For the purposes of the Report, the main plant provisions of the Directive are Article 4 (the exclusion of plant varieties and essentially biological processes) and Recitals 29–32, although it does also discuss, in brief, Article 12.

The Report discusses the decision of the ECJ concerning the challenge to the Directive and affirms the position taken by the ECJ. It reiterates that:

> a patent cannot be granted for a plant variety, but may be for an invention if its technical feasibility is not confined to a particular plant variety . . . plant varieties are defined by their whole genome and are protected by plant variety rights . . . plant groupings of a higher taxonomic level than the variety, defined by a single gene and not by the whole genome, may be protected by patent if the relevant invention incorporates only one gene and concerns a grouping wider than a single plant variety . . . a genetic modification of a specific plant variety is not patentable but a modification of wider scope, concerning, for example, a species, may be protected by a patent.[94]

The Report does not, therefore, offer any new thoughts either on the practice of granting patents over non-variety plant material or on the potential implications of granting such patents. This is a great shame, as some forward thinking as to the potential impact of granting patents on those who are directly affected by them (such as plant breeders with little experience of the patent system) might have provided some reassurance that the Commission is interested in more than just economic consequences.

With regard to Article 12, the compulsory cross-licensing provision, the Report again merely restates the position under both the Directive and Community Regulation, stressing in respect of the latter that such grants are *only* to be made when it is in the public interest. It states that 'the Commission has examined the impact of Article 12 of the Directive on Article 29 of

---

[93] *Ibid*, p 11.
[94] *Ibid*, p 12.

Regulation 2100/94. It has already taken the necessary steps to submit to the Council any suitable proposal for overcoming this difficulty.' As the previous chapter has shown, the result of this activity was a revision of Article 29 to ensure correspondence with Article 12.

The Report does not expand either as to what the difficulties are nor on what steps have been proposed for overcoming them.

## Microbiological Processes

The Report equally does not expand on the exact distinction between a non-essentially biological processes and an essentially biological one. All that it does is to merely restate that there is a distinction, with the former being patentable (subject to the granting criteria being met) and the latter not.

## Threshold for Protection

As with the Directive, the Report only addresses the issue of the threshold required in the context of the patentability of human genetic material.

In respect of both novelty and inventive step, the Report makes it clear that there is no need to refine the ordinary meaning and application of these criteria within patent law. It does, however, make specific reference to the industrial application which must be shown and states that it is essential to the success of an application for an actual, as opposed to speculative, function to be shown.[95] The Report appears to lend full support for a narrow interpretation of sufficiency in keeping with the practice of the EPO.[96] This allows a granting office to reject applications where the claims are too broad or, following discussions with the applicant, to limit the claims to what is actually described in the patent. Patents should only then be granted on the gene sequences essential for the function described, and exclude those that are not indispensable for that function. It is still unclear whether these apply to all genetic material. The same question arises whether the stringency over the industrial application criterion applies for all types of biotechnological inventions or only for those involving human genetic material.

The Report does make a general comment relating to the granting criteria in that it is not sufficient for only one or two of the criteria to be met, but that all three have to be appropriately demonstrated within the patent application—but this merely mirrors existing practice.

---

[95] In so doing the Report approvingly cites the decision of the EPO in *ICOS/SmithKline Beecham*, above ch 5, n 57, which stated that, in respect of a gene sequence, the potential utilisation must not be speculative but specific, substantial and credible.

[96] Art 83 of the European Patent Convention lays down that a European patent application must disclose the invention in a manner sufficiently clear and complete for it to be carried out by a person skilled in the art. Furthermore, Art 84 adds that the claims must be clear and concise and be supported by the description. It should be pointed out that national law on the granting of patents contains numerous provisions identical to those contained in the European Patent Convention.

Cloning Genes

Again within the context of the patentability of inventions involving human genetic material, the Report states that, given the routine nature of cloning genes, it is likely that such clones will not be patentable as they will not meet the inventive step requirement.

Because of the human genetic material context it is not clear if the Commission intends this principle to extend to cloned genes from other living sources.

Deduction of Function via Computer

Within the same context, the Report states that where a computer is used to deduce the function of a gene, this will not comprise an inventive step and the resulting 'invention' will not be patentable. As with the issue of cloned genes, it is not clear if this principle applies only to human genetic material or if it extends across the gamut of living material.

*Ordre Public* and Morality

In an interesting statement the Report states that the morality provisions are modelled on Article 27(2) of the TRIPs Agreement. In so doing it is not clear if this reference is to the Article as a whole or only to paragraph 1; either way, this is an odd claim to make for the two provisions are actually quite different. In respect of Article 6(1) it is much more clearly based on Article 53(a) EPC, in that it simply refers to a general requirement not to grant patents over inventions the commercial exploitation of which would be contrary to *ordre public* or morality—neither Article 53(a) nor Article 6(1) making any further reference to the need to protect human, plant or animal health nor the need to protect the environment. Equally, if the assertion is in respect of Article 6(2) it is still odd, as Article 6(2) focuses on very specific aspects of bioscience research (mainly relating to the use of human genetic material and the need to avoid undue suffering to animals). What Article 6(2) does not do is to mention the need to protect plant health or the environment. It could be argued that the Report is actually referring to the Recitals to the Directive and, in particular, Recital 36, but it does seem rather clumsy drafting not to make this clear in the text of the Report, especially given a) that other Recitals are specifically mentioned and b) there is ongoing confusion over the status of the Recitals.

The Scope of Protection Conferred

The Report provides an exhaustive statement referring to various Recitals within the Directive which can serve to limit the scope of the patent granted. It recognises that there are legitimate concerns over the scope of some patents and in light of technological advances, that there is a need for further review of the scope of protection granted. The Report singles out patents granted on inventions involving DNA sequences, proteins derived from those sequences and those based on ESTs and on SNPs for specific consideration. It does not make any specific mention of plant material.

In its conclusion, the Report reinforces the statements made in the Recitals to the Directive that the Directive both provides appropriate support for European bioscience[97] and also 'takes account of society's concerns.' In so doing, the Articles of the Directive 'comply strictly with the ethical rules recognised in the European Community.'

In summary, the findings of the Report are disappointing, for all that it appears to do is to reiterate the provisions of the Directive, affirm the decision in the Dutch challenge and to reinforce the view that the primary driving force lying behind the patent law initiatives is the need to provide a plethora of European patents for biotechnological inventions which can match the applications and grants made in the US.[98] There is one promising comment, and that is that the Report admits that '[r]egular assessment [of intellectual property rights] will be needed to determine whether the patent system is meeting the needs of researchers and companies.'

What is of more concern is the impression conveyed by the inclusion of several Annexes to the Report which compare European bio-patenting activity with that of the US.[99] The comparison is not entirely favourable, with the Commission focusing on the fact that in the US there has been almost a doubling of patent activity to that in the EPO.[100] In the view of the Commission this means that EU member states are not protecting their European markets as they should. The implication is that the Commission expects the introduction of the Directive to play a critical role in levelling patenting activity by ensuring the grant of more patents over bio-inventions.

The clear commercial focus of the Commission's Report appears to be out of step with views expressed elsewhere that the number of patent grants is, in fact,

---

[97] And in this the Commission directly links the function and effect of the Directive with the needs of the 'life science' industry as set down in an earlier Commission document, *Life Sciences and Biotechnology: A Strategy for Europe*, COM (2002) 27 final.

[98] The annexes to the Report provide comparative tables indicating the differences in both research and patenting practices, with the clear inference that unless a more open patenting practice is adopted across the EU it will fall behind in bioscience research, and by extension, in access to the new products. The fact that by adopting a less rigorous approach to the granting of patents, which arguably will be the result of both encouraging more applications and ensuring an increase in grants, will be a lessening of certainty as to what can be protected and predictability that the right once granted is not overly vulnerable to challenge in the courts.

[99] In assessing the figures provided by the Commission, consideration must be given to the fact that it does focus on EPO applications whilst providing details of US and Japanese grants. Whilst it is still clear that the US is granting more patents, the fact that fewer are granted in Europe does not necessarily mean that Europe is providing an inappropriate patenting environment but can also be attributed to other factors such as attrition, loss of market and merger.

[100] Above n 91, p 34.

likely to decrease as it becomes harder to demonstrate an inventive step.[101] If the Commission is intent on increasing the numbers of patents granted then it can only be presumed that this will be achieved by reducing the threshold for protection. If this is correct, and granting offices comply with the edict to grant more patents, then not only will this mean that patents will be granted over more obvious inventions, but (and possibly more worrying for industry) this could be at variance with the thinking of national courts which might be unwilling to accept a lower threshold for protection. The result could be that any rights granted under such a policy would be more vulnerable to challenge.

## V. OTHER RELATED EU LEGISLATION

As mentioned in chapter 1, the European Commission has recently introduced legislation permitting the extension of a patent term for certain inventions involving medicinal and plant protection products—supplementary protection certificates.[102] This supplementary protection can be sought over medicinal drugs or plant innovations in the form of agrichemicals. The function of the extension is to allow those engaged in these areas to benefit from the patent if the period of exploitation is reduced as a result of the various regulatory approval mechanisms which have to be passed before the product can enter the market place.

Initially, these certificates were introduced to address the problem of providing appropriate protection for pharmaceutical products which only reached the market towards the end of the patent term due to the time taken to secure regulatory approval. The consequence of this protection for the patient is that it may take years before the product actually reaches the market place. In patent law terms this could mean a significant reduction in the value of the patent granted (this usually having been achieved before the drug is presented for approval). In 1992 the EU issued Council Regulation 1768/92 which enables member states to grant a supplementary protection certificate when it can be shown that the delay between the date of patent grant and the date of authorisation is such that the patent holder warrants an additional period of protection. Even where the delay is extensive the maximum period which can be added to the lifetime of the patent is 5 years. The EPC also contains such a provision enabling national patent offices to extend the term of the patent granted, provided, of course, that the original patent concerned has designated that country.[103] This principle has now been extended to agrichemicals. What is as yet uncertain is the extent to which this may have an impact on plant breeding practices—what is clear is that

---

[101] This is also the view of Andrew Sheard (chair of the Intellectual Property Committee for the British BioIndustry Association) and the UK Patent Office, above ch 5, n 63.

[102] Regulation No 1768/92 concerning the creation of a supplementary protection certificate for medicinal products, and Regulation No 1610/96 concerning the creation of a supplementary protection certificate for plant protection products.

[103] Art 63.

those engaged in agrichemical plant research of the kind set out in the Regulation could now look forward to an extension of rights previously available only to the plant pharma industry. Any other invention involving plant material which does not fall within the definition of material covered by the Regulation will not attract the supplementary protection. In order to qualify for the certificate, the applicant has to already have a patent and must also be able to show that they have secured the necessary authorisation. Whatever the value of the invention concerned, the maximum duration of the certificate will be five years (and this is irrespective of the actual duration of the authorisation process). At present these certificates are of only limited value to plant researchers, however, it has been suggested that their use should be extended to transgenic plants,[104] but this is currently only a suggestion and there is no indication that the Commission will further extend protection in this way. If it does so then it would have the effect of providing protection, in certain instances, of a duration roughly commensurate with that provided under the Community Plant Variety Rights Regulation.

As discussed in chapter 2, in 2004, and as a response to the concerns raised at Doha, the EU decided to introduce legislation which would permit member states to issue compulsory licences permitting companies within that territory to manufacture medicinal products which are under patent provided that a) the manufacture is for export and b) that export is to a third country which has insufficient or no manufacturing capacity in the pharmaceutical sector.[105] This new law will, therefore, not apply to the production of pharmaceutical products for use within the European Union.

## VI. THE RESPONSE FROM INDUSTRY

Much has been written about the Directive from the perspective of patent lawyers and the pharmaceutical industry and very little about the reaction of those engaged in plant research. As a result, a myth has arisen that the principles[106] underlying the Directive have not been welcomed by plant breeders. This myth can be dispelled, to an extent, by looking at one of the very few official statements made—this came from the International Seed Federation.[107]

It has welcomed the decision to clarify the position of biotechnological inventions. In its view, patents are 'the most appropriate form of protection' for the results of biotechnological research and it is happy that sequences or partial

---

[104] See Kock, *Intellectual Property Protection for Plant Innovation Conference on Intellectual Property Protection for Plant Innovation* (Frankfurt, 2004); see www.forum-institut.de.

[105] COM (2004) 737, Proposal for a Regulation of the European Parliament and of the Council on compulsory licensing of patents relating to the manufacture of pharmaceutical products for export to countries with public health problems.

[106] As will be seen, whilst there is support for strong protection for the results of plant research, this is tempered by concerns over the impact of these rights on plant breeding in practice.

[107] www.worldseed.org.

sequences of genes are patentable, provided they meet the usual requirements of patentability. It has stated, however, that it is not part of the patent law framework to permit protection for a mere DNA sequence the function of which has not been disclosed. Interestingly, the ISF also welcomes the fact that for a function to be recognised as such it must be specific to the matter claimed and 'that it must be credible for a person of ordinary skill and be practical, meaning attributing a real world value to the claimed invention.' The reason why this is interesting is that this expectation is clearly based on granting office practice and not the Directive, which has no such 'real world value' requirement. The ISF also supports the patenting of material which previously occurred in nature; for some this might appear odd, but actually this is an understandable stance to take. The plant variety rights system specifically permits the protection of previously existing material in the form of discoveries, provided the threshold for protection is met. The approach of the ISF is simply an extension of prior practice. The ISF also supports the extension of rights to material into which the patented technology has been placed, provided it performs the patented function and also to material produced using a patented process, Support for these provisions might lessen in light of the potential impact of these on some of the core European plant researchers, a fact which the ISF has yet to either recognise or acknowledge.

## VII. CONCLUSION

It is clear that the European Commission, on behalf of the EU, is taking a very proactive approach to providing patent protection for all types of bio-inventions. The Directive and the EU Report both indicate a strong commitment to both securing patent protection for the broadest range of bio-inventions as well as ensuring that there is parity of provision across the whole of the EU. What is not so clear is the extent to which this action takes the form of full and unstoppable commitment to patenting more and excluding less, irrespective of the impact on either the threshold for protection or on specific sectors of bio-research. In terms of the former, there would appear to be a conflict between the views of those such as the UK Patent Office who believe that fewer patents will be granted as it will be increasingly difficult to demonstrate an inventive step and that of the Commission, as expressed in the first Report on the Directive, that more patents must be granted as these provide a direct point of comparison between the levels of bioscience research in the EU, the US and Japan. It seems obvious to those involved in patent law that such a growth in patents granted can only be at the expense of the threshold for protection, with possibly indirect (or direct) pressure being brought to be bear by the Commission to encourage granting offices to grant patents even where there is minimal measurable inventiveness. In respect of the impact on a given sector, the Commission has had its focus primarily on providing suitable protection for the pharmaceutical industry. In so doing, the Directive has been drafted to take account of all the various types of activities which this sector might engage in. This ambitious remit has meant that there is little evidence of any attention being paid to the needs of the other key sector reliant on using biological material, plant innovators. As the next chapter will show, in contrast to the pharmaceutical companies, most plant breeders have little prior experience of using patents and there is therefore great potential for a significant impact on plant research. The Directive does contain a number of provisions which could cause concern. In particular, the scope of protection granted by a patent over plant-related genetic material and the derogations to that right (or lack thereof) might have considerable significance for the work of plant researchers (these will be discussed further in chapter 9). There also remains the equally pressing matter of how the Directive will interrelate with the plant variety rights system.

The last set of chapters have shown that the appearance of a coherent and agreed European system of plant protection is deceptive. There is no consistency over the availability of patent protection for inventions involving genetic material (as epitomised by the resistance to the implementation of the Directive). However, the resistance to implementing the Directive is predominantly based on concerns about patenting human genetic material and access to important new medical breakthroughs rather than the modification of plants and the non-medical applications of such plants. The hiatus in providing protection could be detrimental to those seeking to develop, and widely disseminate, new plant-related inventions. However, it is equally correct to state that, notwithstanding the Community Regulation, there is no parity of national practice regarding plant variety rights, with the laws of only seven of the pre-accession date states currently based on the 1991 UPOV Act, the six others being based on either the 1961/72 or 1978 Acts, and one member state, Greece, having no national provision at all.[108] All of these go to create an impression of continuing incoherent provision which, in theory at least, might not serve to provide the appropriate legislative environment breeders might need to carry on with their research work.

In looking at these developments, we have identified a number of issues arising out of the recent legislative initiatives which might cause problems when the policies are put into practice. The question has to be asked, however, whether the concerns raised are shared by breeders. To correlate the academic and the professional opinions, the next chapter will discuss a number of studies conducted both prior to the recent legislative action, and immediately following its introduction, the focus of which was determining the views of plant breeders over plant property provision.

---

[108] Of the ten new Accession States, eight are members of UPOV 91.

# 8

# *The Views of European Plant Breeders*

## I. INTRODUCTION

ONE OF THE justifications for revisions to plant property provision is that it is necessary in order to meet the changing needs of those engaged in research and development. This begs the question whether the needs of European plant breeders have actually been met. For those who have witnessed the increase in plant breeding activity since the 1960s, there is a direct correlation between this growth and the availability of plant property rights.[1] Over the years a number of attempts have been made to assess the use made of the rights and to identify those areas where further legislative activity might be needed. These 'surveys' have sometimes taken the form of legislative overviews (such as that undertaken by the WIPO in 1987) whilst in other instances the studies have looked at the use and attitudes of the breeders themselves. These results of empirical research are important, for they serve to determine whether the issues identified by non-users as potentially problematic are regarded as such by the users themselves. They also demonstrate a continuum of views as to the appropriateness and effectiveness of the systems available to plant breeders. This chapter will outline the results of some of the key studies undertaken.

## II. ASSESSING THE VIEWS OF PLANT BREEDERS[2]

In keeping with the original principle that the rights should reflect the needs of the industry, understanding and responding to the views of plant breeders has played an integral part in the evolution of plant variety rights. To this end the

---

[1] See, eg, www.upov.int and bspb.co.uk. The same correlation can be found on the websites of other organisations representing the interests of plant breeders. What is significant is that whilst there is a further clear increase in private sector plant breeding (and private property rights tend to favour private interests), there is a clear concern to ensure that attracting private sector investment is not at the expense of public sector plant breeding—and this is an issue which needs to be borne in mind when addressing the matter of the effectiveness and appropriateness of plant property provision.

[2] The following studies are included to indicate the types of investigations taking place within Europe during the 1980s, and they not intended to represent all this work.

various organisations which represent the views of plant breeders[3] have been closely involved in the discussions leading up the introduction (and subsequent revisions) of the UPOV Convention as well as in those leading up to the introduction and operation of the Community Regulation. Indeed, the gradual increase in strength of protection provided could be said to underline a growing acceptance of, and need for, these rights by those engaged in the research. On the basis of this it is easy to paint a picture of the plant variety rights system as an inclusive, and therefore sector-reflective, system of protection.

In contrast, the patent system was not designed with a specific sector and type of subject matter in mind, but was in fact predicated on the reverse. It is a system of protection which has been designed *not* to take account of the 'special' nature of either an industry or a subject matter, but instead its function is to treat all innovative activity as the same. It is for this reason that the EPC, for example, is open-textured, with the emphasis on *how* protection can be secured (through demonstrating novelty and so on) rather than on *what* can be protected. This sector-neutral aspect of patent law has, of course, been undermined to an extent through the introduction of the Directive (and its adoption by the EPO) as this, arguably, introduced additional requirements which go beyond that required from other sectors seeking patent protection.[4] What has not altered is the presumption of patentability and the principle that it is the interests of the individual inventor which must be protected.

The recent strengthening (or 'patentisation') of plant variety rights, together with the developments in patent law, have provided a new order of protection, the extent and type of which goes beyond that experienced by many of the plant breeders engaged in European plant breeding work. Ostensibly the justification for each development has been to foster research work and protect the interests of those engaged in bioscience research. Whilst many engaged in plant research have welcomed these developments, the issue remains whether these changes will have the desired effect and continue to provide a suitable environment within which European plant breeders can continue to develop new plant innovations.

As already mentioned, there have been a number of attempts over the years to assess the views of European plant breeders. For example, in 1954 (pre-UPOV), the Organisation for European Economic Co-operation (OEEC) conducted a survey of seed production across Europe.[5] The results of the survey indicated that the differences in national plant variety protection provision were having an impact of the developments of new varieties, and the recommendation of the OEEC was that steps must be taken to ensure that breeders were pro-

---

[3] Such as ASSINSEL, CIOPORA and FIS.

[4] Examples of this include the requirement to demonstrate a specific, substantial and credible function, the exclusion of specific categories of genetic material (irrespective of how beneficial in practice these innovations might be) and the imposition of compulsory cross-licences.

[5] Seed Production, Testing and Distribution in European Countries OEEC Technical Assistance Mission No 106, January 1954.

vided with appropriate protection for their research work. The study did not identify what it thought the form of that 'appropriate protection' should be (whether via patent law or through the introduction of a *sui generis* right); however, as the OEEC report was published at the same time as the first discussions which led to UPOV and the EPC (the initial discussions of which were equally unclear as to the best method to protect plant innovations) this is not surprising. Clearly all interested parties were feeling the way round the issue with caution. Equally, as chapter 3 shows, a number of countries set up national committees to look at the possibility of providing proper protection for plant material, such committees usually comprising an active membership from the plant breeding community (broadly defined).[6]

These studies continued even once the rights were in place. For example, in 1985 the Dutch National Council for Agricultural Research published a study on plant breeders' rights and patent rights in relation to plant genetic engineering.[7] This study did not involve a survey of plant breeders; however, the research team did include a number of plant breeders as well as representatives from the Dutch plant variety rights granting office, the Dutch patent office, and various government and research council members. The study was intended to identify discrepancies in provision between patents and plant variety rights with a view to making recommendations as to possible ways forward. The study was generally supportive both of the new technologies and of the rights used to protect the tangible results. However, it primarily confined its support to those situations where the rights were not used in a way which restricted access to protected material. The modern-day relevance of the study lies in the fact that the main areas of concern that were first raised in the 1950s continue to surround the two systems today. In particular, it raises concerns over the potential impact of patents on the ability of breeders to use patented material in research programmes, the demarcation between excluded and included material within patent law (with resonances of the later EPO decision in *PGS*, the study queried whether an individual plant could be regarded as the first representative of a variety), the problems with the threshold for patent protection and also the potential for using a patent granted over an individual gene to create 'an absolute barrier' for the use of varieties by breeders and growers.

This study (which raised more questions than provided answers) drew five main conclusions. The first was that as, at that time, the use of patents within agriculture was not common, more work needed to be undertaken as to the impact of change within patent law over protectable material on users (and

---

[6] For example, see the UK's Engholm Committee on Transactions in Seeds, which reported in 1960: 'Plant Breeders' Rights Report of the Committee on Transactions in Seeds' (Cmnd 1092, HMSO, 1960). Its advisers included representatives from the Cambridge Plant Breeding Institute, Grassland Institute, Horticultural Institution, National Institute of Agricultural Botany, and National Vegetable Research Station.

[7] Study 14dE, National Council for Agricultural Research, *Plant Breeders' Rights and Patent Rights in Relation to Plant Genetic Engineering* (The Hague, 1985).

specifically scientists and farmers). The second was that where large numbers of patents created barriers to use (primarily use by the farming community) then consideration should be given to assisting farmers to bring opposition proceedings against the grant. The third was that consideration should be given to removing any obstacles to using patented plant material in commercial breeding programmes (and that this should be introduced at the international level). The fourth was that of the issue of novelty and, in particular, problems meeting the disclosure requirement pre-patent filing from the perspective of the academic community (then the dominant type of plant researcher). Finally, the issue of secrecy versus public knowledge needed to be addressed. As can be seen, not one of these recommendations has been heeded within the modern plant protection scheme.

The Netherlands was not alone during this period in trying to evaluate the likely impact of the growth of private property rights on the use of plant material. In 1988 the UK's Common Law Institute of Intellectual Property (CLIP)[8] commissioned a study on the legal protection of plant material. In 1998 the International Seed Federation (in one of its former guises as ASSINSEL) undertook a further study of its members[9] and in 1999 it published a position paper on the Development of New Plant Varieties and Protection of Intellectual Property.[10] Other jurisdictions also indicated interest in undertaking such surveys but it is unclear if such studies actually took place (for example, in 1987 the German Minister of Justice indicated that he wanted a survey conducted of the views of German plant breeders). In addition to these studies, other mechanisms have been used to collect the views of those interested in plant protection. These have included involving organisations representing the views of plant breeders in the giving of evidence to various national committees on the question of patent protection for biotechnological inventions.[11]

As will be seen below, reassuringly for those who have been responsible for developing the modern forms of both rights, each study has found a general welcome within the plant breeding community for the use of strong private

---

[8] In 1995 renamed the Intellectual Property Institute (IPI).

[9] Argentina, Australia, Austria, Belgium, Brazil, Canada, Chile, Croatia, the Czech Republic, Denmark, Finland, France, Germany, the Netherlands, India, Ireland, Israel, Italy, Japan, Kenya, Norway, New Zealand, Poland, Slovakia, South Africa, Sweden, Switzerland, the UK and the US.

[10] www.worldseed.org.

[11] For example, see the 'Report of the UK's House of Lords Select Committee on the European Communities on Patent Protection for Biotechnological Inventions' (HL Paper, 1994), which contains evidence from, amongst others, the Agricultural and Food Research Council, the Bio-industry Association, British Association of Plant Breeders and National Farmers Union. Obviously within such a context views would vary and whilst the studies involving those who represent plant breeders who made most use of plant variety rights wished to keep the exclusion of plant variety rights, those engaged in patent law, such as the Chartered Institute of Patent Agents, made it clear that they would like to see the exclusion removed. See Briefing Paper on the Patentability and EC Proposals on Plant Varieties 1993 submitted to the Select Committee and reproduced on p 61. Other such studies were also being conducted outside Europe; see, eg, Butler and Marion, *The Impacts of Patent Protection on the US Seed Industry and Public Plant Breeding Industry* (University of Wisconsin Press, 1985).

property rights to protect the results of plant research activity. They also all agree that the demarcation between the protectable subject matter under each system should be retained and, in particular, that the express exclusion of plant varieties within patent law should be kept. They all equally stress that a robust use of the patent system to protect plant material other than varieties should not be at the expense of breeders wishing to use this patented material and, in particular, that the issue of the use of patented material in commercial breeding programmes needed to be specifically addressed. The way in which the studies proposed that these matters should be resolved did, however, differ. For example the Dutch study recommended that compulsory licences *should* (emphasis added) be granted in order to enable the breeding and exploitation of new plant varieties whilst, nearly 20 years later, the ISF (using the 1988 ASSINSEL study as its basis), indicated little support for a liberal use of the compulsory licensing provision. However, the ASSINSEL position paper did state that there should be an unrestricted use of the patented technology for *breeding purposes* (whether commercial or not), but that any exploitation of the resulting variety should be subject to a licence[12] (as we saw in chapter 6, the patent system does not draw a distinction between use for commercial research and subsequent exploitation: both are taken to be a commercial use and subject to authorisation from the patent holder).

Of particular interest are three studies, one undertaken within the UK by the Common Law Institute of Intellectual Property in 1988, one conducted 10 years later by ASSINSEL in 1999 of all its breeder members, and a third, which took place shortly after the ASSINSEL study, which was funded by the EU as part of its Fourth Framework Programme which focused on European plant breeders. In addition to their representing local as well as international opinion, these three studies provide an insight into the views of breeders both before- and after-the introduction of the 1991 UPOV Act, the Community Regulation and the EU Directive.

## The CLIP Study

In 1988 the UK Common Law Institute of Intellectual Property Law commissioned the Intellectual Property Law Unit of Queen Mary College, University of London, to look at the legal protection of life-forms.[13] A small survey of the views of the British plant breeding industry was undertaken as part of this project. The findings of the survey have not been published before and the IPI has very kindly given us permission to use the survey information here.[14] The

---

[12] It did not say if this should be automatically granted; however ,as the statement that exploitation of any variety which contains patented traits should be subject to a licence is followed by a clause stating that ASSINSEL members are not generally in favour of compulsory licences, it would seem that the licence to exploit would not be automatic.

[13] The researchers were Dr Noel Byrne and Margaret Llewelyn.

[14] The questionnaire and results can be found in Llewelyn, *The Legal Protection of New Plant Varieties* (PhD thesis, University College of Wales, Aberystwyth, 1990).

conclusions drawn from the results are, however, ours, and should not be taken as reflecting those of either Dr Byrne nor any other person (or organisation) associated with either the survey or with CLIP/IPI. In addition, it is important to bear in mind that such a localised survey should not be taken as indicative of the views of the wider European plant breeding community. As can be seen, the scope of the survey was relatively limited.

The CLIP study was the first time that UK plant breeders had been questioned directly about the legal protection of plant material. The objective of the study was to obtain a snapshot of attitudes towards plant protection and therefore it did not seek to provide any detailed evaluation of either the rights themselves or the attitudes of those who used them. The objective was to identify if there were any matters which CLIP (or other bodies responsible for plant property provision) needed to explore further as part of the then European review of provision. It is not proposed to go into the findings of the survey in great detail, as much of the information is obviously now out of date, and the law, and its use, has moved on considerably in the 16 years since it was undertaken. However, it is useful to briefly outline the then views on the relative merits of plant variety rights (at that time governed by the Plant Varieties and Seeds Act 1964) and patent protection (under the Patents Act 1977) because, as will be seen, there is some correlation between the concerns expressed in the 1980s and those which remain today.

Over 200 companies (which ranged from multinational to independent breeder) were sent a questionnaire; of these 53 replied. The ASSINSEL study does not state how many participated in its survey, but the relatively low return rate mirrors that of the EU study. As will been seen, one of the main reasons for this is the extent to which breeders feel removed from the issues relating to plant property provision—something which most other bio-inventors do not experience as there is a more overt relationship between the intended outcome and patent law, not least because of the need a) to preserve novelty and b) to trace the inventive step. Both the public and private sectors highlighted the need to educate researchers as to the value of intellectual property rights (although not usually defined to include plant variety rights).

Experience and Use of Plant Variety Rights

The majority of the breeders (39) had experience of using plant variety rights. Of these most, 32, were happy with the criteria used to determine grant, although seven did indicate dissatisfaction with the distinctness criterion and wanted the test to be made more stringent. There were concerns that merely cosmetic differences were being used to show a distance between an existing protected variety and one bred from that variety. The breeders so concerned called for greater use to be made of emerging technologies such as genetic fingerprinting.[15] There

---

[15] As has been shown in ch 3, policy makers are still reluctant to use genetic fingerprinting to determine distinctness *at grant*, although it is felt useful in determining whether a variety is essentially derived.

were also calls for the system to be opened up to more species, although this came primarily from the ornamental breeders, with only one agricultural plant breeder making the request. This was an interesting result because at the time of the CLIP survey a number of agricultural crops were excluded from protection[16] and yet breeders were continuing with breeding programmes involving these species. The impression provided by the CLIP survey is that there was little support in the UK for the expansion of protection to all species and yet clearly the signal being sent to UPOV was that such an expansion was both desired and desirable.[17] Of all those surveyed, rose breeders expressed the most dissatisfaction with the existing provision. Their dissatisfaction lay in problems relating to distinctiveness (both in acquiring the right and also in defending it against mere cosmetic variations) and also in the scope of the right granted (which was, at that time, limited to the reproductive material of the variety).[18]

In terms of usage, plant variety rights were widely used by breeders both locally in the UK and abroad. When asked why they used the plant variety rights system the majority of breeders, 27, indicated that they did so because there was no alternative available and not because it was necessarily the best system of protection. Where another form of protection was available, however, only six of these 27 said that they would use plant variety rights in preference to that other system of protection on the basis that it was the better form of protection. In 1988, therefore, there was some evidence that, in the UK at least, not all breeders felt that plant variety rights were the best or most appropriate form of protection for their needs. The 21 breeders who indicated that an alternative system might be better came from a range of plant breeding backgrounds. The questionnaire did not ask them to identify the form of the alternative protection, but some of the additional comments indicated that the breeders felt that the protection they were able to secure was not as robust as that provided under the patent system. There was also little evidence within the responses themselves that the breeders were aware of the activities within either the EU or even UPOV which were intended to strengthen the right provided. Those breeders who did support the use of patent protection did so on the basis that it protected more aspects of the invention and was a more suitable means of preventing companies from producing closely competing copies.

Regarding the seeking of advice in order to obtain and protect their rights, five of the respondents had in-house IP expertise, with the majority, 26, relying on the Plant Variety Rights Office for advice. Of these 26, 12 relied solely upon the Office, with the others (14) seeking additional advice, including consulting patent agents. The responses indicated a heavy reliance upon the advice given, almost to the point that there was no self-awareness of the nature of the rights

---

[16] See ch 3.

[17] As has already been seen this was achieved via the revision of the UPOV Convention in 1991.

[18] This dissatisfaction appears generic to this particular group of breeders, and organisations such as CIOPORA have long sought to secure a remedy. See the views expressed previously by Royon www.ciopora.org.

themselves. For example, many of the 26 breeders appeared confused as to what was protectable subject matter and were not aware of the precise legal status of plant material, and of varieties in particular. The breeders freely admitted this lack of awareness and in all instances stated that this was not a problem but rather that it was more appropriate for them to be guided by the granting offices and legal professionals. That there should have been a lack of detailed knowledge of the law is not surprising nor should any undue emphasis be placed upon it. Most users of intellectual property rights will not be knowledgeable as to the letter of the law. The most important factor is that those who used the system (and for whose benefit the system was introduced) were aware that protection was available and that there were experts whose opinion could be relied upon in securing and protecting rights granted.

The main problems which the breeders identified with the system were mostly to do with administrative or technical issues. The chief complaint with the system was that obtaining and protecting the right was too prohibitive in cost and time terms. The breeders' main suggestions for revising plant variety rights reflected these concerns over cost and time (and related to reducing both the cost and also the extent of the technical examination (this latter being an interesting recommendation given the concerns over permitting protection for varieties with dubious distinctiveness). Only two suggestions were made relating to the technical criteria—and these came from only the handful of breeders (less than ten in total) who identified areas for possible improvement. These were to open up the system to more species and to allow a breeder to provide more of his own research data to granting offices in order to assist in assessing whether a variety is distinct, uniform and stable.

Nearly all those who responded expressed general satisfaction with the plant variety rights system; it was seen as 'working well' and, whilst in need of some amendment, was 'fundamentally fair to breeders, seedsmen and the consumer.' Because of this there was no support for doing away with the plant breeders' rights system, and concern was expressed that if more than one right were available then this would cause confusion: '[i]t is better to maintain one system in order to have the greatest uniformity possible in the laws concerned with plant protection, and avoid problems of interfacing separate methods.' However, the breeders did not totally rule out acquiring patent protection in certain instances. It was recognised that for certain products and processes, patents could provide the type of protection necessary for the inventor, but plant varieties were not seen as coming into this category. The two systems were not seen as mutually exclusive, but rather co-existent, protecting different aspects of plant material, breeders saying that they 'would use both patents and plant breeders' rights . . . the method would depend on the variety/use/market and the breeder's needs.'

Experience and Use of the Patent System

Only nine of the breeders had had any experience of the patent system. In contrast to the popular perception of the patent system, as being only within the reach of the multinationals, those with experience ranged from independent breeders, through agricultural concerns to large pharmaceuticals (with the latter companies admitting that they had, at that time, little involvement in plant *breeding* as such, but nonetheless indicating a growing involvement in plant-related research programmes). Size and business interests do not, therefore, seem to have acted as a barrier to patent protection. There was a similar range to be seen in respect of the type of patented material, from pot plant production, polymer water absorbers, and clips for use on canes to medicine-related products. In total, these nine companies held between them nearly 200 patents, the majority of which had been obtained in the US. Of these, two related to plant genes and 20 to plants and seeds; all of these were US patents. Of the nine companies, two said that they had encountered any problems in using the patent system. This can be compared with seven breeders who said that they had had problems with the plant variety rights system (these problems relating to demonstrating distinctness). In common with breeders' rights, the main problem was the cost and time involved in acquiring a patent. One breeder also specified lack of information over protecting a patent once acquired as a problem, but neither the source (for example whether it was a multinational or an SME) nor the specific nature of this problem was identified in the questionnaire concerned.

The impression provided by the responses to this section was that whilst the actual use of the patent system by plant breeders was limited, this did not necessarily mean that the system was inherently unsuitable for use by the plant breeding industry. Instead, as one then new user of the patent system said, 'it . . . needs to be penetrated in terms of breaking down barriers created through perception and a lack of information . . . . Simply because little or nothing is known about patent protection does not make it wrong for the protection of plant material including possibly plant varieties.' However, not all breeders agreed that a greater use of patent protection should be at the expense of the ban on patenting plant varieties.

Possibly because experience of the patent system was limited, but also perhaps due to the emerging publicity surrounding the issue of patenting living material, the breeders were more vocal in presenting their views on patents than they had been in respect of plant variety rights. In terms of patentable subject matter, 23 breeders said that they wanted patent protection for genes, 15 that the ban on patenting plant varieties should be lifted and 11 said that in the event of the lifting of the ban they would seek patent protection for varieties in preference to the variety right. In contrast, 12 said that they would prefer genes not to be patentable, 17 that the ban should remain and 11 that they would not seek patents in preference to variety rights should that option be available. Ten did not feel able to express an opinion. There was general support for patenting genes but a split as to whether patent protection should be accorded to varieties: an outcome also seen in the EU project.

A number of reasons were given as to why the ban on patenting plant varieties should be removed. These included that, as agriculture is industrial, and the patent system is there to protect novel and inventive industrial applications, then patents should be available for all types of agricultural innovation. In addition, patents provided 'protection to permit commercialization' and were therefore necessary to 'free the market' for plant breeders. Those who supported the extension of patent protection in general also held the view that protection under plant variety rights was limited and did 'not offer protection for gene insertion', nor 'protection for novel material' which the research and development warranted. One breeder did say that his preference for the exclusion to be removed was based on the fact that 'plant breeders' rights doesn't cover the extraction of chemical products [for industrial use]' but added that 'if plant [variety] protection were strengthened to cover this area then he,' 'would support the ban.' This is an interesting statement given that whilst such material was not protectable under plant variety rights it would have been patentable (provided the threshold for protection had been met). Interestingly, only one of the companies calling for the exclusion to be removed was a multinational. Most of those wishing to see the exclusion removed were small groups of breeders involved in specialist breeding. In addition, there was some support for protecting plant species via the patent system. This, as may be recollected, was the view of those drafting the Directive (which took place at the same time as the survey) and it can be seen that there was some support for this within the plant breeding community. However, this support for retaining the divergence of protection has to be read against the then current draft of the Directive which, as shown in chapter 6, at that time provided for the possibility of patenting varieties. There was a common theme to the views expressed supporting a greater use of patent law and that this use was seen as a benefit to breeding programmes and the production of market-valuable new plant products. Those breeders who wished to see the ban deleted envisaged the patent system as an easier system to use. The US system featured as the main influence, which would increase plant breeding activity, making UK breeders more competitive thereby reducing the number of foreign-bred varieties sold in the UK. Patent protection would also remove the farmer's privilege and reduce, if not completely alleviate, unauthorised use of protected material. Income would be increased with the greater use of royalties and licences.

But for every breeder who supported a greater use of patents there was another who wished the opposite. Those who said that the exclusion should remain argued that 'experience shows exercising and enforcing rights under the present system works well, patent law would be expensive in comparison and the existing requirements for patentability do not fit so well when applied to plant varieties. Breeders make use of "state of the art" knowledge. The presence of an inventive step is possibly questionable and industrial applicability is not in issue.' Not only was the ability of plant varieties to meet the patent-granting criteria questioned by the plant breeders, but also the general effects on the industry itself were raised, 'there is a risk that patenting could give too much power and allow control of food' and that patents could 'possibly stop people (trade) growing our protected varieties under licence.' The issue of the ability to use patented material in research was also raised: 'the likely effect on the use of material in future breeding programmes and the likelihood that the restrictions would slow overall scientific progress,' and other replies talked of 'restricting', 'complicating', and 'curtailing access to patented material.' The breeders also mentioned concerns about the impact on the farming community: 'patenting genes will lead to monopoly control by very large multinational organisations and may result in expensive seed to farmers.' 'Too much power in too few hands' was another common theme, and particular concern was expressed over patents being granted for species of plants where the introduction of one gene can be said to be the 'creation' of the patent holder.[19] For others the concern was that adding patent protection to the group of rights available would be 'an unnecessary complication' and cause problems when trying to obtain access to material. Some of the comments coming from the larger breeders indicated concerns that a push towards a greater use of the patent system could cause problems for the small breeders because of the cost implications relating to both acquisition and protection of the right.

The breeders who wanted to retain clear distinctions between the two rights and protectable subject matter fell into two groups, those who wished to retain the breeders' rights system exactly as it was and those who wanted it strengthened.

Those who wanted to keep the status quo gave as their reasons cost-effectiveness and the fact that seed prices could be kept at a reasonable level, thereby increasing the choice of new varieties for farmers and growers. The law also allowed the free availability of protected varieties in breeding programmes, assisting new breeders to engage in further research programmes. Some breeders felt that the system should be minimally extended to include other plant material including genes.

Those who wanted to see a strengthened form of plant variety right gave their reasons as being that it would lead to a greater exchange of germplasm and varieties. The system was seen as less administratively and legally problematic and better geared to the needs of the small plant breeder. Overall, improving the system would mean making plant breeding more worthwhile, as some breeders could not be 'bothered to register new plants as there is hardly any protection at all' but the breeders who expressed this view also made it clear that they would not seek patent protection even if it was available.

---

[19] It is interesting to note that the breeders were aware that a legal distinction could be drawn between a variety which is excluded and a species which could be patented. This awareness was not as visible in the PIP project results.

When asked if, given the option, they would choose plant breeders' rights over patents, the majority said that if they were provided with a strengthened form of plant breeders' right they would choose plant variety rights over patent protection. This is not a surprising response as most of the breeders surveyed had experience of plant breeders' rights but not of patents. It is understandable to opt for the known over the unknown and also to wish to retain the status quo rather than going for change. The reasons for preferring breeders' rights over patents were varied and ranged from general preference because 'plant breeders' rights provides greater protection' to more specific comments such as that breeders' rights allow 'varieties to be used as parents in a breeding programme and insists that varieties are distinct.' However, one breeder did state that the choice as to which system right to acquire would depend on whether the species is one 'where farm saved seed is not important.' Other breeders said that if they had the choice then which system they would use would depend on the particular variety and on where they wished to exploit it. Those who would choose patents over plant breeders' rights gave their reasons as 'wider scope', 'better protection' and 'it would give maximum control over the use of the material.' The need for freedom of access to protected material was central to all answers irrespective of whether the breeder was for or against breeders' rights and concern was expressed by nearly all the breeders that unless this was taken into account the patent system would prove too monopolistic for the plant breeding industry, given its reliance on a wide range of sources for use in new breeding programmes.

In conclusion, the breeders did not commit themselves to one right in sole preference to the other. The main view was that both systems of protection should be available and the breeder allowed a choice as to which is the most suitable for their needs, but this was predominantly contingent on there being a strengthening of the plant variety rights system. It would be wrong to draw this as a conclusive picture of the views of the breeders, as many often contradicted themselves in their answers—one thing is clear and that is in 1989 the majority of those breeders who responded saw *both* rights as having value for the future of plant breeding programmes. One final word of caution was expressed by a multinational. This stated that:

> if plant breeders or other scientists involved in the manipulation of living material wish to make use of the patent system then they will have to contend with the problems and pitfalls of a system not designed for living matter, where compliance with stringent application procedures and legal definitions will be the order of the day. Breeders will have to fit into an established system and its ways not the other way round.

This importance of this need for knowledge is one which we will return to later and in the next chapter.

In many respects, the CLIP study merely outlined the views of a handful of breeders within the UK in the 1980s but, as will be discussed below, the views expressed resonate with those of the breeders who took part in the PIP project 10 years later where breeders from all 15 EU member states expressed similar sentiments. As such, it is possible, by analogy, to view the CLIP survey as indicative of a more general view held by the EU plant breeding industry at that time. In addition, these concerns mirror many of those raised in preceding chapters.

The second key study is that undertaken in 1998 by ASSINSEL.

### The ASSINSEL Study[20]

Ten years later (and seven years after the introduction of the UPOV Act[21]), ASSINSEL conducted a further survey, this time of all its members based across 29 countries[22] (the published version of the study does not detail either the number or the type of plant research organisations involved).[23] The main objective of the survey was to assess availability of protection and to identify any specific areas of concern which might need to be addressed in the future. In summary, the survey found that all its members, irrespective of where they were based, were in favour of a strong system of intellectual property protection. When the specific matter of availability of protection was raised, answers varied according the technical, legal and socio-economic climate of the country concerned. Those which predominantly supported plant variety rights provided protection using either UPOV or a UPOV-type system of protection. Only three countries, Australia, Japan and the US, provided protection for plant varieties via the ordinary patent system, but they all did so in conjunction with a UPOV-type right. There was greater variation in terms of the protection of other forms of plant material—although the general stance of European countries was in keeping with the practice of the EPO as reinforced by the EU Directive.

As the survey has not been published in any great detail, one can only draw a general summary as to its findings based on the ASSINSEL position paper which outlined best practice. The starting point of the paper was that both the patent and plant variety rights systems are legitimate. In terms of deciding appropriate protection, the paper made it clear that it was up to each member state to decide based on its own *local* needs. In other words, member states should not require a specific level of protection to be available in another country unless that level

---

[20] See www.worldseed.org.

[21] The date of the survey is especially interesting as it took place in the same year as the European Parliament voted to adopt the EU Directive on the Legal Protection of Biotechnological Inventions.

[22] These were Argentina, Australia, Austria*, Belgium*, Brazil, Canada, Chile, Croatia, the Czech Republic, Denmark*, Finland*, France*, Germany*, Netherlands*, India, Ireland*, Israel, Italy*, Japan, Kenya, Norway*, New Zealand, Poland, Slovakia, South Africa, Sweden*, Switzerland, the UK* and the US. Those asterisked also participated in the PIP survey, with the additional inclusion of Portugal and Spain.

[23] The study was not therefore confined to an evaluation of European provision.

of protection was deemed by that other country as suitable for its own local plant breeding requirements, which would take into account not only the level of administration in place, and the type and extent of plant breeding, but also the need to attract the transfer of plant-related technology through the reassurance that suitable protection was available (in some respects this is another way of saying that effective protection was provided). ASSINSEL did recommend that for developing countries the use of the ordinary patent system was probably not appropriate and that they should look to introducing a UPOV-type system. In respect of the protection of biotechnological inventions ASSINSEL took a special look at the agricultural implications and came to the conclusion that, whilst it supported the patenting of genetic components which cause a characteristic or trait to be expressed, and of any 'genetic causative agent, when identified, characterized and in a form suitable for use in genetic modification,' where such a use had taken place then it was (and is) the view of ASSINSEL that the patent should remain effective even when the patented technology is introduced into a plant or plant variety. However, partial sequences such as Express Sequence Tags (ESTs) should not be patentable because they are not in themselves inventive and it is difficult to demonstrate utility. In addition, given the limited means of controlling genetic traits and the equally limited range of traits which a breeder might wish to produce, the use of an alternative genetic method to achieve the same trait should not infringe. This issue of the protection of ESTs and the ability of competitors to use an alternative means to achieve the same results is hotly discussed within patent law circles, with varying degrees of support for the ASSINSEL position.

Most critically, ASSINSEL recommended, and this remains the view of the ISF, that a commercially available plant variety which contained patented technology should be freely available for use in further breeding programmes in accordance with the UPOV principle. If that breeding programme produced a non-EDV, and therefore wholly independent variety, then the breeder of the new variety should be free to exploit it. However, there is a caveat to this and this is that where the new variety is an EDV or if it retains the patented technology (in the form of a patented gene), then the exploitation can only take place if a licence is obtained from the breeder of the initial variety or the patent holder. As highlighted in chapter 7, it is not clear from the wording of the ASSINSEL paper if the inclusion of the patented technology within the plant variety has to be on the basis that the material performs the function for which it was patented or if mere passive inclusion nonetheless triggers the need for a licence.

It was against this backdrop that the third study, the EU-funded Plant Intellectual Property (PIP) project, took place.

## The Plant Intellectual Property (PIP) Project[24]

This project was funded for a period of just over two years (from October 1998 until 2001[25]) by the European Union as part of the Fourth Framework Programme. The main project team consisted of the Sheffield Institute of Biotechnology Law and Ethics (SIBLE)[26] (which also co-ordinated the project), the French Société d'Interêt Collectif Agricole des Selectionneurs Obtenteurs de Variétiés Végetales (SICASOV)[27] and the Irish company, Plant Technology Ltd (PTL).[28] In addition, there were three specialist sub-contractors (each responsible for acquiring information relating to a defined group of EU member states)[29] and two expert, independent, consultants.[30] In addition, the project was given invaluable support and assistance from a number of different individuals and organisations including the Community Plant Variety Office, the European Patent Office, the UPOV Office, national patent and plant variety rights offices, law firms, patent agents, collection agencies, nurserymen and breeders' organisations including ASSINSEL, CIOPORA and FIS. As with the CLIP report, the interpretation given to the findings here is the responsibility of the Sheffield team alone and should not be taken as representing the views of either the breeders or any of the other project team members.

As one of the objectives of the PIP project was to identify any areas which the Commission should revisit (and therefore the project was intended to have a direct policy impact), we will outline (in brief) the methodology used as well as detail the results.

## The Objectives of the Project[31]

### Introduction

The project had three main objectives, all of which were directed towards the provision of a platform for European plant breeders from which they could make their views known to the Commission:

[24] The full details of the project (including the questionnaires, and papers from the workshop and conference) can be found at www.shef.ac.uk/uni/projects/pip.

[25] The original project was due to last two years, but the European Commission provided additional funding to extend the project.

[26] Margaret Llewelyn, Mike Adcock and Marie-Josee Goode.

[27] Antoine Alegre de la Soujeole, Jean-Louis Talvez and Marc Lecrivain.

[28] Fintan Moran and Abdullah Sayegh.

[29] Martin Ekvad (Scandinavia), Alexander Krefft (the Germanic countries) and Rosa Manjon (the Mediterranean countries). Any other countries not falling into these broadly defined groups were collectively looked after by the project team and consultant. Dr Adcock was responsible for Ireland and the UK, and the SICASOV team for France.

[30] Geertrui van Overwalle (who was also responsible for acquiring information relating to the Benelux countries) and Tim Roberts.

[31] In the original proposal it was also proposed that the national laws, both before and after the adoption of EU Directive 98/44, would be analysed. It swiftly became clear that financial and time

1) to assess attitudes towards plant intellectual property from within the European plant breeding industry—this was done through the use of two separate questionnaires, a workshop (which took place in Sheffield half way through the project[32]) and an end-of-project Conference (this was held in Angers in January 2001[33]).

2) to examine whether existing European plant intellectual property provision provides a coherent and consistent framework of protection, which is both effective and appropriate. In particular, the project team wanted to look at the various changes which had been introduced into patent and plant variety rights, such as the exclusions from protection, extension of protection to derived material, research use, farm saved seed and licensing;

and

3) to look at European policy and practice, both at the EU and local levels, in the context of the review of Article 27(3)(b) (the optional exclusion of plant varieties from patent protection) of the Agreement on Trade-Related Aspects of Intellectual Property Rights taking place at the World Trade Organisation during 1999–2001. As this proved to be a mere observational review (in that the WTO appears to have only reviewed *whether* the optional exclusion has been taken up and not at whether it *should* be available or extended), the final project concentrated on European provision as good practice.

The Target Audience[34]

Two problems were encountered in defining the target audience. The first was defining a 'plant breeder' and the second was defining a 'European' plant breeder.

With regard to the first, the project team had to take into account the fact that modern plant research encompasses a wide range of different activities. It was, therefore, agreed that it would be impossible (and undesirable) to draw hard and fast lines as to who could be regarded as a 'plant breeder' for the purposes

constraints would not make this possible. It was also proposed to undertake an evaluation of the likely impact a removal of Art 27(3)(b) would have, as part of the WTO 'review' of this provision. As it became clear that the review was going to take the form of noting national legislative activity, it was agreed that this aspect of the project would be dropped. In respect of both decisions, we had agreement from the Commission.

[32] 14 and 15 January 2000. Papers from this meeting can be found on the PIP website.

[33] The papers from this conference were published in *Conference on Plant Intellectual Property within Europe and the Wider Global Community (PIPWEG)*: Llewelyn, Adcock and Goode (eds), *Conference Proceedings* (Sheffield Academic Press, 2002).

[34] Neither the CLIP project nor the ASSINSEL study defined their target audience. For the CLIP study the target group was determined by reference to breeders registered with the then British Association of Plant Breeders (now the British Society of Plant Breeders). For ASSINSEL, participation was defined by references to membership.

of the project. As the objective was to engage with as many types of research users of plant material as possible, it was decided that, whilst the term 'plant breeder' would be used in a generic sense when referring to the participants in the project, participation would not be confined to those engaged in the traditional (or the more obvious) forms of plant breeding. Instead, the target audience would be any user of plant material, where the use of that plant material was primarily for research and development purposes.

The second issue was defining a *European* plant breeder. As with defining 'breeder', the term hides a multiplicity of different meanings: for example, many companies operating in Europe (especially multinationals) are actually foreign companies or companies which appear to operating independently but which are subsidiaries of, later merge with or acquired by, another company which may or may not itself be a European company.[35] Both of these considerations had to be taken into account when determining to which companies the questionnaires should be sent (the Commission agreed that these factors were instrumental in making the study qualitative in nature rather than quantitative) and it was agreed that the term would be taken to mean those individuals and organisations operating within a European context. Given that part of the objective of the Commission in introducing both the Regulation and the Directive was to make Europe a more attractive place within which to engage upon bioscience research, the fact that some of the participating companies were not wholly European in nature was seen as a positive rather than a negative aspect.

In terms of the geographical scope of the project, only those countries which were full members of the European Union in 1999 were included in the survey.

### The Two Questionnaires[36]

As with any survey, the most difficult problem was combining maximum participation with the acquisition of useful information. The former is usually achieved by requiring minimal effort on the part of the respondent, the latter by asking many, detailed, questions. The two do not, however, sit easily together. To try and overcome this it was decided to produce two questionnaires. The function of the first questionnaire was to provide a general overview of the types of plant breeding activity being undertaken, identify particular areas of concern in respect of plant property provision and allow the breeders to rate their

---

[35] There was also the issue of possible duplication with nationally based offices of a single company responding individually. Where possible, we targeted the head office within Europe, but this was not always possible and a significant part of the analysis was spent in cross-referring answers to ensure that there was as little duplication as possible. With regard to smaller companies which were not immediately identifiable as subsidiaries of larger organisations, we found that these tended to notify us of the fact, indicating that they had passed on the questionnaire to their head office for a 'company' response.

[36] The project team was greatly assisted by members of staff at the University of Sheffield in the construction of questionnaires and in the interpretation and evaluation of survey results. In particular, these colleagues were able to both provide guidance on and verify the methodology applied.

own intellectual property awareness as 'extensive', 'good', 'average', 'low' or 'non-existent'. In addition, the breeders were asked if they would be prepared to complete a second, more detailed, questionnaire. As the second questionnaire was only sent to those who had agreed to be involved in the second stage, the return rate for this part of the survey was higher than for the first. The first questionnaire was produced in four of the Community languages: English, French, German and Spanish. In addition, basic information about the project was made available in other Community languages, such as Dutch, Finnish, Greek, Italian, Portuguese and Swedish. This information was posted alongside English language versions of the questionnaire to breeders in relevant countries.

For cost and time reasons, the second questionnaire was only available in English, French, Spanish and German; however, the cultural diversity of the project team (which included Dutch, Greek, Italian, and Scandinavian speakers) meant that, where necessary, assistance could be provided in these other languages. To help participation, both questionnaires were available in hard copy and on the project website.[37] The project team was also fortunate to secure the support of national and international organisations representing plant breeders, all of which encouraged the breeders to participate.

The first part of the survey sought to identify the type of company engaged in plant research, the type of plant breeding activity engaged upon (indicating whether agricultural, ornamental, arboreal, pharmaceutical or herbal, or a combination thereof, and if a combination the extent of that combination in percentage terms), the extent of traditional and/or modern biotechnological research engaged upon, the extent and type of intellectual property used (including the use of confidentiality agreements, propagation agreements and trade marks, as well as the more obvious patents and plant variety rights), the awareness of the umbrella legislation as well as national provision, general satisfaction with the protection provided and more specifically the changes to that protection effected through the revision of the UPOV Convention, the introduction of the Community Regulation and the EU Directive. The second questionnaire built upon the middle set of questions and looked for further knowledge and use of the patent and plant variety rights systems, including detailed questions on concepts such as the exclusion of plant varieties, the notion of an essentially derived variety and scope of protection conferred. In addition, the second questionnaire asked the breeders to provide views on other

---

[37] The returns were not anonymous, although the recording and detailing of the results are. The project team was extremely careful to ensure that there was no duplication of return, eg that a company did not make two returns, one via the website, the other by hard copy. The one area where it was impossible to monitor the source of returns fully was in respect of those companies which are part or wholly owned by another company where both engaged in plant breeding activities, but the actual nature of the relationship was difficult to detect. This problem was exacerbated where the umbrella company owned more than one subsidiary and these subsidiaries were based in different countries. The status of the companies concerned and their relationship to other companies did form part of the second questionnaire, but for some companies this was clearly a sensitive issue and not all sought to answer. It is therefore impossible to guarantee the level of independency of all the returns.

changes which they would like to see made (for example, the introduction of a new single system of protection for all plant material). From this information it was possible to build a picture of a) the range of plant breeding activity across Europe as well as within each member state, and b) the knowledge and use of the systems of protection within each area of plant breeding at the national as well as the European level. The collective views are outlined below. Before looking at these it is worth noting the general picture of plant breeding activity, at the EU level and then within each member state surveyed.

*The Responses*

| | |
|---|---|
| Total number of first questionnaires sent | 2101 |
| Total number of questionnaires received | 449 |
| Percentage returned | 21 |
| Total number of second questionnaires sent | 461 |
| Total number of questionnaires received | 119 |
| Percentage returned | 26 |

A return rate of between 21 and 26 per cent might appear to be very low. Indeed, according to some quantitative methodologies, the return rate achieved would not give the results any value. However, it is important to stress that the study was *qualitative* not *quantitative*. In addition, the fact that the study took place across 15 countries meant that all involved knew that the return rate would be lower than that expected if only a small number of countries had been targeted. From the outset the Commission indicated that it would be willing to accept findings based on relatively low return rate as an *indicator* of *possible* policy routes forward.

Much more worrying was the fact that many of the returns (especially for the second questionnaire) carried minimal information. Indeed, a considerable number (approximately 60 per cent) responded 'Don't know' to most of the substantive questions (these related to knowledge of the patent and plant variety rights systems). There are two reasons why this lack of knowledge is important.

The first is that this, obviously, has the effect of giving greater weight to the information provided by other respondents. When evaluating the responses it must be remembered that those who did comment were in the minority.

The second is that many of those who felt unable to answer gave as their reason a lack of experience of the legal systems (and of patent law in particular). As the previous chapters have shown, those who represent the views of plant breeders have played an active part in the developments within both patent law and, especially, plant variety rights. However, notwithstanding this activity, information about these changes, and their possible (positive and negative) implications for research programmes) had not (at the time of the study) filtered through to the breeders themselves. This general ignorance (within the respondents to the questionnaires) is worrying when looked at in the context of the changes which have been made to both systems of protection.

Because of the limited content of the returns received the survey cannot be taken to indicate *general* views held by all (or most) of those who engage in plant research.[38] It must be stressed, therefore, that the findings should be treated with even greater caution than is usually employed when assessing the representational qualities of statistical information.

There follows an overview of plant breeding activity within the EU in general and then a more detailed breakdown of this activity country by country. The full information relating to each country can be found on the project website.[39] The statistics relating to the number of plant variety rights in force in each year comes from the UPOV website, and the general trend in decreasing national applications needs to be looked at in light of the increase in Community rights granted.[40] There are no equivalent figures for plant-related patent applications, although the EPO and most patent offices publish annually the number of overall applications made and patents granted.[41]

The EU[42]

General Overview[43]

Plant Breeding Activity[44]

Perhaps unsurprisingly, most European plant breeding is concentrated in France, Germany, the Netherlands and the UK, with the bulk of the research

---

[38] For example, the issue of research use is barely raised by breeders, yet it consistently tops the list of issues for attention by organisations such as CIOPORA and the ISF.

[39] Where possible we have indicated the legislation in place at the time the study was conducted.

[40] See ch 4, and www.cpvo.eu.int.

[41] The web addresses of most of the national patent offices are provided below.

[42] There were no research results for either Luxembourg or Portugal. Luxembourg is a member of the EPC but not of UPOV. Its primary patent law is the Law on Patents for Inventions June 1880, last amended in 1978. It has not implemented the Directive. There is no web address for the Industrial Property Office. As there is no national system of plant variety rights there are no statistics relating to the grant of such rights. Equally, there were no statistics relating to the number of patents granted over plant-related inventions for the period of the project. Portugal is a member of the EPC. Its primary patent legislation is contained in the Industrial Property Code, decree Law No 16/95, January 1995. Reports indicate that it implemented the Directive in 2002; however, the basis of the implementation is unclear. Portugal is a member of UPOV 78. In the period during which the PIP project took place, 32 national plant variety rights were granted in 2000, 30 in 2001, and 30 in 2002. There were no equivalent figures for patent grants over plant-related inventions. Only those countries which were full members of the European Union were included in the survey.

[43] These figures are, in the main, based on the survey results. In terms of representation of the scale and type of general plant breeding activity, these figures were agreed by those participating at the workshop and conference to be appropriate indicators of the sector as a whole.

[44] These figures were produced using information provided by the national organisations which represent plant breeders.

activity focused on agricultural plant breeding (the exception to this was the Netherlands where the majority of companies active in plant breeding is in the ornamental sector). Whilst the majority of plant research concentrated on one type of plant-breeding activity (for example agricultural or ornamental), not all do so and a number of companies engage in a number of different activities. This means that there is not necessarily an obvious correlation between the number of responses under the heading 'plant breeding activity' and those under 'type of company'. One company may engage in two or three plant breeding activities.

The largest plant breeding sector in the EU is agriculture, which accounts for 36 per cent of the total plant breeding activity. The second largest sector is floriculture/ornamentals, with 27 per cent, followed closely by horticulture/fruit and vegetables, with 20 per cent. Forestry/arboriculture is the fourth largest sector, with 7 per cent, with pharmaceutical and medicinal, herbs and other plant breeding activities contributing around 3 per cent of the total plant breeding activity. This gradation of activity is important. The interests of the agricultural breeder were, and arguably still are, central to the ethos underpinning plant variety rights (and, as will be seen, they are the most significant users of the plant variety rights system), whereas developments in the pharmaceutical industry have been the primary driving force behind the recent expansion in patent protection.

Type of Company[45]

General information provided indicates that the small-scale and SME breeder comprise approximately 80 per cent of all those engaged in plant-related research. In assessing the weight to be placed upon their views (and also in assessing the potential impact of developments in plant intellectual property provision) it is important to bear in mind that (agricultural breeders aside) not all of these are involved in traditional plant breeding. A significant number of these (especially within France, Germany, the UK, and a number of Scandinavian countries) are involved in biotechnological research, often as start-up companies. These can comprise one or two individuals working on a single inventive concept, the economic potential for which could be considerable (and the need for strong intellectual property protection therefore vital).

In terms of the response rate to the questionnaire, the breakdown of size of company was as follows:

[45] The categories of 'small-scale' and 'small to medium-sized' were defined according to the EU Commission Recommendation of 3 April 1996 concerning the definition of small and medium-sized enterprises: *OJ L* 107, 30 April 1996, pp 4–9. This was revised in 2003: Commission Recommendation of 6 May 2003, *OJ L* 124, 20 May 2005, pp 36–41.

|                                                  | Total responses[46] |
| ------------------------------------------------ | ------------------- |
| Small-scale and Individual Breeders[47]          | 146[48]             |
| SME[49]                                           | 143[50]             |
| National[51]                                      | 111[52]             |
| Multinational[53]                                | 47[54]              |

These figures reflect the general environment, with the majority of replies coming from small-scale and medium-sized businesses (63 per cent). Around 26 per cent of the replies were from large national companies, with the remaining 11 per cent from multinational companies. These figures are very interesting, for it is the latter group which is traditionally presented as pushing for a 'Rolls Royce' system of protection and yet, as will be seen below, it is this group which urged caution over an overly extensive use of patent protection. In contrast, it was the small-scale breeders (not working within the agricultural crop breeding sector) who were pressing for more extensive protection. It was this group which, in general, had the best understanding of *both* systems of protection with the small-scale agricultural breeder feeling confident only about plant variety rights, and the national and multinational companies being more knowledgeable about the patent system.

Of these, the primary plant breeding activity of small-scale companies, or individual breeders, is floriculture and ornamentals, closely followed by agricultural crop plant breeding. Around one fifth of small-scale companies are involved in horticultural, fruit and vegetable breeding. There are also a small number of small-scale companies involved in forestry and arboriculture, pharmaceutical and medicinal and herb plant breeding.

---

[46] The information contained in the general overview is drawn from the responses to both questionnaires. Information provided by local offices enabled identification of both number and type of breeding organisation operating within a given territory. The legislative overview information provided comes from the World Intellectual Property Organisation and UPOV websites (www.wipo.org and www.upov.org) and was accurate as of October 2004.

[47] In so far as the Commission distinguished between SMEs and other 'small enterprises', it defined the latter as one which 'has fewer than fifty employees and—has either, an annual turnover not exceeding ECU 7 million, or an annual balance-sheet total not exceeding ECU 5 million'.

[48] 32% of the overall responses.

[49] 'Small and medium-sized enterprises, hereinafter referred to as "SMEs", are defined as enterprises which have fewer than 250 employees, and—have either an annual turnover not exceeding ECU 40 million, or an annual balance-sheet total not exceeding ECU 27 million".

[50] 31% of the total.

[51] Where the operation of the company is confined to one jurisdiction (the size of the company may, however, be commensurate with that of a multinational).

[52] 26% of the total.

[53] Where the operation of the company is not confined to one jurisdiction.

[54] 11% of the total.

Almost half of the SMEs that replied carry out agricultural crop plant breeding programmes, with a further 40 per cent equally split between the horticulture and floriculture/ornamental sectors. Few SMEs are involved in either forestry and arboriculture, pharmaceutical and medicinal or herb plant breeding.

Almost 60 per cent of the plant breeding activity carried out by national companies is equally split between the agricultural crop and floriculture/ornamentals breeding. The horticulture, fruit and vegetable sector is third largest area of activity, whilst national companies carry out over 60 per cent of all forestry and arboriculture plant breeding programmes. There is also a significant amount of plant research work being carried out by national companies in the pharmaceutical/medicinal and herb plant breeding sectors.

As with the SMEs and national companies, most multinational companies are involved in the agricultural crop plant breeding sector. However, many are also involved in horticulture, fruit and vegetable plant breeding and, to a lesser extent, the floriculture and ornamentals sector. Few multinationals which responded stated that they were involved in either the forestry/arboriculture, or herb plant breeding sectors. Interestingly, and despite the usual picture presented at conferences and within the media, very few of these said that their *plant* research was directed to the production of pharmaceutical/medicinal products (although other aspects of their genomic research was directed towards this).

In terms of use of biotechnology as opposed to traditional plant breeding methods, the majority (between 70 and 80 per cent) of companies in each sector were engaged in traditional plant breeding. Of those who did make use of the modern biotechnology, the greatest use is by floriculture and ornamental breeders, with agricultural breeders (the next main user) some way behind. The country with the largest number of biotech companies is Germany, closely followed by the UK, France, Sweden and Denmark. Greece has the lowest number.

It is clear from this snapshot that, generally speaking, across Europe, and across sectors, the main area of plant research activity is traditional agricultural plant breeding and that those who are most involved in this work fall within the small-scale/SME sectors. This is also supported by the country-by-country breakdown of activity and type of company.

## Country-by-Country Overview[55]

### Austria[56]

*Patents*

Austria is a member of the EPC. Its primary patent law is Federal Law No 259/1970, which has been amended on a number of occasions, most notably in 1984 and 1998. Austria implemented the Directive in June 2005.

*Plant Variety Rights*

Austria is now a member of UPOV 91, however, at the time that the survey was conducted it was still. In the period during which the PIP project took place, 145 national plant variety rights were granted in 2000, 142 in 2001 and 140 in 2002. There were no equivalent statistics in respect of patents for plant-related inventions.

*Response Rate*

| | |
|---|---|
| Total number of questionnaires sent | 53 |
| Total number of questionnaires received | 10 |
| Total number of second questionnaires sent | 10 |
| Total number of questionnaires received | 4 |

*Plant Breeding Activity*

| | Total Responses | Percentage |
|---|---|---|
| Agricultural Crops | 7 | 58 |

---

[55] The statistics provided for each country come from the responses to the first questionnaire. This is because this provides a more general picture of both the type of activity within any given country and also the size of company operating within each country. It is important to bear in mind that the responses to the second questionnaire come from the same companies as participated in the first questionnaire, and the number should not be added to the original 447. The information contained in the general overview is drawn from the responses to both questionnaires. Information provided by local offices enabled identification of both number and type of breeding organisation operating within a given territory. The legislative overview information provided comes from the World Intellectual Property Organisation and UPOV websites (www.wipo.org and www.upov.org) and was accurate as of October 2004.

[56] http://www.patent.bmwa.gv.at, and http://www.lebensministerium.at/.

| | Total Responses | Percentage |
|---|---|---|
| Horticulture/fruit/vegetables | 2 | 17 |
| Floriculture/ornamentals | 0 | 0 |
| Forestry/arboriculture | 0 | 0 |
| Pharmaceutical/medicinal | 1 | 8 |
| Herbs | 2 | 17 |
| Other | 0 | 0 |

*Type of Company*

| | Total Responses | Percentage |
|---|---|---|
| Small-scale/individual | 1 | 10 |
| SME | 7 | 70 |
| National | 2 | 20 |
| Multinational | 0 | 0 |

An analysis of the responses showed that the majority of respondents were SMEs working in the agricultural plant breeding sector.

Belgium[57]

*Legislative Framework*

*Patents*

Belgium is a member of the EPC, its primary patent law is the Patent Law of March 1984. This has been amended on a number of occasions most notably in 1995, 1997, 2001 and 2005. This latter served to implement the Directive.[58]

---

[57] http://www.european-patent-office.org/patlib/country/belgium/index.htm. There was no equivalent website available for the plant variety rights office. Belgium is one of the few EU members which does have national literature on the subject of plant protection; the leading exponent of this work (both in its local and international settings) is van Overwalle. See, for example, van Overwalle, 'Patent Protection for Plants: A Comparison of American and European Approaches' (1999) 39(2) *IDEA* 143; and van Overwalle, 'The Legal Protection of Biological Material in Belgium' (2000) 31(3) *IIC* 259.

[58] Act of 28 April 2005. This amended the Patent Act 1984 and came into force on 23 May 2005.

## Plant Variety Rights

Belgium is a member of UPOV 61/72 and has not yet implemented UPOV 1991. In the period during which the PIP project took place, 529 national plant variety rights were granted in 2000, 433 in 2001 and 373 in 2002. There were no equivalent statistics in respect of patents for plant-related inventions.

## Response Rate

| | |
|---|---|
| Total number of first questionnaires sent | 196 |
| Total number of questionnaires received | 35 |
| Total number of second questionnaires sent | 36 |
| Total number of questionnaires received | 7 |

## Plant Breeding Activity

| | Total Responses | Percentage |
|---|---|---|
| Agricultural Crops | 11 | 24 |
| Horticulture/fruit/vegetables | 7 | 15 |
| Floriculture/ornamentals | 15 | 33 |
| Forestry/arboriculture | 8 | 17 |
| Pharmaceutical/medicinal | 4 | 8 |
| Herbs | 0 | 0 |
| Other | 1 | 2 |

## Type of company

| | Total | Percentage |
|---|---|---|
| Small-scale/individual | 8 | 23 |
| SME | 16 | 41 |
| National | 11 | 36 |
| Multinational | 0 | 0 |

An analysis of the statistics showed that the majority of breeders fell into the SME category and these were most active in the breeding of agricultural crops. However, there was also extensive activity within the ornamental sector, and this work was undertaken by a diversity of small-scale and national companies.

Denmark[59]

## Legislative Framework

### Patents

Denmark is a member of the EPC, and its current patent law is the Consolidated Patents Act No 781 of August 2001 which served to implement the Directive. Denmark implemented the Directive in May 2000.

### Plant Variety Rights

Denmark is also a member of UPOV Act. In the period during which the PIP project took place, 727 national plant variety rights were granted in 2000, 659 in 2001 and 583 in 2002. There were no equivalent statistics in respect of patents for plant-related inventions.

### Response Rate

| | |
|---|---|
| Total number of first questionnaires sent | 108 |
| Total number of questionnaires received | 26 |
| Total number of second questionnaires sent | 27 |
| Total number of questionnaires received | 6 |

### Plant Breeding Activity

| | Total | Percentage |
|---|---|---|
| Agricultural Crops | 15 | 58 |
| Horticulture/fruit/vegetables | 4 | 15 |
| Floriculture/ornamentals | 7 | 27 |
| Forestry/arboriculture | 0 | 0 |

[59] http://www.dkpto.dk/. There appears to be no equivalent website for the Danish plant variety rights office.

| | Total | Percentage |
|---|---|---|
| Pharmaceutical/medicinal | 0 | 0 |
| Herbs | 0 | 0 |
| Other | 0 | 0 |

## Type of Company

The majority of replies were received from small-scale companies (31 per cent) and SMEs (35 per cent), with the remainder of the replies from national (19 per cent) and multinational companies (15 per cent).

| | Total | Percentage |
|---|---|---|
| Small-scale/individual | 8 | 31 |
| SME | 9 | 35 |
| National | 5 | 19 |
| Multinational | 4 | 15 |

Within Denmark the spread of agricultural research work was much more obvious than in many of the other countries surveyed, with clear activity across the gamut of companies surveyed.

Eire (Ireland)[60]

### Legislative Framework

### Patents

Ireland is a member of the EPC, and its primary patent law is contained in the Patent Act No 1, February 1992, as supplemented by the Intellectual Property (Miscellaneous Provisions) Act No 28, July 1998. Ireland implemented the Directive in July 2000.

### Plant Variety Rights

Ireland is a member of UPOV 78. In the period during which the PIP project took place, 100 national plant variety rights were granted in 2000, 85 in 2001 and

---

[60] http://www.patentsoffice.ie. There was no equivalent website available for the Irish plant variety rights office.

78 in 2002. There were no equivalent statistics available relating to patents granted over plant-related inventions.

*Response Rate*

| | |
|---|---|
| Total number of first questionnaires sent | 31 |
| Total number of questionnaires received | 9 |
| Total number of second questionnaires sent | 9 |
| Total number of questionnaires received | 1 |

*Plant Breeding Activity*

| | Total | Percentage |
|---|---|---|
| Agricultural Crops | 6 | 50 |
| Horticulture/fruit/vegetables | 1 | 8 |
| Floriculture/ornamentals | 3 | 25 |
| Forestry/arboriculture | 2 | 17 |
| Pharmaceutical/medicinal | 0 | 0 |
| Herbs | 0 | 0 |
| Other | 0 | 0 |

*Type of Company*

| | Total | Percentage |
|---|---|---|
| Small-scale/individual | 2 | 22 |
| SME | 2 | 22 |
| National | 5 | 56 |
| Multinational | 0 | 0 |

In Ireland the majority of SME and national companies are engaged upon agricultural plant breeding, with the small-scale breeders concentrating on floriculture (for example in the form of micro-propagation[61]).

---

[61] This also being the activity of the partner company PTL.

Finland[62]

### Legislative Framework

### Patents

Finland is a member of the EPC. Its primary patent law is the Patents Act No 550, December 1967, which was amended in 1997 and 2000. Finland implemented the Directive in June 2000.

### Plant Variety Rights

Finland is a member of UPOV 91. In the period during which the PIP project took place, 54 national plant variety rights were granted in 2000, 67 in 2001 and 70 in 2002. There were no equivalent statistics available relating to patents granted over plant-related inventions.

### Response Rates

| | |
|---|---|
| Total number of first questionnaires sent | 6 |
| Total number of questionnaires received | 2 |
| Total number of second questionnaires sent | 3[63] |
| Total number of questionnaires received | 2 |

### Plant Breeding Activity

| | Total | Percentage |
|---|---|---|
| Agricultural Crops | 2 | 100 |
| Horticulture/fruit/vegetables | 0 | 0 |
| Floriculture/ornamentals | 0 | 0 |
| Forestry/arboriculture | 0 | 0 |
| Pharmaceutical/medicinal | 0 | 0 |
| Herbs | 0 | 0 |
| Other | 0 | 0 |

---

[62] www.prh.fi and www.mmm.fi.

[63] The additional response came from a late request from a company which filled in the second but not the first questionnaire.

*Type of Company*

|  | Total | Percentage |
|---|---|---|
| Small-scale/individual | 0 | 0 |
| SME | 1 | 50 |
| National | 1 | 50 |
| Multinational | 0 | 0 |

As can be seen, there was virtually no plant breeding activity within Finland. A check with various organisations indicated that the lack of responses accurately reflected the actual level of activity. What makes this statistic interesting is both the fact that Finland implemented both the 1991 UPOV Act and the Directive very quickly and that their plant variety rights office indicates a good use of the plant variety rights system (with 70 grants being made in 2002). However, these figures do not indicate whether the holders of those rights are companies based within Finland or if they are based elsewhere but have a market in need of protection within Finland.

France[64]

Legislative Framework

*Patents*

France is a member of the EPC; its primary patent law is Law No 92–597, July 1992, which was amended by Decree No 96103, February 1996. France implemented the Directive in December 2004.

*Plant Variety Rights*

France is a member of UPOV 78. In the period during which the PIP project took place, 4351 national plant variety rights were granted in 2000, 4106 in 2001 and 3755 in 2002. There were no equivalent statistics available relating to patents granted over plant-related inventions. At the time of going to press, French law makers were striving to ratify the 1991 UPOV Act, but few details were available.

---

[64] www.inpi.fr/ and http://geves.zarcom.fr.

*Response Rates*

| | |
|---|---|
| Total number of first questionnaires sent | 372 |
| Total number of questionnaires received | 86 |
| Total number of second questionnaires sent | 86 |
| Total number of questionnaires received | 18 |

*Plant Breeding Activity*

| | Total | Percentage |
|---|---|---|
| Agricultural Crops | 37 | 39 |
| Horticulture/fruit/vegetables | 14 | 15 |
| Floriculture/ornamentals | 27 | 29 |
| Forestry/arboriculture | 10 | 10 |
| Pharmaceutical/medicinal | 3 | 3 |
| Herbs | 0 | 0 |
| Other | 5 | 5 |

*Type of Company*

| | Total | Percentage |
|---|---|---|
| Small-scale/individual | 12 | 14 |
| SME | 47 | 55 |
| National | 20 | 23 |
| Multinational | 7 | 8 |

When these figures are broken down it can be seen that the small-scale companies were exclusively involved in floriculture and ornamentals, whereas SMEs were much more actively involved in agricultural, horticultural and fruit and vegetable plant breeding. Of the national and multinational companies who replied, the two main plant breeding activities were agricultural crop production and floriculture/ornamentals. However, these companies also had a small interest in horticulture, fruit and vegetables, and forestry and arboriculture. The most significant aspect of French provision is that so many plant variety rights are granted each year—the significance lies not so much in the success of the system, but in the fact that the French system is based on the 1978 UPOV Act.

## Germany[65]

### *Legislative Framework*

*Patents*

Germany is a member of the EPC. Its primary patent law is the Patent Law, December 1980, which was amended in 1999. Germany implemented the Directive in 2004 (after the completion of the PIP project).

### *Plant Variety Rights*

Germany is a member of UPOV 91. In the period during which the PIP project took place, 3232 national plant variety rights were granted in 2000, 3039 and 2904 in 2002. There were no equivalent statistics available relating to patents granted over plant-related inventions.

### *Response Rates*

| | |
|---|---|
| Total number of first questionnaires sent | 254 |
| Total number of questionnaires received | 61 |
| Total number of second questionnaires sent | 58 |
| Total number of questionnaires received | 17 |

### *Plant Breeding Activity*

| | Total | Percentage |
|---|---|---|
| Agricultural Crops | 38 | 57 |
| Horticulture/fruit/vegetables | 10 | 15 |
| Floriculture/ornamentals | 8 | 12 |
| Forestry/arboriculture | 4 | 6 |
| Pharmaceutical/medicinal | 2 | 2 |
| Herbs | 4 | 6 |
| Other | 1 | 2 |

[65] http://www.dpma.de and http://www.bundessortenamt.de/.

*Type of Company*

|  | Total | Percentage |
|---|---|---|
| Small-scale/individual | 18 | 30 |
| SME | 23 | 38 |
| National | 10 | 16 |
| Multinational | 10 | 16 |

When the figures were broken down it could be seen that small-scale businesses as well as SMEs were involved in agricultural, horticultural and fruit and vegetable plant breeding. National companies carried out the widest range of plant breeding activities, and the responses indicated involvement in all plant breeding sectors. Of the multinational companies which replied, none were involved in horticulture or fruit and vegetable plant breeding, but they did have significant interests in agricultural, floriculture and ornamental, and forestry and arboriculture plant breeding.

Greece[66]

### Legislative Framework

### Patents

Greece is a member of the EPC. Its patent law is contained in a number of laws relating to technology transfer and through various presidential decrees. Greece implemented the Directive in October 2001 (shortly before the completion of the PIP project).

### Plant Variety Rights

Greece is not currently a member of UPOV and it has no national system of plant variety rights. It is, however, in discussions with UPOV regarding possible future membership.

---

[66] There does not appear to be a website for the Greek Patent Office.

*Response Rates*

| Total number of first questionnaires sent | 16 |
|---|---|
| Total number of questionnaires received | 3 |
| Total number of second questionnaires sent | 3 |
| Total number of questionnaires received | 1 |

*Plant Breeding Activity*

| | Total | Percentage |
|---|---|---|
| Agricultural Crops | 3 | 100 |
| Horticulture/fruit/vegetables | 0 | 0 |
| Floriculture/ornamentals | 0 | 0 |
| Forestry/arboriculture | 0 | 0 |
| Pharmaceutical/medicinal | 0 | 0 |
| Herbs | 0 | 0 |
| Other | 0 | 0 |

*Type of Company*

| | Total | Percentage |
|---|---|---|
| Small-scale/individual | 0 | 0 |
| SME | 1 | 34 |
| National | 2 | 66 |
| Multinational | 0 | 0 |

The three Greek companies that replied were principally involved in agricultural crop plant breeding, namely cereals and fodder crops. The low level of plant breeding is reflected in the lack of any national plant variety rights protection—although Greece clearly wishes to be seen as an attractive location for bioscience by virtue of its implementation of the Directive. What is interesting is that Greece has not previously felt the need to provide specific protection in order to attract breeders of plant varieties, presumably on the basis that if protection is required then it can be secured through the Community plant variety rights route.

Italy[67]

### Legislative Framework

### Patents

Italy is a member of the EPC. Its primary patent law is the Law on Patents for Inventions Decree No 1127 of 1939, which was last amended in 1996. Italy will implement the Directive in 2006.

### Plant Variety Rights

Italy is a member of UPOV 1978. In the period during which the PIP project took place, 1681 national plant variety rights were granted in 2000, 1871 in 2001 and the same number in 2002. There were no equivalent statistics available relating to patents granted over plant-related inventions.

### Response Rates

| | |
|---|---|
| Total number of first questionnaires sent | 73 |
| Total number of questionnaires received | 7 |
| Total number of second questionnaires sent | 13 |
| Total number of questionnaires received | 4 |

### Plant Breeding Activity

| | Total | Percentage |
|---|---|---|
| Agricultural Crops | 5 | 63 |
| Horticulture/fruit/vegetables | 2 | 25 |
| Floriculture/ornamentals | 0 | 0 |
| Forestry/arboriculture | 0 | 0 |
| Pharmaceutical/medicinal | 1 | 12 |

[67] http://www.european-patent-office.org/it/. There was no equivalent website available for the Italian plant variety rights office.

|  | Total | Percentage |
|---|---|---|
| Herbs | 0 | 0 |
| Other | 0 | 0 |

## Type of Company

|  | Total | Percentage |
|---|---|---|
| Small scale/individual | 3 | 43 |
| SME | 2 | 29 |
| National | 1 | 14 |
| Multinational | 1 | 14 |

The analysis of the statistics indicated that all companies operating within Italy, regardless of size, were involved in agricultural crop production, with a specific emphasis on the production of cereals. The single multinational company indicated that it engaged upon a broad range of plant-related research activities including horticultural, fruit and vegetable, pharmaceutical and medicinal plant breeding, in addition to its agricultural research work.

The Netherlands[68]

### Legislative Framework

### Patents

The Netherlands is a member of the EPC. Its primary patent law legislation is the Patents Act of the Kingdom 1910, which was last amended in 1998. The Netherlands implemented the Directive in November 2004.

### Plant Variety Rights

The Netherlands is a member of UPOV 91. In the period during which the PIP project took place, 4416 national plant variety rights were granted in 2000, 4385 in 2001, and 4189 in 2002. There were no equivalent statistics available relating to patents granted over plant-related inventions.

---

[68] http://www.bie.minez.nl.

*Response Rates*

| | |
|---|---|
| Total number of first questionnaires sent | 456 |
| Total number of questionnaires received | 80 |
| Total number of second questionnaires sent | 80 |
| Total number of questionnaires received | 18 |

*Plant Breeding Activity*

| | Total | Percentage |
|---|---|---|
| Agricultural Crops | 12 | 13 |
| Horticulture/fruit/vegetables | 20 | 23 |
| Floriculture/ornamentals | 44 | 50 |
| Forestry/arboriculture | 3 | 3 |
| Pharmaceutical/medicinal | 3 | 3 |
| Herbs | 4 | 4 |
| Other | 3 | 3 |

*Type of Company*

| | Total | Percentage |
|---|---|---|
| Small-scale/individual | 40 | 50 |
| SME | 7 | 9 |
| National | 26 | 32 |
| Multinational | 7 | 9 |

Unsurprisingly the analysis of these figures showed that small-scale companies were predominantly involved in floriculture and ornamental plant breeding (63 per cent) (their other plant breeding activities being horticulture, fruit and vegetables and agricultural crops). The majority of SMEs were also predominantly occupied in the floriculture and ornamentals sector (75 per cent) but those that were not concentrated on the production of agricultural crops. In common with the small-scale breeders, the national companies had a much wider interest in plant breeding activities although floriculture and ornamentals still dominated over horticulture, fruit and vegetables and they only indicate a small interest in agricultural plant breeding. Floriculture and ornamentals and agricultural crops also formed the main plant breeding activities of the multinational companies.

Spain[69]

### Legislative Framework

### Patents

Spain is a member of the EPC. Its primary legislation is the Law on Patents and Utility Models No 11/1986, March 1986, which has been amended on a number of occasions since. Spain implemented the Directive in April 2002.

### Plant Variety Rights

Spain is a member of UPOV 61/72. In the period during which the PIP project took place, 1074 national plant variety rights were granted in 2000, 1023 in 2001, and 970 in 2002. There were no equivalent statistics available relating to patents granted over plant-related inventions.

### Response Rates

| | |
|---|---|
| Total number of first questionnaires sent | 85 |
| Total number of questionnaires received | 14 |
| Total number of second questionnaires sent | 14 |
| Total number of questionnaires received | 4 |

### Plant Breeding Activity

| | Total | Percentage |
|---|---|---|
| Agricultural Crops | 4 | 27 |
| Horticulture/fruit/vegetables | 4 | 27 |
| Floriculture/ornamentals | 2 | 13 |
| Forestry/arboriculture | 2 | 13 |

---

[69] http://www.oepm.es/.

|  | Total | Percentage |
|---|---|---|
| Pharmaceutical/medicinal | 0 | 0 |
| Herbs | 2 | 13 |
| Other | 1 | 7 |

### Type of Company

|  | Total | Percentage |
|---|---|---|
| Small-scale/individual | 1 | 7 |
| SME | 1 | 7 |
| National | 10 | 71 |
| Multinational | 2 | 14 |

Again there is a relatively small plant breeding industry within Spain. The analysis of the figures indicated that national companies carried out the widest range of plant breeding activities and these were in horticultural, fruit and vegetables, agricultural and herb research. There was some activity in floriculture/ornamentals and forestry/arboriculture. The multinational companies carried out floriculture and ornamental research, some were also engaged in horticulture, fruit and vegetables plant breeding, but none were involved in agricultural plant breeding. Small-scale businesses and SMEs were primarily involved in horticulture, fruit and vegetables, and pharmaceutical and medicinal plant breeding.

Sweden[70]

### Legislative Framework

### Patents

Sweden is a member of the EPC. Its primary patent legislation is contained in the Patents Act No 837, December 1967, which was last amended in 2000. Sweden implemented the Directive in May 2004.

---

[70] http://www.prv.se.

## Plant Variety Rights

Sweden is a member of UPOV 91. In the period during which the PIP project took place, 323 national plant variety rights were granted in 2000, 336 in 2001, and 329 in 2002. There were no equivalent statistics available relating to patents granted over plant-related inventions.

## Response Rates

| | |
|---|---|
| Total number of first questionnaires sent | 30 |
| Total number of questionnaires received | 4 |
| Total number of second questionnaires sent | 8 |
| Total number of questionnaires received | 1 |

## Plant Breeding Activity

| | Total | Percentage |
|---|---|---|
| Agricultural Crops | 3 | 75 |
| Horticulture/fruit/vegetables | 1 | 25 |
| Floriculture/ornamentals | 0 | 0 |
| Forestry/arboriculture | 0 | 0 |
| Pharmaceutical/medicinal | 0 | 0 |
| Herbs | 0 | 0 |
| Other | 0 | 0 |

## Type of Company

| | Total | Percentage |
|---|---|---|
| Small-scale/individual | 0 | 0 |
| SME | 2 | 50 |
| National | 1 | 25 |
| Multinational | 1 | 25 |

The analysis showed that nearly all the companies (irrespective of size) were involved in agricultural crop breeding, namely cereals, oilseeds, forage and potatoes. However, the national and multinational companies were also involved in horticulture, fruit and vegetable breeding (with one of these engaging in this work to the exclusion of any work in agricultural plant breeding).

## The United Kingdom[71]

### Legislative Framework

### Patents

The UK is a member of the EPC. Its primary patent law legislation is the Patents Act 1977 (as amended in 2004). The UK implemented the Directive in July 2000.

### Plant Variety Rights

The UK is a member of UPOV 91. In the period during which the PIP project took place, 1781 national plant variety rights were granted in 2000, 1622 in 2001 and 1568 in 2002. There were no equivalent statistics available relating to patents granted over plant-related inventions.

### Response Rates

| | |
|---|---|
| Total number of first questionnaires sent | 418 |
| Total number of questionnaires received | 112 |
| Total number of second questionnaires sent | 112 |
| Total number of questionnaires received | 36 |

### Plant Breeding Activity

| | Total | Percentage |
|---|---|---|
| Agricultural Crops | 44 | 32 |
| Horticulture/fruit/vegetables | 39 | 28 |
| Floriculture/ornamentals | 35 | 25 |
| Forestry/arboriculture | 5 | 4 |

[71] www.patent.gov.uk and www.defra.gov.uk.

|  | Total | Percentage |
|---|---|---|
| Pharmaceutical/medicinal | 2 | 1 |
| Herbs | 5 | 4 |
| Other | 8 | 6 |

## Type of Company

|  | Total | Percentage |
|---|---|---|
| Small-scale/individual | 54 | 48 |
| SME | 26 | 23 |
| National | 17 | 15 |
| Multinational | 15 | 13 |

The analysis showed that the main activity of small-scale companies was floriculture and ornamentals, followed by approximately equal activity in agricultural crops and horticulture, fruit and vegetables. The SMEs' primary plant breeding activity was agricultural crops, followed by horticulture, fruit and vegetables, and floriculture and ornamentals. National companies had the most diverse range of plant breeding interests, including pharmaceutical and medicinal, herbs, forestry/arboriculture and floriculture/ornamentals, but agricultural crops and horticulture, fruit and vegetables remained the main areas of interest. Around 50 per cent of the plant breeding activities of multinational companies were concerned with agricultural crops, followed by horticulture, fruit and vegetables (40 per cent), with floriculture and ornamentals making up the remaining 10 per cent.

## Overview of Responses[72]

As might be expected, a project of this size and nature generated a huge volume of information (the complete data extends to several hundreds of pages and hundreds of thousands of words)[73] and it would be impossible to repeat it all here. For this reason, the summary of the results set out below is necessarily brief and should be taken as a global overview of the issues raised by the plant breeders rather than as a detailed analysis.

[72] The full data is available at www.shef.ac.uk/uni/projects/pip.
[73] *Ibid.*

One of the first comments to make is that there were few national variations in content of response. Whilst it had been thought that a country-by-country breakdown might have provided interesting information, the fact that there was such unity of views expressed across the EU rendered making a country-by-country evaluation a rather pointless and repetitive exercise. Where there were disparities these lay not in jurisdictional terms but rather in the views from different sectors of plant breeding activity. In particular, there was a clear difference of opinion expressed by the ornamental breeders and those involved in other areas of plant research, most notably agricultural plant breeding. The ornamental breeders tended to be both more critical of current provision and more experienced in the use of different systems of protection. Breeders in the other sectors tended to have less experience of protection other than plant variety rights and were also less knowledgeable as to those other forms of protection. In expressing these views there was consistency across the ornamental plant breeding sector (irrespective of jurisdiction or size of company) and the same was true of the other groups.

It was possible therefore to make some general points about both the industry itself and the rights which are available to it, highlighting, where appropriate, the differences between the views of the ornamental breeders and those from other sectors. As previously stated, it was the ornamental breeders (and particularly those which fell into the SME category of company) who were most vocal in expressing concerns over provision. It was the small-scale and SME agricultural plant breeders who felt least able to provide information and their returns are peppered with 'don't knows'.

In assessing these conclusions it is also worth noting that there was considerable correlation between the findings of this project and the general conclusions of the surveys conducted by CLIP and ASSINSEL. In the view of the project team, this serves to justify using the limited responses from the survey as an indicator of the general views held across the industry.

The general headings under which the information obtained from both questionnaires will be discussed are:

— Plant Breeding Activity
— Type of Intellectual Property Used
— General Levels of Use and Awareness
— Satisfaction with the Protection
— Research and Development
— Essentially Derived Varieties
— Farm-saved Seed
— Ideal Legislation

## Plant Breeding Activity

As the survey results show, the majority of European breeders are involved in agricultural plant breeding. The main exception to this is the Netherlands where ornamental breeders are in the majority, with agricultural breeders forming the second largest group. For other EU member states, the second most important sector is horticulture (which includes the production of fruit and vegetables) and/or ornamental plant production. Very few breeders who took part in the survey were engaged in other forms of plant research. Only a handful of returns (primarily from France, Germany, the Netherlands and the UK) indicated the use of plants in pharmaceutical or medicinal research.[74] If this is an accurate indicator of the extent of pharmaceutical research involving plants then there could be some cause for concern.

One of the driving forces behind the EU Directive was the argument that the pharmaceutical industry needed the promise of possible patent protection before engaging in lengthy and costly bio-research. If the Directive is looked at solely from the perspective of its impact on plant research, then it could be said that its 'value' would mainly lie in fostering research into developing pharmaceutical applications of plant material for, as has already been shown, its applicability to agricultural plant breeding is relatively small. If the pharma sector of plant research were thriving or showing signs of imminent expansion then the Directive could be justified on the basis that it would both support and foster this work. However, if there is no apparent incentive to direct research to this area then the potential disbenefits of the Directive on the majority of plant breeding activities have to be considered (especially in light of the aggressive patent practices which some bioscience companies have chosen to adopt).

There is a further issue. Slightly more breeders involved in researching into herbs responded to the questionnaires than did those involved in pharmaceutical plant research. If these figures indicate a more general level of research then they could be taken to indicate that there is more research into herbs than into pharmaceutical plants. Obviously one has to be very cautious when suggesting that there is more plant research going on in the herbal, as opposed to pharmaceutical, sector but if this is the case then the introduction of patent protection could have a significant, and potentially deleterious, effect. Most organisations involved in herb research are engaged in research relating to nutrition and health. The techniques used tend to be unsophisticated—for example testing the taste and texture quality of a particular plant by simply brushing the leaves.[75] Very little of the research relates to determining the exact chemical make-up of

[74] However, this does not necessarily mean that there is a minimal amount of research work in this area; it might be that the companies involved do not see this work as related to *plants* but rather that it belongs to broadly defined genetic research.

[75] For a discussion of the type of breeding techniques involved and also the intellectual property issues posed see Franz and Johnson (eds), *Breeding Research on Aromatic and Medicinal Plants* (Haworth Herbal Press, 2002).

a plant with a view to isolating and relocating specific chemical traits through methods other than via traditional breeding. In common with the majority of breeders who responded, the herbal breeders have little experience of using the patent system, nor do they have much interest in using the system. However, it remains perfectly possible for a pharmaceutical company interested in the diverse applications of genetic material found in herbal plants to acquire patents over the genes which can be so used. This could result in the herbal breeders being unable to carry on the breeding programme as that research might now be encumbered by the private rights held by others.

Clearly the majority of European breeders are engaged in agricultural plant breeding. Whilst there is some use made of modern biotechnology techniques, these breeders are primarily reliant on conventional breeding methods in order to produce the uniform and stable crops desired by both farmers and food producers.

## Type of Intellectual Property Used

The majority of respondents primarily used the plant variety rights system to protect their research results although a number (primarily ornamental breeding SMEs based in the Netherlands and the UK) said that they had secured US patents for non-variety plant material and, in a couple of instances, for varieties. There was limited evidence that these breeders had tried to seek European patents for some of the same material but in general the breeders indicated that they had not because whilst the US plant variety rights system was thought to be of little value to the breeder, the European system was seen as both an appropriate and adequate alternative to patent protection. A couple of the Dutch breeders indicated that they had not attempted to secure patent rights (even over parts of plants) because it was thought that the exclusion of plant varieties extended to all plant material. None of the breeders from the other sectors indicated that they had sought patent protection for any of the plant research results.

A few breeders (two or three in the major jurisdictions) said that they also used confidentiality agreements, trade name registration and propagation agreements[76] to protect plant material but this use was invariably in addition to and not instead of plant variety rights. Interestingly, none of those who said that they used these additional methods expressed any dissatisfaction with them.

Most breeders chose to handle their intellectual property 'in house', with very few relying upon external assistance (such as national plant breeders' organisations). A key reason given was cost, but also a number said that the nature of plant variety rights was such that they did not need to involve a third party.

---

[76] These are essentially contracts between breeders and growers which govern the use of plant material by the grower.

Those that did use external organisations predominantly did so in order to secure patent protection, to look after licensing agreements and to advise on royalty payments. There was greater use of external advisers in the UK, the Netherlands and France, where there was also evidence of a more aggressive approach to protecting the intellectual property assets of a company through pursuing licence agreements and threatening litigation in the event of infringement (it should be noted, however, that only one or two companies of all those surveyed said that they had had to resort to the courts in order to protect their plant variety rights).

A number of small-scale companies (mostly from the smaller jurisdictions or those with only minimal plant breeding activity) said that they did not use any form of intellectual property protection but instead solely relied upon propagation agreements. All of these companies only had a local market and did not sell plant material abroad.

The results clearly showed that there was only minimal use made of the patent system, whereas the majority of breeders had experience of the plant variety rights system.

## General Levels of Use and Awareness

The majority of plant breeding companies stated that intellectual property rights were important to their company, with only a few, small to medium-size, companies (most of which were based in Mediterranean countries) stating that they neither used nor had any interest in using either patents or plant variety rights.

Plant Variety Rights.

Most of the breeders (nearly 80 per cent in total) were aware and up to date with developments in plant variety rights, although a significant minority (about 12 per cent) across the EU did not know which version of the UPOV Convention was in force in their jurisdiction. Invariably those who did not know which version was in force, when asked, thought that their national legislation was based on the 1991 Act. There was universal awareness of the existence and substance of the Community Plant Variety Rights Regulation.

Most of the companies who responded held a plant variety right, with the number varying between two and 30 national rights. The size of company made a significant difference as to the number of rights held (for example a small company may have one to three plant variety rights whereas a multinational company may hold up to 30). Where SMEs and multinationals were the same was in the proportion of rights held, with the plant variety rights percentage of the total percentage of intellectual property rights held being roughly the same regardless of size of company with 30 per cent plant variety rights and 70 per cent other intellectual property rights. At the time of the survey, breeders tended to hold more national rights than Community plant variety rights but this was a trend which the breeders said was likely to change, as many indicated that they would opt for Community-wide protection in the future. The main reason cited for the expected change in practice was cost-effectiveness rather than extension of protection.

Few breeders had had an application for plant variety rights rejected at either the national or Community level. Of the tiny handful which had, the reason was generally lack of distinctness or uniformity. None of the breeders affected had any problems with either the examination process or with the decisions reached. There were concerns, however, that a) some national granting offices tended to apply the same notions of distinctness, uniformity and stability to different categories of plants (for example, agricultural crops were treated in the same way as floricultural plants, which may not always be appropriate) and b) that different DUS standards were being applied by different national granting offices.

Nearly all the companies said that they chose to use plant variety rights because they afforded good legal protection suitable for the material concerned. The exception to this view came from the ornamental breeders, and from those in the Netherlands in particular. These breeders were concerned that the current system of plant variety rights did not provide sufficient protection for the end product as opposed to the propagating material. It was from this sector that the strongest support for the use of patent protection came. However, these breeders did indicate that if the possibility to extend plant variety protection to harvested and derived end products was utilised then they would prefer to use plant variety rights over patents.

In summary, and subject to the reservations relating to DUS outlined above, companies from all plant breeding sectors stated their overwhelming support for the plant variety rights system above all other forms of protection.

## Patents

Unsurprisingly perhaps, fewer breeders were aware of the legislation surrounding patent protection (although all were aware that such protection existed). Less than half were aware of the European Patent Convention and only slightly more knew about the existence of the European Directive (the awareness did differ according to size, with multinationals being more aware of the general legislative framework than small-scale breeders). However, aside from the multinationals, such awareness as did exist rarely extended to knowledge about the system itself. There was no difference in level of awareness according to whether the company concerned was based in a member state which had implemented the Directive or one which had not. Indeed, the level of awareness appeared greater in those countries such as France and Germany where there was ongoing debate as to whether the Directive should be implemented.

Very few companies held patents (the figures indicate only between one and ten patents held in any one member state with those patents evenly split between national and EPO grants). Those companies which held patents again spanned the spectrum, and a SME was as likely to hold a patent as a multinational; however, a multinational would have a greater number of patents within its intellectual property protection portfolio. The patents which had been obtained, however, did not necessarily relate to plant material as such. Many of those who hold patents do so over products or processes which can be used in plant research (such as apparatus) but very few were held over plant material itself. Of those who had experience of patent protection, the majority were involved in the modern form of plant breeding.

The breeders who had experience of the patent system did not indicate any particular problems with the granting criteria, and none of the breeders who responded to the sections on patent protection had any problems with either the discovery/invention distinction adopted by patent offices or the definition of plant variety used in *Novartis* and in the Directive (although, as will be seen below, this did not mean that the breeders felt that plant material should be patented). Not one of the breeders who responded was aware of the possible extension of patent protection to material containing patented technology or produced using patented technology, and concern was expressed that the protection conferred as a result of Articles 8 and 9 of the EU Directive would place 'too much power in the hands of those who are best placed to use the patent system.' With respect to the restriction of a right to use patented material beyond the first reproduction, the majority of breeders felt that this would be an inappropriate fetter on their (and other end users') rights to use material legitimately purchased.

When asked, however, nearly all the breeders (with the exception of the Dutch ornamental breeders) said that they did not feel that patent protection in general was suitable for plant material (including plant genes) and this view was shared irrespective of size or location of the company (although the multinationals tended to be less concerned about patenting genes as opposed to whole plants and plant species). The ornamental breeders (most of whom fall into the SME category) were generally supportive of the patenting of all types of plant material; not least they held the view that the protection could extend to material, such as flower heads.

In summary, there was very weak support for the patenting of plants, but also a realisation that there was some plant material, for example, plant genes, which did not fit comfortably into the current plant variety rights system but which nonetheless merited protection. In terms of how to protect this material there was a limited support for allowing plant genes and process involving plant material to be protected by patents. However, there was equal support to look at extending plant variety rights to cover this material. Many plant breeding companies were concerned that an increase in the production and use of genetically modified plants would lead to an increase in patenting within the plant breeding community and that this could have a negative effect on their breeding programmes (this will be discussed further below).

Generally, holders of plant intellectual property rights were able to defend their rights in a reasonably simple way (for example in the form of letters to the infringing party from a lawyer) often resulting in a successful result. However, if this approach failed then it was very rare for companies to take an infringing party to court either because of lack of evidence or excessive cost. There was some support for the plant variety rights offices to play a role in determining infringement, perhaps acting in an arbitrary role before any potential court proceedings. Those who held patents did not indicate any problems with enforcing the rights—although equally they did not indicate if any situation had arisen which might have necessitated bringing an infringement action.

## Satisfaction with the Protection

Two thirds of plant breeders stated that they were satisfied with the level of plant intellectual property rights available. National companies which exclusively used plant variety rights were the most satisfied with the system. However, there was less satisfaction amongst the SMEs and small companies with approximately 50 per cent of both stating that the rights are not suitable for their needs as they are too costly to acquire and protect. Ornamental breeders (and particularly the Dutch breeders) were the most obviously dissatisfied, voicing the views that neither the current patent nor the plant variety rights system adequately met their needs, that there needs to be a greater awareness of the diversity of plant material capable of attracting protection and that a system designed with the needs of one sector in mind should not ignore the needs of others which might benefit from it if the right were allowed to develop with that other sector in mind. These comments were addressed to both plant variety rights (and the emphasis on protecting the results of agricultural plant breeding) and patents (which have tended to look to the interests of the pharmaceutical industry).

Many plant breeding companies, irrespective of sector, stated that the cost of obtaining a plant variety right was excessive. However, when the cost was broken down, only the maintenance fee was generally considered excessive while the application fee, test fee and grant of right fee were considered reasonable. The main concern amongst these groups was that high costs meant that too much control over genetic material was being put into the hands of those who have the most money to spend on the rights. Companies from the agricultural or pharmaceutical plant breeding sectors preferred protection using propagation agreements. However, breeders from both groups said that, not withstanding the cost, they did use plant variety rights, as propagation agreements did not protect the plant material itself

Those who had experience of patents also said that they were satisfied with this system of protection—the concerns over the use of the rights tended to come under the specific sections on the type of material which could be protected (some expressing the view that the exclusion of plant varieties extended to all plant material) and the effect of the right once granted on their ability to use the patented material (with the concerns directed to the need to secure a licence rather than to the lack of a plant variety right research exemption). A few breeders indicated dissatisfaction with the cost of acquiring and maintaining a patent but the number was less than for plant variety rights. This is understandable given that more breeders have used plant variety rights, and the issues of costs in respect of that system are more relevant to them. Of those breeders who did express concern over the cost of patent protection the two areas singled out were the costs of seeking the necessary external advice and the cost of renewal fees. The examination costs were rarely cited as an area of dissatisfaction.

It is interesting to note that the level of satisfaction did not vary according to whether the jurisdiction concerned had implemented the EU Directive or amended their national plant variety rights law to correspond to the 1991 UPOV Act. Instead, all the breeders, irrespective of jurisdiction, raised the same points. A further point to note is that none of the breeders cited the absence of 1991 Act protection as an impediment to commercialising new plant varieties across the EU. However, whilst no actual problems had been encountered in trying to secure protection for patentable inventions, a few breeders (primarily based in the UK and the Netherlands) did indicate concern about the absence of pan-European implementation of the Directive. A further issue, discussed in the next chapter, is that many of the breeders thought that the patent system would only protect the results of microbiological (or the so-called 'modern biotechnology') research and that the exclusion of essentially biological processes meant that the products of conventional breeding programmes, for example, were not patentable. As the 'biscuit' patent obtained by *Monsanto* demonstrated, this is not the case in practice.

### Research and Development

Not all the companies were solely concerned with plant research, with the larger companies stating that half or less of their overall activities were plant research related. The smaller companies tended to be more single breeding programme directed. Equally, larger companies were more likely to use both modern and traditional plant breeding techniques. However, this should not be taken to mean that only the larger companies used modern research methods. A significant number of independent, or SME, breeders were also using this technology. Those that were using these technologies tended to be engaged in ornamental breeding (with some usage within the agricultural breeding sector as well).

Most breeders had used plant material protected by an intellectual property right. However, no companies felt that their plant breeding activities were directed by the availability of intellectual property rights or that their breeding activities had been constrained by an intellectual property right held by a third party. Very few had experienced any problems in obtaining permission to use protected material, and this applied whether the right in force was a patent or a plant variety right. Very few (less than five) had experienced any problems in reaching agreement over the content of the licence. Most companies said that where it was not appropriate to permit free use of protected material they would issue a licence to use that material. On average, companies issued around two to five licences to allow third parties to use plant material, and virtually all the companies stated that they had licensed out protected material. However, because of the limited nature of patent use, and the ability to use protected plant varieties freely in breeding programmes, very few (less than ten) said that they had licensed in technology.

Furthermore, the existence of an intellectual property right held by a third party over plant material did not seem to affect any company's decision to pursue research, although a number did indicate that this might be a problem in the future if there was a significant increase in the numbers of property rights (especially patents) in force over any given plant material. There were concerns raised over identifying who owns the plant material and having possibly to negotiate a number of licences in the event that more than one patent is held over the same material by different organisations or individuals. In addition, there were worries that an increase in rights over plant material might mean an increase in licence fee expenditure. There was a fear also that the licensing system was becoming too complicated and that there was an increasing need to secure the services of lawyers, especially when licensing a Community plant variety right which brought an additional cost.

The majority of companies agreed that all plant material, irrespective of whether it was protected by a plant variety right or patent, should be freely available for research purposes. There was, however, less unanimity as to whether a royalty should be payable once the results of that research are commercialised. Those with little experience of patent law adhered more closely to the plant variety rights notion of free commercialisation, whilst the larger companies, and those with patent law experience, felt that a royalty should become payable. There was, therefore, less consensus on this matter than the results of the ASSINSEL study indicate.

Many of the companies said that it was their policy to make material freely available to competitors, but qualified this by saying that if there was a general change in access (for example, more companies charging for the use of their companies' genetic material) then they would also adopt that policy. This was most clearly voiced by UK and Dutch breeders. Equally, the breeders indicated a less aggressive approach in the event that a competitor used protected material without permission. Nearly all, bar a few multinationals, said that they would not take the alleged infringer to court but would prefer to try and resolve the matter on an individual basis or not at all. A factor for this resistance to litigation was clearly stated to be cost and time, as well as a feeling that breeders should not seek to prevent others from using protected material. Very few (again less than ten) said that they had ever challenged a third party's intellectual property right or been taken to court for infringing a third party's intellectual property right.

Only one or two companies had sought to obtain a compulsory licence (and this was for non-plant related material, for example, a technical instrument for use in a breeding programme). In each instance, the applications were unsuccessful, as in neither instance did the patent office concerned (the Dutch office) feel that the patent holder had acted in an unreasonable manner.

With regard to Article 12 of the Directive (the compulsory cross-licensing provision), the majority of breeders expressed concern over this and in particular over the definition of 'significant technical progress'. Many felt unsure what they would have to demonstrate in order to achieve a licence under this provision, and suggestions as to what it could mean in practice varied from 'generally better than an existing plant, eg, better yield and growth but lower resistance to pests' to 'demonstrably better than any plant already on the market.'

In addition, the majority of breeders did not feel that the compulsory cross-licensing provisions were fairly balanced between the interests of the patent holder and those of other users such as a plant variety rights holder, particularly with regard to when the licence could be sought and more critically as to the impact of the need to show 'significant technical progress' on plant breeding programmes involving patented material.

In summary, the licensing system appeared to be generally working well, with few real problems in obtaining or issuing licences, either for research and development or for commercial exploitation of a protected variety. Compulsory licences are rarely applied for and even more rarely granted. It is argued that this is because the licensing system is working well, rather than because of any fault in the compulsory licence system itself.


## Essentially Derived Varieties

It was this provision, more than any other in either patent or plant variety rights, which caused concern for the breeders. It is relevant to note that the PIP survey took place before the publication of the ASSINSEL position paper or statements of the ISF outlined in chapter 3. It is possible that many of the concerns expressed in the project would be alleviated in light of these proposals—although the main concern, the operation of the provision in practice, will remain until such time as a clear jurisprudence has evolved.

In keeping with the views expressed in the ASSINSEL study, the majority of European breeders were in favour of the introduction of the concept of EDV (although a very few, five out of the whole survey, did say it should be removed as it could hamper further research). However, there was less support for the provision in its current guise. There was a very strong view that the language used in both the 1991 Act and the Regulation lacked clarity and that this would create problems for future breeding programmes. This view was shared across all member states and research areas irrespective of the size of company. The only companies which expressed satisfaction with the current provision were those with experience of the patent system and these likened the EDV concept to the dependency provisions within patent law.

The other area upon which there was general agreement was that the granting offices, and the Community Office, in particular should be more closely involved in deciding if a variety was EDV.

None of the breeders suggested any alternative definitions or methods by which the provision could be clarified.

## Farm-saved Seed

Concerns were also expressed about the farm-saved seed provisions. Whilst all the breeders welcomed the restricted version contained in the Community Regulation a significant minority were concerned about the definition of a royalty sensibly lower than the original price. Their concerns were two-fold. The first was that the figures vary from member state to member state (as each country is responsible for setting its own price[77]) and from species to species. The second was that they felt that they should be more closely involved in determining what that price should be. In respect of the former whilst concern was expressed about the variation, no breeder indicated that they had experienced any problems with this in practice—the issue was more about equity and equivalence of remuneration across the EU.

At the time of the survey very few member states had sent up a system for the collection of remuneration for farm-saved seed. Therefore very few companies were able to monitor the use of farm-saved seed or collect any remuneration. However, since the questionnaire, countries including the United Kingdom, Germany and France have set up systems for the collection of remuneration and from anecdotal evidence these systems appear to be overcoming initial problems and are working.

In contrast to the attitudes towards other breeders using protected material, virtually all breeders said that they would take action against any farmer who retained harvested material from one year to the next without paying the additional royalty.

## Ideal Legislation

The final section of the questionnaire asked the breeders to outline their ideal system of protection and to make general comments on the current provision.

[77] See ch 4 for examples of the differing national royalty rates.

The majority of companies said that the current provision generally met their needs at both the national and European levels. Concern was expressed at the divergence at the international level and at the weakness of other systems of plant variety protection in particular. There was strong support for the standardisation of global plant intellectual property legislation, preferably based on the existing EU system. This last point is of considerable importance given the EU's commitment both to its own internal market and to assisting developing countries. One company said that they would prefer to see UPOV 91 used as the model for all plant variety protection, including within the US, and a reversal of the use of the patent system as an apparent gold standard of protection.

The breeders said that they would like some amendment to national and European provision, most notably in the time and cost of acquiring rights (this applying to both patents and plant variety rights), and that they would like clarification about the EDV provision and also more certainty over the viability of the farm-saved seed provision. Breeders were silent on the issue of the more limited form of research use in patent law. In this there can be seen a stark divergence between the views gleaned from the survey and those expressed by the organisations which represent plant breeders, this latter group having long voiced concerns (including at both the PIP workshop and conference in which breeders as well as breeders organisations participated) over the possible impact of the patent style research exemption on access to plant material. It would be misleading to imply that this difference indicates disunity within the plant breeding community. As both the project workshop, held in 2000, and conference, held in 2001 showed, the lack of comment on the patent law exemption was due more to a lack of experience of the patent law within the wider plant breeding community. This is in contrast to the experiences of the organisations representing their interests which have had greater exposure to the patent system.

In terms of protectable subject matter, there was very little support to open up the patent system to all forms of plant material. Indeed the impression given was that the breeders would prefer a more limited use of the patent system with the plant variety rights system being used to protect a greater range of plant material. The one thing which the breeders all did want to see happen was that there should be greater convergence as to the type and extent of protection across the EU (and for those who market internationally) around the world as well. Whilst they are clearly in favour of plant variety rights (and nearly all support the 1991 UPOV Act form of protection) there is little support for the use of patent protection. Insofar as breeders were able to comment on the possible impact of a growth in patents over plant material they were clearly concerned over access to patented material and the possible effect on breeding programmes. This was of especial concern to the agricultural plant breeders.

Finally, nearly all the companies said that they would like a single body to be responsible for overseeing the regulation of plant property rights although none specified who that body should be nor where it should be based.

Cost

Unsurprisingly, the most pressing issue for breeders was the cost of acquiring and maintaining protection. At the time the PIP study was undertaken (1999) the average cost of acquiring a patent under the EPC was 4300 EUROS (including filing, examination and grant fees). These did not include translation costs, professional representation costs or renewal fees. The average cost of a European Patent, valid in eight member States and in force for a 10 year period (including translation costs, professional representation fees (but not patent agent fees) and renewal fees of 8500 EUROs per year from the 5th to the 10th year was 29,800 EUROS.[78]

A Community Right, for the same period, cost 1000 EUROS for the application fee. Examination fees then differ according to whether the variety falls within one of three groups. Group A (Crops) = 1000 EUROS; Group B (Vegetables) = 800 EUROS; Group C (Ornamentals) = 700 EUROS. These figures do not include renewal fees (which range from 400 EUROs for the first year to 1300 for the final year), nor fees for taking over reports or lawyers fees.[79] The issue of fees has been one that has taxed those charged with administering plant variety rights and in, an unprecedented move within intellectual property law circles, the Community Plant Variety Rights Office in, 1999, reduced its costs. The major unquantifiable figure is the cost of professional (legal) representation. This is subject to market forces and is wholly dependent upon how much a plant researcher wishes to spend on such representation. National rights are subject to local fees and these are determined at the national level.

A further factor to bear in mind is that both a patent and a plant variety right are civil rights which means that they have to be privately enforced (or defended) through the courts by the rights holder. As with any other civil action the cost of pursuing (or defending) an action, therefore, lies with the individual and it is impossible to place a figure on how much an action might cost.

As the issue of fees is primarily an administrative matter, it is not proposed to discuss this further.

For many breeders (from all EU member states) the issue of defending themselves against an aggressive rights holder (and patent holders were particularly singled out) is the most serious concern with some stating that they would prefer to cease breeding activity than face a possible threat of litigation through inadvertently using protected material in a breeding programme. Of significance is the fact that the concerns over aggressive protection of rights granted tended to come from those who said that they had only minimal, or no, legal knowledge. Invariably these were also breeders who only had experience of plant variety rights. Those who had experience of patent law expressed concern but not to the same extent as those whose sole experience was of plant variety rights.

---

[77] The European Patent Office.

[78] The Community Plant Variety Office. These fees have changed since 1999: application fee = 900 EUROS; examination fee = 1020–1200 EUROS; removal fee = 200 EUROS.

A further point to make is that, although this concern was a prevalent theme across plant research sectors, it was most acutely expressed by agricultural plant breeders. This is the largest sector in terms of activity and it is the one with the greatest preponderance of sole use of plant variety rights.

It is clear from the results of the project that the full impact of the developments in plant intellectual property rights has yet to be felt across the European plant breeding industry. Whilst it might be thought that a period of 'bedding in' should be permitted before recommending any changes to the policy and practice, the project concluded that, given the importance of the subject matter being protected, the Commission should specifically look at the potential impact on the plant breeding industry and seek to mitigate any undesirable effects of plant intellectual property provision especially where these are most likely to affect the majority of European breeders (SMEs working in agricultural plant breeding). In particular caution should be exercised in seeking to rely upon the patent system as the most effective and appropriate form of protection for plant material, other than plant varieties, as this may not be in the interests of the plant breeding industry as a whole. Whilst the patent system has provided great benefits for the pharmaceutical industry, and it is recognised that many of these companies now have an active stake in plant research, these companies form only a tiny part of the industry as a whole and it should not be presumed that the same level of use or benefit will inevitably accrue to small to medium sized companies.

## III. CONCLUSION

The various surveys outlined above show that there is general satisfaction with the plant variety rights system although there are concerns over the potential impact of the EDV provision on future plant breeding programmes. With respect to patent protection, the organisations representing the breeders have generally given a warm welcome to the recent developments, however, this has to be tempered by the worrying level of ignorance which exists within the industry itself. It is worth repeating that over 60 per cent of the breeders who participated in the second questionnaire felt unable to answer any of the substantive law questions. Whilst one should exercise caution in using these results as a general indicator of the plant breeding industry as a whole, it is significant that this lack of awareness was not confined to any one sector nor type of company nor jurisdiction. In the absence of any experience it is unsurprising, therefore, that they should prefer an expanded form of plant variety right. Most worrying is the fact that the breeders seemed unaware of the possible scope of patent claims (as exemplified by Article 8 and 9 of the EU Directive) and the impact of patents held by third parties on research. This lack of awareness cannot be ignored. Even if all the others engaged upon plant research who did not participate in the survey have excellent awareness, there remains a worrying kernel of ignorance across the EU[80] which will need to be addressed if breeders are to both maximise their own usage of the system and not be disadvantaged by those more familiar with the systems (and patent law in particular). In addition, it is worth bearing in mind that those breeders who did participate in the project are the ones most likely to have an interest in the subject and it could be argued that the fact that they did participate indicates a greater awareness than those who chose not to be involved on the grounds that 'this is not relevant to me'.[81] For the breeders, the most immediate and pressing issue was the cost implications, as user and receiver, of allowing more intellectual property rights to accrue over plant material. This is of particular concern given that most breeders fall within the EU definition of Small to Medium Sized Enterprise. This is a group which the Commission itself has recognised traditionally has little experience of intellectual property protection and which does not generally have the financial resources available to it to either acquire or protect such rights. However, it is worth repeating that none of the surveys indicate any demand for change in the existing provision, merely clarification within it, and this lack of interest in radical change mirrors both the current political and legal climates.

As previous chapters have shown there is a considerable commitment on the part of the Commission to the provision of a vital intellectual property environment. It is equally apparent that the Commission intends to keep the legislation under review (to ensure that it produces an appropriate environment within which bioscience innovation can take place) and this is to be applauded. However, the findings of the project indicate that there are a number of key issues (in respect of both patent and plant variety rights provision) which will need to be addressed from the specific perspective of the plant breeder. These issues will be discussed in more detail in the next two chapters, but at their heart lies the ability of plant breeders to undertake further research activity.

---

[80]    This is likely to be exacerbated by the accession of the 10 new member states, many of which do not have the same level of intellectual property provision for plants as the pre-2004 cohort.

[81]    This was a common response to the first questionnaire.

# 9

# *Common Ground?*

## I. INTRODUCTION

PREVIOUS CHAPTERS HAVE outlined the substantive provisions of the two main systems of protection, and in each instance the focus has been on the nature of the individual rights. This chapter will draw together aspects of the two rights which it is expected will converge and could potentially collide (such as the research exemption). In looking at the areas of convergence and divergence, we will return to the theme of the justifications supporting each right.[1]

## II. DIVERSITY IN FUNCTION AND EXPERIENCE

As chapter 1 outlined, patent law is, generally speaking, technology neutral and the rationale for granting rights to all forms of industrial property can be traced back to the Paris Convention 1883 and the stipulation that materials from flour to flowers are to be treated as protectable industrial property. As a result, the system does not differentiate between types of technology for the purposes of determining either whether the threshold for grant has been met or the scope of the right to be conferred. The justification for the right is that society's interests are protected by ensuring that only those inventions which can meet the threshold for protection are protected and those inventions which it would be against the public interest to protect (discoveries, plant varieties and essentially biological processes) are excluded. It is only in respect of these categories of excluded material that patent law can be seen not to be technology neutral. This technology-neutral status, together with the twin factors of the overarching presumption of patentability (which patent offices have to adhere to) and the commitment to not fettering the rights of the patent holder,[2] goes to the heart of understanding the patent system's approach to patenting genetic material.

---

[1] Our focus will primarily be the EU provision, and it has to be remembered that national practices will vary according to which version of the UPOV Convention is in force and whether the Directive has been implemented at the national level.

[2] As Cornish said, a 'wholehearted patent system will contain nothing that fetters a patentee's power to act as a monopolist if the market allows it': Cornish, *Intellectual Property*, 5th edn (Sweet & Maxwell, 2003) 7–41.

In contrast, the plant variety right was designed to be sector and technology specific (having only variety-neutral status[3]). The right is intended to take account of the needs of the plant breeding sector as a whole (although the right has at its centre the protection of agricultural plant breeding) as well as the protection of the interests of the individual breeder. This means that whilst the right is also a private right, which serves to protect the interests of the plant variety right holder, there is also the expectation that the grant *and* exercise of the right will serve the interests of the industry as a whole. As a result, provisions relating to both sets of interests, individual and sectoral, are enshrined within the legislation itself.[4] In establishing the right a determined attempt was made to keep it separate from the other forms of intellectual property right. The right was overseen by a separate UN Office (UPOV), and administered by government bodies responsible for agricultural as opposed to trade and innovation concerns. However, the reinvention of the right as a result of both the revision of the UPOV Convention in 1991 and the stipulation in the Community Regulation that this right (although not necessarily any other plant variety rights legislation) is an industrial property right mean that the content of the right now needs to be read alongside, and in conjunction with, it closest comparator within the intellectual property law family—patent law. In particular, consideration has to be taken of whether these changes now mean that the same rationale has to be applied to a Community right as to a patent. If the intention, and effect, is to render the system subject to the same considerations then this could have significance for the application of the substantive law and, especially, for the derogations and limitations to the right.

When the two systems operated independently of each other, as arguably they did until the 1980s and before the advent of patent applications concerning whole plants, there appeared little likelihood of conflict. The perception was that, in so far as the patent system had any relevance to the protection of genetic material it was at the microscopic level, with the Article 53(b) exclusion serving to prevent protection being accorded to higher life forms. The changes in the nature of plant research, however, tested that perception and the case law of the EPO rapidly showed that, whilst there remained some confusion over what was included and what was excluded, plant material of an order higher than a microorganism could be patented. In this, the practice of the EPO merely followed the principle set down in Article 1(3) of the Paris Convention. The result was that the relationship between the protection available for the excluded material and that for the non-excluded became the subject of close examination. Initially, as

---

[3] The one area where the current European system is not variety neutral is in the farm saved seed provision. Art 14 of the Regulation applies only to agricultural plant varieties; all other varieties do not fall into its provision and any rights over these would automatically be infringed if, eg, a nurseryman kept back seed, or other reproductive material, from one year to the next for the purpose of growing further plants.

[4] See, eg, the Mission Statement of the UPOV Office as well as policy statements made by government agencies such as the UK Department for the Environment, Food and Rural Affairs (DEFRA).

the views of those charged with introducing the Directive indicate, there appeared to be an expectation within patent law circles that there would be a 'destructive application'[5] of the exclusion which, unless those charged with overseeing the UPOV system responded effectively, could result in questions being asked 'whether the regime has a viable future.'[6] Both the decision to move the plant variety rights system closer to that of a patent as well as the overt extension of patent protection to higher order plant material (including affecting the uses thereof) has meant that in reality there is a greater likelihood of confusion. At the heart of any attempt to resolve this confusion, and potential conflict, lies the need to understand the technology-neutral and sector-specific nature of each right. Of crucial importance is the impact of the move to bring plant variety rights within the intellectual property law fold.[7]

As has been repeatedly stated throughout this book, the plant variety rights system was originally intended to protect the interests of all of those participating within a given sector. In contrast, intellectual property rights, and patents in particular, are not sector specific but concentrate on protecting the interests of the individual with few fetters on this right—the rationale being that if the threshold for protection has been met then the rights holder deserves strong unencumbered protection. If the plant variety rights system is to be treated as a fully paid-up member of the intellectual property family (with its emphasis on protecting an individual's interests) then it is possible that it could become increasingly difficult to rely on the individual/sector balance enjoyed in the past. Making the right an intellectual property (as opposed to agricultural) right could mean that there will be an expectation held by users that any limitations to that right will be given the same narrow application and interpretation as in patent law and that the paramount consideration will be protecting the monopoly held by the rights holder and not the broader interests of the sector as a whole. This has specific implications for the discussion below of the research exemption (and the relationship between this and the scope of protection afforded by a right) and the compulsory (cross- or otherwise) licensing provisions. In making such an assessment it will be important to bear in mind the fact that, as an industrial property right, any infringement (which would go to issues such as scope and the derogations) is likely to be heard by an intellectual property law court and a judge versed in intellectual property law with all its existing conventions and expectations. It remains to be seen whether judges will choose to retain the different approach (treating a plant variety right as a discrete area of law) or if they will, in light of its reinvention as an industrial property right, use the general principles applicable to other rights within this family, such principles not necessarily directed towards protecting a given sector or technology.

[5] Explanatory Memorandum to the 1988 draft of the EU Directive.

[6] Cornish, *Intellectual Property: Patents, Copyright, Trade Marks and Allied Rights*, 2nd edn (Sweet & Maxwell, 1989).

[7] Either overtly, as in the Community Regulation, or by implication through the provision of a right predicated on protecting an individual's private property rights as, could be argued, the changes to the UPOV Convention indicate.

A further factor to keep in mind is that member states may not treat their own national plant variety rights as an industrial property right, but possibly simply as an agricultural right. This could result in an imbalance in the function and operation of the right at the EU and local levels. It might be that in practice there will be little difference in the way the rights work and, notwithstanding the differences in form—for example 1978 Act versus 1991 Act compliance—granting offices, holders, users and the courts will not differentiate between the two with regard to such matters as compulsory licensing. However, the fact remains that the status of the two types of right (Community and national) is different and the use of the rights could vary according to whether the nature of that status is thought imperative to the operation of the right itself.

One final thought on the issue of function and diversity, with more multinational and start-up companies (both of which traditionally have their long-term security shored up through patent protection) becoming interested in plant research there is a greater likelihood that there will be calls for the right to be strengthened even further. Consideration has to be given to the consequences of these changes for the best long-term interests of the majority of breeders currently engaged in plant variety research.

### III. KEY ISSUES

There are a number of factors within both systems which do not seem especially problematic for breeders; these include the granting criteria,[8] the examination process and issues relating to procedure. Whilst it is recognised that there may be concerns over what constitutes, for example, a novel, or distinctive, plant invention it is clear from the activities at the international, European and national levels that those organisations charged with overseeing each of the systems (the WIPO, UPOV, the EPO, the Community Plant Variety Office and national offices) are actively engaged in trying to set appropriate perimeters—these being set within the context of an ongoing dialogue involving interested parties. It would be unrealistic to imagine that those who administer the systems will be able to take account of all the divergent views on what should constitute a novel or distinct plant invention, but given the level of awareness which exists at the organisational level at least it will behove those involved in the discussions to make sure that both policy and practice reflect, as far as possible, the needs of their constituents. As the plant variety rights system has utilised experts in plant

---

[8] Whilst some commentators have raised the question of what needs to be shown in order to demonstrate the function or application to which the novel and inventive technical effect applies, this has predominantly been in the context of inventions involving human genetic material. It is our understanding that this appears, at the time of writing at least, to be unproblematic in respect of plant inventions. It is also noted that some breeders have experienced difficulties in meeting the threshold for protection in plant variety rights, but as the results of both the CLIP and PIP projects show, this number is so low that it is unlikely to warrant further action.

research from the earliest days there is less doubt over the basis for the decisions it takes. It is likely that as patent offices (at the European as well as national levels) employ more examiners with expertise in plant science then this trust will translate to the patent systems as well. Certainly from the discussion of the operation of the various systems, the PIP project team could not find anything which did not indicate a growing confidence in the patent system—the key factor is having the requisite knowledge about the system. This does not mean that there are no concerns over the threshold for protection. The requirement to provide a substantial, specific and credible function (which does not form part of the language of European patent law) could be challenged on the grounds that it adds a further barrier to protection which the law does not actually permit (and may be contrary to TRIPs). Of more concern are the implications of the European Commission's first Report on the EU Directive, which indicates that it expects more patents to be granted over an array of bioscience inventions. The expectations of patent lawyers are, however, that the number of grants will reduce as the level of knowledge grows. There is a clear contradiction between these two points of view. The only conclusion which can be drawn from the Commission's report is that notions of what is inventiveness will have to be redrawn in order to capture what would otherwise be regarded as obvious advances on the prior art. This will have serious consequences for the whole of the bioscience sector and it is one which the sector (anxious to ensure that those rights granted are not vulnerable to challenge) is unlikely to support.[9] However, whether this push to patent more will happen in practice remains to be seen. Many of the patent offices consulted as part of the PIP project said that they would not jeopardise the expectation of patent holders that, once granted, their rights would stand up to examination in court.

Equally, the changes made to the farm saved seed provision, brought about by the 1991 Act and Community Regulation (which relate to the practices of keeping back, giving away or exchanging/brown-bagging or selling limited amounts of the retained seed) do not appear to have caused problems in practice for either farmer or plant breeder. However, this does not mean that this is an unproblematic provision and it should be remembered that there can be significant variation in the level of equitable remuneration levied in each member state;[10] in addition within each country there may be variation in amounts payable between species. This is an area which will require monitoring to ensure

[9] It is interesting to note that to date, in the UK, at least, no biotechnology patent has been upheld as valid when tested in court. The most common reason is a failure to demonstrate inventive step. As discussed in ch 5, the discrepancy between the judgments of the granting office (which would have found inventiveness) and the courts is understandable given that the latter will have had access to the full range of information at the disposal of the patent holder and opponents to the patent. The former will have had access only to published material. It should also be noted that only a handful of biotechnology patents have been litigated and the fact that those that have, within the UK at least, have been held invalid in whole or in part does not mean all biotechnology patents will be regarded in the same way.

[10] See ch 4, and also http//www.grain.org/seedling/seed.

that the operation of the provision in practice does not adversely affect either breeder or farmer, but the principle itself appears unproblematic.

Finally previous chapters have outlined the concerns relating to the new EDV provision and we will not rehearse these again.

There is one area where it will be relevant to discuss the farm saved seed provision and that is in respect of the scope of the rights and the *use* made by farmers of protected material and, in particular, apparently unauthorised use. This will be discussed further below when looking at the scope of the rights granted.

As already noted, the main concerns for breeders lie in the cost of acquisition and enforcement. In respect of patent law these are matters which patent law administrators are attempting to control; however, it is difficult because of a) the need to secure the services of a third party to draft the patent specification, b) the problem of translation costs and c) the difficulties in controlling the cost of litigation through the national courts (which would again require the services of a third party professional). In respect of plant variety rights, the reduction of costs at the CPVO had only just taken effect at the time of the survey (and it is not clear as to the extent to which this has reduced the concerns raised) and the biggest cost is often using third party expertise to protect the intellectual property in the variety, for example, by way of licence. We do not intend to discuss the issue of cost further other than to mention that, whilst recognising the need to protect the research outputs, it should also be recognised that protection conferred (whether in the form of a patent or plant variety right) is an anti-competitive device and as such should come at an appropriate price. The balance which has to be struck is between making protection available, but not at such a low price that spurious applications can be made nor so high that it excludes all companies other than the very prosperous.

It is against this background that the following issues will be discussed:

— defining the subject matter,
— scope [strength] of protection and infringement,
— exempted acts, and
— compulsory licensing.

## Defining the Subject Matter

There are two concerns here—that which is a) protect*able* and b) protect*ed* under each system of protection.

### Protectable Material

There are three issues which need to be addressed. The first relates to the definition of a plant variety. The second relates to the definition of an essentially biological process. The third relates to what can be captured by the right and this will be dealt with in the section on scope of protection.

Defining 'Variety'

At the policy level it would seem that the plant variety rights system protects only varieties, with the patent system protecting all other types of plant material. The continued reliance on specific categories of excluded material appears to indicate that there is a clear distinction between that which is protected under patents and that under plant variety rights. However, as has been demonstrated, the language used both in the legislation and in case law shows that the boundaries are not as easy to draw in practice and it is on these that this section will focus.[11]

On the face of it, the legal situation appears clear. Plant varieties are excluded from patent protection, but protectable under plant variety rights. All other plant material is protectable by a patent. As discussed in chapter 7, the Directive clearly states that excluded plant varieties are defined according to the definition contained within the Community Regulation.[12] As has already been discussed at some length in chapter 1, there are two problems with using this definition.

The first is that the Community Regulation definition recognises two types of plant variety—varieties which are capable of protection and varieties which are not.[13] The function of the definition is to enable plant variety rights granting offices to use plant groupings (which are not wholly uniform but sufficiently stable) as controls when determining whether another plant grouping is distinct or of common knowledge and therefore protectable.

What is unclear is whether the patent law reference to the plant variety rights definition relates to only those varieties which are capable of protection under the Regulation or if it also applies to those varieties which are *not* protectable under plant variety rights. If the former approach is taken then it would mean that certain types of varieties are patentable and the exclusion, far from being absolute, is only relative—the relativity being determined by capacity to be protected under plant variety rights. For some, this might make a nonsense of an

[11] The specific issue for Europe (as demonstrated in the literature, the case law and the results of the various studies) appears to be one relating to the demarcation between patentable plant material and plant *varieties*, rather than between micro-organisms and plants and other higher life forms. There seems to be less concern as to either the inherent patentability of plant material (provided the threshold for protection is met) or the patentability of plant material other than varieties. Both these could be taken as indicators of a modern recognition of plant research as predominantly a commercial activity.

[12] As discussed in ch 6, the practice of the EPO, following *Novartis,* is also to use the plant variety rights definition when applying the Art 53(b) patent law exclusion.

[13] Under Art 5(2), variety means

a plant grouping within a single botanical taxon of the lowest known rank, which grouping, irrespective of whether the conditions for the grant of a breeder's right are fully met, can be—defined by the expression of the characteristics that results from a given genotype or combination of genotypes, distinguished from any other plant grouping by the expression of at least one of the said characteristics and—considered as a unit with regard to its suitability for being propagated unchanged.

[14] As stated by the EPO in *Novartis,* and the Directive in Rec 32.

exclusion which has been stated to apply to *all* plant varieties.[14] However, there
is also a problem in saying that the exclusion applies to all varieties irrespective
of capacity for protection under plant variety rights, and that is how to determine if a plant grouping is a variety if it does not conform to the conditions
required for a grant under plant variety rights. If the definition were to be
applied fully then it could mean that any plant grouping which exhibits a degree
of stability would be regarded as a variety and therefore unpatentable. Taken to
its logical conclusion this could result in all plant groupings within which there
is some degree of stable conformity (for example in the expression of a single
gene) being excluded. If this is the approach to be taken then it could herald a
return to the immediate post-*PGS* situation and would result in there being three
types of plant groupings: those protectable under patent law (not being a variety in either sense recognised under plant variety rights, such groupings being
very small in number); those protectable under plant variety rights; and those
which are not protectable under either. It is unlikely that this was the intention
of the legislators and yet one wonders if this were not to be an interpretation
why the Directive (and the EPO) did not make specific reference to *capacity* for
protection under plant variety rights.

A further concern is that there remains the possibility for claims to be drafted
which do not refer to varieties as defined in Article 5(2) and yet, through the use
of alternative language, a variety is being claimed. The worry is that this will
mean that the exclusion of varieties will be decided by the 'verbal skill of the
patent attorney,'[15] and this has already been raised by the EPO itself. Because of
the nature of the patent system, where the skill of the patent agent manages to circumvent the examination process (and it is accepted that this will be less likely the
more expert in plant science the examiner is), the burden of rectification will fall
on those challenging the patent.[16] This might be an unwarranted concern, as there
appears to be a general commitment within granting offices to the spirit of the
exclusion, and examiners will be expected to look behind the language used to
assess the material intended to be captured by the patent to assess if the invention
claimed could be a plant variety.[17] However, not all granting offices might follow
this approach and it will be necessary to monitor practices across the EU.[18]

The second problem with using the definition is that a difference can be
drawn between that which is protect*able* under plant variety rights (plant

[15] A fear expressed by the Technical Board of the EPO in *Novartis/Transgenic Plant* [1999]
*EPOR* 123 at 133.

[16] As shown in the *Edinburgh patent* even where the EPO itself later recognises that an incorrect
grant has been made it cannot correct the position; instead, an opposition has to be lodged.

[17] The use of the singular is important as patent law permits claims which encompass more than
one variety; it is only claims to a variety which are prohibited. An example of this can be found in
the UK Guidelines for Examination of Biotechnological Inventions 2003, which make clear that
where all the examples provided in the application are 'directed towards modifying a single variety'
then 'there *could* be a presumption that the invention is specifically for a plant variety' (emphasis
added) www.patent.gov.uk.

[18] This might be especially necessary for those newly accessed states which permit patent protection for plant varieties.

groupings which are distinct, uniform and stable) and that which is protec*ted* (the variety constituents which, as was shown in chapter 4, includes genes). Because genes are patentable there is the possibility that both systems of protection could be used to protect the same material. This might not be thought problematic in practice as it is accepted that more than one intellectual property right may exist over the same material. However, given that the two systems are routinely said to protect different material, and therefore exclusive of one another, the fact that in practice the same material could be protected by both systems needs to be considered, not least because of the differing derogations or limitations which exist. It is possible that a plant gene (which codes for a particular characteristic) the expression of which has been honed in a variety through years of breeding (but which has not been isolated from the plant itself) could be protected by plant variety rights as a variety constituent, and could be captured by a patent where another breeder isolates or recreates just that gene for use within a multiplicity of breeding programmes.[19] Where that gene codes for a very specific, desirable, trait there may be a conflict between the right of the variety rights holder to allow others to use his protected variety in further breeding programmes and that of the patent holder to protect his interests in that gene. The concern is that a) a patent right could be granted over a gene the expression (and utility) of which is known and has been harnessed albeit in a natural rather than isolated form and b) the protection of the reasonable expectations of the patent holder will take priority over any other rights, including those of the holder of a plant variety right.

There is a question whether it is necessary, or desirable, to further delineate the subject matter protected under each right. Supporting such a stance is the argument that if the two rights really are intended to protect different subject matter then there should be a more precisely worded exclusion (for example by inserting into the patent law definition a statement equivalent to an exclusion of plant varieties *capable* of protection under plant variety rights). In addition, if the separation of protection extends to that which is protected as well as that which is protectable then any overlapping references should be removed (for example by removing the reference to variety constituents within plant variety rights, thereby making it clear that that material which makes up a variety constituent, such as a gene, is protectable under patent law alone). This does, however, have the effect of limiting the protection available, particularly with regard to the rights granted under plant variety rights.

The counter argument is that the lack of exclusivity works in favour of the person relying on the rights. An overlap of rights could provide more choice (and protection) rather than less. Whilst this is an attractive argument, however, we would urge caution with this proposal. It might extend optionality for the innovator but it might also make it more difficult for a third party to know which right, and therefore which derogations/limitations to that right, applies.

---

[19] As stated in ch 7, Art 3 of the Directive permits patent protection over previously occurring natural material which has been isolated from its natural environment.

More sharp-eyed observers might ask if such cumulative protection would be permitted under Article 92 of the Regulation. The answer appears to be yes. Article 92 prevents additional protection (either in the form of a national plant variety right or a patent) for a variety where that variety is the subject matter of a Community right. At first reading this seems to say that the variety constituents (which, independent of a collective entity, do not constitute a variety) can be protected by an additional right. However, this depends on what the courts take the term 'subject matter of a Community right' to mean. The wording used appears to refer to that which is protect*ed* by the Community right—in other words that material which *is* the subject manner of a Community *right* not that which *can* be the subject matter of a *grant*. If this is the case then the subject matter of a grant includes the variety constituents, and the dual protection prohibition may operate. The interpretation given will depend on the extent to which the courts will wish to allow the extension of protection under plant variety rights to prevent the acquisition of a patent over the constituents of that variety which are not themselves a distinct, uniform and stable plant grouping but which, when taken collectively, provide the characteristics which define that grouping. It could be that the term 'variety constituents' is intended to only refer to all the constituents of that variety taken collectively, but the fact that Article 5(3) of the Regulation defines a plant grouping as consisting of either 'entire plants' *or* 'parts of plants . . . capable of producing entire plants' (which in modern biotechnology parlance can include single genes) does provide an alternative argument. If this is the case then Article 92 can serve to prevent patents over plant genes. If this is the case then, depending on how the notion of a plant variety is defined (according to that which is capable of protection or that which is recognised as a variety), the only type of plant material which might remain patentable would be whole plant species.

Whilst there is an argument that patent law should make clear that it is only those varieties capable of protection under plant variety rights which are excluded from patent protection, there are also some problems with applying such a principle. The first is that it will depend on which system of protection is used to determine what can be protected. For example, whilst the Regulation and the 1991 UPOV Act require varieties from *all* species to be protected, the 1978 Act does not. If the former are used this could result in the situation where a variety will be deemed unpatentable in a jurisdiction where it is also, for national purposes, unprotectable by a plant variety. However, the variety will be capable of protection by a Community right and, as we have seen in chapter 4, all EU member states are required to give effect to a Community right irrespective of the level of local plant variety right provision. On this basis it would seem that it is expected that the provision of protection at the Community or 1991 UPOV Act level will be used as the benchmark. This does, however, take away from member states the right to use Article 92. For example it might be thought that a variety right is appropriate for agricultural varieties, but not for varieties grown for pharmaceutical or cosmetic purposes. A member state, which is a party to the 1978 UPOV Act, may chose to exclude only those plant varieties which are capable of protection under its national plant variety rights law and provide patent protection for all others. The second problem is that using such a definition could mean that only *varieties* are deemed to be excluded from protection. Again as we have seen above, the fact that the Community plant variety rights system provides for the possibility of protection to extend to material of the variety (either contained within it or produced from it), raises the question does the exclusion extend to only the grouping as a whole or to all those parts of it which will be protected by the right? It would seem, therefore, that the issue of what is a variety remains a live issue and one which will need further attention before it is truly possible to say that there is actual clear blue water between the material protectable under each right.

Essentially Biological Processes

This provision was introduced to ensure that private rights were not granted over i) those processes which occurred naturally and ii) those processes commonly used by plant breeders which might involve some human intervention but which predominantly rely on nature to effect the desired result. However, as chapter 6 indicated, there remains some confusion over the precise scope of the exclusion.

The first matter for consideration is the fact that some believe that the patent system only protects the results of modern biotechnology and not the results of conventional plant breeding.[20] The apparent basis for this belief lies in part in the perceived inability of such products to meet the patent law threshold of novelty and inventive step, but it also lies in a misunderstanding of the scope of the exclusion of essentially biological processes. The problem with the exclusion of essentially biological processes is that it is thought (in some quarters) to extend to the results achieved through the use of an essentially biological process.

Article 4(1)(b) of the Directive refers to 'essentially biological processes for the production of plants or animals.' Article 4(3) then states that Article 4(1)(b) will not prejudice the patentability of inventions which involve a microbiological or other technical process or the products obtained by means of such a process. For many coming new to patent law (and this included many of the breeders surveyed for the PIP project), the juxtaposition of the two types of processes together with the references to the 'production of plants' and 'products thereof' has meant that both phrases have been taken to have the same effect. On this reading, the reference to the exclusion of essentially biological processes for the production of plants is taken to mean that the exclusion applies

---

[20] For example in 2003 the President of the CPVO, Bart Kieweit, stated that '[t]he clear demarcation line between the scope of the patent and PVP system in Europe had the effect that in principle only the results of modern biotechnology are the subject of European patent applications.' As can be seen from the use of the phrase 'in principle', Kieweit recognises that the practice might be different: Kieweit, *Relation Between PVP and Patents on Biotechnology* (UPOV, 2003).

to both the process *and* the products produced by that process. However, a closer examination of the provision itself and of the practice of granting offices (such as that of the EPO in *Monsanto*[21]) shows that the provision only excludes essentially biological processes and not the products of an essential biological process. This means that the results of a conventional (or essentially biological) breeding process are patentable provided that they can meet the ordinary threshold for protection.

Breeders, however, appear to be unaware that the fact that they engage in conventional breeding programmes is not a barrier to obtaining patent protection over any plant material resulting from that programme—provided, of course, that the patent does not claim a variety.[22]

The second issue (discussed at length in chapters 6 and 7) relates to the degree of technical intervention necessary to turn an essentially biological process into a microbiological one. As has been shown previously, it is unclear whether a minimal technical intervention would be sufficient to take a process outside the exclusion. For the EPO, if it continues to follow *Lubrizol*,[23] any application involving potentially such a process

> has to be judged on the basis of the essence of the intervention taking into account the totality of human intervention and its impact on the result achieved . . . . Human interference may only mean that the process is not a 'purely biological' process, without contributing anything beyond a trivial level. It is further not a matter simply of whether such intervention is of quantitative or qualitative character.

The degree of intervention and extent of impact are important, however, and these remain unclear notwithstanding the jurisprudence of the EPO. Using the current case law it would seem that it is possible for a patent to be granted over processes which involve a low level of intervention but which, nonetheless, have a significant impact on the product produced. This could be a cause for concern for those engaged in plant research working at the borderlines between conventional and microbiological breeding. The open nature of the definition means that there could be some areas of plant research, which might have been thought to be essentially biological, but which might not be regarded as such for patent law purposes. The crux of the problem is whether the reference to 'essentially' means that the process must in the main be biological but it need not be wholly biological in form or function. The extent of technical intervention will therefore be critical to determining if the process is caught by the exclusion or not. On the other hand the provision could be interpreted to exclude only those

---

[21] As discussed in ch 6, the case concerned the grant of a patent over wheat which produces soft-milling flour that covers not only the flour, which was produced using 'conventional crossing techniques', but also 'the wheat, the flour, and dough obtained from and resulting foodstuffs.'

[22] This is evident not only from the results of the PIP project but also from the fact that, as the comment by Kieweit indicates, there remains the perception that the exclusion serves to exclude all forms of plant material howsoever produced.

[23] As was shown in ch 6, the decision has been approved in *PGS* and *Novartis*.

processes which are entirely composed of natural steps. On this basis any non-natural intervention will be sufficient to move a process out of the realms of the exclusion. The Directive would appear to support the latter reading. It states that 'a process for the production of plants and animals which consists *entirely* of natural phenomena such as crossing or selection'[24] will be considered to be an essentially biological process. What is worrying for those concerned that patents might be granted over processes involving low level technical intervention is that the Directive does not reiterate the thinking of the EPO. In particular, it does not state that the process must involve 'at least one essential technical step which cannot be carried out without human intervention and which has a decisive impact of the final result'[25] or that the intervention had to go beyond 'a trivial level'.[26] In order to provide clarification, and to ensure that minor interventions do not serve to render the exclusion ineffective (which could have disastrous implications for breeders operating at the borderline between traditional and modern plant breeding), it is to be hoped that national granting offices, courts and, ultimately, the ECJ, will follow the two-step practice of the EPO and require that the process consists of i) a non-trivial intervention which ii) has a decisive impact on the end result.[27] The fact that there is human intervention is not on its own enough to show that the process is not essentially biological; it is the impact of that intervention which is important.

If these issues are mapped onto the question of what the right is intended to protect then a further, simple question arises. How flexible is the notion of what is protectable intended to be? Put a different way what would be the reasonable expectations as to the definitions of the terms 'invention' or 'plant variety'? If the two rights are to continue to be treated separately with distinct individual rationales then it is easy to say that the expansive notion applies to patent law, as that system is predicated upon protecting the individual interests of the holder of the right who, arguably, would expect an inclusive and not an exclusive definition to be used. On this basis, the plant variety rights system would use a more restricted notion as it is intended to serve two interests: those of the breeder who holds the right, but also those of the industry itself, the overall interests of which would probably lie in having a more restricted notion of protected material. If the latter were used as the benchmark then protected and protectable material would be only that which can be recognised as a variety and the notion of 'variety constituents' would be taken to mean a global as opposed to severable construct. However, the Community right now describes itself as an industrial property right. Does this mean that the more flexible approach to

---

[24] Art 2(2) emphasis added.

[25] 'Plant Genetic Systems/Glutamine synthesise inhibitors' [1995] *EPOR* 357.

[26] Lubrizol, above ch 6, n 14.

[27] This approach has been followed by the UK Patent Office, which states in its Guidelines for the Examination of Biotechnological Inventions that the extent to which a process is held to be essentially biological (excluded) or microbiological (included) depends on the 'totality of the human intervention and its impact on the result achieved': www.patent.gov.uk.

that which is protectable should also apply to the subject matter of a Community plant variety right? If (and we accept that this is not necessarily a universally agreed principle) an industrial property right is intended to protect the reasonable expectations of those who seek and secure the right then, by extension, a breeder might reasonable expect that the notion of that which is protectable and protected by his industrial property right should equally be given an expansive interpretation. On this basis, and giving variety constituents a broad interpretation, a breeder can expect his rights to cover the individual components which make up the plant variety, as well as these components collectively as the whole variety itself. This would have significance for the industry as a whole. This then moves to the question—what is protect*ed?* This is closely related to infringement as the scope of the right granted will determine whether a particular activity involving the protected technology falls within or without the patent.

## Scope of Protection and Infringement

In looking at the question of scope it is worth bearing in mind that there is little in the literature (either academic or practitioner) about the precise implications for plant-related technologies. There has been some discussion in the context of genes *per se* but whilst a few have attempted to predict how this issue should be dealt with by the courts, most commentators reach the same conclusion, namely that this is ultimately a matter for the courts and any attempt to predict or pre-empt decisions at the national or EU levels should be treated with caution.[28] The problem with this approach is that the absence of any jurisprudence will provide an unclear and uncertain platform upon which breeders will be required to make decisions about future research work.

### Scope and Plant Variety Rights

For the most part the protection provided by a plant variety right has proved unproblematic in practice and breeders appear relatively happy with its extent. The exception to this are the ornamental breeders who wish to see the principle in Article 13(4) of the Regulation (the extension of protection to 'specific cases' relating to 'products obtained directly from material of the protected variety') applied in practice so that cut flowers may also be covered by the right. Even then there are concerns over the fact that the operation of this principle will not be automatic and will depend upon such products having been obtained without the authorisation of the breeder *and* the breeder not having had an

---

[28] White, 'Gene and Compound per se Claims—An Appropriate Reward? Part I' and White, 'Gene and Compound per se Claims—An Appropriate Reward? Part II'; and Crespi, 'Gene and Compound Claims: Another View' (2002) 3(5) *CIPA Journal* 255.

opportunity to exercise his rights over this material. This is felt to be an inappropriate restriction on the ability of ornamental breeders to protect, and recoup, their investment.

At present, however, there appears to be little political will to adopt such a practice and it is interesting to note that even the Dutch, where the majority of breeders work in ornamentals, have not sought to exercise this option. The reason is simply a fear of extending the protection beyond that which can be reasonably recognised as a variety and giving breeders too much power in the market place. However, it does seen very strange that whilst the UPOV 1991 Act and the Community Regulation both have recognised that rights lie both in the constituent elements of the variety and in any material which closely corresponds to the material protected, they should have shied away from allowing protection to extend automatically to both the material which makes up the variety as well as that which is made from it. It is unclear why this discrepancy remains, although it could be said to reflect the statement within the Paris Convention that flowers are to be regarded as industrial property which is properly protected by a patent. Such a view, based on an absolute separation between that which is protectable under patent law and that under plant variety rights, would be inconsistent with the fact that variety constituents appear protectable under both.

As has been seen, protection under plant variety rights extends to the constituent elements which, collectively, make up the distinct, uniform and stable plant grouping over which a variety right may be sought. The right does not extend to any other types of material such as the process used to produce the variety and under no interpretation can the right, as granted, be held to include any other such material.

The reference to the variety constituents begs the question whether a breeder can exert any rights over a *single* variety constituent. As the results of the PIP project indicate, some breeders are interested in a possible extension of plant variety protection to material other than the variety itself and the language of Article 13 begs the question whether this is already possible.[29] Central to this issue is the right which is granted.

Article 13 of the Community Regulation states that only the rights holder has the right to perform certain acts 'in respect of variety constituents or harvested material' of the protected variety. These acts relate to production or multiplication, conditioning, offering for sale, selling (or other marketing), exporting from or importing into the Community and stocking for any of these purposes. The Article does not say that these acts have to relate to the *variety* but does say that they relate to the variety *constituents*. Nor does the Article state that the *use* of the protected material would infringe the right held, as is the case in patent law. On this basis, the production or multiplication, condition-

---

[29] None of the bodies responsible for variety rights or organisations which represent the views of the breeders have, to date, looked at this matter, indicating that for the present, at least, protection applies only to the collective and not to the individual parts.

ing, offering for sale, selling (or other marketing), exporting from or importing into the Community and stocking for any of these purposes of variety constituents would be an infringement of the variety right. The question is whether infringement occurs when all or only some of the variety constituents are used: for example, does the right to produce or sell apply to each constituent separately or only when taken together collectively? In particular, would the production and sale of one constituent, in the form of a gene, for use in plants other than the variety protected for which the variety right has been granted be an infringing act. The answer is probably not. Not only does the Regulation refer to constituents in the plural indicating that it is those collective elements which make the plant grouping distinct, uniform and stable to which the right applies but also the current environment, where the plant variety right system focuses on the phenotypic rather than genotypic nature of plants, means that it is unlikely that a court would hold that the use of a single gene (no matter how important to the variety protected) would constitute an infringement of a *variety* right. If a variety is dependent upon one gene for its distinctive qualities then the breeder is well advised to seek (if available) patent protection.

In terms of defining the protection accorded by a plant variety right, it is first and foremost a right over that particular variety. The means of producing the variety are not protectable, nor (subject to certain caveats) does the protection extend to any use made of the protected variety. The caveats are that the right does extend to uses made which relate to the production of dependent or essentially derived varieties and to the retention of harvested material for the purposes of resowing (these will be discussed later).

In understanding the right it is important to appreciate that protection does not go beyond those acts outlined in Article 13. Other uses do not fall within the scope of the right granted. In contrast, protection under the patent system does include the use made of the patented technology. This means that the right goes beyond simply protecting the thing. CIOPORA has raised the question whether the omission of 'uses' within the texts of both the 1991 UPOV Act and the Community Regulation constitutes non-compliance with TRIPs.[30]

As chapter 2 discussed, Article 28 of TRIPs states that protection conferred by a patent over a product shall allow a patent holder to prevent third parties from 'making, *using*, offering for sale, selling or importing' the patented product. Where a member state of TRIPs chooses not to use the patent system to protect plant varieties then it may use another system, provided that the alternative takes the form of an 'effective' right. It is the contention of CIOPORA that in order for a right to be effective it must provide the same scope of protection as that set out in Article 28 and that the absence of 'uses' within both the UPOV and Community systems means that neither is an effective form of provision for the purposes of TRIPs provision. Whilst this is an understandable stance to take, it is not one which has found support elsewhere and, as chapter 2

[30] 'CIOPORA Green Paper on Plant Variety Protection: Policy Statement', November 2002.

indicated, the WTO is on record as agreeing that the benchmark for determining an effective alternative to patent protection is the UPOV Act. The WTO has not commented on what it believes to be the appropriate markers indicating an effective system, but the fact that it does not regard the absence of 'uses' as a barrier to the 1991 UPOV Act serving as the benchmark indicates that this is not necessarily a pre-requisite in formulating the scope of protection to be granted. Indeed, as will be discussed below, the scope of the right granted can be seen to equate with the patent law notion of 'use'.

Scope and Patents

In contrast to the protection accorded by a plant variety right, patent protection extends to the thing as described in the specification. The scope of the right is determined by reference to the claims. This means that both the protection accorded to the holder and the ability of third parties to engage with the patent technology will depend on how those claims are interpreted (the general principles relating to claims and their interpretation have been outlined in chapter 6). In assessing the impact of patent law on plant science it must be remembered that the ordinary rules on interpretation will apply and that these are based on the technology-neutral status of patent law. This means that any overarching interests (real or perceived) relating to a specific sector (such as plant breeding) will have little significance in determining how these principles are to be applied to a plant-related invention.

It is also relevant to remember that interpretation in patent law is by way of references to the claims made and not to the physical thing protected. Whilst it could be argued that some of the principles being established by the ISF and others in respect of determining physical infringement (in respect of EDVs, for example) could be applied in a patent infringement context, this is not the traditional approach and could prove problematic in an environment which operates on the basis of a legal/scientific rather than scientific/legal hierarchy.

The basic rule of interpretation is to provide protection commensurate with the inventive contribution made by the invention. The determination of the contribution, and therefore the appropriate scope of protection, is made by reference to the claims as supported by the description of the inventive activity. In addition to protection for the basic invention (which is governed by the EPC), protection extends to any biological material produced by a patented biological invention *and* to any material into which patented technology has been placed. This extension is permitted by Article 64(2) EPC and, where implemented, through the EU Directive. The Directive also, for the first time, specifically relates the general practice to biological material. In so doing the Directive broadens the concept to take account of not only specific uses of the patent material but, possibly more importantly, specific outcomes resulting from that use. This could mean that not only would any resulting plant variety be covered by the patent but ultimately any derived products such as a vaccine developed using the plant variety.

To date, little attention has been given to the potential impact of the scope of protection accorded to the holder of a plant-related patent. In general, a nod is given to the fact that patent protection is stronger than a plant variety right, but this is justified on the grounds of the likely financial investment involved in producing patentable inventions. The breeders' organisations also have tended not to delve too deeply into the matter, possibly because whilst there may be concerns over the strength of the right granted, the fact remains that this right may prove extremely beneficial to some breeders. However, as discussed in chapter 7, the scope of patent protection will extend into and down through future research programmes in a way which could (if not carefully monitored with the use of appropriate safeguards) detrimentally affect future plant research.

The general principles will not be rehearsed here, but it is worth remembering that neither claims drafting nor claims interpretation is a precise science and that there may be variation not only at the jurisdictional level but also across technological areas. Whilst the granting of a patent may indicate the territory claimed, until such time as those claims are tested in the courts the actual extent of that territory will remain uncertain. What is certain is that plant breeders will have to be increasingly mindful that a patent may exist, the interpretation of the claims of which, may affect (or even capture) their research work.

A number of key factors arise. The first relates to the function of the description. The general issues relating to the function of the claims and claims interpretation have been discussed in chapters 5 and 6 and will not be rehearsed again here; instead, attention will be directed towards the question of the extent to which a patentee can claim as yet unidentified applications or undisclosed functions of the invention. The second lies in determining the precise impact of Articles 8, 9, 10 and 12 of the EU Directive. This is essentially a concern over the breadth of claims being made.

As indicated in chapter 6, the issue of broad patent claims (which attempt to catch both disclosed and undisclosed applications of the novel technical effect protected) is one of the most controversial within patent law. Critical to understanding this 'problem' is the fact that both granting offices and the courts will require the patent specification to *support* the extension of the claims to any expected or unspecified applications. This means that the patent specification must contain sufficient information to allow a person skilled in the art to a) replicate the disclosed innovative technical effect and b) understand that the patent extends to both the disclosed and undisclosed uses of the technical effect. Where the claims do not support this extension then the subsequent applications will not fall within the scope of the patent. If the invention is capable of general application then it may be permissible for the claims to be also couched in general terms; however, they must not be so general that a person skilled in the art who reads the specification does not understand what the claims cover. If the claims are too general then they might lead to objections[31] that the breadth of

---

[31] Either during opposition proceedings or as a counter to an action for infringement.

protection granted is greater than the invention described. In patent circles it is generally held acceptable that the greater the inventive leap forward (for example, pioneering advances) the greater the protection which the patentee can claim. Correspondingly, minimal inventive steps forward only warrant narrow claims.[32] The art for both the patent agent drafting the specification and those interpreting it is to ensure that there is a fair balance between protecting the interests of the patent holder and ensuring that this is not done at the expense of future research work. Because this is essentially a matter of interpretation it is impossible to draw hard rules as to how this can or should be applied in practice. Patent applicants need to be aware that whilst they might seek a breadth of protection which they feel is commensurate with the invention produced, patent offices (now operating in an era of increasing reluctance to protect more than has been achieved) might not agree and even where they do, if litigation ensues, the courts might not uphold such a grant. Patentees (potential or actual) also need to be aware that practices are likely to differ between jurisdictions within the EU (up to such time as the ECJ provides a definitive judgment) and externally within the international arena.

In the early years of bioscience patenting there were concerns that patents were being granted over purely speculative applications of genetic material—in other words, where the patentee had not demonstrated *any* (or merely minimal) application(s) of the claimed genetic material, but was claiming all uses of material discovered. If the patent was granted (and initially some grants were made) then competitors would be required to take out a licence in order to use the material to produce an actual application. As patent offices have gained in knowledge and experience in the science, so too has their ability increased to understand what is being claimed and to spot if the claimed material relates to an actual or speculative application.[33] As discussed in chapter 5, the practice of the EPO, and some national offices such as the UKPO, is to require the applicant to include at least one specific, credible and substantial function within the specification. The problem with this approach is that it does imply that provided the

---

[32] See, eg, the decision of the EPO in Case T–29/85 *Genentech I/Polypeptide Expression* [1989] *OJ EPO 275*. In this case the EPO upheld a patent on the grounds that if at least one way of achieving the result is demonstrated in the patent then it is also possible for the patent to extend to other ways of achieving the same result. In this instance, the patent claimed, amongst other matter, recombinant plasmids, and the Board of Appeal held that the disclosure need not 'include specific instructions as to how all possible component variants within the functional definition should be obtained.' The Board went on to say: 'Generally applicable biological processes are not insufficiently described for the sole reason that some starting materials or genetic precursors therefore . . . are not readily available to obtain each and every variant of the expected result of the invention.' Obviously the extent to which it is appropriate to interpret the patent in this way will depend on precisely what the patentee is aiming to protect.

[33] That it has taken time for granting offices to reach this position is not surprising (nor should it be criticised), for patent examiners do not emerge fully versed in all the scientific nuances of a new area of technology but are as new to the area as those engaged in the research itself. In addition, it takes time to recruit those versed in the area in order to properly examine. In the beginning bioscience applications were examined by chemists, whereas now the situation is that most patent offices have examiners who are bioscience specialists.

one specific, credible and substantial function is shown then the applicant may still claim other functions (provided that the specification supports such claims). In the past the main concerns have been about patents relating to human health—either on the basis that they involve human genetic material or because the patented technology has significant health implications (such as the Myriad breast cancer testing kit[34]). But there are issues which affect plant research. These are exemplified by the Monsanto biscuit patent (discussed in chapter 6[35]) where the patent extends not only to the flour but to any products developed using that flour. The grant of such a patent will give the holder immense power not only within the market place but also with respect to controlling the work of others using the patented technology (it is worth mentioning that if Monsanto had secured a plant variety right over the plants then it is possible that it might have secured equivalent protection by virtue of Article 13(4) of the Regulation—the extension of protection to products derived from the harvested material (subject to the qualifications mentioned in chapter 4).

The Directive made only an attempt of sorts to deal with this matter, but (as discussed in chapter 7) it is not clear whether even this attempt will apply to plant-related inventions.

Whilst Article 5(3) of the EU Directive states that *a* function must be disclosed, it does not state that *only* one function may be claimed but simply that one function must be specifically disclosed. This mirrors the practice of most patent systems, which allow a patentee to claim a multiplicity of functions (some of which may be speculative, or undisclosed, at the time of filing). The only requirements are that a) the patentee must show that he is not claiming more than he has invented and b) a reasonable person skilled in that area of technology would, when reading the patent, understand that it extended to those undisclosed applications. There has been some discussion as to whether it would be appropriate to limit the ability of patentees to claim more than one function[36] but until recently this has not been introduced into patent law. One exception to this is Germany which, in December 2004, amended its national patent law (in order to comply with its obligation to introduce the EU Directive). One aspect of the new legislation is to limit the ability of the patent holder to claim anything other than the disclosed function(s) but only where the application applies to *human*[37] genetic material.[38]

---

[34] Above ch 5, n 64.

[35] Above ch 6, n 70.

[36] See 'The Report of the Nuffield Council on Bioethics' (*The Ethics of Patenting DNA*, July 2002) at www.nuffieldbioethics.org/publications/pp_0000000014.asp.

[37] An interesting question is the point at which the German patent office and/or courts will decide that a patent relates to human genetic material, as opposed to a gene, protein, etc which is common to other life forms. The question is whether broader applications would be permitted where the application does not specifically relate to human genetic material as such or whether the office and courts will look behind the language used to see if it pertains to human genetic material. This is an issue both practical and philosophical.

[38] This has met with sharp criticism, not least from Straus who has stated that the restriction to one disclosed function could mean that the German law is in conflict with both the EU Directive and

In addition, the Directive does not make any mention of whether the function has to be described in such a way which indicates a specific, credible and substantial function. This is probably not surprising, given that the introduction of this concept into US patent law was in 2001 and the Directive was adopted in 1998. However, given the unease which had been expressed throughout the 1990s over the types of claims being made, it is odd that the Directive made no attempt to steer practice (for example by requiring more than just speculation as to possible uses for the claimed technology).

The final matter is that it is unclear to which types of bio-inventions the requirement applies. Article 5 sets out the patentability of *human* genetic material. Article 5(3) is the last paragraph of that provision. The question here is whether the requirement to disclose a function applies only to human genetic material (which its place within Article 5 would appear to indicate) or whether it applies to all genetic material (in which case it seems odd that it does not fall within any of the general provisions). There is a lack of clarity on this matter— the UK position (as set out in its Examination Guidelines for Patent Applications relating to Biotechnological Inventions 2003)[39] indicates that the requirement applies to *all* genetic inventions. However, this is on the basis that other, undisclosed functions can be captured by a patent, provided that the disclosure made supports the extension of protection to those previously undisclosed applications. The new German law of 2004 also supports this position and whilst it restricts claims relating to inventions involving human genetic material to only one function it allows patentees to claim additional undisclosed functions in respect of other non-human related genetic inventions.

It is clear that all plant innovators (whether producers or receivers of patentable material) will need to be aware of how a relevant patent could be interpreted. The concern for the majority of current European plant breeders is that they do not have a tradition of relying on patent lawyers to assist in interpreting patents to assess whether they have an impact on research programmes. In light of the probable growth in plant patents this is a matter which will change and, given the sectoral bias towards SMEs, it is an issue which those charged with policy will need to address to ensure that these breeders are not adversely affected by aggressive patent practices.

Scope of Protection—The Directive

As discussed in chapter 7, the Directive makes explicit the extension of protection to biological material:

i) derived from the protected material (where the derived material possesses those same characteristics as are claimed) (Article 8(1));

international patent laws such as TRIPs. The result could be a reference to the ECJ. See www.bio medicalcentral.com/news/20041209/01. The same is true of the French implementation.

[39] www.patent.gov.uk.

ii) any product directly obtained through the use of a patented process (as well as any other material derived from that directly obtained material), again provided both possess the same specified characteristics (Article 8(2));

iii) all material (except the human body) in which the genetic material protected by the patent is contained which performs its function (Article 9).

The only limitations to the protection are contained within Article 10 (protection does not extend to the first propagation or multiplication) and Article 11 (the farm saved seed provision). The scope of protection necessarily determines what will be infringing activity.

Article 8(1) states that where an invention has given rise to biological material which possesses specific characteristics then the protection conferred on biological material extends to any other biological material derived from the patented material, provided that the derived material possesses 'those same characteristics' as described in the patent. The effect of Article 8 is to provide protection for the process, products directly produced using the process and any subsequent derived material with no apparent exhaustion point.

The Article specifically mentions that the derived material can be either identical or in a divergent form, the critical matter is whether the same characteristics are present in both the material produced using the patented invention and in the material derived from it. As discussed in chapter 7, the provision raises two questions. The first is whether the phrase '*possessing* the same characteristics' is intended to refer to active or passive possession. The second relates to the relationship between this provision and the exclusion of plant varieties.

The use of the term 'possesses' indicates that there is no need for the resulting plant material to exhibit those characteristics in any manifest form. It is probable that this will not be a problem in first uses of the patented technology, as it is likely that the initial material, incorporating the patented material, will be sought specifically because of the patented characteristics. However, there might be a problem with 'down the line' uses where the plant material produced using the patented material might itself be useful despite the presence of the patented material, and a subsequent plant researcher may wish to use it for purposes other than to benefit from the patented material. It might prove difficult to eliminate the patented material, and the second, third, or fourth uses may still contain or possess the same characteristics as the first use but this possession might only be a minimal aspect of the resulting plant. Should the holder of the initial patent be able to claim these subsequent uses as covered by his patent—on the fact of it, Article 8 would seem to indicate that he can. Plant researchers therefore need to be aware, as both patent holders and end users, of the potential scope of their patented material to 'reach through' multiple uses of the patented technology to any product within which the characteristics as specified in the original patent can be found.

An example of how this might operate in practice would be where Inventor X produces a genetically modified gene sequence which, when incorporated into plants, ensures a particular trait is expressed and this sequence is then used by other breeders in their breeding programmes. The gene sequence is patented. As a result of Article 8(1), any plants (or plant varieties) produced which incorporate the patented sequence are covered by the patent over the sequence, provided that the plants exhibit the characteristics claimed in the patent as resulting from the use of the sequence. The patent holder does not have to specify anything more in the patent other than that the sequences when incorporated (type of incorporation unspecified) will result in certain, specified, characteristics being expressed. *Any* material produced by Breeder B (whether single plants, plant varieties or plant genes) which includes the patented gene sequence will be protected by the patent over the sequence, provided that the material produced by Breeder B possesses the same characteristics apparently *irrespective* of whether the characteristics perform any specific function within that material. Furthermore, the work of Breeder C, who uses Breeder B's material in the production of Variety D, will also be held to fall within the ambit of the protection granted to Inventor X, and so on. The only qualification to the extent of protection afforded to Inventor X is that the material produced by any user of material which contains the patented invention has to have the same characteristics as those claimed in the patent as resulting from the use of the patented invention.

With regard to the protection of plant varieties, the effect of Article 8 would be to extend protection to any plant variety which contains the patented material. This serves to underline the point made in chapter 1 that whilst the patent system excludes plant varieties as protect*able* subject matter, it does not prevent them from being protect*ed* through the scope of the right granted. The fact therefore that patented material has been used to produce a plant variety will not prevent that plant variety being covered by the patent granted over the biological material incorporated within that variety, provided that the resulting variety expresses the same characteristics as described in the patent. Obviously if the resulting plant variety does not bear the same characteristics then the breeder is free to use the variety, but this absence may only become clear once the breeding programme is under way and up until such time, under the more restrictive research exemption in patent law (discussed later), the breeder will be liable to pay a licence fee or face an infringement action.

Article 8(2) goes further to underline the differences between protectable subject matter and scope of protection. This provision extends the rights of the holder of a patent over a process to any material which is produced using that process and, indeed, in a cascade effect, to any material derived from the directly produced material. For some this could be regarded as a form of 'reach-through'. Suppose that Inventor Z has a patent over Process W. Breeder C uses the process to produce Variety K. Variety K is the property of Inventor Z. Breeder D uses Variety K to produce Variety M. Variety M is also the property of Inventor Z, and this will apply even where Breeder D has not used patented Process W. Even though the patent held by Inventor Z does not claim a variety as such, the scope of protectable material which might be claimed could encompass plant varieties, and neither the Directive nor the EPO precludes such an interpretation being given to a patent (although it should be noted that this has yet to be tested at the local level through the national courts).

As can be seen, Article 8 gives substantial power to the patent holder, this power only being circumscribed in the event that Article 14 of the Directive (the compulsory cross-licensing provision) is held to apply. The strength of the protection provided is even more evident when Article 8 is read alongside Article 9.

Article 9 states that the protection conferred by a patent over a product containing or consisting of genetic material shall extend to *any* material (other than the human body) into which the product, and therefore the genetic information, is incorporated, provided that the genetic information performs the function specified in the patent. As with Article 8(1), this provision applies to all plant material from genes through to species.[40]

What is not clear from the language used is the extent to which the patent information has to perform its function. The Article merely requires that the patented material has to perform *its* function within the new host, but this is not quantified. Nowhere in the Directive is mention made of what effect that function must have on the new host material—in other words, it does not say whether the function has to make a significant or non-significant contribution to the new end product. The current wording would indicate that minimal functional effect within the new host would be sufficient to extend the patent right. This would mean that a patent holder's rights extend to any material produced using a patented product or process where that material contains specified characteristics even where those characteristics play little part in defining the global characteristics of the resulting plant material.

As pointed out previously, the effect of both these Articles is to permit the scope of the patent granted to extend to material which cannot itself be the subject of a patent application—for example a plant variety. This means that if an inventor has a patent over a gene which codes for a particular characteristic and a breeder (whether by use of modern or traditional breeding techniques) includes that gene within a variety then that variety (irrespective of whether or not the variety expresses the gene in an active form) will be covered by the patent. A further question, and one which will be addressed later when looking at the issue of licensing, is the extent to which the extension of protection provided under Article 8, and Article 9, affects the compulsory cross-licensing provisions ostensibly included to allow both a variety rights holder and a patentee to use material which the other holds rights over.

One matter which has yet to be addressed in either the academic literature or jurisprudence is whether the patent holder has to sufficiently disclose the extension of protection (in the circumstances outlined in the two Articles) in the

---

[40] And, of course, the open language used in both Articles means that the principle applies to all living material, the only exception being the human body.

patent specification (in such a way which supports the extension of protection) or whether the mere fact that both these Articles state that the rights will extend to this material means that the patent will automatically extend to this material irrespective of whether the claims support this extension or not.

The issues raised above do not merely apply to those who use protected plant material for research purposes, but also affect other end users such as farmers. In this respect, Articles 8 and 9 need to be read in conjunction with Articles 10 and 11.

Article 10 states that a patent shall not extend to 'biological material which has been obtained through propagating or multiplying biological material placed on the market with the authorisation of the patent holder.' This is subject to two conditions. The first is that the patented material must have been placed on the market for the purpose of permitting a third party to propagate or multiply it, and the second that the propagated or multiplied material is not then itself used for further propagation or multiplication. The effect here is that where patented material is placed on the market and the purpose for which it is bought is for propagation or multiplication then the right to do so only applies to the first propagation or multiplication. Any second or further use would constitute an infringing activity. The effect of this is to allow, for example, an ornamental breeder who holds a patent over a gene coding for a particular characteristic to prevent further replication of his protected plants without authorisation. However, any impression that this provision exacts an absolute moratorium on any subsequent replication of the protected material has be tempered.

A number of considerations need to be borne in mind which could have serious implications for end users of protected material, for example, farmers, when determining whether a given activity falls within or without the scope of the patent.

The first is the emphasis on the need to show that the *first* multiplication or propagation must *necessarily* result from the application or use of the material, that being the purpose for which it was placed on the market. This implies that any inadvertent second multiplication or propagation could be an infringement—for example where patented material is sown in a field and transfers to a neighbouring field where it replicates itself.

The second, which is closely related to the first, is that it is unclear whether the right to first multiply and restrictions on second use apply only to the person who bought the material or whether they apply to any users irrespective of a commercial connection to the person who brought the material to market.

It is possible that the Article will be interpreted as applying only to commercial uses which prevent the patent holder having the full enjoyment of the monopoly conferred. Indeed, it would be perverse (not to mention difficult to police) if the effect of this provision were to prevent *bona fide* purchasers of plant material intended for domestic use from both growing the crop from the plant and also (as is often the case with plant material such as seed potatoes) from retaining part of the harvest for sowing the next year. This use could be deemed 'private use' and held to be an exempted activity, as is the case in many national patent laws. On this basis it could be argued that the function of Article 10 (when taken with Article 11) is to prohibit wide-scale production which is intended for commercialisation. However, the fact that the Directive does not make this clear indicates that it could be interpreted as applying to all uses. As the practice in patent law is to provide the interpretation which best meets the reasonable expectations of the patent holder, it is probable that Article 10 will be deemed to prohibit the repeated production of patented plant material unless the use falls within Article 11 (this is the farm saved seed provision which incorporates into EU patent law the same notions as are contained within Article 14 of the Community Regulation).

The function of Article 11 is to provide a brake, in certain circumstances, to the protection conferred by Articles 8, 9 and 10. This means that any use not falling within the scope of the exception to the right as set out in Article 11 will be subject to the full force of protection conferred by the Directive and liable to litigation proceedings. The farm saved provision permits farmers to retain harvested material from certain species subject to paying an equitable remuneration. The use of any variety not on the stated list is subject to the full payment of the required royalty. The only group exempt from payment appears to be those farmers who fall within the EU definition of a 'small farmer' (however, as discussed in chapter 7, there is a question mark whether even their use might constitute infringement under Article 10). All others, including ordinary uses and re-uses (irrespective of by whom) of protected plant material are subject to the provisions of the Directive (and Regulation).

It is possible that the concerns raised above may prove to be merely academic. If, as the experts predict (and discussed in chapter 7), fewer patents will be granted over inventions involving genetic material because inventive step will be increasingly difficult to demonstrate then breeders are unlikely to be faced with a proliferation of rights affecting their ability to carry on with plant-related research programmes. However, if this does happen (and it is important to bear in mind the Commission's edict that more rather than fewer grants should be made, which may result in a rethinking of the level of inventiveness necessary for a grant to be made) then instances where inventiveness is shown are more likely to involve significant breakthroughs in genetic science. It is possible that these 'blockbuster' developments may be deemed worthy of greater protection than mere minor advances in the knowledge. If this were to be the case, then breeders, as users, may find themselves affected not only by any rights granted over the breakthrough technology but also by any extension of those rights to future developments. In the event that this occurs, then there may be an issue for the courts over the extent to which any sector-specific issues should or could be relevant. Again, the type of research activity (agricultural or cosmetic, pharmaceutical or ornamental) may play a key role in such a determination.

Infringement[41]

The scope of protection conferred by either a patent or a plant variety right extends to a right to use the protected technology.[42] This means that any person other than the holder may not use the protected technology without the consent of the rights holder.

Whilst neither system specifically states that in order for an act to be an infringing act it has to be a *commercial* use, in practice it would seem that the activity has to have some commercial element to it. Both Article 15 of the Regulation and Article 31(b) of the CPC (as adopted by many EU countries) permit private and non-commercial use by parties other than the rights holder.[43] This means that, in addition to determining whether the activity falls within the scope of the patent or plant variety right, it is also necessary to determine if the use is commercial or not. There are two matters which need to be determined: the first is what constitutes 'commercial' and the second is what is 'use'. In discussing this it is important to bear in mind the different notion of permitted acts—the next section will discuss *research* use. This section will concentrate on other uses—and in particular on the use made by farmers.

With regard to deciding what is 'commercial' the issue seems to be whether the use is such that it deprives the patent holder of his ability properly to exploit the market place.[44] In respect of what constitutes 'use' the question is the extent to which the user has to know (or ought reasonably to have known) that they have been using patented technology. The jury appears still to be out on this, for the patent system does not make any reference to the need to know that patented technology is being used (which implies that ignorance is no defence). However, when taken in conjunction with the emphasis on commercial use, it would seem that the use has to be such that it constitutes a commercial disadvantage to the patent holder—implicit in this is that there must be an intention to commercially use material containing patented technology. In this it would appear that ignorance of the rights held over the material is no defence, the issue being one of whether the user reasonably ought to have known that the technology was protected.[45] As will be seen in the next section on research use, the mere

---

[41] Infringement occurs only in the territory for which the patent has been granted. In respect of a nationally granted patent, it will be valid in that territory alone; if it is a patent granted under the EPC then it will be enforceable in those jurisdictions designated in the patent.

[42] Although Art 13 of the Regulation does not specifically refer to a right to use, the rights granted to the holder are sufficiently comprehensive that they equate to a right to use. Art 13 of the 1991 UPOV Act recognises that there may be other acts which a partly may wish to bring within the scope of their national plant variety rights; in terms of the scope of protection, the EU has not sought to go further than the rights provided under the 1991 Act.

[43] And the plant variety rights system obviously goes further in that it also permits use within a commercial breeding programme.

[44] For a general discussion of this see Cornish, *Intellectual Property*, 5th edn (Sweet & Maxwell, 2003) 1–6; and Bently and Sherman, *Intellectual Property*, 2nd edn (OUP, 2004) ch 22.

[45] As mentioned in ch 1, it is not a requisite under either patent or plant variety rights law to indicate that the material is protected. As both are registered rights, the burden of seeking out this information is held to lie with the user.

presence of a commercial purpose to the use may be sufficient to hold that use as falling within the scope of the patent. To a considerable extent, the determination will depend on how aggressively the rights holder wishes to protect the invention and on the impact (actual or likely) of financial detriment resulting from that use.

To date, the only plant-related case which addresses the twin issues of the commercial nature of the use and the intention lying behind that use is the Canadian case of *Schmeiser*.[46] Whilst this has no precedent value within the EU, the reasoning of the Canadian Supreme Court might be of value in assessing how the courts might interpret the term 'use'. This case involved a patent, but as will be shown below, it has resonances for plant variety rights.

In *Schmeiser*, a farmer (Schmeiser) had grown canola[47] on his farm which was found to contained the patented genes and cells used to produced the glyphosate herbicide tolerant 'Roundup Ready Canola' owned by Monsanto. Schmeiser had not obtained a licence to grow 'Roundup Ready Canola' and the patent holders brought an action of infringement against him. One of the questions facing the Supreme Court was what the word 'use' in section 42 of the Canadian Patent Act 1985 meant. For the Court the question was whether the defendant's activity deprived 'the inventor in whole or in part, directly or indirectly, of the full enjoyment of the monopoly conferred by law . . . [in such a way which furthered] a business interest.'[48] In respect of the argument that the patent only protected the claimed genes and cells (plants not being patentable subject matter in Canada) the Court held that 'a defendant infringes a patent when the defendant manufactures, seeks to use, or uses a patented part that is contained within something which is not patented [eg, a plant variety].'[49] In this instance, the presence of the genes within the plant crop being grown by Schmeiser was 'use' and the commercial nature of the growing meant that it was an infringing use. In determining the state of mind of the person using the patented material, the Court reiterated the general principle that intention is irrelevant. However, it said that intent could be relevant if, as was being argued here, the defendant was arguing that he did not know the genes were present in the crop. As he did not know they were there he could not be using them. The presumption at law (and this would be the position in most European jurisdictions) is that the mere presence of patented material carries with it a presumption of an intention to use which the defendant will have to rebut. Certainly Article 8 of the Directive would support such an interpretation. A rebuttal would need to show that the defendant had no intention of using the material in any manner which would be

---

[46] *Monsanto Canada Inc v Schmeiser* [2004] SCC 34. For further discussion of the case see Sherman, 'Biological Inventions and the Problem of Passive Infringement' (2002) 13(3) *Australian Intellectual Property Journal* 146; Lee and Burrell, 'Liability for the Escape of GM Seeds: Pursuing the "Victim"?' (2002) 65(4) *Modern Law Review* 517. The official Percy Schmeiser website also provides some useful insights: http://www.percyschmeiser.com.

[47] Canola is a variety of rape.

[48] *Monsanto Canada Inc v Schmeiser*, above n 46, pp 35 and 37.

[49] *Ibid*, p 42.

to his advantage. In this instance it was held (albeit by a 5/4 split) that 'saving and planting seed, then harvesting and selling the resultant plants containing the patented cells and genes appears, on a common sense view, to constitute utilization of the patented material.'[50] The commercial nature of this use meant that the defendant deprived Monsanto of the enjoyment of the whole of its monopoly. In respect of the defence of a lack of knowledge of the presence of the patented material, the Court said that conduct could go a long way to rebutting the presumption of an intention to use. In this instance the conduct of Mr Schmeiser indicated to the Court that he was aware that some of his plants had acquired the characteristics of the 'Roundup Ready Canola', as he had used the 'Roundup' herbicide in order to isolate the plants, he had harvested these plants, kept them separate from his other harvest and then sowed them in following years to the extent that he ended up with 1003 acres of Roundup Ready Canola. If he had bought sufficient plants to cover the same acreage it would have cost him $15,000. Unfortunately, the court did not comment on the possible outcome if Mr Schmeiser had been able to show that the inclusion of the patented material had been wholly inadvertent and there was no intention to use.

A concern for many farmers within Europe (especially those with a tradition of small farming, with farms located close to one another or with a strong organic farming community) is the extent to which they would be liable if patented genetic material makes its way into their crops either as a result of blow-over from one field to another or via other conventional methods of gene transference which are not controlled by either a breeder or a farmer. There are a number of layers to these concerns, which include whether a non-GM farmer will bear the burden of having to identify whether there is any patented material within the crops he produced. If there is, then would the test for determining liability be one of reasonableness, or would different scales be used depending upon whether the patented trait is observably expressed (such as in colour or resistance) which a farmer should have noted or whether it is impossible to detect the trait without a genetic test (which also could include resistance and traits such as vitamin enhancement). There is also the issue of identifying who owns the patent. The farmer might be aware of new characteristics within his crop; it might also be regarded as reasonable to expect him to realise that the new characteristics might be patented—but how reasonable is it to require him to try and identify who is the owner of any possible patent? There is an argument for requiring any company seeking to rely on a patent over transferable technology to include a marker within that technology (an equivalent to a genetic bar-code) which would identify the owner of any rights over the technology. Official organisations, such as the patent office, variety rights office and those representing the interests of farming communities, could then have access to an official database upon which all the identifying information could be held, enabling a farmer to submit his material for examination to ascertain a) if it is

---

[50] *Ibid*, p 69.

affected by patented technology and b) who the owner of that patent might be. Given that there is an acute need to encourage farmers to use crops bred using the new techniques there is a strong public interest in providing support mechanisms helping them avoid any unnecessary burden resulting from the grant of a patent. Such measures may also help the farmers when assessing levels of GM for the purposes of labelling crop produce.

Given the emphasis in *Schmeiser* on the commercial nature of the use, there is also the question of whether there would be an equivalent emphasis where the alleged use takes the form of transference to a crop which serves to reduce the commercial viability of that crop, as would be the case of the existence of a transgenic gene within an organic crop.

There are also the questions of whether the emphasis on commercial use means mere presence within a crop which, irrespective of the presence of the patented material, is itself commercially valuable (the presence of the gene neither enhancing nor detracting from the commercial value) or whether there has to be added value to the crop being grown and, additionally whether that value added by the patented material has to transfer into the commercialised material itself (for example, if the trait is a nutritional one then the value will move from plant to product, but if it is merely one relating to the qualities of the plant whilst being grown (such as hardiness or yield) then, unless the material produced is itself for sale as seed material, this will not form part of the value of the thing being sold). Also, where patented material has been transferred to a crop, for example, then in order for the patentee to claim infringement does the entire crop have to carry the gene or only some, and if the latter, then how many of the plants must be shown to have the patented material for infringement to take place? This latter point is an important one when determining whether a farmer will know if his crop has been genetically altered. As is recognised within plant variety rights, variation within the plants of a variety is permitted. The genes transferred might result in some of the plants appearing phenotypically different; however, these might only be a small percentage of the plants overall and whilst the farmer might note the differences (and indeed cultivate them) he might put this down to the permitted variations rather than to the presence of patented material. The question here is at what point will a farmer be held to be using the material in a way which infringes the patent.

It could be argued that the same points apply to plant breeders. However, most breeding programmes are now very carefully policed and recorded and there is greater knowledge not merely of the genetic make-up of plants but also of those genetic elements 'developed' by man for use in plants. When taken together with the fact that patents will only be granted over plant material which can be shown to have a demonstrable function (which renders that material inventive) and the likelihood of patent protection being granted over plant genes which have no function when incorporated into a plant will be virtually zero, it means it will be increasingly difficult for a breeder to say that any such incorporation was inadvertent and therefore not an infringing act.

If the Directive were applied then the question which would need to be addressed is whether the extension of protection conferred by Articles 8–10 could be set aside by a defence of non-commercial use. Even if this were an acceptable defence, then the patent holder might still be able to claim royalties on the basis that Article 11 applied. Where the Directive is in force then clearly the key issue is the relationship between Articles 8–11 and the non-commercial use defence. The fact that Article 8 permits an extension of protection through a passive inclusion of patented material would seem to indicate that even where there is no direct commercial use of that technology (although there might be indirect commercial use through the marketing of the technology within which it is passively included) then there may still be an infringement. If the patent is in force in a country which has not implemented the Directive then the critical issue will be how that jurisdiction views the relationship between the general principles relating to scope and any non-commercial use defence.

It is possible that the plants within which the patented technology is included may themselves be protected by a plant variety right. If this is a national plant variety right then the defences available will depend on the national legislation, which may or may not be based on the 1991 UPOV Act. If the right is a Community right then its scope will again depend on the relationship between the provisions relating to scope (including obviously the more restricted form of farm saved seed which may not be in operation at the national level even where a member state has implemented the 1991 UPOV Act as the right further to restrict the activities of third parties is an option which members can choose to adopt) and the non-commercial use defence. If the hypothetical plant variety right was a Community right then a farmer such as Mr Schmeiser would be liable to pay an additional royalty under Article 14. If he would have been liable for the full payment or an equitable remuneration sensibly lower than that originally paid will depend upon whether the canola falls within the list of agricultural plant species contained in Article 14(2) of the Regulation.[51] If he is liable for an equitable remuneration sensibly lower than that originally paid then the extent of that liability will depend on the level of remuneration adopted within the jurisdiction where the saving of the seed took place.

If the person retaining and resowing the protected material is not a farmer then the issue will simply be one of determining the commercial nature of the use. This will be dependent upon local practices (as evolved by national courts and ultimately the ECJ).

There has been increasing correlation between the scope of the rights granted under the two systems. Indeed, the introduction of the essentially derived provision as well as the possibility of extension of protection to products derived from protected material within the Community Regulation could be held to correspond to the Article 8–10 provisions of the Directive. However, for many,

---

[51] The Regulation makes reference to two types of rape species—*Brassica napus* L (partim) and *Brassica rapa* L (partim).

protection under plant variety rights remains less than under patent law, for it is constrained both by the limited nature of that which is protected, and also by the fact that the right primarily relates to physical actions involving the protected material. However, because of this it is more certain and the scope of protection held more evident. In contrast, because the patent system is less concerned with pinning down either the subject matter or the form of the actions involving it, it provides greater uncertainty (and flexibility) as to what is protected. This gives greater scope for defining the territory to be protected, but also means that third parties may remain unclear as to the precise ambit of that territory until such time as they stray (wittingly or otherwise) into it.

As might be realised, the above discussion only scratches at the surface of the potential implications of both the scope of protection and infringement of rights. Unfortunately it is not possible to go into the many and varied possible permutations which might arise, which could relate to type of subject matter or activity and the legal environment within which that activity takes place. The major concern is the fact, as chapter 7 has shown, that the majority of breeders remain ignorant of patent law and, thus, may not be able to protect themselves either from inadvertent infringement or from outside control of the results of their research work where that work has involved the use of patented technology.

The various bodies charged with overseeing provision (such as the WIPO, UPOV, the European Commission and the Community Plant Variety Rights Office) recognise that there could be a problem with the scope of protection—especially with regard to that provided under patent law. However, none has sought to try and curb the scope of protection available but they instead advocate monitoring the situation. In many respects this is understandable as the revised rights bed in. However, it is obvious, as the merest of glances at the patent system shows, that this could have significant implications for future breeding programmes and perhaps any fears that these rights could be used to prevent further research (either on the grounds that the research activity falls within the scope of the claims and outside the research exemption or on the basis that even if the research exemption applies the resulting work will be captured by the patent) should be allayed as quickly and as authoritatively as possible. In the current environment, the impression given is that breeders will be required to fend for themselves within what for many will be unfamiliar and daunting territory. Whilst it is recognised that the patent system may bring great rewards to those who use it, it is imperative that these are not secured to the detriment of others seeking to undertake valuable breeding research.

In respect of the scope of protection, both the patent and plant variety rights system now clearly emphasise the need to protect the interests of the rights holder. In this the rationales for the two rights appear similar. However, it is when the exemptions and limitations are compared that the different approaches taken to protecting the interests of a sector as a whole as opposed to the interests of an individual within it become relevant, and the issue of whether the traditional restricted approach taken within patent law should now be applied to the Community right, as it is an industrial property right, becomes more acute.

## Exempted Acts

As the previous section has demonstrated, the rights granted mean that rights holders have the capacity to control the use of not only the material claimed in the patent or plant variety right but also material into which that protected material has been placed or which is produced by a patented process. The extent, or scope, of the rights is such that it has long been recognised that there is a need to allow use in certain circumstances which will not be held to be infringing. The most important of these for plant innovators is the right to use protected material for research and commercial breeding purposes. As this next section will show, both the patent and plant variety rights systems permit the use of protected material for experimental purposes; however, the basis upon which these derogations are formulated, as well as the way in which they operate in practice, is very different and a possible lack of comparability (and compatibility) between the two is the cause of some concern.

### The Research Exemption in Patent Law

As mentioned in chapter 6, Article 31(b) of the Community Patent Convention permits acts done for private, experimental or non-commercial purposes. Whilst the Convention itself is not in force, most European countries have adopted this provision. The law treats as separate use which is private and non-commercial (for example pure research work in universities, or other public institutions, which is undertaken without industrial backing or commercial purpose) and, on the other hand, experimental use. It is very important to note that there is very little case law on this area, and none which relates to plant innovation. This makes it very difficult to know the precise scope of the exception. In addition, such case law as there is relates to bio-inventions involving pharmaceutical products (which might apply to a new plant-pharma product), and the line taken by the courts might be very different in respect of other types of plant inventions such as agricultural or ornamental plants.

Whilst a first reading of the exemption would appear to indicate that any taint of commercialisation would lead to an action for infringement, it has become increasingly clear that courts across Europe are willing to treat experimental research as non-infringing even where it might have a commercial purpose.[52]

---

[52] For the UK, see *Monsanto v Stauffer* [1985] RPC 515. For recent confirmation of the new approach in France, see *Wellcome Foundation v Parexel International & Flamel* (Tribunal de Grande Instance de Paris, 20 February 2001), *Intellectual Property News Issue*, 17 July 2001. The situation will increasingly change as a result of EU Directive 2004/27/EC.

However, what constitutes experimental use is given a restrictive interpretation and the exemption has been held to apply only where the research involves modifying or improving the patented invention[53]—in Germany at least, this includes providing further information about the properties of the invention, for instance through clinical trials.[54] This interpretation does not extend to research which involves using the patented invention for any other purpose which would affect the right of a breeder to use patented technology in a commercial breeding programme. The classic example of the use of the research exemption in the field of gene patenting is provided by Hoffmann-La Roche's patent on Polymerise Chain Reaction (PCR). Work using the patented material in order to provide an improved PCR would count as an experimental use, but work which simply used Hoffmann-La Roche's PCR as a standard procedural step, for example to amplify genetic material, would not. Equally, the exemption would not cover tests which merely replicate the invention, for example where a generic drug company is seeking evidence for permission from a Medicines Authority to market its version of a drug once the patent on it expires.[55]

From what little case law there is, it would seem that the European exception for experimental purposes is restricted to research which builds upon the knowledge provided by the patent, with the aim of discovering something new about the subject matter of the patent or to test a hypothesis relating to it.[56] The aim is to ensure general demand for the patented material so that the patentee will earn very considerable royalties and other licence fees. Put simply, the exemption permits use *on* but not *with* the patented invention.

One major ambiguity about the experimental use exception as it affects biotechnological patents is how far clinical tests can be regarded as experimental, since treatment and the continuing search for further genetic knowledge often enough go hand in hand. It may well be that they can only be treated as exempt where the latter objective is a dominant motive for the tests but the law remains rather uncertain. The practice in European countries varies. For example, in Holland, Boehringer Mannheim, who were marketing their version of erythropoietin under licence from Kirin-Amgen as patentees, were held entitled to conduct clinical tests of their product for further medical indications.[57] However, questions are raised on what basis Boehringer Mannheim were marketing erythropoietin and how much was for clinical testing and how much was for research. In Germany, a drug company was marketing genetically engineered interferon-gamma under a compulsory licence from a patentee, government authorisation having been given for its use in treating rheumatoid arthritis. It conducted clinical tests for other indications (the treatment of cancer,

---

[53] The exception must also cover experiments to discover whether the invention can be made from its description in the patent specification (essential if the patent is to be challenged).

[54] *Klinische Versuche I and II* [1997] RPC 623; [1998] RPC 423.

[55] Much of the recent case law in Europe goes to this particular question.

[56] See Aldous LJ in *Auchinloss v Agricultural & Veterinary Supplies* [1999] RPC 397, 406.

[57] Court of Appeal of The Hague, 3 February 1994 (Docket No 93/960), affirmed on other grounds by the Netherlands Supreme Court.

Aids, allergies, leukaemia, asthma and chronic hepatitis). To do so amounted to experimental use needing no patent licence.[58] The exception was not limited to experiments on the protein itself, as distinct from its medical uses. They were justified because they would gain information and so would carry out scientific research. The exception would apply whether the purpose was to check statements in the patent specification or to produce further results; and the fact that the work was by an industrial firm which would ultimately seek to commercialise it did not alter the protected legal position of the researcher. Again in Germany, clinical trials of patented erythropoietin were permitted which aimed to produce further knowledge of patient tolerance and side-effects when using the protein for a known indication. The patentee had argued that this testing was taking place after the basic effectiveness of the formulation in humans had already been established, and that therefore the tests were directly related to the commercial potential of the drug and to securing medical authorisation for it. This argument was rejected and the decision stands as highly persuasive authority favouring a broad scope for experimental use in the context of clinical trials.[59] At present this is not an issue which concerns most plant breeders; however, as the use of plants in the production of new pharmaceutical products increases then so too could this issue grow in importance.

Of more immediate concern to plant breeders is that the use of patented material for purposes other than the modification, or improvement of the invention itself is not permitted nor (even where the experimentation relates to improving or modifying) is the commercialisation of the results of that work if the results involve the patented material. These will involve construing the proper scope of the patent claims and determining whether Articles 8 and 9 of the Directive apply. It is clear that there is a stark difference between this position and that under plant variety rights where both the use of protected material in a commercial breeding programme and the commercialisation of the results of that research work are permitted.

At present, most national patent systems do not differentiate between a) types of inventions and b) types of biotechnological inventions for the purposes of applying the research exemption, and until such time as there is a general political will to draw distinctions, plant inventions will be treated in the same way as all other bioscience-related inventions. In the absence of any direct evidence demonstrating that particular types of information should be treated differently, the presumption in patent law is that there should be no differentiation. This in turn makes it the more difficult to suggest that the law on the subject should be substantially revised, as distinct from clarified as to its present meaning.

Many breeders (including those surveyed in the PIP project as well as organisations representing plant breeders) would like to see the notion of experimental use extended to include the use of patented material within a plant breeding

---

[58] German Supreme Court, *Klinische Versuche I and II* [1997] RPC 623; [1998] RPC 423.

[59] *Ibid.* A similar result occurred in *Wellcome Foundation v Parexel International & Flamel*, above n 52.

programme (as per the plant variety rights system). If this were to be permitted then a further question would be whether this should be further extended to permit the breeder freely to commercialise the results of that breeding programme. As will be shown below, there is evidence that some EU member states are looking seriously at the possibility of introducing a patent law equivalent to the breeders' exemption; however, it is extremely unlikely that such an exemption would extend to permitting the free commercial use of the results of the breeding programme where the end product contains the patented material or that there will be a uniform response across the whole of the EU. One problem with such an approach would be determining the status of any submission either for a grant of plant variety rights or for inclusion on the National List. Would the VCU or DUS trials be regarded as clinical trials (and under the existing practice of some countries possibly exempt) or would they be regarding as falling under the heading 'for regulatory approval' and therefore not exempt? Although the two concepts are closely linked, as discussed in chapter 3, it is possible that they might be treated separately for research exemption purposes, with VCU trials falling within the exemption as use *on* the material, in that they serve to assess if the variety does have value for cultivation and use, whereas the DUS trials go to the acquisition of a private property right and might be regarded as use *with* the patented technology.

The existing literature indicates that there seems to be consensus that without an appropriate exception, patents could adversely affect the ability of researchers to carry on R&D. However, those studies which have been undertaken as to the actual impact of the current form of the research exemption[60] indicate that whilst there is concern there is little evidence of any problems in practice. Instead, it appears that those who hold the patents on genetic material are either turning a blind eye to research use, up until such a time as a product comes to market, or they are entering into mutually beneficial agreements with the research users. However, the fact that there is such concern led one EU member state to take direct action to ensure that plant breeding programmes are not adversely affected by the restrictive nature of the patent law exemption.

In November 2004 Germany, as part of its proposed implementation of the EU Directive, attempted to introduce a provision into its patent law which specified that[61]

A patent is not effective in the case of . . .
2a. use of biological material for the purpose of breeding,
discovery and development of a new plant variety.[62]

---

[60] Such as the PIP project and the survey undertaken in the UK by the Department of Trade and Industry which surveyed the UK bioscience industry, including plant as well as pharma research; see UK's DTI study into Patents for Genetic Sequences: The Competitiveness of UK Law and Practice, available at www.dti.gov.uk.

[61] Within §11 of the draft of this law, which has the official number of the German Bundestag (Parliament) Bundestagsdrucksache No 151709 of 15 October 2003, there will be an addition after number 2 which has the number 2a.

[62] 'Die Wirkung des Patents erstreckt sich nicht auf 2a. die Nutzung biologischen Materials zum Zwecke der Züchtung, Entdeckung und Entwicklung einer neuen Pflanzensorte'.

The legislation specifically states that this is intended to ensure that '[b]y the addition of the new §11, sub-paragraph 2a, following the Protocol declaration of the German Delegation within the Common Market Meeting of November 27, 1997 (Footnote 2), the scope of the research privilege in the case of breeding, discovery and development of new plant varieties is defined.'[63]

On this basis it is the development which is freely permitted; the draft was silent on the matter as to whether the resulting variety could be freely commercialised. The context of the exemption would indicate that the breeder would have at least to compensate or pay royalties to the patent holder for any commercial benefit that the breeder obtains as a result of using the patented material.

This amendment to the existing patent practice has been questioned by, amongst others, Joseph Straus.[64] He doubted whether this (together with the restriction of claims to human genetic material to only one function) would be held to be a proper implementation of the Directive.[65] This would be a matter for the ECJ; it is our view, however, that there is nothing within the Directive itself which would preclude the inclusion of such a provision (unless an absolutist position is taken with regard to Articles 8–10—but as such a position would invalidate the existing research/non-commercial use exemption in patent law, it is suggested that the Directive is not intended to be read in such an inflexible manner), but that there could be problems with demonstrating compliance with the TRIPs Agreement and the requirement that there is no discrimination as to field of technology.

Germany is not alone in seeking to extend its experimental use provision. Article 28(1)(b) of the new Belgian Patent Act now states that 'the rights conferred by a patent do not extend to acts that are committed on and/or with the subject of the patented invention for scientific purposes.' This reference to use 'on or with' does not mirror the more usual wording which generally permits use on but not with. It is important that the provision refers to a *scientific* purpose. This implies that a use for a purpose which is not purely scientific, for example use for a commercial purpose, would fall outside the exemption. The critical issue is whether where the scientific purpose is to achieve a commercial result, it falls within the provision or not. It would seem that use of patented plant material in a breeding programme (or for other scientific purposes such as use in the development of new pharma) would fall within the provision. What is not certain is whether it would permit use within a commercial breeding programme. One possible interpretation might be that the use for breeding or within the laboratory would fall within the provision, whereas any use of the

---

[63] Durch den neuen §11 Absatz 2a wird im Anschluß an die Protokollerklärung der Deutschen Delegation im Binnenmarktrat vom 27 November 1997 (Fußnote 2) die Reichweite des Forschungsprivilegs für die Züchtung, Entdeckung und Entwicklung neuer Pflanzensorten geregelt.

[64] Who, it should be remembered, was a key architect of the EU Directive.

[65] At the time of writing it was not clear if the provision had been included in the law which was adopted.

material produced as a result of that work could be caught by patent held over the technology used. This, however, begs a further question as to whether the resulting product has to contain, or be a direct product of, the patented technology. At the heart of this is the question of how this provision will sit alongside Articles 8 and 9 of the Directive, which neither require the use to be commercial nor the resulting material to contain (or be directly produced by) the material claimed by the patent. Other governmental organisations have also unofficially indicated a willingness to look at the issue of the research exemption both in general, bio-patent, terms as well as specifically in the context of commercial plant breeding programmes. In respect of the latter, the interest appears primarily to be directed towards use where the end result, the plant variety, does not include the patented technology[66] (and some members of the patent community are not convinced that use which results in such a product would fall outside the existing exemption).[67] As discussed previously, the problem with the existing provision is that it is unclear if a breeder will be required to take a licence for the duration of the breeding programme until such time as it becomes apparent that the variety will not contain the patented technology or if she will be free to use the technology and only if it is retained in the commercial end product be required, retrospectively, to pay for a licence. In addition, the effect of Articles 8 and 9 of the Directive need to be taken into account providing, as they do, an extension of protection which appears to capture *any* products which have been produced by a patented process or any previous product produced by that process, as well as any material which contains the patented technology irrespective of whether that inclusion is passive or active. Given the emphasis in plant breeding on the external qualities of the plants, it may not be easy, without an internal investigation of the plants' genetic make-up, to know whether a resulting variety contains patented technology or not.

Also the fact that not all those engaged in plant research are doing so from the perspective of producing new plant varieties has to be considered. Current interest in the research exemption appears to be in the production of a plant *variety* and, at present at least, any thinking with regard to extending the research exemption would not include the use of patented technology for the production of any other type of plant innovation. This might give rise to disparities within

---

[66] This mirrors the position of the ISF, which maintains that where a variety is produced which is free of patented technology then the breeder should be able to exploit the variety without recourse to a licence from the patent holder.

[67] Workshop held by the DTI following the completion of its 'Study into Current UK Law and Practice Regarding Patents for Genetic Sequences' (2003), a study carried out on behalf of the DTI by the Intellectual Property Institute in conjunction with the University of Oxford and Imperial College, London, under the guidance of a steering group comprising Leonard, Smith and Llewelyn. One of the key issues for discussion was the research exemption, and this discussion was led by Trevor Cook. He indicated support for the notion that use in a breeding programme should not be an infringing use. This was an interesting stance, as he is not traditionally a supporter of the plant variety rights system: see Llewelyn and Cook, 'Debate' in *Plant Variety Rights: An Outmoded Impediment?* A Seminar Report (Intellectual Property Institute, 1998).

the plant bioscience industry, and any other use of plant material (for example in pharma) might be subject to the general provision.

While the evolving European position on the research exemption does give rise to ambiguities, at least it can be said that a more coherent dynamic prevails in Europe than in the US. It is commonly thought that research is exempt in the US only if it is strictly non-commercial.[68] In its most recent judicial statement, the Court of Federal Appeals said that research is exempt if it is 'solely for amusement, to satisfy idle curiosity, or for strictly philosophical inquiry.'[69] On the other hand, tests to secure marketing authority for generic equivalents to patented pharmaceutical products which take place during the period before the patent expires are now by statute permitted in the US. However, this does only apply to pharmaceutical products and would not apply to any other types of plant invention.

When assessing the research exemption in patent law it is important to remember that a patent is a private property right, and as such, the patent system seeks to enable the patentee to extract maximum value from the exclusive right. This can be achieved either by an aggressive approach to marketing, licensing and enforcing the patent or by working with third parties to maximise the potential of the invention. Whichever approach is taken, the primary interest of the patent holder will be to ensure that general demand for the patented material is such that it repays the original research investment, and ensures that the protection can be maintained.[70] The intention lying behind the patent law research exemption is to encourage future research and development. Any public interest in fostering these new developments is achieved by protecting the interests of the inventor—for it is by ensuring that they have strong protection (thereby ensuring that they maximise controlled access to the patented material) that the public interest element is served. This is very different to the function of the breeders' exemption in plant variety rights, which is intended to protect the interests of the breeding community as a whole rather than only protecting the interests of an individual breeder.

The Breeders' Exemption in Plant Variety Rights

Under the 1978 UPOV Act (which it should be remembered is still in force in some EU member states, most notably France) protected material can be freely used for commercial breeding purposes, but *any* result of that breeding programme could be commercialised unencumbered. The 1991 Act retains this right subject to the condition that where the resulting variety is essentially derived from, or dependent upon, the initial protected variety then the consent

---

[68] The Drug Price Competition and Patent Term Restoration Act 1984 (the Hatch-Waxman Act) permits use for testing that may allow a generic firm's version of a patented product to be licensed by the FDA from the moment of the patent's expiry. The situation in Europe may change as a result of Directive 2004/27/EC.

[69] *John MJ Madey v Duke University* No 01–1587 (Fed Cir, 2002).

[70] With patent renewal fees increasing the longer the monopoly is maintained.

of the owner of the rights over the initial variety must be obtained before commercialisation can take place. It is this latter position which has been adopted by the European Commission in respect of the Community-wide position (it is important, however, to bear in mind that there may be differences at the national level where a local grant has been made). It is also important to note that the breeders' exemption applies only to use within a breeding programme. Any other use or commercialisation is not permitted and may only be undertaken under licence.

The attitude towards the exemption, from within the plant breeding community, has been summed up by the European Seed Association when it called the breeders' exemption '[a] cornerstone of the UPOV Convention'[71] and the first President of the CPVO, Bart Kieweit, has reiterated this, saying that 'it should be emphasised that the breeders' exemption is considered as an essential element of the UPOV intellectual property rights system' to which of course the CPVR adheres. He also quoted Rolf Jörgens (the Secretary General of UPOV) who, in October 2003, said that the research exemption 'recognizes that real progress in breeding relies on access to the latest improvements and new variation. Access is needed to all breeding material in the form of modern varieties, as well as land races and wild species to achieve the greatest progress and is only possible if protected varieties are available for breeding.' This principle not only protects the breeder who has engaged in the conventional norms of plant breeding such as crossing and selection but also takes account of the skilled work necessary to identify the potential of a variant or mutant within an existing plant. The idea is that breeders will collectively benefit from the ability to use protected material freely.

The principle of both free access to protected plant varieties for use in breeding programmes and the unfettered commercialisation of the results is, therefore, fundamental to the system of protection and contrasts sharply with the more restricted concept employed within patent law.

As outlined in chapter 3, the fact that some breeding programmes resulted in only cosmetic changes being made to existing varieties led the UPOV Union to introduce the concept of essentially derived varieties. It is useful to note the current thinking on the relationship between the patent law and plant variety law notions of research use on the part of both the WIPO and UPOV. At a Symposium held in 2002 they issued a joint statement that:

1) Access to plant germplasm, be it patented or protected by plant breeders' rights (PBR) is of key importance for further innovation in plants:
   Within the PBR system this is ensured by the breeders' exemption for entire plant genomes.
   As far as patents for biotechnological inventions (protecting elements or properties in plant material) are concerned and as far as patents for plant varieties *per se* are

---

[71] ESA Statement presented at the WIPO/UPOV Symposium on Intellectual Property Rights, October 2003.

available, access can be assured by a well defined research exemption or experimental use defence.

At present this seems to be ensured by the European system (and comparable systems in the world) but to a lesser extent in the system provided in the United States.

2) The legal framework for the protection of plant innovations must offer efficient (enforceable) and adequate (fair) protection which ensures optimal incentives for investment and good working conditions for further innovation . . . .

3) [The majority of participants] prefer a better harmonization and balancing of the interfaces of the systems by ensuring within the patent system a well defined and broad enough research exemption/experimental use defence . . . .[72]

However, whilst the statement appears to suggest that the 'well-defined' research exemption within Europe is comparable to that within plant variety rights (that is, it provides sufficient scope for ongoing research), concerns were expressed that the existence of the more restricted form within patent law could prove problematic in practice where a breeder wished to use patented technology. From the perspective of the breeders[73] there are two problems. One is that patentees may not permit use of their patented technology unless under licence and (directly linked to this) that the apparent absence of a tradition of paying licence fees could prove too great a financial hardship for breeders. In respect of the latter it is clear from the responses to the PIP project at least that most breeders now license in (and many also license out) protected technologies and that this practice is as widespread amongst small to medium-sized enterprises as it is amongst the multinationals. Whilst having to license great swathes of technology could prove financially difficult, it is probably unrealistic to expect that breeders should have wholly free access to protected technologies and this is recognised by the organisations representing them. The problem with licensing is that this is invariably an individual matter controlled by the holder of the protected material and, as will be seen later, breeders will need to develop licensing strategies to help them both to maximise revenue from their own technology as well as to bring in the best technologies for their own further breeding interests at the most appropriate cost.

The commentary on the Symposium did say that notwithstanding the need for a 'well-defined and broad enough research exemption' any extension of the compulsory licensing provisions would not be acceptable. The issue of compulsory licensing will be discussed later in this chapter. The Symposium did not provide any further guidance on what it thought should be the definition of the research exemption/experimental use provision nor on what it thought constituted a broad enough provision, for example as to whether the existing practice sufficed or required revising. Nor did it try to define what it thought would be an appropriate ordinary licensing environment.

---

[72] This is available at either website: www.wipo.int or www.upov.int.
[73] As outlined in ch 8.

The view at the policy level is that breeders will be expected to pay royalties for the use of patented technologies within their ordinary breeding programmes. The issue, and one where some confusion remains, is at what point breeders will be expected to pay these fees. This confusion can be seen within both the patent and the plant variety rights circles (although there are also many who hold more absolute views such as that the obligation to pay should operate from the moment the patented technology is used, that is, at the start of a breeding programme, which may take between 10 to 15 years to complete, and those who maintain that it should only kick in once a commercial product has been produced, that is at the end of the research and following the trialling to determine VCU which could mean up to 15 years of 'free use'). It is difficult to know where the appropriate line should be drawn. It is possible to envisage a breeder paying to use patented technology within a 10-year breeding programme at the end of which he fails to produces a variety which is capable of being sold as it does not meet the VCU requirements. The patent holder has clearly benefited from his use of the patented technology whilst the breeder has not. The question is one of where the risk should be allocated.

The ISF, for example, would like to see further clarification provided as to the research exemption's use in respect of transgenic plants which contain patented elements. It is the view of the ISF that 'the extension of the protection [by patent] of a gene sequence to the relevant plant variety itself could extinguish this exception' and it recommends that 'a commercially available variety protected only by Breeder's Rights and containing patented elements should remain freely available for further breeding.' In terms of squaring this view with its statement that it supports the extension of protection to material in which a patented technology is incorporated, the ISF says that where a resulting variety (provided it is not an EDV) falls outside the scope of the patent claims (presumably through the patented technology not performing its function) then the breeder should be freely available to exploit the new variety, the corollary to this being that where the new plant variety falls within the scope of the patent claimed then any use of the variety must be subject to the consent of the patent holder.[74] This appears to be a consistent approach to take. The only question which is left is when a breeder is likely use patented technology in order to produce a new variety within which the patented technology does not perform its function. The reality is that few varieties created using patented technology are likely to fall outside the terms of that patent, and the implications of this resonate in the discussion above on licensing and the right to use. The other issue is the recommendation that a breeder should be able freely to use patented material in a commercial breeding programme—it is important to note that this will be a matter for individual patent holders to decide and is not something which either the ISF or individual breeders can unilaterally decide will be the case in practice.

---

[74] Remembering that there is a difference between that which can be claimed and the scope of the claims made, the former being an issue for grant, the latter a matter regarding enforcement.

Showing a worrying disinterest in the issue, Rothley (the member of the European Commission responsible for overseeing the drafting and adoption of the final version of the EU Directive), speaking at an ISF Congress in 1998, said that as the Directive did not provide any answer to this problem, the only way such clarification will be forthcoming will be via litigation. That the matter should be left to courts was a very real cause for concern for the breeders surveyed within PIP, many of whom were unaware that there would be a direct cost implication of using patented technology at the point of use within the breeding 'research' stage. In addition, there have been political concerns (such as that evidenced by the German government with its proposal to make use in commercial breeding programmes non-infringing), which indicate that there is a view that such an important matter should not be left to the potential vagaries of the judicial system. The continued lack of clarity is worrying, not least as the breeders' right encourages the use of discoveries (for example material occurring outside the laboratory) in breeding programmes, and a breeder might make use of plant material found existing ostensibly in a natural environment but which is actually the subject of a patent.

The breeders who took part in the surveys outlined in chapter 8 clearly wish to see an equivalent provision to that contained in plant variety rights included within patent law, as this would mean not only unfettered access to the patented material but also the freedom to commercialise the results of that use. It is extremely unlikely, however, that this will arise, as it is recognised that patent holders (who may very well be fellow breeders) have the right to benefit from uses made of their protected technologies. It is possible that the German proposal might find favour. This seemed to suggest that breeders should be free to use patented material until the point of commercialisation, at which point the obligation to pay a royalty would appear. Whilst there is much to support this, we feel that this is perhaps a little too biased towards the breeders and we would suggest a compromise position based on negotiation between the two parties (with the active involvement of those representing the interests of breeders to ensure that the agreements are fair and appropriately balanced).

Our suggestion is that the breeder and patent holder negotiate a percentage of what would be the normal fee for using the patented technology for the period of the research programme, with the full fee becoming payable at the point that commercialisation becomes possible. At this point the parties should renegotiate on the basis of a) the likely commercial importance of the new variety, and b) the technical contribution to that new variety of the patented technology. It might be that the fee will be increased in order to pay off the outstanding part of the fee owed during the period of breeding (this mirrors in part the position under patent law where the renewal fee increases the longer the right is held—the fee payable here will increase the longer the plant breeder obtains the commercial benefit from using the technology). Such an agreement would, however, have to take account of the impact of Articles 8–10 of the Directive on the relationship between the breeder and the patent holder over the ownership of the variety itself. If it is thought not appropriate to increase the fee then perhaps the patent holder could take a share in the plant variety right itself. The rationale is one of chronology and economics.

Patent holders want to recoup both the cost of the research and development leading up to the production of an invention and the cost incurred in securing patent protection[75] as quickly as possible. A plant breeding programme may last for up to 15 years. A patent term will last no longer than 20 years (unless it involves an agrichemical or pharmaceutical invention which can be shown to meet the conditions for a supplementary protection certificate which can extend the patent term for up to five years but no more). If patented technology is allowed to be used freely in a breeding programme then the patent holder will not be able to obtain a return for their investment until such time as the results of that breeding programme are exploited. That might be near the end of the patent term. The best case scenario would be that the patented technology is utilised in a breeding programme from the moment of grant and the breeding programme takes no longer than 12 to 15 years to achieve a result. That would give the patent holder between 5 and 8 years to secure a return. The worst case scenario would see the patented technology being used at a point in the duration of the patent when it is unlikely that the patent will still be in force at the time that the results of the breeding programme are exploited. However, once a variety has been bred then a variety right can protect it for up to 30 years. If a patent has been granted over material included within that variety, and it has taken 10 years for the variety to be developed, then the patent could be drawing to its end. Giving the patent holder a share in the variety right could provide him with additional protection which extends beyond the term of the patent. In the absence of any ability to reach a contractual position then the compulsory cross-licensing provisions (outlined below) might need to be invoked. In taking a stance which is based on ongoing dialogue between the parties (based on mutual benefit) this would bring the position closer to that suggested in 2004 by the OECD in its draft guidelines for licensing genetic inventions.[76] Such a research strategy might also take note of other factors such as the type of breeding activity. For example, a more lenient approach might be taken with regard to those types of plant research activity which have public benefit outcomes (such as the time-intensive agricultural plant breeding and new pharming, both of which will involve a regulatory, or social control, aspect before they can be brought to market), with perhaps a more overtly protectionist approach being taken over more overtly commercially driven breeding programmes. Obviously such a suggestion will not please all breeders, but we feel that many of the perceived problems could be alleviated if a closer

[75] Bearing in mind that the costs involve the patent agent's fee (which is a matter for the agent and inventor to agree), the examination costs and the renewal fees, which increase the longer the patent is in force to reflect the fact that a monopoly is being allowed to remain in force.

[76] See OECD.org. We have not suggested a wholesale adoption of these guidelines, as they appear predicated upon the need to provide access to inventions involving human genetic material or medicinal products which affect human health. At the time of writing it has not proved possible to evaluate their full potential for the gamut of plant breeding activities.

working relationship were forged between the holders and users of both sets of rights. This could be facilitated by organisations representative of plant breeders and inventors to maximise not only financial but social benefit through greater collaboration. If this were to be undertaken then it might be possible to balance the two types of research exemption.

In discussing the relationship between the two types of research exemption, the application of patented technology into a breeding programme is the most common scenario used. Less often asked is what would be the impact of an inventor using plant variety protected material within a research programme. It is recognised by breeders and inventors alike that this will probably be a less common occurrence. In the event that an inventor were to use a protected variety, or its constituents, in a research programme then he could do so freely only if the research was non-commercial, private, for experimental purposes or was for the purpose of breeding or developing other varieties. The non-commercial, private and experimental purposes have not been tested in the courts and it is unclear if these would cover use of the variety for the purposes of, for example, developing a novel trait within that variety. If the patent law practice were followed then this would be use with, and not on, the protected material, and therefore would be an infringement. If the purpose of research on the variety were to produce another variety, then this would be exempt from infringement. However, it is possible that the work would be to alter *that* variety genetically in which case the exemptions would not operate and the scientist could be liable if it could be shown that his work fell within the scope of protection conferred by the variety right. The relevant provision here is Article 13(1)(a) of the Regulation, which refers to producing or reproducing the variety. The issue for the courts in such an instance is whether work on the genetic, or variety, constituents of the variety will constitute production or reproduction. This could prove to be as thorny a ground as the determination of when a plant grouping is a plant variety.

It can be seen that the breeders' exemption in plant variety rights is a cornerstone of the system. In contrast, the research exemption within patent law is acknowledged as important, but it is a much more limited concept in that it is restricted to acts on, but not with, the protected invention.

Both the scope of rights and the exemptions serve to define that which the rights holder can and cannot control in respect of the protected technology. Normally a right holder will be keen to share his technological developments with others under licence. As indicated in chapter 1, these are privately determined agreements the content of which will be determined by the nature of the relationship which the two parties wish to have. However, in some instances either a patent or a plant variety rights holder may not wish to enter into a licensing agreement and this might be regarded as unreasonable. In such circumstances it may be possible to seek a compulsory licence. Here again it is possible to see differences in function between the basis for granting such a licence.

The final issue to be looked at is that of compulsory licensing.

**Compulsory Licences**

The concept that a granting authority can issue a licence in circumstances where the rights holder has not approved such a grant is fundamental to both the patent and plant variety rights systems, the principle lying behind the grant of a compulsory licence being that a rights holder should not be able to keep third parties from having access to the protected technology unreasonably. However, the notion of unreasonable denial of access appears to differ between the two rights. Within plant variety rights, the question whether a refusal to grant a licence is unreasonable or not centres on the concept of 'public interest'. In contrast, in patent law the focus is first on protecting the reasonable expectations of the patent holder.[77] There is no overt mention of any overarching public interest rationale. To reiterate the comment made by Cornish, the general view within patent law is that a 'wholehearted patent system will contain nothing that fetters a patentee's power to act as a monopolist if the market allows it . . . .'[78] The question which this section will discuss is whether the two approaches to compulsory licensing are different in practice.

The general principle relating to patent law is contained within Article 5 of the Paris Convention (as applied within national patent laws) and Article 31 of TRIPs (as discussed in chapter 2).

In terms of plant variety rights, the principle is governed by Article 17 of UPOV (as discussed in chapter 3).

a) Patent Law

Article 5(2) of the Paris Convention recognises that each member state has the right 'to take legislative measures providing for the grant of compulsory licenses to prevent the abuses which might result from the exercise of the exclusive rights conferred by the patent, for example, failure to work.' Article 5(4) also refers specifically to failure to work the patent or insufficient working of the patent as grounds for granting a compulsory licence. A licence may not be sought before four years have elapsed from the time of filing, or three years from the date of grant—the determining factor is which expires last. The intention behind the time limit is to give the patent holder a definite period within which he can enjoy the exclusive right.[79] The Convention makes it clear that these are minimum limits and that granting offices may permit the patent holder to enjoy a longer

---

[77] And there is extensive jurisprudence from the EPO which indicates that the key relationship is that between the EPO and *users* (that is, holders of rights granted under the EPC) of the European patent system: *Unilever/Good Faith* (G02/97) [2000] *European Patent Office Reports* 73, 76, para 1. Although the EPO is not responsible for granting any form of licence over patented technology, its view on the extent to which a right granted under the Convention can be constrained is obviously persuasive.

[78] Cornish, *Intellectual Property*, 5th edn (Sweet & Maxwell, 2003).

[79] Art 5(4).

period if he can provide good reasons for such an extension (the WIPO cites technical, legal and economic factors). Any licence granted will be non-exclusive and can only be transferred as part of an assignment of that part of the business concerned which has benefited from the use of the patented technology. The patentee remains free to grant other non-exclusive licences.

Implicit in the wording of Article 5 is a recognition that member states may wish to grant a licence for reasons other than non-working or insufficient working but the Convention does not outline what these might be (the *WIPO Handbook*, discussed in chapter 1, mentions the use of excessive pricing by the patent holder as a possible reason for granting a compulsory licence to a third party, but this appears to be dependent on the practice being exceptionally unreasonable). It is left to the WIPO to indicate the circumstances under which a compulsory licence may be granted.[80]

Chapter 18 of the WIPO's *Introduction to Intellectual Property Theory and Practice* details the Paris Convention. It details, at paragraphs 18.52 through to 18.61, the function of the compulsory licence. Firstly it states that it is intended to avoid abuses of the patent grant, such abuses primarily taking the form of either a failure to work the invention or insufficiency of working. Clearly this is a commercial consideration and relates to the manner of use *by the inventor* as opposed to the needs of a third party. Secondly, these licences act as a coercive measure to encourage the patent holder to work the invention in a more appropriate manner, with a principle function being to ensure the introduction and use of the protected technology. The capacity of the inventor to meet this requirement is, as the WIPO acknowledges, an issue of economics and time. For this reason the inventor is given a period post-grant within which he is expected to strive to achieve the appropriate level of working of the invention.

The WIPO makes reference to reasons of public interest which might necessitate the granting of a compulsory licence and, in particular, public health is specifically mentioned. It also states that where dependent technology is involved (this is technology which requires the continued use of other patented technology) which cannot be worked without infringing the patent over the originating technology then a compulsory licence may be granted. Interestingly WIPO merely states that '[i]f the owner of the dependent patent for invention obtains a compulsory licence, he *may* in turn by obliged to grant a licence to the owner of the earlier patent for invention' (emphasis added).[81] Of critical importance is the statement made in paragraph 18.61 that compulsory licences granted for reasons other than non-working or insufficiency of working fall under the heading of public interest. Where member states do exercise this option then 'they are not subject to the restriction provided for in Article 5A[82] [of the Paris Convention]. This means in particular that compulsory licences in the public interest can be granted without waiting for expiration of the time

---

[80] Above ch 1, n 63.
[81] *Ibid*, p 367, para 18.60.
[82] Which is another way of referring to Art 5(4).

limits provided . . . .' However, the granting of a licence on the basis of public interest is not mandated by the Paris Convention and it appears purely optional as to whether a member state uses this as a basis upon which to grant a compulsory licence.

There appear to be three main categories of compulsory licence, with the second of these being further sub-divided.

In addition, a further limitation is provided via Crown/government use. The various grounds for granting a compulsory licence are therefore:

1) Non- or insufficient working (these appears to be the only factors which the Paris Convention appears to require all member states to use as the basis for granting a compulsory licence, and a time limit applies).

2) Other reasons (apparently not binding on member states) are:

    i)    those which are predicated on economic factors such as excessive pricing (no time limit applies but this appears dependent on the reasonableness of the patent holder's actions);

    ii)   those which are non-economic in nature, such as public health (no time limit applies);

    iii)  where a dependent patent exists (no time limit applies, but such a grant *may* require the grant of a compulsory cross licence);

and finally

3)    Crown/government Use—(no time limit. Strictly speaking, this is not a licence as it is an overarching right to use which is exercised by the government over the grant made subject to payment of reasonable compensation).

On the basis of the Paris Convention it would seem that the predominant factors underpinning the grant of a compulsory licence are economic and whilst member states are not prohibited from granting licences for other reasons, this is not prescribed by the Convention. However, where such licences are available then the economic protection conferred on the holder is reduced in that such a licence can be sought at any time following grant. If this is mapped onto types of plant breeding activity then it would seem that a member state might be able to justify the granting of a licence under heading 2(ii) of the above list on the basis of protecting public health. This would certainly apply to any new pharma plant products, as these would fall within the heading of public health, but it is less clear if this could be applied to agricultural plant material and would not seem to be applicable to any other plant-related innovation. However, the application of the Paris Convention is now subject to the provisions of the TRIPs Agreement.[83]

---

[83] Art 2 of the Agreement states that Part II shall comply with Arts 1 through 12 of the Paris Convention. Section V is contained within Part II.

*Article 31 TRIPs*

As discussed in chapter 2, the starting point for any analysis of Article 31 is Article 30. This states that members *may* provide *limited* exceptions to the exclusive rights granted provided that these do not 'unreasonably conflict with a normal exploitation of the patent and do not unreasonably prejudice the legitimate interests of the patent owner, taking into account the legitimate interests of third parties.' The balance here lies between protecting the rights held by the patent owner and safeguarding the legitimate interests of third parties. Article 31 has to be read subject, therefore, to the expectation that there may only be limited exceptions to the rights of the patent holder, and in particular, that such exceptions should not unreasonably conflict with the 'normal exploitation' of the patent. There is no reference within either Article to the public interest. However, if the Agreement is read as a whole then it must be read alongside Article 7 of the General Principles.

Article 7 sets down the presumption that the protection and enforcement of the rights will promote technological innovation and contribute to technology transfer. To this end there must be a balance between providing rights which are to the advantage of the producers and ensuring that these rights are used '*in a manner conducive to social and economic welfare.*' An issue is, if one regards the development of plants for both agricultural and medicinal purposes as being for the social and economic welfare, whether the appropriate balance has been properly struck. As chapter 2 showed, the WTO, in its Doha statement, indicated that Article 7 can be accepted as a basis for permitting greater reliance on the compulsory licensing provisions for the purposes of access to medical products; it is less clear, however, whether this can be relied upon to any great extent a) by developed countries and b) for the purposes of acquiring a compulsory licence for a patent relating to an agricultural or ornamental product or process. Given the general adherence to the principle of non-fettering it is likely that these would be held to fall outside the scope of the provision unless there was an overwhelming public interest which superseded the interests of the patent holder,

The various conditions set down include a requirement that a licence (containing reasonable terms) must have been sought and denied. This requirement is waived in the event of a national emergency, extreme urgency or, useful for our purposes, in cases of public, non-commercial use. However, member states are permitted to ignore these provisions if it is felt that, following due process, the granting of a licence would be anti-competitive. The term of the licence shall be proscribed, non-exclusive, non-assignable, and must predominantly be for the supply of the domestic market of the member state authorising the use. In addition, it can be revoked if the circumstances change and it is subject to an adequate (not necessarily equitable) remuneration (issues of both the grant and form of the adequate remuneration being subject, if necessary, to judicial review).

This would seem to indicate that, notwithstanding the principle that member states of the Paris Convention and TRIPs can use public interest grounds as the basis for the grant of a compulsory licence, their ability to do so in practice is limited. The discussions held on Article 31 have principally centred on the flexibility within it for developing countries (and here the Doha Statement does provide some reassurance) but the question whether any developed country which has a history of operating a sophisticated patent system designed with the protection of the interests of the patent holder in mind can use Article 31 to avoid those rights would seem to have already been answered. What has not been discussed to date is whether a member state of TRIPs could use Article 31 to protect the interests of a particular sector, in this instance plant breeders, which might be adversely affected by the protection conferred by a patent. Here the critical issue is whether (if the research exemption does not apply to a use of patented technology within a commercial breeding programme) a member state could rely on the reference to compulsory licences being available for the purpose of 'public non-commercial use' to enable a breeder to secure a licence to use (where a patent holder had previously refused). This returns us to the matter of what is non-commercial use—this turns on the question of whether the pertinent time is when the material was being used (the breeding period, which could be regarded as non-commercial) or after (when the results of that programme are marketed). It is our view that it would require considerable political will to take such a course of action. On the basis of the hesitancy encountered in seeking to rely on this provision (or rather its equivalent within national patent law) in respect of the *Myriad* patent (discussed in chapter 6) which involved significant issues relating to public health, it is unlikely that European member states would be willing to pursue such a course of action in the absence of any evidence that such patents were actually causing problems to an industry as a whole.

For European purposes, probably the most important provision is paragraph (j) of Article 31 as this is the only provision within this Article which has an equivalent enshrined in European Union patent law (as opposed to implemented at the national level).

Article 31(j) states that where a licence is needed in order to work a second patent, such working being an infringing act without a licence, then the applicant for the licence has to show that the invention protected by the second patent involves an important technical advance of considerable economic importance in relation to the invention contained in the first patent. Where such a licence is granted, then the owner of the first patent will be entitled to a cross-licence allowing him use, on reasonable terms, of the invention protected by the second patent. The compulsory licence can only be assigned if accompanied by an assignment of the second patent. The EU version, contained in Article 12 of the Directive, is different in that it does not apply to *two* patents where the working of one is dependent upon using the other, but rather applies to a patent and a plant variety right.

When looking at the situation, it is important to bear in mind two factors. The first is that Article 31 (j) applies to compulsory cross-licences where two patents are concerned. The second is that Article 12 of the Directive applies to *cross*-licences where a patent and a plant variety right are concerned.

These factors are important because the Regulation has taken the principle set down in Article 31 and applied it to its general compulsory exploitation/licensing provision which refers only to plant variety rights.

### Article 12 of the Directive

There are a number of key elements to Article 12.

Paragraph 12(1) states that a breeder who cannot acquire or exploit a plant variety without infringing a patent may seek a compulsory licence but only 'insofar as that licence is necessary for the exploitation of the plant variety *to be protected.*'

What is unclear here is whether the use of the future tense here indicates that where a breeder already has secured protection for the variety no compulsory licences would be forthcoming and that they are only available for varieties yet to be protected. This would not correspond with the language 'a breeder . . . cannot acquire *or* exploit a plant variety right.' This also does not correspond with the language in Article 12(2): where a patented invention cannot be exploited without infringing a *'prior'* plant variety right, a compulsory licence may be applied. Interestingly, the wording of this section is not limited by the use of 'insofar as that licence is necessary for the exploitation of . . . '. It is not clear if this makes any difference in practice.

Both paragraphs make clear that where a compulsory licence is acquired then it is subject to the payment of an 'appropriate royalty' and that the holder of the variety right or patent which is the subject of the licence is 'entitled to a cross-licence on reasonable terms.' On the basis of existing patent practice any compulsory licence will be subject to national policy and practice in the context of compliance with Article 31, TRIPs. As already noted, the compulsory licensing provisions are, in general, given a very limited application with the focus on protecting the interests of the patent holder first and foremost. Certainly the language of the Article 31 makes it clear that such rights are to be weakened only *in extremis*. However, the language of Article 12 introduces some ambiguity.

Paragraph 3 stipulates some conditions which have to be met before a licence can be sought. It states that 'the person seeking a licence must have unsuccessfully applied to the person holder the variety right or patent for a licence.' This simply restates a common requirement in patent law as reinforced in Article 31. It also underlines one of the basic rationales for the compulsory licensing system, namely to bring a patent holder to the negotiating table in the event that unreasonable licensing terms are being presented. The ambiguity is contained in paragraph 3(b).

This requires the person seeking the compulsory licence to show that their variety or invention 'constitutes significant technical progress of considerable economic interest.'

What is not clear from the language of paragraph 3(b) is whether the requirement to show that the invention or plant variety represents a significant technical progress of considerable economic significance applies to the initial compulsory licence, the compulsory cross-licence or both. The first sentence of paragraph 3 simply states that '[a]pplicants for the licences referred to in paragraphs 1 and 2 must demonstrate . . .', the next two paragraphs outlining the twin requirements of an unsuccessful application and demonstration of significant technical progress of considerable economic interest. No differentiation is apparently drawn. Recitals 52 and 53 provide some clarity, as they indicate that it is granting of the initial compulsory licence which is subject to the requirement that the variety or invention concerned be shown to represent significant technical progress of considerable economic interest. But as has been discussed previously, Recitals are not necessarily binding statements of the law and, therefore, the actual text of Article 12 remains unclear on this issue. It is possible therefore for a member state to hold that both types of licence, the initial compulsory licence and the consequential cross-licence, are subject to this condition.

If the TRIPs Agreement is used as a final arbiter or reference point then it would appear that the condition is intended to apply to the initial compulsory licence[84]—the TRIPs Agreement not extending it to the subsequent cross-licence. However, the lack of equivalent clarity in the Directive means that it remains to be seen if the various national patent offices give it the same restrictive application or if it is argued at any point that the wording of the Directive is such that the two requirements are intended to apply to *both* the original compulsory licence *and* the cross-licence.

A further point of uncertainty lies in whether the provisions of the Directive are intended to be read alongside those set down in the TRIPs Agreement which are not explicitly set down in the Directive itself (Article 31 contains ten qualifying paragraphs relating to either the use of compulsory licensing or

---

[84] Art 31(j) states that

> where such use is authorized [eg the granting of a compulsory licence and possibly also government use] to permit the exploitation of a patent . . . which cannot be exploited without infringing another patent . . . the following conditions shall apply: (i) the invention claimed in the second patent shall involve an important technical advance of considerable economic significance in relation to the invention claimed in the first patent . . . (ii) the owner of the first patent shall be entitled to a cross-licence on reasonable terms to use the invention claimed in the second patent

This makes it clear that only the second invention (that requiring the compulsory licence in order for exploitation to take place) need be shown to be an important technical advance of considerable economic significance. The original patented invention does not have to be shown as such in order for its holder to secure a cross-licence over the second piece of technology.

government use, only two of which, (the requirement to show that a prior application has been unsuccessful and that the technology concerned constitutes technical progress of considerable economic interest) are repeated in the Directive) or if the Directive sets out the *only* requirements for acquiring a compulsory licence over biotechnological innovations within EU member states, all other inventions, including presumably chemical inventions, not falling within the definition of biotechnological being required to comply with the full set of TRIPs requirements.

What is significant about the text of Article 12 is that it focuses primarily on the *economic* importance of the protected variety/patented gene. There is no mention made of any other underlying *public interest* imperatives for granting a licence such as access to medicines or beneficial new agricultural products. Recitals 52 and 53 are notable in their lack of enlightenment, as all they do is to state that the provision is needed in order to guarantee access upon payment of a fee. Commentators, such as Kamstra, *et al*, equally do not provide any illumination, and this issue remains one of considerable uncertainty.

To date there is only one example of a national patent law taking account of any overt public interest element within their patent laws and this is the new Belgian Patent Act 2005. The Act contains a provision which applies specifically to compulsory licences granted in the interest of public health. There is no definition of 'public health' and apparently the background documentation does not provide any explanation as to what this provision is intended to achieve. Such a licence will only be available in respect of patents granted over specified types of medical product,[85] some of which may be produced using plant material. It is relevant therefore for plant scientists to be aware that these may exist where a patent holder is abusing the monopoly privilege granted to him. The language of the provision makes it clear that it is intended to prevent infringement actions against the medical profession. The question which this provision raises is whether it is compatible with Article 31 of TRIPs (the fact that certain requisite elements outlined in TRIPs, such as the need to have first sought a licence on reasonable terms, are omitted means that it could be open to challenge, but a defence could lie by reference to the General Principles of the Agreement as well as in the fact that the ordinary patent law provides for such exceptions to the usual rules governing the grant of a compulsory licence). A further concern is that it might undermine investment in medical research as it could, if overused, result in generic equivalents swamping the market place, potentially seeping out into other EU countries and beyond. This and other unusual implementations will have to be monitored, but serve to underline the continuing uncertainty of the legislative framework within which plant researchers have to operate.

---

[85] A medication, a medical device, a medical or diagnostic product, a therapeutic by-product or a compound therapeutic product; a process or product necessary to manufacture such products; or *ex vivo* diagnostic methods.

The concept of compulsory licensing in patent law appears to be principally concerned with economic factors but this should not be taken to mean that other, non-pecuniary, considerations have no part to play in patent law. As has been shown, the granting of such a licence on the basis of public interest is not precluded but would appear difficult to provide, or secure, in practice. Where such a public interest can be shown then the usual constraints on acquiring the licence (such as the elapse of a specific period of time between grant of right and securing of licence) do not apply and this appears to trump the economic right of the patent holder. Further, it can be argued that the public interest is primarily served by providing strong protection for the patent holder. If he is assured of this protection then he is more likely to place the protected material into the public domain (admittedly not always for free and unencumbered use by third parties) and that once the threshold for protection has been met then he is entitled to control the protected material as he wishes. This, of course, begs the question whether such reasonable use takes place in practice. To date there have been few studies but those which have taken place seem to indicate that most patent holders do license their inventions on third-party friendly terms and that even those who initially do not offer such terms ultimately do so. This does not mean that those charged with policy and practice can be complacent over the potential for adverse effects of an overly aggressive approach to protecting patented material, but rather that the situation will need to be monitored and an open mind given to the possibilities of revising the law in light of actual experience. In this respect the role of the compulsory licence is to act as an incentive to bring parties to the negotiating table. But this underlying public interest role to the compulsory licensing provision is predominantly hidden. This is very different to that within plant variety rights where the principle is explicitly mentioned within the substantive provisions of the law itself.

### b)  Plant Variety Rights

*Article 17 UPOV*

The UPOV Acts have not contained compulsory licensing provisions as such. Instead, Article 17 states that any restrictions on the breeder's right, other than in respect of research or farm saved seed, can only be imposed for reasons of public interest. Where such restrictions are adopted then the breeder must receive equitable remuneration. As mentioned in chapter 3, neither 'public interest' nor the extent of the remuneration are defined in the Acts. In general this principle has been adopted at the national level.[86] In terms of any more general significance to this provision, the World Intellectual Property Organisation's

---

[86] In the UK for example, the equivalent provision in the 1997 UK Plant Varieties Act is held to underline the 'fundamental assumption . . . that breeders should make their protected varieties as

*Introduction to Intellectual Property: Theory and Practice* merely notes (in Chapter Twenty Seven within the section on the 1978 Act), that Article 9 of that Convention only permits an additional restriction for reasons of public interest. The section on the 1991 Act makes no reference at all to Article 17. It is this principle which, if utilised at the national level, will inform national provision. The EU legislation, however, appears to move away from the UPOV concept.

### Article 29 of the Community Regulation

Article 29 of the Regulation states that a compulsory licence can be sought only if it is in the public interest and, if granted by the Community Office, it may be subject to a number of conditions laid down by that Office. These could include a time limitation, payment of an appropriate royalty, and what the Regulation refers to as other 'certain obligations' which are unspecified. The Preamble to the Regulation states that reasons of public interest may 'include the need to supply the market with material offering special features, or to maintain the incentive for continued breeding of improved varieties.' In addition, this provision needs to be read subject to Article 41(1)(a)(6) of the Proceedings Regulation,[87] which states that public interest is to be assessed on the basis of i) the protection of life or health of humans, animals and plants, ii) the need to supply the market with material offering specific features or iii) the need to maintain the incentive for continued breeding of new varieties. This applies to all varieties irrespective of the species concerned.

As discussed in chapter 4, the European Commission has recently amended Article 29 to reflect the obligations undertaken by the European Union as a signatory to the TRIPs Agreement. In so doing, the text has been revised to bring the Regulation in line with the provisions of the Directive, for reasons outlined in chapter 4 (these, in brief, related to a possible imbalance between the provisions within the Directive and those in the Regulation).

The additional new text reads:

The following rules shall apply (by way of derogation from paragraphs 1 to 7);

---

widely available as possible, to those who wish to grow or use them.' The Guide does not elaborate what forms the 'public interest'; it does state that the Controller will not grant a compulsory licence unless it is necessary in order to ensure that the variety concerned is available to the public at reasonable prices, is widely distributed, or is maintained in quality. Additional considerations are whether the applicant is financially in a position to exploit in a competent and businesslike manner the rights to be conferred on him by the licence, and whether the applicant actually intends to make use of the licence granted to him. In addition, it is probably reasonable to assume that the Controller could also take into account those considerations outlined in Art 41 of the Proceedings Regulation. A further example of the flexibility given to member states of UPOV is that the UK Act also imposes a time bar and whilst it states that an application can be made at any time, any licence granted will not come into force until two years after the granting of variety rights.

[87] Council Reg 1768/95 which concerns proceedings before the Office, OJ No L121/37, 1 June 1995.

(a) Where the holder of a patent for a biotechnological invention applies to the Office for a compulsory licence for the non-exclusive use of a protected variety under Article 12(2) of Directive 98/44/EC, the Office shall grant such a licence, subject to the payment of an appropriate royalty, provided that the patent holder demonstrates that

 i) he has applied unsuccessfully to the holder of the plant variety right to obtain a contractual licence; and
 ii) the invention constitutes significant technical progress of considerable economic interest compared with the protected variety.

(b) Where, in order to enable him to acquire to exploit his plant variety right, a holder has been granted a compulsory licence under article 12(2) of the above Directive for the non-exclusive use of a patented invention, the Office shall, on application by the holder of the patent for that invention, grant to him a non-exclusive cross-licence on reasonable terms to exploit the variety.

(c) On granting a licence or cross-licence to a patent holder under sub-paragraph (a) or (b) respectively, the office shall restrict the territorial scope of the licence or cross-licence to the part or parts of the Community covered by the patent.

As chapter 4 outlined, concern has been expressed that this change could have the effect of undermining the public interest basis of the provision. On the face of it, the change does not remove this basis, and Article 29(1) still contains the original statement that a compulsory licence will only be granted on the grounds of public interest (and this is reiterated in Article 29(2)). The issue is the extent to which this is superseded, or constrained, by the patent law principle (which is predicated on economic factors) which is now contained within the new text. Critical to this assessment is the fact that the new text is prefaced with the statement that it is by way of 'derogation' to the preceding paragraphs within Article 29. Does this mean that it is subject to patent or plant variety rights norms? If the former then the provision is likely to be applied using the patent law notions of the economic justification for the licence. This would mean that both the Regulation and the Directive concur, but that this aspect of the plant variety rights systems is now subject to the general principle that the interests of the rights holder are paramount. Or, notwithstanding the reference to 'by way of derogation', is the new text intended to concur with the general principles within plant variety rights (as enshrined in Article 17 of UPOV), namely that the interests of the rights holder are balanced against those of the industry as whole, which could include the interests of those who seek to exploit a protected variety? According to the Kieweit, the President of the CPVO, the new text does not necessarily comply with UPOV *unless* the UPOV Union is prepared to accept paragraph (b) as a reason in the public interest.[88] The UPOV Office has remained silent on this matter and even the news that the EU had joined UPOV as a member did not contain any references as to whether the legislation of the

---

[88] Kieweit, *Principles, Procedures and Recent Developments in Respect of the Community Plant Variety System*, Paper given at the 2004 International Conference on Intellectual Property Protection for Plant Innovation (Frankfurt, February 2004): see www.forum-institut.de.

EU complies with the 1991 UPOV Act. One can only presume that it is taken to so do. However, the lack of a specific statement could indicate that it is not impossible that the Regulation's compulsory cross-licensing provision will be interpreted in accordance with patent law principles. As noted in chapter 4 this seems odd given that the Preamble to the Regulation states '[w]hereas it is indispensable to examine whether and to what extent the conditions for the protection accorded in other industrial property systems, such as patents, should be adapted or otherwise modified for consistency with the Community plant variety rights system,' which indicates that any modification will be to the other industrial property right.

For the purposes of UPOV (and therefore for the application of any national plant variety rights system), the principle of public interest remains central to any restriction on the rights granted in accordance with its provisions. Clearly public interest goes beyond a mere economic or commercial determination of whether it is appropriate to grant a licence and could include taking into account greater social benefits such as access to important, beneficial, new plant products and even protecting the collective interests of the industry as a whole as opposed to the economic interests of the individual. Of course, on a more pragmatic basis the principle may only apply where there is an economic justification for it to do so (and there may be little to distinguish really between it and the patent system), but (and for us it is a significant 'but') the overt reference to 'public interest' indicates that the provision is intended to reflect a principle which goes beyond the merely economic.

The significance of the move towards a patent-based application has not been discussed to any great extent within plant breeding circles, but provides a further example of the conflicting pulls which the move into the industrial property family by the Regulation may engender. It is important to note that, so far, this eliding of patent and plant variety rights principles in respect of the compulsory licensing provisions operates only in respect of a Community plant variety right and does not affect a nationally granted right.

There is a further option available if compulsory licensing (and by extension ordinary licensing practices) does not achieve a desired result: competition law. Competition law, as it has evolved throughout the European Union, applies to both patent law and plant variety rights. All types of commercial and industrial activity are affected by the EC's Rules of Competition both at the overarching EU level and at the national level through national competition (or anti-trust) legislation. The EC Rules of Competition, which are laid down in the EC Treaty, give the European Commission executive responsibility to take certain types of action. Action may be taken in respect of (i) anti-competitive agreements and concerted practices between undertakings; and (ii) abuses of dominant position by undertakings with market power.[89] If the European Commission, or the relevant national body responsible (for example, in the UK

---

[89] EC Treaty, Arts 81, 82.

this is the Director-General of Fair Trading in conjunction with the Competition Commission) finds that a monopoly situation exists then the restrictive terms in a licence may be modified or cancelled, or (where a patent is concerned) it may be subject to a licence of right. Competition law is a useful backstop but a caveat to its use is that once the referral is made then the matter is out of the hands of the granting office, the rights holder and the third party, and any decision a) is subject to the individual vagaries of the competition commission concerned and b) does not deal with the actual issue of the granting of a licence. Where an abuse of market position is found to exist then a fine will be imposed. Under European competition law the European Commission can impose a fine of up to 10 per cent of the company's previous year's profits. The Commission is particularly concerned to eradicate price fixing or the existence of cartels—and these attract the largest fines if found. According to commentators on competition law, 'abuse of a dominant position [which is the type of anti-competitive activity likely to arise as a result of the grant of an intellectual property right], usually result in lower fines, sometimes because the law is not sufficiently clear to allow companies to assess the legality of their practices with sufficient certainty.'[90]

One final comment on licensing and that is that it is important to bear in mind possible time lines which may apply. As has been stated throughout this book it can take up to 15 years to develop a new variety. Once that variety has been produced it is still subject to the various regulatory processes (not all necessarily relating to the granting of a right over the material) which may themselves take a number of years. A patent lasts for up to 20 years. Whether or not a patent remains in force for the entire duration will depend on a number of factors, including commercial viability of the invention, the cost of renewing the patent[91] and also the continued existence of the company/individual concerned and in the event of a merger/acquisition, the objectives of the company taking over or being merged with. If the period of control is only limited then there is a question whether the return would enough to interest a patent holder in issu-

---

[90] Korah, *Intellectual Property Rights and the EC Competition Rules* (Hart Publishing, 2006). The 2004 *Microsoft* decision, [2005] 4 CMLR 965, provides a useful illustration of the level of fine the European Commission can impose where a company has behaved in an anti-competitive manner. In *Microsoft* the Commission fined the company 497 million euros and imposed a number of 'remedies' in respect of certain products. The fine exceeds the 462 million euros fine imposed on Hoffmann La Roche in 2001 in respect of price fixing for vitamins and its role in a market-sharing cartel. In addition, the Commission has, as 'remedies', mandated that Microsoft must disclose interface information, which will allow many servers to interoperate with Windows PCs, and provide some of its competitors with a version of its PC operating system, the version being one untied to Windows Media Player. The *Microsoft* decision is important, for it sends a clear signal to the holders of intellectual property rights that the Commission intends to take a robust line in respect of anti-competitive practices At the time of writing the full judgment was not available, but there is a clear requirement of compulsion within the decision and although it is unclear if either of these 'remedies' is to take place under licence which may or may not have a fee attached, the *de facto* effect is the imposition of a compulsory licence.

[91] Because a patent is viewed as a necessary anti-competitive device, a patent holder has to pay progressively more in the way of renewal fees the longer the patent remains in force.

ing a licence if a granting office has to be convinced that the material utilising
the patented technology represents a significant technical progress of significant
economic interest. It is worth repeating that any patent over either a process or
a product, no matter how minor that invention might be to the breeding work
being undertaken or indeed how minor the user of the patented technology
might feel the innovation concerned to be, *could* require a licence for both its use
in research and any subsequent commercial exploitation. The fact that it *could*
require a licence does not necessarily mean that there will be problems in acquiring a licence—indeed most patent inventions are the subject of reasonable and
mutually beneficial licensing arrangements—nor that where a patented invention is used within a 'research' context the holder of the patent will automatically treat that use as an infringement. Many companies take the practical view
that it is neither physically possible to monitor all uses of their patented technology nor necessarily financially expedient to pursue an infringing act through the
courts. Instead, in the absence of an aggressive protection policy, holders of
patents are likely to wish to enter into some form of agreement with the
'infringer'. Equally, if an infringing act is alleged to have taken place (and the
experimental use defence not offered), there is nothing to stop the person using
the material from claiming that the patent is itself not valid and therefore the use
neither infringes nor needs defending. Although there are societies which
already seek to assist with agreeing and enforcing licences (including collecting
and distributing royalties)—these are currently predominantly in respect of
plant variety rights. Whilst these may extend their services to dealing with
patent licences, many breeders are apprehensive over possible personal involvement in negotiating appropriate terms (both as holders and users). One suggestion for users worried about dealing with strong patent rights, and fearing
difficulties in agreeing licensing terms (something which can be of grave concern
to a small breeder with no or little experience of negotiating a licence), could be
to encourage the setting up of patent buyers' pools. These would involve a
group of breeders collectively entering into a licensing agreement with the
patent holder with the licence negotiated by all on behalf of, and applicable to,
all. The problem with this is it might run into problems with the competition
laws as it might be regarded by some as a form of cartel.

### IV. CONCLUSION

The changes made to the plant variety rights system have, in general, been welcomed by both breeders and intellectual property law commentators alike. There
is a strong sense that the right now provides an appropriate and effective alternative to patent law and that there is no longer any basis for regarding it, in Europe
at least, as 'an outmoded impediment to a logical framework of protection.'[92]

---

[92] Cornish, *Intellectual Property: Patents, Copyright, Trade Marks and Allied Rights*, 2nd edn
(Sweet & Maxwell, 1989).

However, the changes raise further questions over how these are to be applied in practice given the shift in justification from agricultural to intellectual property right. In particular, concerns remain that the Regulation may be subject to the same principles of interpretation which apply to other forms of intellectual property right and patent law in particular (on the basis of the PIP survey this would certainly gain the support of many ornamental breeders). It might be that in the modern plant science era it is appropriate to give a broader interpretation to the subject matter under protection and a more restricted application to any derogations to the right granted. However, as the statements from the ISF, UPOV and the breeders themselves indicate, there is no support for any undermining of the research exemption or diminution of the public interest element. Of course the preceding discussion may prove to be purely theoretical and the practice of granting offices, breeders and courts will continue to adhere to the original principles supporting the grant of a right over plant varieties. However, the fact that the Community right is now a fully fledged intellectual property right, which can be enforced through the intellectual property courts, means that there is a possibility that Community rights at least could be subject to the 'protection of private economic interests' values which underlie patent law. As this chapter has shown this could have serious implications for breeders wishing to pursue further plant-related research. The common ground sought to equate the two rights may have done much to justify the continued existence of the plant variety rights system, but there may be a price to be paid if there is equivalence not only of protection but also of function.

There is another common ground point which is worth making and that is, notwithstanding any merging of function, whether it is appropriate to try and achieve consensus in practice across the European Union. At first glance it might seem desirable to try and evolve a common European position on key issues such as protectable material and derogations from protection; however, differences in the type of plant breeding activity undertaken within each member state, as well as differences in the type and size of companies engaged in such activity, mean that such communality may not be desirable (or achievable) in practice.[93] One of the key reasons for this is that the European legislation primarily mandates general principles relating to grant. What it cannot do is dictate how those principles are interpreted by the national offices nor how the scope is defined by the national courts.[94] Given the diversity of local interests in plant-research activities there may be a strong argument for allowing national differences. Whilst the European Commission appears to be increasingly more

---

[93] The need for diversity of treatment is ostensibly recognised within both the Regulation and Directive but only in respect of end users in the form of farmers (with Art 14 of the Regulation indicating that small farmers are not treated in the same way as larger farming concerns). However, there is no apparent recognition of any need to apply an equivalent sliding scale to breeders according to size of company or type of breeding activity engaged upon.

[94] The power of the EPO in this respect is purely persuasive (and the extent of the persuasion will depend on the extent to which the country concerned wishes to be persuaded).

receptive to such an approach than in the past, it is not clear if it will allow local differentiation in respect of the manner of implementation and enforcement of EU-directed legislation. If direct equivalence is sought then the EU can resort to the European Court of Justice which will serve as the final arbiter of whether the legislation has been properly interpreted, but as mentioned previously, until such time as it has pronounced on all aspects of both systems of protection the environment will permit continuing national variation. This inconsistency was matter of concern for many of the breeders surveyed. However, there is an argument for saying that perhaps it is in the interests of the industry if member states retain a degree of autonomy over how they apply certain provisions (especially in respect of the derogations to the rights), although obviously with the hope that good practice will permeate across all member states (for example on whether the use of patented plant material within clinical trials constitutes research or not). On this basis it might be more appropriate to leave individual countries free to define and apply the various provisions in a manner conducive to their own plant production purposes.[95] The corollary to this is that this will inevitably mean that where a Community right exists, or a European patent is granted which is enforceable across the whole of the EU, then the holder of that right will have to negotiate through these national differences.[96]

In attempting to help plant breeders negotiate through the morass of rights which might potentially affect their ability to conduct further research, we would suggest the following.

— Revisiting the research exemptions within the patent and plant variety laws with a view to clarifying the relationship between the two—in particular, guidance should be provided as to the impact on plant research of Articles 8 and 9 of the Directive, and the relationship between the scope of the right conferred and the ability to use protected material in research programmes.
— Providing assistance for negotiating licensing agreements for those breeders less experienced (or financially less able) to use the services of professional draftsmen, possible by creating a body which can be used to oversee licensing in respect of both sets of rights.[97]

---

[95] The need for this flexibility is underlined by the recent accession of 10 new member states, many of which have differing agricultural and pharmaceutical needs (not least in terms of research and manufacturing capacity) to those of the previous 15. These countries are likely to have a different approach to protecting their indigenous plant research (based on existing administrative infrastructure and a probable need to make significant revisions to bring this in line with other member states) as well as to encouraging breeders from other member states to develop research programmes within their territory.

[96] Bearing in mind that these rights have a pan-biological application, and many courts will be mindful of the type of signals they will be sending in any given case to the whole of the bioscience industry.

[97] Much in the same way as seed associations and, in another context, the Copyright Licensing Authority. This latter possibility (albeit in respect of healthcare provision) has been mooted both by the authors, in Cornish, Llewelyn and Adcock, *Intellectual Property Rights (IPRs) and Genetics: A*

— Ensuring a clear monitoring of any anti-competitive practices (such an operation focusing on the needs of the plant research community as opposed to merely addressing issues of abusive monopolies in general).

— Revisiting the issue of scope of claims with a view to assessing if this issue is likely to cause problems in practice (bearing in mind the consequences for breeding work of allowing rights to extend to end products which are developed using patented technology). In this, possible guidance could be taken from the German implementation of the Directive, which (whilst not applying to plant innovations) could be extended to such end products (the Commission itself is already looking at this matter although purely in the context of patents involving human genetic material).

— Looking at the possible introduction of task forces to address matters relating to parity of practice in those areas outside the control of the granting offices, for example in the determination of EDVs, the public interest or significant technical progress (these bodies could comprise patent experts, experts in plant variety rights, and both generalist and specialist researchers), as well as addressing the interface between the two systems. In this the work of organisations such as the ISF should be recognised and moves taken to ensure that the recommendations made and adopted by the various governing bodies are properly taken into account when determining, for legal purposes, the exact nature of these concepts.

— That the notion of benefit and sharing, as arguably the practice within the plant variety rights system could be described, and enshrined in the CBD, be looked at to ensure that short-term individual gain does not result in long-term collective decline.

Finally and possibly most importantly:

— Action should be taken to ensure that users of plant material have easy access to information about what is protected and who holds the rights—thereby alleviating the considerable burden of having to ascertain this individually. We would strongly argue for a single database to be set up which can be fed into by national, Community and European granting offices with access to expertise in assessing the implications of any sets of grants on breeders.

We would argue that such measures would be crucial to keeping European plant breeders at the heart of modern plant research activity.

*Study into the Impact and Management of Intellectual Property Rights within the Healthcare Sector* (Department of Health, 2003); and in Nicol and Nielsen, *Patents and Medical Biotechnology: An Empirical Analysis of Issues Facing the Australian Industry* (Centre for Law and Genetics, 2003) (available at http://lawgenecentre.org).

# 10

## *European Plant Intellectual Property: Some Concluding Thoughts*

IN CHAPTER 1, we posed the question whether European plant property provision meets the needs of the European plant research community. In other words, do the rights serve the function for which they were introduced? As is clear from chapters 8 and 9, in many respects it is still too early to make such an assessment. The nature of plant research means that the impact of innovations such as essential derivation and compulsory cross-licensing is only like to start surfacing in the next five to 10 years and even then it will take time for case law to emerge and a jurisprudence to become discernible. As a result, the focus remains more on the function of the rights and more precisely on the nature of that function.

At the most basic level, the function can be said to be to protect the interests of plant researchers so that they are encouraged to continue with their research and provide society with new, and improved, plant products and processes. A key consequence of this function is to serve the public interest as society benefits from the work of the scientists (in this 'society' can be taken to encompass all those who can potentially make use of the protected material, such as farmers, consumers and competitors). However, is the function of the rights solely to protect the interests of the plant scientist or does it also mean that these rights be tempered, in certain circumstances, in order to protect a wider interest? It is this aspect of the function of the rights which has taxed legal minds since the Paris Convention first established the general principle that plants and plant products could be the subject of an industrial property right.

Traditionally, patent law has permitted few limitations to the right granted. When it was first mooted that patent protection for plant material was possible this aspect of the rights did not feature as a particular problem mainly because the then prevailing form of plant research, conventional plant breeding using crossing and selection, was unlikely to produce results which could meet the 'manufacture by man', novelty or inventive step criteria requisite for a patent grant. As patent law was not seen as a primary method of protection, the issue of the unfettered nature of the right was not a matter for debate.

In contrast, in the discussions leading up to the introduction of plant variety rights the nature of the right was seen as vital and specific limitations were built into the system. However, this use of limitations to the right was not a commentary on the *patent* system—it was merely an indication of what was thought appropriate within the specific context of plant variety rights provision. Even when the concept of a 'manufacture' was revised following the discussions which led to the EPC, the issue of what patent protection meant for plant research still was not seen as particularly relevant, as molecular biology was still in its infancy. Now that this has changed (with greater swathes of plant research directed towards the molecular characteristics of plant material in general) and as a result of overcoming the hurdle of the granting criteria (and exclusions from patentability) previously thought insurmountable, the issue of the limitations has become crucial.

To a lesser extent the question also applies to the plant variety rights system—in that its revamped guise has brought the right closer to that of a patent (and indeed in the case of the Community Regulation it is now specifically stated to be an industrial property right) and it could be argued that as a result it should operate on a similar basis to patent law. The obvious response to this is that the plant variety rights system is designed to ensure that breeders can continue to develop new plant varieties. As a result, it applies only to uses affecting the variety (for example by prohibiting the production or replication of material 'of the protected variety').[1] Any other use is not prohibited. However, the revisions made by the 1991 Act, as implemented within the Regulation, do indicate a move towards greater restrictions on the rights of others to use than ever before. The most obvious of these is the introduction of the essential derivation provision and revisions to the farm saved seed right, but also indicative of future possible restrictions is the promise of extending rights to any material derived from the protected material (which could be interpreted to include genes as well as material such as fruit and essential oils). At present the breeders' exemption remains a 'cornerstone' of the system, and all the indications are that it will remain so for the immediate future—but this appears to apply only to use for commercial breeding purposes and it can be asked if protected material can be used for non-breeding programme purposes. Crucially important will be the relationship between the public interest provisions and those which define the private rights of the holder.[2]

The increasingly limited amount of use which can be made of protected material is potentially a cause for concern. The issue of whether it *should* be a cause for concern will depend on how the recent changes to the rights are viewed and

---

[1]  Art 14 of the 1991 UPOV Act.

[2]  For example Art 13 of the Regulation prevents the production or replication of the variety constituents of the protected variety without the authorisation of the variety rights holder. The Article does not state that the use has to be for the purposes of producing the protected variety. As discussed in ch 4, variety constituents include genes. It would seem therefore that the production of the genes of the variety for purposes other than to replicate or propagate the variety itself, is prohibited. This prohibition would seem to cover *any* use of the constituents including use for pharmaceutical purposes and this would not even be permitted under the breeders' exemption as this only applies to uses for the purpose of developing new varieties not other types of plant product.

there are a number of different perspectives which might be relevant in making this determination. These include:

— the overarching European[3] response to existing international obligations;
— national legislative responses to these obligations;
— the needs of plant breeders (taking into account the disparate nature of the sector);

and

— broader interests (including those of the wider global community).

## I. OVERARCHING EUROPEAN PROVISION

If the benchmark for deciding whether or not European plant property provision is appropriate is whether it meets international obligations then it is likely that this provision will be deemed suitable. The Paris Convention establishes that plants and plant products can be treated as industrial property. The TRIPs Agreement requires that member states do not differentiate between fields of technology and whilst it does permit the exclusion of plants from patent protection this is by way of an optional exclusion which, on a narrow interpretation of the provision, would seem to apply only to entities in the genetically recognised form of a plant. Parts of plants (which have come to be recognised within patent law as part of the micro-organism family) are mandated as patentable subject matter by virtue of being micro-organisms, and groupings of plants (in the form of a variety) are stipulated as protectable subject matter (with options available under either the patent system and/or an effective *sui generis* system). In respect of the *sui generis* system, the 1991 UPOV Act requires that protection be accorded to all species with the right granted based more on the protection of the general interests of the rights holder and less on the protection of merely the commercial potential of the variety so protected. In respect of both sets of obligations, the policy and practice of both the European Community and the European Patent Office can be said to comply.

Recent EPO case law, together with the Directive, indicates that the option to exclude plants has not been adopted for the purposes of European patent law and that where any such exclusions do exist then these are to be given a restrictive application.[4] Therefore, plant material is patentable provided that it is not expressly excluded and the invention involving this material meets the threshold for protection.

---

[3] 'European' here means both Community action and the policy and practice of the European Patent Office.

[4] This is clear from cases such as *Novartis* and the Recitals to the Directive.

The Community Regulation also appears to be compliant with the 1991 UPOV Act. It does not permit differentiation between varieties as to which may be protected and which may not and, indeed, the Regulation goes further than the UPOV Act in that it has taken up optional elements (such as the restriction of farm saved seed 'privilege') and firmly established these at the EU level.

The result of this is that only minimal plant material now remains unprotected. This would include material, not in the form of a variety, which cannot meet the threshold for protection; essentially biological processes and intangible traits such as the smell or taste of a particular plant[5] are not protected. As the discussions have shown, in theory this actually means that very little falls outside the scope of protectable material. Plant material, not taking the form of a variety, is patentable provided that it is not a discovery—all that appears necessary in order for this exclusion not to apply is that the plant material has been used in a novel and inventive manner. Equally, essentially biological processes are rendered unpatentable if they comprise wholly natural phenomena; technical intervention (of what could be a relatively low order) may therefore be sufficient to permit a patent to be granted and, as has been shown in the recent *Monsanto* biscuit case, even where the process is unpatentable the product may be patentable. In addition, where a process is patentable then the product may be covered by the patent even where the product itself cannot by the subject of a patent application (for example a patent over a breeding process can cover any varieties bred using that process). The exclusion of true intangible (and subjective) traits such as smell and taste can be explained on the grounds that it is less easy to claim these clearly within the specification. However, it is not inconceivable that a time will come when it possible to describe taste and smells in ways that can be directly linked to the patented technical effect and therefore potentially claimable within a patent over that effect.

On the face of it, therefore, if the function of European plant property provision is to reflect international consensus (by way of existing international obligations) then the EU would seem to have achieved the desired result (indeed, the willingness to amend the Regulation to bring Article 29 into line with Article 12 of the Directive, and by extension Article 31 of TRIPs, indicates a commitment to continuing compliance at the highest level). However, it can be argued that uncritical compliance is not necessarily the best method. There are two areas where the EU could be criticised in its eagerness to bring EU legislation into line with TRIPs and the 1991 UPOV Act.

The first is that the EU appears wedded to the view that the provision of strong protection will result in more rights being granted, with the result of greater competition as companies vie to produce better products safe in the knowledge that

---

[5] Although it is possible that in exceptional instances these could be protected under trade mark law. The emphasis here is on 'exceptional', as cases such as *Sieckmann v Deutches Patent und Markenamt* [2002] ECR I–11737 indicate that in practice it can be difficult to provide that a smell or a taste acts as a trade mark (and it is this element, acting (or functioning) as a trade mark which is critical to securing protection).

these rights will be protected once in the market place. A critical reason for taking this line is that studies have shown that countries which provide strong protection for plants (both in the form of patents and plant variety rights) tend to fall into the high-income category of market economies, whilst those that offer little if any protection tend to be low-income economies.[6] On this basis strong rights equate to a strong market economy. There is, however, a flaw in this reasoning and that lies in the nature of plant science. As the genetic make-up of plants (and other life forms) becomes increasingly understood, it becomes correspondingly more difficult to show that the work undertaken in respect of this material is inventive. As indicated earlier, the expectation of local granting offices and patent lawyers is that fewer rather than more patents will be granted over bioscience inventions. The only way in which more rights will be granted is if the threshold for protection is reduced. As discussed in chapter 7, the view expressed by the Commission in its first Report on the Directive, would seem to indicate that this is its expectation. However, reducing the standard for grant, without equally reducing the effect of the grant and especially the extension of protection to capture material produced by or derived from the patented technology, not to mention the effect of a very limited research exemption, is unlikely to be in the interests of those who are affected by the rights. Lowering the threshold for protection is likely to result in more grants being made, but these grants will be more vulnerable to challenge. Patent litigation (either as defendant or claimant) is not a cheap business and it in unlikely that those who currently form the majority of plant researchers would be able to acquire or protect rights (or even interested in doing so) if the threat of litigation is greater than it already is. It is true that for those biotechnology companies who are financially secure enough to have either in-house or easily accessible (and for them affordable) legal advice this is not as great a fear, but even multinationals are likely to baulk at the idea of entering into a market place unsure as to whether the rights they have are at a greater risk of revocation. Where the company concerned does not have ready access to legal advice and support, then the 'attractiveness' of a system of strong protection is likely to wane quite quickly.

Whilst the same is less true of the plant variety rights system, there is concern over the introduction of provisions which are expressly predicated on the need to take legal action before their ambit is fully understood. Obviously no area of law is immune to potential litigation, but in comparison with the patent system there is considerably less jurisprudence in respect of plant variety rights. One of the reasons for this has been the use of expert tribunals which seek to achieve consensus between competing interests in the protected plant material. The fact that organisations such as the ISF are actively engaged in seeking agreement, through the development of models of good practice, indicates that there is still a commitment to working collectively, but even so, there is a greater fear within

---

[6] See Koo, Nottenberg and Parde, 'Intellectual Property Enhanced: Plants and Intellectual Property: An International Appraisal' (2004) 306(5700) *Science* 1295.

the breeding community that redress to the courts will become increasingly prevalent—whether it does so or not in practice does little to remove the perception.

The second area where the EU can be criticised is that its approach to protection appears to be at odds with that of a number of its member states and, as the legislative decisions of countries such as Germany and Belgium indicate, there is a need to take account of local interests rather than merely complying with international obligations. In this there is concern that the EU has failed to acknowledge that the public interest provisions (which can be found in both UPOV and the TRIPs Agreement) can be used to counter any potential inappropriate uses of the rights. Instead, the view seems to be that such issues are to be dealt with on an individual basis through the courts.

## II. NATIONAL RESPONSES TO THE INTERNATIONAL OBLIGATIONS

Clearly the European Commission feels that the function of the rights can only be achieved if the maximum amount of protection is provided. However, this view has not necessarily been replicated at the national level.

In terms of patent protection, differences remain despite attempts by both the introduction of the EPC and the Directive to converge domestic practices. At the most basic level, there are variations in the interpretation of the criteria for protection and exclusions from protection, and despite the best attempts of the EU to direct national practice towards the granting of patents over plant-related technologies, a number of countries remain resistant to the concept of unfettered patent protection. There is a worry, increasingly expressed by the general patent law community, that there is a need to take into account the specific nature of the sector concerned when deciding the operation of the patent system. The most obvious example of this is the apparently increasingly open-minded view taken towards having some form of equivalent to the breeders' exemption within patent law. However, this should not be taken as meaning that there is a general move afoot to constrain patent provision; instead, it is more indicative of the fact that member states wish to retain the right to determine, *at the national level,* the use made of the rights once granted. In terms of the scope of the rights (and given the amount of concern already expressed about breadth of claims and the interpretation given to the claims made), it remains to be seen if the scope of protection conferred as a result of the Directive will be given its full force or if national courts will chose to limit the extent to which a patent can reach through to further plant material produced using or derived from patent technology. In taking control for this provision it could be argued that member states do not see their international obligation (under TRIPs) as paramount, but rather as a tool within which they can develop their own appropriate national systems. The WTO, in its Doha Statement, has clearly said that this is acceptable for developing countries and therefore it remains to be seen if it, and/or the European Commission, will accept this as appropriate activity within a developed country context.

The same is true of plant variety rights provision. The Commission has clearly not only adopted the provisions of the 1991 UPOV Act for Community purposes but it has taken the optional aspects of the Act and implemented them at the EU level fully within the guise of an industrial property right. The same level of commitment to the revised, 'patent-like' right, has not taken place at the national level. There is no uniform commitment to the higher standard of protection.[7] It is unlikely that the failure to revise national plant variety provision in line with the 1991 UPOV Act is purely due to apathy. It is more likely that it is because the extension of protection to all varieties and the subtle changes to the nature of the right once granted are not thought to be in the best interests of the local breeding community and end users. Because of the nature of a Community Regulation, member states are not required to adapt national legislation in order to comply with that Regulation—however, they have to give effect to that Regulation through their national courts. It is possible that those member states yet to update their national plant variety rights provision may have realised that they could not prevent the introduction of the Regulation (this being a matter for the European not national Parliament) but that whilst they would be required to give effect to a Community right that did not mean that they had to endorse this practice by permitting the grant of a commensurate national right.

It is difficult to explain the disparity of provision, both in patent law and in plant variety rights, at the national level with that of the Community other than on the basis that the differences remain for reasons of national interest. Of course there are those member states who have embraced both the 1991 UPOV Act and the Directive—but even in instances such as this, granting offices have reserved to themselves the right to decide when rights will be granted (which may not be wholly in line with the expectations of the Commission[8]).

There is a further factor relating to the retention of flexibility at the national level, which possibly should also inform the activities (and expectations) of the Commission and this relates to the disparate nature of plant research, both in terms of areas of research and also the type and size of company concerned.

---

[7] Of the 15 countries surveyed as part of the PIP project, six are either members of UPOV Acts or have no form of national plant variety right protection. In terms of consistency of provision, there is no correlation between the failure to revise national plant variety rights with non-implementation of the Directive.

[8] An example of this could be the UK Patent Office's *Guidelines on the Examination of Biotechnological Inventions*, which clearly state that it expects fewer patents to be granted in the future—a statement which would seem to be at odds with the Commission's expectation that there will be a growth in bioscience patenting as a result of the Directive: www.patent.gov.uk.

### III. DIVERSITY OF RESEARCH AND ORGANISATION

The work of the Commission has been neutral in that it has sought to provide protection which is specific to neither subject matter nor sector. In so doing it has not sought to differentiate between the use of plants in agricultural breeding, in cosmetic research or in new pharma. In many respects, this has been mirrored in the approaches taken by the EPO and by those national granting offices which subscribe to the technology-neutral basis of patent law. However, as was discussed in the previous chapter, this approach may have detrimental implications for those engaged in plant research. If the function of the rights is to encourage research *and* dissemination then it is imperative that plant researchers can not only protect their research results but, for many the more important aspect, that they can access the results of others. In addition, there is a real public interest element in allowing greater access to certain types of technological developments, for example key new drugs.

At present, access to patented material is dependent upon either the operation of the research exemption (which remains a largely unknown quantity in European patent law) or by licence, which is largely a matter of individual negotiation with the rights holder. As has already been discussed, the way that these principles are used can vary according to the technology concerned. At present, because these are essentially individual matters, to be decided on a case-by-case basis, there is consensus at neither the national nor the EU level. For many who adhere to the mantra that the rights of the patent holder should not be fettered unless *in extremis*, this is an acceptable situation. However, it does leave critical questions unanswered such as whether it is appropriate to leave key questions over what is appropriate access primarily to the holder of the private right. Whilst there is the notion of a compulsory licence present, its use is so rare, and (in the aftermath of the *South African* case when many European politicians sided with the economically powerful pharmaceutical companies) politically sensitive, that its role as an actual instrument to ensure protection of the public interest looks marginal. There perhaps needs to be greater thinking by the Commission as to whether there should be greater activity (of the kind recently engaged upon by the OECD on licensing) which will encompass the gamut of diverse uses—addressing such matters as the public interest in respect of access to agricultural plant research as well as that of more overtly public interest orientated research such as that directed towards healthcare.

Certainly the function of the right can be seen to vary according to the purpose for which the material involved is to be put.

A final thought needs to be given to the types of organisation involved. As already mentioned, most companies involved in plant research fall into the EU's definition of a small to medium-sized company, and yet the patent system (and arguably for some the post-1991 UPOV Act plant variety right) is tuned to the needs of multinational companies. As studies undertaken by the EU have shown, SMEs have a woeful history of using industrial property protection to protect innovation and yet the Commission has taken the determined step to provide the strongest (and most expensive) form of protection for material which is fundamental to the continued success of this industry. As a result it could be argued that the current provision is designed more with large corporations in mind rather than individual breeders and seed companies. Whilst the rights continue to bed in, the question as to whether this provision is wholly suited to the needs of European breeders remains unresolved. Indeed, in some quarters it has been argued whether the realisation of the promise of patent protection expressed within the Paris Convention could be at the expense of the plant variety rights system.[9] However, as Dutfield explains, such a perception is probably misguided as companies are more concerned about realising the intellectual property potential, in all its guises, of plant research rather than holding fast to a prescribed notion of what the right should be. In seeing plant variety protection as part of a modern, vibrant, intellectual property portfolio it can be argued that the plant variety rights system has finally lost its image as an outmoded impediment. The availability of both rights seems secure; however, not only in maintaining this security of provision, but also in ensuring that the benefits of both accrue to as many breeders as possible, it is imperative that the systems are accessible to all and not merely the legally literate few. In our view this should mean introducing short-term measures designed to protect the interests of those not yet in a position to realise and maximise that benefit. Connecting the thinking which lies behind the Directive (with its TRIPs-compliant strong protection) with the type of company primarily engaged in European plant research is not easy and there needs to be some specific work done by the Commission to ensure that its actions in raising the platform of protection to the highest level are not at the expense of those who have made European plant breeding the global leader it is.

## IV. BROADER INTERESTS

In revisiting its provision, Europe would be well advised to think how its actions, at the local and EU levels, play to the wider global audience. It is one thing to be seen to provide protection commensurate with the US and Japan, where the local indigenous plant breeding communities are very different to those within Europe, and another to be seen to provide protection which potentially could decimate that indigenous community through favouring strong rights accessible (and appropriate) only to the financially and legally literate. The European Commission might argue that its actions are designed to ensure the future growth of all plant research activities and that the decision to provide strong rights was intended to draw in all plant breeders and not exclude any.

[9] Dutfield, *Intellectual Property Rights and the Life Science Industries* (Ashgate Publishing, 2003) 193.

However, such an expectation will not find immediate realisation and the Community will have to accept that possibly, in the short term, measures have to be adopted which will protect the public interest inherent in allowing breeders relatively unrestricted access to protected material and the right to exploit on reasonable terms in order for these breeders to achieve the financial and legal security enjoyed by those who are recognised as currently benefiting most from patent law. One of the problems with the adherence to the international obligation as the measure of determining function is that it gives little appearance of recognising sectoral as well as national differences. If Europe (as a whole and nationally) were to propound such an approach it might not only encourage other countries, unsure of what strong private property rights can do for them, to use European provision as a model of good practice. It might also send a clear signal at home and abroad that the primary function of the rights is to take note of and protect all the diverse interests in plant research and not merely individual interests within it.

# Index